D1496423

MILITARY RELIGION IN
ROMAN BRITAIN

MNEMOSYNE

BIBLIOTHECA CLASSICA BATAVA

COLLEGERUNT

H. PINKSTER · H.W. PLEKET

C.J. RUIJGH · P.H. SCHRIJVERS · D.M. SCHENKEVELD

BIBLIOTHECAE FASCICULOS EDENDOS CURAVIT

C.J. RUIJGH, KLASSIEK SEMINARIUM, OUDE TURFMARKT 129, AMSTERDAM

SUPPLEMENTUM CENTESIMUM NONAGESIMUM NONUM

GEORGIA L. IRBY-MASSIE

MILITARY RELIGION IN
ROMAN BRITAIN

MILITARY RELIGION IN ROMAN BRITAIN

BY

GEORGIA L. IRBY-MASSIE

BRILL
LEIDEN · BOSTON · KÖLN
1999

This book is printed on acid-free paper.

Library of Congress Cataloging-in-Publication Data

Irby-Massie, Georgia L. (Georgia Lynette), 1965–
    Military religion in Roman Britain / by Georgia L. Irby-Massie.
        p.   cm. — (Mnemosyne, bibliotheca classica Batava.
Supplementum, ISSN 0169-8958 ; 199)
    Includes bibliographical references and index.
    ISBN 9004108483 (cloth : alk. paper)
        1. Great Britain—Religion—To 449. 2. Soldiers—Great Britain–
–Religious life—History. 3. Great Britain—History—Roman period,
55 B.C.–449 A.D. I. Title. II. Series.
BL980.G7173   1999
292.07'.09362—dc21   99–36882
                                                                                            CIP

Die Deutsche Bibliothek - CIP-Einheitsaufnahme

[Mnemosyne / Supplementum]
Mnemosyne : bibliotheca classica Batava. Supplementum. – Leiden ;
Boston ; Köln : Brill
    Früher Schriftenreihe
    Teilw. u.d.T.: Mnemosyne / Supplements
    Reihe Supplementum zu: Mnemosyne
199. Irby-Massie, Georgia L. : Military religion in Roman Britain.
1999

Irby-Massie, Georgia L.:
Military religion in Roman Britain / by Georgia L. Irby-Massie.
Leiden ; Boston ; Köln : Brill, 1999
    (Mnemosyne : Supplementum ; 199)
    ISBN 90-04-10848-3

                        ISSN   0169-8958
                        ISBN   90 04 10848 3

PRINTED IN THE NETHERLANDS

CONTENTS

PART TWO

CATALOGUE OF INSCRIPTIONS, APPENDICES, AND BIBLIOGRAPHY

ACKNOWLEDGEMENTS

Matters concerning Roman Britain have been much in vogue recently. New archaeological discoveries, especially the wooden writing tablets from Vindolanda, have increased our understanding of the Roman army and Roman society in Britain. The scholarship of E. Birley and Richmond remains essential, and recent studies by Cunliffe, M. Green, and Henig, *inter alia*, are invaluable. Notwithstanding, no systematic study of Roman army religion, incorporating epigraphy and archaeology, has yet appeared. The following pages represent, in part, an effort to consolidate the information on Roman army, religion, and society in the province of Britain and to shed some further light on the role of the army in the acculturation of a provincial population. The results underscore the complexity of Mediterranean religions and society. Contact between different groups was multi-dimensional. Exchanges, borrowings, assimilation, and outright theft in matters social and religious occurred amongst and between different cultural, ethnic, educational and economic classes.

For the pursuit of this endeavor, my debts are manifold. At the University of Georgia, Athens, James Anderson first introduced me to *limesforschung* and the province of Britain, while Naomi Norman sparked my interest in ancient religions. Among those who gave generously of their time in answering questions and discussing problems at the manuscript's various stages, from doctoral dissertation to book, I should like to single out, in Britain, Charles Daniels, Jenny Hall, Mark Hassall, Simon James, John Kent, Martin Millett, Roger Tomlin, and Michael Vickers, whose insights and suggestions helped shape and refine my understanding of the province and its *realia*. Andrew Gregory, Ramsay MacMullen, Ronald Mellor, and John F. Sheah have kindly helped bring into focus larger issues of provincial interaction and cultic practices.

An enormous and incalculable debt of gratitude is owed to Lindsay Allason-Jones, Anthony Birley, Robert Edgeworth, Duncan Fishwick, Kenneth Harl, Martin Henig, and Lawrence Keppie for reading the entire manuscript. Their critiques, comments, corrections, and suggestions have improved both text and argument at every level. Also to my great profit, John F. Finamore and Mary Margolies read portions of the text. Any remaining errors are my own.

Through the Dean's Small Grant Program, the graduate school at the University of Colorado, Boulder, helped make possible two research trips to Great Britain where I was able to examine many of the remains first-hand. The Center for British Studies at the University of Colorado largely underwrote the second of those research trips with generous funding. Furthermore, and certainly not in the least, I owe great thanks to the staff of the Inter Library Loan Office in Norlin Library, University of Colorado, Boulder, who efficiently, cheerfully, and magically filled countless requests for articles from the most obscure journals.

I should also like to express my gratitude to colleagues and friends for their ceaseless support and encouragement: Emily E. Batinski, Mary English, Daniel Gargola, Barbara Hill, P.T. Keyser, Elizabeth Meyer, and Ann Milner, and in general the faculty and staff of the Departments of Classics at the University of Georgia, Athens, and University of Colorado, Boulder, and of the Department of Foreign Languages and Literatures at Louisiana State University, Baton Rouge.

Special gratitude must be expressed to Christoph F. Konrad, a teacher, scholar, and mentor of the highest caliber whose example and guidance helped shape this project in its dissertation stage. Special thanks must also be expressed to my family Keith, Roxie, Fiona, and Agrippa, without whose encouragement, patience, and support nothing would be possible.

TABLES, MAPS, AND PLATES

Plates 1–4 (following the Abbreviations):

Plate 1: Mithras Tauroctony, London: The Museum of London, author's photo.

Plate 2: Birth of Mithras, Housesteads: copyright The Museum of Antiquities of the University and Society of Antiquaries of Newcastle upon Tyne.

Plate 3: Bust of Antenociticus, Benwell: The Museum of Antiquities of the University and Society of Antiquaries of Newcastle upon Tyne, author's photo.

Plate 4: Venus and the Nymphs, High Rochester: The Museum of Antiquities of the University and Society of Antiquaries of Newcastle upon Tyne, author's photo.

ABBREVIATIONS

AA	*Archaeologia Aeliana*
AArchSlov	*Acta Archaeologica Archeoloskivestnik. Ljubljana Académie slovène*
AB	*Analecta Bollandiana*
AE	*L'Année Épigraphique*
AFA	W. Henzen. *Acta fratrum Arvalium*. Berlin, 1874.
AHB	*Ancient History Bulletin*
AJA	*American Journal of Archaeology*
AJP	*American Journal of Philology*
ANRW	*Aufstieg und Niedergang der römischen Welt: Geschichte und Kultur Roms im Spiegel der neueren Forschung*. Berlin and New York, 1972–. Edd. H. Temporini, W. Haase.
AntJ	*Antiquaries Journal*
ArchCamb	*Archaeologia Cambrensis*
ArchCant	*Archaeologia Cantiana*
ArchJ	*Archaeology Journal*
BAR	*British Archaeological Reports*
BBCS	*Bulletin of the Board of Celtic Studies*
BGU	*Aegyptische Urkunden aus den Staatlichen Museen zu Berlin: Griechische Urkunden*
BMC	*Coins of the Roman Empire in the British Museum*. London, 1923–. H. Mattingly (I–V), R. Carson (VI).
BMQ	*British Museum Quarterly*
BNJ	*British Numismatic Journal*
BJ	*Bonner Jahrbücher*
CCID	Monika Hörig und Elmar Schwertheim. *Corpus Cultus Iovis Dolichenus*. Leiden, 1987.
CIL	*Corpus Inscriptionum Latinarum*. Berlin, 1863–.
CIMRM	M.J. Vermaseren. *Corpus Inscriptionum et Monumentorum Religionis Mithraicae*. The Hague, 1956–1960.
CQ	*Classical Quarterly*
CSIR	*Corpus Signorum Imperii Romani.*
	Great Britain 1.1: Corbridge, Hadrian's Wall East of the North Tyne. Ed. E.J. Phillips. British Academy, 1977.
	Great Britain 1.2: Bath and the Rest of Wessex. Edd. B.W. Cunliffe and M.H. Fulford. Oxford, 1982.
	Great Britain 1.3: Yorkshire. Ed. Sergio Rinaldi Tufi. Oxford, 1983.
	Great Britain 1.4: Scotland. Edd. L.J.F. Keppie and Beverly J. Arnold. Oxford, 1984.
	Great Britain 1.5: Wales. Ed. Richard J. Brewer. Oxford, 1986.

	Great Britain 1.6: Hadrian's Wall West of the North Tyne, and Carlisle. Edd. J.C. Coulton and E.J. Phillips. Oxford, 1988.
	Great Britain 1.7: The Cotswold Region with Devon and Cornwall. Ed. Martin Henig. Oxford, 1993.
	Great Britain 1.8: Eastern England. Ed. Janet Huskinson. Oxford, 1994.
DE	E. de Ruggiero, ed. *Dizionario epigrafico di antichità romane.* Rome, 1895–.
DUJ	*Durham University Journal*
EE	*Ephemeris Epigraphica: Corpus Inscriptionum Latinarum Supplementum.* 1872–1913. Edd. E. Huebner, F. Haverfield.
ERML	W.F. Grimes, *The Excavation of Roman and Medieval London.* London, 1968.
ES	*Epigraphische Studien*
FD	Fink, Hoey, and Snyder, "The Feriale Duranum," *YCS* 7 (1940): 1–222.
FGrHist	Felix Jacoby, *Die Fragmente der griechischen Historiker.* Leiden, 1923–1959.
HT	*History Today*
HTR	*The Harvard Theological Review*
ILN	*Illustrated London News*
ILS	H. Dessau, ed., *Inscriptiones Latinae Selectae*, Berlin, 1892–1916.
Jahr RGZM	*Jahrbuch des Römisch-Germanischen Zentralmuseums, Mainz*
JBAA	*Journal of the British Archaeological Association*
JHS	*Journal of Hellenic Studies*
JRS	*Journal of Roman Studies*
JTS	*Journal of Theological Studies*
LS	J.C. Bruce, *Lapidarium Septentrionale.* Newcastle-upon-Tyne, 1870–1875.
M	Pierre Merlat, *Répertoire des Inscriptions et Monuments Figurés du Culte de Jupiter Dolichenus.* Paris, 1951.
MDAI (R)	*Mitteilungen des deutschen archäologischen Instituts: Römische Abteilung*
MGR	*Miscellanea greca e romana*
MHA	*Memorias de Historia Antigua*
MMM	Franz Cumont, *Textes et monuments figurés relatifs aux mystères de Mithra.* Bruxelles, 1896, 1899.
NDO	O. Seeck, ed., *Notitia Dignitatum Occidentalis.* Berlin, 1876.
PBSR	*Papers of the British School at Rome*
PIR	E. Groag and A Stein. *Prosopographia Imperii Romani.* Berlin-Leipzig, 1933–.
PME	H. Devijver. *Prosopographia Militiarum Equestrium Quae Fuerunt ab Augusto ad Gallienum.* 5 vols. Leiden, 1976–1993.
PSAN	*Proceedings of the Society of Antiquaries of Newcastle-upon-Tyne*
PSAS	*Proceedings of the Society of Antiquaries of Scotland*
RCHM	*Royal Commission on Historical Monuments*
RE	*Paulys Realencyclopädie der classischen Altertumswissenschaft.* Stuttgart, 1893–1980.

RevCelt	*Revue Celtique*
RH	*Revue de l'Histoire des Religions*
RIB I	R.G. Collingwood, and R.P. Wright, edd., *Roman Inscriptions of Britain*. Oxford, 1965.
RIB II	S.S. Frere and R.S.O. Tomlin, edd. *Roman Inscriptions of Britain*. Gloucester, 1991–1995.
RIC	P.H. Webb. *Roman Imperial Coinage*. 5 vols. London, 1927–1933.
RMD I	Margaret M. Roxan, *Roman Military Diplomas Published between 1954 and 1977*. London, 1978. *Institute of Archaeology Occasional Publications* 2.
RMD II	Margaret M. Roxan, *Roman Military Diplomas 1978–1984*. London, 1985. *Institute of Archaeology Occasional Publications* 9.
RMD III	Margaret M. Roxan, *Roman Military Diplomas 1985–1993*. London, 1994. *Institute of Archaeology Occasional Publications* 14.
TAPA	*Transactions of the American Philological Association*
TCWS	*Transactions of the Cumberland and Westmorland Antiquarian and Archaeological Society*
TDGS	*Transactions of the Dumfriesshire and Galloway Natural History and Antiquarian Society*
YCS	*Yale Classical Studies*
ZPE	*Zeitschrift für Papyrologie und Epigraphik*
ZRGG	*Zeitschrift für Religions- und Geistesgeschichte*

1. Mithras Tauroctony, London: The Museum of London, author's photo.

2. Birth of Mithras, Housesteads: copyright The Museum of Antiquities of the University and Society of Antiquaries of Newcastle upon Tyne.

3. Bust of Antenociticus, Benwell: The Museum of Antiquities of the University
and Society of Antiquaries of Newcastle upon Tyne, author's photo.

4. Venus and the Nymphs, High Rochester: The Museum of Antiquities of the University and Society of Antiquaries of Newcastle upon Tyne, author's photo.

PART ONE

MILITARY RELIGION IN ROMAN BRITAIN

Map 1: Roman Britain

INTRODUCTION

The Roman Army in Britain

The Roman soldier in Britain occupied his time in many ways. He fought barbarians. He built walls to delineate the borders of empire. He spent his evenings in the bars of the *vici* which inevitably cropped up around permanent forts or at the baths, gambling, or exercising, or gossiping. He might marry a local girl, without the sanction of Roman law. Caracalla's edict ratified such marriages. Upon retirement, he might join the local community as a farmer, a craftsman, a politician. Only the highest ranking officer might return to the home of his birth. The rest would not receive passage home.

The army of Roman Britain was as multicultural as the empire herself. Allied troops stationed in Britain were originally raised from Upper and Lower Germany, the Gallic provinces, Spain, Thrace, Syria, Africa, Pannonia, Dacia, Dalmatia, and Raetia—a microcosm of the empire and an archetype of ethnic and cultural diversity. These troops arrived in Britain during times of crisis and expansion. Fresh units came for Claudius' invasion, to fight Caratacus and Boudicca, to expand Roman hegemony under the Flavians, to draw lines of stone on the Roman imperial map under Hadrian and Antoninus Pius, to fight and hold territory under Severus. Nero's expeditions of 66 saw the removal of one legion. Troops in Britain were depleted by the expeditions of Clodius Albinus, Constantine, Allectus, Carausius.

This standing army enjoyed a diverse heritage. Legions were traditionally raised from Rome and Italy. Although provinces with full rights of citizenship supplied most of the legionary soldiers of the late first and second centuries AD, Italian families are recorded in Britain. Although allied units might continue to receive fresh recruits from the original area of adlection (especially for specialized units of archers or the like), soon the province herself supplied men for the emperor's army. By the third century, Rome's army in Britain was manned by a largely Romano-British force. But the essence of a provincial army hardly became stagnant or entirely local, as units moved into, within, and out of the province.

The Roman soldier, like the rest of the emperor's citizens, was religious, prudent, or simply superstitious. Soldiers and officers in Britain, just as soldiers and officers throughout the empire, worshipped the gods who protected the Roman state, the gods favored by the *princeps*, the gods of their own ancestors. These gods were worshipped discretely and together. To the Roman mind, in the broadest sense that there was anything "Roman," there was no religious conflict of interest, and gods of different traditions—Roman, Eastern, Celtic—co-existed on the same sculpted monuments. Sometimes these gods were authentically local, occasionally they were Romans dressed in ethnic guise.

Soldiers and officers worshipped some gods because they were told to do so, because it seemed prudent, because they wanted to ask favors, because they had vows to fulfill, because they were deeply spiritual or philosophical. Worshipping the gods of the Roman state corporately contributed to a unit's *esprit de corps*. Barbecues improved morale. Public monuments to victories on the battle field or in the construction zone further distinguished units.

Roman religion, whether corporate or individual, was a matter of public record. In dedicating altars or statues or temples to the right gods, a worshipper increased his own esteem among his peers. For the most part, the popular gods, the gods favored by the reigning emperor, received attention from the army. Yet local gods, unknown to Rome or *princeps*, also received attention from high ranking officers as well as enlisted men. A powerful local god in Roman dress might protect the emperor's representatives in that distant outpost. This reflects the practical nature of Roman religion—it is a wise thing indeed to propitiate any deity who might have the power to help or harm.

Army Religion

Was there such a thing as army religion, and if so, what did it entail? The *Feriale Duranum* from Dura-Europus (chapter one) intimates organized state religion in the army.[1] All imperial units would observe state imperial anniversaries.[2] A degree of uniformity in the reli-

---

[1] The document was certainly organized by a central administration: Fishwick, *ICLW* 593–608.

[2] Civilians, also, might observe such anniversaries, especially those seeking favor

gious observances (Mithras, for example, was popular with officers in Britain and along the Danube; the *Campestres* received votives from the *equites singulares* at Rome and from legionary and auxiliary cavalry officers in Britain, Africa, and Germany) suggests universally popular private cults, as well. Army religion, though similar to civilian, had its own purpose. It identified the individual soldier and his legion or cohort with the destiny of Rome; it was the means by which officials maintained a high level of *esprit de corps*; it provided a social structure by establishing a level of discipline, a standard of loyalty, rewards for merit, and explanations of tradition.[3] The soldier was most likely to face danger and probably felt strongly the need to keep the gods happy.

Methods and Evidence

This study will, of necessity, concentrate on material datable to the second and third centuries, whence the best preserved and most abundant material. The state of the evidence reflects the prosperity of the empire during this time: inscriptions from all classes rise sharply from the Flavians to the Severans. Our analysis will show that certain gods are more popular at particular times and that Celtic gods, especially, are attested primarily at local cult centers. Class distinctions also seem evident—officers worshipped the "Eastern" Mithras and the Celtic Cocidius, whereas enlisted men made vows to the Celtic Belatucadrus and Veteris.

This study incorporates various facets (inscriptions, small votives, gems, coins, archaeology) to present a clear picture of the trends and developments of Romano-British military cult.[4] It will, furthermore, show that there existed a balance between public and private religions, as well as between local (Celtic) and imperial (Roman) cults, which runs counter to recent scholarly emphasis on Celtic rites.

---

in larger towns (Pliny *Epistle* 10.100): see most recently, Lendon, *Honour*, especially, 162. Individuals seeking personal gain might erect statues, amphitheaters, altars, temples in the emperor's honor.

[3] Helgeland, "Army religion," 1473.

[4] Seminal works in this area include: MacMullen, *Christianizing the Roman Empire*; Lane Fox, *Pagans and Christians*.

Recent Studies and Trends

Epigraphic and archaeological evidence is fundamental in determining the nature Roman army religion. Valuable work on this subject has already been completed by others: Wissowa,[5] Domaszewski,[6] Helgeland.[7] Religion in the army of Roman Britain, to focus our study, is a multifaceted and complex topic which has inspired much scholarly interest. E. Birley, whose contributions to the understanding of Roman Britain and the Roman army are undeniable, has produced valuable works on Roman army religion. Birley offers an epigraphic cult by cult treatment, with no comprehensive analysis of the development and evolution of Romano-British army religion.[8] Henig's work on gemstones provides invaluable source material,[9] and his work on Roman religion is indispensable but does not fully examine the military contribution to Romano-British religion.[10] Ross' work establishes a firm background for native Celtic religions but ignores the influences of the Roman army.[11] M.J. Green has likewise made important contributions to Celtic religion and the archaeology of military religion, but she does not consistently incorporate epigraphy and numismatics into her work.[12] Additionally, Webster's work is invaluable but proffers the interpretation that religion in Britain was purely Celtic with a thin Roman veneer which disappeared quickly in the fifth century.[13] Furthermore, little new light has been shed on the significance of certain cults venerated by the army in Britain (e.g., the Veteres) since Haverfield.[14]

Focus

The epigraphic data (listed in a catalogue of inscriptions) falls into in three categories: Roman State religion, Eastern "Mystery" rites,

---

[5] Wissowa, *Religion.*
[6] Domaszewski, "Fahnen;" *Religion; Rangordnung.*
[7] Helgeland, "Army Religion."
[8] E. Birley, *Roman Britain and the Roman Army*; "Religion of the Roman Army: 1895–1977;" "Deities."
[9] Henig, "Roman Gemstones: Figuretype and Adaptation;" *Corpus.*
[10] Henig, "Veneration of Heroes."
[11] Ross, *Celtic Britain.*
[12] M.J. Green, *Civilian Areas; Military Areas*; "Iconography;" *Gods of the Celts.*
[13] Webster, *Celtic Religion*; "What the Britons required."
[14] Haverfield, "Di Veteres;" Heichelheim, "Vitires."

and Celtic/Germanic Cults. The most significant and representative discrete cults will be discussed in the text in terms of 1) the concentration of votive material, 2) the social status of the dedicators, 3) comparisons with army ritual and evidence elsewhere, and 4) the mutual assimilation of Roman and native practices.[15] It must be kept in mind that Roman religion was fundamentally syncretic—the adoption of other gods should not surprise. Furthermore, such cultural trades established a point of contact between Roman administrator and local resident.

The interaction of Roman and native in Britain is central. The Roman army, the institution responsible for imposing Roman culture on frontier societies, was itself immensely diverse in ethnicity and culture. The army, despite (or because of) its diversity, enabled locals to interact with Rome *via* veteran colonies, local municipal government, intermarriage, and commerce, as manifested in language, fashion, housing, and religion. Roman and native religions were an important forum for cultural exchange, providing a social organization for civilians as army cults did for soldiers of different cultural and religious backgrounds.

Content

The first chapter addresses Roman Army religion: Calendars, State Cults, State gods, especially Jupiter, the most significant and widely worshipped. Cults which integrated military units into larger imperial structures—the cult of the emperor, the Capitoline triad, and the personified abstractions—tended to be homogenous. Assorted calendars and festival lists show that the Roman government ordained much of the religious activity of civilian and soldier.[16] Bureaucrats presented the cult of the emperor as a focus of loyalty and Romanization.[17] Because the state cults emphasized ritual, rather than belief, spirituality, and salvation, their appeal was limited to official functions.

The second chapter presents Eastern cults (Mithras, Jupiter Dolichenus) which unified legionary and auxiliary units (whose original

---

[15] G. Webster, "What the Britons required;" J. Webster, "Interpretatio."
[16] E.g., Fink, Hoey, and Snyder, "Feriale;" Gilliam, "Military Feriale;" Fink "Hunt's Pridianum;" Fishwick, *ICLW*, 593–608.
[17] For the cult of the emperor, see especially Fishwick, *ICLW*; "Votive Offerings?" "Soldier and Emperor."

ethnic composition varied greatly from place to place) and provided
a social framework through corporate worship.[18] Mystery rites soothed
private anxieties ignored by the state religions.

Local religions are explored in chapters three and four. To fulfill
private, spiritual needs, the soldier stationed in Britain turned also
to the indigenous deities (e.g., Cocidius, Belatucadrus). These horned
warrior cults have much in common with the cult of Greek heroes
in function, iconography, and myth. Whereas the cults of the Greek
and Roman heroes were strictly personal and offered little opportunity for social and religious interaction,[19] native and imported Celtic
cults, in contrast, formed an institutional framework for contacts
between provincial garrisons and native populations. In addition,
many of the most popular cults centered around healing shrines,
where deities were venerated at sacred springs, wells, and other
sanctified bodies of water. The goddess was not merely a healer; she
figured prominently into war-cults as well—inclusion within official
state dedications shows how the native warrior goddess became an
appropriate benefactress of the Roman army.

In chapter five the discussion centers on the introduction of civilian religious epigraphy, archaeology (temple remains and small votives),
religious iconography, and numismatics which point to a melding of
peoples into a uniquely Romano-British community.[20] Sulis Minerva,
our most dramatic example, received a temple at Bath built in the
first century AD.[21] The Roman army continued to patronize these healing springs. In addition, Eastern cults (Cybele, Isis, Jupiter Dolichenus)
are noted in Britain, but popularity is limited geographically and
temporally, coinciding with the Severan dynasty.

In chapter six, evidence for late Romano-Celtic Religion and
Christianity is investigated. Romano-Celtic religions remained vital

---

[18] For Mithras: Franz Cumont, *Textes et monuments; Les mystères*. Beck, "Mithraism
since Franz Cumont." Speidel, *Mithras-Orion*. Ulansey, *Origins*.
   For Jupiter Dolichenus: Merlat, *Répertoire; Jupiter Dolichenus*; Speidel, *Jupiter Dolichenus*;
Hörig, "Jupiter Dolichenus;" Hörig and Schwertheim *CCID*.
[19] Burkert's studies are especially instructive: *Greek Religion; Structure; et alia*. Also
of interest is Henig, "Veneration of Heroes."
[20] For epigraphy: *RIB*, supplemented by annual reports in *JRS* (1956–1969) and
Britannia (1970–present).
   For temple archaeology: Lewis, *Temples*; Rodwell, ed. *Temples*.
   For iconography and art: Toynbee, *Art in Roman Britain; Art in Britain*; Henig, *Art
of Roman Britain; CSIR* 1.1–8.
[21] Cunliffe and Davenport, *The Site*.

in the British countryside. While many temples were converted to
Christian churches on the continent, the contrasting lack of temple
conversion in Britain may be significant. The late antique Christian
community showed strength, as some "pagan" shrines were converted
to Christian use, but the Roman church was not consistent in
Romanized Britain during the Anglo-Saxon hegemony. Augustine of
Canterbury, at the end of the fifth century, would build a Roman
Christian church in southern Britain from the ground up.

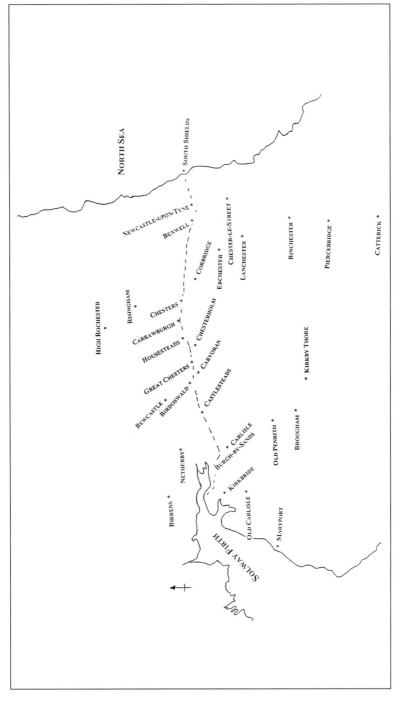

Map 2: Hadrian's Wall

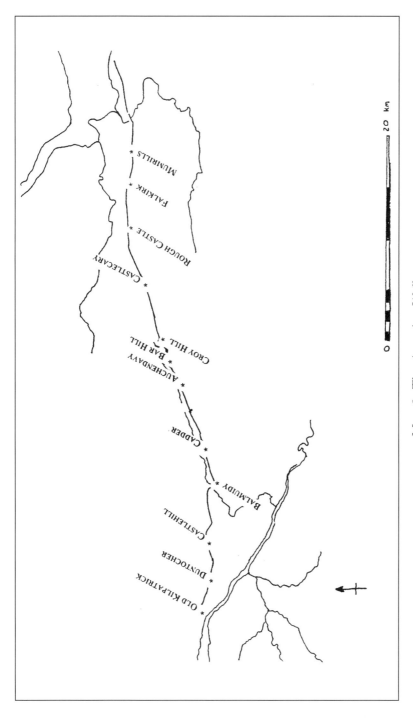

Map 3: The Antonine Wall

CHAPTER ONE

THE ROMAN STATE RELIGION

The Festival Calendar

Roman state religion, rooted in the agricultural calendar, was dominated by fertility and harvest festivals and stemmed from concern to ensure the safety and well being of family and community (especially the community of the Roman state).[1] The Romans, furthermore, were highly syncretic in matters of religion, adapting the Greek pantheon and myth to their own, and borrowing from other cultures as they saw fit. In 204 BC, for example, the Romans imported the cult of the *Magna Mater* from Phrygia in the hope that the goddess would help Rome against Hannibal (Cicero *Har. Resp.* 22–24; Dionysios Halicarnasus 2.19.4; Livy 29.10,14; 34.54.3; 36.36.3; Ovid *Fasti* 4.179–372; Aulus Gellius 2.24).

During the Republic, the state cult or *sacra publica* comprised the *ritus Romanus* and the *ritus Graecus*. The *ritus Romanus* consisted of those cults thought to be native Roman (Mars, Quirinus, the *Lares*, and the *Genii*), or Italic (Venus, Hercules, and the Dioscuri). These cults fell under the charge of the Pontifical College, whose membership, by the end of the Republic, consisted of sixteen Pontifices and the Pontifex Maximus, the *flamen Dialis* attached to the cult of Jupiter, the *flamen Martialis*, the *flamen Quirinalis*, the twelve *Flamines Minores* and the Vestals.

The *ritus Graecus* included cults from Greece (Apollo, for example) and the East (the *Magna Mater*). Temples of these gods were not permitted inside the *pomerium* until the late third century BC. The *Quindecimviri* took charge of the *ritus Graecus* and were responsible especially for keeping and consulting the Sibylline oracles.

Early in the imperial era, a shift in terminology occurred: the *sacra publica* consisted of *sacra Romana* and *sacra peregrina*. The *sacra Romana*

---

[1] Scullard, *Festivals*, 17. Spirits were associated with various parts of the house. Vesta protected the hearth, the *Penates* looked over the *penus*, the cupboards, and the *Lares*, closely associated with the *Penates*, received daily prayers and offerings at the family Lararium.

represented the traditional republican state cult, both *ritus Romanus* and *ritus Graecus*. The *sacra peregrina* included new, foreign (largely Eastern) cults, such as those of Isis, Mâ-Bellona, and Serapis.[2] Although *sacra publica* included both *sacra Romana* and *sacra peregrina*, only temples of those gods worshipped under the *sacra Romana* were built inside Rome's *pomerium*, their rites conducted inside the city walls. The distinction between *sacra Romana* and *sacra peregrina* appears to have been rendered obsolete by the *constitutio Antoniniana* in AD 212.[3]

Much of the information on Roman religious practices survives in the festival calendars, among which the most complete and significant are the *Fasti* of P. Ovidius Naso.[4] The poet's versified account, organized chronologically by month, includes discussion of myth and history, public and private cult practices and festivals, etymology, and the etiologies behind some cultic practices. Ovid's *Fasti* survive only for the months from January to June, ending abruptly at the end of the latter.[5]

Surviving official calendars include the *feriale* attached to the *Fasti Guidizzolenses* (*CIL* I, 253; *ILS* 4917),[6] the *Feriale Cumanum*,[7] the *Feriale* of Oslo,[8] the *Feriale Capuanum*.[9] Of singular importance for the study of Roman military religion, finally, is the *Feriale Duranum*.[10]

The Feriale Duranum

In 1931–32, an excavation team from Yale University recovered a papyrus roll from the temple of Artemis Azzanathkona from Dura-

---

[2] Fink, Hoey, and Snyder, "Feriale," 32. By the reign of Gaius, the cult of Isis was among the *sacra publica* (*peregrina*) (Wissowa, *Religion*, 88 and 351–59). The cult of the *Magna Mater* had been included in the *fasti publici* since Republican times (*Fast. Ant. Vet., Notizie degli Scavi*, 1921, Tav. I and 91–2).

[3] Caracalla built his temple of Serapis on the Quirinal (Wissowa, *Religion*, 355).

[4] Frazer, *Fasti*, English translation and commentary. Bömer, *Die Fasten*, German translation and commentary.

[5] Internal references to later dates in the festival year indicate that the poet intended to complete the *Fasti* to the end of the year (3.57–8; 3.199–200; 5.147–8). Ovid stated that he composed twelve books of *Fasti* dedicated to Augustus, but that his fate (relegation to Tomi) interrupted the work (*Tristia* 2.549–52).

[6] Agricultural workers, primarily, used this private compilation of Augustan date.

[7] *CIL* I, 229; Mommsen, *Gesammelte* 4.259–70. This municipal document dates to AD 3–13.

[8] S.P. Eitrem Osl. III, #77. This calendar, dating to Marcus Aurelius, pertained only to Egypt.

[9] *ILS* 4918; Mommsen, *Gesammelte Schriften* 7.14–24. A local festival list, AD 387.

[10] Nock, "Roman Army," 187–252; Gilliam, "Military Feriale," 183–96; Welles, Fink, and Gilliam, *Final Report*, 191–212.

Europus on the upper Euphrates. This and the other documents recovered from the temple are believed to have belonged to the archives of the *cohors XX Palmyrenorum*.[11] The calendar dates to the reign of Severus Alexander (ii.16–18) and recognized as *diva* Severus Alexander's grandmother Julia Maesa (ii.7), providing a *terminus post quem* of AD 225.[12] Mention, possibly, of Alexander's father-in-law, Lucius Seius, provides a *terminus ante quem* of AD 227 (i.11–12).[13] The document outlines in detail the sequence of religious festivals, sacrifices, and parades to be conducted by the auxiliary troops in Dura.[14] The festival list was written in Latin, the official imperial language, although auxiliary troops stationed in the Greek-speaking East used the calendar. The contents are similar to those of *fasti publici* and to the *Acta* of the *Fratres Arvales*, further proving the official nature of the papyrus.[15] The *Feriale* lacks almost completely local references and offers nothing exclusively applicable to the Eastern legions or provinces. The calendar, composed in Latin and following the model of festival lists issued from Rome, seems to have been an official document which was very likely distributed throughout the empire.[16]

Gilliam argued that Augustus established the military calendar and

---

[11] Rostovtzeff, "Das Militärarchiv von Dura," 351–78.

[12] Welles, Fink, Gilliam, *Final Report*, 191.

[13] L. Aelius Caesar, whose *natalis* is honored in this entry, might be Hadrian's first choice of successor or Alexander's father-in-law. For Hadrian's successor: Hoey ("Feriale," 183, note 870). If our man is Alexander's father-in-law, extensive revisions in the calendar may have been enacted after Alexander's divorce from Gnaea Seia and the execution of her father L. (Gnaeus?) Seius Herennius Sallustius Barbius (*SHA Alex.* 49.3; Jardè, *Sévère Alexandre*, 67–73; Fink, "Lucius Seius Caesar," 326–32; Welles, Fink, and Gilliam, *Final Report*, 205–206). Severus Alexander's downfall may have made this *feriale* obsolete (AD 235; Fink, Hoey, Snyder, "Feriale," 23), or stresses on the *principia* because of invasions from the north (AD 256) may have rendered it untenable (Webster *Roman Imperial Army*, 276; Kettenhofen, *Die syrischen Augustae*, 47–50; Kotula, "Die zwei Frauen," 293–307).

[14] See Welles, Fink, and Gilliam, *Final Report*, 197–202 for text, 202–212 for commentary. Column I contains entries from January to mid-March; column II from *xiii kal. Apriles* to the end of August; column III begins *prid. kal. Septembres*. The third column, highly fragmentary, may have continued into November, and it is likely that the fourth column continued to the end of the year. Lines 7–8 of column IV comprise an entry for the Saturnalia (*xv kal. Jan*), the only indication of the extent of the final column (Welles, Fink, and Gilliam, *Final Report*, 197–212).

[15] Welles, Fink, and Gilliam, *Final Report*, 192.

[16] Fishwick, *ICLW*, 482–483; 593–597. MacMullen, *Paganism*, 110, argues that nothing supports a uniform military calendar issue for the province of Syria, much less the station at Dura, since the Palmyrene cohort worshipped their own gods when off duty, as indeed they did. However, contrary to MacMullen's arguments, the non-Italian Roman soldier worshipped the Roman gods (Jupiter, Mars, *inter alia*) both on duty and off. See also Eck, "Die religiösen und kultischen Aufgaben," 151–161.

probably intended the *feriale* to contribute to a sense of *pietas* among the soldiers, especially the non-citizen auxiliaries, as part of the program to enforce *mores Romani*.[17] The festival list underwent few changes, limited to the additions and substitutions of a few imperial anniversaries.[18] By the reign of Severus Alexander, the military *feriale* may have lost much of its religious significance. Yet, significantly, participation in these festivals helped distinguish the worshipper from civilians and reminded him that he was a Roman soldier.[19]

Nock, who saw no deliberate program of Romanization, suggested that the inclusion of many festivals was intended simply to give the soldiers a holiday. Connecting these holidays with religious observances, wherein free meat and wine would be distributed after the sacrifices, established a link between the soldier's personal enjoyment and his loyalty to the emperor.[20] Nock concluded that, given the nature and intent of the *Feriale Duranum*, the calendar "was not wholly religious, as we should use the word, nor was it the whole of the soldier's religion."[21]

Helgeland argued that the development of the *feriale* stemmed from Augustus' desire to regularize the army.[22] Military units and citizens at Rome celebrated many of the same festivals, including the *Parilia* and *Saturnalia*. Through the calendar of festivals the celebrants helped maintain a veneer of what Augustus considered old republican ide-

---

[17] Gilliam follows Hoey, "Feriale," 32–35, who suggests that the calendar's intent was to enforce Romanization, especially among non-Italian auxiliaries. Such a program of Romanization would explain the inclusion of festivals of limited popular appeal (*Vestalia, et alia*), whose gods, nonetheless, were of vital importance to the welfare of the Roman state. Gilliam, "Military Feriale," 183; Welles, Fink, and Gilliam, *Final Report*, 193–197.

[18] Gilliam, "Military Feriale," 183; Welles, Fink, and Gilliam, *Final Report*, 194–195.

[19] Gilliam, "Military Feriale," 184, 186.

[20] Nock, "Roman Army," 203, 241. The Roman soldier led a life of disciplined, tedious work, which festivals in the *Feriale* alleviated with a change from the routine. There seems to have been no rationalization behind the spacing of the festivals which occurred at irregular intervals—from a day or two to up to two weeks. Evidence from Vindolanda suggests that the army in Britain followed a festival calendar: Bowman and Thomas, *Tab. Vind. II*: #190, referring to food and drink brought in for festivals; #265: referring to a sacrifice on the *dies Kalendarum*; #301, food required for the Saturnalia.

Whether soldiers actually enjoyed these holidays should be questioned. Clearly, essential business, such as guard duty, could not be suspended; and an individual soldier's leave would be left to the discretion of his commanding officer: Gilliam, "Military Feriale," 187; Welles, Fink, and Gilliam, *Final Report*, 196.

[21] Nock, "Roman Army," 229.

[22] Helgeland, "Army Religion," 1487.

ology: the soldiers made sacrifices and observed cultic rites in front of the camp's *praetorium*, symbolizing the *Capitolium* at Rome.[23] The state-ordained calendar of festivals helped give purpose to the soldier's life and constantly reminded him of his duty to Rome.

The festivals prescribed in the *Feriale* fall into three categories: the cult of the *divi* and the emperor; strictly military festivals; and *feriae publicae* and rites of Roman gods. The *Feriale Duranum* includes rites popular in civilian religion: *Quinquatria* (ii.1), *Neptunalia* (ii.22), and *Saturnalia* (iv.7–8); as well as those with little popular appeal: *Natalis Urbis Romae* (ii.5), *Vestalia* (col. ii.15), *Circenses Salutares* (ii.25).[24] Additionally, celebrated by both soldier and civilian, festivals to Vesta, *Salus publica*, and *Roma Aeterna* (symbolizing the power of the state and guaranteeing her continued existence) were closely associated with the prosperity and survival of the Roman state.[25] Paying homage to these powerful symbols would be a high official priority. This crossover of military and civilian religions is to be expected, and similar overlaps will be detected in Britain.

The Cult of the Emperor[26]

Isotheoi timai, inspired by earlier Eastern traditions, were well established in the Hellenistic East by the time Rome aspired to empire. Greek cities in Asia Minor paid obeisance to powerful Romans with altars, temples, sacrifices, priests and games, rites accorded to divinized Hellenistic rulers. In 191 BC, the people of Chalcis, on the eastern Greek shore, voted divine honors to T. Quinctius Flamininus—the

---

[23] *Ibid.*, 1488.

[24] Such events may have been included because of their great popularity (Fink, Hoey, Snyder, "Feriale," 167). The *Menologia Rustica* provide an analogy. Wissowa, *Apophoreton*, 48, pointed out that this particular list, despite its fundamentally agrarian nature, included some festivals of wider interest while excluding some of the old and specifically agrarian festivals. That the *Feriale* from Dura-Europus is of official origin led the original editors to conclude that certain of the more popular *feriae publicae* were included for propaganda reasons.

[25] Welles, Fink, Gilliam, *Final Report*, 195. The calendar itself makes a distinction between carnivals and those days devoted in a real sense to certain gods, for example *dies Quinquatriorum* as opposed to *dies Vestae*. The distinction is made by the mention or omission of the god's name (Fink, Hoey, Snyder, "Feriale," 171 and note 790).

[26] For the Hellenistic background, see especially Fishwick, *ICLW*, 3–82; Price, *Rituals and Power*, 54–62.

first permanent cult awarded to a Roman (Plutarch *Flam.* 17.1) which
still had a priest in Plutarch's day, 300 years later.

After Pharsalus, people in the East, likewise, paid homage to Julius
Caesar. Caesar had enhanced his own divine aspirations by playing
up the family tradition of descent from Venus through Aeneas, emphasized as early as 68 BC, during his funeral oration for his aunt
Julia. By 44, even the senate acknowledged the man's divinity by
granting further honors which confirmed Caesar's sanctified position
in the Roman state. Among these accolades were annual public vows
for his welfare (Dio 44.6.1; 44.50.1) and the introduction of an oath
by Caesar's guardian spirit, his *genius*.[27] Upon his death, Julius Caesar
was duly deified by a vote of the senate, who decreed a temple and
a priest (M. Antonius) in his honor. Rome continued to deify her
beloved deceased rulers until Jovian's death in AD 364. Theoretically,
such honors were to be accorded only to deceased and properly
deified emperors, but, in reality, the question of the ruler cult was
very much an issue for the current, living *princeps*.

In the Latin west, Augustus officially allowed only non-Roman
provincials to observe the imperial cult, and then only in conjunction
with *Dea Roma* (Suetonius *Augustus* 52; Dio 51.20.6–7)—such distinctions were quickly submerged.[28] In 25 BC, the people of Tarraco set
up an altar to Augustus to celebrate the importance of their city in
Hispania Tarraconensis (Quint. 6.3.77). The people of Narbo erected
a similar altar in AD 11 (*CIL* XII 4333 [*ILS* 112]). In 12 BC, in
reaction to disturbances in Gaul caused by the census, Drusus sum-
moned leaders from the three Gauls to a meeting at Lugdunum on
the pretext of a festival (which was still celebrated in Dio's day)
around an altar of Augustus. This altar to Rome and Augustus, at
the confluence of the Rhone and the Saône, incorporated into a
possibly old Gallic festival, may have already been in existence by

---

[27] Alföldi, "Review of Gesche," 170; Weinstock, *Divus Julius*, 214–20; Fishwick,
ICLW, 61. The oath for Caesar's welfare was *pro salute rei publicae et Caesaris*. Since
the *genius* was the guardian only of a living man, after Caesar's death oaths were
sworn *per Caesarem* (Suetonius *Caesar* 85) or *per Iovem Optimum Maximum ac Divum
Iulium* (Dio 47.18.5). Augustus resisted having oaths sworn to his *genius*, as did
Tiberius (Dio 57.8.3). Ovid implied that Augustus allowed oaths to be sworn in his
name: *per te praesentem conspicuumque deum* (*Tristia* 2.54); Ehrenberg and Jones, *Documents*,
117 (Egypt, AD 37): *omnuo Tiberion Kaisara, neon Sebaston*. Caligula made the oath to
his *genius* obligatory and executed those who refused to swear it (Suetonius *Caligula*
27.3).
[28] Fishwick, *ICLW*, 97.

12 (Dio 54.32.1; Suetonius *Claudius* 2; *CIL* XIII 1664–1725).[29] On the banks of the Elbe, ca. 2 BC, L. Domitius Ahenobarbus dedicated an altar to Augustus (Dio 55.10.2–3). This altar's intent was to acknowledge new conquests and victories rather than to propagate the worship of the *princeps*.[30]

Imperial Cult in Roman Britain

Chichester

The imperial cult was a common means by which allies and client kings showed loyalty to Rome, especially in the Greek East. Such may have been the case at Chichester, near the Fishbourne palace which has long been believed to belong to the unswervingly loyal Togidubnus, king of the Regni,[31] who had received Roman citizenship from Claudius (Tacitus, *Agricola* 14).[32] By the king's authority, a guild of smiths erected a temple to Neptune and Minerva in honor of the imperial family (228). The dedicatory plaque was found at Chichester's center, but no trace of the temple itself has survived. Furthermore, the inscription's date is disputed, yet it was likely drafted during the reign of Claudius or Nero.[33] The choice of deities (and

[29] That a festival to Lug coincided with an annual synod of the Gallic tribes celebrating the old festival of Lug-Eisteddfod at Lugdunum (Lyon) is not certain: no direct testimony to Lug has amassed in Gaul, nor is there certain testimony in the Classical period for the celebration of Lug's feast day on 1 August. Nonetheless, annual and semi-annual *concilia* were a native practice: the meeting of 52 BC was held at Bibracte (Caesar, *BG* 7.63). The Druids also met annually in the territory of the Carnutes (Caesar, *BG* 6.13): Fishwick, *ICLW*, 99–102.

[30] Fishwick, *ICLW*, 145.

[31] For a full discussion of the site, see Cunliffe, *Fishbourne*. Whether this estate belonged to Togidubnus is currently disputed.

[32] Cunliffe, *Fishbourne*, 23, 168; G. Webster, *Caratacus*, 25; Boagers, "Cogidubnus," 243–254.

[33] The lettering suggests a date no later than the early Flavian period (Cunliffe, *Fishbourne*, 168). Reference to a *domus divina* suggests that the ruling emperor belonged to a dynasty with at least one deified member; Claudius and Nero qualify, as do Titus and Domitian; Vespasian, however, does not (Barrett, "Cogidubnus," 227–242; G. Webster, *Caratacus*, 25, Fishwick, *ICLW*, 423). Boagers, "Cogidubnus, 254, argues for a Flavian date, since a Julio-Claudian date would render the palace, built ca. 75/80, unexplained. The Flavian Fishbourne palace featured an audience chamber, central in the west wing, indicating Togidubnus' high status. Togidubnus' dynasty would not likely have survived him; the territory probably converted to *civitates* upon the king's death.

the *collegium fabrorum*) suggests shipbuilding—near Chichester were Bosham harbor and the Roman naval base at Fishbourne, and large-scale iron working facilities on the Weald were also associated with this fleet.[34]

The selection of Neptune and Minerva may have been politically tinged. Neither deity is widely attested, and the lack of *interpretatio Celtica*—whereby a Roman god is equated with a native one—(except Sulis Minerva at Bath) suggests that these gods were not widely embraced outside the Roman imperial substructure. Minerva, as a member of the Capitoline triad, was one of the guarantors of Rome's prosperity.[35] Testimony to Minerva in Britain is primarily civilian; the military evidence is limited:[36] cohorts (240), tribunes (235, 236), and record-keepers (229, 231, 232). She was usually invoked alone (229–232, 234, 235, 237–240), but when linked to other deities her associations were purely Roman: Capitoline triad with Mars and Victoria (110), *genius* (236), Hercules Victor (233), Neptune (228). Minerva, especially as *Augusta* (110), protected emperor and empire.[37]

---

[34] Cleere, "Iron Industry," 171–199.

[35] Minerva was especially important to Domitian, who worshipped his divine patroness privately with an almost superstitious awe (Suetonius *Domitian* 15; Dio 67.16): Girard, "Domitien et Minerve," 233–45. She is often depicted (especially on Domitian's coins) bearing Jupiter's thunderbolt: *BMC* II, p. 447; Lestaw, "Minerva," 185–93. Minerva with Jupiter's thunderbolt also appeared on Hadrianic coins (*BMC* III, pp. 298, 379, 564; Fears, "Jupiter," 78). Domitian honored Minerva in the *Quinquatria* at his Alban Villa (Suetonius *Domitian* 4; Dio 67.1.2).

[36] The scant surviving military evidence of small cult objects emphasizes Minerva's military role. Minerva is depicted armed, in bronze at Benwell (M. Green, *Military Areas*, 46, #2), Ribchester (a bronze bust of the goddess with gorgon-shield: M. Green, *Military Areas*, 67), Richborough (armed figurine in bronze, second/third century, converted into a pendant: M. Green, *Military Areas*, 69, #24), and South Shields (bronze head, second/third century). At Chester, a bronze owl, finely engraved, may also indicate Minerva: M. Green, *Military Areas*, 52, #4).

A total of thirty-three gems attest Minerva in civilian and military contexts (Henig, *Corpus*, 227–247, 733, M4–5, App. 14, App. 34, App. 73, App. 123–128). The types include goddess with aegis and plumed helmet (227–230, 242, 243), armed with spear and shield (230–241), goddess with Victory (234–239, 242–244), and with patera (240–241). The gems date from the second century (234, 235), the late third century (238, 246). Military finds include sites in Wales (Caerleon, #234, Dinas Dinlle, Caernarvonshire, #239), Aldborough (Yorks., #232), Richborough (#233), Manchester (#238), Hadrian's Wall (Chesters, #241), and the Antonine Wall—Newstead, 243; and High Torrs, where a cremation burial of a Roman auxiliary soldier yielded #235 as well as late Antonine pottery.

[37] Fishwick, *ICLW*, 446, 448: *Augusta* is a god who protects the emperor. *Augusta*, when linked to the imperial house, comes to mean "royal." See below (pp. 47–54) for "Deified Abstractions."

The epithet is especially appropriate for Minerva as the goddess who inspired wisdom in emperors.[38]

Neptune and the related deity Oceanus (345, 346) may have been especially significant since Britain is surrounded by water, making journeys by sea—travel into the realm of Oceanus and Neptune— necessary to visit the province. That soldiers mutinied (or threatened to) before Claudius' invasion of Britain shows the Roman distrust of the sea (Dio 60.19; cf. Caesar, *BG* 4.25). Furthermore, when Britain finally came under Roman rule, it was declared that Claudius was the first to subjugate Britain and that Ocean had been conquered: *ille Britannos ultra noti/litora ponti/et caeruleos scuta Brigantas/dare Romuleis colla catenis/iussit et ipsum nova Romanae/iura securis tremere Oceanum* (Seneca, *Apocolocyntosis* 12.3.13–18; cf. Seneca, *Octavia* 39, 41).[39] The emperor, in fact, featured Ocean symbolically in his triumphal parade (Suetonius, *Claudius*, 17.3).[40] A third century gem may suggest the continued significance of Neptune *Victor*: the god stands with his foot on a prow, holding a dolphin, similar in type to Victory with her foot on a prow.[41] Neptune received few invocations, has no known Celtic associations, and was usually invoked alone. Most Neptune monuments, excepting those found at forts along the Hadrianic (332–335) and Antonine (336, 337) Walls, have been found near the sea (Lympne: 330; Maryport: 331; Newcastle: 332). The inland dedications to Neptune, originally a fresh-water deity, probably recognized the god in his capacity as a river spirit.[42] The dedication from Castlecary (337), an inland fort on the Antonine Wall, was set up by a part-mounted unit, who may have conflated the Roman Neptune with the Greek Poseidon, a god also of horses and earthquakes. The unit was probably grateful for a safe journey through some body of water

---

[38] Girard, "Minerve," 217.

[39] Claudian propaganda at Rome claimed that Britain was heretofore unknown (Seneca, *Octavia*, 39; *CIL* VI 920). It is true that Claudius was the first to bring the island into the Roman political sphere. Not acknowledging Julius Caesar's efforts is significant. Claudius' public relations people were distancing their emperor from Caligula (C. Caesar) who had certainly disgraced the dynasty and was noted, particularly, for his failure to invade Britain: Stewart, "Inventing Britain," 9.

[40] Caesar, in fact, had featured the rivers Rhine and Rhone, as well as an Ocean of gold in his triumph: Florus 2.13.88.

[41] Henig, *Corpus*, #19. The third century date places the gem within the context of Severan activity in northern England.

[42] One gem (Henig, *Corpus*, #18) from Woodeaton, Oxfordshire seems to depict the river Neptune: Neptune with his left foot on a prow holds a dolphin in outstretched hands.

(the Channel, Irish Sea, or North Sea) and may have hoped for an equally safe return to its home-base.

Both Minerva and Neptune are appropriately associated with ship-building, and this connection must be significant to their shared temple at Chichester. In addition, both were politically important: one, a patroness of the emperor, the other, a god who oversaw travel to and from the island.

Colchester

In Roman Britain, the official cult of the emperor was centered in the "temple of Claudius" at Camulodunum (Colchester). The temple seems to have been exceptionally large. The stone was imported, and the decorations elaborate. There is every reason to believe that money for the project was exacted from the natives, who probably were also drafted to build the temple. The financial drain created by this project would eventually contribute to the local uprisings against Roman hegemony in Britain.

The *colonia*'s purpose (which the cult supported), according to Tacitus, was to indoctrinate the native aristocracy into Roman law, morality, and religion: *subsidium adversus rebellis et imbuendis sociis ad officia legum* (*Annals* 12.32).

The temple was built in the eastern portion of the city perimeter, within the *vicus*, on the site of the military annex to the Claudian fortress.[43] The temple seems to have had no connection with the city forum and other buildings which were usually centrally located.

Accruing archaeological evidence suggests that the building was a eustyle temple with eight columns, of segmental tile with convex fluting typical of the Neronian and Flavian eras, across the front.[44] The podium (31.5m × 24m) is extant under the Norman castle.[45]

In front of the temple, there stood an altar which recalled the Lyon monument, Strabo's description of which (4.3.2) is supported

---

[43] Fishwick, "Provincial Centre," 32–34. The provincial center at Tarraco was, likewise, built on the grounds of a former military installation which lay outside the boundary of the original Roman city: Hauschild, "Tarraco," 213–218, 261–3. The Sarmizegetusa temple also lay at the colonia's perimeter: Étienne, Piso, and Diaconescu, "Les deux forums," 273–96.

[44] Fishwick, "Provincial Centre," 41.

[45] Hull, *Roman Colchester*, 162–8; Crummy, "Roman Colchester," 243–8; Drury, "Temple," 27–28, 34–25; Fishwick, "Provincial Centre," 41.

by an issue of bronze altar coins from the local imperial mint. The coins show a broad, rectangular altar displaying imperial standards and flanked by twin Victories atop columns.[46] A figurine of Victory with two oblong pedestals surfaced at Colchester,[47] along with the base of a large monumental altar, about half the length of the temple, 28 or so meters from the temple's front.[48] Between the altar base and temple, excavators discovered a vaulted drain which may have had "underlay gutters defining the edge of a specially paved area around the altar."[49] The combination of altar and temple is known at no other provincial center, except possibly Sarmizegetusa.[50] Such an altar may very well have been the original cult center in accordance with our earlier examples.[51]

Most provincial centers included facilities for spectacles within easy walking distance. Amphitheaters stood quite close to the provincial centers at Tarraco, Narbo, Sarmizegetusa, Emerita, Corduba, *inter alia*. An amphitheater has not yet been located at Colchester, although Richmond knew of a seventeenth-century record of curving structures in *Insula* 3, within walking distance of the temple.[52] Vestiges of a theater have been excavated immediately west of the "temple of Claudius."[53] Spectacles would have been given in conjunction with imperial festivals, especially the emperor's birthday.

The Colchester evidence does not indicate a positive connection between the emperor and *Dea Roma*, despite Augustus' mandate that western provincial cults should include the worship of *Roma*. There is, however, an utter lack of numismatic and epigraphic evidence to date, an argument *e silentio* not necessarily proving anything. Nor is there positive attestation of a provincial priesthood, although Tacitus (*Annals* 14.31) used the word *sacerdotes*, the technical term for priests of the cult of *Roma* and Augustus, in reference to *templum divo Claudio*.[54]

---

[46] Mattingly, *Coinage*, I, 92ff.
[47] Hull, *Roman Colchester*, 175–77; Fishwick, "Provincial Centre," 43.
[48] Drury, "Temple," 15 and fig. 2.
[49] Drury, "Temple," 27 and fig. 2.
[50] Fishwick, "Provincial Centre," 43; Étienne, Piso, and Diaconescu, "Les deux forums," 297–298.
[51] Fishwick, "Divus Claudius," 23.
[52] Hull, *Roman Colchester*, xxviii, with n. 4; Fishwick, "Provincial Centre," 49. The amphitheater at Lucca was remodeled into a curving row of houses; the same may have occurred at Camulodunum.
[53] Fishwick, "Provincial Centre," 49; Drury, "Temple," 30 and n. 112; Crummy, "Roman theatre," 299–302. The temple seems to have modified c. AD 150–250.
[54] Fishwick, "Provincial Centre," 45.

Such cults were imposed by Rome, and in newly conquered territories, for the most part—the provincial cult of Hispania Citerior is an exception—they took the same form of worship, that of *Roma* and Augustus at an altar.[55] Close analogy with archaeology at Lyon suggests that the Colchester altar was possibly the original site of a cult to *Roma* and Augustus.[56]

In Britain, the cult of *Roma Aeterna* is attested on two dedications found at Maryport (43, 91), and one at High Rochester (1). #1, possibly dating to Gordian III, was set up in honor of the birthday of the city of Rome. In addition, a shrine to the *Dea Roma* stood at Corbridge (*CSIR* 1.1.37–38).[57] The pediment survives, decorated largely with Bacchic imagery—fruited vines frame Romulus and Remus as the wolf nurses them, the traditional symbol of *Roma Aeterna*. Below, Faunus and Pan dance in front of a foliage backdrop. The imagery is intended to emphasize *Romanitas*, peace, and civilization.[58] The significance of the cult of *Roma Aeterna* lay in its connection with the imperial cult, and traces reflect festal celebrations decreed by official calendars. The personification of *Dea Roma* combined with sacrifices and feasting were intended to make a powerful impression on participating troops.[59] Generally, *Roma* was not invoked alone, but she copied Roman imperialistic practices "by invading the sanctuaries of other gods."[60] Likewise, the emperor and Jupiter Optimus Maximus were customarily invoked with other, often native, gods.

The ruler cult at Colchester is so intriguing because the evidence is irregular, controversial, and inconclusive. Seneca referred to Claudius' notions of godhead in his satirical *Apocolocyntosis* (8.3): *deus fieri vult: parum est quod templum in Britannia habet, quod hunc barbari colunt et ut deum orant* morou euilatou tuxein?[61] Tacitus, to the contrary, did not imply that Claudius was motivated by an expectation of godhead. Tacitus in reference to Claudius' cult (*Annals* 14.31) employed only the con

---

[55] Fishwick, "Divus Claudius," 21. *Dea Roma* has been excluded from some provincial cults, notably at Sarmizegetusa (Danube), a later cult dating to Trajan: Fishwick, *ICLW*, 301–307.

[56] Fishwick, "Provincial Centre," 44–45.

[57] An altar from Old Carlisle might suggest a temple to *Roma Aeterna* (Mellor, "Roma," 992): *Deae A[—]ae te[mplum]* | *L. Vater[ius Mar]cellus [praef(ectus)]* | *rest[ituit]* (*CIL* VII 336; *RIB* 886). The goddess could be local.

[58] Hutchinson, "Cult," 138.

[59] Fishwick, *ICLW*, 596.

[60] Mellor, "Roma," 971.

[61] The Seneca passage can be easily misunderstood. The *Apocolocyntosis* presents a debate on Olympus which parodies a debate of the Roman senate which occurred after Claudius' death and in which the senate granted Claudius a decree of deification.

ventional epithet reserved for emperors who had escaped *damnatio memoriae*.[62] Nothing suggests that Claudius was seeking worship as a *praesens deus*. To the contrary, in his letter to the people of Alexandria, the *princeps* indicated his distaste for such displays and rejected temples to himself which he considered necessary in dealing with non-Romans.[63] It is, furthermore, rash to assume that the temple to Claudius could have been in use during his own lifetime. Tacitus emphasized the fact that the temple had been constituted by AD 60, but the historian made no mention of a dedication.[64] The *templum divo Claudio* seems not to have yet been dedicated, therefore not the center of a temple cult, until a good six years after Claudius' death. Furthermore, the temple, begun by AD 54 or later, was still probably under construction in 60.[65]

In AD 60, Camulodunum was destroyed during the revolt led by Boudicca, the widow of the Icenian king Prasutagus. After the revolt, the Romans may have considered withdrawing from Britain: *etiam ex Britannia deducere exercitum cogitavit, nec nisi verecundia ne obtrectare parentis gloriae videretur destitit* (Suetonius, *Nero* 18).[66] The temple, however, was rebuilt, and all traces of the burning removed. This ritual purification may suggest that Colchester continued to be a religious center or that no significant debris had accrued from a building whose construction was in progress.[67] The rebuilding of the temple may have been an object lesson to the vanquished Britons who had destroyed the first temple and, consequently, had to pay the penalty by building a new temple. Reconstruction incorporated a *temenos* clearly defined with mettaled streets and timber buildings (AD 62–80)

The question on Olympus regards ratifying that senatorial decision. Claudius is, at the time of the debate, legally *divus* according to the Roman senate. It is plausible that the senate decreed a temple in Claudius' honor in conjunction with their decree of deification and a priesthood (with Agrippina as priest: Tacitus: *Ann.* 12.69.4—he was clearly *divus* by the time of his funeral and Agrippina was clearly priestess). See further Fishwick "Seneca," 137–138, *ICLW*, 201–203.

[62] Fishwick, "Imperial Cult in Roman Britain," 164.

[63] M.P. Charlesworth, *Documents*, 4, #2, ll. 35–38. Taylor, "Tiberius' Refusal," 87–101; M.P. Charlesworth, "Refusal," 1–10.

[64] Fishwick, *ICLW*, 203.

[65] Fishwick, "Divus Claudius," 15. The colony was created in AD 49, which provides barely five years to constitute and design such a temple, not to mention raising finances, levying workmen and craftsmen, quarrying stone, laying foundations, *et cetera*. The time frame is almost impossibly too short: Fishwick, "Divus Claudius," 13–14; Fishwick, "Provincial Centre," 31.

[66] This story from Suetonius may have been aimed at Hadrian who nearly abandoned Dacia in AD 117/8, as suggested by A. Birley, private correspondence.

[67] Hull, *Roman Colchester*, xxvi; Fishwick, "Provincial Centre," 34.

soon replaced with masonry structures.[68] Although some have suggested that the religious center was moved to London,[69] there is no
parallel for the transference of a provincial cult center, nor would
it be essential for a cult center to coincide with the administrative
headquarters.[70] Any pre-Boudiccan portable votives were likely lost
or destroyed, and little post-Boudiccan evidence has yet come to
light.[71] There is, however, no reason to doubt that the cult flourished
into the fourth century, as it did in, for example, Africa.[72] After the
Edict of Milan (AD 313), the temple façade and columns were
removed as the structure was converted into a basilica, in all prob-
ability not used as a Christian church.[73]

The Cult of the Emperor after Boudicca: genius and numen

Genius

The cult of the *genius* may be one of Rome's oldest, beginning as a
private cult, then extending into the community. By 218 BC, the
genius pR received public sacrifices (Livy 22.62.9).[74]

The *genius* was a protective spirit.[75] Some *genii*—illustrated as togate

---

[68] Fishwick, "Provincial Centre," 34; Drury, "Temple," 25–26.

[69] Wheeler, *Roman London*.

[70] Deininger, "Provinziallandtage," 143; Fishwick, "Provincial Centre," 49 and n. 72.

[71] To take examples from the East where living emperors were honored with
temple cults, in most cases, the cult of an individual emperor did not last long after
that emperor's death, although the Lycian assembly continued to appoint a priest
to Tiberius into the third century (*IGR* III 474): Price, *Rituals and Power*, 61. The
institution continued well into the mid-third century, although it did not fully recover
from the crisis of the third century or the Christianizing efforts which began full-
scale with Constantine (Price, 59–60).

[72] Lepelley, *Les Cités*, I, 367; Wardman, "Pagan Priesthoods," 258. Local dignitaries administered the imperial cult at the municipal level. Romano-British cities
would most certainly have continued to maintain the cult.

[73] Fishwick, "Provincial Centre," 49–50.

[74] *Genius*, cognate with *gens* and *gignere*, was a divinity external to a man, much
like the Greek *daimon*, worshipped with the *Lares, Penates, Manes*, and Olympian gods:
Wissowa, *Religion*, 175–181; Otto, "Genius," 1155–70. Some have argued that the
genius represented the divine embodiment of a man's procreative powers or the spirit
from which he arose: Speidel and Dimitrova-Milceva, "The Cult of the *Genii* in the
Roman Army," 1543; Otto, "Genius;" Nilsson, *griechischen Religion II*, 200–218. Paulus
apud Festum (94L) implied that the *genius* fell between god and man: *Aufustius, "'Genius'
inquit est deorum filius et parens hominum, ex quo homines gignuntur. et propterea Genius meus
nominatur, quia me genuit."*

[75] *deus est qui praepositus est ac vim habet omnium rerum gignendarum* (Augustine *de civitate Dei* 7.13 quoting Varro); *genius est deus, cuius in tutela ut quisque natus est vivit. hic*

Romans holding cornucopias—were identified with men,[76] some with gods,[77] and still others, *genii loci*—often represented as snakes—were equated with places.[78] One would pray to his own *genius*, swear oaths by it, and make offerings to it, especially on his birthday.[79] It is possible for the *genius* to have a *numen*, but the use is undocumented.[80] The *genius* of a *numen* is, however, attested.[81]

Inscriptions[82] and literary sources[83] attest the *genius pR*, a symbol of the old religion contrasted with Christian intolerance. Aurelian, for instance, built a temple to the *genius pR*, and a late third century AD coin issue bore the image of the *genius pR*.[84]

In 14–12 BC, an official state cult of the *genius* was declared, and the *genius Augusti* was honored along with the *Lares Augusti* (Ovid *Fasti* 5.145; Dio 55.8, 6–7; Suetonius *Augustus* 30). A vote of the senate decreed that libations were to be poured in honor of the *genius Augusti* at all banquets: *te multa prece, te prosequitur mero/defuso pateris, et Laribus tuum/miscet numen* (Horace, *Odes* IV.5, 33–35; 14 BC).[85] In AD 5 or 9,

---

sive quod ut genamur curat, sive quod una genitur nobiscum, sive etiam quod nos genitos suscipit ac tutatur, certe a genendo genius appellatur (Censorinus *de die natali* 3.1).

[76] Tombstones record dedications to the *genii* and *di manes* of certain men: *dis manibis, genio C. Iuli Nicero(tis)* (*CIL* VI 4307); *Genio L. Iulio L. f. Magno vixit annis XV* (*CIL* VI 7806); *deis et genio Rhodanis Domitiae Aug ser* (*CIL* VI 8434); *Genio Coeti Herodian(i) praegustator(is) divi Augusti Decessit* (*CIL* VI 9005); and *P. Alfeno Hypano, genio et dis manibus* (*CIL* VI 11429).

[77] The *genius* of Jupiter is acknowledged in the temple of Jupiter Liber at Furfo: *Iovi Libero aut Iovi (Liberi) genio* (*CIL* IX 3513). Petronius referred to the *Priapi genius* (21). There are as well inscriptions naming the *genii* of Jupiter Optimus Maximus (*CIL* III 4401), of Mars (*CIL* XIII 6464), and of Mercury (*CIL* XIII 6425).

[78] Paulus *apud Festum* (95L): *alii genium esse putarunt uniuscuiusque loci deum*; Servius (*ad Aen* V.95) commented: *nullus enim locus sine genio, qui per anguem plerumque ostenditur.*

[79] The *genius Augusti*, for example, received a sacrificial victim, often a bull, as offered to the Olympian gods: Taylor, *Divinity*, 192; Nock "Review of Taylor," 516 expressed doubts concerning the sacrifice of victims to the *genius Augusti*.

[80] Fishwick, *ICLW*, 384 and n. 45.

[81] *genio numinis Priap(pi) potentis polle(nti)s (inv)cti* (*CIL* XIV 3565); *genio numinis fontis* (*CIL* VI 151).

[82] The calendar of Philocalus mentions *ludi Genialici* which occurred quadrennially on February 11 and 12. The *feriale Campanum* cited a *Genialia* which fell on February 11. Some inscriptions include: *genius pR* (*CIL* VI 248, perhaps Aurelian in date); *Iovi Optimo Maximo et genio pR et venalici* (*CIL* VI 29944); *<si> quis hanc aram laeserit, habeat genium iratum populi Romani et numina divorum* (*CIL* VI 30738); *Iovi Optimo Maximo, terrae Daciae et genio p.R. et commerci* (*CIL* III 3650).

[83] Plautus (*Captivi* 977); Terence (*Andr.* 289), Tibullus (4.5.8), Horace (*Ep.* 1.7.94) Seneca (*Ep.* 12.2), Apuleius (*Met.* 8.20) Likewise, Tibullus (3.6.48; 4.13.5), Petronius (25) and the scholiast to Juvenal (2.98) mention women's *iunones*.

[84] Béranger, "Der genius pR," 82–83. This coin issue probably dates to Gallienus.

[85] Horace also referred to the taking of oaths by the *numen* of the emperor: *Praesenti tibi maturos largimur honores/iurandasque tuum per numen ponimus aras* (*Ep.* 2.1.15–16).

Tiberius dedicated the *ara numinis Augusti*.[86] No literary reference describes the cult, but an inscription from Narbo (*CIL* XII 4333 [*ILS* 112]; 22 September, AD 11) to the *numen Augusti* details the cultic rites: the sacrifice of victims and the offering of wine and incense on high feast days; wine and incense offered on lesser days. Pippidi claimed that festivals to the *genii Aug.* and *numina Aug.* were identical.[87] The inscription on an altar to the *numen Augusti* at Forum Clodii (AD 18) invites the *genii* to the altar, clearly indicating that the two must be different.[88] Inscriptions to the *numen* and *genius* of the same person also survive.[89] Epigraphy shows consistently the *genius/genii* of living emperors, never the *genius* of deified emperors, as the object of cult,[90] whereas dedications to *numina* are made to the *numina* of joint emperors or of all emperors, past and present.[91]

Numen

Gods possessed *numina* as quintessential divine powers; he who owned a *numen* was, consequently, a god.[92] Lucretius applied the term to

---

The terms seem to have become interchangeable: Pippidi, "Le *numen Augusti*," 83–111; Taylor, "Worship of Augustus," 132, note 59; *Divinity*, 220, 227, 282. Pippidi (111, note 2) suggested that *numen* was preferred because of its euphony and richness of content.

[86] Rau, "Pann.-dalm. Krieg.," 344–345; Pippidi, "La Date del'Ara Numinis," 435–56; Taylor, "Tiberius' *Ovatio*," 185–93. Tiberius dedicated the altar to Augustus for his Illyrian triumph in AD 13 (Suetonius *Tiberius* 17.2; Dio 56.1.1).

[87] Pippidi, "Le *numen Augusti*," 106–8. The Narbo inscription was dedicated the day before Augustus' birthday, the principal feast day for the *genius*, and a two day festival at Narbo celebrated the birthday (Sept. 22–23). The *AFA*, furthermore, recorded the offering of wine, incense, and victims to the *genius* of a living emperor.

[88] *et ut natalibus Augusti et Ti. Caesarum, priusquam ad vescendum decuriones irent, thure et vino genii eorum ad epulandum ara numinis Augusti invitarentur* (*CIL* XI 3303, ll. 11–13 [*ILS* 154]). Taeger, *Charisma*, 2.145. Also from Forum Clodii, an altar, dedicated AD 18, records the unparalleled form *numen Augustum* (*CIL* XI 3303 [*ILS* 154]). Taylor ("Tiberius' *Ovatio*," 189) interpreted this phrase as referring to a collective deity comprising the *genii* of the emperor and the heir-apparent as well as the *juno* of the empress. The form is probably a variant on the more usual *numen Augusti* (Fishwick, *ICLW*, 380 with n. 23, 385).

[89] *n(umini) et g(enio) L. Caesari(s) [.] Rufinius Adnam(etus) Africani f(ilius) d(edit) d(edicavit)* (*ILTG* 160, from Bourges). It might seem unusual to ascribe a *numen* to L. Caesar, but not unreasonable since he was Augustus' chosen successor (Taylor *Divinity*, 219).

numini Aug(usti) et genio imp(eratoris) Caes(aris) T Ae[l] Hadr Antonini (*CIL* III 3487, from Aquincum AD 138).

[90] Cesano, "Genius," 459–62.

[91] Fishwick, *ICLW*, 385.

[92] Rose, "Numen inest," 237–57; "Numen and Mana," 114; Fishwick, *ICLW*, 385.

human understanding: *ad numen mentis momenque* (3.144); Cicero referred to the *numen* of the senate (*Phil.* 3.32) and of the *populus Romanus* (*Oratio post reditum ad Quirites* 18). The term *numen* soon came to be applied to individual men and, by metonymy, signified a god rather than just his divine essence.[93] The *numen* is not, *per se*, a divinity, but it is a divine property. Nock insisted that to credit the emperor with a *numen* was, in itself, a form of honor, arising from heartfelt gratitude: *deus est mortali iuvare mortalem* (Pliny *NH* 2.18).[94] There is a subtle distinction between being a *numen* and possessing one. The emperors were symbols of divinity, holy but perishable, objects of veneration but not recipients of genuine votives, at least in the early empire.[95] The Roman *princeps*, by virtue of his *numen*, acted as a mediator between men and gods, and so allowed the divine world to act through the agency of human emperors.

The Cult of the Imperial Numina

After Boudicca, the extant evidence suggests that the imperial cult manifested itself in dedications to *numina Augustorum*.[96] The cult included both the reigning emperor together with the *divi* during the second century (before AD 161) as attested for Hadrian (122, 131, 132) and Antoninus Pius (469) in Britain. During the third century, the emphasis shifted to the current emperor(s) to the exclusion of the *divi*, especially from Severus Alexander to Valerian.[97] The British evidence supports this conclusion: Severus Alexander (5, 486, 618, 695–97), Gordian III (24, 212, 692), Valerian and Galienus (150, 216) and Gallienus (193). Stresses on the empire by this time were severe; it only made sense to seek the beneficence of or support for the emperor.

---

[93] Fishwick, *ICLW*, 384; Rose, "Numen and Mana," 114–117.

[94] Nock, "Review of Taylor," 517.

[95] Fishwick, *ICLW*, 385; Nock, "Review of Taylor," 518. See also Fishwick, *ICLW*, 385; "Votive Offerings?" and "Soldier and Emperor," on the emperor as the recipient or prayer in the later empire; Price (*Rituals and Power*, 117–121) on vitality of emperor cult.

[96] For discussions on the expansion of *num. Aug. et sim.* see Pippidi, "Le *Numen Augusti*," 102. Pippidi argued for *numinibus Augusti*. See also Fishwick, *ICLW*, 375–422; "Numinibus Aug(ustorum)." Fishwick (*ICLW*, 405–413) argued that the abbreviations *nn Augg*, *num Augg*, *numinib Aug/Augg/Augustor*, and *numinibus Aug/Augg* are to be expanded to the plural *numinibus Augustorum*, while *n Aug* and *numini Aug.* are the usual abbreviations for *numini Augusti*. The British evidence supports these expansions, which are applicable to the Celtic northwest, though not consistent throughout the Roman world (*ICLW*, 411).

[97] Fishwick, *ICLW*, 416.

The imperial *numina* were rarely honored exclusively (5, 6, 8, 11). More frequently, the emperor's *numen* was invoked with other deities, often native: Antenociticus (535: Caracalla?), Arciaco (538: date uncertain), Belatucadrus (554: Severan), Brigantia (571: Caracalla and Geta), Ocelus (618: Severus Alexander), and Vanauns (625: date uncertain); or imported Germano-Celtic gods: the Alaisiagae (695–697: Severus Alexander), Garmangabis (692: Gordian III), Mars Lenus (469: Antoninus Pius), the Mother Goddesses (486: Severus Alexander; 502: third century?), Mogons (520: date uncertain). Temple cults to the *numina Augustorum* with such local (non-Roman) gods are suggested at York (7: dea Joug-, Severan?), South Shields (10: sancta?, Severan?), and Old Penrith (486: *Matres Tramarines*, Severus Alexander). Many of the aforementioned dedications were erected by troops freshly recruited to Britain, Severus or later.[98] The imperial *numina* are included in dedications to local gods as an act of reverence, since new arrivals would want to appease local, presumably hostile, gods while showing loyalty to the emperor. Many dedicators were auxiliary soldiers, neither native Italian nor native British, neither fully Romanized nor completely local. Such religious expressions allow displaced soldiers to reconcile two foreign cultures, Roman and local, or to bring something of home, e.g., the cult of the *Matres*, to their tour of duty. Hence, non-Mediterraneans and non-Italians could express both fealty to Rome and self-perception as Romans.

These dedications, which include both Celtic and Graeco-Roman deities, have surfaced at legionary forts (Caerleon, Chester, and York) and smaller forts (Corbridge, Risingham), where they were set up by legionary and auxiliary troops alike. The *numina Augustorum* are also frequently attested with Jupiter Optimus Maximus (111, 122, 131, 132, 150, 166, 173–77, 193, 212, 216), on monuments dedicated corporately by detachments of auxiliary troops during annual New Years' celebrations (Tacitus *Historiae* 1.5; Vegetius 2.5). The combination is appropriate since Jupiter, as the god of empire, had close ties with the greatness of Rome.[99] The military New Year's celebration consisted in the commanders taking vows for the welfare and safety

---

[98] Especially the *vexillatio Marsacorum* (478; not attested in Britain before Severus Alexander), the *vexillatio Sueborum Longovicianorum* (692; not known in Britain before Gordian III), and the *cuneus Frisiorum* (695–697; not in Britain before Gordian III). Several *numeri* are attested in the British provinces for the first time in the third century: Holder, *Roman Army*, 17–18; see also appendix of garrisons.

[99] Fishwick, *ICLW*, 595–596.

of the state on behalf of their troops and then erecting new altars inscribed with those vows, formal expressions of allegiance.[100] The altars from the previous year were ceremoniously interred.[101]

Some dedications to the imperial *numen* include purely military associations: *signa* (4), *genius legionis* (24), and *genius cohortis* (32). It is surprising that the *numina Augustorum* appear with the *genius* of a unit in so few dedications,[102] but this may simply speak to the arbitrary survival of the evidence.

Soldiers honored the imperial *numina* with Roman gods and heroes: Mars (245, 272, 280). Hercules (315), Mercury (325), the Parcae (347), Silvanus (352b, 353) and Vulcan (374). It is possible that worshippers invoked such gods on behalf of the emperor. Clearly, all gods of the Roman pantheon, especially Mars and Hercules, were thought to have an interest in Rome's military success.

The imperial cult centered primarily on the *numina* and concentrated on homage to the living emperor. Only a few dedications to the *genius* of an emperor survive in Britain (34, 114, 151), although this was the form of worship prescribed in the Dura calendar and for Roman citizens in Italy. The imperial *genius* shared inscribed altars with other deities, for example, Jupiter Optimus Maximus at Caerleon (114) and Old Penrith (151), and the *signa* of *cohors I Vardullorum* and the *numerus Exploratorum Bremeniensium* at High Rochester (34).

---

[100] Fishwick, *ICLW*, 596.

[101] R.E. Smith, *Post-Marian Army*, chapter 3; Petrikovits, "*Sacramentum*," 178–201. The *sacramentum* probably remained unchanged from Republican to Imperial times, as Vegetius implied. These *vota* were originally sworn on January 1, at least until AD 69 (Tacitus *Historiae* 1.5) and were perhaps moved to January 3 during the Flavian dynasty (Fink, Hoey, Snyder, "Feriale," 50–51, 66). The recruits swore the oath in groups as one chosen representative recited the *sacramentum* entire; the others would say one by one, "*idem in me.*" The oath required the troops to serve the emperor and his generals and obey all orders. The *sacramentum* included a declaration of allegiance to the standards (Dion H. 6.45) and was probably sworn in the camp, in the presence of the *signa* and *imagines*. The precise formula has not survived.

One who deserted or acted with disobedience was considered *nefas* and could be punished with death: *Ex mei animi sententia ut ego rem publicam populi Romani non deseram neque alium civem Romanum deserere patiar: si sciens fallo, tum me Iuppiter Optimus Maximus domum familiam remque meam pessimo leto adficiat* (Livy 22.53). Soldiers might have repeated the oath as necessary. Quintus Fabius, for example, ordered his troops to do so when they retreated to their camp without fighting in the wars against the Veii (Livy 2.45). See also Brand, *Roman Military Law*, 91–93, 95, 101.

Pliny (*Epistle* 10.100) indicated that, at least in Bithynia-Pontus, both troops and provincials joined together in this ceremony of allegiance.

[102] Fishwick, "Imperial Cult in Roman Britain," 215.

Extant evidence does not suggest that any particular *divus* received a cult in Britain.[103] This contrasts with other western provinces where votives to *divi*, individual and collective, have surfaced.[104] Furthermore, the cult of the imperial *divi* is richly represented in the *Feriale Duranum* (twenty-one extant entries). One extant exception in Britain, an inscribed statue base (353) clearly honors the *numina* of the *divi*.[105] At Colchester, however, a third century sculpture depicts a figure wearing a radiate crown and mounted on a winged horse. The statue may represent a deified member of the imperial house.[106] Other statues may have existed as well. At Risingham, two statue bases, found outside the cross-hall of the *principia*, were large enough to support life-size statues.[107] Statue bases have also been found near the *aedes* at Brough-by-Bainbridge[108] and at Bewcastle (*CSIR* 1.6.464).[109] A finger from a colossal bronze statue was recovered at Carvoran (*CSIR* 1.6.364). A bronze mace, typical of Hercules' club, surfaced at a Romano-Celtic shrine, Willingham Fen, Cambridgeshire.[110] Rostovtseff suggested that the bust of an emperor, found with the mace, represented Commodus.[111] The bust, because of its wavy hairstyle, bears a closer resemblance to Antinonus Pius.[112] Additionally, a bronze head of Hadrian (Worlington, Cambridgeshire), and a yew-wood female head (Llanio, county Dyfed, Wales) of either Commodus' wife Crispina or Caracalla's wife Plautilla were mounted on scepters and surely used ceremonially. Like the Willingham Fen piece, the other two may also have belonged to Romano-Celtic shrines.[113] Technically votives to gods, these heads were yet another way to show honor to the emperor who could thence participate in local rural festivals.

---

[103] Fishwick, "Imperial Cult in Roman Britain," 213.

[104] Etienne, *Le Culte impériale*, 294–300. Baetica, Lusitania, and Tarraconensis, for example, are particularly rich in such dedications.

[105] Fishwick, *ICLW*, 396: the monument was meant to include the *numen* of the current emperor, though this is not explicit in the text.

[106] Haverfield and Stuart Jones, "Romano-British Sculpture," 137–38.

[107] Richmond, "Redesdale," 110.

[108] Collingwood, "Brough-by-Bainbridge in 1926," 271.

[109] Richmond, Hodgson, and Joseph, "Bewcastle," 208, and fig. 12, 210.

[110] A. Alföldi, "Bronze Mace," 19–22; Fishwick, "Imperial Sceptre Heads," 399.

[111] Rostovtseff, "Commodus-Hercules," 91.

[112] A. Alföldi, "Bronze Mace," 19.

[113] Henig, *Religion*, 73, 138. Compare *imagines* possibly of Octavian and Livia found at the shrine of a god indigenous to Azailia, Spain: Etienne, *Le Culte impérial*, 390, 400; Gimpera, "Katalonien," 580–600; Fishwick, "Imperial Sceptre Heads," 400.

The Cults of Imperial Women

In the third century AD, imperial women enjoyed genuine power and influence in military matters.[114] Severus Alexander's mother Mamaea, as *mater castrorum*,[115] was recognized by the emperor's troops as the real commander (Herodian VI.8.3),[116] and her tight-fisted control over money matters was a cause of discontent.[117] The entry in the *Feriale* for her *dies natalis* is in a mutilated state (ii.26–27), but a papyrus which describes military and civilian celebrations of Severus Alexander's *dies natalis* or *dies imperii* at Syene indicates a close connection between emperor and mother.[118]

In Britain, the living patronesses of the Roman army (Julia Domna, Julia Mamaea, Sabina) were honored.[119] Julia Mamaea was cited on behalf of the emperor's welfare (18) and victory (22), as was Sabinia (147), Gordian III's consort. Both Julia Domna (14–17) and Mamaea (18–22, 618) were recognized as *matres castrorum*, the living patronesses of the army.[120] Julia Domna visited the province with her husband in AD 208–211 (Dio 72.16.5), and British women copied her hairstyle and clothing.[121] It is unlikely that other empresses accompanied

[114] Livia played no part in the Augustan celebration of the *ludi saeculares*. Julia Domna, to the contrary, led the chorus of matrons during the festivities of AD 204. Faustina Minor (d. AD 175), the wife of Marcus Aurelius, was the first woman honored with a military cult during her own lifetime (Dio 72.10.5), having received the title *mater castrorum*: Mattingly, "Consecration," 147–51.

[115] *Mater castrorum* was part of Mamaea's official titulature (*AFA*, ccxvi). Julia Maesa was not officially *mater castrorum* but was addressed as such at Lambaesis (*CIL* VIII 2564). For titles, cults, and votive evidence, see Kettenhofen, *Die syrischen Augustae*, 156–172. Also, Fink, "*Mater Castrorum*," 17–19.

[116] People offered vows for her victory and return just as for the emperor's, and her image appeared in military contexts with that of the emperor on coins: *RIC* IV, ii, 123, #659, and 662; Cohen IV, 482, #9 and #11, 483, #16, 484, nos. 18–19. Of 53 extant dedications to her, 23 are from military contexts (M.G. Williams, *University of Mich. St., Human. Series* I [1904], 94). Additionally, she received the unique distinction of an eponymous cohort of *vigiles*, the VIIth cohort called *Mamiana Seberiana Alexandriniana* (*CIL* VI 3008).

[117] Hönn, *Heliogabalus und Severus Alexander*, 78, note 172.

[118] P. Par. 96. Wilcken, *Phil* 53 (1894), 80–102.

[119] Fishwick, "Imperial Cult in Roman Britain," 223. Such dedications may be nothing more than an opportunity for a bureaucrat to show diplomatic obeisance to the imperial family.

[120] Such invocations may not have been inspired on religious grounds. Dedicators may simply be flattering the imperial house for purely selfish reasons, hoping for promotions or other favors from the crown.

[121] Allason-Jones, *Women*, 50, 135. Artistic evidence supports this conclusion: reliefs, wall paintings. For example, a tombstone from Lincoln shows in relief a woman with her hair arranged in the Syrian style, crimped waves on each side of the face, rolled into a bun at the back of the head (*RIB* 250).

their husbands to this province, since few other emperors, besides Claudius and Hadrian, actually visited the island. Hadrian's wife Sabina, it was rumored, had illicit affairs with the *praefectus praetorii* and others while in Britain (*SHA Hadrian* 11.3). The wives of Clodius Albinus, Carausius, and Magnus Maximus, who declared themselves emperor of Rome from Britain, were never mentioned in British contexts, nor were the female relatives of Constantius, Constantine I, Gratian and Constantine III.[122]

Conclusions

The imperial cult in Britain centered on the living ruling family, emperor and military patroness. Votive offerings to the emperor's *numen* were almost always made in conjunction with other deities, often Jupiter Optimus Maximus or Germano-Celtic gods. This shows the practical Roman spirit: one dedicates to the *numen* of a living authority who can "get things done" and to a divine authority as a backup, or *vice versa*.

The *Feriale Duranum* points both to the realities of officially sanctioned imperial cult in the third century and to its continued importance. Out of forty-one extant entries, twenty-seven are directly related to the cult of the emperor.[123] The *Feriale* was probably expanded as imperial anniversaries, reflecting the growing importance of the imperial cult and the increasingly close relationship between the emperor and army, were added. Imperial occasions honored by the troops at Dura-Europus included the birthday of Germanicus Caesar (ii.12–13), the popular military leader and avenger of the Varian disaster (Tacitus *Annals* 2.73; Suetonius, *Tiberius*, 52.2, *Caligula* 1–7; Dio 57.5, 57.18.1, 6–8), the birthday of one L. Caesar (i.11–12),[124] the anniversary

---

[122] These men probably were married. Magnus Maximus, at any rate, had a son, Victor, proclaimed co-emperor by Magnus: *PLRE* Maximus 39; Victor 6. *PLRE* indicates no wives for Clodius Albinus or Carausius.

[123] Fink, Hoey, Snyder, "Feriale," 173. This tally excludes the *vota* taken on January 3.

[124] Welles, Fink, Gilliam, *Final Report*, 205–206. The entry calls for the sacrifice of an ox either to the *memoria* of a deceased person or to the *genius* of a living man. The person so honored was not deified. This L. Caesar was probably not the grandson and adopted heir of Augustus, whose birthday was not honored after his death (*FD* 74). Hadrian's adopted son, L. Aelius Caesar, was born on the Ides of January (Philocalus' list of *natales Caesarum; FD* 75). The *SHA* (*Alex.* 49.3) identified a L. Caesar as the father-in-law of Severus Alexander (see above, note 13). Although the *FD* usually reserves the sacrifice of an ox for *divi*, L. Seius Caesar seems the

of Severus' victories in the East (i.14–16), the *dies imperii* of Caracalla (i.17–18). Throughout the year, the units offered sacrifices to observe birthdays and accession days of all the deified emperors and their deified consorts, among them eventually Julius Caesar (ii.21), Augustus (iii.8), Claudius (ii.23), Nerva (iii.4–5), Trajan (iii.4–5), Hadrian (i.13), Antoninus Pius (iii.6), Marcus Aurelius (i.21–22; ii.6), and Septimius Severus (ii.3–4).

Was the cult merely an expression of loyalty or genuinely spiritual? Not all invocations to the *numina Augustorum* point to corporate worship and official New Year's observations. Several altars to the *numina Augustorum* and other gods (Roman, Eastern, and local) were erected at personal expense (32, 111, 245, 347, 469, 570, 619) in fulfillment of vows (353, 378, 465, 529, 692, 696, 697), sometimes on behalf of the dedicator and his family (520, 529, 571), often on behalf of the royal family: *pro salute domus divinae*, et sim. (139, 217, 225, 228, 251, 374, 378, 392, 395, 396, 402, 404, 405, 416, 460, 485, 574, 620). It would be easy to dismiss these testimonies as political expressions, as perhaps are references to Eastern gods (394–6, 402, 404), Brigantia (571, 574), and temple restorations (396, 398). Yet some votive altars were probably sincere, crude and inexpensive monuments subsidized at personal expense by enlisted men. Some monuments invoked deities (excluding the *numina*) on the emperor's behalf: *Fortuna Augusta*, for L. Aelius Caesar (78); Dolichenus for Hadrian's welfare (404); Jupiter Dilectus, for Antoninus Pius (115); Mithras, on Caracalla's behalf (422); for Gordian III, Jupiter Optimus Maximus (147), and Jupiter and Vulcan (165). Interestingly, local gods are excluded from the above list; it was perhaps thought that Roman gods or patron deities were more appropriate or powerful enough to intercede on the emperor's behalf. The emperor's *numen* could ally with local gods who may not have possessed the authority (or strength) to protect the emperor. Finally, some of our worshippers may have thought that the emperor (deceased and duly deified), like the gods with whom he shared these inscribed monuments, had real power to answer prayers (n.b., the formula *votum solvit libens merito*).[125]

---

most likely candidate since the calendar was published before Severus Alexander's divorce from Seia, and the man was named Caesar by Severus. The *AFA* for AD 176 offers a parallel for the sacrifice of an ox to the *genius* of a Caesar, e.g., Commodus.

[125] Price, "Gods and Emperors," 89–93; Fishwick, "Prayer and the Living Emperor," 343; C.J. Simpson, "Real Gods," 264–5.

Military Festivals

In the traditional Roman calendar, March, the month of the renewal
and growth of nature, originally the first month in the Roman year,
was dedicated to Mars, the Roman god of war whose influence
extended to agriculture and the protection of the Roman family and
who was second in importance only to Jupiter (Cato *de Agricultura*
142). On the kalends of March, the *Salii*, priests of the war god,
paid tribute to Mars with a ritual war-dance through the city. With
their swords, they beat the *ancilia*, sacred figure-eight shields, as they
danced accompanied by the *carmen saliare*, an archaic hymn unintelligible even to the priests by the late republic.[126] The day's festivities ended with feasting (Horace, *Odes* 1.37.2).[127] On March 9 (*vii Id.
Mart.*), the priests carried the *ancilia* around the city a second time.
An uninscribed bronze from Barkway seems to represent a youthful, dancing Mars.[128] It is tempting to connect this figure to the *Salii*,
dancing priests at Rome who, in their association with a powerful
agricultural deity, heralded the advent of spring.

   Horse races were conducted during the *Equirria* held on February
27 (*iii Kal. Mart.*) in honor of Mars Gradivus on the Campus Martius
(Ovid *Fasti* 2.857–64) and again during the *Equirria* of the 14th of
March (*prid. Id. Mart.*, Ovid *Fasti* 3.517–22).[129] To date, no Roman
racetrack has been found in Britain.

---

[126] Frazer (*Fasti*, 3.65–69) interpreted beating the shields not as preparation for
the campaign season but as an apotropaic attempt to expel evil spirits; he saw the
Salii's dances as an attempt to promote growth by sympathetic magic.
   Scullard (*Festivals*, 84–86) suggested that, because Mars has both military and
agricultural associations, a primitive agricultural ceremony of apotropaic magic may
have been converted to military purposes.
[127] These rites seem to have been observed only in Rome. In 190 BC, for example, the Roman army, at war with Antiochus the Great, was about to cross the
Hellespont. Scipio Africanus, a Salian priest, refused to cross during the *dies religiosi*
while the priests at Rome carried the *ancilia* in procession (Livy 37.33.6).
[128] Henig, *Religion*, 50–51.
[129] The races would be held on the Caelian Hill if the Tiber had over-flown into
the Campus Martius (Ovid *Fasti* 3.521–22).
   Only a small portion of the entry for March 14 in the *Feriale Duranum* (i.27–29)
survives, referring to the *dies imperii* of Severus Alexander. There is no clear evidence in the *feriale* (or in Roman Britain, for that matter) for the celebration of the
Equirria. It may have been pushed out by the *dies imperii* of Severus (Fink, Hoey,
Snyder, "Feriale," 89). The purpose of these races was to exercise the horses in
preparation for the start of the campaign season after a winter's rest; the horses
were also ritually purified, as were the weapons and war trumpets at other ceremonies scheduled for March.

The *Quinquatrus* (*Quinquatria*) began on the 19th of March (*xiv Kal. Apr.*), lasting five days (Varro *LL* 6.14; Festus 304L). The grammarian Charisius understood the festival as derived from a verb meaning "to purify," *quinquare: a quinquando, id est lustrando*,[130] since this festival to Mars consisted in the annual purification of the *arma ancilia*. Varro stated that the *Salii* had to perform a dance in the *comitium* (*LL* 5.85); the *fasti Praenestini* added that this dance was performed in the presence of the *tribuni celerum*, the officers of the Celeres, the cavalry of the earliest Roman army. These men soon lost their military function, but the institution became religious (Dion. H. 2.64.3). The *tribuni celerum* represented the army in this ritual preparation to the campaign season, while the weapons of both the *Salii* and of the entire army were purified.[131] Gladiatorial shows followed for the next three days. The date and the length of the lacuna at ii.1 of the *Feriale Duranum* very likely indicate that it included an entry for the *Quinquatria*.[132]

On March 23 (*x Kal. Apr.*), at the *Tubilustrium* (repeated May 23), the war trumpets (*tubae*) were purified and the *Salii* continued their dances.[133] Ovid implied that in his day the *Tubilustrium* was considered part of the *Quinquatria* (*Fasti* 3.849: *Summa dies e quinque tubas lustrare canoras*). The festival received no independent mention in the *Feriale Duranum*, probably because it became accepted as part of the extended observations of the *Quinquatria*.[134]

In October, a set of festivals complementary to the March ritual cycle included the *Armilustrium* and the October Horse. On October

---

[130] Keil, 1.81.
[131] Scullard, *Festivals*, 95.
[132] Welles, Fink, and Gilliam, *Final Report*, 207: *xiiii Kal(endas) Apriles ob diem quinq[u]a[trio]r[um] suppl[ic]atio in x ka[l(endas) e]asdem supplic[ationes]*.
The temple of Minerva on the Aventine was also dedicated on this day, hence the close association between Minerva and this festival (Wissowa, *Religion*, 253–4). The festival eventually became one dedicated to Minerva exclusively: *Fasti Praenestini, Fasti Farnesiani*, Tacitus *Annals* 14.12.1. Indeed, the *Menologia rustica* reflect the fact that the entire month of March has been transferred from Mars' control to Minerva's: *Tutela Minervae, CIL* I, 280.
[133] Lydus said that the purification of the trumpets and the dances of the *Salii* on this day were in honor of Mars and a goddess who was called Nerio in Sabine (4.60), whereas Aulus Gellius stated that Nerio was *vis et potentia et maiestas quaedam* of the god (13.23). She was gradually personified and became Mars' wife, eventually identified with Minerva; Frazer (*Fasti*, 3.121–25) argued for an early "marriage" between Mars and Nerio. Ovid stated that the *Tubilustrium* was dedicated to the *fortis dea*, i.e., Minerva (*Fasti* 3.850).
[134] Fink, Hoey, Snyder, "Feriale," 97.

15 (*id. Oct.*) a two-horse chariot race was held in the Campus Martius, after which the *flamen Martialis* sacrificed the winning pair's right hand horse to Mars in the Campus Martius. The rite may have had agricultural (Festus 190L) or military significance.[135] Others considered the sacrifice of the October horse an act of purification of the army returning from campaign.[136] On October 19 (*xiv Kal. Nov.*), sacrifices marked the end of the campaign season. Rites included sounding the *tubae* and purifying the *arma* (after contact with blood) and the *ancilia*, which were then put into winter storage. The dances of the *Salii* are not attested for October, but their performance is not an unreasonable assumption.[137]

It is unfortunate that Ovid's *Fasti* for these rites do not survive and that the *Feriale Duranum* for October is in an extremely poor state of preservation.[138] In Britain two inscriptions date to October 19, 241 (#2–3), but the *Salii* and the *Armilustrium* are not indicated. General political unrest may have inspired the troops to look to state cult and purification rites for extra insurance. It is also possible that the *Armilustrium* was conducted only in Rome or that it, like other traditional festivals, fell into disuse during the third century.

The Cult of the Standards

The cultic activity of the army centered around the *signa* of the smaller military units and the *aquila* of the legion which were kept together in the *principia* at the center of the camp.[139] The *aquila* was so closely connected with Roman military success that the eagle con-

---

[135] Fowler, *Festivals*, 241–2, Frazer, *Golden Bough*, 5.2.42, and Rose, *Roman Quest. of Plutarch*, 208, support the agricultural connection of the sacrifice of the October Horse.

[136] Wissowa, *Religion*, 144–5; Scholz, *Marskult*, 164–167.

[137] Scullard, *Festivals*, 195.

[138] Welles, Fink, and Gilliam, *Final Report*, 211–212.

[139] During times of peace in the Republic, the *aquilae* would be kept in the *aerarium* at Rome (Livy 3.69.8). The Republican legions had five standards: eagle, wolf, minotaur, horse, and boar. The eagle became supreme because of its associations with Jupiter (Pliny *NH* 10.5).

The *signa* served to maintain the unity of the *corps* and to keep the fighting line straight during combat: Caesar (*BC* 1.57.1; 3.75.5; 3.84.3) referred to troops fighting in front and behind the standards as *antesignani*: Parker, *Legions*, 38 suggested that it makes more sense for the standards to be in the front ranks: it is easier to look forward than backward for orders. The *antesignani* were probably a lightly armed body of picked men. Equipped as *expediti*, they likely worked with the cavalry and may have replaced the *velites* abolished by Marius (Sallust *Jugurtha* 46, 105).

tributed to the soldier's *esprit de corps* (cf. Caesar, *BG* 4.25; Tacitus *Annals* 2.17). The *aquiliferi*, second in rank to the centurion, were responsible for records and the regimental strong box stored in the *principia* (Vegetius 2.13). *Imaginiferi* carried images of the emperor (Vegetius 2.7), perhaps to remind the army under whose auspices it fought.[140]

The eagle was common to all the legions; but each unit had its own *vexillum*, often in the form of a zodiac sign representing the birthday of the unit, its founder, or of a commander who led the unit in distinguished service. *Legio II Augusta* displayed on its standards the Capricorn (Augustus' zodiac sign), Pegasus, and Mars.[141] The standards of *Legio XX Valeria Victrix* displayed a wild boar.[142] No Romano-British standard has survived.[143]

A *vexillarius* of a detachment corps carried a *vexillum* (a square flag with fringe at the bottom and hanging from a cross bar or lance), the regular standard of all cavalry units, legionary detachments, and special units attached to the legion.[144] A relief in Britain at Benwell

---

[140] Helgeland, "Army Religion," 1476. These *imagines* often included other members of the ruling house: G. Webster, *Roman Imperial Army*, 136. The Syrian legions, for example, were the only ones not to have on their standards portraits of Sejanus, betrothed to Julia Drusi Caes. f. (Zonaras 11.2; Dio 58.7.5). Tiberius provided funds to supply the portraits (Tacitus *Annals* 4.2; Suetonius *Tiberius* 48).

[141] G. Webster, *Roman Imperial Army*, 135–36. Webster suggests that the legion was founded by Augustus, who was born 23 September (Suetonius *Augustus* 5). Keppie, *Second Augustan Legion*, 3–5, argues that this legion, about whose origins no precise information survives, might be identical with the *Legio II Gallica* known at Aurasio (*CIL* XII 1230).

[142] Parker, *Legions*, 271: the significance of the boar, generally taken to represent Quirinus, with regard to *Legio XX Valeria* is unknown. The relief attached to *RIB* 1284 (*vexillatio Leg. XX V.V. fecit*) displays in detail Mars and Hercules to the sides of the inscription; a boar appears underneath.

[143] A prancing bronze horse found in a civilian house outside Vindolanda was once interpreted as a *signum* but now is identified as a cart fitting: Toynbee and Wilkins, "Vindolanda Horse," 245–251.

Evidence for cavalry units at Vindolanda accrues. The *cohors IIII Gallorum eq.* was *equitata*. The *cohors IX Batavorum* were at Vindolanda 97–105. The *equites I Fida Vardullorum* (Tab. Vind. II, #181.13) was stationed at Vindolanda from 105–ca. 120.

[144] Mayer, *Vexillum*. G. Webster, *Roman Imperial Army*, 138–39. The *vexillum* was the most ancient of the military standards, displayed to summon the people of Rome to vote in the *comitia centuriata* or to fulfill military obligations. The commandant displayed this flag over his tent to signal battle. This standard is well represented in literary sources and on coins, gems, and on triumphal, decorative, and funerary reliefs. The square flags, commonly red (Macrobrius *Saturnalia* 1,16,15; Servius *ad Aen.* 8.1; Plutarch *Fab. Max.* 15; Vegetius 2.1.1), are depicted in the artistic sources as plain pieces of cloth mounted on lances topped with a simple lance head.

(*RIB* 1341) shows a crown on the top of the *vexillum* pole, while a relief at Corbridge (*RIB* 1154; *CSIR* 1.1.86) depicts a *vexillum*-pole crowned by a roundel. At Newburn, a building inscription shows an inscribed *vexillum* at the left, a *signum* at the right, and an eagle in the center (*RIB* 2077). Such variations may represent imperial *dona militaria*.[145] Most *vexilla* bore inscriptions, either painted, embroidered, or interwoven, usually indicating the ruling emperor or the unit to which the flag belonged. Both British examples belonged to *Legio II Augusta*.

The loss of the *signa* was a most serious offense. A late source, the mysterious Ruffus,[146] explained that, if the standards were lost, the *signifer* would be chastised and reduced to the lowest rank in his legion, unless he had been wounded in battle.[147] The loss of the *signa* could result in decimation and the disbanding of the legion, as happened after three legions under Varus' command were completely destroyed in AD 9 (Suetonius *Augustus* 23).[148] In AD 66, in Judea, the *legio XII Fulminata* lost its eagle when the commander, Cestius Gallus, placed all the standards together in one fortified camp, as though

---

The only surviving *vexillum*, now in the Hermitage Museum, St. Petersburg, Russia (*quondam* Leningrad) was found in Egypt, a scarlet linen square (measuring 2,500 cm²). Some fringe remains on the lower edge and a hem for the transverse bar on the upper. A gold image of a Victory standing on a globe is detectable. Rostovtzeff, "*Vexillum* and Victory," 92–106, suggested that this flag (plate 4) was awarded to an officer as a decoration of honor and then buried with him or one of his descendants.

[145] Rostovtzeff, "*Vexillum* and Victory," 96. Other examples can be seen on the Columns of Trajan (a statuette of Victory standing on a crown) and Marcus Aurelius (an eagle atop a *vexillum*-pole), and on the painting of a *vexillarius* found at Dura (a gold crown appears below the lance head).

[146] Ruffus, the author of *Leges Militares*, was a military-legal authority whose identity is conjectural. Some, arguing that the authors of *Strategica* and *Leges Militares* were identical, suggested that Ruffus may have been a general or staff officer who served under the Byzantine emperor Maurice (582) to whom is attributed the work on military science entitled *Strategica* (Vári, "mittelgriechischer Taktiker," 84; Krumbacher, *Byzantinischen Litteratur*, 635). Brand (*Military Law*, 136–7) suggested that Ruffus may have been a pre-Justinian military legal authority not recorded by Tribonian, perhaps because Ruffus was "comparatively 'modern'."

[147] *Si bandum (bandum Romani signum bellicum vocant) ab hostibus, absque iusta quadam et manifesta caussa, fuerit interceptum; iubemus, ut ii, quibus custodia bandi credita fuit, castigentur; et ultimi fiant inter eos, qui ipsis subiiciebantur, hoc est, in iis scholis, ad quas referentur. Si vero quosdam ex ipsis pugnantes sauciari contigerit, hi ab eiusmodi poena serventur immunes* (27): Brand, *Military Law*, 156.

[148] *Legiones XVII, XVIII, XIX* apparently had no *cognomina*, and their numbers were never reassigned. For XVIII, *ILS* 2244; for XIX, *ILS* 2268, 2269, and Tacitus *Annals* 1.60.4. No epigraphic record of XVII survives (Webster, *Roman Imperial Army*, 109). Augustus did mount a campaign to recover the lost eagles and avenge the deaths of the soldiers, but not until AD 41 was the last of the three *aquilae* recovered (Tacitus *Annals* 1.3; 2.25,41).

the entire legion were prepared to fight. Four hundred Roman soldiers defended these standards while Gallus withdrew with the bulk
of the unit. The Jewish army, discovering the trick, destroyed the
four hundred soldiers (Suetonius *Vespasian* 4; Josephus *BJ* 2.18.9,
19.9), but in their honor the legion remained active,[149] and their
standards, when returned to Rome, were placed in the temple of
Mars Ultor.[150]

The standards, integral to a legion's identity, were themselves the
objects of cult. Tacitus (*Annals* 2.17.2) talks of the *aquilae* as *propria
legionum numina*. Tertullian exaggerated: *Religio Romanorum tota castren-
sis signa veneratur, signa iurat, signa omnibus deis praeponit. Omnes illi imag-
inum suggestus insignis monilia crucum sunt; siphara illa vexillorum et cantabrorum
stolae crucum sunt* (*Apol.* 18.8); and *signa adorat, signa deierat, signa ipsi
Iovi praefert* (*Ad nationes* 1.12).[151] It is more likely that the cult of the
standards involved respect rather than literal worship.[152] These rituals also contributed to a unit's morale. However, on the occasions
of religious rites, the standards were anointed with oils, decorated
with garlands (Pliny *NH* 13.3.23; Suetonius *Claudius* 13), perhaps
given battle honors and laurel wreaths.[153] The *signa* also received
sacrifices (Josephus *BJ* 6.6; Herodian 4.4.5). It may be impossible
to determine if sacrifices and sanctified altars to the *signa* were purely
honorific,[154] but surely such events were not empty ceremonies. The
signum, although by no means a national emblem, symbolized a legion
or unit, much like a country's flag as an icon for its citizens. These

---

[149] Helgeland, "Army Religion," 1475. The legion remained in Judea until the
end of the Jewish Wars and was eventually transferred to Cappadocia.

[150] In 20 BC, Augustus built on the Capitoline a small round shrine and was
planning a great temple to Mars Ultor to supplant Romulus' shrine to Jupiter
Feretrius which housed the *spolia opima*. Augustus' small shrine temporarily housed
the recovered standards lost by Crassus and Antony (Augustus *Res Gestae* 21; Suetonius
Augustus 29; Taylor, *Divinity*, 172). Coins and reliefs commemorated the event, and
Horace (*Odes* 3.5) and Propertius (4.10) celebrated it (*RIC* 1.146). C.J. Simpson,
"Mars Ultor," 91–94, doubts the existence of this *aedicula*.

[151] Statius *Thebaid* 10.176; Minucius Felix 29.7. Domaszewski, *Religion*, 12–13;
Renel, *Cultes militaires*; Kubitschek, "Signa," 2342–4; Kruse, *Geltung des Kaiserbildes*.
Tertullian (fl. AD 197–200) did not represent the mainstream Christian church,
whose primary objection was to the idolatrous nature of army religion: Helgeland,
"Christians," 733, 735.

[152] Fishwick, "Provincial Ruler Worship," 1253.

[153] G. Webster, *Roman Imperial Army*, 133. Several reliefs of flowers survive in military contexts in Britain: a building dedication shows a floral wreath surrounding
the inscription *Leg II Aug* (*RIB* 1428); similar engravings have been found at Lanchester
(*RIB* 1093), and Risingham (*RIB* 1227).

[154] Hoey, "Rosaliae," 17.

periodic festivals were, perhaps, similar to the American Flag Day or Veterans Day. The *signum* evoked feelings of pride and allegiance to the unit, the Roman army, and the emperor. Just as honoring the national flag is not a daily religious duty, those who do honor such symbols, nonetheless, express sincere national pride.

At the center of the camp in the *principia*, the standards were kept in a special shrine, the *sacellum*, generally built of stone, even in timber forts, as at Kanovium (Caerhun).[155] An eagle and the emperor's *imago* stood at the center, while the standards of each unit of the legion surrounded these objects.[156] The *aerarium*, holding the military funds, pay chest and savings of individual soldiers, was stored underneath the *sacellum*; attempts at robbery would thus be overshadowed by the greater crime of sacrilege.[157]

It is highly probable that the standards occupied a position of importance during all military ceremonies, as they are, for example, displayed prominently on Trajan's Column. Succeeding Domitian whose divine aspirations were perhaps exaggerated, Trajan was eager to display himself as a religious leader rather than divine ruler.[158] In scenes viii, liii, and ciii of Trajan's Column, representing camp *lustrationes*, the standards are depicted clearly at the center of activity.[159] Literary evidence implies that the standards may have been crowned

---

[155] Baillie-Reynolds, *Kanovium*; Nash-Williams, *Wales*, 56–9. That Flavian timber fort was rebuilt in stone in the Antonine period.

[156] It has been taken on faith that the *princeps'* statue stood in the *sacellum*. Re-examination of archaeological features, especially at Vindolanda, brings this supposition under doubt: Bidwell, *Roman Forts*, 67–68.

[157] G. Webster, *Roman Imperial Army*, 194. Vegetius suggested that the soldier, knowing his savings were kept with the standards, would not consider desertion and would fight more vehemently in defense of the *signa* for which he held great affection (2.19).

The *aerarium* at Brecon Gaer consisted of a stone safe sunk into the ground (Nash-Williams, *Roman Frontier in Wales*, 159). The *aerarium* at Segontium (Caernarvon), reached by a flight of steps, measured 3 by 2.5 by 1.5m and held about 114 coins at the time of excavation (G. Webster, *Roman Imperial Army*, 244, note 1). The *aerarium* at Inchtuthil was found at ground level but with part of the *sacellum* "underpinned by a grid of timber:" Richmond, "Roman Britain in 1943," 85. The *aedes* at Cilurnum (Chesters) and Condercum (Benwell) were accessible only by flights of stairs through the *sacellum* itself (A. Johnson, *Roman Forts*, 115).

[158] Ryberg, *Rites*, 109.

[159] Ryberg, *Rites*, 109–113. The standards are, likewise, prominently displayed on the ceremonial scenes depicted on the Column of Marcus Aurelius, erected by Commodus in honor of his father's campaigns on the Danube, and the Arch of Constantine, on which is displayed a short standard in use in the East under Severus (Speidel, "Eagle Bearer," 124–6).

during the *lustrationes* of the camp (Plutarch *Marcellus* 22; Suetonius *Vitellius* 9), before setting out on campaign (Suetonius *Claudius* 13), and during victories and triumphs (Claudian 10.186–8). A standard, depicted with a large medallion bearing an *imago* of the emperor and with three plumes, one upright and two at right angles to the first, was carved into the first century AD tombstone, now in Hexham Abbey, of a *signifer* of the *ala Petriana*, stationed near Corbridge and then at Stanwix, due north of Carlisle (*RIB* 1172).

Some military cultic activity, however, centered strictly around the standards. The *Feriale Duranum* included two entries for festivals called *Rosaliae Signorum*,[160] dating to May 9 and 30 (ii.8, 14).[161] It was perhaps for such festivals that some military documents mention soldiers' contributions *ad signa*.[162] On festival days, the *signa* were cleaned and anointed. Next to the altar in the courtyard of the *praetorium*, the *signa* were grouped together and decorated with crowns of roses.[163] A *supplicatio* followed. Portable *imagines* of the emperor probably received garlands and wreaths on such occasions.[164]

Rosaliae signorum are connected to the cult of the standards, and

---

[160] Civilian *Rosaliae* or *Rosariae* were of two types: those related to the cult of the dead; and those connected to fertility rites (Nilsson, "Rosalia," 1111–1115). The festival was symbolic of seasonal transition, from winter to summer, and these civilian spring rites were mentioned in the *Feriale Capuanum* under the entry for May 13 (*CIL* X 3792: *rosaria ampiteatri*), a calendar from Pisa (*CIL* XI 1436), the calendar of Philocalus for May 23 (*CIL* I, 264: *macellas [sic] rosa(s) sumat*), and by Pliny (*NH* 21.11). By the third century AD, these spring festivals may have been little more than occasions for merry-making, like May Day (Welles, Fink, and Gilliam, *Final Report*, 208). The festival may have been retained because of its popularity.

[161] Hoey, "Rosaliae," 15–16, pointed out that *signorum* depends grammatically on *rosalias*, not *supplicatio*: throughout the calendar a dative follows *supplicatio*. Since the document is a military one, *signa* can refer only to *signa militaria*, not *signa deorum*.

[162] Premerstein, "Ägyptische Legionsabteilung," 12 for *Pap. Genav. Lat.* 1, line 9, which mentions a contribution of four *drachmas* each *ad signa* by soldiers in an Egyptian auxiliary unit: Speidel, "Pay of the Auxilia," 406. A Vindolanda writing tablet records contributions made *ad sacrum* (Bowman "Military Records," 360–73, plate xxx; cf., nos. 33, 47, and 62, lines 1–9; Bowman and Thomas, *Tab. Vind. II*, #190). Since this document seems to have religious connections (ll. 38–9: *ad sacrum | divae*), this money may to have been set aside for religious purposes, perhaps to fund festivals: Bowman and Thomas, *Tab. Vind. II*, 153. The fact that pay deductions were made for ritual meals at the *Saturnalia* (Fink, *Roman Military Records*, 68.ii.8 and iii.7) provides a parallel.

[163] Hoey, "Rosaliae," 18.

[164] The sources are silent. Tacitus, however, mentions garlanding images during the demonstrations of AD 62 and 69: *Effigies* of Agrippina and Nero (*Annals* 5.4.3); *imagines* of Octavia sprinkled with flowers and placed in the *fora* and temples (*Annals* 14.61.1); *imagines* of Otho decked with bay-leaves and flowers and carried around the temples (*Hist.* 2.55).

offering a *supplicatio* to the *signa* is significant.[165] It has been suggested that such festivals may represent anniversaries (*natalis legionis, natalis aquilae,* or *natalis signorum*) or victories.[166] Military *floralia* may have been the army's equivalents of the cult of the dead, that is, a cult of fallen *commilitones*.[167] More likely, the two *rosaliae signorum* may be the military parallel of increasingly popular civilian *Floralia*.[168] These festivals may be closely related to rites of purification and fertility; by extension to the military sphere, the *rosaliae signorum* indicated the fertility (or power) of the standards.[169]

Despite the fact that no epigraphic evidence survives, three reliefs

---

[165] Hoey, "Rosaliae," 19.

[166] *Ibid.,* 19–20. *CIL* II 2552 (*ILS* 9125) and 2553 (*ILS* 9127) for *natale signorum*. By the early third century AD, festivals to *Victoria* enjoyed great popularity and might have taken the form of rose festivals, wherein the crowning of the standards would be an appropriate part of a victory celebration (Roschers Lexicon, 299–300, *victoria*). Numerous third century depictions show Victory crowning the gods of the army (Jupiter Dolichenus and Mithras, Cumont, *MMM*, I, 319), the emperor, and trophies and *aquilae* (Hoey, "Rosaliae," 20, and note 23). A shield from Dura displays two Victories crowning an *aquila*; a graffito from Dura illustrates perhaps the crowning of a *vexillum* at the *rosaliae signorum* (Rostovtzeff, *Città Carovaniere*, 163 and Brown, *Sixth Season*, ch. XIII; for the graffito, Brown, *Seventh and Eighth Seasons*). According to Republican sources, immediately following a victory the general, his lictors with their *fasces*, the soldiers with their weapons, and the *signa* as well would be crowned in the field (Valerius Maximus 1.8.6; Plutarch *Marius* 22, *Pompey* 31.2; Aemilianus 22.1; Pliny, *NH* 15.133). Coins and other artifacts indicate that these were floral and laurel crowns (Plutarch *Sulla* 27.7; Tacitus *Historiae* 2.70; Ovid *Tristia* 4.2.20).

[167] Trajan instituted such a cult in 101, after the battle at Tapae against the Dacians (Dio 68.8.2). Civilian *rosaliae*, however, were never conducted in honor of more than one or two people. The military *rosaliae* would, thus, differ greatly from their civilian counterparts. The cult acts, moreover, centered around the *signa*, symbolic of the divine protection of the legion. On festival days of the dead, only chthonic deities were invited; all other temples remained closed (Ovid, *Fasti* 2.563, 5.485). A *supplicatio* would not be used in a cult of the dead. Military "Totenkult," finally, took a very different form: Hoey, "Rosaliae," 23–25; Cichorius, *Traianssäule*, plate 91, and 3.99.

[168] Hoey, "Rosaliae," 28–29. Fishwick, *ICLW*, 556. *Rosaliae* festivals seem to derive from civilian practices.

[169] G. Webster, *Roman Imperial Army*, 276. Roses were important flowers in civic and private celebrations. This flower and others were displayed prominently as Commodus (Herodian 1.7.3 and 6) and Septimius Severus entered Rome (Dio 75.1.4), and as Caracalla entered Alexandria (Herodian 4.8.8). Roses were important to public processions in honor of the *Magna Mater* (Lucretius 2.624–8; Ovid *Fasti* 4.346), Elagabal (Herodian 5.6.8), Isis (Apuleius 11.6,9,12), and roses may have been sacred to Mithras (Cumont, *MMM*, 1.194, 195, 205; 2.246, pl. 6). The rose also marked the beginning of spring (*cum rosam viderat, tum incipere ver arbitrabantur*: Cicero *2 Verr.* 5.27), e.g., a mosaic from Cirencester shows in one of the corner roundels a standing female figure, half draped, crowned with leaves and flowers and with a bouquet, the attributes of spring (Toynbee, *Art in Britain*, 269).

found at Corbridge may represent the cult of the standards.[170] The
"*rosaliae*" relief displays a tasseled flag inscribed *Vexillus | Leg II Aug.*[171]
The *vexillum* sits atop a long pole with a curved hand grip. One
roundel, now broken off, seems to have surmounted the *vexillum*.
Pilasters frame the ensign. Composite bases support the pilasters
which have five stopped flutings, the angular caps of which are decorated with a stylized rose, rose-leaf, and rose-bud chaplet, preserved
on the left pilaster.[172] Richmond concluded that this relief comprised
the central feature of the decoration for the *domus signorum* of a *vexillatio* of the *Legio II Augusta.*[173] Some indication of movement, absent
from our relief, should accompany a festival scene. The elegant relief
may be simply decorative.

The cult of the standards is represented in Britain (4, 34, 35); #4
was found in a strong-room, directly below where the standards
would have been kept, at Birdoswald. Nos. 4 and 35 connect the
standards and the emperor of Rome (*Genio domini nostri; numini Augusti*) who, above all others, was responsible for the success of the
Roman army.

Military Genii in Roman Britain

An extensive cult,[174] attested from the first to the late fourth centuries AD,[175] every unit and division of the Roman imperial army

---

[170] Richmond, "Corbridge," 162–65.

[171] Richmond, "Corbridge," 163 and plate XB2; *RIB* 1154; *CSIR* 1.1.86. Haverfield,
Forster, Craster, Knowles, and Meek, "Corstopitum, 1907," 266, argued that the
form *vexillus* was accidental. Dio gave evidence of the impurity of the speech of
legionaries whom Severus had posted to the praetorian guard (75.2.6): the legionaries of the third century were generally noted for their poor pronunciation. The *vexillum* represented on this relief resembles the extant Egyptian *vexillum*.

[172] Richmond, "Corbridge," 163. The upper two thirds was preserved in the
Corbridge parish church; the lower third was discovered in 1908.

[173] Richmond, "Corbridge," 164.

[174] Cesano, "Genius," 475.

[175] A bronze tablet, dedicated by the *legio XI Claudia* at Vindonissa (AD 70–101)
records the earliest known dedication to a military *genius: (centuria) Domiti(i)—TODI
Val(erius) Tertius Genio leg(ionis) XI C(laudiae) p(iae) f(idelis) pullum (dedicavit) v(otum) s(olvit)
l(ibens) l(aetus) m(erito)*: Finke, *Neue Inschriften: Römisch-Germanische Kommission*, 1–107,
198–231, #100; *AE* (1926), 69.

For first century military inscriptions: Ankersdorfer, *Religion des römischen Heeres*,
223–226.

An altar at Singidunum in Upper Moesia preserves the latest extant dedication
dating to Diocletian: *Genio leg(ionis) IIII F(laviae) f(elicis) [et] dd(ominorum) nn(ostrorum)
Dioc[let]iani [et Maximiani] Augg(ustorum) [A]urel(ius) Maxim[. . .]ius ex praef(ecto) leg(ionis)
eiusdem votum posu[it]* (*CIL* III 1646 [*ILS* 2292]).

had its own *genius* (*exercitus, legio, ala, cohors, numerus, vexillatio*).[176] Nothing suggests that the cult of the *genius* was ever formally introduced or that the emperor influenced the nature of the cult.[177] Dedications are official and private, referring to all types of units, implying some religious sincerity.[178] Dedications, made by private soldiers and high ranking officers alike, were not restricted to the regimental shrine but have been found in and outside the walls of the camp, in the baths, at the duty stations, and at veteran colonies.[179] Finally, there seems to have been no decline in the cult of the *genius centuriae* among the empire's soldiers.[180] The *genius* is frequently depicted as a youth, nude and beardless, holding a cornucopia and a patera.

The *genii* of both the second legion (24) and the twentieth (28) were honored in Britain. Several altars to the *genius centuriae* have surfaced at Chester (25–27) and Carlisle (31). A few dedications to the *genius* of a cohort have survived (23, 32, 35). Other units whose *genii* received votives in Britain include an *ala* (36) and a *numerus exploratorum* (34). Also honored was the *genius* of the standard-bearer of *legio XX V.V.* (29) and the *genius signorum* (34). Finally, the *genius praetorii* (30, 33, 37, 179) and the *genius praesidii* (587) were also recognized in Roman Britain.

Dedications to the military *genii* in Britain were both official (24, 34–37, 216), made by a commanding officer on behalf of his unit or by the unit collectively, and private (26, 27, 29, 31–33, 179, 587), dedicated by an individual for his own welfare or for the health

---

[176] Domaszewski, *Religion*, 103–2; Durry, *Cohortes*, 314–16, suggested that the *genius cohortium praetoriarum* was a later creation which reflected the decay. Legions and larger divisions, however, had *genii* early on (Speidel and Dimitrova-Milceva, "Cult of the *Genii*," 1544 and note 7).

[177] Speidel and Dimitrova-Milceva, "Cult of the *Genii*," p. 1545; contra Durry, *Cohortes*, 314, and Beaujeu, *Religion romaine*, 164. Nock ("Roman Army," 223) stated that an emperor might have preferences, but in this area the private citizen could follow or not as he saw fit.

[178] Speidel and Dimitrova-Milceva, "Cult of the *Genii*," 1545. *Exercitus; legio* (*ILS* 2290, 2295); *ala*; auxiliary cohort; *numerus; vexillatio* (*CIL* XIII 7943); praetorian cohort; *cohors vigilum; equites singulares Augusti; centuria/turma*.

[179] Domaszewski, *Religion*, 96. We must be careful here since later inhabitants of a site might move small votives (e.g., coins, jewelry, *et sim.*) from the original dedication site.

[180] Speidel and Dimitrova-Milceva, "Cult of the *Genii*," 1546; contra Durry, *Cohortes*, 317, who saw a decline. The extant evidence for the post-Severan period is poor, but the *genius centuriae* received cult as late as AD 245 among the praetorians (*CIL* III 3457, AD 233; *AE* 1905, 242, AD 245), recruited from the legions at this time. The *genius turmae*, a comparable cult observed by the *equites singulares*, is attested for AD 250 (*ILS* 2190).

and good fortune of family and friends. About half of the dedications are exclusive to a single *genius* (23, 25–31, 33, 37). The *genius*
is, likewise, honored with other deities, including the *numina Augustorum*
(24, 32, 216), Jupiter Optimus Maximus (179, 216), the standards
(34), Cocidius (587), and all the other gods (179). Military *genii* were
honored by officers (24, 27, 32–36, 179, 216) and soldiers (587), by
legions (24, 28, 29) and by auxiliaries (32–37, 216).[181] Many of these
votives are securely or plausibly dateable: Hadrian (587), Antoninus
Pius (46?), Marcus Aurelius (32), Severus Alexander (31), Gordian
III (24, 34, 36), Decius (28), Probus (26). The fact that the cult was
so culturally and socially pervasive indicates its universal appeal and
importance. These spirits watched over the troops during their activities, and the soldiers countered with genuine spirituality or simple
superstition, as is well demonstrated by the soldier's willingness to
cultivate the various *genii* at personal expense and by the cult's steadfast longevity through times of war and peace. In addition, soldiers
invoked gods on behalf of the army. Jupiter Optimus Maximus was
called upon for the *vexillationes* of the *legiones XX et VI* (158). Dedicated
about AD 122, the soldiers, or more likely their officers, may have
been concerned with success in building Hadrian's Wall. A *custos
armorum* invoked Hercules and Silvanus on behalf of his *vexillatio* and
himself (305, date unknown). One might assume that the unit was
either about to embark on a hunting trip or to engage the enemy.
The *Matres Communes* were called upon for the welfare of a *decuria*
(498, AD 22/35). Finally, a successful campaign may be indicated
by an altar, dedicated in fulfillment of a vow, to the Germanic
Garmangabis and the *numen* of Gordian III (692).

Deified Abstractions

Augustan attributes and deified abstractions were likewise represented
in military cult. The personified Virtues, of which the imperial *numina*
were specialized examples, stood between the emperor and the gods;
and the cult of Virtues elevated the emperor's status above that of
ordinary men.[182] These Virtues,[183] including *Virtus, Victoria, Discipulina,*

---

[181] Surviving stone dedications were sponsored primarily by wealthier officers who
could afford costlier votives.
[182] For discussions of the imperial virtues, see, M.P. Charlesworth, "Virtues;"
Wallace-Hadrill, "Emperor;" Fears, "Virtues;" Fishwick, *ICLW*, 455–474.
[183] Some find the terms "abstraction" and "personification" as descriptions of the

and *Fortuna*, were closely connected with the success of the empire through the *princeps*, hence closely aligned with the cult of the emperor. The quality of Victory or Virtue became understood as the effect of that quality. *Fortuna*, for example, brought about good luck. Whatever granted favor to mankind was eventually regarded as divine: *Fides, Mens, Virtus, Honos, Ops, Salus, Concordia, Libertas*, and *Victoria*. The power inherent in these abstractions implied divine governance (Cicero, *ND* 2.60–62).

The Roman cult of deified abstractions had Hellenistic origins (e.g., *Nike, Tyche, Eirene*) in the development of a philosophy of kingship which emphasized god-like qualities of a ruler whose actions ensured a prosperous and victorious state; an emperor derived his power as much from arms as from subjects who believed that the man possessed the right qualities and divine backing for the job; by securing his subjects' honor and trust, the *princeps* fortified his position.[184] According to tradition, in 367 BC Camillus vowed a temple to *Concordia*, thereby establishing a precedent for this new breed of state gods (Plutarch, *Camillus* 42).

Many of the imperial Virtues worshipped in Republican times originated as *vota* made in war: e.g., Q. Fabius Maximus' vowed a temple to *Honos* (Cicero *ND* 2.61) in 233 BC during battle with the Ligurians. The Roman Virtues were formalized under Augustus. The Senate commemorated Augustus' "restoration" of the Republic by placing in the *curia* a shield, supported by two *Victoriae*, in honor of Augustus' *Virtus, Clementia, Iustitia*, and *Pietas* (Augustus *Res Gestae* 34).[185] When Augustus returned from Syria, the Senate dedicated an altar to *Fortuna Redux* (Augustus *Res Gestae* 11). In commemoration of Augustus' return from campaigning in the west, the altar to the *Pax*

cult of imperial virtues imprecise and inaccurate: Fears, "Virtues," 830–32; Fishwick, *ICLW*, 459. Personification, rather broad in meaning, is a modern usage derived from *prosopopöie*, the giving of an actor's mask to a fictitious character (Cicero *Orat.* 3.205). Abstraction is another modern term which makes little sense in Roman usage. The Roman had a concrete conception of divinity. Fears suggested that better terms would be the Ciceronian *pragmata* and *utilitas*, in English "Virtue" whose archaic meaning emphasizes "the power or operative influence inherent in a supernatural being."

[184] M.P. Charlesworth, "Virtues," 105; Fears, "Virtues," 850; Wallace-Hadrill, "Emperor," 299; Lendon, *Honour*, 10, 160–172.

[185] Wallace-Hadrill, "Emperor," 300–307. That four virtues are named is philosophically significant; moral philosophers cite four cardinal virtues: bravery, temperance, justice, wisdom (Plato, Rep. iv.428A), not identical with the virtues listed on Augustus' shield.

Augusta was erected (Augustus *Res Gestae* 12). Reliefs on this altar show the epiphany of *Pax, Felicitas, Concordia,* and *Pietas,* symbolic of Augustus' restoration of order in the Roman world.[186]

The imperial Virtues were heavily exploited for propaganda value,[187] but they signified more. As the cult of abstractions developed, these divinities became personalized, attached to a particular politician rather than to the Roman people *in toto*.[188] The ideology of imperial abstractions enhanced an emperor's charisma, which in turn solidified his *auctoritas*. The cult of Virtues came to represent the actuality of an emperor's actions.[189] The imperial abstractions eventually made their way into honorific and official titles.[190] The abstractions also served to enhance the reputations of imperial ladies.[191] Pliny drew heavily on the imagery of the imperial Virtues in his sycophantic *Panegyric* to Trajan, especially with Trajan's arrival at Rome marking the restoration of *Concordia* (*Panegyric* 7–11), and the epiphany of *Libertas* (*Panegyric* 24.5). Nerva's adoption of Trajan secured the foundation of the Virtues for the *res publica: Libertas et Salus et*

---

[186] Toynbee, "Ara Pacis," 81; Fears, "Victory," 806, n. 330.

[187] M.P. Charlesworth, "Virtues," 105–133; Wallace-Hadrill, "Emperor," 307–317, 323 for emperors and the frequency with which certain virtues were exploited; Béranger, "idéologique," 169–217; Fears, "Virtues;" Mannsperger, "ROM ET AUG," 919–996.

[188] Fears, "Virtues," 875–888; Fishwick, *ICLW*, 456–459. An administration could thus set its own tone. Tiberius' reign, for example, symbolized *Clementia* and *Moderatio*: Downey, "Tiberiana," 98–105; Levick, "Mercy and Moderation," 123–137; the hallmark of Claudius' reign was *Constantia*: Fears, "Virtues," 894; Mannsperger, 951–954.

[189] When Vitellius tried to abdicate, he offered his dagger to the consuls who refused it; the *princeps* then proceeded to lay the dagger in the temple of *Concordia*, until one from the crowd shouted *tu es Concordia; tu es Libertas; tu es Abundantia* (Suetonius *Vitellius*, 15).

[190] Official imperial titles began as legalistic terms (e.g., *tribunicia potestas*) but developed to include honorific terms. The titles "Augustus" and "pater patriae" are terms of veneration rather than terms of function or office: Fishwick, *ICLW*, 85–87; A. Alföldi, "Review of Gesche," 79–88. Trajan, as Jupiter's vice regent on earth, received the titles "Optimus" and "Maximus" which clearly linked him and his rule to Jupiter: Fears, "Jupiter," 80–85, "Virtues," 879. Nerva occasionally acquired the title "Piissimus:" Instinsky, "Kaiser," 348, n. 1; Charlesworth, "Virtues," 113–114. Commodus appropriated the title "Felix," which, along with "Pius" and "Fortissimus" was applied to almost every subsequent emperor. Likewise, *Pius, Felix,* and *Invictus* became part of the regular official imperial titulature in the third century: Erkell, *Augustus*, 115–119; A. Alföldi, *monarchische Repräsentation*, 206–209; Instinsky, "Kaiser," 349; M.P. Charlesworth, "Pietas and Victory," 1; Wienstock, "Victor," 242–246; Mastino, *Titolature, passim*.

[191] Trajan's coinage issued on behalf of the women of his court emphasized traditional Roman ideals of womanhood, *Vesta, Fides, Pietas,* "virtues of the home, hearth, religion, and children:" Fantham *et al., Women,* 351.

Securitas fundabatur (*Panegyric* 8.1). Likewise, the iconography on the
arch at Beneventum reveals Trajan as the epitome of imperial *moderatio*. On the right side of the relief, the *princeps*, on foot, waits for
the *praefectus urbi* to invite him before he enters Rome, while on the
left side, the *genius senatus*, *genius populi Romani*, and *genius ordinis equestris*
await the new *princeps*.[192]

Cults of the imperial Virtues at Rome were as important as the
Capitoline triad. The Arval Brethren, accordingly, invoked the imperial Virtues as frequently as they called upon Jupiter, Juno, and
Minerva; when Claudius accepted the title *pater patriae*, sacrifices were
made to Jupiter, Juno, Minerva, *Felicitas*, *Divus Augustus*, and *Diva
Augusta*.[193] *Providentia*, *Aeternitas Imperii*, and *Honos* received thanksgiv-
ings for the detection of a conspiracy against Nero.[194] There was, in
fact, little difference in cultic observance: heifers were sacrificed to
the Virtues, as to Juno and Minerva, on important state occasions.
Sacrifices *pro salute et reditu et victoria* of Trajan were offered to the
Capitoline Triad, Jupiter *Victor*, *Salus rei publicae populi Romani Quiritium*,
Mars *Pater*, Mars *Victor*, *Victoria*, *Fortuna Redux*, Vesta *Mater*, Neptune
Pater, and Hercules *Victor*.[195]

In Britain, as at Rome, the imperial Virtues were closely connected with the cult of the emperor. *Virtus*, a bare-breasted Amazon
dressed in tunic and helmet, appears as *Virtus Augusta* at Maryport
(107) and Duntocher (109). At Chesters, a monumental relief cites
Virtus Augusti (108). An inscription from Bath implies a temple to
Virtus and the *numen Augusti* (106). This *locus religiosus* was restored
after it was insolently desecrated, perhaps during the political and
military confusion of the third century.

Victoria, an important deity of the state (as the *Feriale* indicates),
associated with the annual *vota* and frequently invoked for the emperor's
welfare, was understandably popular in soldiers' dedications. In 295
BC, Q. Fabius Maximus Rullianus vowed a temple to Jupiter *Victor*
in thanksgiving for his victory at Sentinum (Livy 10.29.14). In the
following year, L. Postumius Megellus dedicated the first temple to
Victory at Rome on the Palatine (Livy 10.33.9). Victory, a logical
imperial attribute, was a prerequisite to strong government[196] and a

---

[192] Fears, "Jupiter," 83, n. 409; Lorenz, *Leben*; Andreae, "Triumphfries," 325–9.
[193] *AFA*, 73.
[194] *AFA*, 121.
[195] *AFA*, 124.
[196] Henig, *Religion*, 77.

personification associated with the emperor, especially on the day of his ascension.[197] As an epithet, it was a banner of pride for *legio VI Victrix* and *legio XX Valeria Victrix*. *Victoria* was personified as a winged maiden—standing on a globe, holding a wreath and a palm branch—and dedications to her were restricted to larger military forts: Maryport, Corbridge, Chesters, Castlesteads, and Birrens.[198]

Victoria often appeared with the Roman god of war along the Hadrianic (249, 253, 271, 272, 276) and Antonine frontiers (281, 283). The Scottish votives seem datable to the Antonine occupation, but the pieces from the Hadrianic *limes* are not securely datable. Mars himself procured the epithet "Victor" (263–265, 267, 274), and Venus in Britain was depicted as *Victrix*.[199]

Victoria was invoked, as well, as *Augusta* (95–97, 99, 102–104, 281). The epithet suggests an intimate tie to the imperial house. *Victoria Augusti* attended particular emperors, and she personified victories of individual rulers.[200] Most of these stones read *Victoria Aug*, and it is a point of debate whether to expand the stones *Victoria Augusta* or

---

[197] Domaszewski, *Religion*, 37.

[198] Fishwick, "Imperial Cult in Roman Britain," 219.

[199] Venus *Victrix* appears at Caerleon (Henig, *Corpus*, #280, ca. AD 125, Venus holds a helmet; #279, 3rd century, she holds a palm of victory and a helmet), Llansadwrn (Henig, *Corpus*, #281, the goddess holds a helm, a shield in the foreground), South Shields (Henig, *Corpus*, #282, late 2nd century, shield and helmet characterize the goddess as *Victrix*), Vindolanda (Henig, *Corpus*, #App. 132, ca. AD 270, Venus rests her left elbow on a column and holds a helmet in her right hand, a shield at her feet), Dumfreisshire (Henig, *Corpus*, #283, 2nd century), Inveresk (Henig, *Corpus*, #App. 56, 2nd century, her left elbow rests on a column; the goddess holds a spear in her left hand, a plumed helmet in her right, a shield at her feet), and London (Henig, *Corpus*, #M6, fourteenth century type ring).

[200] Fishwick, *ICLW*, 466–467; Nock, "*Comes*," 114 and note 105. Under the late Republic, a statuette of Victory would precede an *imperator* (A. Alföldi, "Review of Gesche," 240). Furthermore, inscriptions attest multiple Victories when more than one Augustus held power (*SHA Sev.* 22.3: three plaster Victoriolae inscribed with the names of Severus and his two sons; *CIL* 8 25836 [*ILS* 8926]; *CIL* 8 5290 [*ILS* 5477]; *CIL* 8 25371 [*ILS* 5472]; *CIL* 8 4764 [*ILS* 644].

See Ovid, *Tristia* 2.169–176, who portrays her as the emperor's *comes* who remains close by the commander through whom the emperor does battle:

Sic adsueta tuis semper Victoria castris,
  Nunc quoque se praestat notaque signa petat,
Ausoniumque ducem solitis circumvolet alis,
  Ponat et in nitida laurea serta comis
Per quem bella geris, cuius nunc corpore pugnas
  Auspicium cui das grande deosque, tuos,
Dimidioque tui praesens es et aspicis urbem,
  Dimidio procul es saevaque bella geris.

Victoria Augusti.[201] The question remains whether *Victoria Augusta* and *Victoria Augusti* are identical or have different connotations.[202] Some argue that genitive and adjective have the same meaning.[203] Others suggest that the genitive *Augusti* refers strictly to Victory as a quality of the emperor himself and that the adjective *Augusta*, in a more general way, relates the personification to the imperial system.[204] Two British examples clearly indicate a genitive use by the reduplication of key letters in the inscriptions: 97 (DD NN), 102 (Augg). At any rate, the distinction is a subtle one, semantically and theologically, unlikely in the minds of most worshippers.

Nonetheless, both the genitive *Augusti* and the adjective *Augusta* emphasize the close connection between Victoria and the emperor. The epithet *Augusta* signifies both Victory belonging to the emperor and Victory consecrated and imbued with a *numen*.[205] *Augusta*, frequently added as a stock epithet, became a means by which Victory (or other imperial abstractions) could be invoked for the emperor's protection, as his *comes*.[206] Furthermore, Victoria was called *Victrix* (225) *pro salute imperatoris*. On occasion, a worshipper would invoke

---

[201] Both uses are attested epigraphically; note catalogue #102 where *Victoria Augg* must refer to Victoria Augustorum.

[202] The usages *Victoria Augusta* (or *Pax Augusta*) and *Victoria Augusti* are paralleled and probably inspired by the archaic religious nomenclature: Janus Quirini, Janus Quirinus: Altheim, "Altitalische Götternamen," 163; Kerényi, "Altitalische Götterverbindungen," 18. See also, Fishwick, *ICLW*, 446.

[203] Gagè "Victoria Augusti," 3, n. 3; Latte, *Römische Religionsgeschichte*, 394, n. 1; Schultze, *lateinischen Eigennamen*, 510–11; Nock, "Studies in the Graeco-Roman Beliefs of the Empire," 92–3.

[204] Mattingly, *Coinage*, 160; Also Otto, "Fortuna," 37; Fears, "Virtues," 887, n. 284. Mattingly suggests further that the average Roman and the imperial propagandists did not perceive a difference between the adjectival and genitival use.

The epithet *Augustus* was, additionally, applied to a variety of gods, Roman and non-Roman, local and imported. Roman gods include Jupiter (121), Minerva (110), Mars (256, 277), Hercules (317), and the local spring nymph Coventina (448, 449). Many agree that divine qualifications serve to help define a god's sphere of influence: Radke, *Götter Altitaliens*, 10–12, 24–38; Fears, "Virtues," 886–889; Fishwick, *ICLW*, 447, 462–465. Styling a god "Augustus" would link that deity to the emperor. However, Republican examples of the epithet exist (e.g. *CIL* V 4087: Augustis Laribus, Betriacum, 59 BC) in which the epithet simply implies "sacrosanct." Presumably Augustus picked up the term from earlier usage.

[205] Fears, "Virtues," 888.

[206] Fishwick, *ICLW*, 449, 465. Lucan, *Pharsalia*, 5.510: *Fortuna comes*. Beyond literary references (Ovid, *Tristia* 2.169–176), the epithet *comes* is surprisingly rare for *Victoria*, in particular. It is limited to coin issues of the emperors of Gaul, Postumus (*RIC* 5.2, 355), Victorinus (*RIC* 5.2, 395–96), and Tetricus I (*RIC* 5.2, 403, 407, 413), and II (*RIC* 5.2, 421). Carausius (*RIC* 5.2, 465, 481–2, 502, 527) and Allectus (*RIC* 5.2, 558), emperors in Britain, also used the image of *comes Victoria* on their coins: Fishwick, *ICLW*, 467; Nock "*Comes*," 102, note 3.

a member of the Roman pantheon on behalf of the Victory of a reigning emperor (22, 165).

Victory was closely associated with Roman success in war (eight dedications to her include Mars). Eight dedications (of twenty) were made to *Victoria Augusta/Augusti* emphasizing her tie to the imperial house. Victory was cited only four times without overt association to the cult of the emperor or Mars: the Victory of the legion (94), Victory and Peace (100), and *Dea Victoria* (98, 101).

Discipulina, a prerequisite of Victory, was the greatest virtue of the Roman army and the "empire's strongest bond" (Val. Max. 2.7). Dedications to *Disciplina* (alternatively spelled *Discipulina* in Britain) are common only in Africa, Mauretania, and Britain. These three provinces, at least from the Severan point of view, exhibited questionable loyalty: all had supported the British governor Clodius Albinus against Septimius Severus.[207] Consequently, the Severi vehemently emphasized military discipline, as attested in Africa: *vindex et conditor Romanae disciplinae* (*ILS* 446, cf. *CIL* VIII 9832, 10657). Hadrian, who reformed army discipline and abolished certain excesses (*SHA Hadrian* 10), may have been responsible for the creation of a cult to *Disciplina*.[208] The earliest known dedication to *Disciplina* is from Britain and dates to reign of that emperor (50).[209]

Dedications to Discipline in Britain usually refer to the Discipline of an emperor: Hadrian (50), Antoninus Pius (56, 57), the Severi (52, 55a), Caracalla (55b). This list is, *per se*, interesting since each emperor was active in Britain: their programs included military campaigns or the building and refortification of *limes*. Only one reference to Discipline lacks the qualification *Augusti/Augustorum*—a fragmentary altar from Aesica (54), now lost, which may very well have cited an emperor.

Imperial Virtues with a more general application were also represented in military dedications in Roman Britain. Prominent among these is *Fortuna*, well represented in Britain in inscriptions, statues, coins, and gems, and especially in the bath houses where men, at their most vulnerable when naked, engaging in gambling, were

---

Comes is, furthermore, not a common appellation for other abstractions: Fishwick, *ICLW*, 465–72; Fears, "Virtues," 929.

[207] Richmond, *Roman Britain*, 166–67.

[208] Domaszewski, *Religion*, 44; Henig, *Religion*, 77. *Disciplina* first appears on coins late in Hadrian's reign.

[209] The cult is attested on late Hadrianic coins (E. Birley, "Religion of the Roman Army," 1513–15).

particularly susceptible to mishap or especially interested in Fortuna's favor during games of chance.[210] The cult originated in Hellenistic times[211] when the fate of the individual was first considered significant. *Fortuna*'s familiar attributes include the cornucopia and rudder by which Fate is steered, symbolic of steering the Ship of State. The distinction between imperial fortune and the fortune of the individual was not absolute; ideally, the emperor's good fortune was the good fortune of his people as well.[212] Consequently, *Fortuna Augusta* emphasized the prosperity and success of the state and its people rather than the imperial connection.[213]

Fortuna was not as intimately associated with the cult of the emperor as were other deified abstractions.[214] Augustan Fortune is attested (59, 70, 72, 78), as is *Fortuna Populi Romani* (76). The *dea Fortuna* is invoked with the *numina Augustorum* (86) and with her consort *Bonus Eventus* (61, 63). Most dedications to Fortune invoke the goddess without further qualification (or to *Dea Fortuna*). The evidence is primarily military (60, 62, 64, 65, 67, 69–71, 74, 76–79, 81, 82, 84, 85) and largely associated with the fort bath-house (60–65, 67, 70, 71, 75–78, 84, 85, 88, 89, 92).

Fortuna, *Bonus Eventus* (61, 63), *Concors* (48–49), and *Felicitas* (58), generally cited without reference to the imperial house, emphasized good luck for the dedicator rather than emperor or empire.

Gods of the Roman State

The gods and heroes of the Graeco-Roman pantheon are found in Britain with their usual attributes and seem to have been closely related either to the imperial cult or have been assimilated into Celtic,

---

[210] A number of curse tablets offered to Sulis Minerva at Bath are concerned with the theft of some article of clothing: particularly Tomlin in Cunliffe, *Sacred Spring*, curse tablet 32, which cites the theft of a cloak and bathing tunic: *paxsa(m) ba(ln)earem et [pal]leum*; curse tablet 63, theft of a bathing tunic: *balniarem*; #10, a hooded cloak: *caracellam*; #43, *p]alliu[m]*; #61 *mafortium*; #62, *la[nenam | pa]lleum sagum*; #64, *pallium*, #65, *caracallam*. At the Uley shrine, only one curse tablet discovered to date mentions the theft of clothing: Tomlin in Woodward and Leach, *Uley Shrines*, 116.
[211] D.B. Thompson, *Ptolemaic Oinochoai*. *Tuche* appears on numerous faience jugs which comprised votives to deified queens of Ptolemaic Egypt.
[212] Henig, *Religion*, 78.
[213] Richmond, *Roman Britain*, 205.
[214] Fishwick, *ICLW*, 466, 471. *Felicitas* more often accompanied the emperor. Both brought good luck to the *princeps*.

Germanic, or Eastern religions. The state gods, especially the Capitoline triad, held a formal and official place in imperial religion.
Jupiter Optimus Maximus, Juno, Minerva, and Mars were well represented in the *Feriale Duranum*, receiving sacrifices on January 3 for
the annual *vota* (i.2–6), January 7 for honorable discharge and payment of salaries (i.7–9), and March 13 for Severus Alexander's accession (i.23–26). The cults of the Capitoline triad and of Jupiter Optimus
Maximus, in particular, were especially connected with the welfare
of the Roman state.

Jupiter

According to tradition, the Tarquin dynasty built the temple to Jupiter
Optimus Maximus, and M. Horatius dedicated it during the first
year of the Republic (Cicero *Rep.* 2.24.44; *Verr.* 5.19.48; Livy 1.38.7,
55.1; Pliny *NH* 3.5.70; Tacitus *Historiae* 3.72).[215]

Jupiter, the king of gods and men, the one who bestowed justice
to mankind, was regarded as the basis for *imperium* and came to be
associated with the emperors of Rome, and, in that regard, was frequently mentioned in Augustan panegyric (Horace *Odes* 1.12.49–60).
Jupiter, or rather Zeus, was the traditional patron of kings in the
literary tradition. According to Hesiod, "Kings come from Zeus"
(*Theogony* 94–6). Zeus, granting kingship to Agamemnon, bestowed
the scepter, the symbol of royal power, the right to exact justice
over his subjects (Homer *Iliad* 2.203–6) and the right, to Agamemnon
alone, to lead the Achaean army (*Iliad* 2.100–8). The theme was
echoed in Pindar (*Nem.* 4.67; *Pyth.* 4.105, 5.12), Aeschylus (*Agam.* 42;
Eum. 625; *Pers.* 762), and Sophocles (*Philoc.* 135–43). Zeus played a
prominent role in the royal ideology of the Hellenistic period; the
connection between Zeus and his chosen kings was a common *topos*
in Hellenistic panegyric (Callimachus *Zeus* 73–4; Theocritus *Idyll*
17.71–5). Alexander was also portrayed as Zeus (Callisthenes *FGrHist*
124 #F 14a; Pliny *NH* 35.92; Plutarch *Alex.* 4.2, *de fort. Alex.* 2.2).

Under Nero, Jupiter appeared prominently on imperial coin issues:

---

[215] Coulanges, *Cité Antique*; Fears, "Jupiter," 11 and note 7. Peisistratus and the
cult of Athena at Athens parallel, in political context, the rule of the Tarquins and
Servius: seizure of power (Peisistratus: Herodotus 1.59–64; Aristotle *Ath. Pol.* 13–6;
Tarquinius Priscus: Livy 1.34–5, 41–42; Servius Tullius: Livy 1.41.3; Dion H. 4.4.2),
violent overthrow (Herodotus 5.55–65; Thucydides 6.54–9; Aristotle *Ath. Pol.* 18–19;
Livy 1.57–60), and an attempt to return to power with foreign aid (Herodotus
6.107; Livy 2.6, 10).

the protection of the emperor resulted in the preservation of Rome
herself. Inspired by his uncle Gaius, Nero assumed his princely power
derived directly from Jupiter.[216] Gaius had called himself "Optimus
Maximus Caesar" (Suetonius *Gaius* 60), while others called him "Jupiter"
and "Olympios" (Dio 59.26) and, in the East, "Zeus Epiphanes
Neos Gaios" (Philo *Leg. ad Gai.* 43.346, 29.188; Josephus *AJ* 19.1.4,
19.2.11). With the political upheavals of 68/69 came added importance to divine sanction of the imperial system.[217] Jupiter appeared
on civil war coins which, frequently lacking an imperial image,
honored Jupiter as *Optimus Maximus, Capitolinus, Liberator,* and *Custos,*
invoking him as the protector and liberator of the Roman people.[218]
Vespasian and Titus, like Nero, viewed Jupiter as closely linked
to the emperor. The Flavians displayed on their coins Jupiter, offering
a sacrifice from a *patera.*[219] Domitian honored Jupiter as the supreme
god. In contemporary literature, the emperor was represented as
subsuming his power from Jupiter (Statius *Silvae* 4.3.128–9); in defeat-
ing the Chatti, he fought a *bellum Iovis* (Statius *Silvae* 1.1.79). Pliny
portrayed Trajan as elected by Jupiter (*Pan.* 52.6), while Hadrian
used imperial coinage to portray his investiture by that god[220] invoked
as the agent responsible for earthly stability.[221] Septimius Severus also
imbued legitimacy and authority to his own reign by suggesting his
election as Jupiter's warrior vice-regent on earth.[222] At Rome, one
sees the assimilation of emperor to Jupiter.[223]

The connection between Jupiter and the imperial cult is clear in
Britain where the god was invoked in civilian and military cult, with
and without epithets. Several military inscriptions cite Jupiter Optimus
Maximus with the *numen Augusti/numina Augustorum* (111, 122, 131,
132, 150, 166, 173–77, 193, 212, 216). Further emphasizing Jupiter's
close imperial associations, Jupiter Optimus Maximus was honored

---

[216] Fears, "Jupiter," 71.
[217] Fears, "Jupiter," 74.
[218] *BMC* I, 294–5.
[219] *BMC* II, 49, nos. 276–9; p. 53 nos. 305–9. The type stems from Neronian
issues bearing the legend IUPITER CUSTOS. In both Neronian and Flavian contexts, Jupiter is seen as *custos Augusti*: Fears, "Jupiter," 76.
[220] Fears, "Jupiter," 86. *BMC* III nos. 1203, 1236.
[221] *BMC* III, 438, 442, 444. Fears "Jupiter," 86–87, note 423.
[222] After his victory over Pescennius Niger, Septimius issued *aurei* which showed
the emperor in military dress, standing at Jupiter's height, clasping hands with the
god: P.V. Hill, "Coinage," 16, #74. After 194, the house of Septimius showed
Jupiter as *conservator* of the house: Fishwick, *ICLW,* 337.
[223] Fears, "Jupiter," 97. The ruler in the East is assimilated to Zeus.

on behalf of the emperor's welfare: uncertain (148, 165); Antoninus Pius (139, 142, 225); M. Aurelius and L. Verus (115); Septimius Severus and Caracalla (146); Gordian III (147, 149); Trebonianus Gallus and Volusianus (217).

Jupiter was also cited with various *genii*, including the collective *genius* of Marcus Aurelius and Commodus (114), and the Philippi (151), the *genius loci* (119, 172, 213), the *genius* and the *di custodes* (180), and the *genius praetori* with *ceterique di immortales* (179). Jupiter's other associations included *di deaeque* at York (116), Vulcan at Old Carlisle (149), *Matres Ollototae* at Binchester (154), and Cocidius at Housesteads (172). Cocidius' worship was prominent in the northern military zone but the *Ollototae* (the goddesses of the other folk) are known positively only at Binchester (489, 490). The epithet is vague, providing opportunity to Romans to "hedge their bets;" and the goddesses are obscure, though perhaps more consequential than the surviving evidence attests. These local connections might underscore a Roman attempt to ally Roman with native gods, who, by association with Jupiter, were brought into the Roman pantheon.

Jupiter Optimus Maximus alone received numerous official dedications from military units in Britain. Many of these were probably dedicated during the annual New Year's celebrations, (especially 121–143, Maryport; 144–149, Old Carlisle; 170–178, Housesteads; 185–207, Birdoswald; and 208–214, Castlesteads). The altars were likely associated with the *vota*, but they may not have been propitiatory. The language—e.g., the formulaic *v(otum) s(olvit) l(ibens) m(erito)*—strongly suggests personal (individual and corporate) rather than official worship.[224]

Within the military areas in Roman Britain, Jupiter was strongly associated with the imperial household and the "official" state cult. Most dedications to Jupiter were made by a commanding officer (prefect: 115, 116, 134–136, 139–142, 163, 164, 179; tribune: 125–127, 131–133, 217; *primus pilus*: 114; *princeps cohortis*: 119; centurion: 121, 222, 225; *ordinatus*: 156) on behalf of his unit or collectively (cohort:

---

[224] Mann, "Maryport Altars," 90–91. The condition of the altars buried at Maryport suggests that the items were inhumed hastily, laid diagonally, capitals broken off. Furthermore, the earlier altars were buried above the later ones. The archaeology does not suggest annual internment. The altars were probably buried during some military crisis of the late second or early third century or during a reorganization of the fort or to save the altars from use as whetstones: P.R. Hill, "Maryport Altars," 100–103, and 104 note 48.

120, 122–4, 128–130, 137, 138, 151–53, 157, 162, 173–75, 180, 181, 184–212, 215, 218, 219, 223, 224; *ala*: 144, 145, 147, 155; *numerus*: 150, 216; *vexilliatio*: 159, 160, 221; legionary century: 121, 153, 222; *milites*: 171, 172). In accord with *interpretatio Romana*, Jupiter has Eastern associations as well: Dolichenus (393–412); Heliopolitanus (413).

In addition to the epigraphic evidence, several engraved gems from Romano-British sites depict the classical Roman Jupiter standing, holding a scepter, the symbol of kingly rule, in one hand, a patera or thunderbolt in the other, or seated on a throne and holding a scepter in one hand and a patera or victoriola in the other; on other gems, the deity is seen with his eagle. Many of these gems were discovered at military sites and probably belonged to soldiers.[225]

Religious devotion to Jupiter Optimus Maximus was sincere, and private votives to him throughout the empire out-number those to other gods.[226] One cannot dismiss such numerous dedications as mere expressions of loyalty to Rome and Emperor,[227] as religious feeling and patriotism were not necessarily exclusive of each other, given the theocratic nature of the Roman state and the divine sanction of the emperor. In official dedications, he was likely to be called *conservator, defensor et tutor*, and *depulsor*, but in personal dedications he was *Optimus Maximus*, and it was with Jupiter Optimus Maximus that the Roman pantheon was most frequently associated with native Germano-Celtic and Eastern deities.[228] Jupiter worship extended well into the fourth century, and late antique monuments indicate real love and devotion in the service of Jupiter.[229] This can be proved, in Britain, on the strength of inscribed altars: 120, 147, 149–151, 162–164, 175–181, 185–194, 196b–213, 215–7 are securely datable to the post-Severan period; one of these—196b originally a votive

---

[225] Henig, *Corpus*, #1–17, 813, 814, M1, App. 90, App. 91, App. 121. Many of these gems of seated Jupiters were found in military areas: Coventina's Well (#2), York (#3), Newstead (#5), Carvoran (#6), Castlecary (#7), Chesters (#11); Jupiter with his eagle from Newstead (#14), and Housesteads (#16). The datable *intagli* can be placed between the late 1st and early 3rd centuries: #1, App. 90 (first century); #5 (first/second century); #7, 11, 14, 15 (second century); #4, 12 (late second century); #17 (second/third century); #2, 10, 13 (third century).
[226] Fears, "Jupiter," 100–101.
[227] Fears, "Jupiter," 103.
[228] Fears, "Jupiter," 104.
[229] Henig, "Art and Cult," 110. Henig, *Corpus*, cites twenty-three engraved gems representing the Roman Jupiter with his Roman attributes (eagles, *fulmines*, thrones, scepters).

to the local Cocidius—was rededicated to Jupiter Optimus ca. AD 270. The Romano-British altars and *intagli* represent a purely Roman Jupiter, with one exception.[230] It will, however, be seen that the Roman Jupiter appropriated the iconography of Celtic gods into the "official" votive altars.

Jupiter Optimus Maximus Tanarus

Both in Gaul and in Britain, the wheel-god resembled the Roman Jupiter—a sky and father god. The Celtic wheel god, as the extant iconography suggests, was almost completely Romanized, his attributes including eagle and thunderbolt. The wheel, however, was a Celtic symbol for the sky or sun, a symbol which also took the form of a swastika and a stylized flower with six petals.[231] The sky-god as conqueror assumed the wheel as his primary symbol. The wheel is significant for its implicit motion (since the sun was assumed to travel). Solar symbols and wheel-shaped amulets appear in the context of the cult of the dead, since the sky god was thought to overcome chthonic forces.[232] For example, a small lead shrine from Wallsend, apparently dedicated to Mercury and clearly a personal possession, shows the sun god wearing a radiate crown and his wheel (on the door's pediment) juxtaposed with Mercury, a dolphin and seahorse, suggesting travel to the underworld or a sea-god (set into the shrine's niche).[233]

The evidence for the cult of the wheel god is concentrated in the highly Romanized civilian southeast, and along Hadrian's Wall, "Romanized" early during the Roman occupation.[234] In addition, the wheel symbol was significant to a god worshipped by northern tribes.

Both epigraphy and iconography support a military wheel cult. Tanarus (also Taranis), a Celtic name meaning "the roarer,"[235] is

---

[230] Henig, *Corpus*, #624, invoking a syncretized Jupiter.

[231] The wheel was also a symbol of the sun in Persia where the swastika seems to have originated.

[232] M.J. Green, "Jupiter," 68, 74. Green sees the torc as an extension of the sky-god's wheel attribute. In addition, horses are associated with the conquering Celtic sky-wheel god.

[233] Allason-Jones, "Lead Shrine," 231–232. The uneven workmanship of the item implies that it may have been mass-produced with a relevant detail or two added to order. In fact, the god displayed in the shrine may have been added at the consumer's discretion. Hence, the Mercury in the shrine may have had only a passing association with the sun-god on the cupboard.

[234] M.J. Green, "Wheel God," 354.

[235] Tolkien in Collingwood, *Roman Britain*, 262; Heichelheim, "Vitiris," 408.

attested by name only once in Britain, on an altar from Chester, set
up by an Hispanian *princeps* of the *Legio XX V.V.* (534).[236] On the
side of this altar is a flower with six petals which may represent a
wheel; on the back, a wreath surrounding a rosette may indicate
another wheel-symbol.[237] Other altars to Jupiter Optimus Maximus,
without a Celtic qualification, display wheel motifs (stylized rosettes
and swastikas): 134, 139, 140, 188, 210, 212; and thunderbolts: 210–
12. Frequently, the wheel is the only Celtic symbol on these *vota*.[238]
The worshipper may have seen the god as a true ethnic blend and so
crammed together as many sky-symbols as possible, or he may have
tried to cover all eventualities, in reality honoring two gods: one
native, and one imported.[239]

The wheel-god is also represented in relief. For example, the
Willinghan Fen bronze scepter illustrates a naked youth with an
eagle, a solar wheel, a three-horned bull, and a dolphin: the imagery
suggests a complex myth, a balance between solar elements (eagle,
solar wheel) and chthonic (dolphin—Celts viewed the ocean as a
path to the underworld) as well as Roman and Celtic.[240] One relief
from Netherby shows a god, half-draped, his left hand holding a
cornucopia, his right hand extending a wheel over an altar (*CSIR*
1.6.376).[241] A second relief depicts the god with the same attributes
(a wheel held over an altar) but includes a boar and a tree, thereby
enhancing rural and fertility connections (*CSIR* 1.6.375). These reliefs
seem to depict a wheel god who, after losing solar associations, has
become a local *genius*.[242] From Corbridge, a clay mold shows a warrior god with a club and wheel.[243]

Miniature objects, wheel and swastika brooches—perhaps good
luck charms and sun symbols without reference to wheel gods—are

---

[236] Only a handful of dedications to Tanarus have been found on the continent.
At Scardona Dalmatia, he is attested as *Iovi Taranunco* (*CIL* III 2804). In the Rhineland,
he is cited twice as *deo Taranunco*, at Böckingen (*CIL* XIII 6487) and at Godramstein
(*CIL* XIII 6094).
[237] M.J. Green, "Wheel God," 363.
[238] M.J. Green, "Jupiter," 70.
[239] M.J. Green, "Jupiter," 70.
[240] M.J. Green, *Wheel as Cult Symbol*, plate lxxxi; "Jupiter," 72.
[241] The first figure resembles a *genius*, and the wheel could be taken as a Celtic
version of the *patera*. M.J. Green, "Netherby," 41, suggests that the proportions of
the relief accentuate the wheel—the altar and cornucopia are proportionally small;
the wheel is stressed as the deity's primary symbol.
[242] M.J. Green, "Wheel God," 349.
[243] Forster and Knowles, *Corstopitum*, 224, fig. 6.

known in military contexts from the continent, at Pfünz (*ORL* XIII 26), Tongeren, Juslenville, Hauchlin, Élouges and Lavacherie, and Zügmantel (*ORL* XXXIII pl. x, pp. 17, 27).[244] Small votive objects, wheels, axes, shields, spears, and, swords, have been found in Britain in ritual contexts especially at Woodeaton, Oxon.,[245] Worthington, Kent,[246] and at grave sites in Welwyn, Herts.,[247] and Poundbury, Dorset.[248]

Wheel brooches and studs are common finds in the military zones of Roman Britain and are often associated with Tanarus' cult. Small votive finds include bronze enameled wheel-brooches found at Corbridge and Turret 18B on Hadrian's Wall; a bronze swastika-brooch from Benwell (compare the swastika on 218);[249] part of a large bronze wheel-brooch, from Housesteads, dating to the fourth century;[250] a six-spoked wheel-brooch from the Sewingshields mile-castle (Turret 35A);[251] and a stone mould for miniature wheel-spokes found at Gateshead, near Newcastle. The wheel was also worn as a pendant in gold.[252] The god was also represented in bronze.[253] Jupiter Tanarus' nature was two-fold, this deity elevated to corporate worship retained his broad popular appeal.

Jupiter, like other representatives of the "official" Roman religion, is connected to corporate army worship to ensure military (and polit-ical) success. In their official capacity, the state gods incorporated indigenous religions into official monuments. However, despite the ritualistic and authoritative nature of these deities of state, each cult appealed personally to officers, soldiers, and civilians. Hence, through centrally imposed cults, a balance was struck between securing wel-fare for the state and for the individual.

---

[244] M.J. Green, "Wheel God," 351.
[245] J. Kirk, "Woodeaton," 33–35.
[246] Klein, "Worthington, Kent," 76.
[247] Westhall, "Romano-British Cemetery," 37.
[248] Farrar, "Bronze Hanging Bowl," 98.
[249] Petch, "Benwell," 135–193.
[250] E. Birley and Charlton, "Housesteads," 197.
[251] Woodfield, "Six Turrets," 87–201.
[252] M.J. Green, *Military Areas*, at Backworth (45, #3) and Dolaucothi (59). Both examples are 8–spoked gold wheel pendants. A silver filigree 9-spoked wheel came from Newstead (65, #1).
[253] M.J. Green, *Military Areas*, at Caerleon (48, #2), Ilkley (61, #2), Kirkby Thore (62, #4), Manchester (64, #1), Piercebridge (66, #2), South Shields (71, #2).

CHAPTER TWO

EASTERN CULTS

Introduction

Despite the Roman attitude of religious tolerance, assimilation, and syncretism, Eastern cults were not widely embraced by Rome on an administrative level. Augustus officially discouraged cults from the near East, especially the Egyptian cult of Apis, though he tolerated some ancient cults (Suetonius *Augustus* 93). Tiberius upheld this policy (Tacitus *Annals* 2.85), as did Claudius (Tacitus *Annals* 11.15). Despite the fact that the Flavians favored Isis, Eastern cults were categorically restricted from the official military worship at least through the middle of the third century: they were not included in the camp shrine, excepting a few votives to Serapis and Jupiter Dolichenus, nor were monuments to Eastern deities erected in the courtyards of the *praetorium*, the centers of official army religion; and temples were built outside the camp walls.[1] No Eastern ritual is mentioned in the *Feriale Duranum*,[2] despite the fact that some cults, especially that of Jupiter Dolichenus, most popular under Severus and Caracalla, had enjoyed wide acceptance prior to the issuance of this military festival list, and, furthermore, that a fresco from Dura shows Roman military units venerating local gods.[3]

---

[1] Hoey, "Official Policy," 458. The exception is Dura, a camp which was built around a pre-existing city, an unusual circumstance. Found within the camp walls are the Mithraeum, the joint temple to Mithras and Dolichenus and the temple to Artemis Azzanathcona, all of which were standing before the camp was built: Rostovtzeff, *Dura-Europus and its Art*, 51–2.

[2] Fink, *Roman Military Records*, 421–22.

[3] Dedications made to Jupiter Dolichenus before the Severan dynasty include *CIL* VII 2680 (*ILS* 4311a; M286 [AD 125/6]), M74 (AD 138?), M175 (AD 163), M17 (AD 167–180?), M115 (AD 180–183), *CIL* XIV 110 (M264 [AD 186]), M274 (AD 185–192), *CIL* XIII 6646 (M301 [AD 191]), *CIL* VI 31172 (*ILS* 2193; M238), *CIL* VI 31181 (*CIMRM* 373; M239), M221, *CIL* XIV 22 (M265 [191–192]), *CIL* VI 414 (*ILS* 4315b; M224 [AD 191]).

A fresco from Dura, in the Yale collection, show a Syrian triad dressed in Roman military costume. Julius Terentius, commander of the Palmyrene troop, offers sacrifice for his unit: MacMullen, *Paganism*, 80–81.

Eastern cults continued to thrive, and some of them even received official sanction: Elagabal served as priest of the Sun god; Aurelian included Sol Invictus prominently with the state gods, and Constantine recognized Christianity as an official state religion. Abundant evidence suggests that oriental cults were treated with the widest tolerance. Nonetheless, mystery rites, which offered hopes for an afterlife and potential rewards for service accomplished under rather bleak circumstances of earthly existence, were widely embraced from the second century onwards, especially among the more mobile classes: soldiers, merchants, slaves, and aristocrats in imperial service.

Jupiter Optimus Maximus Dolichenus

The widely worshipped Jupiter Dolichenus attracted senators, governors, traders, and soldiers.[4] The cult of this old Hittite storm deity Teshub—who evolved into a god of heaven and fertility—arose originally in Commagene (Dülük, near Gaziantep, eastern Turkey) between the Taurus mountains and the Euphrates river.[5] Nothing of the god and his cult is known until 64 BC, when Rome annexed Syria, whence, presumably, Dolichenus and his cult diffused into the Roman world (Plutarch *Pompey* 24). A temple building inscription from Lambaesis, Africa provides the earliest positive Roman documentation of his cult, AD 125/6.[6] Provincial governors, it would seem, actively supported the Dolichean Jupiter, and other religions from the near East, including Mithraism, enabling the cults to expand and attract worshippers.[7] The Commagenean cult continued to grow in popularity, reaching its climax under the Severi.[8]

---

[4] Speidel, *Jupiter Dolichenus*, 2.

[5] Lewis, *Temples*, 115; Speidel, *Jupiter Dolichenus*, 1: Hörig, "Jupiter Dolichenus," 2139–2140.

[6] *Pro s[alute] et incolumitate | imp(eratoris) Cae[s(aris) Traia]ni Hadriani Augusti | Iuli[us Maio]r | legatus ipsius pro praetore | templu[m I(ovi) O(ptimo) M(aximo) D]olicheno dedicavit* (*CIL* VIII 2680 [*ILS* 4311a]). Sextus Julius Maior was a Greek senator from Nysa (Tralles) in Asia who grew up closer to the cult than many. Dedicating the temple does not necessarily suggest that Sextus commissioned its building. Interestingly, documentation for the cult of Mithras first appears at about the same time at Histria (*CIMRM* 2296).

No pre-Roman Hellenistic or Persian evidence survives, nor has the site of the original temple on Dülük Baba Tepe been excavated.

[7] Speidel, *Jupiter Dolichenus*, 5.

[8] Speidel, *Jupiter Dolichenus*, 10. Some have argued that Severan support guaran-

The cult's success is, perhaps, attributable to the zealous worship of Easterners,[9] but epigraphic evidence indicates that the cult was not restricted to Commageneans, Syrians, and Parthians.[10] Among non-eastern worshippers were the *Equites Singulares* (*CIL* VI 31172 [*ILS* 2193a; M238]; *CIL* VI 31181 [*CIMRM* 373; M239]; *CIL* VI 31187 [*ILS* 2193]).[11]

The temples were richly decorated,[12] but excavations of modest western sanctuaries reveal no common pattern. No literary text attests cult practices, but inscriptions and archaeology imply that priest-hoods were numerous but temporary. The adherents, *fratres* (M73, 192, 200), gained admission to the sacral feasts only after a period of instruction as *candidati* (M192, 194, 199, 200). The term *colitores* applied to those outside the inner-group (M200). Women could be *colitores*, but there is no positive evidence for a female priest or "*frater*." Additionally, the cult maintained *scribae* and *notarii*; written records were probably important.

---

teed or contributed to the success of the cult (Kan, *Jupiter Dolichenus*, 19; Fitz, "Septimius Severus"; Merlat, *Jupiter Dolichenus*, 26–27). This seems highly conjectural since Jupiter Dolichenus attracted Roman worshippers before Severus, and no primary written source supports the supposition that the Severi sponsored the cult of Jupiter Dolichenus, despite Septimius Severus' supposed *propaganda fidei* (Speidel, *Jupiter Dolichenus*, 71). Furthermore, there is no documentation of any emperor's reaction to Jupiter Dolichenus. If, however, statues from Carnuntum and Chesters are to be interpreted as representations of Severus Alexander and Julia Mamaea in the guise of Jupiter Dolichenus and Juno Dolichena, there would exist at least two traces, albeit late, that provide evidence for Severan espousal of this cult.

Twenty three dedications were made during the Severan period (192–235: Speidel, nos. 6, 7, 8, 12, 13, 35, 38, 42, 44, and M19, M22, M69, M75, M79, M130, M248, M290, M324, M345, *AE* 1957, 327; *AE* 1967, 259; *AE* 1971, 28, *AE* 1972, 505); Six monuments were dedicated after the Severan period (Speidel nos. 50–54).

[9] Cumont, "Jupiter Dolichenus," 1276; Merlat, *Jupiter Dolichenus*, 11; Latte, *Römische Religionsgeschichte*, 348. Many worshippers' names suggest first or second generation immigration: Gordon, "Jupiter Dolichenus," 802.

[10] Speidel, *Jupiter Dolichenus*, 9. Only one monument was set up by a unit from Commagene, at Micia in Dacia (M31). At least one *ala* and six cohorts were levied from Commagene: *Ala I Commagenorum* sent to Egypt in 83, no longer there in 105 (*CIL* XVI 29), sent to Noricum by 106 (*CIL* XVI 52); cohorts I and II *Flavia Commagenorum* were stationed on the Danube (Wagner, *Dislokation*, 123–24; Russu, "Elementele Syriene," 167–86); one cohort was stationed in Numidia by the reign of Hadrian (Cagnat, *L'armée romaine*, 202); one may have served in Cappadocia (Cichorius, "Cohors," 275).

[11] Of sixteen excavated Dolichena, only the one at Heddernheim may owe its origins to a Semitic auxiliary corps (*Cohors I Flavia Damascenorum*). Such a fact argues to the cult's broad appeal (or imperial connections). Haynes, "Romanisation of Religion," 146.

[12] A silver votive tablet from Heddernheim, Upper Germany, was dedicated by a common soldier (*CIL* XIII 734a [M312]).

Dolichenus probably never attained far-reaching popularity.[13] During the reign of Maximinus Thrax (235–38), temples to Dolichenus along the Rhine and Danube were destroyed and pillaged for their treasures (Herodian VII 3.5–4.1).[14] The cult survived the demolition of its temples. In Britain, the latest evidence to Dolichenus is datable to Maximinus (410). Soldiers from other frontiers cultivated Dolichenus until ca. AD 250.[15] The latest civilian monument dates to Gallienus (AD 253–68; M202), during whose reign the Persians invaded Doliche, destroying the city and the primary sanctuary.[16] The fall of the god's city and cult center may have somehow discredited the god in the eyes of potential worshippers to the extent that the fourth century Christian polemicists saw no need to mention the god or his cult. The cult seems to have disappeared completely after Gallienus.[17]

Jupiter Dolichenus, the storm god, is often depicted standing on a bull, an emblem of his power over nature, wearing a Phrygian cap and an anatomical cuirass. He usually holds a double axe and a thunderbolt, symbols of heavenly power. One of the finest representations of this god is a bronze statuette from Noricum (M149).

Domaszewski suggested that Jupiter Dolichenus was the official god of the Roman army, worshipped like Mithras primarily along the frontiers.[18] The cult was concentrated along, but not exclusive

---

[13] Dolichenus' adherents seemed to have belonged to a wealthy and probably highly disliked group. Additionally, the cult never freed itself from its cultural and ethnic characteristics (like the Isis cult). Subsequently, it was never able to attain true universality: Speidel, *Jupiter Dolichenus* 72, 75; Hörig, "Jupiter Dolichenus," 2173–2174.

[14] Tóth, "Ornamenta," 105–9, discusses archaeological evidence for the destruction of these shrines along the Rhine and Danube. Maximinus was notorious for stealing the riches acquired by sanctuaries, according to Herodian (VII.3.5–4.1).

[15] Speidel, *Jupiter Dolichenus*, 73–75. Among these late Dolichean monuments are an altar from Dacia dating between 238 and 244 (*AE* 1971, 381), an altar from Rigomagus in Lower Germany dating to 250 (*CIL* XIII 7786 [M342]), two altars erected in the Dura-Europus Dolichenum in 251 (Speidel, *Jupiter Dolichenus*, 7, nos. 9–10), and four altars from the Dolichenum at Lambaesis in Numidia on which the name of the *legio III Augusta* was erased in 238 but restored in 253, by which date the Dolichenum was still in use (M289–293).

[16] Honigmann and Maricq, *Res Gestae Divi Saporis*, 131–2. Maricq, *Classica et Orientalia*, 53. Speidel, *Jupiter Dolichenus*, 75, note 246. Doliche may have fallen during the same campaign as Dura-Europus.

[17] Speidel, *Jupiter Dolichenus*, 75. Nilsson, *Griechische Religion*, 701, argued that the religion of Jupiter Dolichenus, like all Eastern cults with the exception of Christianity, never attained true universality since it was never able to sever itself completely from its national/ethnic character.

[18] Domaszewski, *Religion*, 60; Cumont, "Jupiter Dolichenus," col. 1276; Kan, *Jupiter Dolichenus*, 40; Swoboda, *Carnuntum*, 132.

to, the military *limes* of the Roman empire.[19] Wearing a cuirass and standing between military standards, accompanied by *Victoria*, he evokes a military image. Both civilian and soldier worshipped the god, and little, if any, difference between civilian and military ritual is detectable. The cuirass, for example, might suggest Dolichenus' military nature. On civilian monuments, however, Jupiter of Doliche wears the cuirass, whereas military relics from Carnuntum (M86) and Brigetio (M106), legionary camps on the Danube, show the god in eastern dress. At Croy Hill in Britain, the god appears in military dress, wearing a tunic but not a cuirass (411). The Greek anatomical cuirass was a standard feature by which gods were represented in Hellenistic and Roman art.[20] Merlat suggested that the cuirass was reserved for higher ranking officers, the emperor, and the gods, and correlated Jupiter Dolichenus more closely to the emperor than to the common soldier.[21] Rarely was the god seen with a shield and frequently the hilt of his sword terminates in an eagle's head, as on reliefs from Carnuntum. Association with the eagle suggests Jupiter Dolichenus as emperor rather than soldier.[22] Gods were often dressed in Roman costume, by which soldiers assimilated the attributes of emperor (political *dominus*) to god (spiritual *dominus*). Such *interpretatio Romana* may have been seen as more impressive and dignified than native guises, lending greater authority and sobriety to the cult.[23]

Several reliefs show Victory offering a crown to Dolichenus; *Victoria* often represents military—and moral—triumph.[24] No dedication to *Victoria*, however, is known to be associated with the Dolichean cult.[25]

Jupiter Dolichenus was also known as "the god from where the iron grows," especially at Apulum (M24, 26), Rome (M176–245), Heddernheim (M312–23), and Pfünz (M1169–174). Iron, the material for weapons, might connect the god with army religion, but the two uses of the formula *ubi ferrum nascitur* which reveal the dedicators' identities were both civilian (*CIL* VI 30947 [*ILS* 4302]; *CIL* III 11927 [*ILS* 4301; M170]). The formula should, consequently, refer to the mythology of the god's origins rather than his martial nature.

---

[19] Speidel, *Jupiter Dolichenus*, 38 and map.
[20] Will, *Le relief cultuel gréco-romain*, 255–71; Merlat, *Jupiter Dolichenus*, 33–34, suggested that the adoption of the cuirass was a Roman rather than a Hellenistic feature.
[21] Merlat, *Jupiter Dolichenus*, 33.
[22] Dolenz, "Jupiter Dolichenus;" Speidel, *Jupiter Dolichenus*, 41–42.
[23] Kantorowicz, "Gods in Uniform," 368–98.
[24] Speidel, *Jupiter Dolichenus*, 43.
[25] Speidel, *Jupiter Dolichenus*, 44.

Iron smelting furnaces have been discovered at Commagene,[26] and the Dolichenus monuments in Britain correspond to sources of iron ore.

Dolichenus is frequently represented with standards. The *signa* may be cult standards, which lack Graeco-Roman parallels but were common in Syrian and Mesopotamian cults. These ensigns closely resemble the military *signa* in shape: stones from Kömlod (M65) and Mauer-an-der-Url (M153) show standards surmounted by eagles, suggesting legionary or praetorian *signa*;[27] and one such *signum* is associated with Serapis.[28] They may have been assimilated to Roman military ensigns as an expression of loyalty to Rome.[29] Such cult standards, however, were also known at Hatra, an old and bitter enemy of Rome.[30]

Jupiter Dolichenus, often shown without a sword, may have personified cosmic victory. He was frequently invoked on behalf of the emperor (395–6, 398, 402, 404–5), and his worshippers included as many civilian as soldiers. He was *conservator totius mundi* (M195). His popularity with the army may stem from the fact that his attributes were those of the emperor, and his monuments revealed a vision of power. He was the Cosmic Emperor who would protect all his adherents.[31]

Jupiter Dolichenus in Britain

No Dolichena survive, but inscriptions and scattered sculpted relics testify to the worship of Jupiter Dolichenus in Britain, where, however, he was restricted to the northern frontier, except for a relic from Caerleon (393) and a dedication slab from York (394); both were legionary bases. Jupiter Dolichenus was an iron-working god, and his worship in Britain corresponds with ore deposits and iron-working centers. The supply station at Corbridge, a rich source for Dolichean material, was an iron working depot, giving Dolichenus local appeal.[32] Slag from Roman iron-working has been noticed at

[26] Merlat, *Jupiter Dolichenus*, 72–73; Richmond, "Corbridge," 179 made a strong military connection between Dolichenus and his cult at Corbridge.

[27] Speidel, *Jupiter Dolichenus*, 58. One auxiliary standard bears a tiny eagle attached to the middle of the pole rather than the top (Domaszewski, *Fahnen*, 72).

[28] A bronze standard head found at Flobecq, Belgium, shows Serapis: Faider-Feytmans, "Enseigne Romaine," 3–43.

[29] Rostovtzeff, "*Vexillum* and Victory," 92–106; Fauth, "Simia," 699–700.

[30] Maricq, *Classica et Orientalia*, 1–26; Ingholt, "Parthian Sculptures," 29. Speidel, *Jupiter Dolichenus*, fig. 15.

[31] Speidel, *Jupiter Dolichenus*, 41–44.

[32] Richmond, "Corbridge," 180.

Bewcastle,[33] where a temple to Jupiter Dolichenus may have stood (398). Epigraphic evidence indicates the cult at Risingham (402–3), just north of the Redesdale iron ore deposits, mined to supply the Roman workshops at Corbridge.[34] Coal and iron deposits have been found in south Durham, near Yorkshire at Piercebridge (399–400). The Caerleon monument may imply iron mines in the area (393).[35]

Since Dolichena were systematically destroyed during the reign of Maximinus Thrax, few remains survive, and only sixteen temples have been located and excavated along the Rhine and Danube frontiers. Furthermore, these richly decorated temples standing above ground were less likely to survive than partially subterranean Mithraea. The cult of Jupiter Dolichenus first appeared in Britain by Antoninus Pius' reign (404) and reached its peak under Septimius Severus, as elsewhere.[36] None of the god's temples in Britain have been excavated,[37] but temples are attested at Bewcastle (398) and Old Penrith (396).

An interesting collection of Dolichean material has come to light at Corbridge. This cache reveals much about the cult, its pantheon, and the general Roman attitude of religious tolerance. An extended pantheon, an unusual feature in oriental religions, included Apollo and Diana, Sol Invictus and Luna, Castor and Pollux, and Juno Dolichena. The cult, enjoying Severan imperial patronage, willingly incorporated Roman ritual precepts, and unlike occult mysteries (Cybele and Mithras), its appeal was both personal and corporate.[38] The emperor could offer the cult as a basis for imperial unification.

One fragmentary frieze (*CSIR* 1.1.52; *CCID* 568) was recycled as a paving stone on a Constantinian floor of workshop III of the west military compound. The find spot and the dates during which the workshop was employed suggest that the piece was destroyed late in the third century. The frieze shows a youthful rider, beardless and with curly hair, wearing knee-breeches, tunic, cloak, and a radiate crown—Sol Invictus. He rides through the air on a winged horse and grasps with his right hand the horse's forelock, the source of its magic power. Sol guides his mount towards a pillared building, richly decorated with foliate antefixes on the roof and a beribboned swag hanging from the eaves. Inside the temple stands a Dioscurus,

---

[33] Bruce, *LS*, 378.
[34] Bruce, *LS*, 308; Richmond, *Roman Britain*, 159.
[35] Camden, *Britannia*, col. 605.
[36] Speidel, *Jupiter Dolichenus*, 72; Lewis, *Temples*, 115.
[37] Lewis, *Temples*, 115.
[38] Richmond, "Corbridge," 181.

wearing a Phrygian cap and facing front. Just having finished or about to start his celestial journey, he holds his horse in check with his left hand and leans upon a lance.[39] At the far right of the building stands a large deciduous tree, and beyond the tree a youthful figure, muscular, nude, with flowing hair: the god Apollo gazing at the scene to his right.

Sol appears subordinate, smaller in scale, off-center. The missing figure in the center of the frieze was no doubt the god Jupiter Dolichenus, with his familiar double-headed ax, thunderbolt, and bull.[40] Apollo, shown on a larger scale than the other figures, probably represents the center of the scene. It seems unlikely that Sol would ride away from the center. Finally, the colonnade as it appears is L-shaped, an unusual form. Colonnades with two projecting wings were common in sacred precincts, and such a form would be consistent with artistic balance and symmetry. The central group of figures would have included Jupiter Dolichenus and Juno Caelestis, Apollo (who is shown), and perhaps Diana. The missing right hand section of the panel may have depicted the corresponding colonnaded wing, the second Dioscurus to the right, and Luna, in apposition to Sol Invictus.

Three sculpted fragments (*CSIR* 1.1.55; *CCID* 569) from a second monument, dating to the third century and destroyed in 297, represent a Dioscurus. In high relief, a youth faces front and holds in check a horse, with a plume on his head, facing right. The youth wears a Phrygian cap (fragmentary), and a light cloak covers his left shoulder and upper arm. He holds a spear in his right hand and raises his left hand towards the horse's head as if grasping a bridle, not cut into the panel but perhaps painted onto it later. The scene is traditionally Dioscuran—nude, Phrygian cap, spirited horse.[41] The other Dioscurus probably appeared on another panel.

A third sculpted panel (*CSIR* 1.1.56; *CCID* 570), also dating to the third century, was found in the fourth century floor of the east granary. In high relief, a large bust of Sol, draped at the neck, wears a radiate crown. There was probably an accompanying relief of Luna.

A severely and deliberately damaged bull survives as fragments of

---

[39] Richmond, "Corbridge," 183; see Collingwood and Richmond, *Archaeology of Roman Britain*, fig. 65. The rider beginning or ending his journey is appropriate both to the myth and to the balanced composition of the piece.
[40] Richmond, "Corbridge," 184–5; Toynbee, *Art in Britain*, #92, fig. 95.
[41] Richmond, "Corbridge," 186–7.

the animal's hindquarters and midsection (*CSIR* 1.1.57; *CCID* 566).
This piece may have supported a statue of the god. The Dolichean
bull denotes creation; he is the proud leader of the herd, not the
"moribund sacrificial bull of Mithras."[42]

A fragment from the Dolichean panel shows a Pegasus, a head
and part of one wing below a row of garlands hung from *bucrania*.
(*CSIR* 1.1.53; *CCID* 571). The plume on the horse's head and the
bucrania were crudely executed, little more than blobs; rosettes were
cut into the center of the garlands. Another fragment (*CSIR* 1.1.54;
CCID 570), which may belong to the same collection, shows part of
an ox-head and garland, deeply incised—similar in execution to the
other pieces.

An interesting dedication from Corbridge deserves some attention
(401). The stone was dedicated by a centurion, and the man's name
and titles were inscribed over a deliberate erasure, the correction of
a stonemason's error or the rededication of the altar.[43] The text invokes Brigantia, a deity politically fabricated by the Severans, who
was assimilated to Juno Dolichena and invoked here as Caelestis.[44]
The affinity between Juno Caelestis and Brigantia Caelestis may have
been intended as a compliment to the Severan Dynasty, especially
Julia Domna.[45] Furthermore, the invocation includes *Salus*, not otherwise associated with Dolichenus, invoked for the personal well-being
of the worshipper.[46] The Corbridge material accords with temple
accoutrements.[47]

From Chesters a headless Juno Regina, in the round and of fine
workmanship, has survived.[48] The body, wearing a long-sleeved ankle-
length tunic—a broad piece of cloth bordered in bands with a running wave design—tied at the waist and draped around her thighs,
was broken off at the shins. The heifer, on which she stood, survives as another headless fragment. A flat base, with the hooves of

[42] Richmond, "Corbridge," 191.
[43] Richmond, "Corbridge," 193.
[44] Richmond, "Corbridge," 195–197. The cult of Dolichenus was conducted by
a priesthood who saw the need to make their religion attractive to large number
of people thereby ensuring their own livelihood: 399. See also Joliffe "Brigantia,"
43–45.
[45] Jolliffe, "Dea Brigantia," 44, 53.
[46] Speidel, *Jupiter Dolichenus*, 35. Although priests did not habitually add gods to
their pantheon at random, simply to attract new worshippers, they did engage, to
some extent, in propaganda to attract worshippers (Tóth, "Sacerdotes Iovis Dolicheni").
[47] Richmond, "Corbridge," 196.
[48] Bruce, *LS* 149; Budge, *Chesters*, 300; Merlat, *Répertoire*, 276.

a bull crushing a serpent, probably belonged to a complementary statue of Jupiter Dolichenus.[49]

Sculptured remains have been found at Croy Hill on the Antonine Wall, the northernmost point recorded for the worship of the god. An inscribed relief of Dolichenus and Juno (411) may have belonged to the *principia*.[50] Above a framed inscription are the remains of fore-legs and haunches of a cow facing left. A smaller fragment preserves part of a relief of a male torso wearing a tunic. The intact relief would have shown Dolichenus standing on a bull, in his familiar pose, and his divine consort poised on a heifer.[51]

The divine pair at Chesters may be Severus Alexander and Julia Mamaea, if statues of Severus and his mother found in the *principia* at Carnuntum can be interpreted as representing Jupiter Dolichenus and Juno Dolichena.[52] The Carnuntum Juno Regina wears a cloak with a border decorated with the same wave design found on the Chesters statue. Both pieces wear the imperial mantle, which equates the empress with the goddess.[53] Speidel, proffering no argument, is unconvinced that these statues represent members of the imperial family.[54] It is, however, possible that, even if Severus Alexander did not publicly support this cult, his subjects might nonetheless envisage their emperor in this guise of this god and honor the emperor by association with the deity: e.g., the Dolichenus temple at Voreda was restored *in honorem domus divinae* (396).

The cult of Jupiter Dolichenus was deeply personal: two dedications were set up *ex iussu dei* (399, 401), perhaps evidence of prose-lytizing priests. The distribution of the Doliche material in Britain reflects the military nature of the cult, in contrast to evidence for other Eastern cults, which tends to coincide with the presence of soldiers with eastern heritages.[55] The cult's decline did not necessarily follow the collapse of the Severan dynasty. Most monuments were destroyed in the invasions of AD 296/7 or recycled in Constantinian contexts (401, 402, 407; *CSIR* 1.1.52, 55).[56]

---

[49] Cumont, "Groupe de Marbre," 187; Bosanquet, thought that he had found a torso of the god in a pile of stones at Chesters: cited by Merlat, *Répertoire*, 270, n. 4.

[50] Robertson, *Antonine Wall*, 7, 37; Harris, *Oriental Cults*, 63.

[51] Harris, *Oriental Cults*, 63.

[52] Richmond, "Juno Regina," 50; Harris, *Oriental Cults*, 64.

[53] Richmond, "Juno Regina," 51.

[54] Speidel, *Jupiter Dolichenus*, 65; Hoey, "Official Policy," 462; Swoboda, *Carnuntum*, 195.

[55] Harris, *Oriental Cults*, 96.

[56] Constantius oversaw wholesale reconstruction along the length of Hadrian's

Mithras

Origins

Mitra (Mithras), one of the oldest attested Indo-European deities, was invoked as a guarantor of a treaty between the Mitanni and the Hittites (fourteenth c. BC).[57] The god is also mentioned in the Rig Veda, ca. 1400 BC, by which time a joint cult to Varuna and Mitra had been established in India. In Persia, Mitra and Varuna came to be known as Mithra and Ahura (Ahura Mazda, Ahura the Wise). Though Ahura was supreme, Mithra, the protector of his people, the vengeful warrior god, was nearly his equal. The reforms of Zarathustra (Zoroaster), a semi-legendary prophet, traditionally dated to 628–551 BC, tried to exclude all the gods, except Ahura Mazda, from the pantheon. However, by the reign of Artaxerxes II (404–358 BC), Persian religion was once again officially polytheistic, and Mithras gained a position of prominence among the Achaemenid kings in Persia and their Hellenistic successors, the Seleucids,[58] and in Commagene, Parthia, and Pontus, the kingly name Mithridates recalls the god. Eventually a modified form of Zoroastrianism included Mithras and other deities of the old Persian pantheon. Mithras, the "Lord of Light," likened to the sun and moon, the origins of all beneficial light, is still worshipped in India and Iran today.[59]

Persian God or Greek Hero?

In the Roman world, Mithras was frequently depicted wearing a Phrygian cap and Persian dress, suggesting an Iranian origin.[60] In his comprehensive study of the cult, Cumont argued that the western cult was an offshoot of Zoroastrian dualism. Mithraism, as practiced

---

Wall, including Corbridge, Risingham, and Great Chesters: Richmond, "Redesdale," 107; Frere, *Britannia*, 333, 348, n. 14.

[57] Speidel, *Mithras-Orion*, 1; Ulansey, *Origins*, 4–14.

[58] Antiochus I of Commagene (69–34 BC) called Mithras the bulwark of his throne (*CIL* III 3; *MMM*, II, 89, #1) and commissioned a relief which shows the god and the king shaking hands.

[59] Speidel, *Mithras-Orion*, 1; Daniels, *Mithras*, 3. With the Islamic conquest of Persia, Zoroastrianism was suppressed in the seventh century. But small groups of followers still practice the faith at Yazd and Kerman in central Iran. In the eighth century, a second group fled to northern India where the Parsees of Bombay continue to practice a modified form of Zoroastrianism.

[60] Cumont, *Mystères*, 1–3.

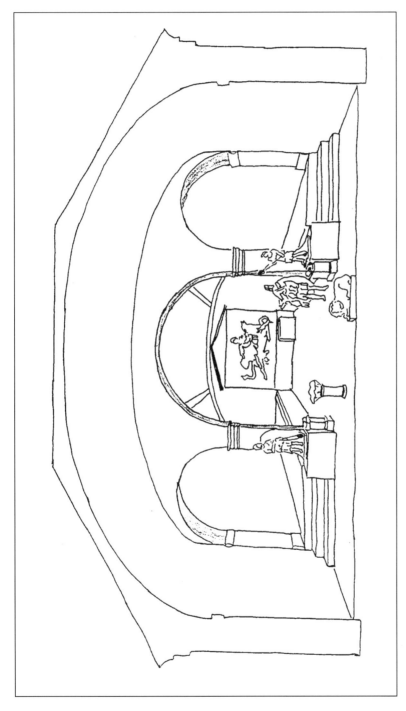

Figure 1: The Temple of Mithras at Carnutum, Austria, after Daniels, *Mithras*, Figure 10.

in the west, was a mystery religion,[61] a cult element not characteristic of Persian worship until after AD 150.[62] According to Wikander,
the western Mithras was a Baltic god.[63] Mithras in the Graeco-
Roman cult was a mediator and a creator deity, indeed similar to
the Persian Mithras, but not identical. The Persian Mithras influenced
the Roman god, yet western Mithraism was not simply a Romanization
of the Persian cult: the Roman Mithras was supreme in his pantheon, and mysteries were not associated with the original Persian
rite.

According to Speidel, the Roman Mithras, was closely related to
the Greek hero Orion, a suitable hero for the Roman army. According
to popular belief, soldiers and officers were born under the constellation of Orion and consequently took on his heroic characteristics—
strength and power with which they could subdue barbarian tribes
in foreign lands.[64] Orion, a son of Mars, was a fierce warrior and
leader of armies.[65] Furthermore, the constellation Orion, so it was
thought, portended war when the stars in his sword flared brightly
(Lucan *BC* 1.665); it is no secret that astrology affected the Roman
soldier (Tacitus *Historiae* 2.78; Dio 74.14.4). Mithras carried the sword
of Aries (the sign of Mars) and rode Taurus (the sign of Venus),
both of which were associated with Orion (Porphyry *de antro Nympharum*
24). The constellation of Orion, Speidel concluded, closed the gap
between Taurus and the other summer constellations.[66]

Ulansey, more convincingly, connects the Roman Mithras with
the hero Perseus. Both Perseus and Mithras wear similar costumes
(especially Phrygian caps) and use similar weapons (scimitars).[67] Like
Perseus who looks away from the Medusa, so Mithras looks away
from the bull as he kills it.[68] Mithras' Persian origins have already

---

[61] Beck, "Mithraism since Franz Cumont," 2006.
[62] Gordon, "Cumont," 217.
[63] Wikander, "Mithras," 46.
[64] Teukros (F. Boll, *Sphaera*, 43); Hermes Trismegistos (Gundel, *Hermes Trismegistos*,
54, 12–17); Speidel, *Mithras-Orion*, 38–39. Orion was swift (Homer, *Iliad* 18.486;
Pindar 1.3–4.67; Germanicus *Aratea* 322), armed with a *gladius* (Vergil, *Aeneid* 3.517;
Germanicus *Aratea* 3301; Ovid, *Fasti* 4.388). He wore the *cingulum* (Avienus *Aratea*
1375) and was the master of the military art of hunting (Horace *Satires* 2.2.9–16),
the epitome of *virtus* (Eratosthenes *Catasterismi* 32) and of a warrior (Vergil *Aeneid*
10.763–67).
[65] Wehrli, "Orion," 1079.
[66] Speidel, *Mithras-Orion*, 19.
[67] Ulansey, *Origins*, 26–7, 36.
[68] Ulansey, *Origins*, 30. This observation dates back to Saxl, *Mithras*, 14.

been noted. Perseus, furthermore, has a strong legendary connection to Persia: his son Perses, according to Greek tradition from the fifth century onwards, was the eponymous founder of the Persians (Herodotus 7.61.3). Perseus himself had an important cult center at Tarsus, the capital of Cilicia, of which Perseus was the legendary founder.[69] Furthermore, Mithras' position in relation to the bull in the tauroctony correlates to the position of the constellation Perseus above Taurus the bull.[70] It would seem that the Mithraic tauroctony might be a star map, and the cult mysteries might be related to the precession of the equinoxes.[71] In the Graeco-Roman era, Taurus was the last constellation in which the spring equinox occurred. The death of the bull (apparently tied to the precession of the equinoxes during which the entire sky seemed to move) seemed to usher in a new age. The constellation above the bull, Perseus, whose connection to Mithras has been demonstrated, was apparently responsible for the new age.[72]

Mithras and Rome

In 331 BC, after Alexander's overthrow of the Persian empire, the cult of Mithras spread throughout Asia Minor. Rome first encountered the cult in the first century BC, when, according to Plutarch (*Pompey* 24), Pompey subdued Cilician pirates who worshipped Mithras. When Tiridates of Armenia came to Rome during the reign of Nero, he brought the Magi (the official Persian clergy), who initiated the emperor into their banquets, presumably the mysteries of Mithras (Pliny, *NH* 30.1.6; *MMM*, II, 239).[73] Late in the first century AD, the poet Statius referred to the taurine and cave imagery of Mithraic cult (*Thebaid* 1.717).

The *legio XV Apollinaris* brought the cult from the East to the

---

[69] Fonterose, *Python*, 279–80; Ulansey, *Origins*, 42–45. Perseus is featured on the coins of Tarsus, and it will be remembered that Cilician pirates introduced the cult to the Romans.

[70] Ulansey, *Origins*, 26.

[71] Astrological interpretations of the Mithraic cult have gained currency over the past few decades. See Beck, *Planetary Gods*, for a useful analysis.

[72] Ulansey, *Origins*, 83–84.

[73] *MMM* I, 279, note 2; Cumont, *Mystères*, 85; Daniels, *Mithras*, 3, indicated that it is difficult to determine if this interpretation is correct. Such an interpretation, that Nero wished to be initiated into the mysteries, is quite reasonable, given this emperor's flair for the dramatic and exotic.

Danube frontier in the late first century AD.[74] Merkelbach argued
that the Roman cult of Mithras stressed the god as a protector of
oaths and treaties, a significant point for soldiers and customs officers
who swore the *sacramentum*.[75] As the cult gained popularity among
imperial soldiers and civil servants, the emperors tolerated and
endorsed the cult in varying degrees. Commodus was himself an initiate; Septimius Severus used Mithraism as the basis of religious syncretism, and his son Caracalla likewise favored the cult.[76] The Mithraic
high water-mark, politically at least, was perhaps AD 307/8, when
the emperors Diocletian, Maximianus, and Galerius made dedications to Mithras as *Fautor imperii sui* while they were attempting to
solve the problems of imperial succession (*CIL* III 4413 [*ILS* 659];
cf. 415). Private dedications from civilians fall off in the early third
century, a fact which makes a marble inscription from London, dating to AD 310/11, all the more remarkable (415).[77]

Myth and Ritual

The literary sources for the cult are sparse and, for the most part,
hostile. Christian writers deliberately misled their readers regarding
the beliefs of non-Christians, especially Mithraists, whose rites they
regarded as "Satanic mimicries" of the Christian faith (Justinian
Apology 1.66; Tertullian *de praescr. haer.* 40). Plutarch described the
Persian cult theology (*De Iside* 20) as a dualistic conflict between good
and evil. Ahura Mazda (Ormazd), Lord of Creation and Goodness,
reigned supreme in celestial serenity. Angra Mainyu (Ahriman), the
Lord of Darkness and Evil, opposed Ahura and constantly sent his
agents to corrupt and destroy mankind. Mithras stood between the
two, at war with the forces of evil and always the savior of mankind,
and hence *Invictus*. The Iranian Mithras, god of truth, was the warlike defender of righteousness.[78]

In the Romanized version of the cult, Mithras was paramount,
not subordinate to Ahura Mazda, but the Roman myth derives from
the Persian. Mithras was born, fully formed, from the cosmic egg

---

[74] *MMM*, I, 252–3; see Daniels "Role of the Army," 249–74.
[75] Merkelbach, *Mithras*, 153–156.
[76] *MMM*, I, 281 and note 5; A. Birley, *Septimius Severus*, 82; Grosso, *Commodo*,
131–132.
[77] Sauer, *End of Paganism*, 15. This plaque does not necessarily support a revi-
talization of the cult in southern Britain.
[78] Cumont, *Mystères*, 2–4.

or life-giving rock. He challenged and overcame the sun, regarded as an agent of desiccation and torment.[79] The two became allies, and Mithraic reliefs frequently show Mithras returning the Sun's radiate crown (epigraphically, Mithras is often cited as Sol Invictus: cat. 430, 431, 434). Mithras created the inanimate world.[80] He pursued the bull, Ormazd's creation of brute force, and dragged it back to his cave where he slaughtered it, thereby releasing its powers for humanity's benefit.[81] After the bull's slaughter, the torchbearers, the raven, and other attendants served the Sun and Mithras a celebratory feast of the bull's flesh and a drink,[82] the event commemorated by the Mithraic sacral feast.[83] After the banquet, Mithras and Sol mounted the Sun's chariot and ascended into the sky. Mithras continued to guide men, whose faith he has gained since he himself once suffered in mortal form on earth.

A fine, though fragmentary, relief from Housesteads shows the typical appointments of the cult. Mithras, in the central scene, wearing his Persian costume of tunic and breeches, Phrygian cap and short cloak, has forced the bull to the ground. Mithras presses his left knee into the bull's back. He pulls the bull's snout back with his left hand, a dagger in his right, as he stabs the bull's shoulder. A dog leaps at the bull's wound, from which a vine sprouts. The bull's tail terminates in stalks of grain. A snake slithers up to the bull, and a scorpion, sent by Ahriman, snaps at the bull's genitals. A raven, the Sun's messenger who relayed the command to slay the bull, perches atop Mithras' billowing cloak. To the god's right stands a torch-bearer, the *dadophorus* Cautopates, with his torch turned down and a sorrowful gaze, and to the god's left stands Cautopates' counterpart, Cautes, with up-turned torch. Cautes and Cautopates may represent, respectively, the rising and setting of the sun. Luna appears above Cautes, Sol above Cautopates. A zodiac surrounds the central bas-relief. Over five hundred Mithraic tauroctonies, displayed as the central scene in every Mithraeum, have surfaced—in bas-relief,

---

[79] Daniels, *Mithras*, 6.

[80] *MMM*, I, 294.

[81] Cumont, *Mystères*, 136-7.

[82] The herb *haoma* may have been an ingredient in the drink: Flattery and Schwartz, *Haoma and Harmaline*; Daniels, *Mithras*, 6.

[83] Evidence for such ritual feasts survive for the Mithraeum at Dura where fragmentary food accounts survive. Mithraic reliefs, such as the one from Konjic (Sarajevo) in the former Yugoslavia (*MMM*, II, 335, #234), and wall paintings illustrate such feasts in progress. The plant *haoma* was presumably unknown in the west where wine was substituted for the drink made from *haoma*.

sculpted in the round, and painted in fresco—with few variations in the cult iconography.[84]

As icons of the Mithraic cave, the excavated Mithraea, many of which are underground or partially sunken, as in Britain, follow a standard pattern. The initiate passed through a shallow antechamber to enter the sanctuary. Raised benches were placed at each side of the inner chamber. At the end, the *reredos*, the relief depicting the god's slaying of the bull, sat on a raised dais, around which worshippers placed votive altars and reliefs. The sanctuary's furniture might also include a flowing stream or an urn of water (e.g., Carrawburgh I, Housesteads). The shrines were often built near streams, indicative of the importance of water for purification, and many have become waterlogged. Because the sanctuary was usually sunken and windowless, the interior would be dark, lit with lamps or candles (Firmicus Maternus *De errore profanarum religionum* 5.2). Candlesticks have been found at Caernarvon, Carrawburgh,[85] and London; lamps have been recovered from the Caernarvon, Carrawburgh,[86] and Rudchester Mithraea. Smoking pine cones and incense would supplement the aura of the temple.[87] Pine cones and an incense shovel have been found at the Carrawburgh Mithraeum;[88] an incense burner was excavated at Rudchester.

Mithraic Grades and Initiation

Mithras' worshippers were divided into seven grades of initiation into the mysteries of the cult. Only after strenuous training and tests, the followers entered successively higher grades, a list of which Jerome recorded: *Corax, Nymphus, Miles, Leo, Perses, Heliodromus*, and *Pater* (*Ep.* 107 *ad Laetam*).[89] These grades of initiation reflect a sophisticated cult philosophy: Origen's planetary ladder with seven gates may correlate to the seven grades (Hieron. *Ep. 107 ad Laetam*).[90] Wall paintings, especially those from the Mithraeum at Santa Prisca in Rome (*CIMRM*

---

[84] The Mithraic relief at Dura, for example, shows the sun above to Mithras' right and the moon to his left.
[85] Richmond and Gillam, "Carrawburgh," 84–85.
[86] The Carrawburgh lamps disappeared soon after excavation. Lindsay Allason-Jones brought the existence of these artifacts to my attention.
[87] Lewis, *Temples*, 99.
[88] Richmond and Gillam, "Carrawburgh," 84–5.
[89] It is clear that Mithraism involved sophisticated cult philosophy and astronomy.
[90] Ulansey, *Origins*, 18–19.

476) and the floor mosaics from the Mithraeum of Felicissimus at Ostia (*CIMRM* 299), reveal much about the costumes and symbols of the various grades of worship. Further, a bronze tablet discovered at Virodunum, on display in the Landesmuseum für Kärnten at Klagenfurt, lists a sodality of followers of Mithras, including those who have died from the plague.[91]

Ceremonies varied according to the grade of initiation, and since our sources are hostile, and much of the information seems outrageous. One initiation ceremony may have involved binding the initiate's hand with chicken gut. He was blindfolded and had to leap across a trench of water, after which a single sword stroke liberated him (Ambrose, *Commentarii in XIII epistolas Beati Pauli ad Rom.* 22–23). Initiation might have entailed tortures and branding (Gregory Nazianzen, *adversus Iulianum* 1.70), washing away sins (Tertullian, *de baptismo* 5; *MMM*, II, 50), or live burial—a stone structure at Carrawburgh was just large enough for a prostrate man; a cylindrical silver canister from London shows a man emerging from a coffin-like chest in the midst of a beast fight or, more likely, after enduring a Mithraic initiation—effecting rebirth in imitation of Mithras' birth from the cosmic egg.[92] Initiation and testing may have included ordeals of heat, cold, and fasting, according to Nonnus (*MMM*, II, 27–28); supporting Nonnus' claim, narrow benches have been installed very close

---

[91] Piccottini, *Mithrastempel.*

[92] Toynbee, *Art in Britain*, #110, pls. 111–12; Toynbee, *A Silver Casket; ERML*, 114–16, figs. 26–7; Toynbee, *Temple of Mithras*, #16, Pl. XIII, pls. 22–25, 29, figs. 1–4; Shepherd, *Temple of Mithras*, VII/IX/X.1. Merrifield in Shepherd, *Temple of Mithras*, 233–236, provides complete description and discussion of these very complex scenes. On the side of the container, one can see a man, his head covered (with the veil of the *nymphus*, presumably), emerging from an oblong wheeled box (Toynbee, *Temple of Mithras*, 50). Another figure with a pointed hat helps the initiate from the box as he clasps right hands with him. The initiate seems to hand over a purse. The scene apparently displays three separate events: the emergence of the initiate; the oath he swears while clasping right hands with his mentor; and the payment of his initiation fee. The lid shows, *inter alia*, two griffins about to be trapped. According to Toynbee, the scenes on the box are analogous to scenes of hunting, capturing and transporting wild animals (and griffins), presumably for the arena, found on mosaics in a villa near Piazza Armerina in central Sicily: Gentili, *villa romana di Piazza Armeni*; "mosaica," 33–46; *villa erculia*; Kähler, *Villa des Maxentius*; Pace, *mosaica di Piazza Armerina*. Toynbee argued that the silver casket represents the hunt. Merrifield suggested that the scene can be taken in a strictly Mithraic (rather than decorative) context. Mithraic philosophy emphasized the progression of the soul which had endured danger with steadfast courage. These scenes could represent Mithraic philosophy: the struggle between man and nature (Merrifield in Shepherd, *Temple of Mithras*, 234).

to large fireplaces in some British Mithraea (Carrawburgh). Simulated fear was yet another element, as attested by the tradition that Commodus committed murder at a point in the ceremony when fear was called for (*SHA Comm.* 9). Initiation may have been a painful and dangerous ordeal. Some suggest that drugs may have been used to effect the appearance of death and to give the candidate a chance of survival.[93]

As a Roman god, Mithras attracted primarily civil servants and soldiers, an educated class to whom the cult's esoteric ritual and theosophy appealed. Tertullian (*de Corona* 15.4) viewed the cult as inseparable from army life because it promoted the camaraderie of the men. Women were not admitted. Reliefs show no goddesses; and no votives bear the name of a woman as dedicator.[94] Mithras' lessons included fortitude and restraint, skills necessary for a soldier. His cult demanded a complete and lifelong commitment from worshippers, just as military service does, but Mithras tolerated other deities. Occasionally, votives to other gods found sanctuary in his temples (i.e., the Mother Goddesses at Carrawburgh). The cult may have promised redemption, salvation, and ever-lasting life.[95] As the cult developed in the west, Mithras became more closely associated with the sun until the two were fused as indicated by the address *Deo Invicto Soli Mithrae.*[96] As such, Mithras was worshipped in Britain (430, 431, 434, 435).

Mithras in Britain

Although the evidence for Mithras in Britain is extremely localized, this Roman version of a Persian deity is attested more widely than other Eastern gods in Britain, indicative of Mithras' wide appeal.

The large frontier army supported the cult in Britain where five

---

[93] Merrifield in Shepherd, *Temple of Mithras*, 233. Merrifield interprets a silver casket (Shepherd, *Temple of Mithras*, fig. 209) and strainer (Shepherd, *Temple of Mithras*, fig. 210) as an infusion kit for such a drug. The small silver strainer, too fine to strain honey used for purification of the lion grade, shows a triple bar at the top identical with Roman containers for measuring dry, loose materials, such as grain. The silver casket, just barely larger than the strainer, was probably a storage container for this valuable implement (Merrifield, 233).

[94] *MMM*, I, 329–30.

[95] Cumont, *Mystères*, 143; Ulansey, *Origins*, 125.

[96] Halsberghe, "Sol Invictus," 117–22.

Mithraea, most cut into hillsides (in imitation of the Mithraic cave), have been excavated.[97] The elaborate Mithraeum in London may have been used primarily by civilians, but soldiers from the Cripplegate fort and veterans likely patronized the temple—a legionary veteran is the only worshipper of Mithras at London whose name is known (415). The other four British Mithraea are strictly military. All stood within 180m of their respective forts, built into the sides of valleys, to simulate the world cave, and all were near water sources.[98] Most, perhaps all, of the Mithraic material in Britain is military.

Augusta Londinium (London)[99]

The Walbrook Mithraeum was discovered in 1953 on the east bank of the Walbrook, a stream which has long since dried up, west of and partially underneath the current Walbrook street. The temple, about 516.75m east of the stream, measured about 18.3 by 7.6m, excluding the apse at the west end and the narthex at the eastern end.[100] It was the most elaborate and largest of the British Mithraea.[101] The temple followed the general basilical plan, its interior divided into a nave and side aisles. A double-door set into the east wall led into a narthex whose floor was roughly .75m above the nave. A stone sill and two steps originally led into the Mithraeum: effecting a sense of descent recalling the *Mithraic* cave. By the fourth century, the floor level had risen so that the steps were completely covered. The nave, 3.35m wide, was flanked by sleeper-walls supporting seven stone colonnades at each side, perhaps symbolizing the seven grades of initiation.[102] One fragmentary base and the plaster settings of the other bases survive, the columns removed in antiquity.[103] Wooden benches occupied the aisles beyond the sleeper walls. The semicir-

---

[97] Harris, *Oriental Cults*, 1. Elsewhere, Mithraea were subterranean, but such a construction in the wet British climate would have been extremely difficult.

[98] Lewis, *Temples*, 102.

[99] For a complete discussion of the temple and site see, most recently, Shepherd, *Temple of Mithras*.

[100] Lewis, *Temples*, 100. The London Mithraeum is among the largest, surpassed only by two Mithraea in Ostia and one in Rome (Santa Prisca). The apse is also an unusual feature for a Mithraeum.

[101] Lewis, *Temples*, 100. Strictly military Mithraea are generally of rougher construction than the commercial sanctuaries.

[102] Lewis, *Temples*, 100; W.F. Grimes, in Toynbee, *Temple of Mithras*, 1.

[103] The surviving fragment is of rough oolite limestone, Guildhall Museum, #18500; Richmond, "Roman Britain in 1954," 138.

cular apse at the western end was elevated about a meter above the nave. At the southwest corner stood a square timber-lined well. The floors and benches were wooden.

The temple was originally constructed AD 240–250, as the evidence of pottery attests.[104] As the temple aged, the floors were built up, perhaps in reaction to the damp conditions near the Walbrook stream. Eight floors successively installed eventually concealed the sleeper walls. Numismatic evidence suggests that the temple's use continued until ca. 350, after some of the Mithraeum's finer marble pieces had been buried. No inscribed altars were found in the Walbrook temple, nor were any of the marble sculptures associated with the cult found *in situ*. The marbles, found in the 1954 excavations, were unearthed in two caches near the eastern entrance of the shrine.

Among the strictly Mithraic objects belonging to the temple is a tauroctony, of saccharoidal marble in bas-relief, dedicated by an *emeritus* of *legio II Augusta* (415). The tauroctony shows the usual scene of Mithras slaying the bull (see above, description of Housesteads tauroctony). The bull-slaying scene is framed by a roundel featuring the twelve signs of the zodiac. Outside the roundel in the upper left hand corner, Sol drives his team of four horses towards the right. Sol's head has broken off; a headless Luna, in the upper right hand corner, steers a pair of bulls towards the right. Boreas and Zephyrus appear in the lower corners.[105] A marble panel, dedicated in 310/11 to *Deus Mithras et Sol Invictus* (416), was found reused in the Mithraeum floor.[106] A marble bust, representing the god as the handsome bearded youth wearing a Phrygian cap, shows a cut on the neck but is otherwise undamaged and probably did not fall victim to iconoclasts.[107] The temple probably featured a marble colossus of Mithras Tauroctonus.

---

[104] Shepherd, *Temple of Mithras*, 221; Merrifield, *London*, 183; Grimes in Toynbee, *Temple of London*, 1; Sauer, *End of Paganism*, 11. Some pieces of sculpture (Toynbee, *Art in Britain*, #20, 24, 29, 32, 38) date to the second century and were probably in private hands before coming into possession of the Mithraeum: Toynbee, *Art in Britain*, 142.

[105] The workmanship is probably Italian. *CIMRM* 801–11, fig. 218; Toynbee, *Art in Britain*, #69, pl. 73; Toynbee, *Temple of Mithras*, #10, Pl. X; Shepherd, *Temple of Mithras*, IX.46.

[106] Shepherd, *Temple of Mithras*, IX.47.

[107] Richmond, "Roman Britain in 1954," pl. 44, fig. 1; *CIMRM* 815, fig. 252; Toynbee, *Art in Britain*, #36, pl. 42; *ERML*, 106, pl. 44; Toynbee, *Temple of Mithras*, #1, pls. 1–3. Sauer, *End of Paganism*, 26–27, 52; Shepherd, *Temple of Mithras*, IX.38. The workmanship is Italian.

A detachable marble hand, late second century, about twice life size, grasps a cylindrical hilt, broken off.[108] The left hand and forearm of a limestone statue of Mithras Tauroctonos (third century) was found just northwest of the temple.[109] A third century limestone Cautopates, in high-relief and much damaged, surfaced just outside the south wall of the temple. Extant is the lower portion, from the waist downward, of Cautopates, standing with his right leg crossed over his left. The down-turned torch is clearly visible.[110] The silver casket (described above) exhibits a hunting scene on its outer wall, an appropriate image: Mithras is occasionally rendered as a mounted hunter who slays forces of wickedness and death.[111]

Other pieces of statuary found on the temple site reveal the syncretic nature of the cult. A removable marble head from a statue of Minerva dates to the second century.[112] A second century marble head of Serapis, also removable, with a *modius* was found deliberately buried together with the Mercury group and the colossal hand of Mithras Tauroctonos.[113] A fine-grained marble sculpture in the round shows Mercury sitting on a rock, with his money bag, tortoise

[108] Richmond, "Roman Britain in 1954," pl. 45, fig. 2; Toynbee, *Art in Britain*, #37, pl. 40; *ERML*, 108, pl. 50; Toynbee *Temple of Mithras*, #5, pl. 12; Shepherd, *Temple of Mithras*, IX.41. The statue seems to have been of Italian workmanship. There are no known parallels for such hands in other Mithraic contexts.

[109] Richmond, "Roman Britain in 1954," pl. 48, fig. 2; Toynbee, *Temple of Mithras*, #11, pl. 16–17; Shepherd, *Temple of Mithras*, IX.43. Henig, "Sculptors from the West," 97, suggests that the sculptor was a native of the Cotswolds and used limestone quarried locally.

[110] Richmond, "Roman Britain in 1954," pl. 48, fig. 1; Toynbee, *Temple of Mithras*, #12, pl. 18.

[111] For example, on a two sided slab from Dieburg, Mithras is depicted with three hunting dogs; the prey is not shown: Behn, *Mithrasheiligtum*, 11–16, pl. 1. On the reverse of a slab from Rückingen is a similar scene: Birkner, "Mithraskultes," 349–62, pl. 24; *CIMRM* 1137, fig. 297. From Osterburken, one of the small scenes framing the tauroctony shows Mithras taking aim with bow and arrow; again, the quarry is not shown: *MMM*, 350, #246, pl. 6. Mithras as a rider, not necessarily a hunter, appears in relief at Neuenheim: *MMM*, #310, fig. 357; *CIMRM* 1289, fig. 338. On the Tauroctony from Neuenheim, in two small bordering scenes along the top, Mithras appears as an unmounted archer: *MMM* #245c, pl. 5; *CIMRM* 1238, fig. 337. A mural painting from the Dura-Europus Mithraeum shows Mithras accompanied by a lion and a snake in pursuit of five wild animals: Rostoftzeff, ed., *Dura-Europus: VII–VIII*, 1939, pls. 14–15; *CIMRM* 52, fig. 24.

[112] Richmond, "Roman Britain in 1954," pl. 44, fig. 2; Toynbee, *Art in Britain*, #24, pl. 28; Merrifield, *ERML*, 107–8, pl. 46; Toynbee *Temple of Mithras*, #2; Shepherd, *Temple of Mithras*, IX.39. The workmanship is Italian. This piece is the only known example of Minerva in a Mithraic context: Shepherd, *Temple of Mithras*, 167.

[113] Richmond, "Roman Britain in 1954," pl. 45, fig. 1; *CIMRM* 818, fig. 253; Toynbee, *Art in Britain*, #38, pl. 43; Merrifield, *ERML*, 108, pls. 47–8; Toynbee,

and ram. The second century piece is fractured in several places. Now missing are the god's right hand and the caduceus which it probably held.[114] A limestone relief, reminiscent of the Dioscurus at Corbridge (*CSIR* 1.1.55), shows a Dioscurus standing in front of his horse whose hindquarters only survive.[115] The figure, holding a staff in his left hand, rests his weight on his right leg and wears only a cloak fastened at the right shoulder and a pointed cap covering his curly locks.[116]

Local deities are also represented. A marble sculpture in the round represents a reclining water deity, whose head and upper torso survives; the nose has cracked off.[117] Since Mithras was significant to sailors (pirates, *inter alia*), as were star maps, water *genii* do not surprise.[118] A half draped *genius*, whose head has snapped off at the neck, holds a cornucopia and a prow. He holds a patera in his right hand, a snake coils around his right wrist.[119] One of the most intriguing finds is a fourth century circular marble plaque of Danubian rider gods, possibly a *votum* to Mithras.[120]

The finds from the London temple are among the most elegant

Temple of Mithras, #3, pls. 8–9; Shepherd, *Temple of Mithras*, IX.40. Serapis is attested at Mithraea in Merida, Spain (Paris, "Mithra en Espagna," 11–13, #11, fig. 9) and Rome (Santa Prisca: Vermaseren and van Essen, *Santa Prisca*, pl. 104, 105, 107) and Dura-Europus (Rostovtzeff *Dura-Europus: VII–VIII*, pl. 29, fig. 2; pl. 30; *CIMRM* 40, fig. 15).

[114] Richmond, "Roman Britain in 1954," pl. 46; Toynbee, *Art in Britain*, #20, pl. 31; Merrifield, *ERML*, 108, pls. 48–9; Toynbee, *Temple of Mithras*, #4, pls. 10–11.

[115] It has been argued that the Dioscurus may have belonged to another temple or to a Bacchic rededication of the London Mithraeum. However, the Dioscuri can be correlated to the Mithraic *dadophori* since both sets of twins frequently wear Phrygian caps, stand with their legs crossed and symbolize the equinoxes and the rising and setting of the sun: Ulansey, *Origins*, 112–116. Furthermore, Bacchus was very popular with Mithraists in the fourth century: Sauer, *End of Paganism*, 27.

[116] Richmond, "Roman Britain in 1957," pl. 21, fig. 2; Toynbee, *Art in Britain*, #61, pl. 69; Toynbee, *Temple of Mithras*, #13, pl. 19.

[117] *CIMRM* 813, fig. 220; Toynbee, *Art in Britain*, #29, pl. 35; Toynbee, *Temple of Mithras*, #8; Shepherd, *Temple of Mithras*, IX.44. The marble and workmanship are Italian.

[118] Parallels for water deities in Mithraic contexts are to found at Dieburg (Behn, *Mithrasheiligtum*, pl. 2 and *CIMRM* 1247, fig. 324), Virinum, Noricum (*CIMRM* 1430, fig. 366), Heddernheim (*CIMRM* 1083, fig. 274), Santa Prisca, Rome (*CIMRM* 478, fig. 131; Vermaseren and van Essen, *Santa Prisca*, pl. 18, figs. 1, 19), and Merida, Spain (Paris, "Mithra en Espagna," 8–9, #8, fig. 6; *CIMRM* 273, #778, fig. 212).

[119] *CIMRM* 812, fig. 219; Toynbee, *Art in Britain*, #32, pl. 25; Breeze, "*Optio* and *Magister*," 130, pl. 20b; Toynbee, *Temple of Mithras*, #9, pl. 15; Shepherd, *Temple of Mithras*, IX.45. The marble and workmanship are Italian.

[120] *CIMRM* 819; Toynbee, *Art under the Romans*, 167–8, pl. 42; Harris, *Oriental Cults*, 4–5, note 7; D. Tudor, *Equitum Danuvinorum* i, pl. 79, #181; Toynbee, *Temple*

art pieces associated with any Mithraeum. All the pieces seem to have been of foreign craftsmanship, probably from Mediterranean workshops, and these exquisite votives indicate that the followers of the London cult were wealthy and sophisticated. The remains point to syncretism in Mithraic cult. All the gods who shared the Walbrook temple with Mithras were harmonious with the Mithraic concerns for the beatitude and after-life of his followers. Minerva, patroness of arts and crafts, the source of wisdom, could bestow immortality, and as a martial deity she conquered death. Accepted as a god of fertility and the underworld, the bestower of abundance on earth and in the after-life, as a savior, like Mithras, Serapis is called Sol and Invictus.[121] By the first century BC, Mithras was identified with Mercury/Hermes, who as *Psychopompos* guided souls on their journey after death.[122] A Cautes at Housesteads holds a caduceus in addition to his up-turned torch (p. 94, below), providing another link between Mithras and Mercury. Water gods, a common motif in Roman funerary art, remind one that the soul must travel the river of death to the Isles of the Blessed. Water, furthermore, is an agent of purification and fruitfulness. The *genius* also brings to mind other-worldliness with his patera and snake, an image of the living-dead.[123] The Dioscuri's roles included guarding tombs.[124] Finally, Bacchus, a popular theme for Roman tomb-art, seems, in Mithraic contexts, to stress the mortality of humanity and the transitory nature of life on earth.[125] The deliberate burial of these pieces, possibly after AD 330,

---

of Mithras, #14, Pl. XI; Mackintosh, *Divine Rider*, 60, and plate V; Shepherd, *Temple of Mithras*, X.1. The roundel features two horsemen facing a central female figure who stands behind a tripod table on which lies a fish. The left horseman is clear: he wears a short tunic and a Phrygian cap; his right hand is raised as if to strike the prostrate figure beneath his horse's hooves. The right-hand figure is fragmentary. Beneath the main scene, one can detect a leaping hunting dog, a crater, and an object which might have been a bird or a scorpion. Rider gods evoke the Dioscuri (Toynbee, *Temple of Mithras*, 37). No extant Danubian rider monument bears an inscription.

[121] For example at Rome: *invicto deo Serapidi* (*CIL* VI 574); at Sentinum: *Iovi Soli Invicto Serapidi* (*CIL* XI 5738).

[122] At Nemrud Dagh in Commagene, Mithras was identified as Apollo Mithras Hermes during the lifetime of Antiochus I (69–34 BC): *CIMRM* 33. Nb. Mercury as patron of the Mithraic *Corax*.

[123] Toynbee, "Genii Cucullati," 330, pl. 20b.

[124] Will, *Le relief cultuel gréco-romain*, 89–90.

[125] Toynbee, *Temple of Mithras*, 62. These pieces are described in chapter 5 (p. 163). Some argue for a rededication of the London Mithraeum to Bacchus: Hutchison, "Cult," 152; Toynbee, *Temple of Mithras*, 60; Henig, *Religion*, 107–109; Merrifield, "Art and Religion," 375–382, 396–97. However, it was not uncommon

illustrates the worshippers' concern to protect their cult implements from iconoclasts.[126]

The cult of Mithras seems to decline in London in the fourth century. It is also clear that the Mithraists left the temple before the building was abandoned. Several points support a conclusion of abandonment: collapse of part of the building (and subsequent rebuilding); removal of the colonnades which resulted in a more open floor plan; burial of cult icons in the temple floor and a subsequent new floor-plan.[127] The building may have been converted to use as a Bacchus temple. The early sculpture only was Mithraic; later pieces represent the Dioscuri, the Danubian rider gods, and the Bacchus cult.[128]

Legionary Forts (Caerleon, Chester, York)

An inscribed column base, dedicated to Mithras Invictus (417) implies a Mithraeum at Caerleon. The extra-mural temple, perhaps of third century construction, has not yet been located.[129]

From Chester, a fragmentary Cautopates stands with legs crossed and holds a down-turned torch (*MMM*, II, 268; *CIMRM* 830).[130] A bas-relief shows a *dadophorus*, presumably Cautopates, dressed in the Phrygian style, his legs crossed, and resting on an unrecognizable

---

for Mithraists to worship Bacchus in the fourth century: Collins-Clinton, "Liber-Pater," 38–45; Bloch, "Pagan Revival," 203. The fact that the marbles and three silver pieces which had been buried were not retrieved does not prove that the temple changed hands. As long as the threat of iconoclasm remained, it would be unwise to remove these pieces from their hiding places. The threat may have been Christian, though common soldiers probably delighted in destroying officers' temples: Sauer, *End of Paganism*, 56.

[126] Saur, *End of Paganism*, 37–38. The temple eventually collapsed because the foundations had been built on shifting sediment.

[127] Shepherd, *Temple of Mithras*, 227–229. The icons may have been buried as an act of reverence by the congregation as the building was converted from Mithraeum to Hall.

[128] Henig in Shepherd, *Temple of Mithras*, 230–232. Of particular interest are a fourth century marble Bacchic group, (Shepherd, *Temple of Mithras*, X.59); and a marble Bacchus inscribed: *Hominibus Bagis Bitam* (Shepherd, *Temple of Mithras*, X.58). Trevor Brigham in Shepherd, *Temple of Mithras*, 237–240, discusses architectural changes which support the conversion of the temple to a *bacchium* or *sacrarium*. The very nature of Roman religion was syncretic, and there is no reason to suppose that Mithras would have excluded Bacchus.

[129] Boon, *Caerleon*, 41. Epigraphic evidence also suggests extra-mural temples to Jupiter Dolichenus (393) and Diana (297).

[130] Watkin, *Roman Cheshire*, 191.

object in his right hand (*MMM*, II, 269a; *CIMRM* 831; Wright and Richmond, *Cat. Chester* no. 169). This relic suggests either Cautopates or a mourning Attis.[131] No temple site has been identified.

A Mithraeum may have been attached to the Micklegate fort at York, but the temple site has not been located. A weathered limestone relief of the tauroctony is extant but uninscribed (*MMM* II, 270; *CIMRM* 835; *CSIR* 1.3.23). The *dadophori* stand on either side of the central scene, Cautes much damaged. A bust of Sol appears to the left of Mithras' head, Luna to his right. An unidentifiable figure stands at the extreme right. Below the central scene, three episodes from the life of Mithras are illustrated (from left to right): Sol kneels before Mithras who places his hands upon the other; Sol and Mithras recline at a covered table and share a meal; Mithras steps into Sol's chariot. In addition, the Mithraic god Ahriman is attested at the site (418).

Segontium (Caernarvon)

A Mithraeum, discovered in 1958, stood 137m east of the eastern corner of the Roman fort at Segontium.[132] Built near the bottom of a marshy valley,[133] the temple probably dates to the early third century.[134] Abandoned by the end of that same century, it measured 14.6 by 6.5m, overall, with an interior of 10.6 by 5.5m. A rectangular niche, 2.4 by .45m, was set into the north wall. At the south end, the narthex, 1.8 by 5.5m, was almost completely destroyed. At the side, steps approached the nave, flanked by benches.

Four altars, badly damaged, also survived; at least one was inscribed but only the last line survives: *SCOC*, perhaps the *tria nomina* of the dedicator followed by the centurial sign.[135] The other altars were smashed. No statuary survived except for a fragmentary pedestal which at one time may have held a *dadophorus*. Fragments of at least twelve oil lamps were associated with the temple's first phase; an

---

[131] Harris, *Oriental Cults*, 44. Wright and Richmond, *Grosvenor Museum*, #169, preferred to interpret the figure as Cautopates.

[132] Boon, "Mithras at Caernarvon," 136–72, for a full description of the excavations; Sauer, *End of Paganism*, 24–26.

[133] Harris, *Oriental Cults*, 36–37. In Roman times, a stream seems to have flowed through this marsh.

[134] Boon, "Mithras at Caernarvon," 144.

[135] Boon, "Mithras at Caernarvon," 166; J. 1960 #4. The dedicator may have been a centurion of the *cohors I Suncicorum*.

iron candle-holder with a central finial and a socketed base, dates
to the temple's final phase, as does a candlestick.

The limited finds from the temple make an assessment of its cult
difficult. A layer of humus suggests that the temple was abandoned
for a time and later burned (late fourth century), probably deliberately, though whether the temple was used as a Mithraeum at the
time of its destruction by fire is uncertain.[136] It may be significant
that archaeologists have recovered no statuary or *vota* unambiguously
Mithraic from the site. Only the temple floor-plan supports the
Mithraic identification.

Vindobala (Rudchester)

In 1844, farmers at Rudchester found five altars and a statuette
(*CIMRM* 843c; *CSIR* 1.1.229), which they recycled as a drain cover.[137]
The findspot, a little more than 137m southwest of the Roman fort,
was later judged to be the location of the Rudchester Mithraeum,
of which nothing can be seen today.[138]

The temple, following the usual plan, stood in a much drier locale
than other Wall Mithraea, and therefore was not subject to constant
renovations. The spring to the east and the "Giant's grave," a tank
cut into rock, are too far distant from the temple site, about 137m
to the southeast, to have been ritually connected to the shrine.

The temple was rebuilt according to the original plan and size,
without the ante-chapel. The benches were lengthened towards the
sanctuary (to accommodate a larger congregation?) and wooden roof-
posts were erected along the faces of the benches. A raised dais with
a grooved slab was built into the western apse, probably for the tauroctony. An undated inscribed altar (424) attests the restoration, probably late third or early fourth century.[139] No direct evidence suggests
that either the first or the second Mithraeum was ever abandoned,
and, furthermore, nothing suggests that any length of time elapsed
between the collapse of Mithraeum I and the construction of Mithraeum II.[140] Late fourth century pottery which accumulated as debris

---

[136] Boon, "Mithras at Caernarvon," 137–138; Saur, *End of Paganism*, 26.
[137] "Proceedings of the Committee," 385.
[138] Gillam and MacIvor, "Rudchester," 176–219.
[139] Gillam and MacIvor, "Rudchester," 196.
[140] Gillam and MacIvor, "Rudchester," 218.

on the floor of the abandoned temple, argues for a mid-fourth century abandonment date.

Four inscribed altars (423–426) and one uninscribed altar surfaced in 1844; one inscribed and four uninscribed altars (*CIMRM* 843b) were found against the northern bench in 1953, all of which probably date to the third century. That three were dedicated by prefects, one of whom dedicated an altar in honor of the temple's restoration, indicates that officers actively cultivated Mithras along the Wall. Also of interest is the altar dedicated by Aponius Rogatianus, who equated Mithras with Apollo (425).[141]

Heads of the *dadophori* (*CIMRM* 843d; *CSIR* 1.1.226–7), one still wearing his Phrygian cap (*CSIR* 1.1.226), were found in the eastern part of the nave, together with a limb (*CIMRM* 843d; *CSIR* 1.1.228). The two heads, made of different materials, probably did not form a pair.[142] Perhaps the Rudchester Mithraeum had two sets of *dadophori*, as did Carrawburgh.[143] The utter destruction of the statuary contrasts with the relatively good condition of the altars.[144]

Other finds include an oval stone water basin (*CIMRM* 843e), set in the narthex against the northern bench side two thirds of the way along the nave,[145] three lamps found near the south bench, a terracotta object pierced with small openings, perhaps an incense burner or thurible,[146] and an iron cleaver probably used in preparation of food for the ritual meals. No trace of the tauroctony has survived, but fragments of a large grooved slab (the slab is 61cm wide, 21.6cm thick, 86.4cm in length; the central groove 23cm wide and 2.54cm deep) suitable for supporting the base of such a *reredos* have been discovered south of the apse.[147]

---

[141] Also interesting is the Greek *Anicetus* for the Latin *Invictus*, found only once more on an altar from Dacia (*CIL* III 1436, Sarmizegetusa), suggesting that the dedicator had some Greek education (Bosanquet *History of Northumberland*, XII 38–9).

[142] Gillam and MacIvor, "Rudchester," 201.

[143] Harris, *Oriental Cults*, 28.

[144] Gillam and MacIvor, "Rudchester," 201, 206; Harris, *Oriental Cults*, 28, note 2. The damage to the altars is comparatively recent. The altar of Sentius Castus (426), with its rock birth and Mithras with the bull, could hardly have seemed as innocuous to the Christians as the radiate busts of the Sun god spared at Housesteads and Carrawburgh.

[145] Daniels, *Mithras*, 19. Parallels for such placement from other cults suggest a ritual significance to the placement of the water basin.

[146] Gillam and MacIvor, "Rudchester," 214–15.

[147] Gillam and MacIvor, "Rudchester," 210–11.

Brocolitia (Carrawburgh)

In 1950 Richmond and Gillam excavated the Carrawburgh Mithraeum,
built 27.4m southwest of the fort, on the east bank of a small marshy
valley. The temple, discovered in 1949, originally was a free-stand-
ing structure, not set into the hillside.[148]

The first temple, early third century, measured 8 × 5.6m overall,
and 5.3 × 4.6m internally.[149] Below the floor of the narthex, a drain
ran from the north-east corner of the narthex to the west side of
the door. This drain, from which it was possible to draw out running water for ritual use, carried a small feeder spring into the valley. Nothing implies that water was ever drawn from the spring—it
was possible to do so only during the earliest stage of the temple
since, in subsequent renovations, the pavement of the narthex floor
completely covered the drain.[150] This tiny temple was soon enlarged;
construction extended the building 4.3m northward, adding an apse
at the north end.

This second temple underwent at least two internal refittings,
including a change in the position of roof supports and ante-chapel
screen. Mithras may not have attracted a consistent congregation at
Carrawburgh, and the temple may have fallen into temporary periods of disuse. Alternatively, commanding officers may have imposed
personal tastes on subsequent renovation.[151] The first of the internal
renovations included the installation of an ordeal pit, a stone-lined
coffin-like recess in the floor (described above). The ordeal pit was
removed during the second renovation and replaced with a large
stone bench, as in the original plan. In both plans, a large stone
hearth was very close (38cm to the south) to the pit and the bench.
The Mithraic tests of endurance included subjection to the ordeals
of heat and cold (*Suda*, s.v. *Mithrou*; Gregory Nazianzen *adv. Iul.*

---

[148] Richmond and Gillam, "Carrawburgh," 1. The temple was oriented at 321
degrees, in accord with the natural contour of the hillside. Similar orientations at
Housesteads (260 degrees) and at Rudchester (307 degrees 5') may be purely coin-
cidental (Harris, *Oriental Cults*, 17, note 3). Gillam and MacIvor, "Rudchester," 182,
do not find astronomical or religious significance in the orientation but find the
coincidence of Mithraic orientation on the Wall interesting.

[149] Comparable in size are Mithraeum I at Poetovio (5.60 by 5.57m; Abramic,
Poetovio, 163) and Dura I (4.65 by 5.80m; Rostovtseff, ed. *Dura-Europus, VII–VIII*,
64, fig. 32).

[150] Richmond and Gillam, "Carrawburgh," 5–6.

[151] Harris, *Oriental Cults*, 19.

i.70),[152] including an element of terror (*SHA Commodus* 9). Comparable tests of endurance could have occurred in both bench and pit.[153]

The dilapidated second-phase temple was destroyed by fire during the invasions of AD 296/7. Renovators then enlarged the building (to accommodate a larger congregation),[154] completely restructured at a higher floor level. The walls were rebuilt fully. The internal measurements remained constant, but the apse was reduced to .46m in depth (formerly 1.7), and the narthex increased to 2.5m. A stone and clay platform held the hearth. Soon thereafter, the temple was destroyed: the roof was torn off, the tauroctony was removed, and the statues of the *dadophori* were smashed. That no Constantinian coins have appeared at the site indicates a late third/early fourth century abandonment.[155]

The three principal altars were dedicated by prefects of the *cohors I Batavorum*. Each altar belonged to a different period of the temple's use, but all were found in the ritual deposit and were originally on display in the apse. 428 is the earliest, belonging to the first temple; 427 dates to AD 213–222, the second phase of the Carrawburgh Mithraeum. 429 cannot be dated precisely but is of great interest because of the relief—originally painted, above the inscription—which represents the epiphany of Mithras as Sol. The rays of the radiate crown were pierced for illumination from behind by lamps placed in a recess carved at the back of the altar. In addition, the dedicator of 429, Simplicius Simplex, was seemingly a Romanized Celt, suggesting the cult's broad appeal.

Other pieces from the Mithraeum's narthex include a statuette of a seated Mother Goddess (*CIMRM* 850; *CSIR* 1.6.164)[156] and small pot for offerings from the ante-chapel. The *Mater*, excluded from the main chapel, was relegated to the narthex; and it is clear that the statue, heavily eroded from exposure to the open air, had previously

---

[152] Similar features have been found in one of the rooms of the Santa Prisca Mithraeum (Vermaseren and van Essen, *Santa Prisca*, 140–41). Gregory Nazianzen, *adversus Iulianum* i.89, refers to an ordeal by hair pulling.

[153] Richmond and Gillam, "Carrawburgh," 19.

[154] Richmond and Gillam, "Carrawburgh," 28.

[155] Richmond and Gillam, "Carrawburgh," 34; Harris, *Oriental Cults*, 23. The coins found in Mithraeum III include an illegible *denarius* of Severan date; some slightly worn coins of Victorinus (268–70; *RIC* 57; Cohen 90), Claudius II (268–70) and Tetricus (270–73; *RIC* 113; Cohen 119); and a nicely preserved *follis* of Maximinius I (296–308).

[156] A statue of a Mother Goddess nursing a child was found in the narthex of the Dieburg Mithraeum (Behn, *Mithrasheiligtum*, 35, #14; *CIMRM* 1262).

been in use elsewhere. Additionally, this local Mother Goddess was acceptable to Mithras in his fertility aspect (Porphyry *de antro nympharum* 6): n.b. the *nymphus* grade of initiation.[157]

At the ends of the benches in the nave, Cautes (*CIMRM* 849; *CSIR* 1.6.109) was found beheaded, Cautopates (*CIMRM* 849; *CSIR* 1.6.112) completely smashed and removed from the temple, except for his feet. Each statue and its bases were carved from a single piece of stone. The rough backs suggest that the statues originally stood against a wall, and the signs of damage and repair are clear. These pieces, sculpted from local stone, date to the third century. The existence of a second pair of *dadophori* at Carrawburgh may be inferred from pedestals found at the south end of the nave.[158] A Cautopates in high relief (*CSIR* 1.6.113), on display at the Chesters museum, is thought to have belonged to Carrawburgh.[159] Four small altars, personal votives to the god, were also found in the nave. The tauroctony relief, whose original position in the temple is still indicated by a grooved slab in the apse, survives in one small fragment, showing the bull's horn (*CSIR* 1.6.124).

The violent destruction of the statuary contrasts with the relatively decent state of preservation of the altars. The statuary was subjected to one of three fates. Some pieces were deliberately removed, as was the tauroctony; others were violently desecrated on the spot, for example, the *dadophori*; finally, some pieces (i.e., the statue of the Mother Goddess) were altogether left alone. If the worshippers had removed the tauroctony, it is unlikely that they would have left the statues of the *dadophori*. It is, furthermore, unlikely that stone robbers would have ignored the altars while pillaging the statuary. It is not surprising that the Mother Goddess statue survived: four Mithraea on the German frontier—Stockstadt, Saarburg, Königshofen, and Neuenheim—suffered similar destruction of Mithraic icons while those pieces associated with other cults were spared.[160] Furthermore, the altars, less suggestive of idolatry, may not have been as offensive to the Christians—if Christians are to be blamed for the temple's destruc-

---

[157] Richmond and Gillam, "Carrawburgh," 30–1. One *Matres* altar was recycled into the temple's bench (499), but an altar to the Nymphs and *Genius loci* may have taken refuge in the narthex (341, found near the temple).

[158] Richmond and Gillam, "Carrawburgh," 32.

[159] Daniels, "Housesteads Mithraeum," 114–15; Harris, *Oriental Cults*, 23. Perhaps a third pair is to be associated with the final construction of the temple.

[160] Richmond and Gillam, "Carrawburgh," 42–3.

tion[161]—as were the other Mithraic monuments (statues, reliefs).
Curiously, no positive evidence attests Christianity at Carrawburgh,[162]
and the local water nymph Coventina enjoyed worship well into the
Christian era.

After worshippers abandoned the Carrawburgh temple, the building was incorporated into a garbage dump—animal bones covered
it as it sank into the marshy peat.

Vercovicium (Housesteads)

The Mithraeum at Housesteads, facing east, about 274m south of
the fort, just to the west of a rocky ridge called Chapel Hill, was
built early in the third century. All that can be seen today is a slight
depression in the ground. In 1822, after workmen found altars belonging to the sanctuary (discovered in 1809), John Hodgson excavated
the site, finding the fragments of the tauroctony, a headless statue
of Cautes, and several altars.[163]

The temple itself measured about 13 by 4.9m internally, most
likely consisting of a nave with raised benches, a sanctuary and an
ante-chapel to the east, almost completely destroyed. Benches, approx-
imately 1.5m wide, flanked the nave's central aisle, paved with
flagstone, 2m wide. The nave's rough walls invoked the Mithraic
cave as the floor level deepened towards the west.[164] Traces of the
upper floor survive: oak planks and small birch logs on stone chip-
pings, raising the floor above the water table. Within the temple, a
spring rose into a stone tank with two channels to carry off excess
water. Perennial springs are common to Mithraea for ceremonial
purification.[165]

To the west, the sanctuary measured 3.9 by 3m. The tauroctony
was probably displayed in a recess (.76 by 2.1m) at the west end of
the sanctuary. The Housesteads tauroctony, the largest extant British
Mithraic bull-slaying relief, roughly 2.13m square, survived in 6 small
fragments (*CIMRM* 853; *CSIR* 1.6.127), which comprise less than a

---

[161] Sauer, *End of Paganism*, 41–42, 56–57.
[162] One shard of glass seems to bear the image of a swimming fish, which may
have a Christian connection: Allason-Jones and MacKay, *Coventina*, #137; Mawer,
Christianity, C6.G1.5.
[163] Hodgson, "Housesteads," 274.
[164] Bosanquet, "Housesteads," 257–8.
[165] Harris, *Oriental Cults*, 31.

quarter of the original. At the right hand edge of the scene, in three fragments Cautes holds his upturned torch and a caduceus and stands next to the foreleg of a bull.[166] Other fragments show part of Luna's crescent moon, bits of the bull's head, Mithras' right hand holding his dagger, the god's right shoulder, the edge of a tunic, and much of the dog. The piece was so large that it must have taken up the end wall of the sanctuary and may have been constructed in several panels.[167]

The Housesteads Mithras Saecularis (*CIMRM* 860; *CSIR* 1.6.126)— unusual in showing Mithras' birth from an egg (the cosmos, before the creation of the world), not the customary rock—is the only such example from Britain and one of four known in the Roman empire.[168] The base is plain; the upper frame is an egg-shaped border decorated with zodiac signs. Within the frame, Mithras rises, holding a sword in his right hand, torch in his left. The piece was probably intended to be viewed against a lighted backdrop.[169]

---

[166] The caduceus is an unusual feature though not without parallel. A relief from Fiano Romano shows Cautes in a feast scene striking the ground with a caduceus to produce fire or water (*CIMRM* 641, fig. 180; Daniels, "Housesteads Mithraeum," 108). The caduceus also brings to mind Hermes Psychopompus (Cumont, "bas-relief mithraique," 189).

[167] Daniels, "Housesteads Mithraeum," 108.

[168] The relief from Trier (*CIMRM* 985, fig. 237) shows Mithras as a child holding a sphere in his hand while leaning through the orbit of the zodiac. The relief from Modena (*CIMRM* 695) depicts Mithras fully grown, standing with one half of the egg under his feet, the other half on his head. He has goat horns and wings and holds a staff and a torch. A snake encircles him while a zodiac frames the entire scene. Daniels, "Housesteads Mithraeum," 109, takes that scene to represent the Orphic Phanes. The third is a fragment of an oval border from the former Yugoslavia (*CIMRM* 1870). See also Beck, *Planetary Gods*, 34–42, for a discussion of the astrological significance of the Mithras Sacularis at Housesteads. The arrangement of the signs of the zodiac on this piece suggest the planetary arrangement within those signs. That the zodiac is arranged by planetary house further suggests that the theme of the Mithras Saecularis is nothing less than the birth of the universe. The planets were first set in those houses when the universe was created: Firmicus Maternus, *Math.*, 3.1; Macrobius, *In Somn.* 1.21.23–27. At the top of the scene, above the nascent Mithras, are Cancer to the left, Leo to the right. The significance of the Cancer-Leo boundary might derive from an ancient theory whereby the "return" of the planets to a single point of longitude would occur in the sign of Cancer. Universal conflagration or deluge would ensue: Beck, *Planetary Gods*, 40–41; Seneca, *Nat. Quaest.* 3.29.1. Although Cancer (summer solstice) was the usual point of entry for souls and Capricorn (winter solstice), the point of exit (Porphyry *de antro* 21), Varro did know of a variant which provided for three gates: Scorpius, used by Hercules; a boundary between Aquarius and Pisces; and one between Leo and Cancer (Servius *ad Georg.* 1.34). The Cancer-Leo boundary might then serve as an access point for souls: Beck, *Planetary Gods*, 42.

[169] *CIMRM* 695; Toynbee, *Art in Britain*, #71, pl. 74; Daniels, "Housesteads

The two altars flanking this sculpture were dedicated to Mithras Saecularis (430, 431), indicating a connection with the Orphic cult. Mithras as Saecularis was closely connected to Aeon, the bull-slaying warrior son of Jupiter (Ahura Mazda), who became conflated with the Supreme Deity (First Cause, Aeon, Saeculum, Chronos). Aeon yielded Jupiter, goodness incarnate, and Pluto (Ahriman), the embodiment of Evil. The supreme deity, he was also called Phanes in the Orphic cult.[170] The egg from the Housesteads birth of Mithras also recalls Orphism. Orphic influence indicates that, especially on the Wall, highly educated senior officers, sophisticated religio-philosophical leanings, cultivated Mithras.[171]

A headless Cautes (*CIMRM* 856) was found in 1822; no companion Cautopates has been recorded. A second pair of *dadophori* (Cautes: *CIMRM* 857; *CSIR* 1.6.111; Cautopates: *CIMRM* 857; *CSIR* 1.6.114) were uncovered by Bosanquet, both greatly damaged, the head of Cautopates missing. Catalogue 431 (AD 252) might indicate a rededication of the shrine since this altar's material differs from the stone of the tauroctony, birth scene, and *dadophori*.

An altar to Sol (432), a deity not unexpected in Mithraic contexts, was found on the site. An additional three altars, found in the temple, invoke Cocidius (172, 587, 588). In addition, Mithras at Housesteads gave refuge to an altar dedicated to Mars and Victory (271). It is possible that the local shrine to Cocidius was destroyed in the invasions of 297, and that sanctified objects were thereafter accepted into the Mithraeum (n.b., the *Matres* at Carrawburgh).[172]

Typically, very little survives of the Housesteads Mithraeum.[173] Unlike other Wall Mithraea, the Housesteads temple was not rebuilt after the barbarian invasions of 296/7.[174]

Mithraeum," 108–13; Harris, *Oriental Cults*, 34. As were the Bacchus group from London and an altar from Carrawburgh.

[170] Daniels, "Housesteads Mithraeum," 110–11.

[171] Daniels, "Housesteads Mithraeum," 111; H. Jackson, "Leontocephaline," 20–21; Ulansey, *Origins*, 120. Although Mithras appealed only to officers, as far as we know, in Britain, this was not the case elsewhere especially the German provinces where epigraphy and archaeology suggest a broader base of worshippers: Sauer, *End of Paganism*, 56.

[172] Daniels, "Housesteads Mithraeum," 106. The Cocidius altars have suffered heavy weathering, supporting the suggestion that they were left exposed to the weather for some time.

[173] Harris, *Oriental Cults*, 36.

[174] Lewis, *Temples*, 106.

Other Evidence from the Wall Area

A few scattered pieces from other sites along or near Hadrian's Wall attest Mithras. Three inscribed altars (433–5) suggest a Mithraic congregation at Castlesteads, although a temple site has not been located. Attributable to Carlisle is a fragmentary Cautes, consisting of an inscribed pedestal and the figure's right foot (419). A large stone slab from High Rochester, the most northerly point at which Mithraism has been recorded, commemorates the building of a temple, early third century (422).

Conclusions

Mithraism in Britain was localized, and most of the evidence can be placed firmly within military contexts datable to the third century. It has been taken on faith that Mithraism fell victim to Christianity. This supposition, however, is problematic for Roman Britain since, for a large part, Mithraic cult icons were destroyed and temples abandoned by the late third century, before the official Christianization of the empire. Pre-Constantinian evidence for Christianity in Britain is isolated, mostly civilian, mostly southern. Christian influence over soldiers and officers of the Roman army in Britain before Constantine was, at best, limited. However, we should not dismiss the possibility that on occasion a Christian officer might have ordered the destruction of a Mithraeum on Hadrian's Wall.

It will be remembered, furthermore, that Diocletian, Maximianus, and Galerius invoked Mithras as *fautor imperii sui* (*CIL* III 4413) in 307/8. One must ask why this cult fell out of favor in our province while it still enjoyed imperial patronage.[175] Britain's rather homogenous (Romano-Celtic) population did not, as the lack of Mithraic evidence outside the military zone in Britain (*contra* Germany) suggests, cultivate Mithras, a completely foreign god. Iconoclasts, Christian or not, may have met with little resistance.[176] Furthermore, the

---

[175] 415 was dedicated 310/11 from London. The governor's staff certainly would have maintained closer ties to the central imperial administration. The Caernarvon temple, if it can be identified as Mithraic, survived well into the fourth century. Caernarvon was strategically important, on the route to Anglesey, but in a remote, economically weak, and relatively un-Romanized corner of Wales: Sauer, *End of Paganism*, 57.

[176] Sauer, *End of Paganism*, 58.

timing of the cult's demise corresponds to the implementation of Diocletian's reforms in army organization, recruitment and administration.[177]

Mithras' appeal in Britain was clearly limited. If the late third century army was comprised primarily of local recruits, those recruits probably found greater spiritual solace in local, familiar gods. Additionally, education may have been a factor. Britain was an isolated province, and local enlisted men may not have received the type of education which would have made them amenable to this esoteric and philosophical cult.

Furthermore, both Mithras and Dolichenus appealed to soldiers as well as officers; both gods were Eastern, retaining vestiges of their exotic origins in cult iconography and ritual while maintaining a Mediterranean veneer which lent greater dignity and authority to the religions. Both cults involved catechism and initiation; both cults consisted of sacral meals. The followers of both gods probably, Mithraism certainly, subscribed to an esoteric cult philosophy which would further distinguish the group of worshippers from non-worshippers. Such social and "secret" activities allowed adherents of each of these gods to distinguish themselves from the larger group; "reticence was not merely a means of self-protection: it was an essential part of their appeal."[178] On the one hand, group worship enhanced *esprit de corps*; on the other, cultic isolation contributed to a sense of importance and distinction for an elite group of worshippers.

The popularity of both gods depended on imperial patronage and worship fell off dramatically once emperors embraced Christianity.

Neither Mithras nor Dolichenus, as will be seen with other Eastern gods (notably Isis), gained lasting popularity in Britain. Roman Britain never sustained a large Eastern population, which might have enhanced the popularity of Eastern gods, but which was restricted to the military zone and London, the seat of the provincial government as well as a center for trade. Native gods remained popular, answering the spiritual needs of Romano-British worshippers. The local population probably did not distinguish these Eastern rites from more purely Roman rites.

---

[177] Sauer, *End of Paganism*, 57. Changes in recruitment of soldiers and officers may have affected the dynamics of minority cults, though further speculation is unprofitable.

[178] Gordon, "Authority, salvation and mystery," 45.

CHAPTER THREE

CELTIC RELIGIONS, HORNED WARRIORS, AND GRAECO-ROMAN HEROES

The horned warrior cults, as the Roman soldiers observed them, pose certain problems: extreme localization and class stratification, both aspects reflective of Celtic, rather than Roman, practices. The localization, and to a lesser extent class stratification, are reminiscent of Greek hero cults, which provide a better model for the interpretation of our Celtic gods than do the deities of Graeco-Roman civic rites.

Sources and Problems

The Romano-Celtic religions owe their survival almost exclusively to the epigraphic record. The literary record is sparse, and all accounts stem from the lost works of Posidonius. Caesar's discussion merely underscored the Roman attitude that all men, Roman and foreign, worship the same gods, albeit under different names (*BG* VI.16–17, cf. Tacitus, *Germania*, 9). The Celts, so the Roman believed, worshipped Mercury foremost, they venerated Mars and Hercules with animal sacrifice, they also recognized Isis, and they did not generally construct permanent, roofed temples on *loci consecrati*. The prominence of the Druid class and the Celtic practice of human sacrifice were the only differences of substance between Roman and Celtic ritual, according to the prejudiced Roman.[1] Lucan (1.445–6) cites three divine names, Teutates, Esus, and Taranis, respectively equated with Mars, Mercury, and Jupiter. Other sources include Strabo (4.4.4–5), Athenaeus, and Diodorus Siculus (5.28.6), as well as Pomponius Mela (3.2.18–19), Pliny (*NH* 16.249–51, 30.13), Dio Cassius (60.20.6–8), and Ammianus Marcellinus (15.9.4,8), all of whom follow Posidonius. There is only an occasional passing refer-

---

[1] For the Druids, see Piggot, *Druids*, especially 13–33, where the author discusses the problems connected with archaeological and written sources. More recently, Lonigan, *Druids*.

ence to Celtic and Germanic deities by Christian writers who, for the most part, reserved their invective for the state religion and Eastern cults.

Nor is the epigraphic record helpful. In most cases, Celtic gods of the Roman era are attested by a single inscription, and little more can be said other than what the stone itself tells us; but the find spot (within the camp, outside the camp, or in the civilian *vicus*) and accompanying votive offerings, if any, provide further clues. Virtually all of our evidence comes from military contexts. Since the material is erratically preserved, gaps in the record constitute another problem with the source material. The Christian sweep of non-Christian religious sites in the fourth century, in particular, caused great archaeological loss and destruction. We shall never know what has vanished or how much.

Celtic Religion

The Celtic pantheon differed from the Roman in several important aspects. Since there was no unified Celtic state, there was, consequently, no organized Celtic religion, which was ordered instead at the local tribal level rather than regionally or "nationally." Second, whereas the Roman Jupiter was universally recognized in the Latin speaking world, Celtic gods were mostly localized. Some Celtic gods were recognized widely: Lug, corresponding to Caesar's Mercury, was commemorated in place names throughout Europe (especially Lugdunum) and survived as the Irish Lugh and Welsh Lleu; Epona the goddess of horses was likewise attested throughout the Celtic ethnic areas (pp. 154–155). The cultic range of a god could be rather large, extending along Hadrian's Wall (Belatucadrus to the west, Veteris towards the east), common throughout a region (the *Matres* in Gloucestershire), or quite small—a single spring or well (Mars Nodens at Lydney and Cockersand Moss, Lanc., Coventina at Carrawburgh, or Sulis at Bath). Each tribe likely had its own sky or war god, yet these tribal Celtic gods shared a number of characteristics which makes it possible to discuss them according to type.[2] For example,

---

[2] Ross, "Horned God," 63, 65. Ross sees patterns of worship. The tribal god is a multi-functional deity who protects his tribe in war, provides for the fertility of humans, stock, and fields, who oversees law, religion, and the administration of

a worshipper of the healer god Mars Nodens would find the cult to the Treveran healer god Lenus Mars familiar. Third, Roman deities were more specialized in function than their Celtic counterparts, so the survival of our evidence would suggest. Mars was seen primarily as a god of war (though he was in origin an agricultural, protective deity); his Celtic counterparts, the various horned-gods, were concerned not only with war but also with fertility, healing, protection, law and justice, and prosperity, as suggested by the iconography. The same Celtic deity could easily assimilate to different Roman gods: Cocidius Silvanus (588) on the eastern part of Hadrian's Wall, Cocidius Mars (596, 598) in the west.[3] This, however, does not suggest monotheism. In addition, androgyny in Celtic deities suggests further ambiguities—not only are the gods multi-valent, but worshippers viewed them with sexual ambivalence depending, one imagines, on what the dedicator required.[4]

Nonetheless, many Celtic deities have been equated with Graeco-Roman deities by the process of *interpretatio Romana* (n.b., Tacitus *Germania* 43). The Romans saw characteristics of their own deities in native gods, or they used the veneer of native gods to expand the geographic scope of Roman gods.[5] *Interpretatio Romana* manifested itself epigraphically and iconographically by representations of Celtic gods according to Roman aesthetics. The gods, for the most part, remained completely Celtic. Before the Roman occupation of Britain, Celtic gods maintained a status of anonymity since worshippers did not affix names to illustrations of their gods.[6] In the more developed religious iconography of the Roman period, attributes indicated function and provenance, but the divine name was rarely attached to a

---

justice. The tribal god's consort is tied to the land rather than the tribe, and she has the powers to influence war and agriculture by virtue of her magic, rather than through interference.

[3] The attitude survived into post-Roman Irish myth. For example, the chthonic deity Dagda, whose name means the "good one," though not in a moral sense, addressed a council of war with the declaration, "All that you promise to do, I will do, myself alone." Dagda, *Ruad Ro-fhessa*, the "Lord of Great Knowledge," was the omniscient, all-powerful warrior-artist: Dillon and Chadwick, *Celtic Realms*, 139.

[4] Examples of possible androgyny include the *deae Vitires* (632, 633). Veteris is usually *deus* (e.g., 627, 628, *et alia*). A horned, possibly antlered, goddess decorates a piece of locally-made pottery from Richborough, Kent (M.J. Green, *Military Areas*, 67, #3). Horns are common for gods. A horned god from Burgh-by-Sands (*CSIR* 1.6.373), carries a spear, but his pronounced hips give him an effeminate appearance.

[5] Henig, "Art and Cult," 108.

[6] Caesar, *BG* 6.14.3, implied that the Celts (the Druids) were in fact literate, at least in the Greek alphabet. Ross, "Horned God," 83–84, cites an Old Irish Oath:

portrayal.[7] The difference between Roman and Celtic iconography was one of approach: Roman art aimed at realism, whereas Celtic iconography was schematic. *Interpretatio Romana* can be seen in the cult statue of Antenociticus from Benwell on Hadrian's Wall (pp. 112, 117, below). The deity's native British characteristics have been understated to fit a more Roman model, making him appear less Celtic. The process, however, worked both ways, and Roman gods were superimposed onto equivalent Celtic cults by *interpretatio Celtica*.[8] For example, divine Celtic couples are more common in Celtic religion than in the Mediterranean world. The male god, retaining his Celtic name, assumed a Roman appellation (Mars Loucetius and Nemetona; 470), but the goddess remained predominantly Celtic, to emphasize her territorial role.[9]

The Horned God

Perhaps the most prevalent type was the horned god, whose headgear indicates the intimate connection between hunter and prey. Closely associated with the horned god are various horned animals including the stag which figured prominently in Celtic art, attested as early as the eighth century BC. A brooch from Rovalls, Gotland (eighth century BC), clearly illustrates the accoutrements of the horned warrior: a serpent with a bull-horned human head, which in turn is surmounted by a ram head, forms the piece.[10]

I swear by the gods by whom my tribe swears (*Tongu do dhia tonges mo thuath*)—the gods are unnamed, but understood; the oath is binding. The name-taboo remained strong through Celtic culture and history.

[7] Ross, *Celtic Britain*, 158. Perhaps a god's true name was a carefully guarded tribal secret. The true name of a god is a dangerous thing—n.b. Yahweh whose true name was kept secret because it was too powerful and dangerous. Enemies with such knowledge could exercise an unfair advantage over the tribe. By analogy, consider Oedipus' words to Theseus (Sophocles, *Oedipus Colonus*, vv. 1522–1533). Oedipus enjoined the king of Athens to keep his grave site secure, so that the Theban can protect the people who buried him. Possession of a hero's bones ensured protection for that community and danger for enemies. On the basis of an oracle, the Spartans, seeking divine help against Tegea in the mid-sixth century, retrieved the coffin of Orestes (Herodotus, 1.68). The Athenian Cimon would later (475 BC) bring the "bones of Theseus" from Skyros to Athens on the authority of a similar oracle (Arist. Fr. 611.1; Plutarch, *Theseus* 36, *Cimon* 8): Herter, "Theseus," 1224; Burkert, *Greek Religion*, 206, and n. 38–39.

[8] M.J. Green, "Iconography," 120.

[9] M.J. Green, "Iconography," 37.

[10] Ross, "Horned God," 65–66; Sprockhoff, "Urnfield Culture," fig. 10.6.

Also of significance are the rock carvings at Val Camonica. The valley itself is a mountain pass, a natural migration route for wild herd animals, a convenient kill-site.[11] Hunting scenes dominate the rock carvings: ithyphallic hunters are aided by their dogs in snaring and striking down birds, deer, and other prey. One figure (seventh century BC) appears to be fully stag, with excessively large antlers, and half human (the body of the stag is complete, but perched on his back is the torso of a man).[12] Another carving (late fourth century BC, at which time the Celts controlled northern Italy), shows an antlered figure wearing a long garment; he holds a torque on each arm, and a serpent curls up his left arm. An ithyphallic figure propitiates our antlered deity. In addition, the Gundestrup Cauldron (found in Denmark), a first century BC fabrication, showcases an antlered deity squatting next to his stag and holding a large ram-headed snake. The Gundestrup god wears one torque and holds another.[13]

The stag is represented throughout the Celtic world in both pre-Roman and Roman times. Dating to the seventh century BC, from Strettweg, Austria, a bronze cult wagon shows a goddess accompanied by soldiers and two small stags with exaggerated antlers. The scene may indicate a ritual hunt.[14] A gold bowl from Altstetten, Zürich (sixth century BC) shows stags, among other (unidentifiable) animals and astronomical symbols (suns and moons).[15] Other examples are to be found at Balzars, Lichtenstein (third century BC)[16] and Saalfelden, Austria (first century BC). Horns mark the animals' functions—strength, fertility, and potency.[17] Furthermore, the stag is a prominent theme on Celtic coin issues.[18] The horned god of the Brigantes might also be the horned god of the Carvetii, the "stag people."[19]

---

[11] Anati, *Camonica Valley*, 126.
[12] Megaw, *Art*, #2. The conflation of hunter and prey underscores the intimate and symbiotic relationship between the two.
[13] Ross, "Horned God," 69–70; The Gundestrup Cauldron may, in fact, be Thracian in origin: Bergquist and Taylor, "Gundestrup Cauldron," 10–24, argue that the cauldron's symbolism is Eastern rather than Celtic; Kaul, *Gundestrupkedelen*, places the piece in a south-eastern European silver-smithing tradition. See also Davidson, "Mithraism," 494–506, who discusses the piece in terms of Mithraic iconography.
[14] Megaw, *Art*, #38; Mohen, Duval, and Eluère, *Trésors des princes celtes*, #27.
[15] Megaw, *Art*, #4.
[16] Anon., *Kelten in Mitteleuropa*, #76.
[17] M.J. Green, *Symbol and Image*, 135.
[18] Laing, *Coins and Archaeology*, 163.
[19] A. Birley, "Celts, Romans, Picts," 188–192.

The stag god is represented in Britain at Cirencester and Verulamium. The Cirencester relief shows an antlered stag god holding
ram headed serpents by the neck (the relief could show Hercules
and the serpents). An antlered head decorates the centerpiece of a
mosaic from Verulamium (this piece may represent Neptune with a
lobster claw).[20] The ram and horned serpent, constant companions
of the horned warrior, indicate war and fertility in Celtic contexts.[21]
Furthermore, the horned warrior, ram, and serpent trio is intimately
connected to the Celtic warrior class who are shown wearing horned
helmets on the Gundestrup Cauldron and on the triumphal arch at
Orange.[22] Celtic warriors wore the emblems of their hero gods just
as Greeks and Romans looked to the attributes of their heroes: men
wore armor and gems decorated with scenes from the myth of a
favorite hero.[23]

The stag cult image influenced the development of the Celtic
deity Cernunnos, "the horned one."[24] Cernunnos was attested iconographically in the La Tène III (ca. 100 BC) period in Romania,
Germany, and Spain.[25] The cult of Cernunnos is too widely attested
for full discussion here, but studies show that this Celtic Lord of
Animals (the iconography indicates an intimate connection between
stags and serpents) provided a prototype for the Christian figure of
Satan.[26] Yet this deity's pre-Christian associations evince his role over
prosperity and health. The correlation between Cernunnos and Apollo
underscores the Celtic deity's therapeutic concerns: Apollo with his
lyre accompanies Cernunnos, who is represented at curative springs.[27]

---

[20] Ross, "Horned God," 70. Close examination of the head, traditionally interpreted as an Oceanus, reveals that it is, in fact, antlered.

[21] Ross, "Horned God," 72.

[22] Ross, "Horned God," 73.

[23] The extreme example is, of course, the Roman emperor Commodus who had
commissioned a statue of himself styled as Hercules.

[24] Ross, *Celtic Britain*, 135.

[25] The Romanian piece is a fragment of a bronze sword scabbard illustrated with
three human forms, each with a triple set of horns: Ross, *Celtic Britain*, 131 and fig.
91. The German piece, from Waldalgesheim, shows a ram-horned figure with hands
outstretched in prayer fashion: Ross, *Celtic Britain*, 131 and fig. 92. The Spanish
example comes from Numantia. The crudely painted horned-figure stands with
hands outstretched in prayer: Ross, *Celtic Britain*, 131 and fig. 92.

[26] Bober, "Cernunnos," 13–51. See also Ross, *Celtic Britain*, 131–153; M.J. Green,
Symbol and Image, 86–96. Perhaps this deity's popularity served as a focal point for
Christian change whereby Cernunnos was made into the ultimate evil, Satan.

[27] For Cernunnos with Apollo: Espérandieu, *Bas-Relief*, #3653 (Riems), and 1539
(Vendoevres). Cernunnos is attested at a healing spring at Genaiville: Mitard, *La
Sculpture gallo-romaine*, 56–71; and at Néris-les-Bains: Espérandieu, #1566.

Cernunnos is also depicted with the horn of plenty and is seen as a Mercury-figure, emphasizing his role over prosperity.[28]

Cernunnos may have provided the prototype for other horned warriors. Though less prominent on the continent than in Britain, unnamed horned figures have been found in Germany[29] and Gaul.[30] The motif is also found on coin issues. Tetradrachmas from Hungary show horned horsemen.[31] A coin from Massilia displays an ithyphallic horned figure.[32] Cunobelinus' coin issues (ca. AD 40, Colchester) also depict horned figures.[33] The horns emphasize the god's attributes—aggression, war, fertility, i.e., power over every aspect of tribal life.

The horned god, powerful over agriculture, prosperity, justice, health, war, and death,[34] functionally overlapped warrior and sky gods. The non-Celtic Roman soldier, however, appears to have worshipped the horned gods—and other local gods as well—in a limited capacity, primarily as warrior gods. Yet other functions do occasionally surface. A Priapus relief from Scotland (348) shows that Roman fertility deity with horns (drawing a clear connection between horned god as bestower of fertility and protector of the home; compare the Greek herms). A figurine votive to Mercury at Uley depicts a horned figure;[35] via *interpretatio Celtica*, Mercury became the Celtic horned god of retribution. It should also be kept in mind that Mercury *psychopompos* traveled between the worlds of gods and men, living and dead—an afterlife association is implicit.

Several local Celtic warrior gods are known by name, and their epigraphic record, concentrated along Hadrian's Wall, reveals interesting patterns of worship. Especially enlightening are five gods worshipped on Hadrian's Wall, where the Roman army was concentrated—Veteris, Belatucadrus, Mogons, Cocidius, and Antenociticus. The order

---

[28] Espérandieu, #1539 (Vendoeuvres), 3015 (Blain), 2083 (Beaune). A relief from Lyon shows a horned Mercury type counting money; another from Riems depicts the god with caduceus and purse: Green, *Symbol and Image*, 95.

[29] For the Holzerlingen piece, see Megaw, *Art*, #14. The janiform head wears a double-horned crown. Another horned figure, a Mercury with purse and caduceus, was found at Unterheimbach: Espérandieu, #6009. A third German example of the Mercury type comes from Staufenberg: Benoit, *Art et dieux*, pl. 145.

[30] A relief from Beire-le-Châtel with triple-horned bulls, and human figures with triple and double sets of horns: Espérandieu, #3622. For horned figures from Selle Mont Saint Jean (northwest Gaul) see Espérandieu, #3001.

[31] Allen, *Coins*, #479, 480.

[32] Laing, *Coins and Archaeology*, 156.

[33] Allen, *Coins*, nos. 477, 478.

[34] Ross, "Horned God," 65.

[35] Henig in Woodward and Leach, *Uley Shrines*, 98–99, fig. 85.2.

of the evidence roughly follows the social rank of the dedicators, starting with *humiliores*, then officers. Within these two groups (*humiliores* vs. *honestiores*), the deities are presented according to geographic extent of worship, beginning with those most widely attested. Each god will be introduced briefly, and a comparative analysis will reveal patterns of worship (geography, social status of worshippers, orthography, and iconography).

Veteris

The deity Veteris is well attested along Hadrian's Wall from the east to the central region, but not to the north of the wall (map 4; table 5). Nearly a quarter of the known dedications are concentrated at Carvoran, the probable cult center. The crude physical state of the altars and the names of the dedicators indicate that Veteris appealed primarily to enlisted men rather than wealthier officers.

This god, never subjected to *interpretatio Romana*, is once equated with the Celtic Mogons (519). Veteris is attested by numerous variant spellings which suggest that this mysterious deity was known as an individual god, as a plurality, and as both male and female (632). Invocations to *Di Veteres* may imply that some worshippers regarded the group as a trio: triads are common in Celtic religion (e.g., Nymphs, *Matres*, and *Genii Cucullati*); the number three has magical properties in Celtic religion and is perhaps apotropaic.[36]

The name has defied interpretation.[37] It has been argued that Veteris was a German god whose name (*vithrir*) became an epithet of Odin, a weather god.[38] E. Birley suggested that the distribution,

---

[36] Ross, *Celtic Britain*, 375.

[37] Some have tried to connect Veteris with the Latin *vetus*—"old." These dedications would then have been made in honor of the old gods in contrast with Christianity which began to gain acceptance in the fourth century. But the intrusive "h" on several altars, including a nicely cut one from Vercovicium (652), weakens such an argument, as does the fact that our evidence pre-dates wide-spread acceptance of Christianity. One could argue that the "H" is a late-Latin version of the letter "N" used as an abbreviation for "numen," but the spelling "Vheteris" on the altar from Catterick (628) argues against this conclusion. Ross, *Celtic Britain*, 374, tentatively suggests that the appearance of the -H- in this deity's name reflects an attempt to record a pre-aspiration utilized in the vocative form of the name, as with the modern name Hamish derived from the aspirated vocative form of the Gaelic name Seumas. See also Heichelheim, "Vitiris," 408, 411–12.

[38] Hodgson, *History of Northumberland*, 140, 200. Haverfield, "Di Veteres," 36–37, agreed with the German origin of the intrusive "H," characteristic also of Old Irish phonology and morphology.

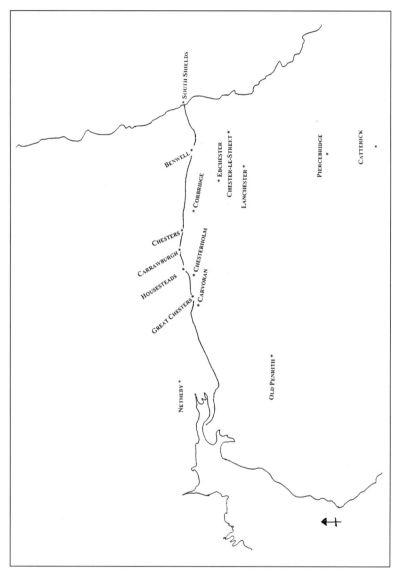

Map 4: Veteris Distribution

and the fact that many of the dedicators have native British, not Germanic, names implies a British origin for this god.[39] Vitiris may derive from *hvethr-*, an epithet of Loki, the Germanic equivalent of Vulcan.[40] Hence, Veteris could be a god of smiths. The cults of Veteris and Jupiter Dolichenus, an Eastern iron and weather god, overlap in northern England.[41] In fact, one Dolichenus monument (397) was rededicated to Hveter, perhaps by the original worshipper. Finally, the divine name could have derived from a stem related to the Old Norse *hvitr*, "white," or "shining."[42]

The altars, about twenty of which do not name a votary, are small (the largest of them 40.6cm tall) and crudely cut. The names of the worshippers who have been identified are unusual and for the most part non-Roman, probably Celtic.[43] Most of these names could easily have belonged to provincial auxiliary soldiers of the late empire (and probably did since most of the altars were discovered within or near the walls of auxiliary forts). Few of the altars were decorated, and the god himself was never illustrated on his altars. Based on the iconography, Veteris could have been one of the horned gods found frequently in the north, since serpents and boars, sacred to the Celtic horned god, are found on altars to the *Di Veteres*. The cult to Veteris seems to have been particularly significant to men, even though a woman figured among his worshippers (668),[44] and the goddesses Veteris received two dedications (632, 633).

---

[39] Birley, "Deities," 63.

[40] Webster, *Celtic Religion*, 78–79.

[41] York: Dolichenus (394), Veteris (627). Corbridge: Dolichenus (401), Veteris (640–3). Piercebridge: Dolichenus (399), Veteris (639). Benwell: Dolichenus (404), Veteris (644–5). Chesters: Dolichenus (405–6), Veteris (646–9). Great Chesters: Dolichenus (407–8), Veteris (667–9). Carvoran: Dolichenus (409), Veteris (670–82). Furthermore, the cults of Veteris and the Celtic smith god overlapped at Corbridge: Richmond, "Corbridge," 179–196; Leach, "Smith God," 35–45; *CSIR* 1.1.51–57.

[42] A. Birley, *People*, 108.

[43] Andiatis (674); Aspuanis (653) a name recalling Aspuna, the name of a town in Galatia; Uccus (650); Dada (677); Duihno (631) which is suggestive of Duina, the ancient name of a river near Verdun; and Senaculus (660): Haverfield, "Di Veteres," 34.

[44] Wright, "Roman Britain in 1961," 192, #6. Ivixa (681) and Mocuxsoma (685) may be female names, increasing our count of female worshippers to three: A. Birley, *People*. 107.

Belatucadrus

The worship of Belatucadrus, whose name might mean "the fair, shining one" or "fair slayer,"[45] was confined to the northwest of Roman Britain (map 5; table 6). The dedications are concentrated at Brougham, south of the Wall, in northwestern England. Most of the altars dedicated to this god are small, rarely leaving enough space for the worshipper's name.

Belatucadrus, probably represented as a local warrior, was linked with Mars (554, 557, 558, 562), but never with Rome's more peaceful deities, such as Apollo or Silvanus. He was never invoked with a consort. Belatucadrus' emphatic martial associations obscured other probable functions (healing, fertility) which are clearly seen in other Celtic warrior gods (i.e., Mars Nodens), functions which this god may have fulfilled for the local population.[46] For the soldiers of the Roman army, Belatucadrus was strictly a warrior god.

Mogons

Mogons (map 2; table 7), "the powerful one" or "the great one," may have come to Hadrian's Wall from Upper Germany (see 518). Limited evidence (seven inscribed altars) is widely scattered to the north and south of the central region of Hadrian's Wall. The worshippers of this god included low ranking officers (520, 523).

Cocidius

This god's name may derive from the Welsh stem *coch* or *cocco*, meaning "red," an appropriate color for a god of war.[47] Cocidius' probable cult center was Bewcastle, north of the western end of Hadrian's Wall, where his votives are concentrated (map 6; table 8). This same

---

[45] Tolkien in Collingwood and Myers, *Roman Britain*, 262, 265, 269; Ross, "Horned God," 72. Ross, *Celtic Britain*, 371, suggested that this armed warrior may have had solar origins. The interpretation of the name is far from certain.

[46] Indeed, the link with Mars underscores the deity's ability to cure serious deficiencies: G. Webster, "What the Britons required," 59.

[47] Tolkien in Collingwood, *Roman Britain*, 103–4; Ross, *Celtic Britain*, 169–70. Ross' objection to this interpretation is that the name Cocidius is spelled consistently with a single internal -c- where one might expect the -c- to double (internal gemination). But the color red is associated with warrior gods. Words meaning red in Goidelic dialects (*dearg* and *ruadh*) also mean "strong," "swift," and "turbulent." *Da Choc* or *Coca*, a Irish god, may be comparable to Cocidius. Rudiobus, a deity from

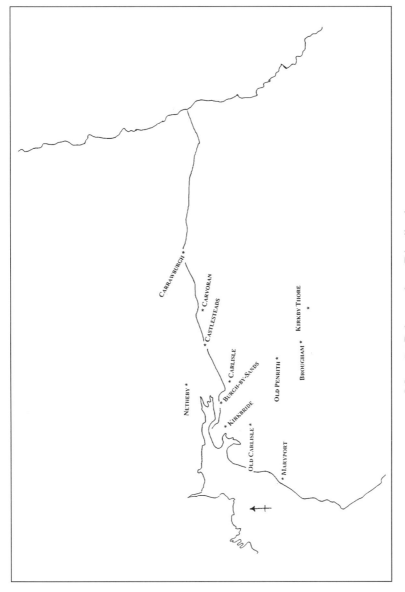

Map 5: Belatucadrus Distribution

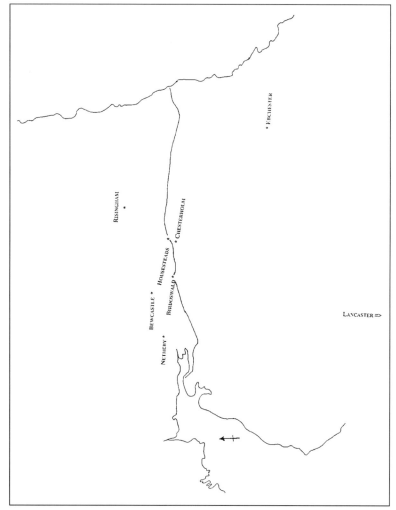

Map 6: Cocidius Distribution

site may be the *Fanococidi* mentioned in the *Ravenna Cosmography*.[48] In addition, the god may have overseen a shrine at Yardhope, east of the High Rochester fort, where an image of a warrior was carved within a countersunk area in the north wall of a squarish chamber of natural bedrock. The warrior stands, arms outstretched, holding a spear in his right hand, a small round shield in his left. The helmeted figure, otherwise naked, is non-phallic. The identification of this figure as Cocidius is not certain.[49] Cocidius was apparently a native British god who, as attested epigraphically on Hadrian's Wall, attracted high ranking worshippers, including legionary soldiers and senior auxiliary officers.

The god underwent moderate *interpretatio Romana*, equated in the west with the war god Mars (577, 584, 596, 598), and in the east with the hunter-warrior Silvanus (586, 588).[50] In the east, Cocidius was the benign god of hunting for sport (and economy); he was a warrior in the more unsettled west. Cocidius, however, was also conflated with the Celtic deity Vernostonus at Ebchester (585), via *interpretatio Celtica*—perhaps an attempt to identify one tribal god with another.

Antenociticus

A temple to Antenociticus stood outside the south-east angle of the Roman fort at Benwell (map 2; table 9). Votive offerings of coins found within the temple precinct, dating to Marcus Aurelius and earlier, provide a *terminus ante quem* for the temple. The joint emperors

---

Gaul, and Rudianus, whose names contain the stem meaning "red," are associated with the Roman war god Mars. Richmond and Crawford, "Ravenna Cosmography," 34, suggested that ancient orthography was careless with doubling consonants and that the derivation of Cocidius from the word meaning "red" is quite reasonable. Other possibilities make less sense: *cog* (cock), *cogor* (croaking), *cog* (round stack or snail shell), *cogail* (distaff).

[48] Richmond and Crawford, "Ravenna Cosmography," 34. The *Ravenna Cosmography* was a geography compiled in the seventh century from earlier sources. The *fanum Cocidi* seems to be within a triangular region between Bewcastle, Netherby, and Stanwix.

[49] Since no epigraphy accompanies this figure, the identification is far from certain. Charlton and Mitcheson label the Yardhope deity as Cocidius because the shrine falls within his geographic area of concentration: "Yardhope," 143, 149. Cocidius was depicted as an armed god without horns at Bewcastle (580–1).

[50] Silvanus, spirit of the trees, guardian of woods and forests, represents the hunter as protector (n.b. 686: Vinotonus Silvanus): G. Webster, "What the Romans required," 59.

referred to in two inscribed altars found within the temple (535, 537) could have been Marcus Aurelius and Commodus or a later pair (Severus and Caracalla, perhaps).[51] At the same site, the god is portrayed in a sophisticated but badly damaged life-sized statue on whose head stylized horns form the decorative hairstyle of his frontal locks (*CSIR* 1.1.232). The statue is influenced by Graeco-Roman models but native elements are discernible, including lentoid eyes and the remains of a torque around the neck.[52] It is interesting that Tineus Longus, *quaestor designatus* and on orders from the emperors, appealed to an obscure god from northern England (537). Antenociticus seems to have found imperial favor, probably from the house of Marcus Aurelius.

Ross suggested that Antenociticus may have been imported from northern Spain or southern Gaul, since Spanish garrisons were stationed at Benwell.[53] But no strong Spanish connection can be made.[54] The meaning of the god's name has defied explanation.

Assessment of the Evidence

Geography

The clustering of votives suggests a geographic concentration for these gods—indicating a localized or tribal origin. Yet the cults were diffused from centers of worship by the army (maps 2, 4–6; tables 1–4).

Dedications to Veteris are concentrated at the center of Hadrian's Wall (Housesteads, Great Chesters, Carvoran) and fan out eastward. The *Di Veteres* are not attested west of Carvoran. In proximity to Veteris and the central region of Rome's occupation of northern England is Cocidius, whose cult evidence is concentrated north of the Wall (Bewcastle) and the Wall fort of Housesteads. The same deity is well attested along the Wall between Castlesteads and Carlisle.

---

[51] Richmond and Simpson, "Benwell," 36, n. 136. The temple may have been destroyed by AD 197.
[52] Ross, *Celtic Britain*, 163, 377.
[53] Ross, "Horned God," 81.
[54] The evidence is simply too sparse for judgement. If Antenociticus was imported, it is highly unlikely that he was native to the Astures. Instead, the German cohort, responsible for the cult's diffusion, may have venerated this horned warrior, or the deity was simply local and popular with the officers stationed at Benwell.

Scant and scattered evidence in the eastern regions suggests that the cult was widely diffused. Dedications to Mogons seem to circumscribe this nexus (Veteris and Cocidius) in an ellipse. It is curious to note that Mogons is not positively attested at a fort on the Wall. Belatucadrus' cult center may be Brougham, south of the Wall in Westmorland. For the most part, dedications extend northward and westward. Belatucadrus is not attested south of Kirkby Thore (Westmorland) north east of Carrawburgh. The surviving evidence shows the cult of Antenociticus to have been the most limited (attested positively only at Benwell).

Overlap

As widely scattered as these cults were, overlap of the discrete gods seems to have been limited, as worship moved away from the cult center into the territory of another tribal god, reflecting cult localization.[55] The distribution and overlap may indicate that these discrete gods filled similar or identical roles. Roman soldiers and officers might have regarded them as identical gods invoked variously in separate tribal territories (e.g., 519: Mogons Vitiris).

There is some overlap between Veteris and Belatucadrus (at Carvoran and Carrawburgh) and between Veteris and Cocidius at Housesteads, a site reasonably close to the supposed "cult centers" of each god, and at Ebchester (south of the wall). Cocidius and Belatucadrus are attested together only at Netherby (north of the wall), well north of the native range of worship for each god. Cocidius and Belatucadrus may have been, on the tribal level, exclusive of each other, as the cults of Jupiter Dolichenus and Mithras seemed to be in Britain.

Social Stratification of the Worshippers

Most of these gods (especially Veteris and Belatucadrus) seem to have been worshipped by soldiers rather than officers, while few had any wide appeal across social rank. Veteris' appeal was greatest among *humiliores*: thirty stones (of sixty-one total) give Celtic names without

[55] Austen, *Bewcastle and Old Penrith*. Mithras and Jupiter Dolichenus are not attested at the same sites in Britain. Elsewhere the cults of Mithras and Dolichenus overlapped to the extent that they shared a temple at Dura-Europus.

rank, twenty-four stones provide no name at all, five stones are too fragmentary to determine if a name was ever cut. Two altars, however, indicate men with some official rank in the Roman army: *princeps* (636) and *imaginifer* (673). Much of the evidence dates to the third century, and the dedicators whose names have survived seem to be native to Britain.[56] Belatucadrus' votaries, likewise, were predominantly *humiliores*, including the *optio* Julius Civilis (549), the *miles* Peisius (569), and the *veteranus* Aurelius Tasulus (550).[57] Despite the fact that most stones dedicated to either Veteris or Belatucadrus were found within fort walls, no unit is named, nor is there any indication of corporate worship. The one exception is the altar which Julius Pastor, an *imaginifer* of the *cohors II Delmatarum*, set up to *Deus sanctus Veteris* (673). Furthermore, about half of those worshipping Veteris or Belatucadrus did not identify themselves by name. The votives seem to be purely private: *pro se et suis* (543, 566), *pro sua salute* (544, 568), *votum solvit libens merito* (543, 545–546, 549–551, 558, 561, 564, 569). Although the evidence for Mogons is too scant for accurate interpretation, this divinity seems also to have been more popular with the lower ranks. Mogons' worshippers with rank comprise a decurion (523) and a *beneficiarius consularis* (520).

The cults of Cocidius and Antenociticus offer a contrast to the above pattern. Roman citizens who offered dedications to Cocidius included soldiers of all three legions stationed in Britain and senior officers of auxiliary cohorts. Cocidius, a god who protected the army and ensured the safety of the unit, rather than just the individual soldier, received corporate dedications from soldiers of each legion in Britain (*Legio II*: 592, 598; *Legio VI*: 587, 594, 597; *Legio XX*: 593). The *cohors II Nerviorum* (from *Gallia Belgica*: 590), and the *cohors I Aelia Dacorum* (from Dacia: 591) also worshipped Cocidius corporately. The

---

[56] Haverfield, "Di Veteres," 38, suggested that the cult of Veteris was imported. That the worshippers were native would seem to dispute that theory: A. Birley, *People*, 107–108.

[57] The votary on 549 (Maryport) brings to mind the Batavian chief who organized his people in a revolt against Rome during AD 69–70. There is no positive evidence of a Batavian cohort at Alauna (the *cohors I Batavorum eq.* is attested at Carrawburgh for the third and fourth centuries [*RIB* 1553; *NDO* XL 39]), yet other units raised from Lower Germany recorded their presence at Maryport, e.g. *Cohors I Baetasiorum CR ob virtutem et fidem* during the late second century (*RIB* 830).

The *nomen* Aurelius is attached to three of Belatucadrus' worshippers: Aurelius Tasalus (550), Aurelius Diatova (551), and Aurelius Nicanor (558), perhaps providing a clue to time or geography. These Aurelii probably became citizens as a result of Caracalla's edict.

tribune Paternius Maternus of the *cohors I Nerviorum* (578) and the prefects Q. Florius Maternus (*cohors I Tungrorum*: 588) and Decimus Caerellius Victor (*cohors II Nerviorum*: 590) may have honored Cocidius on behalf of their troops. Dedications of a more private nature include those by the legionary centurion Annius Victor (579), a legionary soldier (587), equestrian officers (588, 590), an auxiliary centurion (596), and a *beneficiarius consularis* (577), as well as non-Romans: a certain Virilis, a German (585), Vabrius (589), and others (196a, 474, 586). The limited evidence for Antenociticus reveals a similar pattern of worship by officers from both legionary and auxiliary units. A legionary centurion erected one of the extant monuments (535), and a second piece was set up corporately by the *cohors I Vangionum* (536). Even more interesting is the fact that all three dedicators were Italian officers, rare enough on the Wall.

These men enjoyed a higher social status than did the worshippers of Veteris, Belatucadrus, and Mogons. The cult iconography for Cocidius and Antenociticus shows greater Roman influence (as will be shown below), and the orthography is regular and Latinate compared to Veteris and Belatucadrus. The officers who worshipped these gods seem to have Romanized them. Subsequently, worshippers imposed a more "sophisticated" and hence "Roman" or even "Mediterranean" veneer on those deities. The gods became appropriate to the officers' social class and cultural experiences and proved themselves suitable intercessors for the emperor's frontier representatives.

Such social stratification might seem strange upon first glance. Yet parallels are to be found in mystery rites and in the later Celtic traditions, though not in strictly Roman/Mediterranean practices.[58] Mithras, for example, was primarily an officers' cult in Britain.[59] Because it was an inexpensive cult, Christianity found early popularity among the *humiliores*—the lower urban classes, craftsmen, merchants, slaves and ex-slaves, the urban poor who did not have the same outlets for socialization enjoyed by the wealthy.[60] A similar

---

[58] MacCanna, *Celtic Mythology*, 16. The Ulster Cycle, which told the deeds of great heroes (e.g. Cuchulainn) and exalted universal heroic virtues, was held in the highest esteem by the priests (filidh). In contrast, the Fionn cycle which related the deeds of roving bands of hunter-warriors, was more popular with the common people.

[59] Mithras received cult from the less privileged classes elsewhere, especially Noricum: cf. p. 95 note 171.

[60] Wilcken, *Christians*, 35.

stratification may be exhibited in the rider god monuments prominent along the Danube. Inscriptions are altogether lacking, but the
iconography bears a superficial resemblance to Mithraism: e.g., grades
of initiation.[61] The votive material varies widely (e.g., *CSIR* 1.2.114;
1.7.123), yet some elements remain constant: initiation, secrecy,[62] and
popularity with the Roman army. It is possible that worshippers were
drawn from local recruits who continued to cultivate the gods of
their ancestors (like Celts in Britain who preferred to worship local
deities). It is also possible (though not provable) that the Danubian
rider gods appealed to troopers who might have preferred their own
ethnic god over Mithras.

Iconography

The horned god, the warrior god of fertility and hunting, is seen on
numerous uninscribed altars from Hadrian's Wall. Dedications to
hunting gods and hunting scenes etched in relief are concentrated
in the eastern region of Hadrian's Wall: Chesters, Corbridge, and
High Rochester.[63] The stag is associated with Cocidius who appears
as a hunter on an altar from Risingham (586). A frieze on the capital of the altar shows the god with his dog hunting a stag.

Hunting scenes are evident on monuments to other gods attested
in the north-east. Specifically, Maponus, equated with the youthful
Graeco-Roman god of the hunt and of the lyre—Apollo (see 460,

---

[61] Tudor, *Equitum Danuvinorum*, vol. 2, 72–73.

[62] *Ibid.*, 279. The secret nature of the deities and their rites is underscored by
the lack of inscribed votives and the absence of votive altars. The gods possessed
nomina arcana, and worshippers may have been forbidden to speak or inscribe the
divine names.

[63] One uninscribed stone from Chesters depicts a stag approaching a net (*CSIR*
1.6.389). A relief from Carlisle shows a horned figure (or winged Mercury—the
execution of the stone is classical), naked except for a cloak around his shoulders,
resting his left foot on a rock as he holds a small animal over an altar: Ross,
"Horned God," 78–79; *CSIR* 1.6.482.
The civilian, and relatively leisured, Cotswolds has also yielded a number of
hunter god monuments, all of which show the deity wearing a conical, "Phrygian"
cap (*CSIR* 1.7.110–115). A funerary relief (*CSIR* 1.7.115) may have intended Attis
rather than the Celtic hunter. Such a detail (conical caps) may suggest a fusion of
Oriental mystery practices with native customs—an indication, in civilian religion
at any rate, that the hunter god's functions included fertility and afterlife or rebirth.
Warrior gods, in civilian iconography, also demonstrate a clear function of fertility
by association with mother goddesses: *CSIR* 1.7.133, showing three warriors, each
armed with shields, standing to the right of a mother goddess (compare *CSIR*
1.7.101–104). Heroes (Heracles, Theseus, Perseus, *et alia*) are hunters, and their cults
demonstrate the same provenance over fertility, life, and death.

462 for Maponus as hunter).[64] Maponus, "the youth," has survived in Welsh tradition as Mabon, the mighty hunter in the *Mabinogion*. Silver votive plaques from Bewcastle portray Cocidius as an armed warrior without horns (580, 581).[65] Cocidius the warrior god is possibly depicted at Birdoswald where a relief-fragment shows a muscular male figure, largely nude, with a cape, sandals, and belt. He holds a rectangular shield, decorated with a large fish (*CSIR* 1.6.162; n.b. 587). This armed warrior may also have appeared at Yardhope (p. 111).

With the possible exception of Maponus (460), Antenociticus was the only Celtic god in the area of Hadrian's Wall who, so far as the extant evidence attests, received a cult statue. The god appears youthful and beardless. His hair is elaborately sculpted to suggest stylized stag horns, and the eyes are Celtically lentoid. The statue, influenced by Graeco-Roman models, recalls archaic Greek sculpture, but native elements are discernible, including the treatment of eyes and mouth and the remains of a torque around the neck.[66] Ross noted that the Graeco-Roman influence renders Antenociticus an atypical Celtic horned warrior.[67]

No surviving altar preserves a depiction of Belatucadrus (n.b. 547), and no other iconography of the god exists, but it is possible that Belatucadrus was one of the horned deities pictured on numerous uninscribed altars from the Hadrianic *limes*,[68] since his votives coincide roughly with the horned god monuments. A relief of a naked and armed horned god was found near an altar dedicated to Belatucadrus at Maryport.[69] At Netherby, where Belatucadrus was honored with a dedicated altar (558), a ram-horned head is distinguished by its gouged-out hollow eyes suggestive of the eyes of the dead,[70]

---

[64] Maponus the hunter may have been worshipped in Scotland, near Birrens, where an inscription of possible Antonine date displays the etching of an animal, ears erect, a collar around its neck (466). This creature could be Maponus' hunting dog.

[65] Ross, *Celtic Britain*, 158, 165. The horned helmets, familiar as part of the Celtic battle uniform, were worn in honor of the horned warrior gods venerated by the Celtic fighter.

[66] Toynbee, *Art in Britain*, #41 and frontispiece; Ross, *Celtic Britain*, 163, 377; *CSIR* 1.1.232; Allason-Jones and McKay, *Coventina*, #12. Also found with the head were fragments of a forearm and lower leg. The statue seems to have been a life-sized cult statue.

[67] Ross, "Horned God," 81.

[68] E. Birley, "Deities," 61.

[69] Burgh-by-Sands; Wright and Phillips, *Carlisle Museum*, #194.

[70] Allason-Jones, *Guide*, #89.

supporting a connection between the horned god and the cult of the dead. Reliefs of horned deities together with undecorated invocations to Belatucadrus (565–568) have also surfaced at Burgh-by-Sands.

The iconography from altars can shed some further light. The evidence falls into two categories: implements associated with sacrifice (knives, axes, paterae, wreaths—as in Roman cult) and theriomorphic illustrations which might indicate function (boars, serpents, quadrupeds). Sacrificial implements appear on altars to Veteris (644, 670), Cocidius (587, 593, 594), and Antenociticus (535), but not on monuments dedicated to Belatucadrus or Mogons. Such details would increase the cost of the altar, and it has already been seen that Belatucadrus and Mogons were more popular with the lower and less wealthy classes.

A greater amount of evidence attests Veteris, who was popular with the same less privileged class. Veteris, like the Celtic horned god, is associated with serpents. A scene from Netherby (630) shows Hercules and the apples of the Hesperides—which might point to Veteris' link with death, the afterlife, and immortality. A boar and dolphin have been incised into an altar from Carvoran (682; n.b. 587 to Cocidius, which also shows a dolphin). Veteris' connection with the boar is emphasized at Ebchester, where that animal is sculpted into the right side of an altar (637), and at Weardale, where an altar records the death of a large boar in a hunt (359b). Cocidius also is tied with the wild boar (593). The boar, perhaps indicating some connection with *legio XX Valeria Victrix*, was venerated by the Celts. The animal is frequently attested as a Celtic war standard. Heroes hunted boars and this animal survived as a symbol in the Pictish folk tradition. The boar also had a supernatural association because its favorite food was the acorn, from the oak, a tree sacred to many Celts, and was symbolic of war and fertility in Celtic tradition. Cocidius' and Veteris' tie to this sacred animal may underscore their connection with death and the afterlife.

Orthography

The orthography of divine names offers some clue to the status and appeal of various gods. Cocidius and Antenociticus enjoyed regular orthography, a reflection of their dedicators higher education and higher socio-military status. Veteris and Belatucadrus are altogether a different matter. One might ask if the variant orthography, at the same time puzzling and intriguing, does, in fact, reflect local pronunciations, the difficulties of rendering a foreign name from an unwritten Celtic language into Latin (not all names were as troublesome, e.g., Cocidius), or simply reveal limited literacy.[71] Problems with grammar and orthography may, simply, result from an unsupervised stone mason.

Veteris' name was the most troublesome (table 1)—seventeen variations attested on fifty-six stones. The stem *Veter-* (singular and plural), our most common spelling, appears on twenty-three stones. This root, not localized, is found in auxiliary forts extending the width of Hadrian's Wall. The Hv/Hu variation is restricted to the west. *Vitir-* is concentrated in the east and at Carvoran. The variant spellings may imply regional pronunciation. In addition, many of the dedications are marred by blatant grammatical errors.[72]

Twenty-seven stones confirm fourteen variations in the spelling of "Belatucadrus" (table 2). "Belatucadrus," the most common variant, is found on altars throughout the range of dedications; other types only appear once or twice. When Belatucadrus is equated with Mars, the orthography is more regular—suggesting, possibly, a more thoroughly Romanized (or literate) worshipper.

The limited evidence to Mogons indicates a similar problem (table 3). Seven inscriptions attest four variant spellings.[73]

The orthography closely parallels social patterns of worship. The higher ranking dedicators honor their gods with regular spelling, lower ranking deities are plagued by variable orthography and poor grammar. The problem of orthography might also be connected to the degree of literacy or Romanization of the stone cutters commissioned: lower ranks might not be able to afford more competent workmanship, or lesser skilled craftsmen may have compounded a slip of the chisel with spelling mistakes.

Deus Sanctus

All of the gods discussed above were commonly invoked as *Deus* or (less frequently) as *Deus sanctus*. Other Celtic deities worshipped in

---

[71] Green, "Iconography," 111.

[72] Ross, *Celtic Britain*, 371. For example: the singular *deo* with the plural Veteribus (654) and *pro et suis* for *pro se et suis* (653), both at Housesteads.

[73] Jackson, cited by Ross, *Celtic Britain*, 375, suggested that Mogons and Mogunus are two separate and distinguishable deities.

the same region are identified in similar terms: Deus sanctus Apollo
Maponus (Ribchester: 460), Deus Maponus Apollo (Corbridge: 463),
Deus Maponus (Vindolanda: 464), Deus Maponus (provenance
unknown: 465), Deus Mars Condatis (Piercebridge: 607), Deus Mars
Condatis (Concangis: 608). Worshippers added these titles to honor
strictly Celtic and Roman hybrid spirits. This clarification of status
(as divine) could suggest that these Celtic deities were foreign to the
men and women making the dedications.[74] The dedicator may have
wanted to ensure that the offering would indeed be received by a
local *deus* who would have the appropriate powers to fulfill the dedicator's request. *Deus/dea* was an uncommon appellation for Roman
gods and deified abstractions, excluding archaic concepts—*Di Manes,
Lares, Penates.*

Yet most of the worshippers have non-Roman names. Perhaps
native worshipper, like Roman, saw his own gods and heroes in the
religions of others. Once the Celtic speaking world of Britain was
conquered, and business was transacted in Latin, perhaps it was
thought that the native divinities also began to speak Latin and even
became Roman (Macrobius 3.9.7–8). Another possibility is the supposition that native worshippers felt it necessary to clarify to non-
Celtic passers-by that his dedication was addressed to a deity, rather
than a friend or relative.

Celtic God and Greek Hero Cult

The horned warrior gods bear little resemblance to those of the
Graeco-Roman pantheon, and our Celtic deities may not, in origin,
be gods at all. The worship and ritual of the Celtic horned god may
have developed along lines similar to the cults of Greek and Roman
heroes, mythical characters victorious in epic battles, who have been

---

[74] The clarification "deus" is often added to local gods: Fishwick, *ICLW* 450. As
an epithet, "deus," attested after AD 124, suggests a god's importance and omnipotence. Hercules, Mercury, and Silvanus are most commonly addressed as "deus:"
Vaglieri, "Deus," 1716–26; M. Raepsaet-Charlier, "datation," 232–82; *eadem* "A propos des premiers," 204–08; Mancini, "Deo-Deae," 173–78. Delehaye, "Sanctus,"
145–200.
Delehaye, "Sanctus," 145–200; Palmer, *Roman Religion*, 223; Dorcey, *Silvanus*, 29.
According to Palmer, the epithet "sanctus" derives from the consecration of a
statue—the epithet is transferred from votive to deity. "Sanctus" on epitaphs indicates chastity.

elevated to semi-divine or fully-divine status.[75] In both cases, cults were highly localized, worshippers maintained personal relationships with deities, and there were indications of an after-life. Romano-Celtic soldiers cultivated native gods in the same way that Roman soldiers worshipped the heroes Achilles, Hercules, Orion, *et alia*, who, as *local* heroes, were honored with a cult of the dead, thus providing continuity with the past and perhaps the future, as well.[76] A Celtic soldier (whether from Britain or some other area of Celtic culture) in the Roman army would reasonably look to familiar religious practices and adapt them as he saw fit, thereby incorporating a Celtic after-life element into a Roman military environment.

Several factors, many of which are indicated in the Romano-Celtic tradition, distinguish the cults of the Graeco-Roman heroes. Heroic cult observances, festivals and rituals, were localized to a grave at a particular site. The *heroon* was marked off as a special precinct, where sacrifices and votive gifts accumulated. This localization of the hero cult contrasts with the omnipresent Olympian gods. As the cult and ritual were centralized, so were the powers of the hero and the tie between demi-god and worshipper: "The bond with the hero is dissolved by distance."[77] And so the cult of the Greek hero provided a measure of community cohesion and group identity. It has already been noted that worship of Celtic warrior gods was either strictly localized (Antenociticus at Benwell) or regionalized around a cult center (Cocidius at Bewcastle), as worship expanded more widely because of the increased mobility of worshippers and new demands on the gods. None of the Celtic gods discussed above is attested significantly north or south of the Roman occupation of Hadrian's Wall.

The horned warrior was significant as a founding ancestor who protected pastoral peoples.[78] Caesar, in fact, states that all the Gauls

---

[75] Many horned warriors are called *divi sancti* by Romanized worshippers, implying that the worshipper, who has to identify the recipient of his votive as a *deus*, may not fully understand the *numen* to which he pays homage. Romans saw their own gods in the deities of foreigners, but the match was not always exact—the same Celtic god could be identified with the Roman Mercury, Mars, or Apollo, deities of vastly different function and interpretation, i.e., Cocidius Mars (577), Cocidius Silvanus (588).

Greek heroes are called *isotheos*, emphasizing their semi-divine status: *Iliad* 3.310; 4.212; 11.412, 472; 15.559; 16.632; 23.569, also *isotheos phos*: 2.565; 7.136; 9.211; 11.428, 644; 23.677.

[76] N.b. the tradition of the isles of the Blest: Homer, *Odyssey* 11; Vergil, *Aeneid* 6.

[77] Burkert, *Greek Religion*, 206.

[78] Ross, "Horned God," 82.

believed that they were descended from Dis Pater (*BG* 6.18.1). By comparison, Greek heroes were ancestral founders of cities: Theseus, the national hero of Athens; Heracles, the legendary ancestor of the Dorian, Spartan, Lydian (Plutarch, *Quaest. Graec.*, 301e), and Macedonian (Herodotus 8.137) kings.[79]

That Celts believed in life after death is not disputed. Caesar (*BG* 6.14) claims that Druids believed in the transmigration of souls and that the promise of reincarnation removed the fear of death in battle, emboldening the Celtic soldier—Caesar may be attributing Orphic practices to Celtic rites he did not understand. Cult iconography supports the theory of a blessed Celtic afterlife—both Veteris and Cocidius are linked with the wild boar (593, 637), a supernatural animal in Celtic lore. Dolphins, in classical myth, symbolized the journey of the soul across the sea to the Isles of the Blessed and are noted iconographically on altars to Celtic gods (587, 682; cf. 451), perhaps evoking rebirth after death. Moreover, the theme of life after death recurs in later Irish, Welsh, and Germanic myth (all of which Greek epic and Celtic myth probably influenced), with stories of battles between great heroes and sumptuous feasts afterwards.[80]

Similarly, Greek hero cult is closely identified with the cult of the dead. Heroes were worshipped at grave sites with chthonic rituals (*contra* Olympian rites). Their myths frequently involved travel to and return from the underworld (e.g., Odysseus, Aeneas, Heracles). Likewise, the Celtic deities (n.b. 630). In addition, the Roman god Mercury, like the Greek hero, traveled between the worlds of the living and the dead. In Britain and Gaul, the horned deity was readily correlated to Mercury:

> deum maxime Mercurium colunt. Huius sunt plurima simulacra, hunc omnium inventorem artium ferunt, hunc viarum atque itinerum ducem,

---

[79] Burkert, *Greek Religion*, 211.

[80] Ross, *Celtic Britain*, 357. The otherworld in Celtic mythology transcended human time and space. A mortal hero could remain youthful (ageless) during a visit to the underworld but would age immediately upon return (e.g., *Voyage of Bran*). The otherworld was thought to lie beneath the earth or sea or to exist as a series of islands. It could appear in the form of a house or a grass covered hill and disappear with equal suddenness. The otherworld was reached through caves, lakes, mists, insights (MacCanna, *Celtic Mythology*, 125) and was viewed as a serene place, full of wisdom, peace, and harmony, where heroes could fight and feast to their hearts' content. The gods of the otherworld frequently lure heroes to fight their battles, e.g., the Welsh Pwyll and the Irish Cuchulainn.

These tales, which sound Homeric, may in fact be the creation of literate monks inspired by classical epics.

hunc ad quaestus pecuniae mercaturasque habere vim maximam arbi-
trantur (Caesar, *BG* 6.17.1).

The large number of small bronzes and reliefs of the god, found
throughout Britain, testify to Mercury's popularity. Mercury, without *interpretation Celtica*, seemed fully Celtic in his own right.[81] About
fifty examples are from civilian areas,[82] and another twelve from
camps and forts.[83] A silver-plated bronze figurine from the amphitheater at Caerleon renders a naked god wearing a winged hat
(suggestive of the horned helmets worn by certain warriors), his ankles
winged, and carrying a tri-lobed purse. A lead plaque from Chesters
crudely delineates a deity with wings on his head (*CSIR* 1.6.76).[84] A
small lead shrine from Wallsend, fourth century, also suggests Mercury: within the cupboard, a nude male wears a winged head-dress;
a dolphin and a bridled sea-horse curl around his feet.[85] A small
bronze Mercury from Verulamium renders the god accompanied by
his Roman attributes, cockerel, tortoise, and ram, but wearing a
silver torque, a purely Celtic attribute.[86] A relief from Great Chesters
portrays a crude horned-god, ithyphallic (recalling the classical herms)
with a pronounced navel. He holds a caduceus in his left hand and
a circular object in his right.[87] Where the classical Mercury (whose
winged helmet resembles the Celto-Germanic horned headdress, at
least in appearance if not in function) overlapped the Graeco-Roman
heroes, so did the Celtic horned warriors as chthonic liminal deities,
protectors of flocks.

The cult of the dead is linked to the moral conquest of good
(light) over evil (dark) as divine epithets will elucidate. Celtic Mars

---

[81] Hassall, "Altars, Curses," 83.
[82] M.J. Green, *Civilian Areas*, 31.
[83] M.J. Green, *Military Areas*, 10. Green suggested that, given this god's function
as a trader, small cult objects of Mercury may have belonged to civilians somehow
attached to the military, rather than to the soldiers themselves.
[84] M.J. Green, *Military Areas*, 11. Lead is the material more commonly used for
curse tablets than votive plaques. In this case, lead may emphasize Mercury's netherworld connections. See also Sieburg, *Goldamulet*, 123–53.
[85] Allason-Jones, "Lead shrine," 231–232. The portable shrine, 75mm by 36mm,
takes the form of a cupboard with two rectangular doors. Above these doors, a
semicircular projecting pediment shows a bust in radiate crown flanked by a whip
and wheel symbols—the sun god. The dolphin, associated with river gods, suggests
the cult of the dead (n.b. Hermes *Psychopompos*) while the sea-horse indicates, perhaps, travel on the sea, or possibly to the realm of the dead (as the dolphin designates). Lead was a material used in coffins and again seems to emphasize netherworld
properties.
[86] Henig, *Religion*, 58, 60, 61.
[87] Ross, "Horned God," 77.

epithets often refer to light: Belatucadrus (fair shining one, or fair slayer), Loucetius (brilliant—*CIL* XIII 3087), and perhaps also Veteris (*hvitr*, "white," or "shining").[88] Lucan mentioned both Teutates and Esus, whose name means "lord." Mars Caturix is the "master of fighting." Mars Camulos is "powerful" as is Mogons. Mars Segomo is "victorious." Rigisamus is the "greatest king." Mars Albiorix is "Master of the World."[89]

Their names recall the heroes of the Homeric cycle:[90] Shining Achilles (*dios*), Lord Agamemnon, king of men (*Iliad* 1.172: *anax andron*), the kingly Atreides, Hector of the flashing helmet (*Iliad* 6.112: *koruthaiolos*), warlike Trojans, Patroclus' shimmering bronze, royal lord Patroclus, powerful Lycurgus (*Iliad* 6.130: *krateros*). Cocidius' name, "red," may be descriptive of the armor worn by the aristocratic warrior class, either by virtue of the flashing bronze or of the armor's blood-stained appearance. Indeed, it is hoped that Hector shall return with the blood-stained armor of his enemies (*Iliad* 6.480: *enara brotenta*). The force of the Greek word *erythros* transcends "red." This adjective, which describes the color of blood, wine, gold, copper, and bronze (*Iliad* 9.365), implies a quality of brightness and reflectiveness.[91]

These epithets of brightness may refer to the color of the hero's hair, as, for example, Cocidius.[92] Boudicca, as Dio tells it, sported "a great mass of bright red hair down to her knees" (Dio 62.2.4). Cuchulainn is among the many Irish and Welsh heroes described as red, auburn, or yellow-haired. Compare the Greek heroes whose hair color is similarly auburn or yellow (*xanthos*), especially "red-haired" Menelaus: *xantho* (*Iliad* 10.240; 11.125), and Achilles whose locks are

---

[88] M.J. Green, *Gods of the Celts*, 111–112, argues that a Celestial Mars is intended. The sky god, or ruler deity, would be but one of the numerous functions fulfilled by the all-purpose Celtic tribal god. Associations with light are not restricted to sky deities: Athena is frequently called "of the flashing eyes," and Apollo is "golden" in the Homeric tradition. Athena is a deity of technology and military science, Apollo is the archer *par excellence*, a useful trait in battle (Odysseus' specialty).

[89] de Vries, *Religion des Celtes*, 65.

[90] Though we must be careful with stock epithets which serve metrical and mnemonic purposes, their use is consistent enough that they must also provide, to some degree, contextual significance.

[91] The idea is emphasized in Vergil's descriptions of Aeneas' battle gear: *loricam ex aere rigentem/sanguineam* (*Aeneid*, 8.621–622). Aeneas' armor is described as blazing (*refulgit*: 8.623; 12.168).

[92] It is possible that the name Cocidius is derived from an Indo-European root meaning, "scarlet" (compare the Greek *kokkinos* and Latin *coccineus*). The similarity might be mere coincidence.

"red-gold:" *pures xanthon* (*Iliad* 23.141). Red-haired heroes are considered divinely touched. Indeed when Cuchulainn, who had tri-colored hair (brown, red, and blond), entered battle, he was overcome by a berserk state (his *ríastarthae*), in which he attained a mode of super-human strength. In his *ríastarthae*, the Irish hero's hair would drip red with blood at the tips, making the hair appear even more red and reflective, like bronze armor, either clean or freshly stained with blood.

Most importantly, ritually appeased heroes were expected to provide all good things—bountiful harvests, healing, military success—for the community,[93] paralleling the multi-valent Celtic tribal god. The Greek hero, unlike the Olympian god, was close to his worshipper (again, Celtic gods are more accessible). Heroes (especially the Dioscuri)[94] were called on in times of personal crisis, and Heracles was honored with a healing shrine at Boeotia, where the sick could receive cures (Pausanias 9.24.3). The one who averted evil, the mortal who was accepted at the banquets of the Olympians, Heracles gave the common man hope for immortality.[95]

Similar elements are to be found in Celtic art wherein the warrior, mortal or divine, fights on horseback (Mars was rarely viewed as a horseman), e.g., a bronze from Westwood Bridge, Peterborough, shows a mounted soldier in panoply;[96] a stone relief from Margidunum (Nottinghamshire: *CSIR* 1.8.30) features a mounted warrior with spear

---

[93] Burkert, *Greek Religion*, 207. Greek literature provides numerous examples. The Lokrian Ajax, the hero who defied the gods has traditionally proven himself a reliable comrade in arms in closing a gap in the phalanx during the Lokrian victory over Kroton: Pausanias 3.19.3; *FGrHist* 26 F 1.18.

Telamonian Ajax has become identified with the protective battle shield. The Athenians called upon the protection of this hero together with Aiakos before the battle of Salamis (Herodotus 8.64; Plutarch, *Themistocles*, 15). Polygnotus' painting of the battle of Marathon shows the hero Marathon and Theseus, Attica's first king, rising from the earth to help their people (Pausanias 1.15.4). Oedipus declared the value of his grave, a secret site which will offer greater protection than shields and mercenaries. Oedipus' grave would protect Athens (Sophocles, *Oedipus at Colonus*, 1524–1533). See note 7, *supra*.

[94] Burkert, *Greek Religion*, 213. The Dioscuri especially rescued those in danger at sea. Ancient seamen regarded St. Elmo's fire (an electrical discharge from a ship's mast caused by a thunderstorm) as the epiphany of the heavenly twins (*Aet.* 2.18 = Xenophanes *VS* 21 A 39; Metrodorus *VS* 70 A 10). The sparks and the brothers themselves were compared to stars (Euripides, *Hel.*, 140; Plutarch, *Lysias*, 12). Like Heracles, the Dioscuri were initiated at Eleusis (Xenophon, *Hell.*, 6.3.6) and were thought to provide a guiding light to those seeking immortality.

[95] Burkert, *Greek Religion*, 211.

[96] Mackintosh: *Divine Rider*, 14.

and shield;[97] and, on a relief from Stragglethorpe, a mounted and armed warrior spears a serpent (*CSIR* 1.8.29).[98] The Celtic horseman fights evil, offers protection against the "dark forces" of the underworld, as the guardian against evil, the protector of territory and tribe.[99]

So too the Greek hero protected community and conquered malevolent forces from horseback. Greek gods did not share these equine affiliations.[100] For example, the Dioscuri, who rode white steeds, parallel the Vedic Asvin, shining, fraternal horsemen,[101] recalling the shining (Belatucadrus, Loucetius) equestrian gods of Celtic myth. Bellerophon tamed Pegasus (with Athena's help—Hesiod, *Theogony*, 318; Apollodorus 2.3.2; Pindar, *Olympian*, 13.63; Pausanias 2.4.1). Achilles' horses were semi-divine (*Iliad* 19.408–417). The equestrian Diomedes of Argos fought the gods from his chariot.[102] Diomedes of Timavon (near Venice) was renowned as a master of animals, and in his groves animals lived peacefully together (Strabo 5.194).[103]

Hero cult has been compared with the Christian cult of the saints, and indeed there may be direct continuity as well as structural parallels.[104] Each is honored with an annual feast day, real or symbolic. According to the later, recorded tradition, the Celtic comparison holds up: multiple functions, near to hand, mythic feasts. Heracles, himself a voracious eater, was especially honored with annual meat banquets,[105] reminiscent of the feasts which would be enjoyed by German gods and heroes.

Greek heroes were ultimately warriors who could provide military protection for their communities. As warriors, they were also hunters who protected their communities from starvation, the warrior-hunter associated with his prey.[106] In relief, Cocidius hunted stags (586).

---

[97] Todd, "Romano-British Warrior God," 238 and plate xxxiii A.
[98] Ambrose and Henig, "Roman Rider Relief," 135–136. Mackintosh, *Divine Rider*, 18–19.
[99] M.J. Green, *Gods of the Celts*, 116–117.
[100] The exception is Poseidon, the mythical father of horses, including Pegasus (Pindar, *Pythian Odes*, 6.50; Pausanias 8.25.3–5; Apollodorus 3.6.8).
[101] Burkert, *Greek Religion*, 212.
[102] Burkert, *Structure*, 95; *Iliad* 5 (passim).
[103] Wolves, who were also considered masters of animals, are said to have brought horses to the groves: Meuli, *Gesammelte Schriften*, 810; Burkert, *Structure*, 95.
[104] Burkert, *Greek Religion*, 207.
[105] Burkert, "Buzyge und Palladion," 356–368.
[106] Chiefs of American Plains Indian tribes wore ceremonial head-dresses adorned with the horns of the buffalo which provided these same tribes with food and clothing.

Celtic warrior gods and chiefs were distinguished by their head-dresses of rams' and bulls' horns. The connection is not altogether lacking in the classical tradition. Though not commonly, Greek heroes wore horned helmets, the most famous, Odysseus' boar's tusk helmet (*Iliad* 10.261–271), representative of gear from Mycenaean sites and apparently the oldest type of helmet found on the Greek mainland.[107] This particular helmet had a row of boar's tusks around the outside. Agamemnon wore a more traditional horned helmet, forked with twin horns (*Iliad* 11.41). Achilles owned a similar helmet, worn by Patroclus (*Iliad* 16.795), and Hephaistus provided Achilles with a second four-horned helmet (*Iliad* 22.315) to replace the one looted by Hector.

Greek heroes assumed, furthermore, other symbols from the world of hunting. Heracles wore, as a badge of honor, the skin of the Nemean lion. Heracles hunted cattle, deer, and boar, wild animals which destroyed crops and human livelihood yet were useful and welcomed sources of meat and warmth. Theseus also hunted one destructive bull. Furthermore, Nestor's cattle rustling expedition (*Iliad* 11.674–683) recalls Cuchulainn's exploits.[108] In addition to agriculture, these horned animals personify fertility, strength, and power, characteristics desirable for a warrior.[109]

Are Greek heroes faded gods or ritually honored mortals?[110] Perhaps the same question can be asked of the Celtic warrior god. Are the

---

[107] Nilsson, *Homer and Mycenae*, 138; Lorimer, "Homer and the Monuments," 212–214.

[108] Cuchulainn, the hero of the *Táin Bó Cuailgne* ("Raiding the Cattle of Cooley") and a master of wild beasts (Ross, *Celtic Britain*, 235), resembled Achilles (Nutt, *Cuchulainn*; Squire, *Celtic Myth*, 158; Sergent, "Celto-Hellenica.") and Heracles (Rhys, *Arthurian Legend*, chapters 9, 10; Squire, *Celtic Myth*, 158).

[109] Many societies, including the twentieth century U.S., correlate sexuality and virility with strength and success in battle and hunting (or sports). The Germans of the Roman era felt that excessive or premature sexual activity hindered growth and the development of strength and prowess in battle (Caesar, *BG* 6.21.4). Myth reflects similar taboos. Enkidu became powerless over animals after he slept with the prostitute (*Gilgamesh* I.iii–iv). The Hurrite hunter Kessi failed because of his excessive devotion to his wife. The hunter Hippolytus kept himself chaste in honor of Artemis. In contrast, Adonis, who left Aphrodite's bed for the hunt, had to fail because of his lack of chastity and "purity:" Burkert, *Structure*, 118; Frazer, *Golden Bough*, vol. III, 191–200; Meuli, *Griechische Opferbräuche*, 226, Burkert, *Homo Necans*, 72–73.

[110] Burkert, *Greek Religion*, 205. Usener, *Götternamen*, 252–273 and Pfister, *Reliquienkult*, 377–397 argue that the heroes were in origin gods. J.E. Harrison, *Themis*, 260–363 perceives the heroes as pre-Olympian *daimones*. Those who argue to the contrary, that hero-cult arose from ancestor worship or that heroes are ritually elevated men include Foucart, "Le culte des héros," 1–15; Farnell, *Greek Hero Cults*, 280–285; and Rohde, *Psyche*, 157, n. 170.

Celtic warrior gods lesser tribal deities, below the rank of the tribal sky god,[111] or are they great heroes who died spectacularly and were hence elevated to cult status?

Graeco-Roman Heroes

Since the relationship between Celtic horned gods and Graeco-Roman heroes has been delineated, a brief discussion of the military evidence of the cults of classical Heroes may prove useful. Gemstones, primarily, attest to Hero worship. In antiquity, rings carved or cast, were often worn to reflect the personality or occupation of the owner. Augustus, for example, wore the representation of a sphinx to stress his enigmatic character (Suetonius *Augustus* 50). Among engraved gemstones found in military contexts in Britain, some depict heroes of Graeco-Roman myth. Theseus with his father's sword appears on a small red jasper stone found at Walbrook, London, very likely belonging to a soldier, and possibly cut by a provincial artisan.[112] A nicolo, mounted on an iron ring, depicts a formalized Theseus (late in the first century or early second, Corbridge).[113] A third gem, an oval carnelian from East Wretham Heath, Norfolk, is not associated with a fort but could have belonged to a soldier, perhaps lost after the Boudiccan revolt.[114]

Achilles, likewise, appearing on several gems, was more popular as the Ideal Hero. Several examples show him with the armor of Thetis.[115] At Caerleon, a large, finely worked red jasper represents the hero wearing his chlamys, plumed helmet, and spear.[116] A carnelian gemstone from the legionary fortress at Eboracum (York) illustrates the rape of Cassandra—perhaps a warning to soldiers to avoid sacrilege and impiety.[117]

---

[111] M.J. Green, "Wheel God," 345–367; Leach, "Smith God," 35–45.

[112] Henig, "Heroes," 250–1; *Corpus*, 79, #455.

[113] Henig, *Corpus*, #456.

[114] Henig, *Corpus*, 79, Appendix #75.

[115] Henig, *Corpus*, #460 from Caerleon set in a silver ring; #457 from Corbridge set in a silver ring; #459 from Heronbridge, Cheshire; #458 from Chalgrave Bedfordshire set in a silver ring; Appendix #39 from Cirencester; Appendix #154 from Watercrook Westmorland; #461 from Atworth, Wilts.; #462 from Standish, Lans. found with a hoard of 200 denarii and two gold rings.

[116] Henig, "Veneration of Heroes," 254.

[117] Henig, "Veneration of Heroes," 257.

Other events from the Trojan War were commemorated on gems and worn by soldiers: after the desecration of the Palladium at Troy, Diomedes climbs over the altar of Apollo in his attempt to escape;[118] Achilles drags Hector's corpse behind his chariot (Hartburn, Northumbria);[119] Ajax carries Achilles' dead body (London);[120] the hound Argus recognizes Odysseus (Brecon).[121] Many soldiers in Britain probably hoped for a safe return home, though the state is unlikely to have funded the return trip.

Hercules' popularity among the soldiers in Britain is attested by the sixteen dedicated altars, two of which (307, 317) suggest temples; he also appears on numerous *intagli*. The great appeal of this deified hero may lay in his double nature, as hero and god, two aspects which are often difficult, if not impossible to distinguish.[122] A handful of gems, found at Caerleon, Corbridge and Colchester, represent Hercules as a god.[123] In addition, a statue at Rudchester shows Hercules with the apples of the Hesperides (*CSIR* 1.1.189).

Hercules was frequently represented engaged in his labors as examples of valor to which the owner might aspire: the hero overcoming Cerberus (Dorchester, Dorset);[124] wrestling Antaeus (Richborough);[125] fighting the Nemean lion (Caerleon).[126] Other Hercules scenes include the infant strangling the serpents,[127] and the queen of Lydia, Omphale, dressed in his skin and holding his club.[128]

Parade armor also points to the popularity of heroes. On a sword

---

[118] Henig, *Corpus*, #441 (Dorchester), #442 (Lincolnshire). An *intaglio* from Verulamium (#444) shows Diomedes about to seize the Palladium.

[119] Henig, *Corpus*, Appendix 72.

[120] Henig, *Corpus*, Appendix 153. An intaglio from Wadden Hill, Dorset shows the same scene (#447).

[121] Henig, *Corpus*, #446; "Veneration of Heroes," 256–7.

[122] Richmond, "Corbridge," 171. Henig, *Corpus*, 72, suggested that to distinguish the hero from the god was nearly as difficult in antiquity as it is today. But this ambiguity was convenient to someone like Commodus who wanted to "indulge in the trappings of divinity without claiming it specifically."

[123] Henig, *Corpus*: from Caerleon a late third century cameo (#732), and late second/early third century intaglio (#430), late second or early third century intaglio from Corbridge (#428), late second or early third century intaglio from Colchester (#429).

[124] Henig, *Corpus*, #436.

[125] Henig, *Corpus*, #437.

[126] Henig, *Corpus*, #431. The ring dates to the third century. The labor of the Nemean lion continued to be a popular as represented on third century nicolo pastes (#432, 433) from Verulamium and Springhead, Kent, respectively.

[127] Henig, *Corpus*, Appendix #152, from Wroxeter.

[128] Henig, *Corpus*, #439, from Fox Hill, Kent, first century.

scabbard found in the Thames at Fulham, there appears the image
of a she-wolf suckling the legendary founders of Rome, Romulus
and Remus.[129] Such scenes are found in military contexts throughout the empire. Mythical heroes such as Hercules, Achilles, Odysseus,
Theseus, and Romulus provided examples which the soldier might
follow.

Heroes were associated with healing, salvation and rebirth, since
many (i.e., Odysseus, Theseus, Heracles, Aeneas) travel to and return
from the underworld. Many worshippers thought that heroes had
real power to influence events on earth. It would only make good
sense for a worshipper to keep the image of a protector hero on an
amulet as a piece of jewelry.

Conclusions

That native rites became popular with soldiers of the Roman army,
both native Celts and men and officers from abroad, demonstrates
several aspects about Roman religion and the attitudes of the soldiers. First, Rome had no desire to offend any divine spirit and was
eager to welcome all into her pantheon. Second, the worshippers
may have felt that native gods possessed greater power on Hadrian's
Wall than did Roman gods, so far from home. Third, Celts and
perhaps soldiers of diverse origins looked to these native Celtic traditions which, unlike the Roman "state religion," offered the promise
of an afterlife to their adherents, a component which goes far in
explaining the increasing popularity of Eastern mystery cults at the
same time (third century AD). This same quality has already been
noted as a prominent factor in Greek hero cults (n.b. Heracles and
the Dioscuri) as well as in the Celtic horned warrior rituals.

Celt and Roman worshipped these gods, and with different effect.
The Romanized worshipper exploited only the martial aspects of
these local tribal gods. The cult of the horned warrior god may have
been the Romano-Celtic soldier's answer to mystery rites from the
East which gained in popularity from the first century AD onwards,
perhaps as self-induced "cultural exclusion." Mithras, Isis, and the
Dea Syria were worshipped in Britain, but their followers were either
Oriental (the Syrians alone cultivated their native goddess at Carvoran)

---

[129] Henig, "Veneration of Heroes," 263.

or fully Romanized, perhaps even Roman (as the officers who worshipped Mithras throughout the empire's frontiers). There is little evidence pointing to local Celts worshipping these popular deities from the East. Why is cultural isolation evident? We may never know, but reasonable causes are numerous. It is unlikely that local, Celtic soldiers were the victims of cultural prejudice, especially since shrines to Mithras protected cult objects sacred to other gods (including statues and votives to the Mother Goddesses, and altars to Cocidius) in the fourth century.[130] Perhaps Eastern cults were too expensive. Perhaps local Celts in the Roman army simply resisted Graeco-Roman religious culture—Romanization in northern England was opposed, the Brigantes to the west were never fully comfortable with Rome's presence, and the Picts remained always hostile. It is reasonable to assume that these staunch Celts were fiercely traditional, a trait the Romans prided in themselves, in preserving their own gods. As Burkert suggests within the context of Greek hero worship (note 77), these regionalized local cults provided a focus for cohesion of the group, and the group could include the civilian community or men at arms who shared a cultural (Celtic) upbringing.

---

[130] A statuette of a Mother Goddess was recovered from the narthex of the Romano-British Mithraeum at Carrawburgh (*CIMRM* 850; *CSIR* 1.6.164); from the sanctuary in the narthex of the Dieberg Mithraeum there was found a statue of a Mother Goddess nursing a child (Behn, *Mithrasheiligtum*, 35, #14; *CIMRM* 1262).

TABLES

Key to the tables:
  xxx: information is not given on the stone
  ???: information may have worn off the inscription
  the chart of place names is arranged geographically, proceeding roughly
    south to north and east to west

Table I: Distribution of Celtic Gods South of Hadrian's Wall in the East

Eboracum (York)	Veteris:	1
Cataractonium (Catterick)	Veteris:	1
Piercebridge, Co. Durham	Veteris:	1
Longovicium (Lanchester)	Veteris:	2
Concangis (Chester-le-Street)	Veteris:	3
Vindomora (Ebchester)	Veteris:	2
	Cocidius:	1

Table II: Distribution of Celtic Gods South of Hadrian's Wall in the West

Lancaster	Cocidius:	1
Bravoniciacum (Kirby Thore, Westm.)	Belatucadrus:	1
Brocavum (Brougham, Westm.)	Belatucadrus:	7
Voreda (Old Penrith, Cumbria)	Belatucadrus:	4
	Mogons:	2
Alauna (Maryport, Cumbria)	Belatucadrus:	1
Maglona (Old Carlisle, Cumbria)	Belatucadrus:	3
Luguvalium (Carlisle, Cumbria)	Belatucadrus:	1
Kirkbride	Belatucadrus:	1

*Table III: Distribution of Celtic Gods along Hadrian's Wall and forts within
3 miles south*

Arbeia (South Shields)	Veteris:	1
Corsiosopitum (Corbridge)	Veteris:	3
Condercum (Benwell)	Veteris:	2
	Antenociticus:	3
Cilurnum (Chesters)	Veteris:	4
Brocolitia (Carrawburgh)	Veteris:	2
	Belatucadrus:	1

(Table III cont.)

Vercovicium (Housesteads)	Veteris:	6
	Cocidius:	3
Vindolanda (Chesterholm)	Veteris:	9
	Mogons:	1
	Cocidius:	1
Aesica (Great Chesters)	Veteris:	3
Magnis (Carvoran)	Veteris:	14
	Belatucadrus:	3
Thistleton, Rutland	Veteris:	1
Aballava (Burgh-by-Sands)	Belatucadrus:	3
Milecastle 52	Cocidius:	2
Milecastle 55	Cocidius:	2
Banna (Birdoswald)	Cocidius:	2
Milecastle 59	Cocidius:	1
Milecastle 60	Cocidius:	1
Milecastle 65	Cocidius:	1
Hadrian's Wall (unspecified)	Veteris:	1
Camboglanna (Castlesteads)	Belatucadrus:	2

Table IV: Distribution of Celtic Gods North of Hadrian's Wall

Habitancum (Risingham)	Mogons:	2
	Cocidius:	1
Bremenium (High Rochester)	Mogons:	1
Fanum Cocidi (Bewcastle)	Cocidius:	7
Castra Exploratorum (Netherby)	Veteris:	3
	Belatucadrus:	1
	Mogons:	1
	Cocidius:	1

Table V: Veteris: Orthography and Worshippers

Location	Orthography and titles	Dedicator	rank/unit	cat. #
Eboracum	Deus Veteris	Primulus Vol(usianus)		627
Cataractonium	Deus sanctus Vheteris	pro salute Aureli Muciani		628
Voreda	Vicres	T.S.		629
Castra Exploratorum	Mogons Vitiris Sanctus	Aelius Secundus		519
	Deus Huetiris	xxx		630
	Deus Iu[--]ter sanctus	Fortunatus		397b
Concangis	Deus Vitiris	Duihno		631
	Deae Vitires	Vitalis		632
	Deae Vitires	???		633
Arbeia	Deus Vitiris	Cr?		634
Longovicium	Deus Vitiris	xxx		635
	Deus Vitiris	VNTHAV	princeps	636
Vindomora	Deus Vitiris	Maximus		637
	Deus Vitiris	???		638
Piercebridge	Deus Veteris	xxx		639
Corsiosopitum	Deus Veteris	xxx		640
	Deus Vitiris	xxx		641
	Vitiris	Mitius		642
	VM deus	?		643
Condercum	Deus Vetris sangtus	xxx		644
	Vitires	xxx		645
Cilurnum	Deus sanctus Vitiris	Tertulus		646
	Di Vetere	xxx		647

(Table V cont.)

Location	Orthography and titles	Dedicator	rank/unit	cat. #
	Di Vitires	xxx		648
Brocolitia	Deus Votris	xxx		649
	Deus Veteris	Uccus		650
	Di Hviteres	xxx		651
Vercovicium	Deus Hueteris	Superstes et Regulus		652
	Deus Huitris	Aspuanis		653
	Deus Veteres	xxx		654
	Veteres	Aurelius Victor		656
	Di Veteres	xxx		655
	Di Veteres	xxx		657
Vindolanda	Veteris	-tin-		659
	Deus Hvitiris	xxx		665
	Deus Veteris	xxx		658
	Deus sanctus Vetiris	xxx		663
	Deus Ve --	???		664
	Veteres	Senaculus		660
	Veteres	Senilis		662
	Vitres	xxx		666
Aesica	Di Veteres	Longinus		661
	Deus Vetiris	xxx		667
	Di Veteres	Romana		668
	Di Vetere	???		669
Magnis	Deus Veteris	Necalames		670
	Deus Veteris	Necalames		671
	Deus Viteris	NO???		676

(*Table V cont.*)

Location	Orthography and titles	Dedicator	rank/unit	cat. #
	Deus Vitiris	Menius Dada		677
	Deus Vitiris	Milus et Aurides		678
	Deus Vitiris	Necalimes		672
	Deus Vetiris	xxx		675
	Deus sanctus Veteris	Iulius Pastor	*imaginifer*	673
	Deus Vetiris sanctus	Andiatis		674
	Veteres	xxx		679
	Di Veteres	xxx		680
	Di Vitere	IVIXA		681
	Di Vitires	Deccius		682
Hadrian's Wall	Deus Veteris	xxx		680
	Huitires	xxx		684
Thisleton, Rutland	Deus Veteris	Mocuxsoma		685

Table VI: Belatucadrus: Orthography and Worshippers

Location	Orthography and titles	Dedicator	rank/unit	cat. #
Bravoniciacum	Deus Belatucadrus	-iolus		541
Brocavum	Blatucairus	Audagus		544
	Deus Belatucadrus	Iulianus		545
	Deus Belatucadrus	-inam		546
	Deus Balatucairus	Baculo		543
	Deus Balatucadrus	-tinus		542
	Sanctus deus Belatucadrus	xxx	ex cuneo	547
Alauna	Belatucadrus	Iulius Civilis	optio	549
Maglona	Deus Belatucaurus	-cipa		552
	Deus Belatucadrus sanctus	Aurelius Tasalus		550
	Deus Sanctus Belatucadrus	Aurelius Diatova	veteranus	551
Voreda	Deus Balatocadrus	xxx		555
	Deus sanctus Belacairus	xxx		556
	Deus sanctus Belatucadrus	xxx		553
Luguvalium	Deus Mars Belatucadrus	Iulius Augustalis	actor praefecti	554
	Deus Mars Belatucadrus	xxx		557
Castra Exploratorum	Deus Mars Belatucadrus	[A]ur(elianus) [Ni]ca[n]or?		558
Brocolitia	Deus Belleticaurus	Lunaris		559
Magnis	Deus Baliticaurus	xxx		560
	Deus Blatucadrus	xxx		561
Camboglanna	Deus Mars Belatucairus	xxx		562
	Deus Belatugagrus	Minervalis		563
Aballava	Deus sanctus Belatucadrus	-ullinus		564
	Balatucadrus sanctus	Censorinus		568

(*Table VI cont.*)

Location	Orthography and titles	Dedicator	rank/unit	cat. #
	Deus Belatucadrus	xxx		565
	Deus Belatocadrus	Antronius Aufidianus		566
	Mars Belatucadrus sanctus	xxx		567
Kirkbride	Deus Belatocairus	Peisius M.		569

Table VII: Mogons: Orthography and Worshippers

Location	Orthography and titles	Dedicator	rank/ unit	cat. #
Voreda	Deus Mogons	xxx		518
	Deus Mountis	xxx		522
Castra Exploratorum	Deus Mogons Vitiris sanctus	Aelius Secundus		519
Habitancum	Deus Mogons Cad.(?)	M. Gavius Secundinus	beneficiarius cons.	520
	Deus Mounus Cad (?)	Iuuentius Do[ ]		524
Bremenium	Di Mountes	Iulius Firminus	decurio	523
Vindolanda	Deus Moguntis	Lupulus		521

Table VIII: Cocidius: Orthography and Worshippers

Location	Orthography and titles	Dedicator	rank/unit	cat. #
Lancaster	Deus sanctus Mars Cocidiu	Vibenius Lucius	*ben. cons.*	577
Castra Exploratorum	Deus sanctus Cocidius	Paternius Maternus	*trib. coh. I Nerv.*	578
Fanum Cocidi	Deus Cocidius	xxx		580
	Deus Cocidius	Auentinus		581
	Sanctus Cocidius	Aurunceius Felicessemus	*trib. ex evocato*	582
	Deus sanctus Cocidius	Annius Victor	*centurio leg.*	579
	Deus sanctus Cocidius	Q. Peltrasius Maximus	*trib. ex corniculario*	583
	Deus Mars Cocidius sanctus	Aelius Vitalianus		584
	Mars Cocidius	Vitalis		474
Vindomora	Deus Vernostonus Cocidius	Virilis Germanus		585
Habitancum	Deus Cocidius	Seu --		586
Vercovicium	Cocidius	Valerius	*miles leg. VI*	587
	Deus Cocidius	Vabrius		589
	Deus Silvanus Cocidius	Q. Florius Maternus	*praef. coh. I Tung.*	588
Vindolanda	Deus Cocidius	Decimus Caerellius Victor	*praef. coh. II Ner.*	590
Banna	Deus Cocidius		*coh. I Aelia Dacorum*	591
	Deus Cocidius	xxx		196a
Milecastle 52	Deus Cocidius		*milites leg. II Aug.*	592
	Deus Cocidius		*milites leg. XX VV*	593
Milecastle 55	Deus Cocidius		*vex. leg. VI V*	594
	Deus Cocidius	xxx		595
Milecastle 59	Deus Mars Cocidius	-martius,	*centurio coh. I Bat.*	596
Milecastle 60	Deus Cocidius		*milites leg. VI VPF*	597
Milecastle 65	Mars Cocidius		*milites leg. II Aug.*	598

Table IX: Antenociticus: Orthography and Worshippers

Location	Orthography and titles	Dedicator	rank/unit	cat. #
Condercum	Deus Antenociticus	Aelius Vibius	centurio leg. XX	535
	Deus Antenociticus		coh. I Vangionum	536
	Deus Antenocitus	Tineus Longus	praef. eq.	537

CHAPTER FOUR

CELTIC HEALER AND WARRIOR MAIDEN

Celtic gods served the tribe in matters of war and peace, justice and fertility, salvation and healing. As fully-fledged tribal deities, they did not entirely engage the interests of the soldier on the Roman frontier, but some divine aspects were relevant and desirable. We have already seen the Celtic god as horned warrior. It remains to consider native gods and goddesses as healers. The ill relied as much on the supernatural as on empirical medicine, inextricably linked with religion.[1] Consequently, physicians and priests were on staff together at most healing shrines, Graeco-Roman as well as Celtic (i.e., 614).[2] Most healer gods are associated with water and curative springs; as will be seen, some have connections with curses and retribution (Sulis at Bath, Mercury at Uley).

Warrior God and Healer

Under numerous epithets, Mars was thoroughly assimilated into Celtic cults known both on the continent and in Britain alone: Camulus (467), Lenus (468, 469), Loucetius (470), Toutates (474). Celtic gods equated with Mars in Britain emphasize the god's regal and military character:[3] Alator, the huntsman (603–604), Belatucadrus (Fair Shining One: 554, 557, 558, 562, 567),[4] Rigisamus (most kingly: 472), Segomo (Victor),[5] Toutates (Ruler of the people: 473, 474), Barrex (Supreme).[6] Occasionally his role as healer surfaces, especially

---

[1] Allason-Jones, *Women*, 156.

[2] For example, Asclepius' incubation shrines at Cos and Epidaurus. For Celtic examples, priests and physicians attended the sick at the *Fontes Sequana*, where the water spirit who personified the river Seine dwelled (Deyts, *Sanctuaire*) and at Bath where Sulis Minerva presided over a healing sanctuary (Cunliffe, *Sacred Spring*, 359–62).

[3] Ross, *Celtic Britain*, 183.

[4] Tolkien in Collingwood, *Roman Britain*, 262; K.H. Jackson, *Language and History*, 431.

[5] Ross, *Celtic Britain*, 172.

[6] Ross, *Celtic Britain*, 182.

at Bath (Loucetius; 470), Caerwent (Lenus and Ocelus; 469), and Lydney (Nodens: 611). Condatis (606–608), associated with springs, may have been honored with a healing cult in county Durham. His votives were private, and one (607) was dedicated *ex iussu*—Condatis may have healed Attonius Quintianus in a dream or vision. An altar to Ialonus Contrebis (459), found near a spring probably sacred to the god, might suggest a healing role. Furthermore, Lenus' association with dogs links him to the Greek healer Asclepius to whom the dog was also sacred.[7] Even though Roman medicine was relatively advanced, the soldier, whom Tacitus characterized as superstitious (e.g., *Annals* 1.25), may have preferred not to trust his medical health entirely to the camp physicians. Some soldiers clearly took comfort in calling upon local healer deities to supplement available medical treatment.

Mars Nodens

The remains of the temple of the healer god Mars Nodens lay on high ground overlooking the river Severn at Lydney, where inscribed altars attest him (611–614). A second cult center may have stood at Cockersand Moss, where another two inscriptions (615–616) have surfaced. Finds from the site suggest a third century date, though the mosaic floors (not part of the original décor) belonging to the entrance-lobby of the "Abaton" can be dated to the fourth century on stylistic grounds.[8] E. Birley preferred an earlier date (AD 150–300) because of the good quality construction of the precinct buildings.[9] The superior workmanship does not necessarily preclude the traditional date, and the temple may have been restored in response to Julian's edicts of religious tolerance (AD 361–3).

The temple contained three small shrines at its north-western end.[10] Two small niches formed small chapels in each side-aisle. Near the temple, other fourth-century buildings included a square courtyard house, a bath-suite (AD 354–6), and a narrow building with numerous cubicles. The third building is probably the *Abaton*, where Nodens,

---

[7] G. Webster, "What the Britons required," 58, 61.

[8] Grew, "Roman Britain in 1980," 357. Coins, dating predominantly to the third and fourth centuries, but into the fifth century as well, e.g. Honorius and Theodosius, were buried through a floor and do not necessarily provide evidence for a later phase of the temple.

[9] E. Birley, "Deities," 90.

[10] The rectangular temple, 18.3 × 24.4m, faced southeast.

visiting patients in their sleep (by analogy with Asclepius at Epidaurus: Pausanius II.27) would effect cures.

Nodens' healing properties are further indicated by cult-objects: bronze and stone dogs and pins of various materials (n.b. *CSIR* 1.7.161–162). Dogs, linked to Asclepius' cult, were thought to heal wounds by licking them. About nine bronze canine figurines have surfaced at Lydney. A large number of bronze and bone pins (ca. 320) also point to a healing cult. Greek women often dedicated pins to goddesses after a successful childbirth.[11] In addition, brooches and bracelets, again common offerings to deities concerned with female healing, have been excavated at Lydney. Finally, articles representing the sun and water were appropriate to healing cults.[12]

The god's name is etymologically related to the Irish Nuada, the most famous of which is Nuada Argit-kain, of the silver hand, a legendary and early king of Ireland.[13] The name may be cognate with Germanic "neut-", to catch, entrap.[14] Hence, Nodens may also be a deity of hunting or fishing. Temple decoration suggests association with the sea: the cella's mosaic pavement showcases sea monsters and fish; one bronze fragment designates a sea-god holding a shell in one hand, an anchor in the other; another bronze fragment represents a fisherman and tritons with conch-shells and anchors. The healer with maritime associations also evokes the cult of the dead.[15] Nodens' hunter aspects recall another Celtic Mars with Silvan associations, Mars Rigonemetos (619). The three *sacella* in the temple may have been set up to accommodate the god's ternary nature (healer, hunter, ocean-deity).[16]

---

[11] Rouse, *Greek Votive Offerings*, 252–253; Whatmough, "Rhetia," 212.

[12] Wheeler, "'Romano-Celtic' Temple," 300; Lewis, *Temples*, 88–92; Richmond, *Art and Archaeology*, 157. The dog was closely associated with Nodens. The connection between dogs and healing cults may be strengthened by dog bones found in wells and rivers are generally associated with healing cults) with votive objects (Ross, *Celtic Britain*, 340). In addition, Apollo Cunomaglus, "the hound prince," oversaw a healing shrine at Nettleton: *JRS.*1962 #8. Jenkins, "Dog in Romano-Gaulish Religion," 60–76.

[13] Lewis, *Temples*, 90. Irish settlers in the third century may have influenced both Lydney and Lancaster, further strengthening Nodens' Irish connection.

[14] Tolkien in Wheeler, *Lydney park*, 132–137; K.H. Jackson, *Language and History*, 306, 313, 619.

[15] Dolphins and other maritime images are connected to travel to the underworld. Furthermore, Gods often control complementary (Apollo: plague and healing, e.g.) or contradictory (Artemis as virgin and goddess of childbirth) spheres.

[16] Lewis, *Temples*, 89.

Apollo Maponus

A cult of Maponus is attested, in six British inscriptions, four of which equate the god with Apollo and were made by members of the sixth legion (460–466).[17] The deity's musical aspects were emphasized in Roman iconography, perhaps reflecting a bardic tradition of a god's ability to heal through musical enchantment.[18] High-ranking officers patronized Maponus' cult, significantly the only British cult to attract prominent attention at Corbridge.[19] The deity survived in Welsh myth as the heroic hunter Mabon who, in the "Mabinogion," was abducted from his mother at birth and imprisoned until Culwch's companions rescued him. His name might derive from the Old Celtic *maqono-s* meaning "boy" or "youth." Maponus, it is generally agreed, was more widely cultivated than our epigraphic sources imply.[20]

There are no clear Celtic images of the god. Richmond labeled a Corbridge head, whose expression is somber and mature, as Maponus (*CSIR* 1.1.122).[21] The figure appears too mature to suggest a youthful Apollo Maponus. A figure etched into the back of an altar from Corbridge might portray Maponus (462). Further, Maponus may be sculpted on an altar to Apollo at Whitley Castle (292). Many have thought Maponus purely British. MacDonald called him Brigantian.[22] Yet evidence outside Britain suggests our god. Ross argued that Maponus was attested in Gaul on a potter's stamp dating to the first century AD. An eleventh century document belonging to the abbey of Savigny, Rhône, furthermore, referred to *Mabono fonte*, indicating that a Gaulic spring may have been dedicated to Maponus.[23] This suggests a healer Maponus in Gaul.

---

[17] E. Birley, "Deities," 55, note 286a, cites a Celtic inscription found at Chamalières, France which shows that Maponus was an Avernian deity.

[18] Richmond, "Corbridge," 209–10.

[19] Richmond, "Corbridge," 206–10. Votaries at Corbridge include a prefect from the sixth legion (461), a tribune (462), and a centurion of the sixth legion (460).

[20] An inscription from Birrens (466) may refer to Maponus and would, indeed, corroborate this supposition.

[21] Richmond, "Two Celtic Heads," 11; *CSIR* 1.1.122.

[22] MacDonald, "Maponi," col. 1413.

[23] Ross, *Celtic Britain*, 368.

Mother Goddesses and Related Triads

Matres

The *Matres* are well-represented on inscriptions at Rome, Gallia
Lugdunensis, Upper and Lower Germany, and Britain. In addition,
epigraphic evidence has surfaced in north and south-west Gaul, Spain,
Africa, and in the Illyrian provinces, but the cult seems to have been
native to the Germanies. German soldiers, especially, worshipped the
Matres. The goddesses broad appeal is underscored by the fact that
the *equites singulares* at Rome were responsible for sixteen dedications
to the *Matres*.[24]

Germans recruited for the army probably imported these goddesses
to Britain.[25] The highest concentrations of votives appeared in Lower
Germany, perhaps the original seat of worship.[26] The epithets with
which they were widely invoked suggest foreign (non-British) cults:
Afrae (481), Communes (498, 500), Domesticae (480, 483, 508, 509),
Gallae (476, 481), Germanae (476, 511), Italae (476, 481), Italicae
(475), Ollototae (478, 489, 490), Patriae (494), Suae (482, 503, 510),
Tramarinae (486, 487, 493, 494, 507). However, it is likely that distinct but similar cults to Mother Goddesses existed among both Celtic
and Germanic people, since both groups are known to have worshipped ternary deities. Perhaps because of the migrations of the
Celtic and Germanic peoples in the second and first centuries BC,
two cults, Celtic and Germanic variations, were fused, retaining the
vestiges of original differences.[27] The cult of the *Matres* flourished
from the reign of Gaius to that of Gordian (238/44), weakening in

---

[24] For the *equites singulares*, see, most recently, Speidel, *Riding for Caesar*. They
accompanied the emperor to the front during wartime. The *equites singulares*, an
auxiliary equivalent of the praetorian guard, were kept up to full strength by transfer of men chosen from the *alae* in the provinces and recruited from the provinces.
Hence, this detachment included a greater mixture of races and cultures than other
auxiliary units. It was appropriate that the *equites singulares* worshipped a variety of
deities both Roman and Gallic (E. Birley, "Marcus Cocceius Firmus," 100). A series
of altars dedicated by the *equites singulares* at Rome include votives to Jupiter Optimus
Maximus, the *Genius singularium Augusti*, Mars, Minerva, the *Matres*, the *Campestres*,
Hercules, Epona, Victoria, Silvanus.
[25] Haverfield, "Mother Goddesses," 314.
[26] Haverfield, "Mother Goddesses," 317. Moreover, the sculptures from this area
are most characteristic, suggesting that the worship of the Matres is indigenous to
Lower Germany. Furthermore, the fruit basket serves as an attribute of the Batavian
goddess Nehalennia, further linking the *Matres* to Lower Germany.
[27] Haverfield, "Mother Goddesses," 318.

the late third century. The cult was commonly recognized (e.g. *Matres Communes*: 498, 500; *Matres omnium gentium*: 506), and worshippers may have thought that the Mother Goddesses were universally power-ful.[28] Otherwise it might seem strange to worship gods connected to other lands (they would be less powerful further from their cult cen-ters).[29] Such invocations may represent the soldiers' poignant desire to return home after a successful tour of duty. Or worshippers may have attempted to transfer their own gods to a new seat of power; just as foreign gods could become Roman (n.b. Macrobius 3.9.7–8), consequently Roman (and allied) gods could become British.

The Mother Goddesses were almost always invoked in the plural and usually depicted as a seated triad. Each of the three often holds in her lap an emblem of fertility (plates of fruits or breads): from Culver Hole Cave, Gower, a bronze figurine of a Mother Goddess holds two children.[30] Stone reliefs of the three Mother Goddesses are concentrated in the Cotswolds (Cirencester and Bath: highly Romanized centers), Hadrian's Wall, Lincolnshire, and London.[31]

The *Matres* unqualified received numerous votives throughout Romanized Britain. Civilian dedications have been found in London (*RIB* 2), Daglingworth near Cirencester (*RIB* 130), Doncaster in Yorkshire (*RIB* 618), Adel in Yorkshire (*RIB* 629), Old Carlisle for the welfare of Severus Alexander and Julia Mamaea (485), and Bowness (*RIB* 2059).[32] Troops in units of Celtic origin, including the

---

[28] Barnard, "*Matres*," 244, argues that these universal *Matres* (e.g., *communes*) are a manifestation of catholic gods among non-Christians. These attestations are too early (Severan—early third century), though, for Christianity to have affected the *Matres* cult in Britain. To be sure, the *Matres communes* and *omnium gentium* show catholic tendencies, but perhaps as Mithras, Isis, Jupiter Dolichenus, or other (non-Christian) Eastern mysteries influenced Celtic religions. Assimilation of Isis rites, for example, to Celtic manifestations will be noted in chapter 5 (pp. 180–181).

[29] Burkert, *Greek Religion*, 206.

[30] Collingwood, "Roman Britain in 1935," pl. XLIII.

[31] M.J. Green, "Iconography," 140. These areas (with the exception of London) correspond to areas with good quality stone.

[32] Britain has yielded twenty three dedications to the *Matres* unqualified from civilians and soldiers, thirty seven to the *Matres* with various epithets.

The dedication slab from Bowness preserves a poem in catalectic trochaic tetram-eters, divided on the inscription at diaeresis or verse-end: *[Matribus deabus aed]em | [Ant]onianus dedico: | [se]d date ut fetura quaestus | suppleat votis fidem; | aureis sacrabo car-men | mox virtitim litteris.* The three metrical lines may have been inspired by Vergil, *Ecl.* vii 35, 36 (to Priapus) as suggested by Heurgon to Richmond (April 22, 1951, cited by Wright, *RIB*, 631):

nunc te marmoreum pro tempore fecimus; at tu,
si fetura gregem suppleverit, aureus esto.

Astures (479) and Vardulli (496) of Spain and the Tungrii (501, 512) from Gallia Belgica, honored the *Matres* with inscribed altars.

In addition to epigraphic testimony and reliefs in stone, the *Matres* received a silver ring at Carrawburgh. At Backworth (Tyne and Wear), another ring in gold, dedicated to the *Matres Coccae*, was discovered in a silver patera, the handle of which was also inscribed with a dedication to the *Matres* (*RIB* II.3.2422.9). This patera also contained coins, including two brasses dating to Antoninus Pius, another gold ring, three rings with gems, and two chains with wheel shaped pendants, linking the worship of the mother goddesses with that of the wheel-god, as consorts of the solar deities or as vanquishers of evil.[33] Civilian evidence supports a connection between the two cults. In Britain, one *Matres* relief (found at Easton Gray, provenance unknown) also shows wheel-symbols.[34] A wheel-symbol in the gable above surmounts three *Matres* in relief (*CSIR* 1.7.119).

Temples to the *Matres* are implied epigraphically at Old Penrith (486) and Castlesteads (506). Milecastle 19 incorporates a third altar (496) suggesting a *Matres* temple. Yet no traces survive. The implication, though, is significant. These sites are military, and the fact that the *Matres* were honored with temple cults underscores their broad appeal and importance.

The *Matres* triad illustrates the fundamental Celtic belief in the ternary power of gods—fertility, war and protection of the community, medicine and healing. The three are related to the Macha, a trio of war-goddesses, and the three Brigits of Irish lore. Furthermore, they shared attributes with other Celtic goddesses including Epona and Coventina (who was represented in three-fold form at Carrawburgh: *CSIR* 1.6.93; compare 444). Like many other Celtic deities, their spheres of influence included the battlefield and horses (also connected with war); they were, however, most significant as deities of fertility and childbirth.[35] The *Matres* were not identical with the *Parcae*, nor the *theoi meteres* of Sicily (Diodorus Siculus iv, 79.7), but these goddesses were often confused with the *Parcae* in Middle Ages,[36] which may argue to the *Matres*' powers over fate.

---

[33] M.J. Green, *Military Areas*, 17.
[34] Green, *Civilian Areas*, 18, 190, pl. XVe.
[35] Ross, *Celtic Britain*, 206–8.
[36] Haverfield, "Mother Goddesses," 319. From a German book of questions to be asked of penitents, dating to the eleventh century: Hast thou done, as do some women at certain seasons, preparing a table in thy house and meat and drink thereon, that the three Sisters or *Parcae* may come and be refreshed therewith?

Invoked without qualification but with geographic epithets, the *Matres* may have lacked proper names (contra Juno, Minerva, or Diana); instead, they represent a god-type, in this respect resembling the horned warrior gods. A soldier travelling from one area of the empire to another would recognize the triad of goddesses, whose tribal names changed, yet who remained mother protectors. Our soldier could assume these goddesses to be his own, and so used the very process by which the Romans understood non-Roman religions—*interpretatio Celtica*.

Genii Cucullati

The distribution of the *genii cucullati* in Britain largely overlaps the Mother Goddesses.[37] In Britain, these deities appeared as a triad of dwarf-like creatures dressed in loose hooded cloaks (*cuculli*); to the contrary in Germany the *genii cucullati* were usually represented individually as giants.[38] Their associations link them with prosperity, fertility and healing, as they were found with the Mother Goddesses in Gloucestershire, and with Mercury and "Rosmerta" in Bath.[39] About ten groups of *genii cucullati* are known in the south of England, concentrated in Gloucestershire (*CSIR* 1.7.95, 97–100, 102, 105–107).

The *Genii Cucullati*, in their capacity to heal, were connected to the Celtic warrior gods, as suggested by finds from Gloucestershire. For example, a relief from a well from Lower Slaughter, Gloucestershire, shows a divine warrior god standing beside three *genii cucullati*. The god is not armed, but he wears the short kilted tunic of the Celtic war god, and two birds, possibly ravens though the species is uncertain, appear above the human figure (*CSIR* 1.7.98). A second relief from the same well represents only the *genii cucullati* (*CSIR* 1.7.95). A relief from Bath shows a horned god and his seated consort (*CSIR* 1.2.39). Below the pair is a large horned male animal— perhaps a ram, symbolic of war in Celtic iconography—and three small hooded figures.[40] A bone *genius cucullatus* was among the votives recovered from a healing shrine at Springhead. *Genii Cucullati*, often

---

[37] Heichelheim, "Genii Cucullati," 187–195. The distribution is the Cotswolds in the western areas of the province and the northern *limes* (Hadrian's Wall).

[38] M.J. Green, "Iconography," 144.

[39] M.J. Green, *Civilian Areas*, 187, pl. XVIIIa.

[40] Ross, *Celtic Britain*, 188, 300, pl. 55a. The ram, an animal of war, also has healing associations in Celtic mythology.

found in wells, were frequently linked to water deities and healing cults: Bath, Springhead. R. Egger once suggested that the central figure might represent Telesphorus, the flanking figures depicting the other sons of Asclepius, Machaon and Podaleirius or Akesis and Euamerion, or the healing sisters in the cult of Asclepius.[41] The epigraphic record to Telesphorus does not support such an hypothesis. Heichelheim saw syncretisation with Roman *penates*.[42]

This enigmatic trio is attested along the military *limes* of Roman Britain. At Housesteads, they are depicted with rough features, facing front and wearing heavy hoods, while their cloaks, concealing the arms and hands of the figures, reach to the ankles (*CSIR* 1.6.152). The middle figure of the Housesteads relief appears male, his face squarish, while the two outer figures, whose faces are more oval and effeminate, seem to be feminine but could be young boys.[43] The relief was found with five *denarii*, perhaps votive offerings, in a small shrine. The coins date to 220–229.

A sculpture from Carlisle once bore three hooded figures in relief (*CSIR* 1.6.485, second/third century). Two *genii cucullati* appear in the recess of the votive plaque, each dressed in short hooded cloaks; the arms are completely muffed. The legs, mostly worn away, are barely visible underneath the cloaks. The figure on the right has since worn off. The central figure seems to be male, the surviving flanking figure may be female, although Toynbee found no basis for that conclusion.[44] The workmanship is crude and local.

A relief found at Netherby shows three male figures standing, facing front and each wearing a *cucullus* and tight fitting trousers (*CSIR* 1.6.155). The right-most and central figures hold egg-shaped objects (perhaps eggs, stones, or fruit). The right hand of the left figure is missing, but it is likely that he also held an egg-shaped object. These eggs could represent the Orphic-Bacchic egg, symbolizing the creation of the world, as some have suggested.[45] A simpler and more

---

[41] Egger, "Genius Cucullatus," 313.

[42] Heichelheim, "Genii Cucullati," 187–94.

[43] Heichelheim, "Genii Cucullati," 187; Toynbee, *Art in Britain*, #77; Ross, *Celtic Britain*, 380, pl. 90.

[44] Heichelheim, "Genii Cucullati," 188; Toynbee, "Genii Cucullati," 460. The figure on the left could be female, since it is smaller, thinner and shorter than the middle figure. The face is more oval with very pronounced cheekbones in contrast to the central figure's square and severe features. Contrast, however, *RIB* 685, where Flavia Augustina is shown taller and fatter than her husband; the difference in size may simply reflect the sculptor's lack of skill.

[45] Heichelheim, "Genii Cucullati," 188.

likely explanation, eggs are widely recognized images of life and fertility.[46] The fertility/egg association is not an isolated instance: in relief, a single *cucullus*, holding an egg, stands next to a mother goddess carrying fruit (*CSIR* 1.7.104, Cirencester).

At Birdoswald, a statue in the round, of crude workmanship, represents a single *cucullus* (*CSIR* 1.6.154).[47] The face is pear shaped, the eyes lentoid, the nose wedge-shaped, the mouth wide and irregular. The cloak, ending at the waist, conceals arms and hands. Below the waist, the sculpture assumes the shape of a pillar. The artifact was perhaps a soldier's dedication in a shrine attached to the fort. This superficial resemblance to a herm may be an attempt to classicize the *cucullus*, a protective deity like Hermes/Mercury. A relief from Cirencester suggests the protective nature of the *genii cucullati* (*CSIR* 1.7.103). Three *cucullati*, the outer two armed with swords, accompany a mother goddess, seated and holding fruit or cakes in her lap.

These curious deities were associated with fertility (*Matres*, eggs), healing (springs and water deities at Bath and Springhead), and war (especially the warrior-healer). These three aspects make the *cucullati* attractive to the soldier who fights and requires physical healing. The appeal of fertility is universal. Their hooded and shrouded heads suggest the mystery of death and of the Otherworld, an universal concern, no less to one who could lose his life in the line of duty. The *cucullati* survived as dwarfs and hobgoblins.[48] According to tradition, three dwarfs created Thor's hammer Mjollnir. This suggests that the *cucullati* might be related to the Celtic smith god. *Genii cucullati* and Tanarus monuments overlap, especially at Maryport, Castlesteads, and Netherby. Monuments to the *genii cucullati* have not yet been found at Corbridge, where smith gods (Celtic and Eastern) and the *Matres* are known (*CSIR* 1.1.62, 63). The iron-working association stems from the *cucullati* as warrior-healers and protectors (they are depicted with swords at Birdoswald). Furthermore, the *cucullati*, abnormally short and stout, appear misshapen, a characteristic they share with creator-gods in other traditions, namely Vulcan (Hephaistos), the club-footed, unattractive god who created objects of great beauty.[49]

---

[46] Toynbee, *Art in Britain*, 177.

[47] Toynbee, *Art in Britain*, 105.

[48] Heichelheim, "Genii Cucullati," 194. Dwarfs and trolls are mysterious creatures, with overtones of evil, frequently depicted in myth as a triad. In later traditions, dwarfs developed metallurgy: mineral and agricultural wealth both derive from the earth, linking *genii cucullati* as fertility *daimones* to metallurgy.

[49] Anthropologists have studied pre-literate societies in which artisans are customarily

Additionally, the *cochull* (hood), common in Irish myth, frequently embodied supernatural characteristics.[50] The dwarfish characters in Celtic and Germanic myth, both of the Roman and the post-Roman periods, seem to be antitheses of the gods, malformed creatures of short stature in contrast to the tall and (presumably) handsome gods.

Warrior Maidens

It has been argued above that Celtic horned warriors closely resemble Greek heroes in myth and cult. The warrior god has also appeared as healer, and attribute shared by the tribal mother goddesses. True gods of war seem, in Medieval Irish Celtic lore, to have been female, comparable perhaps with Athena who developed scientific warfare (contra Ares bloodlust) and trained and protected heroes (e.g., Odysseus, Heracles). The Irish (Celtic) deities who controlled warfare were female: the triple Mórrígan, Macha, and Badbh, among other goddesses driven by maternal, territorial, and military instincts. In addition, heroes were taught the arts of war by women. In the "Wooing of Emer," the Irish hero Cuchulainn received his training from the prophetesses Scáthach and Aife, and the Welsh hero Peredur was trained by the nine *gwiddonod* of Gloucester.[51]

Campestres

The *Campestres* (36, 283, 512, 515–17), worshipped originally in Gaul, came to be known, by a Latin name, in the Latin speaking

---

maimed: on the principle that only those who are physically crippled can create objects of beauty (beauty and the beast), and crippling a craftsman would make it difficult for him to take his skills to another community.

[50] Ross, *Celtic Britain*, 380.

[51] Dillon and Chadwick, *Celtic Realms*, 145–146; MacCanna, *Celtic Mythology*, 86–93. The *gwiddonod* seem to be divinely inspired prophetesses. They wear armor and train their students, including Peredur, in chivalry and military technique. They also supply their students with armor and horses. The number nine has magical properties in Celtic and Greek cultures, and their number brings to mind the Muses, the daughters of Zeus and Mnemosyne, who inspire men to great feats of art (heroic fighting or dueling is a highly developed art form). These *gwiddonod* do, in fact, serve the same purpose as the Greek Athena who trains, arms, inspires and emboldens her hero-soldiers, and is always at the ready to help her proteges out of tight spots. In other cultures, goddesses likewise control warfare, for example, the Germanic Campestres who would become the Valkyries. See Irby-Massie, "Campestres."

world through the auxiliary cavalry recruited in Gaul.[52] These goddesses were cultivated almost exclusively by the cavalry and were associated with the exercise ground (*campus*), which Epona, the patroness of horses and their riders, also protected.[53] Like the *Matres* proper, the *Campestres* received several votives from the *equites singulares* at Rome.[54]

The *Campestres* were represented in Roman Britain on six inscriptions and are twice defined as *Matres*, at Benwell (36) and at Cramond (512). As one might expect, all these dedications were clearly made by soldiers from units which were mounted or part-mounted, with one possible exception (512).

The other dedications to the *Campestres* in Britain include one to the *Tres Matres Campestres* and the *Genius alae* (36), one to the *Campestres* and *Britannia* (Castlehill: 517), and one made by M. Cocceius Firmus (283), a centurion of the second legion, who probably served as an *eques singularis* in Rome before earning his commission as a legionary officer.[55]

Campester or *Campestris* was an epithet for Mars at Tarraco (AD 182; *CIL* II 4083 [*ILS* 2416]) and Nemesis at Rome (*CIL* VI 533 [*ILS* 2088]). Both dedicators were *campidoctores* associated with the *campus* or practice field. Domaszewski took Mars Campester as a god for Roman citizen units equivalent to the Celtic *Campestres* cultivated by allied units.[56] Perhaps the *Campestres* were the Celtic cousins of the Germanic Alaisiagae who are considered to be the ancestors of the Valkyries (the choosers of battle). Two of the Alaisiagae have been named on an altar from Vercovicium (697) as Baudhillie (ruler of battle) and Friagabi (the giver of freedom).[57]

---

[52] E. Birley, "Campestres," 108.

[53] Domaszewski, *Religion*, 50–51.

[54] At Rome: *CIL* VI 533 (*ILS* 2088); VI 768 (4776); VI 31158 (*ILS* 2213); VI 31171; VI 31139; VI 31140–6; VI 31148–9; VI 31157; 31161; 31167; and III 7904 (*ILS* 2417, Dacia).

[55] It seems that others had been promoted from the *equites singulares* to the rank of legionary centurion. Among these was M. Ulpius Martialis who is attested on an altar dedicated by the *equites singulares* at Rome (*CIL* VI 31158 [*ILS* 2213]). When Martialis was promoted from decurion in the *equites singulares* to centurion in the *Legio I Minervia*, stationed at Bonn, Lower Germany, he erected an altar in honor of Jupiter Optimus Maximus, Juno, Sol, Luna, Hercules, and the Campestres, similar to the text of 283.

[56] Domasewski, *Religion*, 52.

[57] Bosanquet, "Alaisiagae," 185–192. Further, Speidel ("Dii Campestres," 118) noted the conflation of the *Dii Campestres* with Aulisua, a Berber cavalry and horse god, worshipped by the by the *ala exploratorum Pomarensium* at Tlemcen.

Epona

Epona (283, 456–458) was an Indo-European horse goddess whose cult is attested by inscriptions and sculpted monuments, concentrated along the Moselle near Autun, on the Gallic side of the *limes* between Gaul and the Germanies. She was a Celtic goddess, the equivalent of the insular Riannon (a divine mother and nurturer of the gods),[58] represented as a Graeco-Roman deity and associated with the mare and with fertility.[59] Sculpted in stone, Epona was most frequently represented mounted side-saddle.

A few Epona monuments have been found in Britain, one of which shows Epona seated, a horse facing her.[60] On a cheek piece, she was depicted standing next to a horse and holding the reins in her right hand, a cornucopia in her left.[61] A figurine from Caerwent may portray Epona.[62] A wooden statuette from Winchester (ca. AD 150/160) depicting a figure holding a key may represent Epona (*CSIR* 1.2.115). A fragmentary stone sculpture of an equestrian figure from Colchester may also depict the goddess, as evidenced by the long drapery worn by the figure (*CSIR* 1.8.14).[63] A bronze, found in Wiltshire (provenance unknown), depicts the goddess seated between two foals or ponies. Large ears of grain fill her lap and the patera in her left hand, thus clearly showing her association with fertility.[64] These sites are civilian.

The goddess, most popular in the least Romanized areas of Gaul and Germany, remained Celtic. The bulk of votives, distributed along the western frontier, were offered by Gallic recruits in the Roman cavalry who may have adopted her cult as a substitute for other military rites, for example Mithraism.[65] The goddess was funereal (perhaps an after-life deity), since many votives were recovered near or in water (suggesting both healing properties and routes to the underworld) and within burial mounds.[66]

---

[58] Ross, *Celtic Britain*, 227, 267, 326. Riannon also has connections with horses.

[59] For Epona: S. Reinach, "Epona," 163–195 and "Divinites Equestres," 225–38; Thévenot, *Inventaire*; Magnen, *Epona*; Benoît, "Des chevaux;" and "Les mythes;" Linduff, "Epona," 817–37; Oaks "Epona," 77–84.

[60] Magnen, *Epona*, #46. A second statue (#76) was made in Belgica; a third (#175) is badly damaged.

[61] Ross, *Celtic Britain*, 198, 224.

[62] Thévenot, *Inventaire*, 130–2.

[63] Hull, "Epona Sculpture," 19, 198.

[64] Johns, "Epona," 37–41.

[65] Linduff, "Epona," 823, 2825, 831; Magnen, *Epona*, #13, 18, 22, 29, 32, 130, 152, 182, 187; see also Oaks "Epona," 78.

[66] Magnen, *Epona*, #113–114, 173, 190; Linduff, "Epona," 835.

Epona was clearly a familiar cult in an alien environment, and her worshippers probably wanted to emphasize her dignity rather than her association with fertility.[67] Her cult did, however, spread widely, and she was worshipped by muleteers and ostlers as well as cavalrymen. Apuleius, in fact, mentioned the goddess in *The Golden Ass* (3.27): Lucius, after being turned into an ass, saw an image of Epona in a stable's shrine garnished with fresh roses—the literary record testifies that shrines to Epona would have been placed in stables. Like the *Campestres*, she was an appropriate protectress of mounted units.

Coventina[68]

It was previously believed that the nymph Coventina was cultivated exclusively at Carrawburgh on Hadrian's Wall. Three altars, however, from Galicia in Hispania Citerior are dedicated to a goddess Coventina, identifiable with our nymph at Carrawburgh.[69] Coventina received fourteen dedications in Britain (440–453), all found in the well in the precinct of Coventina's temple during the excavations of 1876. A water deity, Coventina may have been chthonic and oracular.[70]

---

[67] For example, mounted troops were always the most valuable military resource, and horse ownership implied power, wealth, and maneuverability (Oaks "Epona," 80). In addition, the horned warrior, associated with solar symbols, was also connected with horses. The horse represents sovereignty, and the mounted warrior can be interpreted as the vanquisher of chthonic forces (M.J. Green, "Jupiter Taranis," 74; see chapter 3, pp. 125–126).

[68] For the name, see Allason-Jones and McKay, *Coventina*, 3–6. C.R. Smith ("Roman Wall, Procolitia," 125) tried to connect the goddess the Convenae of Aquitania, an area rich in springs. Joliffe, "Dea Brigantia," 58, suggested that the goddess derived from *conventus*: goddess of a community of German soldiers stationed at Carrawburgh, hence an usurper of the sanctuary. K.H. Jackson argues that the name is Celtic: KOWENTINA, derived from KONWENTINA. The element -vent remains enigmatic, but the Latin termination -ina suggests that the goddess has been Romanized (*Language and History*, 481). This water deity may be related to Covetena, Cuhvetena (Hispania Tarraconensis) or Convertina (Gallia Narbonensis). Allason-Jones and McKay, *Coventina*, 4.

The various spellings of her name (Conventina, Coventina, Covetina, Covotina, and Covventina) reflect barbarisms: Clayton, "Procolitia," 10–11.

[69] *AE* (1950), 24; (1954), 251; (1957), 322. The first inscription reads: *Conv|etene | e(x) r(editu) n(ostro)*. The third line was subsequently expanded *e(x) r(esponsu) n(uminis)*: Lambrino, "Coventina," 73.

J.R. Harris, "Coventina's Well," suggested that this Celtic deity survived as Quentin, a male saint with aquatic associations, honored in the Low Countries. If this thesis is true, it suggests that the cult disseminated from Britain with lasting impact or originated on the continent.

[70] Lambrino, "Coventina," #1, #3, 74–87.

The temple, seemingly a square Romano-Celtic type,[71] had an enclosing wall 0.9m thick and dimensions of 13.4 by 14m, with a large opening in the west side of the *temenos*. The size was normal for a Romano-Celtic temple, but no other such temples have been found on or near a military frontier, nor did any other Romano-Celtic temple in Britain have a west door. The well, 2.6 × 2.4m, lies in the center of the temple. No *cella*, which may have been missed by the excavators or plundered away before the excavations were conducted, was found. The *cella*, if it existed, may have been wooden,[72] or the well may have replaced the *cella* symbolically but not architecturally. Since column shafts were seen next to the well in 1817, the sacred spring may have been open to the sky with just a parapet to cover it.[73] The apparently short outer wall may have merely served as a *temenos* boundary. The thick foundations recall the roofless mausoleum at Shorden Brae; and temples from Gaul, furthermore, provide parallels for open air wells.[74]

The goddess had a strong Germanic following. The three cohorts represented among her votaries were raised in Lower Germany and sent directly to Britain (441, 442, 452, 453). Germans were also among the votaries (443, 444, 450). Her broad appeal is further noted by Celtic (446) and even African (451) worshippers. Epigraphy suggests both corporate (452, 453) and private (440–451) votives. Especially touching is 449, an incense burner which the worshipper made *manibus suis*.

One would like to assume that Coventina was a healer because of her association with the well and her identification as *nympha* (444, 445). However, as far as is known, she received no *ex votos*.[75] Nor

[71] Richmond, *Roman Britain*, 196.

[72] One *cella* from a Romano-Celtic temple at Colchester was wooden: Lewis, *Temples*, 17–18. It is not known which cults were venerated at the Chedworth or Colchester temples.

[73] Hodgson, *History of Northumberland* II.iii (1840), 183. Springhead 3, to provide an analogy, was a rectangular Romano-Celtic temple whose walls date to between 150 and 160. Pottery from the temple indicates late second to the early third century use. To which cult this temple belonged is uncertain: Lewis, *Temples*, 92. In addition, at Housesteads excavators found two uninscribed altars and coins (dating from Faustina II to Constantine I) and pottery (dating from the mid second to the early fourth centuries). A spring on the site is enclosed by a well which is in turn surrounded by a square temple with a curved north wall. The site is clearly sacred, but one must ask: to whom? Lewis, *Temples*, 73, 145.

[74] Lewis, *Temples*, 87. Gallic parallels come from Fontaines Salées (Grenier, *Manuel d'archéologie Gallo-Romaine* 4, 2, 453), Montbouy (Lewis, 152, note 5 [p. 87]), and the source of the Seine (Lewis, 152, note 6 [p. 87]).

[75] Allason-Jones and MacKay, *Coventina*, 9.

can a bronze terrier-type figurine be assigned without doubt to the precinct.[76] Pins were favored votives to healing deities, yet only two have been found in the well.[77] The votaries are predominantly male and, for the most part, attached to the army, which by no means precludes a healing shrine. A small bronze horse may identify Coventina as a cavalry goddess, and members of the *cohors I Batavorum*, which was *equitata*, were among her worshippers (452–453).[78] A stag brooch, of Rhenish workmanship, may suggest a hunting cult (appropriate to a cavalry cult or fertility and strength).[79] A number of brooches from the well take the form of discs, wheels, or solar symbols.[80] These wheels might connect Coventina to the solar wheel god, vanquisher of dark forces, possibly as his consort. The well itself probably linked Coventina to the underworld, a goddess of death, a vanquisher of death. The evidence points to a predominantly military cult: soldiers worshipped the goddess, and wheel votives imply a vanquishing deity.

Altars and other votives were preserved in the sacred well, probably for safe-keeping.[81] Coins date consistently from the beginning of the Roman occupation to the end of the fourth century suggesting that the goddess enjoyed the continuous and long-lived veneration of her Roman wards.[82]

---

[76] Allason-Jones and MacKay, *Coventina*, 9–10, 21–22, #38.

[77] Allason-Jones and MacKay, *Coventina*, 10, 36, #108–109, both in bone. Clearly, *Coventina* could have received more pins.

[78] Allason-Jones and MacKay, *Coventina*, 23, #39. The relic is crudely executed, perhaps a mass-produced trinket to be affixed to the shrine's wall (Thomas, "Animal Art," 25), or a locally crafted item from a piece of furniture (Toynbee, *Art in Britain*, 125).

[79] Allason-Jones and MacKay, *Coventina*, 23, #40.

[80] Allason-Jones and MacKay, *Coventina*, 23–25, #41–47.

[81] Coins, whose copper concentrated in so limited a space would have spoiled the water supply, may have been tossed into the well as votives—this occurred at Bath and other water-cult sites. However, it is unlikely that altars would have been offered into the well. It is also unlikely that the Romans, being suspicious of a new goddess, would have blocked off the sacred spring as derogatory to Roman religion: *Vana superstitio, veterumque ignara Deorum* (Vergil *Aeneid* 8.187); Rome was usually tolerant.

[82] Allason-Jones and MacKay, *Coventina*, 50–76, for a complete catalogue of the numismatic remains.

CHAPTER FIVE

THE ROMANIZATION AND POLITICIZATION OF CIVILIAN RELIGION

Interpretatio

Interpretatio Romana, as already noted, is the Roman articulation of an alien religion,[1] the Roman attempt to make sense of foreign practices and beliefs (Tacitus, *Germania* 43).[2] Roman soldiers identified Celtic (473) and Eastern (425) gods with their own deities, and native Britons saw Roman gods as manifestations of indigenous Celto-Germanic cults (470). J. Webster argued that name pairing was mostly performed by Romans and Romanized Briton (e.g., 469).[3] This practice was seen as essential to avoid ambiguities: Apollo must be addressed by his *local* name.[4]

Three points deserve emphasis. First, *interpretatio* was an ancient process, by no means confined to the northwest frontier.[5] Romans

---

[1] J. Webster, "Interpretatio," 153, 156. Webster interprets the process as a one-sided power play, initiated by the in-comer.

[2] This leaves a broad margin for misinterpretation. A misunderstanding of native deities can lead to erroneous, misleading equations, and it has been seen that Celtic deities can be equated with more than one Roman god (e.g., Cocidius Mars, Cocidius Silvanus). These equations are probably meant to emphasize one function or another. One must keep in mind that Roman gods are not as obviously multivalent as deities of non-Roman pantheons (n.b., Cato, *de Agricultura* 139–141). It must also be noted that Roman gods had complex and overlapping functions, and a soldier could just as easily misinterpret his own gods as those of his enemy.

[3] J. Webster, "Interpretatio," 159. Webster claims that name pairing was conducted by Roman not Celt. Many but not all worshippers, who utilized *interpretatio* were Romanized. Mars is equated with non-Roman gods by Celts (470, 472, 474, 603, 606, 613, 616), and by Romans, soldiers worshipping corporately (597, 598), by Roman, with the *tria nomina* (520, 588, 604, 605, 614, 619) and without (554, 558, 577, 584, 611, 615, 617). An overwhelming majority of inscriptions, with and without *interpretatio*, omits the dedicator's name. The two most interesting cases are 519 and 585 in which two Celtic gods are equated. A Romanized Aelius Secundus worshipped Mogons Vitiris (519); Vernostonus Cocidius received homage from Virilis who identified himself as *Germanus* (585).

[4] Henig, *Religion*, 66. Consider also the detailed prayer formula, which invokes a god by all his names (or whatever name he wishes at this time) and uses his proper address (or wherever he happens to be), thus avoiding ambiguity and loopholes, in case the god does not wish to be bothered or will not expend the energy to collect his mail: Burkert, *Greek Religion*, 73–75.

[5] Henig, *Religion*, 66.

had already adapted Greek myth, equating their own gods with the Olympians. Nor was Etruscan influence lacking.[6] Second, *interpretatio* was not merely the process by which the Roman imperialist religion replaced indigenous practices. Both systems were changed. Military victory resulted in the defection of local gods who would, in turn, become Roman, hence the ritual procedure of *evocatio* (Macrobius 3.9.7–8):

> Si deus, si dea est, cui populus civitasque Carthaginiensis est in tutela, teque maxime, ille qui urbis huius populique tutelam recepisti, precor venerorque veniamque a vobis peto ut vos populum civitatemque Carthaginiensem deseratis, loca templa sacra urbemque eorum relinquatis, absque his abeatis eique populo civitati metum formidinem oblivionem iniciatis, proditique Romam ad me meosque veniatis, nostraque vobis loca templa sacra urbs acceptior probatiorque sit, mihique populoque Romano militibusque meis praepositi sitis ut sciamus intellagamusque. si ita feceritis, voveo vobis templa ludosque facturum.
>
> In eadem verba hostias fieri oportet auctoritatemque videri extorum, ut ea promittant futura . . .

For example, wheel iconography was incorporated into Jupiter Optimus Maximus monuments (134, 139, 140, 188, 210, 212), and many local deities received temple cults in accord with Roman practices (e.g., Antenociticus, Cocidius, Sulis Minerva). The resulting ritual was mostly Roman in form (dedicated altars, cult statues, temples) and tone (the epigraphy survives in Latin), and many of the worshippers are Roman or Romanized (*tria nomina*, Latinate *gentilica*); non-Roman flavor surfaced in iconography and symbolism. For example, Mithraism differed much from its Persian roots.[7] Mithras of the Roman army was a Roman god, wholly acceptable to the gods of the Capitoline. Finally, the average worshipper probably did not distinguish between Roman and non-Roman gods, or even "official" and "private."[8] Officers and soldiers often worshipped "foreign" gods, treating them as fully Roman. Furthermore, few enlisted men (that is, the majority of the standing army) would have enjoyed the benefits of an elite, classical education—unlikely would they have made subtle distinctions in myth or theocracy. Our soldier, like his

---

[6] Dumézil, *Roman Religion*, 625–696. Etruscan religion did not entirely shape Roman practices, which derived from a well-structured Indo-European belief and ritual system. Yet Romans considered much of their practice Etruscan, notably *haruspicium* (Cicero *Div.* 2.49).

[7] Gordon, "Cumont," 215–248.

[8] MacMullen, *Paganism*, 80–81; Henig, *Religion*, 88–94; Henig, "Throne," 228.

British counterpart, was keenly aware of the spiritual world around him. Roman, Celt, and Oriental thought it prudent to acknowledge, propitiate and seek the protection of local gods, as indeed they invoked numerous *genii loci*.[9]

Military Influence

In the first century AD, Roman soldiers provided the only real point of contact between Roman and native. With the army came Roman customs, Roman gods, and the Latin language. As the army moved northward after the Flavian period, others took the soldier's place, and military influence on the province as a whole was indirect (through trade contacts, building contracts, *et alia*). Roman culture, shared institutions and shared symbols comprised the cultural language common to soldier, trader, and bureaucrat.[10] Popular religion assumed its own character, expressing itself through the Romano-British cults of Bacchus, Mars, Mercury, Silvanus, Venus, *et alia*. Nonetheless, the Roman army remained Rome's representative in the British provinces, not only protecting *civitates* but also fuelling the economy. The elite society in southern Britain depended on Roman political and military commitment to the extent that, in the fifth century, troop and bureaucratic withdrawal undermined the aristocratic power-base, resulting in the collapse of local governments.[11]

Vici

Soldiers were concentrated along Hadrian's Wall, the Antonine Wall, and—in the fourth and fifth centuries—the forts of the Saxon Shore. Around these centers, camp followers, soldiers' families, merchants, and others settled in nearby *vici*.[12] In these civilian settlements, most the accoutrements of civilized Mediterranean life could be found: *vicani* at Housesteads issued Roman-style decrees (*RIB* 1616), *vicani* at Vindolanda commissioned an offering to Vulcan and the divine House (374). Excavations at Corbridge, an arsenal under the Severans, indicate a raised aqueduct near *horrea*, strip-buildings (shops and work-

---

[9] G. Webster, "What the Britons require," 57.
[10] Hopkins, *Conquerors and Slaves*, 242.
[11] James, "Britain and the Late Roman Army," 182–183.
[12] See Sommer, *Military Vici*.

shops), a winged corridor villa terraced into a slope (probably a *mansio*), and an unfinished courtyard building which may have been intended as a *civitas* forum.[13] Catterick, between Corbridge and York, was established as an auxiliary fort during the Flavian era. The site included a *mansio*, with courtyard, an ornamental fountain, and baths supplied by the fort's aqueduct. Open-fronted shops and workshops lined the streets. The *vicus* and its expanding suburbs grew and prospered during the third and fourth centuries.[14]

Genius Loci

The ultimate dynamic of Romanization was manifested in cults to unknown local gods (*genii locorum*) whose inherently powerful names remained secret.[15] Despite (or because of) not knowing the name, soldier and civilian worshipped these gods to gain their goodwill. The widespread military evidence for the cult of the *genius loci* in Roman Britain—legionary fortresses and auxiliary camps—includes generic and specific local *genii*. The *genius Eboraci* (42) is cited at York, while a centurion of the second legion, M. Cocceius Firmus, honored the *genius Terrae Britannicae* (46) at Auchendavy (ca. AD 150) on the Antonine Wall. The soldiers of the second legion honored the *genius huius loci* with Jupiter Optimus Maximus and the native Cocidius at Housesteads (172, Hadrianic). An unknown member of the sixth legion erected an altar to the *genius loci* in fulfillment of a vow at Bath (38, after AD 122). The twentieth legion dedicated an altar to the *genius loci* for the welfare of the imperial family at Chester (39, Severan). Auxiliary troops also honored the *genius loci*: a *princeps* of a cohort at Clifton, Westmorland (119), a tribune at Maryport (43), *vexillarii* at Carrawburgh (45, 2nd century) and a prefect of *cohors I Batavorum* at the same site (341). In addition, the *di cultores huius loci* at Risingham (379) were, in spirit, similar to *genii locorum*; and invocations to generic, unnamed *di deaeque* (110, 116, 293, 375–383) were intended to secure the beneficence of local, unknown spirits. The *genius loci* was associated with local deities: Mogons at Vindolanda (521), and Cocidius (172).

---

[13] Burnham and Wacher, *Small Towns*, 59–61; Richmond, "Corbridge;" Gillam and Daniels, "Roman Mausoleum;" Rivet and Smith, *Place Names*, 323.

[14] Burnham and Wacher, *Small Towns*, 111–117; Hildyard, "Roman and Saxon Site;" R.E.M. Wheeler, *Stanwick Fortifications*; Hildyard, "Cataractonium, fort and town."

[15] See Henig, *Religion*, 55; Alcock, "Concept of *Genius*," 113–133.

Small cult representations of the *genius* are few and typical in exe-cution, mostly dating to the second and third centuries: a small bronze with cornucopiae, found unstratified at Bewcastle,[16] a third century bronze *genius*, draped and holding a patera (Carrawburgh),[17] a bronze figure of a draped *genius* with cornucopia and patera (Papcastle),[18] a second century *lar* (Richborough),[19] a mural-crowned *genius* on the rim of a gray ware pot (Corbridge).[20] Perhaps the most interesting, a bronze *lar* in Romano-Celtic style; he wears the local costume of boots, kilt and cloak (Carley Hill Quarry).[21] The evidence of gemstones is similarly scant: six depict the *genius loci* holding cor-nucopiae;[22] one shows the *genius pR* (early third century).[23] The *genius* was tied to the land, and our evidence suggests that the *genii locorum* received cult as troops were garrisoned to Britain or restationed within the province under Hadrian, Antoninus Pius, and Septimius Severus.

Bacchus

Hutchinson thoroughly discusses the cult of Dionysus-Bacchus in Britain.[24] Her catalogue of the evidence according to its origins included *Dionysiaca* from the military sphere.[25] Our remains consist of bronze statuettes of Bacchus, *intagli* of satyrs, bronze Sileni, bronzes and *intaglios* of Maenads, bronzes and *intagli* of Pan, images of Priapus in stone and bronze, stone and gem reliefs of masks, *thyrsoi* and *can-thari*, Bacchic cupids and *genii* on bronze and gems, and bronze images of panthers, griffins, and leopards. The evidence dates from the mid-first century AD to the fourth century.[26]

---

[16] M.J. Green, *Military Areas*, 46.
[17] D.J. Smith, "Shrine of the Nymphs," 80; M.J. Green, *Military Areas*, 51.
[18] D. Charlesworth, "Papcastle," 114; M.J. Green, *Military Areas*, 66, #2.
[19] M.J. Green, *Military Areas*, 68, #8.
[20] M.J. Green, *Military Areas*, 57, #26.
[21] Petch, "Roman Durham," 28; M.J. Green, *Military Areas*, 50.
[22] Henig, *Corpus*, #104–108, App. 116; Vindolanda, #104, third century; South Shields, #106, second century. Alcock, "Concept of Genius."
[23] Henig, *Corpus*, #103.
[24] Hutchinson, *Bacchus in Roman Britain*.
[25] *Ibid.*, Table 1, 89–108; the other categories include the evidence from major towns (table 2, 109–122), from villages, small farms, and rustic shrines (table 3, 123–132), and evidence from the villas (table 4, 133–139).
[26] Increased use of jet in the third and fourth centuries is linked to the rise in popularity of the Bacchus cult at York: Allason-Jones, *Roman Jet*, 16.

Of particular interest is a Priapus piece (348) from Birrens. This crude stone slab shows an ithyphallic horned god etched above the inscription. The god, Celtic in form, is recast as Roman. Priapus, an Hellenistic god of fertility, often decorated gardens. Here, it seems, Priapus shows broader significance. The horned ithyphallic figure suggests a strong, aggressive protector recalling, in function, the herms of classical Athens. Unfortunately, the dedicator is unknown, but the monument's crude workmanship implies that his status was not high. The piece may have been a charm for a soldier or a local indirectly connected with the army.

The London Mithraeum may have been rededicated to Bacchus during its last pre-Christian phase. The god was rarely depicted in Mithraea, according to the extant evidence, yet some Bacchic statuary was found in the London temple debris.[27] A marble group, possibly late second century, shows the god grasping a large snake whose tail curls around the deity's right arm. A cluster of grapes hangs beyond the god's left shoulder. Much of a tree trunk, on which Pan perched, has disappeared. One shaggy leg and hoof and the lower part of his hairy torso remain. A headless Silenus, sitting on a little donkey, holds a large wine goblet in both hands. A maenad, also headless, wears a long robe and stands at the right, while a leopard, crouching in front of her, looks up at Bacchus and the Silenus.[28] The Bacchus group, like many of the marble Mithraic pieces, was sculpted from saccharoidal marble, possibly from Carrara, Italy. This piece, and other Bacchic statuary, might suggest Dionysus' elevation to an extraordinarily high status in the Mithraic hierarchy.[29] Numerous *intagli* further indicate the cult's vitality into the third and fourth centuries.[30]

---

[27] Hutchinson, "Cult," 136; and Merrifield, "Art and Religion," 382. Two second century Bacchic torsos, apparently deliberately chopped up, were found in the temple debris reused as building material: Toynbee, *Temple of Mithras*, #6, #7, pl. 14. For arguments in favor of rededication see p. 85 note 125 and Henig in Shepherd, *Temple of Mithras*, 230–232.

[28] Richmond, "Roman Britain in 1954," pl. 47; Toynbee, *Art in Britain*, #12, pl. 34; Grimes *ERML*, 109–10, pl. 51; Toynbee, *Temple of Mithras*, #15, Pl. XII, pl. 21; Shepherd, *Temple of Mithras*, X.59, 230.

[29] Vermasseren, *Mithras*, 113–114: Hutchinson, "Cult," 137.

[30] Henig, *Corpus*, #144–180, App. 99–101. These gems date primarily to the second and third centuries. First century: #157, 160, 166, 171, 178.

Mars and Mercury

Roman and Celtic Mars in military contexts assumed a warlike char-acter, as appropriate to army religion, as seen above (p. 142). Yet Mars was popular in civilian religion as well. In the south and east, Mars was the peaceful, protective god of agriculture, in accord with his origins as an agricultural deity. For example, Mars Olludius, "the great tree," was shown at Custom Scrubs as a *genius* with a double cornucopia (471). Surprisingly, not many small Mars votives came from military areas where Mercury seemed more popular.[31] Mercury and Mars were apparently confused in Britain and elsewhere (i.e., the Berne scholiast on Lucan *Pharsalia* 1.391–465). Their inter-changeability points to an overlap in function: Mercury (as influenced by his Greek counterpart) was a god of young men (soldiers are often young), and of travelers (the army travels). Mars, as the god of soldiers and war, governed a dangerous occupation, potentially resulting in a violent death (Mercury was the herdsman of the dead, *psychopompos*). Both gods were concerned with liminal groups and danger/death. The Celtic conflation of Mars and Mercury followed, and it should be noted that any equation lacks exactitude since gods on both cultural sides were complex in function and form.

In Britain, Mars had sixteen Celtic counterparts; Mercury, with-out *interpretatio Celtica*, was usually paired with a tribal goddess ("Rosmerta" at Cirencester, her name is not attested positively in Britain: *CSIR* 1.7.78–82). Mars was a healer, a ruler (see p. 142), and a bestower of wealth and fertility: e.g., Mars as *genius* with cor-nucopiae.[32] Bronze and inexpensive pipe-clay pieces depict Mars the equestrian, mounted warrior and vanquisher.[33] *Intagli* denote Mars as victor in war, purely Roman in image.[34] Caches imply (though

---

[31] M.J. Green, *Military Areas*, 13.

[32] M.J. Green, *Civilian Areas*, 162. About twenty-one examples survive in stone, another thirty-two in bronze. Mars is scantily represented at military sites: Burgh-by-Sands (bronze: 48, #1), Burgh Castle (bronze plaque: 48, #3), Corbridge (bronze helmeted head: 56, #7), Richborough (fragmentary statue in bronze: 70, #43), South Shields (incised on a sword: 71, #13).

[33] M.J. Green, *Civilian Areas*, 29–31. The Roman Mars was not an equestrian god (see chapter 3; p. 125).

[34] Thirty three *intagli* (Henig, *Corpus*, #70–94, App. 13, 29, 33, 62, 71, 86, 98, 214c) have been found mostly, though not exclusively (#72: Verulamium; #74: Cirencester), in military contexts: Wales (#71, 77: Caerleon), London (#80, 90); York (App. 62, App. 86) and Hadrian's Wall (South Shields: #87; Corbridge: #79; Chesters: #94; Housesteads: App. 98; Vindolanda: App. 29, 33). The earliest dates

do not prove) temples at Stony Stratford, Bucks. and Barkway, Herts.[35] Two pieces of particular interest come from Netherby, Cumbria and Custom Scrubs, Glouc. The Netherby piece shows a Mars with a wheel (symbolizing solar deities: n.b. Jupiter Tanarus: pp. 59–61) and a cornucopia (fertility); thus two god-types are conflated on one monument.[36] The Celt Gulioepius dedicated an altar at Custom Scrubs to Romulus (350) which shows an armed Mars. Gulioepius may have seen Mars Romulus as the all-conquering legionary, and our worshipper likely welcomed the prosperity that often followed Rome.[37] Epigraphically, Mars was popular in military zones: forty-four inscriptions attest Mars without *interpretatio* (241–284). His epithets are political (Augustus: 256)[38] and military (Conservator: 247; Militaris: 254, 255; Pacifer: 248; Ultor: 262; Victor: 263–265, 267, 274). Most of these are private votives.[39] The Roman Mars is addressed as *Deus* (241–247, 249–51, 253, 257–59, 261–62, 266–67, 269–70, 272–73, 275–77, 279, 280, 284) and *sanctus* (270, 279, 280, 284). Corporate worship is indicated (250, 254, 255, 262, 269, 274, 275, 281), and Mars was invoked on behalf of the imperial household (245, 248?, 251, 261, 272, 280). The rich epigraphic record may suggest Mars' official nature, a powerful and popular god who protects not only the individual, but the state as well.

In contrast, Mercury's popularity is not reflected epigraphically. Although Mercury was invoked on behalf of the state (325), his power

---

to the first century (App. 71), most date to the second (#70–74, 76–77, 80, 82, 90, App. 29, 62, 86, 98) or late second/early third (#78–79, 88, 93) centuries, early to mid third century (#83–87, 91, App. 33). The most commonly represented type is Mars Gradivus, helmeted and armed, carrying a trophy (#70, App. 71), or crowning one (#77). On one gem (#78), *Roma* appears with an armed Mars, another gem (#93) shows a sceptered Mars. Though gems may not have military significance, they indicate that the Mars of the private soldier, if we can assume that most of these items belonged to soldiers, was warrior, victor, and vanquisher.

[35] Henig, *Religion*, 51. Silver *ex votos* invoke both Mars at Vulcan at both sites.

[36] M.J. Green, "Celtic god from Netherby," 43.

[37] Henig, "Throne," 234. Henig, *Corpus*, 156, Romulus as a vanquisher wears a plumed helmet, and carries a spear and *tropaeum*, late first century, found near Corbridge.

[38] Dorcey argued that *Augustus* does not necessarily link the cult to the imperial house. It may simply imply that the god was revered: Dorcey, *Silvanus*, 29. For *deus* and *sanctus*, see p. 120, note 74. A god called "Augustan," though, probably did operate within the emperor's sphere as his protector. A local god would hardly steal an imperial epithet.

[39] *Militaris* seems redundant, but the *cohors I Baestasiorum* probably considered the epithet significant since in their homeland Mars was often a healer: Richmond, "Roman Army and Roman Religion," 193.

was petitioned privately through portable objects, *intagli* and reliefs. Mercury is represented in small bronzes,[40] on lead plaques,[41] and in pipe-clay.[42] Small cockerels in bronze also evoke Mercury,[43] in relief on terracotta,[44] and in pipe-clay.[45] *Intagli* also evince Mercury's wide popular appeal.[46]

Political Religions I: The Flavians

The highly politicized state religion was Rome's mainstay in peace and war, and when the gods were neglected, divine anger caused military disaster and even civil war (see Horace *Odes* 3.6). As Rome vanquished city-states, conquered gods abandoned their peoples and became Roman (Macrobius 3.9.7–8, p. 159). Additionally, Rome often imported new gods to help against natural disasters (e.g., foreign wars, plagues) and maintain public morale (Asclepius: Isidorus *De Viris Illustribus* 22; Cybele: Livy 29.24.10–14).

Sulis

Political intent may surface in the cult of Sulis Minerva, a healer and goddess of retribution, worshipped at a magnificent bath complex in southwestern England. The Roman baths, originally constructed in the 60's and 70's, after the revolt of Boudicca, were

---

[40] For bronze Mercuries, M.J. Green, *Military Areas*: Benwell (46, #5: head), Caerleon (49, #3: silver-plated, bronze figurine from the amphitheater), Carlisle (51, #10: head), Corbridge (56, #3: nude figurine with purse and winged head), Aesica (60, #1: figurine), Lanchester (62, #2: head), Monreith, Perth (64: a dancing Mercury), Piercebridge (66, #7: figurine), Richborough (68, #21: figurine), St. Donats (70: figurine), St. Ninian's (70: figurine), Stelloch (72: figurine); York (75, #29: figurine; #31: bust with winged cap).

[41] M.J. Green, *Military Areas*: Chesters (55, #16). The piece possibly came from a shrine.

[42] M.J. Green, *Military Areas*: Corbridge (57, #11: figurine with caduceus, purse, and cloak; the original head is missing).

[43] For bronze cockerels, M.J. Green, *Military Areas*: Chester (52, #6), Chesterholm (54, #4), Colchester (56, #2), Corbridge (57, #13), Aesica (60, #4).

[44] Corbridge: a cockerel stands at the side of an armed figure (M.J. Green, *Military Areas*, 56, #1).

[45] Talgarth: M.J. Green, *Military Areas*, 72.

[46] Forty-two gems show Mercury (Henig, *Corpus*, #11, 36–69, App. 9, App. 32, App. 66, App. 94–97, App. 208), dating from the first century (#36) to the third (#46). Sixteen *intagli* representing cocks also suggest Mercury (#677–684, 781, 805, App. 46, 82, 182–185).

funded by Rome and organized by the army, and the sophisticated engineering reflects Roman technology and Gallic workmanship. A Roman military presence near these baths has long been suspected but never confirmed, but the hypothesis is by no means unreasonable, given the military involvement in the building of the baths, military tombstones found at Bath, and military dedications from the sacred precinct.[47] The military presence validated the official Roman status for and authorization of the cult of Sulis Minerva at Bath.

Pre-Roman interest in the hot springs at Bath is evident. Celtic coins dating to the early first century AD have been recovered from the King's Bath Spring.[48] Moreover, the name Sulis Minerva strengthens the connection. Sulis is etymologically related to the Suleviae,[49] a Celtic triad originally worshipped in Germany as goddesses of fertility and prosperity, as well as of water and healing, evocative of the divine duties of Sulis at Bath—fertility, prosperity, regeneration, healing, protection, death. In her healing aspect, Sulis can be identified with Minerva Medica.

The presence of a *haruspex*, L. Marcius Memor, at Bath points to official Roman interest in Sulis' temple.[50] Such *haruspices* were usually found in Rome and other Italian cities; that one was so far from Rome, paying homage to a local deity, only underscores the importance of the cult and the official support for the temple of Sulis Minerva. It is possible, however, that our L. Marcius Memor was simply seeking a cure at the shrine. In addition, the tombstone of C. Calpurnius Receptus, *sacerdos deae* (*RIB* 155), underscores sophisticated cult practice: the shrine may have employed full time priests. Furthermore, the repetitive tone of the curse tablets implies temple scribes on staff. Mistakes, as Cunliffe notes, could be dangerous.[51]

---

[47] Cunliffe and Davenport, *The Site*, 9–10; Burnham and Wacher, *Small Towns*, 165. Military tombstones represent veterans from the *Legio II Ad. p.f.*: *CIL* VII 48 [*RIB* 157]; the *Legio XX VV*: *CIL* VII 49 [*ILS* 2429; *RIB* 156], *CIL* VII 50 [*RIB* 158], *CIL* VII 51 [*RIB* 160]; and the *ala Vettonum cR*: *CIL* VII 52, addit., 306 [*ILS* 2517; *RIB* 159].

[48] Cunliffe, *Sacred Spring*, 1.

[49] M.J. Green, *Gods of the Celts*, 140.

[50] Salway, *Roman Britain*, 487. The inscription, on a statue base, reads *deae Suli | L. Marcius Memor| Haruspex | d.d.*: Wright, "Roman Britain in 1965," 217. The *haruspex*, an officer of the Roman state cult, divined the will of the gods by reading the entrails of sacrificial animals according to the ancient Etruscan tradition.

[51] Cunliffe, "Sanctuary of Sulis Minerva," 9. It also seems necessary for the worshipper to write out his request for himself: *carta picta persc[ripta]*: Tomlin in Cunliffe, *Sacred Spring*, 118–119, #8, line 6.

The temple and bath complex, classical in form, encouraged Romanization and loyalty to Rome. The Roman baths may have even been intended as atonement in the aftermath of the uprising led by Boudicca, a speculation which can account for the deliberate and official conflation of Celtic and Roman deities. Cunliffe suggested that monumentalizing this ancient Celtic sanctuary and melding its presiding goddess with a Roman deity legitimized Roman presence and modeled the peaceful syncretization of Roman and native cultures.[52]

Sulis, a native British deity whose cult was exported to the Rhineland (see 526), was equated with the Roman Minerva (529, 533), while the remaining inscriptions offered no *interpretatio Romana* (526–528, 530–532). Of these votives, two (526, 527) were made by freedmen on behalf of their patron, a centurion of *legio VI Victrix*. Curse tablets confirm the pattern of *interpretatio*: six *defixiones* cite Sulis Minerva, of these, only two worshippers identify themselves, and both have Celtic names.[53] One *defixio* cites Minerva without *interpretatio Celtica*.[54] Eighteen *defixiones* attest Sulis without *interpretatio Romana*.[55]

In contrast, the head of the cult statue, purely classical in form, completely lacks Celtic attributes. The temple pediment, the curious relief typically described as a gorgon's head centered within a shield supported by two winged Victories, likewise points to the cult of the Roman Minerva.[56] Her symbols, as depicted on the pediment, include two helmets, indicative of Minerva's martial prowess and the domineering military presence of Rome. The right helmet supports a little owl, the symbol of Minerva's wisdom. The winged Victories are appropriate to the martial theme. At the center of the temple's

---

[52] Cunliffe, "Sanctuary of Sulis Minerva," 1–2; Salway, *Roman Britain*, 87.

[53] Cunliffe, *Sacred Spring*, #32 (Solinus), #34 (Docca), #35, 46, 60, 65.

[54] Cunliffe, *Sacred Spring*, #70.

[55] Cunliffe, *Sacred Spring*, #8, 10, 19, 20, 21, 42, 44, 45, 49, 50, 54, 62, 63, 66, 69, 90, 94, 108. Also invoked are Mars (#33, 97) and Mercury (#53). Most of the curse tablets are in too poor a state of preservation for accurate interpretation.

[56] For twin Victories on the altar of the three Gauls, see Fishwick, *ICLW* 111–118. Double Victories appear at Rome as early as Marius who erected a statue of himself between two Victories on the Capitoline. Sulla tore down the statue which Caesar restored in 65 (Plutarch *Caesar* 6.1; Velleius Paterculus 2.43.4; Val. Max. 6.9.14; Suetonius *Caesar* 11). See Fears, "Victory," 788. Two Victories, it seems, occupied the spandral of the arch decreed in Augustus' honor in 19 after Parthians returned Crassus' *signa*: Weinstock, "victor and Victory" 2524, 2526. Victory, in both the public and private spheres, became a central part of Augustus' program of propaganda: Zanker, *Power of Images*, 265–278.

pediment, a "Gorgon," as it is frequently described, sports a beard and masculine Celtic facial features.[57] The pediment clearly mixes Roman and Celtic symbols and images.[58] Our "Gorgon" could be a water deity, as indicated by the two Tritons at the lower corners of the pediment. The flame-like hair may be an attempt to represent the sun god. The complex of images might represent the dual nature of the spring, water and heat, or the child—that is the hot spring—produced by the union of the sky god and earth goddess.[59] Henig suggested that the mix of Neptune and Minerva images on the pediment supports the notion that Togidubnus was involved in building the temple.[60]

Of other deities, a few remains indicate Mercury, Asclepios, and Diana (probably a local huntress with a Roman name). More common are Celtic divinities: Loucetius Mars and Nemetona and the *genii Cucullati*, triads of hooded dwarfs with an underworld association. Hence, the divine collection at Bath takes on a predominantly non-Roman, local, Celtic flavor, which the epigraphic record supports.

Public bathing establishments, such as the one at Bath, were common centers for relaxation and socialization in large and small towns, central fortresses, and isolated military outposts throughout the empire. The temple at Bath, however, was different. Roman baths did not usually center around major healing shrines.[61] This practice reflects Celtic notions, recalling springs sacred to Apollo Cunomaglus and Mars Nodens—healer gods honored from pre-Roman times through

---

[57] The "Gorgon" would be *apropos* to the cult of Minerva, but the traditional interpretation is problematic. Cunliffe, "Sanctuary of Sulis Minerva," 8.

[58] Salway, *Roman Britain*, 486–487; Boardman, *Diffusion of Classical Art*, 308–9.

[59] Our "gorgon" resembles the Oceanus at the center of the Mildenhall Siver Dish, calling to mind, perhaps, Claudius' conquest of Britain and Ocean (see chapter 1). Hind ("Whose Head?" 359–360) has argued that the Bath "gorgon" illustrates Typhoeus, son of earth, defeated by Zeus. Typhoeus' burial mythically explained the preponderance of volcanic activity in the Bay of Naples, a site also rich in hot springs. Since, as Hind argues, Typhoeus personified geothermal activity, he might be the wild element figured at the center of the Bath pediment. The connection between Typhoeus and hot springs needs to be firmly established before such an identification can be accepted.

[60] Private communication. The theory is argued in a forthcoming *festschrift* for John Boardman. Togidubnus was a client king loyal to Rome and was probably involved to some extent on the Roman side in the Boudiccan uprising after which Togidubnus' territory was enlarged (*quaedam civitates Togidubno regi donatae* [*is ad nostram usque memoriam fidissimus mansit*]: Tac. *Agr.* 14.1). Togidubnus, a royal and influential local patron, would have had the clout to engage his own clients in the building effort: Henig, "Review of Cunliffe," 102.

[61] Salway, *Roman Britain*, 347.

the fourth century. As centers of socialization, bathing complexes were popular sites for games of chance. Votives to Fortune and gaming pieces abound in the archaeological remains of most Roman public baths. Fortune, however, is almost completely absent from the remains at Aquae Sulis.[62]

The votives seem unusual. Coins and altars, as found at Bath, are stock offerings at any religious center. Unexpected, though, is the paucity of *ex votos* representing ailing body parts, prevalent at shrines to the Greek Asclepios and Celtic Sequana.[63] Cunliffe suggests that such offerings may not have been necessary since both deity and worshipper understood that the primary reason for contact between the two was curative.[64] It is also possible that Sulis Minerva was not primarily a healer, as springs are often depositories for *defixiones*; the Uley Mercury, clearly a healer, was also a god of retribution, as curse tablets invoke him; and this underscores the typical sense of balance which most deities represent.

Dedications to Sulis, instead, consist in *defixiones*, intended to hand over the victim to the powers of the underworld, an ancient form of primitive magic. The formula is standard—the goddess is addressed, the grievance stated, a horrible fate requested (i.e., impotence and death), and a list of suspects supplied.[65] The curses themselves are strongly linked to disease—punishments involve fertility, sleep, blood— the goddess can bestow or deprive health.[66]

The practice of dedicating curse tablets is universal, attested in both the Graeco-Roman and Celtic tradition. It is, however, Mercury or Nemesis (compare 327–329), not Minerva, upon whom a Roman

---

[62] The finds from the spring include small votives (masks, a few representations of body parts, and offerings in pewter and silver), personal objects (gemstones, jewelry including bracelets, brooches, and pins, which are found as votives at other healing shrines: Lydney, Uley), curse tablets, and a large number of coins. For a complete catalogue and discussion see Henig, Brown, Sunter, Allason-Jones, and Baatz in Cunliffe, *Sacred Spring*, 5–54.

The absence of *Fortuna* may prove nothing.

[63] Many votive offerings were made of organic material which has simply not survived. It may not be remarkable that few *ex votos* remain at *Aquae Sulis*: Henig, *Religion*, 147.

[64] Cunliffe, "Sanctuary of Sulis Minerva," 10.

[65] For the complete collection of curse tablets, with transcripts, translations, and commentaries, see Tomlin in Cunliffe, *Sacred Spring*, 59–278.

[66] M.J. Green, "Celtic Goddess as Healer," 35. Green also questions the identification of Sulis primarily as a healer. Nonetheless, the duel function of healing and retribution does not surprise: Artemis, and goddesses in general, who can both grant life, and take it away.

would call when issuing a curse. The practice at Bath, peculiar from a Roman point of view, may shed light on important facets of the local cult and the interaction between native and Roman. Mercury, a liminal god, protected transient groups and crossed boundaries between gods and men (as Jupiter's messenger) and between life and death (as *psychopompos*). According to ancient practice, curse tablets were buried near fresh tombs or on battlefields, where the dead could take power over their victims, or they were tossed into wells, springs, and rivers, wherein the link between the worlds of the living and the dead existed.[67]

Sulis' duties paralleled Mercury's. The very nature of the hot springs made the place liminal, where the worlds of the living and the dead, of gods and mortals, came into contact, and where communication between goddess and worshipper was facilitated. Sulis functioned as a goddess of curses and healing, of death and of immortality.

The springs flourished well into the fourth century AD. Cow bones found on the site might suggest that sacrifices to the goddess continued.[68] In the middle of that century, the last substantial renovation included reflooring the area in front of the temple. In the last decade of the fourth century, the colonnades were pulled down, and secular buildings began to encroach into the *temenos*. The temple may not have been abandoned at this point, but mud and refuse accumulated in the sacred precinct until, sometime in the fifth century, the altar was dismantled and the sculpted blocks from the pediment were used as paving slabs. The temple façade either collapsed or was demolished, and it is currently impossible to determine if early Christian use respected the sanctity of the space.[69]

Political Religions II: The Severans

Orientalizing cults are often associated with the imperial house. Severan sculptures and coinage demonstrate that Egyptian gods,

---

[67] van der Leeuw, *Religion*, 395–396; Luck, *Arcana Mundi*, 18; Henig in Cunliffe, *Sacred Spring*, 5; M.J. Green, "Celtic Goddess as Healer," 35. We still toss coins into wishing wells.

[68] Grant in Cunliffe and Davenport, *The Site*, 164–171, esp. 169–170. Most cattle bones at the site date from the fourth to sixth centuries. Other bone remains include sheep, pigs, dogs, cats, horses, red and roe deer, hares and rabbits, birds and fish.

[69] Cunliffe, "Sanctuary of Sulis Minerva," 12.

including Zeus Ammon, Apis, and Serapis, were significant to that
house.[70] It must be emphasized that these gods, despite their Egyptian
trappings, were generally presented in Alexandrine guise, as Hellenized
gods. A carnelian gem from Castlesteads depicts Severus as Serapis,
in bust, facing right; the emperor wears a *modius* which connects him
unquestionably to the god. On either side of the bearded god and
facing him are busts in profile, figures who may represent the Dioscuri:
each of the two is clean-shaven and crowned with an eight rayed
star. Castor and Pollux frequently symbolized the emperor's two
sons.[71] Serapis' connection to the imperial house is further demonstrated on an iron ring, stylistically datable to the third century,
which shows Serapis with an eagle and double *signa* with Victories.[72]
A Severan connection might also explain the Kirkby Thore dedication (437) and the temple at York (436),[73] as well as the Carvoran
poem (388) in honor of the *Virgo Caelestis*.[74] At Chesters, a statue,
perhaps of Julia Mamaea as Juno Regina—the identity is far from
certain—could echo Severus Alexander's choice of Dolichenus and
Juno Regina as his patron deities.[75]

---

[70] L'Orange, *Apotheosis*, 73–86 and notes 31–33. Serapis became the tutelary divinity of the house of Severus. See also Gagé, "Serapis," 145–168; Mastino, *Titolature*,
68, note 311; Fishwick, *ICLW*, 317–350, especially 339–340. The god's association
with the emperor seems to have enhanced the mystique of the position.

Early third century evidence shows an association between Severus and Jupiter,
Bacchus and Heracles (whom Septimius emphasized as the divine patrons of Lepcis
Magna: Squarciapino, *Leptis Magna*, 52) as well as Serapis, the Egyptian god of the
dead who offered salvation and immortality. These divine associations suggest emperor
as savior, as *cosmocrator*, an emperor who instigated a new *saeculum* celebrated by the
games of 204: McCann *Portraits*, 53, 64, 110; Mundle, *Religionspolitik*, 147; A. Birley,
Septimius Severus, 224–225; Fishwick, *ICLW*, 340.

[71] Henig, *Corpus*, 229–30, #358. The Gem, inscribed in Greek EZS (EIS ZEUS
SARAPIS), probably belonged to a trader or a soldier. Henig, Religion, 181; Fishwick,
ICLW, 340.

[72] Henig, *Corpus*, #357. The ring is from Gloucestershire. For double Victories,
see note 56 above.

[73] Fishwick, "Imperial Cult in Roman Britain," 225; Richmond, *Roman Britain*,
208.

[74] Halsberghe, "Dea Caelestis," 2203–2223. Fishwick, "Soldier and Emperor,"
69–72 for discussion of a Caelestis inscription at Mainz (*CIL* XIII 6671) in which
Julia Domna is addressed as the *dea Caelestis*. There is no reason to suppose, as
once believed, that the Carvoran piece refers to Julia Domna: Kettenhofen, *syrischen
Augustae*, 98. Nor does any evidence prove that the empress herself endorsed the
cult. The Severi expressed greater interest in other gods, and it was not until the
reign of Elagabal that the *Dea Caelestis* officially entered the state cult: Mundle, "Dea
Caelestis," 228, notes 2–4.

[75] Domaszewski, *Religion*, 65. A pair of statues found in the legionary headquarters at Carnuntum on the Danube represents the emperor and his mother as Jupiter

There was, however, little Eastern influence in Britain, and the appearance of Serapis and other oriental deities in Britain stemmed from a personal association with a particular emperor,[76] as in restorations of temples to Isis (392) and Jupiter Dolichenus (396) both *in honorem domus divinae*. Dolichenus, especially, thrived under imperial Severan patronage and favor. The cults of the *Dea Brigantia* (deliberately manipulated by the Severans), Cybele, and Isis in Britain demonstrate similar imperial connections.

Dea Brigantia

The cult of the goddess Brigantia, officially encouraged by ca. AD 210, was closely related to the imperial house. Brigantia is once cited with the imperial *numina* (571) and once, as *nympha*, invoked for Caracalla's health and well-being (574). One statuette was produced on imperial command (575).[77] Brigantia was twice called *Victoria* (571, 572) and once represented as Victory (575), an important imperial virtue. She is shown in relief with a turreted crown, the wings of victory, a gorgon, aegis, spear and shield; her globe suggests universal rule. Brigantia was probably a local manifestation of the Severan Juno Caelestis. As with many Celtic goddesses, she was a warrior-mother and native river deity whose name, meaning "High One" or "Queen," is mirrored in the tribal name of the Brigantes, the Braint of Anglesey, a stronghold of Druidism (Tacitus *Annals* 14.30),[78] and the Brent of Middlesex.[79] Close, thus, were her ties to the Irish Brigid and the triple Brigit, the daughter of Dagda whose cult associations included fertility, culture, and medicine.[80] Brigantia was worshipped by a *procurator Augusti* (574), a centurion of *Legio VI* (401) and by an *architectus* (575). The elevated position of the goddess Brigantia, invoked as *Caelestis Brigantia* at Corbridge (401), may reflect the high status of women in Celtic society. Boudicca, queen of the Iceni whose name means Victory, invoked the goddess Andraste (Invincible) during her conflict with the Romans (Cassius Dio 62.6,1–2).

Dolichenus and Juno Regina. There may have been a similar pair at Chesters: Richmond, "Juno Regina," 47–52.

[76] Richmond, *Roman Britain*, 208.

[77] Birrens, where the statuette was found, was, however, abandoned by about 184: Breeze and Dobson, *Hadrian's Wall*, 144.

[78] Ekwall, *English River Names*, 51; Ross, *Celtic Britain*, 358, 366.

[79] Stokes, "Prose Tales," 315.

[80] Ross, *Celtic Britain*, 226, 232.

The Roman cult of Brigantia appears to be a local interpretation of the *Dea Caelestis*, a goddess with strong Severan associations (n.b. 388). The local goddess may have been an official Severan creation,[81] as our extant evidence dates primarily to that dynasty (571: to the *numina* of Geta and Caracalla; 574: for Caracalla's welfare).

Dea Syria/Cybele and Attis

Cybele, the *Magna Deum Mater Idaea*, was Eastern in origin but had been included among the gods of the Roman state cult since the late third century BC (imported on the advice of the Sibylline books in 204 BC to help against Hannibal: Livy 29.14.10–14). The festivals, held in April (Ovid *Fasti* 4.183–7), were noisy and public.[82] Her aspect as Mother Goddess, with sway over fertility and animals, had much in common with Roman (Diana) and Gallic practices. In Britain, she was worshipped by the tribune M. Caecilius Donatianus at Carvoran who composed a poem in iambic senarii (388) identifying her as the empress Julia Domna. The verses were written in honor of the *Virgo Caelestis*—the apotheosis of Julia Domna—identified with *Mater Divum* (Cybele), *Pax, Virtus,* Ceres, and *Dea Syria.* Donatianus almost certainly intended an apotheosis of Julia Domna, and it is possible that the poem was attached to a statue of the empress depicted with divine attributes.[83] The poem reflects both loyalty to the empire as well as genuine religious enthusiasm.[84]

The darker side of Cybele's myth included the self-castration of her faithless consort Attis. Consequently, members of her priesthood,

---

[81] Joliffe, "Dea Brigantia," 55; Henig, "*Ita intellexit*," 161. Compare Isis Noreia at Noricum for Oriental elements in native territorial goddesses: G. Alföldy, *Noricum*, 194, 240, plate 14. However, note #575 from Birrens, abandoned before the Severan dynasty (*supra*, note 77).

[82] For the chronology of March *Magna Mater* festivals (*CIL* I² p. 260): Fishwick, "Cannophori," 193–202.

[83] Collingwood, *Cat. Newcastle*, 22–3 (#55).

[84] Henig, *Religion*, 110. The political connection is strong. In AD 203/4, the Severans issued coins with the legend: *Indulgentia Augg. in Carthagine.* Caelestis symbolized Carthage. Three events are significant. Coin issues commemorated the 400th anniversary of Cybele's arrival in Rome, the celebration of the *ludi Saeculares* (in 204, the centenary celebration of Rome who traced her origins to Troy, Cybele's region), and the elevation of Carthage, Utica, and Lepcis Magna to *ius Italicum* (current prosperity could be attributed to an emperor from a once hostile territory): Vermaseren, *Matrem in leone sedentem*; Grant, *Roman Anniversary Issues*, 119–120; Vermaseren, *Cybele and Attis*, 138–139. The poem also suggests a link between dreams and the cult of the emperor: Allason-Jones, "Visions and Dreams," 21–22.

the *Galli*, were eunuchs (Catullus 63; Ovid *Fasti* 4.183–185; Lucian *De Dea Syria* 27; Julian *Oratio* 5.168D). Castration clamps for the gelding of horses have been found at Chichester in Britain and are depicted on a relief at Aix.[85] A bronze castration clamp found in the Thames near the London bridge is ornamented with busts of Cybele and Attis, the deities of the week, and the protomes of horses at the top, and bulls and lions on the handles.[86] The elaborate decoration hints at the cultic value of this piece which was deliberately damaged. Found nearby, a bronze figurine of Attis wears a short tunic and trousers open at the front to reveal the *vires*.[87] The London evidence is probably civilian rather than military.[88] It is not known, furthermore, if Cybele had a temple in London, as she probably did, nor where that temple might have stood.[89]

Evidence suggests a shrine to Cybele at Corbridge. An altar invokes the *Dea Panthea* (386, third century), who can be identified with the Phrygian *Magna Mater*. On each side of the altar appears a youth wearing a Phrygian cap, his head held downcast in mourning. The head of a young Hermes, wearing a winged cap, can be seen in a niche at the back of the altar. The mourning youths represented Attis and Men, the Phrygian moon god. Hermes appears as *Hegemonios*, guiding the initiates through the mysteries of the cult.[90] Also found at Corbridge, the upper part of a ram's head corbel, "one of the

---

[85] Vermaseren, *Cybele and Attis*, 96.

[86] Vermaseren, *Cybele and Attis*, 356; Harris, *Oriental Cults*, 109–12.

[87] C.R. Smith, *Illustrations of Roman London*, 69, pl. XVII. A terracotta head of Cybele with a mural crown is not indigenous to the site: *Catalogue of the Guildhall Museum*, 70.

[88] Richmond, "Corbridge," 199.

[89] In fact, no temple precinct of the *Magna Mater* in London has been positively identified. In 1933, however, excavations at Verulamium revealed a "triangular" temple within the town walls and immediately north of the triumphal arch on Watling street. Because of its shape and the discovery of seeds of Italian pine associated with pottery deposits found within the building, the temple was thought to have some connection with the cult of Cybele: Collingwood and Taylor, "Roman Britain in 1933," 208; Wheeler, *Verulamium*, 113–20, pl. XXXIV. But this association is by no means certain (Richmond, *Roman Britain*, 191). The shape of the temple may in fact be attributable to the fact that it was built in a fork between Watling Street and a street in the grid plan of the city (Harris, *Oriental Cults*, 97; Lewis, *Temples*, 95). The temple, built early in the second century and last restored late in the third, has a superficial resemblance to the temple of Cybele at Zugmantel. Imported pine cones might indicate a connection with an oriental cult (Lewis, *Temples*, 95–96). Harris, *Oriental Cults*, 97, concluded that the temple suggests a Romano-Celtic shrine adapted to fit into the triangular space.

[90] Richmond, "Corbridge," 198.

most vigorous pieces of carving at Corbridge and . . . difficult to place among ordinary conventional ornamentation," is reminiscent of a *criobolium* and could easily have been part of the decorations of a shrine to the *Magna Mater*.[91] A 1909 excavation report from Corbridge referred to two statuettes in white clay, one of Cybele with a mural crown and one of Mercury, "both executed in good classical style."[92] The "Cybele" statue, however, could be a mother goddess.[93]

The most familiar manifestation of the cult was the mourning Attis on sepulchral monuments. A gritstone relief from York shows Attis standing in a niche and wearing Phrygian dress, resting his head on his left hand as if in a posture of grief.[94] Examples are found also at Chester (see also p. 87, for a possible Attis or Cautopates). A fragmentary tomb block shows a cloaked figure, in a mourning pose, leaning against a pedestal.[95] Fragments of two corresponding door jambs from a circular sepulchral monument show the middle thirds of two figures in mourning.[96] On the damaged base of a tombstone, an inscribed panel is supported by a figure in cloak, tunic and Phrygian cap.[97] The mourning Attis on funerary monuments was probably decorative.

The cult was not completely localized, though it can hardly be claimed that the appeal of Cybele and Attis was broad.

Isis

The cult of Isis, a traditional Egyptian goddess, was introduced to the Greek-speaking world in Hellenistic times under the Ptolemies, who exploited the goddess' popularity to establish their rule in Egypt and to unite their Greek and Egyptian subjects under one religion. Alexander himself took advantage of the indigenous religion by sacrificing to the bull Apis at Memphis where he was enthroned as the new Pharaoh. Alexander's entourage included a retinue of scholars who helped him understand how the Nilotic culture could aid him in his goals.[98] Ptolemy Philadelphus wished to systematize Egyptian

---

[91] Richmond, "Corbridge," 199.
[92] *AA* ser. 3 6 (1910), 271; cited by Harris *Oriental Cults*, 99.
[93] Harris, *Oriental Cults*, 99.
[94] Collingwood and Taylor, "Roman Britain in 1927," 190.
[95] Wright and Richmond, *Grosvenor Museum*, 51 (#133), pl. XXXIII.
[96] Wright and Richmond, *Grosvenor Museum*, 53 (#154–5), pl. XXXVIII.
[97] Wright and Richmond, *Grosvenor Museum*, 28 (#50), pl. XVI.
[98] Witt, *Isis*, 46–7.

religion, and so employed the Egyptian priest Manetho and the Greek Timotheus, who together produced an *Interpretatio Graeca* of Egyptian religion. Philadelphus, who married his sister Arsinöe in imitation of Osiris and Isis and of the Pharaohs of Egypt,[99] also instigated a program of expanding and building temples to Isis, Osiris, and Horus, "the guarantors of Divine Order."

Ptolemy Philadelphus sent an embassy to Rome in 273,[100] and the Egyptian cults were introduced soon afterwards. An inscription from Puteoli (*CIL* X 1781 [*ILS* 5317 1.6]) indicates that by 105 BC a temple had been built to Serapis, the Hellenistic fusion of Osiris and Apis. The cult of Isis, however, was not well-received by politicians at Rome. The worshippers of Isis were tolerated by Sulla, at which time a college of the servants of Isis, the *pastophori*, was founded at Rome;[101] but the Isea at Rome were destroyed on consular order in 58, 50, and 48 BC. Augustus' disapproval of Eastern cults has been noted (p. 62). Nero was the first emperor to favor this cult.

Nonetheless, the popularity of the Egyptian rites grew. Under this personal and interactive religion, offering hope of an after-life to initiates rich and poor, temples would open for two services daily.[102] The goddess' multi-valency is evident in her assimilation to several Graeco-Roman deities: Ceres, Venus, Minerva.[103] Her epithets also reveal universal appeal: Hygieia, Fortuna, Pelagia. The goddess was most widely identified with Fortuna, Serapis with Jupiter, and Horus (also Harpocrates, the son of Isis and Osiris) with Cupid.

In the Roman world, Isis was worshipped with other Egyptian gods. Isis herself, holding dominion over all things, was commonly depicted wearing a vulture head-dress surmounted by a pair of horns, either of the cow of Hathor or of the ram associated with Osiris; between the horns was a solar disk. Osiris, her husband-brother, god of the sea and the underworld, was viewed in the Roman world as the Egyptian Bacchus (Diod. 1.25).[104] The falcon-god Horus, holding

---

[99] Such brother-sister and even father-daughter marriages within the royal house in Pharaonic Egypt also occurred in imitation of Isis and Osiris. The king set himself apart from his subjects by marrying his sister. This act, by no means common, stressed the divine aspect of kingship in imitation of the gods: Robins, *Women in Egypt*, 27.

[100] Witt, *Isis*, 70.

[101] Mau, *Pompeii*, 169.

[102] Mau, *Pompeii*, 169.

[103] Witt, *Isis*, 20.

[104] Hart, *Dictionary*, 151. In fact, the Romans thought that the rites of Bacchus and Demeter closely resembled those of Isis and Osiris (Diod. 1.25).

sway over the sky, was an heroic figure, who avenged the death of his father Osiris (Serapis), and who, in mortal guise, was represented by the pharaoh.[105] Anubis, the jackal god, deity of embalming and cemeteries, acted as an intermediary through whom mankind communicated with the gods. He frequently carried the caduceus, Mercury's attribute.[106]

The cults of the Egyptian gods attracted prominent followers, including Apuleius, whose *Metamorphoses* are an essential source for these cults, and Plutarch (*de Iside et Osiride*).[107] The cults from Egypt gained great popularity in the Roman world late in the Julio-Claudian dynasty and in Flavian times, as many Easterners came west.[108]

Isis, Serapis, and the Egyptian Cults in Britain

Worshippers of the Egyptian cults were primarily Egyptians and other Easterners, and it does not surprise that evidence for the cult of Isis in Britain is meager, mostly small personal items (gemstones and statuettes) which may have little bearing on religion. Isiac relics may simply be curiosities and collectibles, or, as in the case of the occasional Serapis relic, a compliment to Severus.[109]

Fragmentary evidence attesting Isis in London includes an inscribed jug (391).[110] The inscription implies the existence of a temple to Isis in Southwark,[111] but the jug may have been associated with a wine-

---

[105] Hart, *Dictionary*, 87–88.

[106] Hart, *Dictionary*, 21–22; Witt, *Isis*, plate 48.

[107] In 69, during the civil war between Vitellius and Vespasian, while the riots plagued the city of Rome, an Isiac priest protected Domitian, who eventually escaped disguised as a young devotee (Suetonius *Domitian*, 1; Tacitus *Historia*, 3.74).

[108] MacMullen, *Paganism*, 114–18.

[109] Harris, *Oriental Cults*, 74–75; L'Orange, *Apotheosis*, 76–77; Richmond, "Juno Regina," 51, suggests that the verses at Carvoran (388) may have been paired with a corresponding poem in honor of Septimius Severus as Serapis.

[110] Henig, *Religion*, 113. The jug, found at Tooly street, might originally have come from elsewhere in London. The graffito was etched into the clay after manufacture: Harris, *Oriental Cults*, 79–80; Marsh, "Arrentine Ware," 129, note 27.

The jug is usually dated ca. AD 75: Harris, *Oriental Cults*, 79. While there is evidence for a Flavian occupation of the Southwark area, the date is not impossible, but the jug could have been manufactured later: Kenyon, *Excavations in Southwark*, 12; *VCH, London I*, 136–42. Collingwood and Taylor, "Roman Britain in 1923," 283, #13, date the jug to the second century. A second century date seems more likely, as merchants followed troops freshly recruited to Britain and London's significance increased.

[111] Collingwood and Taylor, "Roman Britain in 1923," 283, #13; RCHM, *Roman London*, 177, pl. 53; Wheeler, *London in Roman Times*, 25, 51, pl. V.

shop or tavern near a temple of Isis.[112] The jug's condition suggests that it had been buried, perhaps because, in its defiled state, it was no longer suitable to contain holy (Nile) water. Purification by water was an essential element in the Isiac rite, and the goddess was frequently depicted with a *situla* (water bucket) and *sistrum* (rattle).[113] An altar (392), found reused in the foundations of the Roman wall at Blackfriars, records the restoration of a temple to Isis in the third century.[114] Other London Isiac relics include a bronze figurine of a seated goddess, previously identified as Demeter,[115] a bone pin terminating in a hand which holds a bust of the goddess,[116] a bronze steel-yard weight with a bust of Isis,[117] and a bronze ring with a glass *intaglio* of Isis-Fortuna, perhaps third century, found in the Roman Wall.[118] A marble head of Serapis was found in the London Mithraeum.[119]

Epigraphy and archaeology point to a Serapeum built outside the York fortress to the southwest (late second century). The temple, 3.65 × 8.23m, featured an apse at the southeast and a curved step at the northwest.[120] A bull with a fish tail in mosaic decorated the mosaic floor. The foundation inscription for the York Serapeum (436) tells us that the temple was built on the order of the legate of the sixth legion, a man with an eastern name, Claudius Hieronymianus. The date is too early for the temple to have been built in honor of Severus' enthusiasm for Serapis, who likewise held wide appeal among merchants.[121]

A dedication to Serapis from Kirkby Thore (437) does not necessarily imply a Serapeum connected to that fort. The Kirkby Thore altar is among the dedications to Serapis, like some to Jupiter

---

[112] Catullus 37; *CIL* XIV 4291; *CIL* VI 9824; Squarciapino, *Ostia*, 28; Kleberg, *Hôtels*, 59, 128–9, note 47; Firebaugh, *Inns*, 160–1.

[113] Henig, *Corpus*, #359. an *intaglio* shows Isis or her priestess holding a *sistrum* in one hand and *sistula* in the other (Wroxeter).

[114] Hassall, "Inscribed Altars," 196–8, #2; A. Birley, *Fasti*, 176–78. Recycling might suggest the rejection of a cult in favor of Christianity.

[115] Henig, *Religion*, 114.

[116] Wheeler, *London in Roman Times*, 103–4, fig. 32.

[117] Wheeler, *London in Roman Times*, 47, pl. XIX.

[118] Wheeler, *London in Roman Times*, 100–101, fig. 31.

[119] Toynbee, *Art in Britain*, 43, #38; *Temple of Mithras*, #3; *CIMRM* 818, fig. 253.

[120] Lewis, *Temples*, 117; Harris, *Oriental Cults*, 76.

[121] Harris, *Oriental Cults*, 75–6; RCHM *Eburacum*, 53–4; A. Birley, *Fasti*, 263–5; Henig, *Religion*, 114. Henig suggests that the temple date to as early as 170 or as late as 190.

Dolichenus, which were placed in the *principia*, in honor of Severus.[122]

Two Harpokrates figurines come from London, one in bronze, the other in silver, each depicting the god with his right hand raised to his lips in a gesture of silencing the initiates not to reveal the mysteries of the faith. The bronze figurine shows the god with the cornucopia. The silver piece shows the Egyptian god conflated with Cupid.[123] A tiny Harpokrates figurine was found at the Chester amphitheater.[124] Pliny (*NH* 33.41) mentioned that images of Harpokrates were employed as devices on bezels of rings. The presence of Greek physicians at Chester (*RIB* 461) may explain the Harpokrates figurine.

Magical amulets from Romano-British military centers pertain to the Egyptian cults.[125] A gold *lamella* (10 × 2.5cm), discovered 18m south of the fort at Caernarvon,[126] bears a largely unintelligible inscription, with references to the sun and moon and the Egyptian god Toth.[127] A fragmentary gold *lamella* was recovered from York (2 × 2.5cm). The first of the two extant lines seems to consist of magical symbols, the second line reads *phnebennouth*, perhaps transliterated from the Coptic, "the lord of the gods."[128] A nicolo bezel from a bronze ring (Great Chesters)[129] depicts a cock-headed anguiped. A carnelian *intaglio* from Castlesteads is engraved with a triple head which has feet, masks of a cock, an eagle, and a horse.[130] From Chesterholm a triangular relief shows a cock and other magical symbols.[131]

Finally, the cult of Jupiter Ammon, though not attested at military sites, is relevant for its assimilation to Celtic cults. Jupiter Ammon was, perhaps tacitly, identified with the native horned god or with the Celtic cult of the head.[132] A horned Jupiter Ammon, cut in high relief into a carnelian, was found at York.[133] A lamp disc of fine clay, stamped "Probus," depicts Jupiter Ammon, probably decora-

---

[122] Harris, *Oriental Cults*, 77.
[123] Henig, *Religion*, 114.
[124] M.J. Green, *Military Areas*, 52, #10.
[125] Harris, *Oriental Cults*, 93–4.
[126] Wheeler, *Segontium*, 129–30, fig. 52.
[127] Bonner, *Magical Amulets*, 136, 187.
[128] Bonner, *Magical Amulets*, 56–7, 199; Harris, *Oriental Cults*, 94.
[129] Harris, *Oriental Cults*, 94. The piece was found in the western guardroom of the south gate.
[130] Henig, *Corpus*, #382.
[131] Harris, *Oriental Cults*, 94.
[132] Harris, *Oriental Cults*, 83.
[133] Johns, *Jewellery*, 81; Henig, *Corpus*, #352.

tive, not religious.[134] The piece was found in a Roman grave at Borough Green, near Ightham, Kent.[135] The head of Jupiter Ammon decorated a pottery shard found in a tumulus in Wiltshire.[136] From Canterbury, the rim of light buff-ware a bowl shows the molded head in relief.[137] From Clifford Street, York, a fine relief of Jupiter Ammon appears on a large buff ware vessel.[138]

---

[134] Harris, *Oriental Cults*, 83.
[135] Payne, "Catalogue," 9.
[136] Cunnington, "Wiltshire Exhibits," 289; VCH *Wiltshire*, I, 131.
[137] Kirkman, "Canterbury Kiln Site," 119, 132–3, pl. I.
[138] Home, *Roman York*, pl. opposite 158.

CHAPTER SIX

ROMAN RELIGION IN LATE AND
POST-ROMAN BRITAIN

Issues

It has long been thought that the Roman influence on Britain was a mere gloss which quickly disappeared as the Romans gradually left the island. It is true that the Celtic substratum remained strong, as already seen in the Romanized Celtic names which appear in religious dedications (e.g., 619). Furthermore, mixed marriages were frequent, and Latin may have remained a second language for many. In addition, native, that is Celtic, gods (Sulis Minerva, Coventina, Belatucadrus, *et alia*) remained popular among both Roman and Celt. Yet the Roman element also proved strong, as seen in the continued relevance, popularity, and vitality of Roman cults: Jupiter, Mars, Mercury.

Language

Inscriptions imply that, at least in the earlier years, Latin was a language learned at school, rather than spoken at home. British Latin was archaic in tone, compared with other provinces, and this may simply indicate the remoteness of the island, as some have argued.[1] Yet pre-Roman ties with Gaul and Roman-era trade contacts between Britain and much of the continent do not bear out the thesis of isolation.[2] Romanization of the British languages occurred in the incorporation of Latinate words into Celtic languages for concepts and items foreign to pre-Roman Britain—e.g., *fenestra-* for window.[3] To

---

[1] Mann, "Spoken Latin," 219.
[2] C. Smith, "Vulgar Latin," 947. The problem is complex. Most societies have at least two levels of spoken language, a colloquial dialect and a more formal, literary diction. Inscriptions, by their official nature, fall into the latter category. We are further handicapped by the fact that no true vulgar Latin texts exist from Britain; even *defixiones* are formulaic: C. Smith, "Vulgar Latin," 936, 944. However, some rather rude graffiti do survive: *RIB* 2447.16.a–d; 2447.28a, 28d.
[3] S. Johnson, *Later Roman Britain*, 54. See also Rhys, "Welsh words;" Güterbock,

be sure, many of these Latin loan words entered Celtic languages at a late date, *via* the Church, whose official language in the west was Latin, a strong influence of southern Britain after the seventh century.[4] Furthermore, Celtic names appear in Latin inscriptions to Roman (95, 105, 134, 185, 213, 224, 239, 245, 257, 266, 279, 295, 299, 334, 353), Eastern (412, 423, 429), and Celtic (e.g., 442, 533, 589, 631)[5] gods; this may suggest a bilingual society. Finally, it must be noted that eventual Saxon domination led to the eradication of Celtic languages which survived in the Celtic fringes, beyond Anglo-Saxon hegemony (Cornwall, Ireland, the Scottish highlands, Wales). Our limited knowledge for post-Roman, pre-Saxon England survives in non-Celtic and late-Celtic (ninth century) sources: Gildas, *de excidio et conquestu Britanniae*, sixth century; Nennius, *Historia Britonum*, ninth century.

Coinage[6]

Carausius, the Belgian overseer of the defense of the *litus Saxonicum* and one-time imperial contender against Diocletian and Maximian, established an imperial mint in London, and perhaps another at Colchester, when he needed ready funds to pay donatives to the troops who made him emperor (Eutropius 9.21).[7] Allectus used the London mint, which was kept in operation until ca. 326 (Eutropius 9.22.2),[8] and Magnus Maximus revived the mint briefly, to keep his troops financially happy.[9] For the most part, Britain relied on shipments from the continent for hard currency. Roman bronze coins found in Britain predate AD 402/403. Gold and silver appears no later than AD 406, and none of these are struck after the fall of

---

lateinischen Lehnwörter; Vendryes, *Hibernicis Vocabulis*; Loth, *mots latins*; Pedersen, *Vergleichende Grammatik*, i.189–242; K.H. Jackson, *Language and History*, 76–121; Evans, "Language Contact," 960–963.

[4] C. Smith, "Vulgar Latin," 945–947.

[5] Celts also worshipped the Severan deity Brigantia (572, 573). Romans venerated local gods (e.g., 687), as noted above. A Numidian, interestingly, honored Mars Braciaca (605).

[6] Casey, *Caurausius and Allectus*, 55–88.

[7] *RIC* V.2; Casey, *Caurausius and Allectus*, 58. The bulk of Carausius' coins bear the legend "Pax Aug(usti)" to proclaim and celebrate the blessings of Carausius' peace.

[8] *RIC* V.2, 562; Casey, *Caurausius and Allectus*, 83–84, 86–88. London together with unmarked mints (probably Colchester) produced the majority of coin issues for both Carausius and Allectus.

[9] *RIC* IX, 2; Salway, *Roman Britain*, 466.

Constantine III. The central administration habitually sent coins in bulk to pay the provincial troops, and the lack of coins (which may prove nothing) seems to imply that bureaucrats and soldiers in significant numbers no longer occupied the British provinces. Honorius did have a serious currency shortage and may have simply stopped paying imperial employees in Britain, or the island may have been garrisoned by German confederates who accepted land in exchange for military services.[10]

Military Withdrawal[11]

Roman Britain remained peaceful until the crisis of ca. 342/3. The situation was serious enough to warrant a visit from the emperor Constans. Though the details are vague, sources suggest internal threats of rebellion from supporters of the murdered Constantine II, threats of invasion from Picts and perhaps Scots with mutinous *areani*, frontier scouts, and, further, potential threats along the *litus Saxonicum* (Firmicus Maternus, *de Errore Profanarum Religionum* 28.6; Libanius, *Oration* 59.139 and 141; Ammianus 28.3.8). Magnentius, attempting to usurp the purple, withdrew troops from Britain in 350 (Ammianus Marcellinus 14.5.6–8)—leaving the island vulnerable to raids from Picts and Saxons from the north, and the Scotti and the mysterious Attacotti from Ireland (ca. 360, Ammianus Marcellinus 26.4.5).[12] Barbarian threats to Britain, AD 367, were quelled in a series of naval expeditions under the direction of the elder Theodosius, father of the future emperor (Claudian *de Consulatu tert. Honorii* 51–6, *de Consulatu quart. Honorii* 24–33; Pacatus *Panegyr. Theod.* 5.2; Ammianus Marcellinus 28.3).

After Valentinian's death, AD 375, the western empire passed to his sons Gratian and Valentinian II. Under Gratian, relations between

---

[10] The sources are too sketchy for tenable answers. It is also possible that military problems in Italy and Gaul prevented the safe transport of funds to distant provinces: Salway, *Roman Britain*, 300.

[11] The following is hardly an attempt to solve the manifold problems of late Roman Britain, all the more distressing because of the unreliable witness of near contemporary literature (e.g., Gildas). A synopsis will prove efficacious in determining troop strength and the influence of those garrisons on the native populations. For a discussion of the numbers of soldiers posted to Britain in the fourth and fifth century, see James, "Britain and the Late Roman Army," 162–172. The troop strength may have reached about 35,000.

[12] G. Webster, "Possible Effects;" Tomlin, "Barbarian Conspiracy;" M. Jones, *End of Roman Britain*, 245.

the emperor—a feeble administrator who left government duties to incompetent favorites—and the army deteriorated to such a degree that a civil war took place in AD 383 when Magnus Maximus, "almost against his will," was declared emperor by his troops in Britain (Orosius 7.34.9). Magnus Maximus withdrew troops to fight on the continent; Gratian's defeat followed. Maximus, demanding a truce and offering allegiance, sent an embassy to Theodosius (Orosius 7.34.9–10; Zosimus 4.35–37). Maximus continued to campaign, gathering troops of Britons, Gauls, and Celts (Germans) under the pretext that he was trying to prevent innovations in the "national" religion (Christianity) and ecclesiastical order (Sozomenus *Ecclesiastical History* 7.13).[13] The final armed engagement between Theodosius and Maximus occured at Aquileia in AD 388. Theodosius, taking Maximus by surprise, besieged and defeated the usurper (Prosper Tiro *Chronicon* 1191; Orosius 7.35.3–4). Maximus' escapades resulted in the removal of troops from Britain (Gildas *de Excidio Britanniae* 14–15), but, because of threats from the Saxons and the Picts, Britain was reinforced late in the fourth century (AD 396–398) as Stilicho, Honorius' general, campaigned against the sea-borne incursions of Scots, Picts, and Saxons (Claudian *De consulatu Stilichonis* 2.247–255).

As the course of events in the rest of the empire deteriorated, Hadrian's Wall was abandoned, and troops were withdrawn from Britain, ca. 400, to fight against the Visigoth Alaric (Zosimus 6.1).

Troops remaining in Britain took it upon themselves to elect their own emperor in 406, the short-reigned and enigmatic Marcus, who was soon replaced by a certain Gratian, a town councillor (Zosimus 4.2.1–2; Orosius 7.40.4). Late in 406, Germanic tribes from across the Rhine mounted a large scale invasion of Gaul (Prosper Tiro, *Chronicon Gratiani* 1230). Troops in Britain, fearing that Germanic migrations might affect Britain, deposed Gratian and elevated Constantine III, a common soldier (Zosimus 4.2.2, 6.3.1), who, in the following year, crossed over to the continent with British troops (Zosimus 6.2–5), once again leaving the island vulnerable to a Saxon invasion in 408. He intended either to stave off invasion or to reestablish ties with Rome, perhaps both. Constantine III was recognized as legitimate Augustus by Honorius.

Saxon attacks on the British island in 408 devastated the Britons

---

[13] Maximus alleged that the Church was being subjected to intolerable treatment (*Chronicle of 452*, for AD 387): Ireland, *Roman Britain*, 161–162.

who took up arms in their own defense, freed their cities from Saxon
invaders, rebelled from Roman hegemony, expelled Roman officials,
and established a sovereign constitution (Zosimus 4.5.2; Gallic Chronicle
of the year 452, *Chronica Minora* 1.654).

In 410, the Britons appealed to the emperor Honorius who told
them that they must look to their own defenses (Zosimus 6.10.2).[14]
The Britons may have asked for military or diplomatic help, or their
intent may have been to re-establish ties with Rome.[15] A supposed
Roman reoccupation of Britain (ca. 417–425), as implied in the
Notitia, is highly improbable.[16]

Nothing tells us what happened to any troops remaining in Britain
after AD 409. The much-quoted example from Noricum (470's),
however, may suggest the actions of any remaining British garrisons.
The Noricum unit sent a deputation to Italy to collect back pay.
When the embassy failed to return, the unit disbanded itself (Eugenius,
Life of St. Severinus). By default, the frontier was abandoned, and a
neighboring king crossed the Danube and established military control over former Roman cities. Something similar could have occurred
in Britain. In any event, standing troops were probably drawn from
the local population, and at least one late unit, the *Cohors I Cornoviorum*,
was raised from a British tribe. It is likely that such troops would
have remained on the island.

By the third century, fresh recruits for most garrisons were local.

[14] Wood, "The Fall of the Western Empire;" Jones and Casey, "Gallic Chronicle
Restored;" Thompson, "Britain, AD 406–410." R.W. Burgess ("Dark Ages," 185–195)
refutes Jones and Casey. Zosimus 6.10.2 may not refer to Britain (Brettania) but
rather to Bruttium (Brettia/Bruttia): Bartholomew, 1982, 261–70.
[15] S. Johnson, *Later Roman Britain*, 136–138. Allegiance to the emperor at Rome
was a necessary precursor to financial and military help. Two conflicting political
factions are indicated: pro- and anti-Roman. Those who were disenchanted with
Roman authority probably felt the burden of public duty to the state as well as
the disappointment at Rome's failure to help against the Saxons in AD 408. British
successes fueled the movement for political independence.
[16] Scullard, *Outpost*, 176. The *Notitia Dignitatum*, surviving in several late antique
illuminated manuscripts, preserves lists of Roman officials and their insignia and
includes records of the garrison of Britain. The document, its date and nature much
discussed, was edited by Seeck, *Notitia*. Britain in the *Notitia* has been discussed by
E. Birley, "Beaumont Inscription, the *Notitia Dignitatum*," 190–226, and Hassall,
"Britain in the Notitia," 103–118.
The *Notitia*, compiled ca. AD 395 and haphazardly updated in the 420's, probably reflects the military situation in Britain for the late fourth century, as British
garrisons probably remained on the books because of administrative inertia or in
case the information might someday be useful again: Stephen Johnson, *Later Roman
Britain*, 38; Salway, *Roman Britain*, 309.

Provincial governors were responsible for keeping garrisons under their jurisdiction up to strength (only specialized units, e.g. Thracian archers, continued to receive troops from the original province of recruitment). Sons of soldiers followed their fathers into service, and, as with most professions, military service became an hereditary obligation in the late Roman empire. In addition, German confederates, manning the fourth century Roman army, accepted Roman citizenship and land in frontier zones in exchange for military services. The Burgundians, Vandals, and Alemanni are attested in Britain (Zosimus I.68), and Crocus, "the king of the Alemanni," at York in 306, enthusiastically advised Constantine I to make his bid for the purple (Pseudo-Victor, *Epitome De Caesaribus*, 41.2).[17] There is, however, no direct evidence that *laeti* (federates) contributed to the fourth-century standing British army.[18] Some units were sent to Britain late: the *Ala Herculea*, the *cuneus Frisiorum Aballavensium*, the *numerus Barcariorum Tigrisensium*, the *numerus Exploratorum Bremeniensium*, and the *vexillatio Sueborum Longovicianorum*.

Foreign Pressures

Britain was not immune to the foreign stresses which weakened other Roman frontiers. A series of civil wars and imperial pretenders launching their causes from Britain has been mentioned above. As Roman troops were withdrawn from the island, threats increased on all borders: Ireland from the west, Picts from the North, and Saxons from the east. Irish sources indicate that the high king of Ireland, Niall of the Nine Hostages, attacked the southern coast of Britain, perhaps in AD 405. Vortigern, whose name means "high king," invited Saxons to England in the 420s and had established contacts with a Saxon king, Hengest in Kent—an isolated incident of cooperation between Anglo-Saxons and Britons. In the 440s, some British families emigrated to Armorica (Brittany) at the invitation of the Gauls in their quest for help against the Visigoths.[19] As the Saxons advanced

---

[17] Otherwise, evidence for Germanic tribes settled in Britain is scant, though it is to be expected that settlers quickly assumed the cultural benefits of their new province: Stephen Johnson, *Later Roman Britain*, 52.

[18] James, "Britain and the Late Roman Army," 171–172; Johnson, *Later Roman Britain*, 173. Furthermore, few fourth-century remains can be identified as Germanic. For example, fourth century animal-style military belt fittings—a sign of rank and service—were produced in local Roman, not Germanic, factories.

[19] Morris, *The Age of Arthur*, 90. Gildas implies that the Britons were fleeing the

(from the 440's), Ambrosius Aurelianus organized the resistance, and
led the Britons to a decisive victory at Mt. Badon, temporarily halting Saxon expansion (Gildas, *de Excidio Britannia* 25–26).

Administrative Reorganization

No clear evidence speaks to a large-scale overhaul of politics, culture, and daily life after the British split from Rome: when the bishop
Germanus of Auxerre visited southern Britain in 428/9 and 448, he
met church dignitaries and civic leaders, and saw all the outward
trappings of normal Roman life (Constantine, *Vita Sancti Germani* 3.14).
It is likely that local public policy and private life continued much
as before for a few generations. Immediate Saxon take-over is, at
best, unlikely.[20] The transition could not have been smooth since the
island was probably short of men who could administer Roman-style
towns after local (anti-Roman) factions purged themselves of Constantine
III's administrators. By the 440's, a distinctly post-Roman society
had emerged. No Roman reconquest is evident—Rome simply did
not have the strength and manpower to launch such an expedition
in the northwest.[21] Besides, Britain was no longer useful or cost-
effective enough to make a reconquest worthwhile.

Archaeology indicates that life continued above subsistence level
at several sites, including Bath and Cirencester, where the forum
was maintained well into the fifth century, and Verulamium (St.
Albans) where civic leaders functioned in the 430's.[22] Yet subsistence
is evident in most places. Taxation and pottery production stopped.
Agricultural economics was disrupted, and villas, for the most part,
had fallen into ruins. Old iron-age forts were reoccupied, and new
tribes may have emerged around the nucleus of a rich or powerful individual who could provide protection.[23] Britain was fundamen-

---

Saxons, an unlikely supposition since the migrations occurred gradually into the
sixth century: Johnson, *Later Roman Britain*, 154.

[20] Saxons began to arrive ca. 449 (Bede; *Gallic Chronicle of 452* dates the Saxon
take-over to AD 441), but their progress was slow and halting. Not until the sixth
century was Anglo-Saxon control over southwest England secure.

[21] Nonetheless, several forts on Hadrian's Wall were clearly occupied and even
refortified in sub-Roman Britain: South Shields, Housesteads, Chesterholm, *inter
alia*. These sites were reused by locals and possibly provided centers of operation
for Anglo-Saxon mercenaries: Dark, "Sub-Roman Redefence?," 111–20.

[22] Salway, *Roman Britain*, 321.

[23] Wilmott, *Birdoswald*, 227, 228.

tally integrated into Roman society to the extent that separation was detrimental.[24]

Though political ties with Rome had been severed, religious ties remained. Germanus bishop of Auxerre visited Verulamium twice (AD 429, 448) to deal with remnants of the Pelagian heresy (Constantius, *Vita Germani* 12–27). The Briton Pelagius studied law at Rome in the 380's, where he converted to Christianity, took holy orders, and taught religion (AD 394–410). Pelagius' teachings resulted in a dispute with Augustine of Hippo over the sinfulness of mankind. Augustine maintained that man was always sinful in God's eyes, and that grace depended entirely on God's mercy and forgiveness (Augustine, *Confessions*, 10.29). Pelagius countered that men possessed freewill, the correct use of which enabled them to live free from sin and to gain justification in God's sight through their own efforts. Augustine, among others, denounced Pelagius in 410, and by 418 Honorius declared him an heretic.[25] Pelagius left Rome in 409/410 for Carthage and Palestine. Myres suggested that Pelagian doctrine was a central cause of the British revolt from Roman rule in 410.[26] Morris argued that Pelagius' followers were active in Britain since the late fourth century, recommending an egalitarian social and political agenda.[27] Yet nothing clearly proves Pelagianism as a political movement, nor can the heresy be securely placed in Britain much before Germanus' visit in 429. By all accounts, Pelagianism was developed in Rome and subsequently exported to provincial sees.

Survival of Celtic Paganism

Worshippers in Britain extended old temples and built new ones to pagan gods while Constantine was trying to Christianize the rest of the empire.[28] Constans in 341 (*Codex Theodosius* 16.10.2) and Constantius

---

[24] James, "Britain and the Late Roman Army," 182–183; Salway, *Roman Britain*, 334.

[25] Ferguson, *Pelagius*; Evans, "Pelagius;" Morris, "Pelagian Literature;" Rees, *Pelagius*; Thomas, *Christianity in Roman Britain*, 53–60.

[26] Myres, "Pelagius and the End," 26.

[27] Morris, "Literary Evidence," 61–73.

[28] The evidence is both military and civilian. A temple at Brean Down, Somerset, underwent two remodelings during Constantine's tenure: Richmond, "Roman Britain in 1958," 129. The temple was built ca. AD 340, but went out of use by 370. Temples at Worth, Kent and Pagan's Hill, Somerset were also modified and enlarged

in 357 (*Codex Theodosius* 16.10.3) both ordered pagan temples closed. Yet Christianity struggled in the British urban centers while older religions flourished in the countryside, remaining popular and vital. In the late fourth century, native styles and languages were revived in Syria and Egypt, in connection with the Christian church. In Britain, Christianity helped give new meaning to older styles of religion, especially healing cults, already seen in the late survivals of Mars Nodens (pp. 143–144) and Coventina (pp. 155–157) and Sulis Minerva (pp. 166–171).[29] Venus with Christianizing influences appears at Silchester: a fourth century *intaglio*, showing a female bust, is inscribed *VE|NUS*; the gold hoop reads *Seniciane Vivas in De(o)*.[30] The Christian inscription was secondary and may have been added as an owner came to identify Venus with Mary. VENUS possibly refers not to the goddess but perhaps to an abbreviated personal name (Venustinus, Venustinius, Venusta). The Celtic belief in an afterlife and struggles between the Celtic equestrian god of light and forces of darkness (e.g., the serpent of *CSIR* 1.8.29) rendered Celtic religion open to syncretism with Eastern mystery rites: the Egyptian Apis and the Celtic cult of the head may have been considered equivalent. It has also been seen that "pagan" vitality was not restricted to Celtic cults. Jupiter, especially, remained popular. One monument to a Celtic god, for example, was rededicated to Jupiter Optimus Maximus late in the fourth century (196b).

---

after Constantine's death: Klein, "Roman temple," 76–86; Rahtz, "Roman Temple at Pagan's Hill," 112–142. Sites at Lydney, Frilford, Woodeaton, Bourton Grounds, Farley Heath, and Pagan's Hill flourished into the fifth century.

[29] Frend, "Romano-British Christianity," 8; Thomas, *Christianity in Roman Britain*, 118. Consider, for example, the Christian poet Ausonius (AD 310–390), Gratian's tutor (AD 365–375), who continued to show enthusiasm for classical literature as well as his ancestral connections to Druidism (Ausonius, *Commemoratio Professorum*, 4.7–10, 10.22–30).

Additionally, fourth-century British mosaics blend popular mythical scenes with Christian themes. For example, the Europa and the Bull mosaic (Constantinian) at Lullingstone is inscribed: *Invida si t[auri] vidisset Iuno natatus | Iustius Aeolias isset adusque domos. Invida* is significant since this word begins several verses attached to Constantinian mosaics of both Christian and non-Christian value in Africa: Frend, "Religion in Roman Britain," 14–15. Such verses are meant to turn the "evil eye" away from the home.

[30] Henig, *Corpus*, #789; Mawer, *Christianity*, D3.Go.14. A Senicianus also issued a curse at Lydney (*RIB* 306), and Henig suggests that the ring owner and curser are quite possibly the same man.

Apollo at Nettleton[31]

Romans developed an interest in the site in the first century AD, though stone axes, Belgic pottery, flint tools indicate pre-Roman use. The Roman cult possibly absorbed a pre-existing Celtic one. A circular shrine was built ca. AD 69, followed by a large hostel along the Fosse Way. An octagonal podium encircling a small shrine was erected ca. 230, at which time the construction of a larger hostel suggests growing interest in this pilgrim's cult. Twenty years later (ca. 250), the original shrine was destroyed by fire, but the cult continued to grow as buildings were enlarged. The site fell into disrepair ca. 330. After the 330s, increased industrial activity (pewter casting, bronze and iron smelting) hints that the shrine could no longer sustain the local population. The temple may have been converted to Christian use until 370 when it became a homestead, and a portion of the central shrine was revived for pagan worship. In the late fourth century, buildings deteriorated through disuse and fire. The site came to a violent end—bones were slashed with swords and decapitation is apparent—perhaps at the hands of raiding Irish pirates from across the Bristol Channel, or at the hands of Christians who had defaced other pagan sites.[32]

Mercury at Uley

Early in the second century AD, Mercury received a Romano-Celtic temple in stone at Uley. Numerous buildings around the temple precinct, modified and rebuilt over the years, provided living quarters for priests, hostels for worshippers, and temple shops. The site's limestone cult statue, figurines, and altars attest Mercury. Late in the fourth century, the temple partially collapsed but was modified and used for a short time into the fifth century, at which time temple remains were obliterated and votive objects deliberately buried. As at Nettleton, the temple site was converted into a Christian church, recycling Mercury votives into the Christian structures. The Christian center was not abandoned until the seventh or eighth century.

---

[31] Wedlake, *Apollo at Nettleton*, for a complete discussion of excavations, finds, and history of the site.

[32] Lewis, *Temples*, 143–145; Thomas, *Christianity in Roman Britain*, 136. Consider cat. 106 which seems to allude to the restoration of a temple after Christian desecration (after 313): Cunliffe, *Roman Bath*, 4.

A limestone cult statue, classical in form, Antonine in date, represents the Uley Mercury. The god sports curly hair, wings sprout from his head. A chlamys drapes from the left shoulder; the god is otherwise nude. Mercury holds his classical accoutrements: a caduceus in his left hand, money bag in his right. His cult animals stand beside him: a cock at his left leg, a ram at his right.

Votives are numerous and varied. Typical are figurines of Mercury, the infant Dionysus, and cockerels. Interesting are spears and other weapons, which underscore the possibly martial nature of the earlier, non-Romanized cult.[33] Celts conflated the Roman gods Mars and Mercury (pp. 164–166). Furthermore, Mercury and Celtic horned gods overlapped to some extent in form and function (p. 164). The site has also yielded several caducei, a predictable offering to Mercury and healers. Interestingly, several caducei have been deliberately bent, as if in ritual sacrifice to Mercury.[34] Healing functions may be implied by brooches and pins, and one fragmentary plaque which shows a breast with enlarged areolar glands (as in pregnancy).[35]

The lead tablets (about 140) recovered from the shrine resemble those from Bath and other healing shrines: Caerleon, Lydney, Brean Down, Pagan's Hill.[36] Most follow standard formulae with complaints of theft and promises to devote recovered property to the god.[37]

That there were Christians at Uley is implied on bronze figured plaque, carefully folded, apparently sheeting from a casket. Only four scenes are discernable, and each illustrates a biblical episode. The top left scene shows Christ and the centurion (*Matthew* 8:5–13). On the top right, Christ heals the blind man (*Mark* 8:22–25; *John* 9). The bottom scenes are taken from the Old Testament: Jonah in the bottom left, the sacrifice of Isaac at the right (*Genesis* 22). This plaque does not prove active Christianity at Uley, and it is reasonable to suppose that the worshippers simply used a Christian object

---

[33] Henig in Woodward and Leach, *Uley Shrines*, 131–147.

[34] Henig in Woodward and Leach, *Uley Shrines*, 103. Killed swords (deliberately bent or broken) are typical for the cult of dead, and broken bracelets indicate divorce. The "killed" caduceus may suggest a thank offering for a healed body.

[35] Henig in Woodward and Leach, *Uley Shrines*, 107.

[36] Eighty-seven tablets, inscribed on one or both sides, are generally in bad physical condition, and difficult to decipher: Tomlin in Woodward and Leach, *Uley Shrines*, 114.

[37] The Uley collection attests to embezzlement, the only evidence in Britain for a crime widespread on the continent: Tomlin in Woodward and Leach, *Uley Shrines*, 130, #78.

in a "pagan" burial, or that they integrated the old religion with Christianity, a new sect which enjoyed imperial patronage and must, consequently, have been exceptionally potent.[38]

Christianity

By most accounts, Christianity came to Britain with the army. Evidence for Christians in the Roman army, however, is limited.[39] Constantine's legendary vision at the Milvian bridge before his battle with Licinius resulted, from Constantine's point of view, in victory for Constantine and caused the eventual Christianization of the empire, including the army, upon whom he imposed an obligatory oath to the vague *summus deus* (Eusebius, *Life of Constantine* 4.20).

Christians in the Army

Early Christians avoided the draft for several reasons: the church opposed bloodshed and war; a soldier's unconditional oath of service to the emperor conflicted with the Christian's unquestioning loyalty to the Church (Origen, *Contra Celsum* 7.67, ca. 178); the army rigidly observed the cult of the emperor; military religion dictated that officers make animal sacrifices and that soldiers participate (Hippolytus, *Apostolic Tradition* 16.17, third century); the worship of the *signa* amounted, in Christian eyes, to idolatry; and traditional off-duty distractions (gambling, off-color jokes) conflicted with the Christian ethic.[40] Ironically, after the death of Stilicho, pagans were, for a time,

---

[38] Henig in Woodward and Leach, *Uley Shrines*, 108–110. The casket may have presented two registers, Old Testament scenes on the bottom, New Testament episodes on the top. The four surviving scenes share the theme of absolute faith.

[39] Helgeland, "Christians," 766. Evidence comes primarily from church historians Eusebius and Lactantius, martyr accounts which are embellished and exaggerated, and inscriptions which provide little information beyond the basics of rank, unit, and (rarely) the date of death.

[40] Harnack, *Militia Christi*, 46–47; Helgeland, "Christians," 728. Idolatry is the most serious point of contention. Tertullian (fl. 197–220), who did not speak for the mainstream church, recognized that Rome secured her glory through her wars, though not without destruction (*Apology* 25.14). Tertullian disapproved of Christian service in the Roman army, not so much because of potential bloodshed, but rather exposure to amoral influences (pick-pockets, extortioners, pimps, gamblers: *De fuga in persecutione* 13.3; Luke 3:14) and the idolatrous nature of Roman army religion (*De Corona; Apology* 16.8). Tertullian, in fact, considered idolatry the most grievous sin against God, worse than murder: *atquin summa offensa penes illum*

excluded from army service because of questionable loyalty to the
currently Christian state.

In Britain, traditional religions remained strong among soldiers
and officers. The healing cult of Coventina, for example, flourished
until the late fourth century—late pagan cults were often, but not
always, healing centers. There is little to suggest strong Christianity
in the ranks. No Christian churches have surfaced along Hadrian's
Wall, though possible churches have been identified at South Shields
and Housesteads.[41] Possibly Christian tombstones at Carvoran (*RIB*
1828),[42] Chester (*RIB* 508),[43] and York (*RIB* 690)[44] and the bishopric
at York suggest some Christian activity in the northern military zone.
Furthermore, a number of non-Christian altars and statuary frag-

---

idololatria (*De spectaculis* 2.9, 9.6). Minucius Felix considered Roman religion useless:
the *auspicia* had brought destruction to Rome and her armies (*Octavius* 26), and it
was pointless to worship the gods of conquered people since those same gods could
not grant protection against Rome (*Octavius* 25). Origen argued that Christians did
their share of service to preserve the empire through their prayers which were,
according to Origen, far more effective than armies (1 *Timothy* 2:1–2).

Clement of Alexandria, a contemporary of Tertullian, exhibited a more balanced
opinion. His occasional references to Christian army service suggest that he considered soldiering merely another job (*Protrepticus* 10.100) and recognized military
discipline as a cogent example for the Christian life (*Stromata* II.83.3–4). Clement
did not forbid Christians from enrolling in the service, nor does he give the impression that he thought about military life as systematically as Tertullian: Helgeland,
"Christians," 745. Cyprian, ca. 250, employed military metaphors in describing the
Church: the church is the camp, martyrs are the soldiers of God (*Epistles*, 10.1;
28.2; 57.4–5; 58.3).

The Christian mandate against military service seems to have been relaxed after
Constantine: Lactantius, nonetheless, lamented the horrors of killing and warfare
(*Divine Institutes* 3.17, 4.20, 5.18; *Epitome* 63), but nowhere did he openly condemn
Christians enlisting (Helgeland, "Christians," 759); the highly patriotic Eusebius of
Caesarea consistently praised Constantine's achievements and his army whose suc-
cesses only proved God's favor (*Life of Constantine* 1.1).

[41] Crow, *Housesteads*, 96–7.

[42] *D.M. Aur. T. f. Aiae d. Salonas Aur. Marcus cent. Obseq(uentis) coniugi sanctissimae
quae vixit annis XXXIII sine ulla macula.* Third century. *Sine ulla macula* may not prove
a Christian connection since pagan parallels exist: Watson, "Christianity," 52; *CIL*
VI 22657, VI 9663.

[43] *Dis Mani|bus Q. Vib|ius Secun|dus Annie(n)s|is Cremon|a miles leg(ionis) XX | V.V.
c(enturia) Octavia[ni]|.* The tombstone shows in triplicate eight-pointed stars enclosed
in concentric circles, a symbol which could be identified as a monogramatic cross
(cross-pattée): Furlonger, "*RIB* 508," 225–226. The three crosses may refer to the
trinity. The stone dates to the third century.

[44] *D.M. Simpliciae Florentine anime innocentissime que vixit menses decem Felicius Simplex
pater fecit leg. VI V.* The legionary title has been cut roughly as a secondary graffito
(Wright, *RIB*, p. 232). The Christian identification depends on the phrase *anime
inocentissime* for which there are numerous pagan parallels: G.R. Watson, "Christianity,"
52–53; Toynbee, "Christianity," 23, n. 4.

ments became bedding for a military road built at Corbridge ca. AD 369 (cat. 421).[45]

Christian objects from military sites are few in number, and whether these objects belonged to soldiers, their families, or merchants cannot be determined. These items are identified as Christian by various symbols: chi-rhos and crosses; fish; and inscriptions (e.g., VIVAS). A glass bottle from Catterick, dating to the first/second century, displays an inverted "rho-cross" with an oblique cross-bar, a symbol not commonly used by Christians until the fourth century.[46] A pottery lamp from Newcastle (now lost) which was described as bearing a "chi-rho" might have a Christian connection.[47] Clearly Christian is a samian-ware bowl (third/fourth century) from Richborough which shows a graffito, incised on the lower wall, resembling an inverted rho-cross with an oblique cross-stroke.[48] Six chi-rho symbols, each within a square compartment, were etched onto the rim of a silver bowl found at Corbridge.[49] A chi-rho monogram appears on a bronze ring from Brough-under-Stainmore.[50] A jet ring from Chesters has a possible Christian connection. A symbol resembling the chi-rho is inscribed on the smaller bezel. The larger bezel is engraved: "QUIS SEPA(RABIT). The inscription continues on the two sides of the hoop: MEUM ET TUUM | DURANTE VITA. The piece could be a marriage or betrothal ring without Christian significance.[51] A fourth century polygonal bronze ring from Richborough displays a five-stroke chi-rho framed by an alpha and omega (on the bezel). Eight of the nine facets of the hoop are inscribed: IU|ST|IN|EVI|

---

[45] Similar monument recycling occurred where Christians asserted themselves, as at Gaza, where the Christian population openly demonstrated its rejection of the past (Paul the Deacon, *Life of Porphyry of Gaza* 76). Saturn altars were used as building material by the people of Cuicul in Mauretania Sitifensis in the fourth century.

In Britain, a number of monuments were recycled before and after Christianity's rise to privilege. At Housesteads, a Hadrianic altar was recycled into a Severan guard chamber (170, cf. 402, 407, 417). Post-Constantine recycling includes 506, 600, 634. That some sanctified pieces were reused during Severan rebuilding raises the question of how long a votive should remain inviolate. The Housesteads altar to Jupiter Optimus Maximus might suggest that after a while, New Years' dedication monuments became fair game to builders.

[46] Mawer, *Christianity*, C7.Gl.3. Mawer rejects a Christian connection on the basis of the discrepancy between the bottle's date and the Christian usage of the symbol.

[47] Mawer, *Christianity*, B6.Po.13.

[48] Mawer, *Christianity*, C8.Po.24.

[49] Mawer, *Christianity*, C2.Si.1.

[50] Mawer, *Christianity*, D3.Un.2.

[51] Mawer, *Christianity*, D3Je.2

VA|SI|ND|EO (*Iustine vivas in deo*), a common early Christian for-
mula.[52] A bronze medallion from Richborough has a possible Christian connection. This fragmentary medallion (fourth century) seems
to represent Magnentius in bust, beardless, bare-headed, holding a
chi-rho in front of his face.[53]

Fish and fisherman were widely used Christian symbols since, *inter
alia*, Clement of Alexandria recommended fish as acceptable decorations for Christian jewelry to suggest Christ as the fisher of souls
or the apostles as fishers of men (*Paed.* 3.59.2; *Matthew* 4.19). The
imagery also appears in pagan iconography: fishing Cupids elicit
prosperity or the joys of Paradise, and fish evoke the journey of the
soul to the Isles of the Blessed. As Christian icons, fish were often
found with anchors or palm trees.[54] Glass items and rings with fish
from military zones cannot be positively identified as Christian. A
glass fragment from Caerleon shows a palm branch and a fish facing
left, date unknown.[55] Cup fragments from Chesters[56] and Coventina's
Well[57] show swimming fish. A fish appears on a cup from Corbridge.[58]
A second century red jasper from Caerleon shows fisherman with
three fish.[59] A silver ring from Chester (second/third century) was
set with a pale carnelian stone engraved with a fish. The fish could
be a Christian or pagan symbol, evoking the Isles of the Blessed.[60]

Certain epigraphic formulae using the present subjunctive "vivas,"
inscribed on rings or other implements, may suggest Christianity.
A gold ring from Brancaster is inscribed *Vivas in deo*.[61] From Corbridge
several items suggest Christian influence: a silver beaker inscribed
Desideri Vivas; a bone plaque inscribed *S(o)ror ave | Vivas | in | Deo*.[62]
A bone tablet from Richborough reads *Vivas*, possibly but not certainly Christian.[63]

---

[52] Mawer, *Christianity*, D3.Br.3.
[53] Mawer, *Christianity*, F1.Br.6.
[54] Mawer, *Christianity*, 72, 77. Compare also the Christian acrostic IXTHUS (Iesus
Christos THeou Uios Soteros), which spells out a Greek word for "fish:" Leitzmann,
History, 2.106–7.
[55] Mawer, *Christianity*, C6.Gl.1.
[56] Mawer, *Christianity*, C6.Gl.2.
[57] Mawer, *Christianity*, C6.Gl.5.
[58] Mawer, *Christianity*, C6.Gl.4.
[59] Mawer, *Christianity*, D3.Ge.2.
[60] Mawer, *Christianity*, D3.Si.3.
[61] Mawer, *Christianity*, D3.Go.2.
[62] M.J. Green, *Military Areas*, 57, #17–18.
[63] Mawer, *Christianity*, E2.Bo.1.

Gildas tells us that at least three Christians, connected with the army in Britain, were martyred under Diocletian's persecutions (*De Excidio Britanniae* 10): *sanctum Albanum Verolamiensem . . . Aaron et Iulium legionis urbis*. The date is far from certain (Gildas admits his conjecture: *ut conicimus*), and some have tried to push that martyrdom to AD 209,[64] though Decius' persecutions (AD 250s) may be more likely.[65] St. Alban is, *per se*, significant because his cult extended broadly at an early date. Constantius (ca. 480) did not detail Alban's life, assuming his readers knew the story (Constantius *Vita Germani*), and a number of post-Roman local German saints bore similar names. Since feast days overlapped, some of the older sites (Albansberg, Mainz) may honor the British martyr.[66] The martyr's grave at Verulamium was honored without interruption to Augustine's day (Bede, *HE*, 1.7). Alban's martyrdom, at the very least, attests Christianity in the Romano-British army by the third century.

Christianity in Britain

Tertullian (ca. AD 200) claimed that Christianity spread quickly and widely, reaching even beyond Romanized Britain: *Britannorum inaccessa Romanis loca Christo vero subdita* (*adversus Judaeos* vii). Origen (ca. AD 240) argued that Christianity unified the Britons: *quando enim terra Britanniae ante adventum Christi in unius dei consensit religionem?* (*Homily iv in Ezek. Hieron. interpr.*). Despite patristic exaggeration, Christianity did strengthen the late Roman state, aiding in the preservation of *Romanitas*, its benefits extending to the British provinces.[67] Christianity is only implied in Britain during the early years, namely St. Albans' martyrdom at Verulamium, and the third century provides little evidence beyond the ROTAS SATOR square found at

---

[64] Morris, "Date of St. Alban," 1–8.

[65] Williams, *Christianity in Early Britain*, 103–109; Thomas, *Christianity in Roman Britain*, 48–50; G.R. Stephens, "Martyrdom of St. Alban," 20.

[66] Thomas, *Christianity in Roman Britain*, 49.

[67] M. Jones, *End of Roman Britain*, 174. Christianity was a double-edged sword. On the one hand, the Church provided a new intellectual vitality to a stagnant civilization. Yet, manpower and resources were drawn away from the state and into the church; Christian apocalyptic expectations increased instability; the official church violently tried to eradicate Christian heresies and non-Christian practices; allegiance was subtly undermined through alternative focuses of loyalty, e.g., Augustine's *de civitate dei*: Jones, 175–176.

Cirencester.[68] Christianity was not a grass roots movement in our province.[69]

Official Christianity came to Britain by the fourth century: three British bishops from York, London, and Lincoln (or Colchester) attended the Council of Arles in 314 (Eusebius, *Hist. Eccles*, x.5.21), and the Council of Rimini in AD 359 (Sulpicius Severus, *Chronica*, II.41). Development and organization in Britain was consistent with other western provinces.[70] However, whereas as other regions engaged in large-scale Christian inspired building programs (e.g., Aquileia and Trier: Athenasius, *Apologia ad Constantium imperatorem* 15), no equivalents have been found in Britain. In fact, the small urban church at Silchester could accommodate a congregation of only about fifty,[71] and a small church at Verulamium marked the site of St. Albans' grave.[72] Continental interest in the British church remained strong, as implied by the embassy of Victricius of Rouen to Britain in 394/5 to settle ecclesiastical disputes (*De Laude Sanctorum* 1.1).

Some argue for an uninterrupted tradition of British Christianity, Roman in origin, organization, and creed.[73] Others maintain that the

---

[68] The ROTAS SATOR square (*RIB* 2447.20), found etched on the painted wall of a house at Corinium, reads: ROTAS/OPERA/TENET/AREPO/SATOR, "The sower Arepo holds the wheels carefully." The words can be rearranged to form a cross reading "PATER NOSTER," with the letters "A" and "O" flanking each beam of the cross. This cryptogram also appears at Dura (before AD 256) and Pompeii (before AD 79). The Corinium rebus has been tentatively dated to the third or late second century: Fishwick, "ROTAS SATOR," 39–53; Liversidge, *Britain*, 455–6. See also Mawer, *Christianity*, C8.Po.21, for the Cirencester word square and a second example of a "ROTAS SATOR" graffito from Manchester, late second century. These items may not be Christian since "Pater Noster" was not an exclusively Christian formula and not used commonly until later. Nor was the cross suggested by the anagram an acknowledged Christian emblem until the late Roman and Byzantine periods.
[69] Frend, "Christianization of Roman Britain," 38.
[70] Frend, "Romano-British Christianity," 5.
[71] Radford, "Christian Origins;" Boon, *Silchester*, 173–184; Frere, "Silchester Church."
[72] Frere, *Verulamium*, 24. It seems certain that a martyrium to Alban existed in the fifth century, and that shrine may now be covered by the modern town's Abbey. During excavations in 1963/4, archaeologists found the traces of a small apsed building which was consistent in form with martyria: Anthony, "Verulum Hills Field," 49–50. No grave survived, nor is the building's function known. It may have been a chapel or a mausoleum (Frere, 24).
Other intra-mural congregational churches may have stood at Caerwent (the evidence is inconclusive), Canterbury (possibly in continuous use down to Augustine's visit), Colchester, Exeter, Lincoln, Richborough: Thomas, *Christianity in Britain*, 166–170.
[73] Toynbee, "Christianity," 24.

Christian church failed to survive in recognizable form in southern (the most Romanized) Britain.[74] In Gaul (370's-380's), Martin, an ex-soldier from Pannonia, set up a mission in the ruins of a villa outside Tours, whence he directed a tireless anti-pagan campaign in the countryside "where Christianity had hardly before penetrated" (Sulpicius Severus 13.7). Martin effected "miraculous cures," he convinced non-Christians that the Christian god was more powerful, and he occasionally used brute force to convert skeptics.[75] As Christianity spread into rural Gaul and Spain, cults of martyrs and their relics also gained momentum: Paulinus of Nola attested to the growing popularity of a local martyr's shrine in northern Spain, since he and his wife buried their infant son there (*Carmen*, 31.605–614).

The efforts of Martin and others secured Christianity in the Gallic countryside, but they had no imitators in Britain. Ninian's mission among the southern Picts in the 390's failed to establish a long-term center (Bede, *HE*, 3.4). Hence, Christianity failed to penetrate rural Britain where it could attract Celtic worshippers. Romano-Celtic healing shrines continued to hold loyalties which elsewhere were transferred to cults of Saints, Martyrs and relics.[76] The British Church failed because it neglected to proselytize. Christianity was an urban religion, it required a population center for its survival, and these centers often took the form of estate villas (n.b. Martin), as at Chedworth, Hinton St. Mary, Lullingstone, Mildenhall where Christian remains date to the fourth/fifth centuries.[77] As villas fell into disrepair, Christian influence waned. It should also be noted that Patrick's missionary efforts were not to Roman Britain; instead, he went outside Roman hegemony to Ireland.[78]

---

[74] Causes for the failure of Christian survival include a language barrier (Latin remained the official language of Christianity in the west for centuries), deep-seated antagonism between British and English, non-coincidence of individual Christian states, and the refusal of the British Church to evangelize and proselytize the Anglo-Saxons (Bede, *HE*, 2.2, 5.33): Thomas, *Christianity in Roman Britain*, 353.

[75] Rouselle, "Sanctuaire au thaumaturge."

[76] Frend, "Romano-British Christianity," 10.

[77] Frend, "Religion in Roman Britain," 7; Painter, "Villas and Christianity," 166.

[78] Patrick, it will be remembered, was born into a Christian family ca. AD 410 (his father was a deacon, his grandfather a presbyter): Patrick, *Confessio* 1, *Epistula* 10. Irish pirates captured a teenage Patrick in a raid, but the youth escaped, studied perhaps at Rouen under Victricius, then was consecrated bishop. The Christian communities in Ireland were already thriving. See further, L. Bieler, "St. Patrick."

Even more telling is the failure of British Christians to convert the Saxons.[79] British Christianity, as we have seen above, did not supplant more traditional styles of religion.[80] The Christian question remains key in determining the extent of Romanization and British loyalty to Rome, if not politically and diplomatically, then at least culturally and socially.

The failure of Christianity in the Romanized portions of Britain is evident in Augustine's mission to the island in AD 597, when Pope Gregory, knowing little about the British kingdoms or their people, sent Augustine of Canterbury to convert the Anglo-Saxons (Bede, *Historia Ecclesiastica gentis Anglorum* 1.29): The priest was sent to uphold Rome's authority against the proselytism of the Celtic church. Augustine found no parish organization, no ascetic colonies, in other words, Augustine's mission began essentially from scratch.[81] Vague traces remained: Aethelbert's subjects remembered a St. Sixtus,[82] ruined churches could be restored to Christian use (Bede, *HE*, 1.26), and St. Alban's shrine still enjoyed uninterrupted veneration (Bede, *HE*, 1.7). Although Christian sees in the seventh century arose on or near old Roman *civitates* (which had served as sees in the fourth century), these sites were, for the most part, unoccupied in the seventh century. Many of these *civitates* were geographically outside Anglo-Saxon influence, but no Christian activity is positively attested for fifth and sixth centuries.[83] It is likely that no conscious plan to re-establish old sees existed, but the geographic centrality and importance of the sites was evident. The old *civitates* retained potential economic and political importance. The fourth century sees perhaps served in the continuous practice of Christianity through post-Roman Britain. Nonetheless, the Medieval English Church was not a Celtic creation, instead it reflects Augustine's efforts to establish a Christian Church in England on the Mediterranean, not Celtic model.[84]

---

[79] M. Jones, *End of Roman Britain*, 177. In the west, for the most part free of Anglo-Saxon dominance, monastic Christianity dominated. Jones argues that Christianity remained a fringe religion in Britain, and this fact implies the weakness of Romanization, intimately interwoven into the Christian church in the fourth and fifth centuries. Christianity may have been confined to the urban, noble, Latin-speaking circles: Painter, "Villas and Christianity."

[80] Henig, *Religion*, 230.

[81] Frend, "Ecclesia Britannica," 129–144.

[82] Ewald and Hartmann, *Gregorii I Pape Registrum Epistolarum*, 11.64.

[83] Bassett, "Churches in Wrocester," 228–230.

[84] Frend, "Romano-British Christianity," 11.

Christianity failed to take root, while Celtic healing cults flourished. The popularity of cults at Uley, Nettleton, Bath, Carrawburgh, and Lydney (*et alia*) distracted worshippers' loyalties from cults of saints and saints' relics (similarly, healing and miracle cults) which grew, expanded, and flourished in continental centers because of the evangelism of Gallic and Italic churches, a factor utterly absent from British sees.

CONCLUSIONS

This discussion of military cults has dealt with a large number of cults observed over a significant span of time and geography. Some cults enjoyed greater popularity with officers, others with enlisted men. Some appealed to legionaries, others to auxiliaries. Roman citizens worshipped local gods, and Romanized Celts conflated their own deities with Roman divinities.

Such a collection of material may raise more questions than it answers, and it would be difficult, if not impossible, to bring such a study to a final conclusion. However, trends have emerged and some significant questions remain. We shall first address the larger patterns of worship, then we shall turn, briefly, to questions of spirituality.

Three major patterns have emerged. First, votives are concentrated temporally and geographically. Second, trends regarding the social status of dedicants have been detected: some cults were more popular among the enlisted men, others appear to have been exclusive to the officers. Third, this collection demonstrates how the Romans assimilated native cults, a process which was not entirely mutual.

Temporal Patterns

It quickly becomes clear that some cults were favored at certain times. First, it should be noted that inscriptions on stone were prevalent from the beginning of the Roman occupation until about the mid-third century. Dedications in stone fell off dramatically in the late third century. Two factors might explain this phenomenon, one economic, the other psychological. Economic instability characterized the third century crisis, resulting in less disposable income to devote towards ethereal and spiritual concerns.[1] Although we should expect our ancient worshippers to make every effort to gain the goodwill of the gods in such turbulent times, Roman and Celtic religions were,

---

[1] Sauer, *End of Paganism*, 10.

to be sure, practical matters, and it has been noted in the discussions of individual cults that small votive offering (coins, pipe-clay figurines, *et alia*) often date to later antiquity. Furthermore, psychological shifts occurred in the late third century population. Stone altars were meant to be lasting (eternal) memorials, yet the events of the late third century showed that some stone votives could have a very short life: some pieces were destroyed, others were recycled as building material. Finally, one of the religious trends of late antiquity was a shift from public religion to private. Stone altars were public displays which, possibly, had less religious force than before.

Our categories of religion include cults from Rome, the Eastern Mediterranean (Eastern), and the north-western provinces (Celtic and Germanic). From each of these categories, some rites are clearly public and political, others are private. Some are a little of both. Roman cults, as we have seen, blended political and private elements. The emperor, worshipped in Britain from Claudius to Valerian and Gallienus, may have been thought to have real power to hear and grant prayers. It is interesting to note that emperors are attested epigraphically with a concentration in the Severan Dynasty: the troops and officers in Britain felt obligated to demonstrate their loyalty to Severus after the civil wars of the 190's. Jupiter Optimus Maximus, whose temporal range extended from the first through fourth/fifth centuries in Roman Britain was not only the guarantor of Rome's strength, he was also a personal savior. The cult of the *genius* (especially the *genius loci*), which seems to be a Roman interpretation of unknown and unnamed local (presumably Celtic) deities, correlates to the importation of fresh troops to the island and troop transfers within the island.

A clearer temporal pattern emerges for the Eastern cults, peaking in Britain, as elsewhere, during the Severan dynasty. Dedications to Jupiter Dolichenus were made as early as the reign of Antoninus Pius (404, 407, 408). Mithras is attested epigraphically in Britain no earlier than the beginning of the reign of Septimius Severus (428, 430) and no later than the early fourth century (416). Most Eastern evidence dates to the Severan dynasty (Dolichenus: 394–96, 405), and most of these cults were observed in Britain because the Severi favored them (Dea Caelestis, Isis, Serapis).

Dating is more difficult for Celtic cults, but the same temporal pattern manifests itself. Celts who worshipped local gods tended to preserve their own and their gods' anonymity. Names, dates, and official connections appear with greater regularity on monuments dedicated by Romans and Romanized natives who took credit, publicly, for their religion and who showed fealty, publicly, to the Roman central administration. The Celtic attitude was different. Celts tended to withhold vital statistics, exacerbating the problems of dating. The worship of Coventina does not seem to be restricted temporally, with the earliest evidence from AD 140 (452), and the latest datable to the third/fourth centuries (453). The same holds true for Cocidius, who is represented as early as the reign of Hadrian (587, 592, 594, 596–98) and as late as the fourth century (583, 588, 591). It has been noted, however, that local Celtic religions, especially healing and spring cults, enjoyed a revival in late antiquity (fourth century: Mars Nodens, Mercury at Uley, *inter alia*) while the rest of the empire converted to Christianity. Christianity in Britain was unique in its lack of proselytism and the establishment of cults of saints and their relics which served as healing cults in continental Europe. British Christianity was, likewise, strongly tied to urban centers and grand villas which could not maintain their influence over a largely rural population in the ensuing barbarian threats of the fifth century.

The great majority of the dedications in stone are datable to the early-mid third century (especially the Severan dynasty and Gordian III) during a reasonably peaceful—as regards Britain—era, a phenomenon observable empire-wide. However, archaeology and small votives suggest the continuing relevance and vitality of both Roman and Celtic cults (though not Eastern). Unlike other provinces in the Roman empire, the ethnic make-up of the civilian population was probably largely Romano-Celtic. Furthermore, the ethnic make-up of the army was probably similarly homogenous, especially as the standing army was kept up to strength by increasing reliance on local recruits. By the third and fourth centuries, Easterners, though not completely unknown, were probably a rarity in Roman Britain. Roman and Celtic religious practices were sufficiently similar, and sufficiently melded over the centuries, that the mix was a happy one. Eastern rites were significantly foreign in tone and practice to relegate Isis, Dolichenus, Mithras, and other "curiosity" mystery gods to fringe worship. The one remarkable exception is the resurgence of Bacchus' popularity in the late third century especially at London.

Geographical Patterns

As one might expect, the vast majority of military dedications have been found where the Roman army was concentrated, that is, from the forts along Hadrian's Wall.[2] There is no particular geographic concentration of votives to the state cult. Six dedications to military *genii* come from Chester (25–30). Series of altars to Jupiter Optimus Maximus have been unearthed at several auxiliary forts in the north of England, including Maryport (121–143), where three dedications to Victoria (95–97) were also discovered, Old Carlisle (144–149), Housesteads (170–178), Chesterholm (179–183), Birdoswald (185–207, where the Roman Mars was also popular), and Castlesteads (208–214). Most of these altars represent the annual renewal of the *vota*, oaths of loyalty to the emperor. It is quite likely that similar altars were dedicated at other forts throughout Roman Britain, but simply did not survive for various reasons: weathering, reuse as building stones, etc. Most dedications to Minerva have been recovered from sites along or near Hadrian's Wall, but three have been found at High Rochester (234–236). Mars was especially popular at Housesteads under his Roman (268–273), Celtic (587–589; cf. 577) and Germanic veneers (695, 696). Dedications to Neptune, the Nymphs, and Oceanus are found primarily in well-watered areas (Nymphs: 338–344), or coastal regions (Neptune: 330–332; Oceanus: 346). Silvanus was found in the north-eastern part of England in well-wooded areas with good hunting (354–367) and in Roman Scotland (368–371).

Dedications to Eastern gods generally coincide with sites where Eastern units were stationed. For example, the *cohors I Hamiorum* worshipped the Dea Hammia (385) and Dea Syria (387–388) at Carvoran. The worship of Dolichenus, found primarily along the Hadrianic *limes*, coincides with British iron-ore deposits in Wales and Co. Durham (393, 399–400) and iron-working stations at Corbridge (401). Votives to Mithras have been found primarily where temples to him have been constructed: London, Caernarvon, Rudchester, Carrawburgh, and Housesteads. Mithras is also represented at each of the legionary centers, but evidence suggests that a temple may have existed only

---

[2] The concentration of votives in the north is, in part, a factor of geology. In the southern areas, there were few convenient sources of stone suitable for inscribed altars, as a result of which numerous civilian votives in the south had been made on bronze: E. Birley, "Deities," 103.

at the York fort (*MMM* II, 270; *CIMRM* no. 831). It is interesting that, in Britain, Mithras and Jupiter Dolichenus are not once represented at the same site (contrast their shared temple at Dura).

The worship of Celtic deities tended to be localized around a cult center: e.g., Antenociticus at Benwell (535–537), Coventina at her well at Carrawburgh (440–453), Mars Nodens at Lydney (611–614), Sulis Minerva at Aquae Sulis (Bath, 526–533), Vinotonus at Bowes (686–691). The cults of the horned warrior gods enjoyed a slightly wider distribution but were still restricted to the region of Hadrian's Wall. Dedications to Cocidius, concentrated at Bewcastle, are more evenly distributed than those to other horned gods. A *fanum Belatucadri* is not known, but votives to this god are concentrated in the northwest of England (Cumberland, Westmorland) and do not overlap Cocidius' centers. Mogons was worshipped in Cumbria, Durham, and Northumberland. There seems to have been a *fanum Veteris* at Magnis (Carvoran) whence nearly a quarter of the votives were recovered, but he is also represented in Durham, Yorkshire, and Northumberland, though not in Westmorland.

Most military dedications have been found along Hadrian's Wall and in legionary fortresses. There seems to have been little concentration of Roman gods, except where it might have been appropriate for personal needs (as with Silvanus in hunting regions). Celtic cults show the most localization, with a god's worship concentrated around his cult center, but Eastern cults (Mithras and Jupiter Dolichenus) were also concentrated around centers of worship.

Legionary vs. Auxiliary

Most of the religious material from the military zone was found in auxiliary contexts. Legionary evidence is limited. An examination of the dedications from the legionary sites will demonstrate to what extent the Roman army adapted local religious customs on an official level (by the time the Romans got to Britain, few legionaries would have been Italian). An examination of dedications made by auxiliary cohorts will illustrate to what degree non-Italian soldiers practiced religious syncretism.[3]

---

[3] For religion of the auxiliary troops, see Haynes, "Romanisation of Religion," 141–157.

The gods of each of the three legions are primarily Roman. Yet soldiers and officers of each legion also cultivated Eastern gods and Romanized Celtic gods. Soldiers from the second legion corporately worshipped the Concord of their legion (48), Augustan Discipline (52), *Fortuna* (84), Jupiter Optimus Maximus (150, 171, 172), Silvanus (362), Mars Camulus (467), the *Matres* (514), and Cocidius (592, 598). Centurions of the *legio II* cultivated the *Genius Terrae Britanniae* (46), and Sulis Minerva (529). A *primus pilus* claimed responsibility for a dedication to the *numina Augustorum* and *Genius loci* (24). Dolichenus (393, 404) and Mithras (415) received attention from this legion. Centurions of the second legion commanded auxiliary cohorts which erected dedications to Jupiter Optimus Maximus (153, 162, 191).

Members of the *legio VI Victrix* made corporate dedications to *Fortuna* (84), Jupiter Optimus Maximus (158), Mars Ultor (262), Mercury (326), the Nymphs (340, 344), Oceanus (346), Sol Invictus (421), and Cocidius (594, 597). Officers, primarily centurions, from this legion were responsible for inscribed monuments to the *genius loci* (38), *Fortuna populi Romani* (76), *Fortuna Conservatrix* (87), Hercules (308), Silvanus (343), Dolichenus (401), Mithras (426), Apollo Maponus (460, 463, 461: *praefectus castrorum*; 462: *tribunus*).

Members of the *legio XX Valeria Victrix* made corporate dedications to Jupiter Optimus Maximus (158), the Nymphs and fountains (338), and Cocidius (593). Legionary centurions oversaw dedications to Fortuna (79), Jupiter Optimus Maximus (222), Diana Regina (300), Silvanus (368), Dolichenus (407), and Antenociticus (535). Other officers responsible for dedicated altars include a *tribunus militum* (*genius loci*: 39; Jupiter Optimus Maximus: 110), and a *princeps legionis* (Jupiter Optimus Maximus Tanarus: 534). Auxiliary cohorts erected altars to *Victoria* (105) and the *Matres Alatervae* and *Campestres* (512) under the auspices of centurion commanders from the twentieth legion.

Legions combined efforts for some corporate dedications: the legionary Concord (48: legions II and XX; 49: legions VI and XX), to Fortuna (79: legions II, VI, and XX; 84: legions II and VI).

The legions, it would seem, largely restricted themselves to gods of the state religion. The surviving evidence suggests that the legions cultivated Celtic and Germanic cults which were Roman in form and appealed to Romanized worshippers (Antenociticus, Cocidius, Maponus). Indicated, perhaps, are differences of religious attitudes. It may simply be that soldiers worshipped the gods he was likely to know from his homeland or those he was advised to worship.

From Roman Britain, a few auxiliary dedicators claimed the honor of Roman or Latin citizenship on their stone altars. The gods worshipped in this category are strictly Roman: Disciplina Augusta (53, 56), *Victoria Augusta* (96), Jupiter Optimus Maximus (156, 210, 211, 212), Minerva (240), Mars Militaris (254), Asclepius and Salus (287), and Neptune (337), It was appropriate, perhaps, for auxiliary troops to claim the honor of citizenship while worshiping the gods of the *sacra Romana* as, possibly, a show of loyalty to Rome and worthiness of calling themselves *cives Romani* or *Latini*.

The auxiliary soldiers recruited from throughout the empire worshipped the entire array of gods (a complete catalogue would here be tedious; see the appendix of garrisons for full cross references to the catalogue of inscriptions). A few words should suffice. The state cult was homogenous—especially Jupiter Optimus Maximus and the *numina Aug.*—since all soldiers from all over the empire observed the rites called for in the festival calendars.

Analysis of the origins of auxiliary troops and their gods shows that soldiers tended to worship the gods of their homelands. One must keep in mind that, as these units were sent to Britain, their members would have been born in the tribe or country of the unit's origin. However, as certain units continued to serve in our province over several generations, replacements may have been recruited from the local population—a fourth century unit was more ethnically Romano-British than its first or second century forebears recruited from continental *provinciae*. However, it is reasonable to assume that, over the years, a god might become the traditional patron for a certain unit. The *cohors I Hamiorum* and the worship of the Syrian goddesses at Carvoran has already been mentioned. Auxiliaries originally from both Lower Germany (Batavi: 427, 428) and from Spain (Vardulli: 422) worshipped Mithras.

Germans individuals (443, 444, 450) and German auxiliaries (*cohors I Batavorum*: 452, 453; *cohors I Cubernorum*: 442; *cohors I Frixiavonum*: 441) cultivated the local goddess Coventina on Hadrian's Wall, as did an African individual (451). Members of units from Spain (*ala II Asturum*: 479; *cohors I Vardullorum*: 496), Gallia Belgica (*cohors I Tungrorum*: 501), and Germans (*vexillatio Germanorum*: 487) made dedication to the *Matres*. Cocidius received votives from Gallic auxiliaries (*cohors I Nervana*: 578; *praefectus cohortis II Nerviorum*: 590; *praefectus cohortis I Tungrorum*: 588) as well as Dacians (*cohors I Aelia Dacorum*: 591) and Germans (*centurio cohortis I Batavorum*: 596). Thracians offered dedications to Vinotonus (686–688). Auxiliaries from Gallia Belgica (Tungri) dedicated altars to the Germanic Hercules Magusanus (693), Ricambeda (698), and Viradecthis (700).

Officers vs. Enlisted Men

Numerous votives were erected by officers, who had the financial means to do so. Many of these votives were erected by tribunes or prefects on behalf of their units, as has been seen frequently in the case of the annual *vota* to Jupiter Optimus Maximus. Many private cults especially popular among the officers included Jupiter Dolichenus, Mithras, Cocidius, Maponus. Perhaps there was a property or class qualification, since there is absolutely no evidence that the enlisted men ever engaged in such cults in Roman Britain (continental evidence suggests that Mithraism was open to wealthier enlisted men and middle range bureaucrats). The cult accoutrements, especially from the temples of Mithras, are elaborate and exquisite, suggesting that wealthy patrons supported these temples. Statuary attached to the cults of Cocidius and Mogons is of much higher quality than has been found in association with the cults to Belatucadrus and Veteris, for example.

Only a few examples represent enlisted men. Votives made by *milites* include an altar to Jupiter Optimus Maximus dedicated by the *milites* of *legio II Augusta* (171); an altar to Jupiter Optimus Maximus with Cocidius and the *genius loci* erected by soldiers of the second legion (172); two altars to Cocidius erected by the *milites legionis II Augustae* (592, 598); an altar to Mercury set up by the *milites* of the sixth legion (326); an altar to the *Matres* dedicated by a *miles* of *legio VI* and a *gubernator* from the same legion (481); an altar to the *Matres* erected by *milites* from a vexillation of *legio VI* or II (514); an altar to Cocidius and the *genius praesidi* dedicated by Valerius, a *miles* from *legio VI* (587); an altar to Cocidius set up by the *milites* of *legio VI Victrix* (597); an altar to Cocidius erected by the *milites legionis XX V.V.* (593).

Auxiliary dedications include an altar to the Roman Mars dedicated by the commander and the soldiers of the *numerus Barcariorum* (250) at one time stationed on the river Tigris; an altar to Coventina set up by an auxiliary *miles* from a cohort whose name has since weathered off (447). Coventina also received altars from the Germans

Crotus (443, 450) and Maduhus (444). Other auxiliary dedications made by soldiers include an altar to the *Matres* dedicated by a *miles* called Quartus (499), perhaps a German; an altar to all the gods and goddesses dedicated by Frumentius, a *miles* belonging to the *cohors II Tungrorum* originally raised in Gallia Belgica (383); an altar to Ricambeda dedicated by Vellaus who fought in the *cohors II Tungrorum* (698); and an altar dedicated to Viradecthis by a man from the Condrusi who was fighting with the *cohors II Tungrorum* (700). The German Virilis worshipped Cocidius (585). The Germans Durio, Ramio, Trupo, and Lurio set up an altar in honor of Maponus (465). Congenniccus (a Celt?) worshipped Brigantia (573), as did M. Cocceius Nigrinus (574). Belatucadrus' worshippers, who never indicated their units (if we can assume that they were soldiers) and rarely indicated their names, include Baculo (543), Audagus (544), Julius Civilis (549), Aurelius Nicanor (558), and Lunaris (559). Veteris' worshippers, likewise, rarely indicated unit, and many of their names, seem to have been Celtic (non-Roman): Duihno (631), Vitalis (632), Mitius (642), Uccus (650), Aspuanis (653), Senaculus (660), Senilis (662), and Necalames (670–672). Men with Latin-sounding names who worshipped Veteris included Primulus Volusianus (627), Tertulus (646), Aurelius Victor (656), and Julius Pastor the *imaginifer* from the *cohors II Delmaturum* from Dalmatia (673). Most of these dedications seem to have been made privately, as there would have been little need for the Roman government in Britain to call for votives to local tribal gods. All but a few dedications were made by a pair or group of soldiers, perhaps sharing expenses, as indicated above. The worship of Belatucadrus and Veteris seems to have been restricted to *humiliores*, perhaps including enlisted men, though dedicators to these gods rarely reveal their status.

Prosopography

That men of Roman origin (who revealed themselves as such by their *tria nomina*) worshipped Roman gods is by no means surprising. Nor is it alarming, given the syncretic and superstitious nature of Roman religion, that our Roman citizens worshipped local Celtic gods, as we have seen in the discussion of individual cults.

Peoples of other ethnic and "national" origins demonstrated similar religious cross-pollination, though there is a remarkable preference to worship familiar gods from one's cultural traditions. Greeks predominantly worshipped Roman (Nemesis: 329; Ocean and Tethys: 345; Silvanus: 369) and Eastern (Silvanus Pantheus: 363; Hercules Tyrius: 390; Dolichenus: 401; Arimans: 418; Sol: 432; Serapis: 436) gods. Greeks also cultivated the Celtic Sulis (526, 530, 531) and Britannia (576) as well as the mysterious Arecurius (539) who may very well not be Celtic at all. Sulis, it has been noted in chapter five, enjoyed political endorsement.

Africans, similarly, preferred Roman (Jupiter Optimus Maximus: 123, 129, 147, 195, 216, 223, 229; Mars: 280; Apollo: 295; Hercules Invictus: 311; Vulcan: 373) and Eastern (Dea Syria: 388; Dolichenus: 407; Anicetus: 425) gods. They did, however, worship the local nymph Coventina (451) and Mars Braciaca (605).

Germans, who like Africans comprised a significant minority in Britain, showed a tremendous preference for Celtic and Germanic cults (see above, pp. 208–209). Roman gods to attract Germanic attention include Fortuna (89), Apollo (294), and Hercules Invictus (307).

Men with Celtic names naturally worshipped gods of Celtic origin. They did not, however, neglect Roman or Eastern gods. Celts dedicated inscribed stone altars to the Roman Jupiter Optimus Maximus (185, 213, 224), Minerva (239), Mars and the *numina Aug.* (245), Mars (257, 266), Mars Victor (267), Sangtus (sic) Mars (279), Apollo (295), Diana (299), Regina (349), Romulus (350), and Silvanus (353, 354, 366). Dolichenus (407) and Mithras (423, 429) were the Eastern mystery gods who received Celtic attention.

In short, worshippers preferred to trust in familiar gods. Although Celts may have believed that a god's power was tied to the land or tribe, others trusted in the omnipotence of the gods of their fathers over space and time.

Military vs. Civilian Cult

The religion practiced by the Roman soldier can be expected in some degree to differ from the civilian cultic practices. Religion as practiced by the Roman soldier and the Romanized civilian in the south varied only a little. In terms of small personal votive objects, for example, the difference between military and civilian, north and south, is practically non-existent.[4] The state cult is well represented

---

[4] Green, *Civilian Areas*, 117.

in both spheres. Roman military units did, of course, make dedications to deities and abstractions not represented in the Romanized civilian sphere. These include dedications to the *genius legionis, genius centuriae, genius signi, genius praetorii, et alia.*

The largest difference between military and civilian cults can be discovered in areas where the civilian population was not highly Romanized. The cults of the horned warrior gods provide the clearest example. It has already been seen how the soldiers on Hadrian's Wall cultivated these local gods where the barbarian threats would be the greatest. The predominance of these same gods worshipped by the local civilians demonstrates their own resistance to the Roman presence.[5]

Mutual Assimilation

Most of the evidence with respect to the assimilation of cults shows a bias towards the Roman side. The literary tradition is purely Roman, until Celtic mythological accounts from the Celtic point of view were written down in the tenth century. However, there is evidence for some mutual assimilation of cults in Britain, a result of the deliberate policy of Romanizing the native Britons (especially during the governorship of Agricola: Tacitus *Agricola* 21). Positive Roman influence on native practices was limited to iconography and temples—which are known in Britain only after the Roman conquest and which were cast into a uniquely Romano-Celtic mold.[6] The representation of Celtic gods as a manifestation of the Romanization of Celtic cults has already been discussed (chapter 4). Before the Roman occupation of Britain, Celtic holy places, for the most part, were natural sacred sites: wooded areas, streams, hill tops, *inter alia.*[7] The Romans brought to Britain the idea that enclosed temples could demarcate a sacred site. As with the representation of Celtic gods, the temples in Britain took on a more typically Celtic appearance. The classical style of temple—columns, pediment, and

---

[5] Ross, *Celtic Britain*, 181–182.
[6] Green, "Iconography," 120.
[7] Suetonius Paulinus, for example, attacked the sacred groves at Anglesey (Tacitus *Annals* 14.30), and Boudicca's troops were tortured in the groves sacred to Andraste (Dio, 62.7).

high podium—and the Eastern basilical temples are infrequently represented in Britain.[8] More common is the Romano-Celtic temple type which seems to be based on Celtic architectural patterns, i.e., rectangular earthworks thought to have been sanctuaries, dating to the first century BC and found widely on the continent.[9] The pattern varies but often takes the form of a double rectangular box, with clerestory lighting and an outer portico enclosing the inner shrine which might be square, rectangular, polygonal, or circular. There is, however, no evidence that religious practices within a Romano-Celtic temple differed from those in a classical one.[10] In general, the worship of Celtic gods by Celtic Britons survived in a form separate from that of the Roman gods, as local civilian iconographic traditions imply.[11] This assumption is further supported by the fact that, during the Roman era, the locals continuously used their ancestral hill-fort sanctuaries, some of which were even rebuilt during Roman times according to Roman models.[12]

Celtic influence on Roman cultic practices was more comprehensive in that the Romans practiced a policy of religious toleration and syncretism to begin with, as long as the local cults were not exclusive (i.e., Christianity and Judaism) or secretive, thereby posing a threat to Rome, or "barbaric" in Roman eyes (i.e., human sacrifice). The most famous example of a Romanized Celtic cult is to be found in the cult of the local water nymph Sulis, who was assimilated to Minerva at Aquae Sulis (Bath). The Romans completely took over the local deity and made her their own. Her temple and baths are Roman in design, and her cult statue, of which only the head remains, is purely Roman. Other local cults were embraced by the Roman army, for example Cocidius, Antenociticus, Mogons, Maponus, Mars Nodens, and Coventina. Many of these cults were made acceptable to Roman state practices as these gods were included on dedications to the *numina Augustorum*: Mars Lenus or Ocelus (469); Mars Ocelus (618); Mars Rigonemetos (619); *Matres* (486, 502); Mogons (520); Sulis Minerva (529); Antenociticus (535); Ariaco (538); Belatucadrus (554); Bregans (570); Brigantia (571); Maponus (465); Vanauns (625);

---

[8] The temple of Sulis Minerva at Bath shows classical features as does a temple at Wroxeter.
[9] Scullard, *Outpost*, 160.
[10] Henig, *Religion*, 114.
[11] Ross, *Celtic Britain*, passim; Green, *Civilian Areas*, 117; Henig, *Religion*, 114.
[12] Webster, *Celtic Religion*, 140.

Garmangabis (692); Mars Thincsus and the Alaisiagae (695–697). Local deities were also invoked with the epithet *Augusta*, appropriately the god's powerful emblem, which was meant to imply a close connection between the deity and the imperial household: for example Coventina Augusta (449). Some local deities had been invoked for the welfare of the imperial household: for example Matunus (620).

What did the Soldier Believe?

Despite our separation, by nearly two millennia, from the men who served the emperor on the British frontier, it is possible to reconstruct, however tentatively, religious beliefs and expectations. Religion, a universal phenomenon, speaks to "mental, social, and spiritual needs."[13] That the same gods were worshipped in Britain by invaders and locals alike for four centuries, despite cultural and social pressures which helped usher in Christianity, suggests that these gods, in the eyes of their worshippers, wielded real power. Gods who lost their numinous quality were abandoned. Two categories will shed further light on the question of what soldiers believed. Dream inscriptions will elucidate positive spirituality. Recycled altars will suggest which gods seems no longer efficacious to their potential worshippers.

Dreams

That gods visit men and women through dreams and waking visions is an inherent characteristic of literature (e.g., Homer, *Iliad*, 1.62–7) and the religious experience, especially in conjunction with healing cults (e.g., Asclepius: Aristophanes, *Ploutos*, 654–747; Pausanias 2.27.1–3). The richest source of *ex visu* and *ex iussu* dedications comes from the East, concentrated in Egypt during the second and third centuries AD. Much of the Egyptian evidence stems from the blurred distinctions between prophecy, medicine and magic. Many of the monuments (from Egypt and elsewhere) were found in the contexts of healing cults. These recorded dreams imply an intense level of personal belief in the real powers of those gods who send dreams and visions. *Ex visu* and *ex iussu* dedications also point to the flexibility

---

[13] Sauer, *End of Paganism*, 9.

and continuing relevance of older cults and, furthermore, provide an effective means of spreading new cults without missionary fervor.[14]

From the military zone of Roman Britain, epigraphic evidence has produced an interesting array of gods who communicated directly with their worshippers. These gods were Roman: Fortuna Augusta (78), Fortuna Servatrix (66), and Nemesis (328); Eastern: Jupiter Dolichenus (393, 399, 401); and Celtic: the Nymphs (339), and Mars Condatis (607). These dedications underscore the vitality of Roman, Eastern, and Celtic religions. Dreams and divine commands, both in the east and in the west, derived from political expediency, connections to healing cults, divine retribution as a form of magic, and salvation.

Political expediency is suggested in an *ex visu* dedication to Fortuna Augusta on behalf of Hadrian's heir, L. Aelius Caesar (78). The prefect who received that dream probably hoped that this dream would be taken as proof of his loyalty, and that he would benefit accordingly. An *ex iussu* dedication which connects Brigantia to the cult of Dolichenus might suggest a Severan affiliation (401).

Most dream inscriptions, however, resonate with sincerity. Sincere communication between worshippers and their gods is suggested in the Dolichenus cult (399), on an *ex iussu* inscription dedicated *pro se et suis*. Nemesis came to a Romanized Celt *ex visu* (328). A woman, possibly a slave, appealed to Fortuna Servatrix *ex viso* (66).

Physical healing is indicated in the worship of Mars Condatis and the Nymphs, both associated with springs which, in Celtic lore, indicate the power to heal. The fact that the dedication to the Nymphs (339) takes the form of two hexameters is significant in regard to the perception of music as a healing agent. The metrical form of this inscription may suggest that our soldier consulted a professional dream interpreter, since poetry was the common medium used by those who deciphered visions and oracles.

Mars Condatis, a local healer god at Piercebridge, appeared to a Romanized Celt *ex iussu* (607). This piece is particularly interesting since the Latin reads "ex iussu," the same phrase read on an altar to Dolichenus at the same site (399). The formula is common in the Dolichenus cult but rare in Romano-Celtic epigraphy. It seems that the cult of Dolichenus, at least at Piercebridge, may have influenced the ritual of a native god.

---

[14] Lane Fox, *Christians and Pagans*, 165.

Recycling

Several dedications in stone from the military zone of Roman Britain were recycled in antiquity. These pieces were either recut and subsequently dedicated to different gods or were reused as building materials in late antique construction. The practice was not altogether uncommon in deliberate attempts to profane once sacred pieces which, for whatever reason, had lost their sacred nature.

Only a handful of pieces were rededicated; the sample is too small for meaningful conclusions. Silvanus benefited from the erasure of one altar possibly to Jupiter (352) and another to the imperial *numen* (359). Interestingly, Silvanus "Invictus" replaced the emperor who fell out of favor. One altar to the Celtic Cocidius was rededicated to Jupiter (196), while the Celtic Veteris replaced the Eastern Jupiter Dolichenus on another piece (397).

Nor can any useful trends be gleaned from the array of pieces which were recycled as building material. The gods are Roman, especially Jupiter (155, 170, 209), Neptune (330), and Silvanus (352), Eastern (Dolichenus: 402; Mithras: 417) and Celtic (*Matres*: 499, 506; Apollo Cunomaglus: 600; Veteris: 634). On the one hand, old altars provide a convenient source of hewn stone, and there may very well have been a statute of limitations on the sanctity of an object. However, very few altars were put to such use in antiquity (from Medieval times onwards, this practice was quite common), that one must wonder if these particular gods lost power at those particular sites. The recycling of Dolichenus and Mithras pieces seems reasonable in the light of Christian assumptions, and Jupiter would have been especially threatening to Christian sensibilities. Local healing cults (Cunomaglus) also threatened the spread of Christianity. Christians, nonetheless, provide too easy a scapegoat.

Roman Army Religion in Britain as a Model

The study of the Roman army cults in Britain may be useful as a model for other areas of the empire. Since a large army occupied the frontier in Britain, the finds have been rich, revealing much about many aspects of military life in the Roman empire, from camp construction to private religion.

Although evidence concerning military cult in Roman Britain

may appear abundant, only some small portion of the evidence has survived. One can never know if what we surmise is correct or merely conjecture. What remains, however, is a model for the study of life and cults in other areas of the Empire. Rome, in the guise of the Empire, was not an insular community, with ideas and cultures specific to its location and environment. Instead, the Roman Empire was a myriad of cultures, combining those aspects of Rome herself with the native ideas and superstitions of the frontiers. Although determining factors differ from province to province (i.e., Britain was less Romanized than the Danube provinces, and Greek culture strongly influenced the eastern provinces), Britain can serve as a model for other provinces according to which one can set up a framework within which to investigate larger questions concerning the Roman Empire.

PART TWO

CATALOGUE OF INSCRIPTIONS,
APPENDICES, AND BIBLIOGRAPHY

ANNOTATED CATALOGUE OF INSCRIPTIONS:
INTRODUCTION AND INDEX

The inscriptions in the catalogue are arranged by cults as shown in the index below. Within each section, inscriptions are arranged geographically, following the pattern established by *RIB*: London, southern Britain, Wales, Cheshire, Yorkshire, northern England, Hadrian's Wall (east to west), Scotland and the Antonine Wall (east to west), and milestones. Where inscriptions were discovered after 1954 (the cut-off date for inclusion in the *RIB*), the following notation is used. Those inscriptions included in the annual reports published in *JRS* are noted thus: *JRS.* followed by the year of the journal issue and the numbers (#) of the inscription in the report; e.g., catalogue 57 = *JRS*.1959 #6, published in the 1959 volume of *JRS*. Inscriptions published after 1969 appear in the annual volumes of *Britannia* and are noted as follows: *Britannia.* year of the journal issue, number of the inscription in the annual report: e.g., 12 = *Britannia*.1985, #11, first published in the 1985 issue of *Britannia*.

The commentary for individual inscriptions has been kept to the minimum. Each piece is briefly described, including significant iconography (i.e., animals, wheel-motifs, sacrificial implements), but not decorative moldings unless the monument is especially elaborate (thereby indicating great expense). The physical state of the stone, particularly if it has been deliberately destroyed in antiquity, is also pertinent. The find-sites have been included only if germane to the religious or military nature of the stones, e.g., pit burials indicate deliberate protection; camp ruins provide a clear military context. Details concerning rededications, desecration in antiquity, and recycling in antiquity have also been provided. Every attempt has been made to date each piece. The probable ethnic origins of dedicators are also offered, a moot point in the late empire. The bibliography has been limited to the primary catalogues: *CIL, ILS, RIB, CSIR*. For further bibliography and history, consult *RIB* or the various fascicles of *CSIR* (wherein many, but not all, monuments are cited).

Contents of the Catalogue of Inscriptions

Deified Abstractions

Graeco-Roman Deities

Celtic Deities Found Only in Britain

Germanic Deities

CATALOGUE

State Cults

Parilia

Bremenium (High Rochester)
1. *D(eae) R(omae) s(acrum)* | *dupl(icarii) n(umeri) Explor(atorum)* | *Bremen(iensium)* *aram* | *instituerunt* | *n(atali) eius c(urante) Caep(ione)* | *Charitino trib(uno)* | *v.s.l.m.* (*CIL* VII 1037, *addit.* 312; *ILS* 2631; *RIB* 1270).
   Statue base. Gordian?
   Caepio Charitinus: *PME* C34. Italian?

Armilustrium?

Cockermouth Castle, 1.6 km northwest of Derventio (Papcastle, Cumberland)
2. ---*in cuneum Frisionum Aballave]nsium [---*| *ex v(oto) p(osuit) (ante diem) XIIII* *[Kal(endas)]* | *et XIII Kal(endas) Nov(embres)* | *v.s.l.m.* | *[G]ordiano II e(t) Pompeiano* *co(n)[s(ulibus)]* (*CIL* VI 416; *RIB* 882).
   Altar fragment. Top, back, and portion of left-side chiseled off. Regular lettering. October 19–20, AD 241.

3. --- | *l]eg(at.) Aug(usti) in c[u]* | *neum Frision* | *um Aballav* | *ensium [Philip* | *p(iano-* *rum]] (ante diem) XIIII Kal(endas) et (ante diem) XIII Kal(endas)* | *Nov(embres)* *Gor(diano) II et Pompei(ano)* | *co(n)s(ulibus) et Attico et Pre[te]* | *xtato co(n)s(ulibus)* *v.s.l.m.* (*CIL* VII 415; *ILS* 2635; *RIB* 883).
   Altar fragment. Partially erased. Oct. 19–20, 241 and 242.
   Curiously, the stone attests two separate years.

Cult of the Standards

Banna (Birdoswald)
4. *Signis* | *et N(umini) Au[g(usti) coh(ors) I]* | *Aelia [---* (*CIL* VII 829; *RIB* 1904).
   Statue base. Neat lettering. Probably set up the *cohors I Aelia Dacorum*. Third/fourth century.

Numina Augustorum

Gwaenysgor, Flintshire
5. *Num(ini)* | *Aug(usti) Im* | *p(eratoris) Cae* | *s(aris) M A* | *ur(elio) S* | *evero Alex* | *and[r]o* *<A> Pi* | *o Fel(ice)* | *Aug(usti) T* | *rib(unicia) pot(estate)* | *[P]roco[s]* | *[---* (*JRS.*1957 #19).
   Milestone. AD 231–235.

Ty Coch, Pentir
6. *Num(ini) Aug(usti)* | *imp(erator) Caesar M.* | *Aurel(ius) Antoninus* | *Pius Fe[l]ix Aug(ustus) Arab(icus)* | *---] IX* (*CIL* VII 1164; *RIB* 2264).
Milestone. From Segontium (Caernarvon), 11.3km southwest Ty Coch. AD 212–217.

Eboracum (York)
7. *Numinib(us) Aug(ustorum) et deae Iovg[---|---] sius aedem pro parte di[---* (*CIL* VII 239; *RIB* 656; *CSIR* 1.3.2).
Fragmentary tablet. *Pelta* with rosettes on the left. No earlier than AD 161, the first pair of joint emperors (Marcus Aurelius and L. Verus).
The goddess was probably local.

Voreda (Old Penrith)
8. *[Num(inibus) A]ug(ustorum) vex(illatio)* | *[leg(ionis) X]X [Val(eriae)] Vic(tricis)* | *[---* (*RIB* 940).
Dedication slab. After 161 (#7).

Castra Exploratorum (Netherby)
9. *Imp(eratori) Caes(ari) M. Aurelio* | *Severo Alexandro Pio [F]el(ici) Aug(usto)* | *pont(ifici) maximo trib(unicia) pot(estate) co(n)s(uli) p(atri) p(atriae) coh(ors) I Ael(ia)* | *Hispanorum m(illiaria) eq(uitata) devota numini* | *maiestatique eius baselicam* | *equestrem exercitatoriam* | *iam pridem a solo coeptam* | *aedificavit consummavitque* | *sub cura Mari Valeriani leg(ati)* | *Aug(usti) pr(o) pr(aetore) instante M. Aurelio* | *Salvio trib(uno) coh(ortis) imp(eratore) d(omino) n(ostro)* | *Severo Alexandro Pio Fel(ice)* | *Aug(usto) co(n)s(ule)* (*CIL* VII 965; *ILS* 2619; *RIB* 978).
Dedication slab. AD 222.

Arbeia (South Shields)
10. *[---] sanct(a)e et Numini[bus* | *Aug(ustorum) (---)] Domitius Epictet[us ---| --- cum] commilitonibus templu[m restituit]* (*RIB* 1056).
Fragment of frieze. Found inside the fort. After AD 161 (#7).
The goddess may have been a deified abstraction or a local divinity.
The worshipper, probably a prefect of *cohors V Gallorum*, might have been Italian (*PME* I.329, #D.21, cf. *CIL* XIV 2886, Praeneste).

Habitancum (Risingham)
11. *Numini(bus)* | *Augustor(um)* | *coh(ors) IIII Gal(lorum)* | *eq(uitata)* | *fec(it)* (*CIL* VII 1001; *RIB* 1227; *CSIR* 1.1.215).
Dedication slab. A richly carved border surrounds the inscription; *peltae* appear on either side of it, relief knots below the *peltae*, masks above. To the left of the inscription, a winged Victory, framed by an arch, stands on a globe and holds her usual accoutrements, a wreath and a palm branch. A crane is etched below her. To the right of the inscription, Mars, fully armed, stands within an arch. A goose corresponds to Victory's crane. Both are Celtic war birds. Late second century.

Magnis (Carvoran)
12. *Deo M[---]* | *et Numinibu[s Aug(ustorum)]* | *Iul(ius) Pacatus e[t---]| et Pacutius C[---]* | *et V..VAL [---| ccus a solo [--- fec]|er(unt) v.s.* (*CIL* VII 755; *RIB* 1786).
Slab fragment. Uneven lettering. Mars?
Pacatus: Kajanto, *Cognomina*, 67, 261.

Blatobulgium (Birrens)

13. *et?] numin[ibus Aug(ustorum)? --- | ---]ente D [---] (Britannia.1992 #19).*
    Slab fragment. Found 5km. WSW of fort. Lettering is regular and square, typical of inscriptions of *cohors II Tungrorum* at Birrens (Hassall and Tomlin, *Britannia*.1992 #19, note 34). ca. 158?

Imperial Women: Julia Domna

Arbeia (South Shields)

14. *[---] | [ac c]astr(orum) [ac senat(us) ac] | [pa]triale pro pietate] | [a]c dev[otione] | [com]muni c[urante] | [G(aio) Iul(io) Marco] | l[eg(ato) Aug(usti) pr(o) pr(aetore)] | [coh(ors)] (V) Ga[ll(orum) pos(uit)] (Britannia.1985, #11).*
    Dedication slab. AD 213.
    C. Iulius Marcus: *PIR* IV.3, 234, #405.

Castra Exploratorum (Netherby)

15. *---] Iuliae Au[g(ustae)] | [M] matri Au[g(usti) | nostri M. Aur]|eli[i] Anton[ini] | et castr(orum) [et] | senatus et | patriae pro | [pietate ac] | devotione | [communi] | num(ini) eius | [curante G(aio) Iul(io)]| Marc[o] l[eg(ato) Aug(ustorum)] |pr(o) pr(aetore) coh(ors) [I] Ael(ia) | [Hisp(anorum) m(illiaria) eq(uitata)] | posuit (CIL VII 963; RIB 976).*
    Dedication slab. Found 4.8km south of fort. AD 213.

Habitancum (Risingham)

16. *[Imp(eratori) Caes(ari) di]vi Sept(imi) [Severi Pii Arabici Adi]abenic[i Parthici Maxi]mi Bri[tannici Maxi]mi filio di[vi Antonini Pii | Germanici] Sarmati[ci nepoti divi Anton]ini Pii pro[nepoti divi H]adriani a[bnep(oti) divi Traian]i Partichi et [divi Nervae adnep(oti)]| M. Aurelio] Anton[ino Pio Fel(ici) Aug(usto) Parth]ico Maxim[o Britannico Maximo Germanico Maximo] trib(unicia) potesta[te XVI imperatori II | patri pat]ri(a)e proconsuli pro [pietate ac dev]otione com[muni e]t Iul[iae Domnae Piae Fel(ici) Aug(ustae) Ma]tri August[i nostri item | castroru]m senatus [h]ac patri(a)e pro [pi]etate [h]ac d[evoti]one [communi curante / / / / / / / / / / leg(ato) Aug(ustorum) pr(o) pr(aetore) | coh(ors) I Van]gionum item Raeti Gae[sa]ti et Expl[oratores Habitancenses] posuerun[t d(evoti) n(umini) m(aiestati)q(ue) eorum (CIL VII 1002, addit., 311; RIB 1235).*
    Dedication. Found in the *principia.* AD 213.

Pons Aelius (Newcastle)

17. *Iulia[e Aug(ustae)] | NO[--- matri] | [imp(eratoris) M. Au]|reli Anto[nini ac] | cas[tr(orum) ac senat(us)] | ac pat[riae pro pietate] | ac dev[otione] | [curante G(aio) Iul(io) Marco] | leg(ato) Aug(usti) pr(o) [pr(aetore) coh(ors) (I) Ulpia] | Traiana C[ugernorum] | c(ivium) R(omanorum) [posuit] (Britannia.1980 #6).*
    Altar. AD 213.

Imperial Women: Julia Mamaea

Bremetenacum Veteranorum (Ribchester)

18. *---p]ro | [sa]l(ute) im[p(eratoris) Caes(aris) Al]ex[andri Aug(usti) N(ostri) et | Iul(iae) Mamaeae ma]t[r]is D(omini) N(ostri) et Castr(orum) su[b cura] | Val(eri) Crescentis Fuluiani leg(ati) eius pr(o) [pr(aetore) | T. Florid(ius) Natalis c(enturio)*

leg(ionis) praep(ositus) n(umeri) et regi[onis] | *templum a solo ex responsu [dei re]|sti-tuit et dedicavit d[e suo]* (*CIL* VII 222; *RIB* 587; *CCID* 581).

Dedication slab. Reused as flagstone in southeast area of the fort. AD 227/235.

The legion was possibly the sixth: A. Birley, *People*, 81.

Bremenium (High Rochester)
19. *Imp(eratori) Cae[s(ari) M(arco) Aur(elio) Seve]|ro Alex[andr]o P(io) F(elici) [Aug(usto)] ---* | *--- matr(i)]* | *i[mp(eratoris) Caes(aris) et ca]s(trorum) coh(ors) I F(ida) Vard(ullorum)* | *m(illiaria) S(everiana) A(lexandriana) ballis(tarium) a solo re[sti]t(uit)* | *sub c(ura) Cl(audi) Apellini le[g(ati)] Aug(ustorum)* | *instante Aur(elio) Quinto tr(ibuno)* (*CIL* VII 1046, *addit.* 312; *RIB* 1281).

Dedication slab. Found at the fort's center (*principia?*). Fractured and severely defaced. AD 222–235.

20. *matri --- Alex]andr[i felicis* | *for]tissimi Aug(usti) [nos|tri] et castror(um) senat[usque* |*---* (*CIL* VII 1047; *RIB* 1282).

Fragment of dedication slab. 222–235.

Julia Domna or Mamaea

Calleva Atrebatum (Silchester)
21. *Iuliae Aug(ustae)* | *matri se|natus et* | *castror(um)* | *M. Sabinius* | *Victor ob|* *[---* (*CIL* VII 7; *RIB* 68).

Dedication. Found west of north gate.

22. *Pro Salute* | *et Victoria* | *invicti imp(eratoris) Mar(ci)* | *Aur(eli) Sever(i) Ant|onini P(ii) F(elicis) Aug(usti) et Iul(iae)* | *Aug(ustae) matri(s) D(omini) N(ostri) et cas(tro-rum)* | *[---|---] Se(m)pr(oni-* (*CIL* VII 226; *RIB* 590).

Altar. Vine scroll on each side.

Caracalla was styled as Antoninus, but not as Severus. Severus Alexander was not normally styled Antoninus. Could refer to Elagabal.

Military Genii

Kingsholm
23. *Deo* | *Genio c(o)ho(rtis) cunc(tae)* | *Oriuendus* | *---VAV* (*RIB* 119).

Altar, badly damaged. E. Birley's reading ("Deities," 26). Before 66/70.

Isca (Caerleon)
24. *N.N(uminibus)* | *Augg(ustorum)* | *Genio leg(ionis)* | *II Aug(ustae)* || *in hono|rem [aquilae?]* |*---|---|---|---|---*| *p(rimus) p(ilus)* | *d(ono) d(edit)* || *d(e)d(icatum)* | *VIIII* | *Kal(endas) Octob(res)* | *P[e]r[e]gr(ino)* | *e[t Ae]m[i]l(iano)* | *co(n)s(ulibus)* | *cur(ante) Urso* | *actar(io)* | *[l]e[g(ionis) e]ius|[dem* (*CIL* VII 103, *addit.* 306; *RIB* 327).

Several fragments of a pilaster or door-jamb. Found in the *principia*. September 23, AD 244 (Augustus' birthday).

A legion with *Augusta* in its title would probably observe Augustus' birthday as its own, and would make such dedications to the eagle in honor of the day (Domaszewski, *Religion*, 77).

Deva (Chester)
25. *Genio | c(enturiae) (RIB* 446).
   Altar. A patera on the left side, a jug on the right.

26. *Genio | c(enturiae) A(ureli) Verin(i) | Iul(ius) Quin|tilianus (CIL* VII 165;
RIB 447).
   Altar.
   An Aurelius Verinus is attested at Birdoswald under Probus (AD 276–282):
#207; Kajanto, *Cognomina,* 254.

27. *Genio | sancto | centurie | Aelius | Claudian(us) | opt(io) v.s. (CIL* VII 166;
RIB 448).
   Altar. An axe and knife carved into the right side, jug and patera into
the left.

28. *Genio [leg(ionis) XX] | V.V. D[ecianae] | T. Vet[--- (RIB* 449).
   Door-jamb fragment, probably from the fortress' *principia.* Decius (AD
249–51).

29. *Genio signi[f(erorum)] | leg(ionis) XX V.V. | T. Fl(avius) Valerianus | collegis
d(ono) d(edit) (RIB* 451).
   Semi-circular white marble base to hold a *genius* statuette.
   A Flavius Valerianus *(cohors I milliaria Hemesenorum)* is attested in Moesia
Superior, AD 167 *(PME* I.382, #F.80; Kajanto, *Cognomina,* 157).

30. *Theois | tois tou ege|monikou prai|toriou Skrib(onios) | Demetrios (CIL* VII 62;
ILS 8861; *RIB* 662).
   Bronze plate, originally silver-plated.
   The dedicator (#345) may have been the same Demetrius, Plutarch's
interlocutor in *de defectu oraculorum* (AD 83–84), who had recently returned
from a trip to Britain where he had voyaged to the western islands of
Scotland on imperial instructions (Plutarch 419E).

Luguvalium (Carlisle)
31. *Geni[o cent]uria[e] | [c(enturia)] Bassi[li] Cresce[ntis]| don[o d]onavit (RIB* 944).
   Statuette, dressed in a toga, wears a mural crown and holds a cornu-
copia in his left hand, a patera in his right.
   P. Bassilius P. filius Crescens, *tribunus cohors Germanorum,* AD 218/22:
CIL XIV 160 *(PME* I.180, #B.17, Ostia).

Longovicium (Lanchester)
32. *Num(ini) Aug(usti) et | Gen(io) coh(ortis) I F(idae) | Vardullorum | c(ivium)
R(omanorum) eq(uitatae) mi(lliariae) sub An|tistio Aduen|to leg(ato) Aug(usti) pr(o)
p[r(aetore)] | F(lavius) Titianus trib(unus) | d(e) s(uo) d(edit) (CIL* VII 440; *RIB*
1083).
   Altar. Erected between AD 175 and November 27, 176, when Marcus
Aurelius made Commodus Augustus *(SHA M. Aur.* 27.5).
   Flavius Titianus: #289; *PME* I.381, #F.78. For homonyms: *CIL* II 4076
(governor of Africa, *praeses Hispaniae Citerioris),* 4118, VIII 7045.

33. *Genio praetori | Cl(audius) Epaphroditus | Claudianus | tribunus c(o)ho(rtis) |
I Ling(onum) v.l.p.m. (CIL* VII 432; *RIB* 1075).

Statue base; third century.

Claudius Epaphroditus: *PME* I.250, #C.140, A Greek name, possibly from an Italian family.

Bremenium (High Rochester)

34. *G(enio) d(omini) n(ostri) et | Signorum | coh(ortis) I Vardul[l(orum)] | et n(umeri) Explora | tor(um) Brem(eniensium) Gor(diani) | Egnat(ius) Lucili | anus leg(atus) Aug(usti) pr(o) pr(aetore) | curante Cassio | Sabiniano trib(uno)* (*CIL* VII 1030, addit., 312; *RIB* 1262).

Altar. From the strong room of the *principia*. AD 238–241.

For Cassius Sabinianus, *PME* I.231, #C.97.

35. *Genio et Signis | coh(ortis) I F(idae) Vardul(lorum) | c(ivium) R(omanorum) eq(uitatae) m(illiariae) | T. Licinius Valeri | anus [t]rib(unus)* (*CIL* VII 1031, addit., 312; *RIB* 1263; *CSIR* 1.1.188).

Altar, burnt, and split vertically; from the bath house. Mid-third century.

Licinius Valerianus, an Italian, related to Valerian: *PME* II.533, #L.21.

Condercum (Benwell)

36. *Matr(ibus) Tribus Campes[t]r[i]b(us) | et Genio alae prim(ae) Hispano | rum Asturum [--- | ---] Gordi[a]nae T(itus) [Fl.] | Agrippa praef(ectus) templum a sol(o) res | tituit* (*CIL* VII 510; *ILS* 4828; *RIB* 1334; *CSIR* 1.1.237).

Dedication slab. Inscription flanked by *ansae* with curved edges. AD 238–244.

The stone has been partially erased, a secondary "Gordianae" was incised. Hübner suggested "Severianae Alexandrianae" for the missing text; Mommsen conjectured "Pupienae Balbinae" (*CIL* III 6953), which, when combined with "Gordianae," would date the text to March/June AD 238 (*CIL* VIII 10365; *ILS* 496); Haverfield saw *[PUPIENAE | BALBIN]A[E]* (*AA* ser. 2, 16, 1894, 323).

Vindolanda (Chesterholm)

37. *Genio | praetori | sacrum Pi | tuanius Se | cundus prae | fectus coh(ortis) IIII | Gall(orum)* (*CIL* VII 703; *RIB* 1685; *CSIR* 1.6.24).

Altar. An axe, knife and ox on the left side; a patera, jug and cone on the right. Found in the *praetorium*. Third/fourth century.

From an Italian family? *PME* II.643, #P.37.

Genius loci

Aquae Sulis (Bath)

38. *Genio loci | ---IA..N.P | [--- | --- | .] leg(ionis) VI [V(ictricis)] | Forianus | v.s.l.l.m.* (*CIL* VII 1351; *RIB* 139).

Altar. Split into two pieces, much damaged. After AD 122.

Deva (Chester)

39. *Pro sal(ute) Domin | [oru]m NN(ostrorum) Invi | ct[i]ssimorum | Augg(ustorum) Genio loci | Fl[a]vius Long[us] | trib(unus) mil(itum) leg(ionis) XX [V.V.] | [et] Longinus fil(ius) | eius domo Samosata | v.s.* (*CIL* VII 167; *RIB* 450).

Altar. Third century lettering. On the right side, a *genius* holds a cornu-copia in his left hand and a patera in the other one (now broken away). The left side displays a vase with acanthus leaves, and the back features fruit on a draped cloth. In the focus, a mask faces the back of the altar.

For speculation on the emperors, see Wright, *RIB*, 149. The dedica-tors are natives of Commagene. Samosata, Syria: *PME* I.370, #F.55.

Eboracum (York)

40. *[D]eo* | *Genio* | *loci* | *v.s.l.m.* (*ILS* 3647; *RIB* 646).
    Altar fragment.

41. *Genio loci* | *feliciter* (*CIL* VII 235; *ILS* 3650; *RIB* 647).
    Fragmentary building stone.

42. *Num(ini) Aug(usti)* | *et Gen(io) Eb[or(aci)* (*RIB* 657; *CSIR* 1.3.3).
    The top of an altar.

Alauna (Maryport)

43. *Genio loci* | *Fortun(ae) Reduci* | *Romae Aetern(ae)* | *et Fato Bono* | *C. Cornelius Peregrinus* | *trib(unus) cohor(tis)* | *ex provincia* | *Maur(etania) Caesa(riensi)* | *domo Sald[i]s* | *d[e]c(urio) v.s.l.l.m.* (*CIL* VII 370, *addit.*, 308; *ILS* 3657; *RIB* 812).
    Altar. Found at the fort's northwest corner. On the backside, two fluted columns flank an axe and knife, above which is the inscription: *Volanti vivas.* The capital has been damaged, but a human bust with animal heads to either side appears in the center of the front part.
    Saldae was a *colonia* in Mauretania Caesariensis; *PME* I.300, #C.244.

Luguvalium (Carlisle)

44. *Genio* | *lo[c]i* (*CIL* VII 923 *addit.* 311; *RIB* 945; *CSIR* 1.6.468).
    Altar. On the left, a goddess holding a cornucopia in her right hand, a patera in her left, sits in a projecting niche. On the right, a genius, who might have once worn a mural crown, holds a patera in his right hand, cornucopia in the left. Second/third century.

Brocolitia (Carrawburgh)

45. *Genio* | *hu(i)us lo|ci Texand(ri)* | *et Suue(uae)* | *vex(illarii) cohor(tis)* | *II Nervior|um* (*ILS* 2556; *RIB* 1538; *CSIR* 1.6.20).
    Altar. Found in the fort's center as recycled building material (for later fort renovations). Second century.
    Texandri and Suevae may be geographical (R.P. Wright, *RIB*, 490). Suuivesela or Suivesela is the Roman place name for the modern Sysseele, east of Bruge.

Auchendavy

46. *Genio* | *Terrae* | *Brita|nnicae* | *M. Coccei(us)* | *Firmus* | *c(enturio) leg(ionis) II Aug(ustae)* (*CIL* VII 1113; *ILS* 4831b; *RIB* 2175).
    Altar. Split across the die. Found in a pit southwest of the fort. Ca. AD 150? Perhaps erased and recut.
    See #225, 283, 301; E. Birley, "Marcus Cocceius Firmus," 97–101. A widely attested *nomen*, including a Roman emperor (M. Cocceius Nerva) and a British procurator (M. Cocceius Nigrinus).

Unspecified Genii

Vindomora (Ebchester)
47. *Genio [---|---IV|---]rieius* | *[---|[p]r[a]ef(ectus) v.l.s.* (*RIB* 1099).
    Altar. Badly weathered; on the left side, patera and jug; knife and eagle
on the right.

DEIFIED ABSTRACTIONS

Concors

Luguvalium (Carlisle)
48. *C[o]ncord[iae]* | *Leg(ionis) II Aug(ustae) et XX V.V.* (*Britannia*.1989 #4).
    Base of inscribed relief. Two legionary soldiers, now largely worn away,
are carved in high relief. Could date to Hadrian.

Coriosopitum (Corbridge)
49. *Concordi|ae leg(ionis) VI* | *Vi(ctricis) P(iae) F(idelis) et* | *leg(ionis) XX* (*RIB*
1125; *CSIR* 1.1.1).
    Dedication slab. Found at Hexham. Possibly Hadrianic, but both legions
were active in the north in the early third century.

Disciplina

Cilurnum (Chesters)
50. *[D]iscipulinae* | *Imp(eratoris) Had(riani) Aug(usti)* | *Ala Aug(usta)* | *[o]b*
virt(utem) appel(lata) (*Britannia*.1979, #7).
    Altar fragment. Found 150m southeast of fort. Ca. AD 122.

Fanum Cocidi (Bewcastle)
51. *Discip(linae)* | *Aug(usti)* (*RIB* 990; *CSIR* 1.6.8).
    Altar. Primary text chiseled off. On the front, ox-head above altar
flanked by two dolphins. Discovered in the *aerarium principiorum* with fourth
century debris.

Coriosopitum (Corbridge)
52. *Discipuli|nae Augustorum* | *leg(io)* | *II* | *Aug(usta)* (*RIB* 1127).
    Statue base. Found in the Severan strong-room. Probably early third
century.

53. *[Disci]p(linae) August[orum* | *milit]es coh(ortis) I [F(idae) Var|dullo]rum m(illiariae)*
[c(ivium) R(omanorum) eq(uitatae) | *quibus] praees[t Pub(lius)* | *Calpur]nius Vic[tor*
tr(ibunus) (*RIB* 1128).
    Fragmentary dedication slab. The restoration is highly conjectural: *coh.*
I [ ]rum m. could refer to any number of units (e.g., *coh. Germanorum m.,*
coh. Hispanorum m., coh. Tungrorum m.); *[ ]nius* can be expanded to about
thirty plus *nomina; Vic[ ]*, likewise, is one of many possible expansions.
Furthermore, the presence of the Vardulli at Corbridge is not certain

(Holder, *Roman Army*, 124). Datable to the late second century if *]nius Vic[* (#462) is the same man; *PME* I.215, #C.64.

Aesica (Great Chesters)
  54. *Disc[i]p[ulinae---* (*RIB* 1723).
    Top of an altar.

Camboglanna (Castlesteads)
55a. *Discipu|[l]inae | [A]ug[gg]|ust(orum)* (*CIL* VII 896; *RIB* 1978; *CSIR* 1.6.7).
    Altar. AD 209–11 (Severus, Caracalla, and Geta).

55b. *Discipu|[l]inae | [A]ug[gg]|usti.*
    Caracalla's sole reign (AD 212–217).

Blatobulgium (Birrens)
  56. *Discip(linae) | Aug(usti) | coh(ors) II Tungr(orum) | mil(liaria) eq(uitata) c(ivium) L(atinorum)* (*RIB* 2092; *CSIR* 1.4.2).
    Altar. On the left side, a patera with a ram's head handle; on the right, a knife and axe. Found in the well of the *principia*'s courtyard. Ca. AD 158.

Bertha, Perthshire in Scotland
  57. *Discipul|inae | Augusti* (*JRS*.1959 #6).
    Dedication slab. Found on south bank of River Almond, facing the fort. Second century lettering.

Felicitas

Bravoniacum (Kirkby Thore)
  58. *[F]el(icitati) eq(uitum) L(---) Aurelius M|arcus dec(urio) alae v.s.l.l.m.* (*RIB* 765).
    Stone base. Found east of the fort. Third century (A. Birley, *People*, 96, 185; *RIB* 1828).

Fortuna

Augusta Londinium (London)
  59. *For(tuna) Augg(ustorum)* (*Britannia*.1985 #35).
    Oval die. Seal displays Fortuna standing and facing left; she holds a cornucopia on her left arm; in her right hand, she holds a rudder which rests on a globe. After AD 161 (#7).

Isca (Caerleon)
  60. *Deae | [F]ortu|nae | [I]ulius | [B]assus | praef(ectus) | castror(um)* (*CIL* VII 96; *RIB* 317).
    Dedication with molded border. Found in bath building.

  61. *[Fort]un(a)e et Bono Eve|nto Corneli(us) Castus et Iul(ia) | Belismicus coniuges | po[s(u)er(unt)]* (*CIL* VII 97; *RIB* 318; *CSIR* 1.5.1).
    Dedication slab. Above the inscription, a weathered Fortuna holds a cornucopia in her left hand, and *Bonus Eventus*, wearing a toga, apron, and

high boots, holds in his right hand a patera over a small altar. Found in bath building. Early third century.

Slack

62. *Fortunae | sacrum | C. Anto(nius) Modes(tus) | c(enturio) leg(ionis) VI Vic(tricis) P(iae) F(idelis) | v.s.l.m.* (*CIL* VII 199; *RIB* 624; *CSIR* 1.3.20).

   Altar. Patera shaped focus. Found just south of the bath building.

Eboracum (York)

63. *Bono Eventu]i et F[ortunae* (*RIB* 642; *CSIR* 1.3.9).

   Dedication fragments. Molded sides. Found just south of the baths.

64. *Deae | Fortunae | Sosia | Iuncina | Q. Antoni | Isaurici | leg(ati) Aug(usti)* (*CIL* VII 233; *RIB* 644).

   Altar. Trimmed down (for reuse). Found in the baths. Antonius Isauricus, cos. AD 143: A. Birley, *Fasti*, 247.

Lavatris (Bowes)

65. *D(e)ae Fortunae | Virius Lupus | leg(atus) Aug(usti) pr(o) pr(aetore) | balineum vi | ignis exust|um coh(orti) I Thr|acum resti|tuit curan|te Val(erio) Fron|tone praef(ecto) | eq(uitum) alae Vetto(num)* (*CIL* VII 273; *RIB* 730).

   Altar. Found in baths. AD 197–202.

   One wonders if the baths were burned because of stresses deriving from the civil war or barbarian threats.

Bravoniacum (Kirkby Thore)

66. *[F]ortunae | [S]ervatrici | Anton[i]a | Stratonis | ex viso* (*CIL* VII 296; *RIB* 760).

   Altar.

67. *Fort[un]a[e] | Bal[n(eari)] | n(umeri) m(ilitum) S(yrorum) s(agittariorum) | C. Cale[d]i|us F[ro]|ntinus | NOIV* (*RIB* 764).

   Altar. *C. Cale[d]ius Florentius*: E. Birley, "Deities," 25, n. 50.

   Our guy probably hoped for good luck at the gambling table.

Luguvalium (Carlisle)

68. *vo[t]um [Fo]rtunae libens meruit meru[---* (*Britannia*.1993 #6).

   Capital and upper die of a miniature votive altar. Found among Trajanic debris.

   Dedicated after a gambling win?

Vinovia (Binchester)

69. *[F]ortunae | sanctae | M. Val(erius) Fulvianu[s] | praef(ectus) eq(uitum) | v.s.l.l.m.* (*CIL* VII 423; *RIB* 1029).

   Altar. Engraved with a jug on the left side, patera on the right.

   Valerius Fulvianus may be related to a governor of 225/235 (A. Birley, *Fasti*, 194). *PME* II.815, #V.13.

Longovicium (Lanchester)

70. *Fortunae | Aug(ustae) sacr(um) | P(ublius) Ael(ius) Atti|cus praef(ectus) | v.s.l.m.* (*CIL* VII 433, *addit.* 308; *RIB* 1073).

   Altar. From the baths.

   PME I.57, #A.24 for Ael. Atticus, of *cohors I Lingonum*.

Habitancum (Risingham)
71. *Fortunae | sacrum C. | Valerius | Longinus | trib(unus)* (*CIL* VII 982; *RIB* 1210; *CSIR* 1.1.186).
Altar; a jug on the left side, patera on the right. Found in the baths. Third century.
Cohors I Vangionum. PME II.817, #V.18, *CIL* III 14507 (Dacia): C. Valerius Longinus, honorably discharged in 195, perhaps the father of our man? See #310.

72. *Fortunae | Aug(ustae) | Ael(ia) | Proculina | v.s.* (*CIL* VII 983; *RIB* 1211).
Altar.

Onnum (Halton Chesters)
73. *Deae | Fortu|nae [---| CVR[---|HD[---* (*CIL* VII 558; *RIB* 1423; *CSIR* 1.1.184).
Altar. Patera engraved on each side. Perhaps of Eastern workmanship or native British: crow-stepped gables, as seen on this altar, are common to both. Second/third century.

Brocolitia (Carrawburgh)
74. *Fortunae | coh(ors) I Batavor(um) | cui praeest | M. Flaccinius | Marcellus praef(ectus)* (*CIL* VII 617; *ILS* 2549; *RIB* 1536; *CSIR* 1.6.10).
Altar. Wreaths adorn each side. Third century.

75. *D(e)ae For(tunae) | Vitalis | fecit | lib(ens) mer(ito)* (*RIB* 1537).
Altar. Found at the baths.
Vitalis: #354, 474, 538.

Vindolanda (Chesterholm)
76. *Fortunae | p(opuli) R(omani) | C. Iul(ius) Raeticus c(enturio) leg(ionis) VI Vic(tricis)* (*CIL* VII 702; *RIB* 1684; *CSIR* 1.6.11).
Altar. Knife and patera on the left side, patera on the right. Found in the bath hypocaust. Second/third century.
Iulius, probably born in Raetia.

Aesica (Great Chesters)
77. *D(e)ae F]or[t]u(nae) | vexs(illatio) G(aesatorum) R(a)eto(rum) | quorum cur|am agit Tabe\llius Victor | c(enturio)* (*RIB* 1724).
Altar. Much weathered. From bath building. Third century.

Magnis (Carvoran)
78. *Fortunae Aug(ustae) | pro salute L(uci) Aeli | Caesaris ex visu | T. Fla(vius) Secundus | praef(ectus) coh(ortis) I Ham|iorum Sagittar(iorum) | v.s.l.m.* (*CIL* VII 748, addit. 310; *ILS* 2551; *RIB* 1778; *CSIR* 1.6.12).
Altar. Found in the *apodyterium* of the bath house. L. Aelius Caesar, Hadrian's heir, died AD 138.
Flavius Secundus, a *grammateus* at Pergamum under Hadrian (*IGR* IV 349, 386): *PME* I.377, #F.69.

79. *Fortun[ae] | Audac(ilius) Ro|manus c(enturio) | leg(ionum) VI XX | (II) Aug(ustae)* (*CIL* VII 749; *RIB* 1779; *CSIR* 1.6.13).
Altar. Patera on the left side, jug and knife on the right. AD 122/6.

Banna (Birdoswald)
80. *Deae* | *Fortu*|*nae* (*CIL* VII 805; *RIB* 1873).
    Altar.

Blatobulgium (Birrens)
81. *Fortunae* | *coh(ors)* I | *Nervana* | *Germanor(um)* | *m(illiaria) eq(uitata)* (*CIL*
VII 1063; *RIB* 2093; *CSIR* 1.4.3).
    Altar. AD 142/57.

82. *Fortunae [pro]* | *salute P. Campa[ni]* | *Italici praef(ecti) coh(ortis) I[I] Tun(gro-*
rum) Celer libertus | *[v] s.l.l.m.* (*CIL* VII 1064; *RIB* 2094; *CSIR* 1.4.4).
    Inscribed pedestal for a statuette. Ca. AD 158.
    For Campanius Italicus, see *PME* I.219, #C.70, from the west.

83. *Fortu*|*nae vo*|*tum* | *[---*|*---]* (*RIB* 2095).
    Altar.

Castlecary
84. *Fortunae* | *vexilla*|*tiones* | *leg(ionis) II Aug(ustae)* | *leg(ionis) VI Vic(tricis)* |
P(iae) F(idelis) p(osuerunt) l(aetae) l(ibentes) (*CIL* VII 1093, *addit.* 313; *RIB* 2146).
    Altar. Found in the baths. A statuette of Fortune was found nearby.
AD 139/42.

Balmuldy
85. *Deae Fortunae* | *Caecilius Nepos* | *trib(unus)* (*RIB* 2189).
    Altar. Found in the baths. See *PME* I.195, #C.17.

Provenance unknown
86. *Deae* | *Fortunae* | *et* | *Numini*|*bus Augusto*|*rum* (*RIB* 2217).
    Altar. Four round objects, probably fruits, were sculpted into the focus.

Fortuna Conservatrix

Mamucium (inside modern Manchester)
87. *Fortunae* | *Conserva*|*trici* | *L. Senecia*|*nius Mar*|*tius c(enturio) leg(ionis)* | *VI*
Vic(tricis) (*CIL* VII 211; *RIB* 575).
    Altar; patera on the right side, a jug on the left. Found near the river,
outside the fort. Dates to after 122.

Castra Exploratorum (Netherby)
88. *Deae sanct*|*ae Fortunae* | *Conservatrici* | *Marcus Aurel(ius)* | *Saluius tribun*|*us*
coh(ortis) I Ael(iae) Hi|*spanorum* | *m(illiariae) eq(uitatae)* | *v.s.l.m.* (*CIL* VII 954;
RIB 968).
    Altar. Found in the fort's baths. Ca. AD 222.
    M. Aurelius Salvius, perhaps Italian: *PME* I.159, #A.253.

Cilurnum (Chesters)
89. *D(e)ae* | *Fort(unae) Co*|*nservatr*|*ici Venenu*|*s Ger(manus) l(ibens) m(erito)* (*RIB*
1449; *CSIR* 1.6.9).
    Altar. On the front, Fortuna stands in niche. She holds a cornucopia
in her left hand. The position of her right suggests that she held a rudder,

of which there is no trace. By her right leg is a patera (instead of a globe: the sculptor seems to have worked from a drawing which he did not understand: *CSIR* 1.6.9). Found in the baths. Third century.

The dedicator is German.

Fortuna Redux

Deva (Chester)
90. *Fortunae Reduci | [A]esculap(io) et Saluti eius | libert(i) et familia | [T.] P[o]mponi T. f(ili) Gal(eria tribu) Mamilian[i] | Rufi Antistiani Funisulan[i] | Vetton[i]ani leg(ati) Aug(usti) | d(ederunt) d(edicaverunt)* (*CIL* VII 164; *RIB* 445).

Altar. On the left side, a festooned swag with a ladle crossed by caduceus. Below are two flesh hooks, a sacrificial knife and the handle to something now flaked away. On the right are Fortuna's rudder atop a cornucopia.

Pomponius Mamilianus, cos. AD 100, a friend to the younger Pliny (*Epistles* 9.25; A. Birley, *Fasti*, 234–235), was perhaps, but not necessarily, of Spanish origin (Galeria). For Funisulaunus Vettonianus: *PIR* III, 224, #570, compare #190 (a descendant?).

Alauna (Maryport)
91. *Romae | Aeternae | et | Fortunae | Reduci* (*CIL* VII 392; *RIB* 840).
Votive pillar.

Habitancum (Risingham)
92. *Fortunae Reduc[i] | Iulius Severinus | trib(unus) explicito | balineo v.s.l.m.* (*CIL* VII 984; *RIB* 1212; *CSIR* 1.1.185).

Altar; knife and axe on the left, jug and patera on the right. Found in the baths. Early third century (*RIB* 1236).

Iulius Severinus (*PME* 1.487, #I.124) perhaps related to #221.

Salus

Isca (Caerleon)
93. *Saluti Re|ginae P. Sal|lienius P. f(ilius) | Maecia (tribu) Tha[la]|mus Had[ria] | pr(a)ef(ectus) leg(ionis) II A[ug(ustae)] | cum fili(i)s suis | Ampeiano et Lu|ciliano d(ono) d(edit)* (*CIL* VII 100; *RIB* 324; *CSIR* 1.5.6).

Altar. Cracked through the middle. Early third century.
Hadria, Picenum.

Victoria

Tunshill Farm, Milnrow
94. *Victoriae | leg(ionis) VI Vic(tricis) | Val(erius) Rufus | v.s.l.m.* (*CIL* VII 217; *RIB* 582).

Silver plate attached to silver statuette of Victory. Probably looted from York.

Alauna (Maryport)
95. *Victoriae Aug(ustae) | coh(ors) I Baeta|siorum c(ivium) R(omanorum) | cui praeest | T. Attius Tutor | praefec(tus) | v.s.l.l.m.* (*CIL* VII 394; *RIB* 842).

Altar. Found in a pit northeast of the fort, perhaps interred during the annual new year's celebrations. Late second century.

For Attius Tutor (from Noricum), see #137, 254; *CIL* III 5331 (*ILS* 2734); *PME* I.134, #A.191. The name is Celtic (A. Birley, *People*, 69).

96. *Victoriae Aug(ustae)* | *coh(ors) I Baetasior(um)* | *c(ivium) R(omanorum)* | *cui praeest* | *Ulpius Titia|nus praefect|us* | *v.s.l.l.m.* (*CIL* VII 395; *RIB* 843).

Altar. Found in a pit northeast of the fort. Third century lettering.

For Ulpius Titianus, see #255; *CIL* III 4422 (Carnuntum, Upper Pannonia); *PME* II.803, #U.17.

97. *Victoriae* | *Aug(ustorum)* | *DD(ominorum) NN(ostrorum)* (*CIL* VII 396, *addit.* 308; *RIB* 844).

Dedication slab. Two winged Victories hold a wreath. Third/fourth century.

Longovicium (Lanchester)
98. *D(eae) Victorie* | *vot(o)* | *s(uscepto) Ulpiu|s po(suit)* (*CIL* VII 443, *addit.*, 309; *RIB* 1086).

Altar. Patera on the left side.

Coriosopitum (Corbridge)
99. *Victoriae* | *Aug(ustae)* | *L. Iul(ius) Iuli[anus|* *leg. Au]g. [--- (*CIL* VII 480; *RIB* 1138).

Altar fragment.

L. Iulius Iulianus: A. Birley, *Fasti*, 265–6. Ca. AD 205?

Possibly a monument to Severus' civil war victory.

Bremenium (High Rochester)
100. *Victoriae* | *et Paci Iul(ius)* | *Me[l]anic[us] pro b[ono]* | *publico* | *(v.s.l.m.* (*RIB* 1273).

Altar. Found north of fort.

A. Birley reads the piece tentatively: *Melanio tr[i]b* | *[i]mp Volusiano et* | *Publico cos.* ("Altar from Bremenium," 13–23). AD 253.

Northumberland; Provenance unknown
101. *Dea* | *[---]* || *Victoria* | *[---]* (*Britannia.*1985 #12).

Altar inscribed on left and front.

Condercum (Benwell)
102. *Victoriae* | *[Au]gg(ustorum) Alfe|no Senecio|n[e] co(n)s(ulari) felix* | *ala I Astu(rum)* | *[---] M pra(efecto)* (*CIL* VII 513; *RIB* 1337; *CSIR* 1.1.219).

Dedication slab. Two winged Victories flank the inscription. Found in the ruins of the fort's walls. Ca. AD 205–208 (Septimius Severus and Caracalla; *PIR* I, 88, #521; A. Birley, *Fasti*, 157–161). A monument to imperial victories in Britain?

Aesica (Great Chesters)
103. *Victoriae Aug(usti) coh(ors) VI* | *Nerviorum cui praeest G.* | *Iul(ius) Barbarus praefec(tus) v.s.l.l.m.* (*CIL* VII 726; *RIB* 1731).

Statue base. Hadrianic.

PME I.442, #I.33, Iulius Barbarus, an African?

Camboglanna (Castlesteads)
104. *Vict(oria)* | *Aug(usti)* (*CIL* VII 891; *RIB* 1995).
Sculptured block. A winged Victory, with her left foot on a globe, holds a wreath in her right hand, rudder in her left.

Rough Castle
105. *Victoriae* | *coh(ors) VI Ner|viorum c(uius) c(uram agit)* | *Fl(avius) Betto c(enturio) leg(ionis)* | *XX V.V.* | *v.s.l.l.m.* (*CIL* VII 1092; *RIB* 2144).
Altar. Found about 183m south of fort. Antoninus Pius.
Betto (var. Vetto?) is Iberian or Celtic: Holder, *Alt-celtischer* III.266–271.

Virtus

Aquae Sulis (Bath)
106. *Locum reli|giosum per in|solentiam e|rutum* | *Virtuti et N(umini)* | *Aug(usti) repurga|tum reddidit* | *C. Severius* | *Emeritus c(enturio) reg(ionarius)* (*CIL* VII 45, addit., 306; *ILS* 4920; *RIB* 152).
Altar. Third century?

Alauna (Maryport)
107. *Virtuti* | *Augustae* | *[---.]iana* | *Quinti filia* | *Hermionae* | *v.s.l.l.m.* (*CIL* VII 397; *RIB* 845).
Altar.
Hermione may have been an officer's wife: #227.

Cilurnum (Chesters)
108. *[S]alvis Aug[g](ustis)* | *[f]elix ala II Astur(um)* | *[Antoniniana]* (*RIB* 1466).
Monumental relief, below which is the helmeted head of a *signifer* holding a *vexillum* inscribed *Virtus Aug(ustorum)*. Found in the *principia*. Elagabalus and Severus Alexander (AD 221/2).

Duntocher
109. *Imp(eratori) C(aesari) T(ito) Aelio Hadr|iano Aug(usto) p(atri) p(atriae) vex(illatio) leg(ionis) VI* | *Victric[i]s P(iae) F(idelis)* | *opus valli p(edum) MMMCCXL f(ecit)* (*CIL* VII 1135; *RIB* 2200, pl. XIX).
Commemorative tablet. Two winged Victories, standing on globes, support the inscribed panel. Mars Victor appears to the left, Virtus Augusta to the right. Virtus holds in her left hand an inverted sheathed sword, and in her right a vexillum inscribed: *Virtus* | *Aug(usta)*. Her right breast bare, she wears a tunic and a helmet. Found 1.1km southeast of the fort. AD 138–161 (Antoninus Pius).

GODS AND HEROES OF THE ROMAN STATE

Capitoline Triad

Luguvalium (Carlisle)
110. *I(ovi) O(ptimo) [M(aximo)]* | *Iunon[i Reginae]* | *Miner[vae Aug(ustae)]* |*Marti P[atri Vic]|toriae c[eteris]* | *diis dea[busque]* | *omnibus [M. Aur(elius)]* | *M. f(ilius)*

Ulp(ia) Syrio [Nico]\poli ex [p]rov(incia) Trh[ac(ia)] | *trib(unus) mil(itum) leg(ionis) (XX) V.V. Antoninianae* | *[---] (Britannia.*1989 #5).

Altar. On the left, a pair of clasped hands within a wreath. Below the wreath, an eagle has snatched Ganymede, wearing a Phrygian cap. Perhaps dedicated during the *vota* ceremony (January 3). *Antoninianae* suggests a Severan date.

M. Aurelius Syrio, from Thrace, may have been *evocatus* from the praetorian guard. Tomlin, "Roman Altar," 77–91.

Minerva Augusta: *AE* 1973 #635.

Jupiter Optimus Maximus

Dorchester

111. *I(ovi) O(ptimo) M(aximo)* | *et N(u)minib(us) Aug(ustorum)* | *M. Vari(us) Severus* | *b(eneficiarius) co(n)s(ularis)* | *aram cum* | *cancellis* | *d(e) s(uo) p(osuit)* (*CIL* VII 83; *ILS* 5458; *RIB* 235).

Altar. Found buried at a depth of 1.8m.
Cancelli: CIL VI 5306 (*ILS* 7930).

Goldmanstone

112. *I(ovi) O(ptimo) [M(aximo)]* | *Tit[inius]* | *Pine[s]*\ *l[[eg---]* | *V[---] v.s. [l.m.]* (*JRS.*1965, #2).

Altar. Found 6.4km NNW of Dorchester fort. The legion was probably *XX V.V.*, stationed at Chester: R.P. Wright, "Roman Britain in 1964," 221.

Isca (Caerleon)

113. *I(ovi) O(ptimo) M(aximo)---* (*RIB* 319).
Altar.

114. *[I(ovi) O(ptimo) M(aximo) et] G(enio)* | *[Imperator]um* | *[Antonini] et* | *[Commodi A]ugg(ustorum)* | *[aedem a so]lo* | *[restituit] T. Es[u]*\ *[vius ---]N[---* | *[l]eg(ato) A[ugg(ustorum)]* | *[p]r(imus) p(ilus) d(edit) [d(edicavit)]* (*Britannia.*1970 #3).

Slab. Found at basilica northwest of the *principia*. AD 177–180 (Marcus Aurelius and Commodus): A. Birley, *Fasti,* 202–203.

Verbeia (Ilkley)

115. *[Pro salute* | *imperato]**rum Caes(arum)* | *Augg(ustorum)* | *Antonini* | *et Veri* | *Iovi dilect(ori)* | *Caecilius* | *Lucanus* | *praef(ectus) coh(ortis)* (*CIL* VII 209; *RIB* 636).

Altar. AD 161–69. E. Birley, "Deities," 19, suggests that "Dilector," a late and mainly Christian epithet (*TLL*, sub "dilector"), is nonetheless not unsuitable for Jupiter whose inferred relationship to M. Aurelius and Verus was benevolent.

Caecilius Lucanus (*PME* I.195, #C.16).

Eboracum (York)

116. *I(ovi) O(ptimo) M(aximo)* | *Dis Deabusque* | *Hospitalibus Pe**natibusq(ue) ob con**servatam salutem* | *suam suorumq(ue)* | *P. Ael(ius) Marcian**us praef(ectus) coh(ortis)* | *ARAM SAC F NC D* (*CIL* VII 237; *ILS* 3598; *RIB* 649; *CSIR* 1.3.6).

Altar. On the right side, a figure holds a staff in his left hand; on the altar's left side, a figure, wearing a tunic, holds a large animal and faces right.

The inscription is preserved only in Lister's letter to R. Hooke (*Philosophical Transactions* iv, 92). Hübner suggested that ARAM represents the name of a cohort misread (*CIL* VII 237). E. Birley, "Review of Wagner" 139, suggested *coh. I Augusta Bracarum*, cited with P. Aelius Marcianus (*ILS* 2738; *PME* I.65, #A.44) who hailed, perhaps, from Mauretania Caesariensis.

Bravoniacum (Kirby Thore)
117. *I(ovi) O(ptimo) M(aximo)* | *RI[---* (*CIL* VII 296a; *RIB* 761).
    Altar.

Brocavum (Brougham)
118. *I(ovi) O(ptimo) M(aximo)* | *Ann[ius]* | *VISL* | *SSAC* | *v.s.l.m.* (*CIL* VII 297; *RIB* 778).
    Altar.

Clifton
119. *I(ovi) O(ptimo) M(aximo)* | *Gen(io)* | *loci* | *Su<u>br(ius) Ap|ollina|ris prin|cep(s) c(ohortis) I V[* (*CIL* VII 302, *addit.* 307; *RIB* 792).
    Altar. A jug on the left; a patera on the right. Perhaps *cohors I Vangionum*, garrisoned at Risingham in the third century.

Gabrosentum (Moresby)
120. *I(ovi) O(ptimo) M(aximo)* | *coh(ors) II Tra(cum)* | *eq(uitata) c(ui) p(raeest)* | *Manili|us Nepos pra|ef(ectus)* (*RIB* 797).
    Statue base. Found immediately west of the fort. Third/fourth century. E. Birley's reading (*PME* #M.19).
    Manilius Nepos, perhaps Italian (*PME* II.558, #M.19).

Alauna (Maryport)
121. *Iovi Aug(usto)* | *M. Censorius* | *M. fil(ius) Voltinia* | *[C]ornelianus c(enturio) leg(ionis)* | *[X Fr]etensis prae|[posi]tus coh(ortis) I Hisp(anorum) ex provincia* | *Narbone[n(si)] domo* | *Nemauso [v.]s.l.m.* (*CIL* VII 371; *RIB* 814).
    Altar. Mid-second century.
    M. Censorius (*PME* I.235, #C.106) from Gallia Narbonensis. Nemauso (Nîmes).

122. *I(ovi) O(ptimo) M(aximo)* | *et num(ini)* | *Aug(usti) coh(ors)* | *I Hispa(norum)* | *pos(uit)* (*CIL* VII 372; *RIB* 815).
    Altar. Found 320m northeast of the fort. Hadrianic.

123. *I(ovi) O(ptimo) M(aximo)* | *coh(ors) I His(panorum)* | *eq(uitata) cui praeest* | *L. Antistius L. f(ilius)* | *Quirinia Lupus* | *Verianus praef(ectus)* | *domu Sic|ca ex Africa* (*CIL* VII 373; *RIB* 816).
    Altar. Found 320m northeast of the fort. Second century.
    Perhaps Antistius, from Africa, is related to the L. Antistius Rusticus, from Cordoba, governor of Cappadocia in the 90's (*AE* 1925 #126; *PME* I.103, #A.126; A. Birley, *People*, 48).

124. *I(ovi) O(ptimo) M(aximo) | coh(ors) I | Hispano(rum) | cui pra|est |
C. Cab(allius) | Priscus | trib(unus)* (*CIL* VII 374; *RIB* 817).
    Altar. Found in a pit 320m northeast of the fort. Second century.
    Caballius Priscus: #125–127; E. Birley, *Roman Britain*, 90–91; *PME*
I.189, #C.3. For a private of the praetorian cohort with the same name
(from Verona), not our tribune: *CIL* VI 3888, 38889.

125. *I(ovi) O(ptimo) M(aximo) | C. Cabal(lius) | Priscus | tribunus* (*CIL* VII 375;
RIB 818).
    Altar.

126. *I(ovi) O(ptimo) M(aximo) | G. Cabal(lius) | Priscus | trib(unus)* (*CIL* VII
376; *RIB* 819).
    Altar. Found 320m northeast of the fort.

127. *I(ovi) O(ptimo) M(aximo) | G. Caba|llius P|riscus | tribun(us) | [---* (*RIB* 820).
    Altar. Found 183m northeast of the fort.

128. *I(ovi) O(ptimo) M(aximo) | coh(ors) [I Hisp(anorum)] | eq(uitata) c(ui) p(raeest)
Pub. Corn[elius] | Pub. fil(ius) | Gal(eria tribu) V[---] | [p]raef(ectus) F(---) | P
ROMAN | v.s.l. [m.]* (*CIL* VII 377, *addit.* 308; *RIB* 821).
    Altar. Second century.

129. *I(ovi) O(ptimo) M(aximo) | coh(ors) I | Hispa(norum) | cui pra[e(est)] |
Helstri|us Nove[l]|lus prae|fect(us)* (*CIL* VII 378; *RIB* 822).
    Altar. Found 320m northeast of the fort.
    Helstrius Novellus (#373; *PME* I.416, #H.4), possibly Italian or African.
Helstrius, as an Etruscan *nomen*, is not found outside Italy. As a *cognomen*,
Novellus is common in Africa (Kajanto, *Cognomina*, 289).

130. *I(ovi) O(ptimo) M(aximo) | coh(ors) I His(panorum) | cui prae(est) |
M. Maeni|us Agrip(pa) | tribu(nus) | pos(uit)* (*CIL* VII 379; *RIB* 823).
    Altar. Found at the fort with a sundial set into its capital. AD 130/135
(*CIL* XI 5632 [*ILS* 2735]).
    M. Maenius Agrippa: #131–133; *PIR* V.2, 141, #67; Pflaum, *Carrières*,
#107; *PME* II.551, #M.5; A. Birley, *Fasti*, 292–94; Jarrett, *Maryport*, 17–18.

131. *Iovi Op(timo) M(aximo) | et num(ini) Aug(usti) | M. Mae(nius) Agripp(a) |
tribun|us | pos(uit)* (*CIL* VII 380; *RIB* 824).
    Altar. Found in a pit 320m northeast of the fort. AD 122/126.

132. *I(ovi) O(ptimo) M(aximo) | et num(ini) Aug(usti) | Mae(nius) Agrip|pa tri-
bun|us pos(uit)* (*CIL* VII 381; *RIB* 825).
    Altar. Found 320m northeast of the fort. AD 122/126.

133. *I(ovi) O(ptimo) M(aximo) | [--- | ---] | Maen(ius) [Agrip(pa)] tribu[n(us)]*
(*CIL* VII 382; *RIB* 826).
    Altar. Found in a pit 320m northeast of the fort. AD 122/126.

134. *I(ovi) O(ptimo) M(aximo) | [L.] Cammi|[u]s Maxi|mus prae(fectus) | coh(ortis)
I His(panorum) | eq(uitatae) e(t) tri(bunus) XVIII | cohor(tis) Volu(ntariorum) |
v.s.l.m.* (*CIL* VII 383; *RIB* 827).

Altar. Patera on each side. Wheel on the back. Found 320m north-east of the fort.

Cammius Maximus (from Noricum) a Celtic name: #135–136; *CIL* V 961; *PME* I.217, #C.68; A. Birley, *People*, 69. Mid to late second century.

135. *I(ovi) O(ptimo) M(aximo)* | *L. Cammi*|*us Maxim*|*us praefec*|*tus coh(ortis) I Hispano(rum)* | *eq(uitatae) v.s.l.l.m.* (*CIL* VII 384; *RIB* 828).
   Altar. Found 320m northeast of the fort.

136. *I(ovi) O(ptimo) M(aximo)* | *L. Cammi*|*us Maxi(mus)* | *pr(a)efe(ctus) coh(ortis)* | *I His(panorum) eq(uitatae)* | *v.s.l.m.* (*CIL* VII 385; *RIB* 829).
   Altar.

137. *I(ovi) O(ptimo) M(aximo)* | *coh(ors) I Baeta*|*siorum* | *c(ivium) R(omanorum) cui prae*|*est T. Attius* | *Tutor praef(ectus)* | *v.s.l.l.m.* (*CIL* VII 386; *RIB* 830).
   Altar. Found 320m northeast of the fort.
   Attius Tutor: #95, 254.

138. *I(ovi) O(ptimo) M(aximo)* | *coh(ors) I Da*|*lmatar(um) cui* | *praeest L. Cae*|*cilius Veg[e]*|*tus praefec(tus)* | *v.s.l.m.* (*CIL* VII 387; *RIB* 831).
   Altar. Found 320m northeast of the fort.
   Caecilius Vegetus: *PME* I.200, #C.28.

139. *Iovi Optim(o) Maxi(mo)* | *Capitolino* | *pro salut(e) An*|*tonini Aug(usti)* | *Pii Postumi*|*us Acilianus* | *praef(ectus) coh(ortis) I Delm(atarum)* (*ILS* 3009; *RIB* 832).
   Dedication slab. Symmetrical *peltae*, each underneath a rosette, flank the dedication. Found in a pit. AD 138–161.
   Postumius Acilianus (Hispania Baetica): #140, 142, 376, *RIB* 847. Perhaps a descendant of Trajan's procurator (Pflaum, *Carrières*, #62; *PME* II.676, #P.100; A. Birley, *People*, 69).

140. *I(ovi) O(ptimo) M(aximo)* | *Acilianus* | *praefect(us)* | *<P>* (*CIL* VII 388, *addit.* 308; *RIB* 833).
   Base. Rosettes on front, sides, and back of the capital. AD 138/61.

141. *I(ovi) O(ptimo) M(aximo) p[r]o [--- | --- | --- | --- | --- | ---]* | *praef(ectus) coh(ortis)* | *fecit* (*RIB* 834).
   Altar.

142. *pro sa[lute imp(eratoris) Caes(aris)]* | *Antonin[i] Aug(usti) Pii p(atris) [p(atriae)]* | *[P]aulus [P(auli)] f(ilius) Palatina* | *[Postumi]us Acil[i]anus* | *praef(ectus) c[o]h(ortis) I Delmatar(um)* (*CIL* VII 400, *addit.*, 308; *RIB* 850).
   Dedication slab in three fragments. Possibly to Jupiter Optimus Maximus. AD 138/61.

143. *Iov[i O(ptimo) M(aximo)] et V[---]* | *Cr[--- (CIL* VII 389; *RIB* 835).
   Upper left hand corner of an altar.

Maglona (Old Carlisle)
144. *I(ovi) O(ptimo) M(aximo)* | *ala Aug(usta) o[b]* | *virtut(em) appel(lata) cu[i]* |

[pr]aeest Tib(erius) Cl(audius) Tib(eri) fi(lius) | INGM Iustinu[s] | praef(ectus)
Fuscian[o] | II Silano II c[o(n)s(ulibus)] (*CIL* VII 340; *RIB* 893).
Altar. AD 188.
Ti. Claudius Justinus, from Gaul? *PME* I.254, #C.147.

145. *I(ovi) O(ptimo) M(aximo) | ala | Aug(usta) ob virtutem | [a]ppellata cu[i]*
prae\[e]st P. Ael(ius) Pub(li) fi(lius) Ser\gia (tribu) Magnus d(omo) Mursa ex Pannon(ia)
| Inferiore praefec(tus) | Aproniano et Br[a(dua) co(n)s(ulibus)] (*CIL* VII 341; *RIB*
894).
Base. AD 191.
P. Aelius Magnus, from Lower Pannonia: *PME* I.64, #A.42.

146. *[I(ovi)] O(ptimo) M(aximo) | [p]ro sal[u]te L. Septi[mi | S]everi et M. Aur(eli)*
Anto\[nini Aug(ustorum)--- (*CIL* VII 343; *RIB* 896).
Altar fragment. Found 183m east of the fort. AD 198–211.

147. *I(ovi) O(ptimo) M(aximo) | pro salu[te] imperatoris | M. Antoni Gordiani P(ii)*
[F(elicis)] | Invicti Aug(usti) et Sab[in]iae Fur\iae Tranquil(lin)ae coniugi eius to\taque
domu divin(a) eorum a\la Aug(usta) Gordia(na) ob virtutem | appellata posuit cui
praest | Aemilius Crispinus pref(ectus) | eq(uitum) natus in pro(vincia) Africa de Tusdro
sub cur(a) Nonii Ph\ilippi leg(ati) Aug(usti) pro pre[to(re)] | [At]tico et Praetextato |
co(n)s(ulibus) (*CIL* VII 344; *ILS* 502; *RIB* 897).
Altar. AD 242.
Aemilius Crispinus, North African: *PME* I.80, #A.76; Jarrett, "Eques-
trians," 153, n. 10.

148. *I(ovi) O(ptimo) M(aximo) C(onservatori) | [p]ro salut[e] ---] MI [---|---] V [---*
|---|---|---|c]onsec[ra]v[it (*CIL* VII 345; *RIB* 898).
Altar.
The epithet could also be Capitolinus, which is much rarer: #139.

149. *I(ovi) O(ptimo) M(aximo) et | V(u)lk(ano) pro sa\lute d(omini) n(ostri)*
M. Anto(ni) | Gordiani P(ii) | F(elicis) Aug(usti) vik(anorum) | mag(istri) aram |
a(ere) col(lato) a v(ikanis) d(edicaverunt) (*CIL* VII 346, addit. 307; *RIB* 899).
Altar. Jug on right side; patera on the left. AD 238/44.

Luguvalium (Carlisle)
150. *[I(ovi)] O(ptimo) M(aximo) | [et N(uminibus)] D(ominorum) N(ostrorum)*
Va\[leri]ani et G\[allie]ni et Vale\[ria]ni nob(ilissimi) C(a)es(aris) p(iorum) | [f(eli-
cium)] Aug<g>ustor(um) | [nume]rus [---]TVO[.] | [s(ub) c(ura) G. C]arini Aureli(ani)
| [c(enturionis) leg(ionis) II] Aug(ustae) voto do\[n]avi(t) (*RIB* 913).
Altar. Found 6.4km southwest of Carlisle, on a road to Old Carlisle
where the *ala Augusta* was based. The restoration is not certain. The stone
could have read *M]arini* or *V]arini*; *Aureli* could be expanded *Aureli[ani praef.*
alae] Aug.: E. Birley, "Review of *RIB*," 229. AD 255/9.

Voreda (Old Penrith)
151. *I(ovi) O(ptimo) M(aximo) | et G(enio) DD(ominorum) NN(ostrorum) Phi\lip-*
poru[m] | Augg(ustorum) coh(ors) | [II] Gallo[r(um) (*CIL* VII 315; *RIB* 915).
Altar. AD 244/9.

152. *I(ovi) O(ptimo) M(aximo) | coh(ors) | II Gal(lorum) eq(uitata) | T. Dom[i]ti|us Heron | d(omo) Nicomedia | praef(ectus)* (*CIL* VII 317; *RIB* 917).
    Altar. Late second century. Now lost.
    The prefect was from Bithynia (*PME* I.330, #D.22).

Fanum Cocidi (Bewcastle)
153. *I(ovi) O(ptimo) M(aximo) | coh(ors) I Dac(orum) [---| ---]at[.]e[.]t centur(io) | leg(ionis) II [Aug(ustae) | v.s.l.m.]* (*CIL* VII 975; *RIB* 991).
    Altar. Hadrianic?

Vinovia (Binchester)
154. *I(ovi) O(ptimo) M(aximo) | et Matrib|us Olloto|tis sive Tra|nsmarinis | Pomponius | Donatus | b(ene)f(iciarius) co(n)s(ularis) pro salute sua | et suorum | v.s.l. a(nimo)* (*ILS* 4785; *RIB* 1030).
    Altar. On the right side, a patera and jug; on the left, a knife and axe. Found 73m south of the fort.
    "Ollototae" means "from the other folk." (Ihm, "Matres Ollototae," 257). The *Matres* may have had a temple here, but there is no archaeological proof: Lewis, *Temples*, 125.

155. *[I(ovi) O(ptimo) M(aximo)?] | [al]a Vet[to|nu]m c(ui) p(raeest) [---] | [---]oniu[s] | [R]ufu[s pr|aef(ectus) v.s.l.m.* (*Britannia*.1992 #10).
    Altar fragment. Reused in rebuilt furnace of the *praetorium* bath-suite.

Longovicium (Lanchester)
156. *[I(ovi)] O(ptimo) M(aximo) | [ord]inati coh(ortis) | [I F(idae)] Vard[ul]lor(um) | c(ivium) R(omanorum) eq(uitatae) m(illiariae) | v.s.l.l.m.* (*CIL* VII 435; *RIB* 1076).
    Altar. Later second century.

157. *[I(ovi) O(ptimo) M(aximo)] | [coh(ors) I] Ling(onum) | [e]q(uitata) c(ui) p(raeest) | [.] [F]ulvius | [Fel]ix praef(ectus)* (*Britannia*.1988 #10).
    Altar: Found in the *vicus*, south of the fort's southwest angle. AD 218/22: Tomlin, "Ignotus," 145–47.

Coriosopitum (Corbridge)
158. *I(ovi) O(ptimo) M(aximo) | [p]ro salut[e] | [v]exillatio|num leg(ionum) XX [V.V. | e]t VI Vic(tricis) mi[lites | a]ge[n]t(es) in p[---* (*RIB* 1130).
    Fragment of dedication slab or altar. Jug and patera on left; patera on right. Perhaps AD 122/6.

Habitancum (Risingham)
159. *I(ovi) O(ptimo) M(aximo) | v[e]xi[l](latio) G(aesatorum) R(aetorum) | q(uorum) c(uram) a(git) | Aemi(lius) Aemilianus | trib(unus) coh(ortis) I Vang(ionum)* (*CIL* VII 987; *RIB* 1216; *CSIR* 1.1.197).
    Altar. Knife and axe on right side. Third century.
    Perhaps the tribune would be the emperor of 253 (*SHA Gallieni* 4.1, 5.6, 6.4; *PIR* I, 50, #330; *PME* I.78, #A.72).

160. *[I(ovi)] O(ptimo) M(aximo)? | ve]xi[l](latio) G(aesatorum) R(aetorum) | q(uorum) c(uram) a(git) | Iul(ius) Victor | tr[i]b(unus) coh(ortis) I V|angionum* (*CIL* VII 988; *RIB* 1217).

Altar. Third century.

Iulius Victor: #379, 483, 493; *PME* I.445, #I.140.

161. *I(ovi) O(ptimo) M(aximo) O|IOVIOM* (*CIL* VII 989; *RIB* 1218).

Altar. Found 0.8km southeast of the fort.

Segedunum (Wallsend)

162. *I(ovi) O(ptimo) M(aximo) | coh(ors) IIII Lin|gonum eq(uitata) | cui attendit | Iul(ius) Honor|atus c(enturio) leg(ionis) II | Aug(ustae) v.s.l.m.* (*ILS* 9151; *RIB* 1299).

Altar. Found 274m west of fort's allotments. Third/fourth century. Haverfield, "Altar from Wallsend," 79.

For a Iulius Honoratus: *PIR* IV.3, 222, #356.

163. *I(ovi) O(ptimo) M(aximo) | Ael(ius) Rufus | praef(ectus) coh(ortis) | IIII Lingo|num* (*CIL* VII 493; *RIB* 1300; *CSIR* 1.1.193).

Altar. Jug, bucranium, axe, and knife on the left; on the right a patera with snakes on either side; on the base, Hercules with two snakes. Third/fourth century. *PME* I.71, #A.57.

164. *[I(ovi) O(ptimo)] M(aximo) | [Cor]nel(ius) | Celer pr|aef(ectus) coh(ortis) | IIII L[ing(onum) | --- (RIB* 1301; *CSIR* 1.1.194).

Two fragments of an altar. On the left side, a fragmentary belted figure. Knife and hatchet on the right. Found at the fort allotments. Third/fourth century.

Pons Aelius (Newcastle)

165. *I(ovi) O(ptimo) M(aximo) | pro salu|te et victor|ia Aug(usti)* (*RIB* 1316; *CSIR* 1.1.195).

Altar. On the left, a jug; a patera on the right. May date to Caracalla: *pro salute et victoria* (compare #22).

166. *[I(ovi)] O(ptimo) M(aximo) et | [Nu]mini [---|---| [D]is Hospital(ibus) |--] S [---] AE | [--- (RIB* 1317; *CSIR* 1.1.196).

Altar. The name of an emperor has been erased (about 10 letters); not earlier than Commodus, the first emperor to suffer *damnatio memoriae* since the building of Hadrian's Wall.

Hadrian's Wall, Benwell to Rudchester

167. *Iovi O(ptimo) M(aximo) | [--- (CIL* VII 505; *RIB* 1366).

Small altar (14 × 17.8cm) inscribed on three sides.

Cilurnum (Chesters)

168. *I(ovi) O(ptimo) M(aximo) | C---O | ---IIS | --- | --- | --- (CIL* VII 577; *RIB* 1450; *CSIR* 1.6.37).

Altar. Garland on left; jug and patera on right; double garland on back. Second/third century.

169. *I(ovi) O(ptimo) M(aximo) | --- | ---OIN --- (CIL* VII 578; *RIB* 1451; *CSIR* 1.6.38).

Altar. Second/third century.

Vercovicium (Housesteads)

170. *I(ovi) O(ptimo) M(aximo)* | *[--- (CIL* VII 636; *RIB* 1581).
Altar. Reused in a guard-chambers of the fort's north gate. The fort was expanded under the Severi. Probably Hadrianic.

171. *I(ovi) O(ptimo) M(aximo)* | *milites* | *leg(ionis) II A[ug(ustae)]* (*CIL* VII 637; *RIB* 1582).
Altar. Found on the hillside south of milecastle 37. AD 122/6.

172. *I(ovi) O(ptimo) M(aximo)* | *et deo Cocidio* | *Genioq(ue) hui(u)s* | *loci mil(ites)* *leg(ionis)* | *II Aug(ustae) agentes* | *in praesidio* | *v.s.l.m.* (*RIB* 1583; *CSIR* 1.6.39).
Altar. Found in the Mithraeum. AD 117/138?

173. *I(ovi) O(ptimo) M(aximo)* | *et Numinibus* | *Aug(ustorum) co(hors) I* | *T[un]gror(um)* | *cui praeest* | *Q. Iul(ius) Maxi|mus praef(ectus)* (*CIL* VII 638; *RIB* 1584; *CSIR* 1.6.40).
Altar. On right side, jug underneath a fillet; on left, patera beneath a fillet. Found on Chapel Hill, south of the fort. Third century?
Q. Iulius Maximus: *CIL* II 112 (governor of Gallia Narbonensis); *PIR* IV.3, 237, #424; *PME* I.468, #I.85; Iulius Maximus *sacerdos Digenis*: #455.

174. *I(ovi) O(ptimo) M(aximo)* | *et Numinibus* | *Aug(ustorum) co(hors) I* | *Tungr[orum* | *cu[i] prae(e)st* | *Q. Iulius* | *[---]sus praef(ectus)* | *v.[s.l.m.]* (*CIL* VII 639; *RIB* 1585; *CSIR* 1.6.41).
Altar. Found on the hill south of the fort. The reading of the cognomen is extremely uncertain. Third century?

175. *I(ovi) O(ptimo) M(aximo)* | *et Numinibus* | *Aug(ustorum) co(hors) I* | *Tu|ngro-rum* | *mil(liaria) cui praee|st Q. Verius* | *Superstis* | *praef[ec]tus* (*CIL* VII 640; *ILS* 2550; *RIB* 1586; *CSIR* 1.6.42).
Altar. Found on Chapel Hill. Third/fourth century.
Verius Superstis (*PME* II.849, #V.70), a German? Compare *CIL* III 12574, VI 32627.

176. *I(ovi) O(ptimo) [M(aximo)]* | *et Numinibus* | *[---|---|---|---]rius* | *[.]upe[---* | *p]raefectu[s]* (*RIB* 1587).
Altar. Third/fourth century.
Probably Q. Verius Superstis (#175; Wright, *RIB*, 505).

177. *I(ovi) O(ptimo) M(aximo)* | *[et Numinibus A]ug(ustorum) ---|---|---|---|p]rae-fectu[s]* (*CIL* VII 641; *RIB* 1588; *CSIR* 1.6.43).
Altar. Found on Chapel Hill. Third/fourth century?
Cohors I Tungrorum, inferred from "*praefectus*" (Collingwood, *RIB*, 505).

178. *I(ovi) O(ptimo) M(aximo)* | *pro salute* | *Desidieni Ae|[mi]liani praef|[ecti] et* *sua su[or|u]m posuit vot|[um]q(ue) solvit libe|ns Tusco et Bas|so co[(n)s(ulibus)]* (*CIL* VII 769, *addit.* 310; *RIB* 1589).
Altar. AD 258.
Desidienus Aemilianus from Dalmatia (*PME* I.321, #D.6).

Vindolanda (Chesterholm)

179. *I(ovi) O(ptimo) M(aximo)| ceterisque | diis immort(alibus) | et Gen(io) prae-tor(i) | Q. Petronius | Q. f(ilius) Fab(ia) Urbicus | praef(ectus) coh(ortis) IIII | Gallorum | --- | ex Italia | domo Brixia | votum solvit | pro se | ac suis (CIL* VII 704; *RIB* 1686; *CSIR* 1.6.45).

Altar, found in the *praetorium*. On the left side a stork with a chick, on the right a stork. Third/fourth century.

Brixia, between Verona and Milan.

180. *I(ovi) O(ptimo) M(aximo) | et Genio | diisq(ue) cus|todi(bus) coh(ors) II[II] | Gall(orum) et Ve[---]| Caecil[.] E[.]I | OP CELER [---] (CIL* VII 705; *RIB* 1687; *CSIR* 1.6.46).

Altar. Found in the *praetorium*. Third/fourth century.

A. Birley offers a new reading (via e-mail correspondence): *I.O.M. | et Genio | diisq(ue) cus|todib(us) coh(ors) IIII | Gallorum M. | Caecilius M. f(ilius) | (tribu) Quir(ina) Celer Praefect(us) (dedicavit)*. This makes the dedicator a prefect of the fourth cohort of Gauls, and a full Roman citizen as the full Roman nomenclature suggests. Birley also suggests that the prefect came from Lusitania. For *praefect(us)* see #181.

Domaszewski (*Religion*, 101) suggested *genius praetorii*.

181. *I(ovi) O(ptimo) M(aximo) | [c]oh(ors) IIII G[al]l(orum) | [cu]i p[rae]est L. [.] | [.]gius Puden|[s] pr[a]efect(us) | [a]ram [p]osuit | v.[l.] m.s. (RIB* 1688; *CSIR* 1.6.44).

Altar. Bucranium on the right side. Third/fourth century.

182. *I(ovi) O(ptimo) M(aximo) | AVG |---|---l(ibens) m(erito) (RIB* 1689).

Altar. Found 110m west of fort.

183. *I(ovi) O(ptimo) M(aximo) | [--- (RIB* 1690).

Altar.

Aesica (Great Chesters)

184. *[I(ovi) O(ptimo)] M(aximo) | ---Gal(l)or(um) | ---N (RIB* 1727; *CSIR* 1.6.49).

Altar. Fluted pilasters flank inscription. Jug on right side.

No *cohors Gallorum* is positively attested at Aesica.

Banna (Birdoswald)

185. *I(ovi) O(ptimo) M(aximo) | co(hors) I Aelia | Dacorum | qu(i)b(us) pr(a)eest | Ammonius | Victorinus | trib(unus) (CIL* VII 806; *RIB* 1874).

Altar. Third/fourth century.

Perhaps a Celtic name: Holder, *Alt-celtische* I, 131; or Egyptian: Schulze, *Eigennamen*, 121; *PME* I.96, #A.112. Compare *RIB* 2213 (Ardoch, Perthshire), an epitaph to Ammonius, son of Damio, centurion of *Cohors I Hispanorum*.

186. *I(ovi) O(ptimo) M(aximo) | [co]h(ors) I Ael(ia) | Dac|o[rum] | c(ui) p(rae)est | [A]urelius Fa(u)s|[t]us trib(unus) | Perpetuo | co(n)s(ule) (CIL* VII 808; *RIB* 1875).

Altar; dedicated in 237.

Cornelius, the second consul, may have been omitted by mistake. Aur. Faustus (*PME* I.148, #A.225). Homonyms: *CIL* XI 4082 (Oriculum); *CIL* III 12595 (Dacia, a veteran).

187. *I(ovi) O(ptimo) M(aximo) | [c]oh(ors) I Ael(ia) Da[c(orum)] | c(uius) c(uram) agit A|urel(ius) Sa[t]urn[inus---* (*CIL* VII 809; *RIB* 1876).
Altar. Third/fourth century.

188. *I(ovi) O(ptimo) M(aximo) | c[o]h(ors) I Aelia | Daco[r]|um Aug(usta) | [cui] p(raeest) Aur(elius) | [---* (*CIL* VII 825; *RIB* 1877; *CSIR* 1.6.50).
Altar. Wheel symbols and swastika on the focus. Third/fourth century.
The dedicator may be identical with #186 or #187, though Aurelius is a common *nomen* in Britain.

189. *[I(ovi)] O(ptimo) M(aximo) | [coh(ors) I A]el(ia) Da|[corum] c(ui) p(raeest) F[l(avius) [---* (*RIB* 1878).
Altar. Third/fourth century.

190. *I(ovi) O(ptimo) [M(aximo) | coh(ors) I Ael(ia)] | Dac(orum) cu[i pr]|aeest [.] | Funisul[an]|us Vetto[ni]|anus t[ri]|b(unus) v.[s.]l.m.* (*CIL* VII 811; *RIB* 1879).
Altar. Third/fourth century.
The Funisulauni Vettoni were an Italian family, of whom one was a prominent senator (1st c. AD). Perhaps a distant descendant: *PIR* III, 224, #570; Tacitus, *Annals*, 15.7. See #90. From Caesaraugusta (Saragossa, Spain): Syme, *Roman Army Papers IV*, 82, 151.

191. *I(ovi) O(ptimo) M(aximo) | coh(ors) I Ael(ia) Da|cor(um) c(uius) c(uram) a(git) Iul(ius) | Marcelli|nus c(enturio) leg(ionis) II | Aug(ustae)* (*ILS* 9150; *RIB* 1880).
Altar. Third/fourth century.
RIB 2172, a tombstone to a C. Iulius Marcellinus, prefect of *Cohors I Hamiorum*, at Bar Hill (occupied by Agricola and the Antonine army). A relative? *PME* I.466, #I.80. A Iulius Marcellinus was prefect of Egypt, AD 271 (*PIR* IV.3, 234, #403). Homonyms: *CIL* V 3329 (*ILS* 544, AD 265), 7234.

192. *I(ovi) O(ptimo) M(aximo) | c(o)ho(rs) I A[el(ia)] | Dac(orum) cui p[rae]|est Iuliu[s] | Saturnin[us] | tribun[us]* (*CIL* VII 812; *RIB* 1881).
Altar. Third/fourth century.

193. *I(ovi) O(ptimo) M(aximo) | et N(umini) Aug(usti) | coh(ors) I Ael(ia) | Dac(orum) c(ui) p(raeest) M(arcius) | Gallicus | trib(unus)* (*CIL* VII 821; *RIB* 1882).
Altar. AD 259/268 (#194; *PME* II.562, #M.28).

194. *I(ovi) O(ptimo) M(aximo) | coh(ors) I Ael(ia) Dac(orum) | Postumi[ana] | c(ui) p(raeest) Marc(ius) | Gallicus | trib(unus)* (*CIL* VII 820; *ILS* 2553; *RIB* 1883).
Altar. Found 91.5m east of the fort. AD 259/68 (Postumiana).

195. *coh(ors)* | *I] Aeli[a Dac(orum)* | *c(ui)] p(raeest) Oc[tavius* | *H]onor[atus]* | *tri[b(unus)]* (*RIB* 1884).

    Fragment of dedication.

    Octavius Honoratus, African? *CIL* III 14698 (*ILS* 2655); *PME* II.612, #O.8.

196a. *Deo Co[c]i[dio.*

    Altar. Original text.

196b. *I(ovi) O(ptimo) M(aximo)* | *coh(ors) I Ael(ia) D[a]c(orum)* | *Tetricianoru\m c(ui) p(raeest) Pomp[on\i]us D[eside]\rat[us---*] | *t[rib(unus)* (*CIL* VII 823; *RIB* 1885).

    AD 270/73 (Tetriciani). The reading is not certain, tribune could read: *Pompe[i]us M[ode]rat[us], et alia.*

197. *I(ovi) O(ptimo) M(aximo)* | *coh(ors) I Ael(ia)* | *Dacoru[m]* | *Postum[i]\ana c(ui) p(raeest)* | *Prob(ius) Au\gendus* | *trib(unus)* (*CIL* VII 822, addit. 310; *RIB* 1886).

    Altar. Found 91.5m east of the fort. AD 259/68 (*Postumiana*).

    Probius Augendus: *PME* II.681, #P.108.

198. *I(ovi) O(ptimo) M(aximo)* | *coh(ors) I Ael(ia)* | *Dac(orum) c(ui) p(raeest)* | *Stat(ius) Lon\ginus trib(unus)* (*CIL* VII 813; *RIB* 1887).

    Altar. Third/fourth century.

    An Italian senatorial family: *CIL* IX 338 (*ILS* 6121, AD 223); *PME* II.755, #S.76

199. *[I(ovi)] O(ptimo) M(aximo)* | *[coh(ors) I A]el(ia) Dac(orum)* | *[cui pr]aeest* | *[---]us Con\ [---t]rib(unus)* (*CIL* VII 814; *RIB* 1888).

    Plaque. Third/fourth century.

200. *I(ovi) O(ptimo) M(aximo)* | *coh(ors) I Ae(lia)* | *Dac(orum) c(ui)* | *[p]raees[t]* | *[---* (*CIL* VII 815; *RIB* 1889; *CSIR* 1.6.51).

    Altar. Third/fourth century.

201. *I(ovi) O(ptimo) M(aximo)* | *co(hors) I Aelia* | *Dacorum* | *cui pr(a)ees[t]* | *[---* (*CIL* VII 816; *RIB* 1890).

    Altar. Third/fourth century.

202. *I(ovi) O(ptimo) M(aximo)* | *coh(ors) I Aelia* | *Dac[or(um)] c(ui) p(raeest)* | *[---* (*CIL* VII 817; *RIB* 1891).

    Altar. Third/fourth century.

203. *I(ovi) O(ptimo) M(aximo)* | *coh(ors) I Aeli[a]* | *Dac(orum) Anto(niniana)* | *[---* (*CIL* VII 818; *RIB* 1892).

    Altar. Third/fourth century.

204. *I(ovi) O(ptimo) [M(aximo)]* | *coh(ors) I Ael(ia)* | *Dac(orum) Gordi\ana [ ] c(ui) p(rae)est* | *[---* (*CIL* VII 819; *RIB* 1893).

    Altar. AD 238/44.

205. *I(ovi) O(ptimo) M(aximo)* | *co[h(ors)] I A[el(ia)]* | *[Dac(orum) ---* | *---* |

M --- | *NV* --- *A* | --- *S* | ---*]rin(.)* | *b(ene)f(iciar.)* *v.s.l.m.* (*CIL* VII 824; *RIB* 1894).

Altar. Third/fourth century.

206. *I(ovi)* *O(ptimo)* *M(aximo)* | --- | --- | --- | ---*]s tri(bunus)* (*RIB* 1895).

Altar. *Cohors I Aelia Dacorum*? Third/fourth century?

207. *I(ovi)* *O(ptimo)* *M(aximo)* | *coh(ors)* *I Ael(ia)* | *Dacorum* | *Probiana* | *c(ui)* *p(raeest)* *Aur(lius)* | *Verinus* | *trib(unus)* (*JRS.*1961, #12).

Altar. Found near milecastle 49. AD 276/82 (*Probiana*).

Aurelius Verinus: #26.

Camboglanna (Castlesteads)

208. *I(ovi)* *O(ptimo)* *M(aximo)* | *coh(ors)* *IIII Gal|lorum eq(uitata)* | *cui pr[ae(e)]s[t]* | *Ca[.]s [---* | *Ir[---* (*CIL* VII 878; *RIB* 1979; *CSIR* 1.6.54).

Altar. Moldings on back and sides have been chiseled off. Found 0.8km west of fort. Third century.

209. *I(ovi)* *O(ptimo)* *M(aximo)* | *coh(ors)* *IIII* | *Gallorum* | *c(ui)* *p(raeest)* *Volcaci|us Hospes* | *pr(a)ef(ectus)* *eq(uitum)* (*CIL* VII 877; *RIB* 1980; *CSIR* 1.6.53).

Altar. Reused as a sundial. Third century lettering.

Volcacius Hospes, possibly Italian: *PME* II.881, #V.123.

210. *I(ovi)* *O(ptimo)* *M(aximo)* | *coh(ors)* *II Tungr(orum)* | *m(illiaria) eq(uitata)* *c(ivium)* *L(atinorum)* *cui* | *praeest Alb(ius)* | *Severus pr|aef(ectus)* *Tung(rorum)* *in|sta(nte)* *Vic. Severo* | *principi* (*CIL* VII 879, *addit.* 310; *RIB* 1981; *CSIR* 1.6.55).

Altar. Thunderbolt on the left, wheel on the right side. Found south of the Wall. Third century.

Albius Severus, possibly Italian: *PME* I.90, #A.98.

211. *I(ovi)* *O(ptimo)* *M(aximo)* | *[c]oh(ors)* *I[I]* *Tung(rorum)* *[m]|il(liaria) eq(uitata)* *c(ivium)* *L(atinorum)* *cu[i pr]|aees[t]* *Aure[lius]* | *Optatus p[raef(ectus)]* | *Tun(gro-rum) instan[te]* | *Mes(sio) Opse[quente]* | *p[r]inc[ipe]* (*CIL* VII 880; *RIB* 1982; *CSIR* 1.6.56).

Altar. Thunderbolt on the left. Third/fourth century.

Aurelius Optatus, *PME* I.156, #A.247.

212. *[I(ovi)* *O(ptimo)* *M(aximo)]* | *et Numi[ni Aug(usti)]* | *n(ostri) coh(ors)* *II Tu[n]|gror(um) Gor(diana) eq(uitata)* | *c(ivium)* *L(atinorum)* *cui prae|est Ti(berius) Cl(audius) Clau|di[anus] pra|ef(ectus) instante [P(ublio)]* | *Ael(io) Mart[i]n[o]* | *princ(ipe) K(alendis) Ian(uariis)* | *I[mp(eratore) d(omino) n(ostro)] G(ordiano) Aug(usto) II [et Po]|mpeiano co(n)s(ulibus)]* (*CIL* VII 882; *RIB* 1983; *CSIR* 1.6.57).

Altar. Thunderbolt on left; wheel of Nemesis on right (the attributes also of Tanaris). AD 241.

Ti. Claudius Claudianus, *PME* II.247, #C.131.

213. *I(ovi)* *O(ptimo)* *M(aximo)* *et Genio* | *loci G. Ve|recundius* | *Severus* | *v.[s.]l.[m.]* (*CIL* VII 881; *RIB* 1984; *CSIR* 1.6.58).

Altar, patera on the left, jug on the right. Third century.

The name is Celtic (A. Birley, *People*, 110).

214. *Iovi O(ptimo) M(aximo)* | *vo[tu]m* (*CIL* VII 883; *RIB* 1985; *CSIR* 1.6.59).
Altar fragment. Second/third century.

Aballava (Burgh-by-Sands)
215. *I(ovi) O(ptimo) M(aximo)* | *coh(ors) [I] Nervan[a]* | *Germanorum* | *mil(liaria)*
eq(uitata) | *cui praeest* | *P. Tusc[i]l(ius) CLND|asinianu[s] [t]r[ib]u[n(us)]* (*CIL*
VII 937; *RIB* 2041).
Altar. Third century.
PME 169, A.278: *Claud. (tribu) Claud(ia) Asinianus?*

216. *[I(ovi) O(ptimo) M(aximo)* | *e]t Numinib|us Augg(ustorum) G(enio) n(umeri)* |
Maur[o]rum | *Aur(elianorum) Valer|iani Gallie|niq(ue) Cael(ius)* | *Vibianu|s trib(unus)*
coh(ortis) | *[p(rae)]p(ositus) n(umeri) s(upra)s(cripti) i(n)st|[a]nte Iul(io) R|ufino*
pri|ncipe (*RIB* 2042).
Altar. AD 253/5.
Caelius (Flavius) Vibianus: *PME* I.384, #F.84, from Lepcis Magna?

Maia (Bowness-on-Solway)
217. *I(ovi) O(ptimo) M(aximo)* | *pro salute* | *DD(ominorum) NN(ostrorum) Galli* |
et Volusiani Augg(ustorum) Sulpicius | *Secundian|us trib(unus) coh(ortis)* | *[p]osuit*
(*CIL* VII 949; *RIB* 2057).
Altar. Found southeast of Bowness fort. AD 251/3.
Sulpicius Secundianus: *PME* II.765, #S.87.

Hadrian's Wall; Provenance Unknown
218. *I(ovi) O(ptimo) M(aximo)* | *coh(ors) IIII Gal(l)or(um)* | *et Naevius Hilarus* |
praef(ectus) cur[am ag(ente)] | *Firm[---]* (*RIB* 2062; *CSIR* 1.6.47).
Altar. On the left, a draped figure blowing a trumpet; on the right,
a wreath and foliage. Probably from Vindolanda. Late second/early third
century.
Naevius Hilarus, possibly Italian: *PME* II.593, #N.2.

Blatobulgium (Birrens)
219. *I(ovi) O(ptimo) M(aximo)* | *coh(ors) I* | *Nervana* | *Germanor(um)* | *m(illiaria)*
eq(uitata) cui | *praeest L. Faeni|us Felix trib(unus)* (*CIL* VII 1066; *RIB* 2097).
Altar. AD 138/150.
Faenius Felix, Italian: *CIL* VI 1762, 35218; *CIL* X 1975; *PME* I.356,
#F.21.

220. *[I(ovi)] O(ptimo) M(aximo)* | *[---ia]inius* | *[---] fe[c]it pr(o) ---* (*CIL* VII
1067; *RIB* 2098; *CSIR* 1.4.5).
Altar. Patera on right side; jug on left. Found in vicinal camp on
banks of the Kirtle, 4km east of Birrens. First/second century.

Cappuck
221. *I(ovi) O(ptimo) M(aximo) ve[x]|il(l)atio Reto|rum Gaesat(orum)* | *q(uorum)*
c(uram) a(git) Iul(ius) | *Sever(inus) trib(unus)* (*ILS* 2623; *RIB* 2117).
Altar. AD 139/42. See #92.

Trimontium (Newstead)
222. *I(ovi) O(ptimo) M(aximo)* | *C. Arrius* | *Domitianus* | *c(enturio) leg(ionis) XX*
V.V. | *v.s.l.l.m.* (*RIB* 2123; *CSIR* 1.4.47).

Altar. Found in the well of the *principia*. Before AD 158.
C. Arrius Domitianus: #300, 368.

Cramond

223. *I(ovi) O(ptimo) M(aximo)* | *coh(ors) V Gall(orum)* | *cui praeest* | *L. Minthonius* | *Tertullus* | *praef(ectus) v.s.l.l.m.* (*CIL* VII 1083; *RIB* 2134).
    Altar. AD 193–211?
    A fabricated *nomen*, North African in origin (n.b. *CIL* VIII 5256, 23401 [*ILS* 4142], 23429, 23437, 20177; E. Birley, "Equestrian Officers," 166; *PME* II.579, #M.64).

Old Kilpatrick

224. *I(ovi) O(ptimo) M(aximo)* | *coh(ors) I Bae|tasiorum* | *c(ivium) R(omanorum) cui pr|aeest Publicius* | *Maternus praef(ectus) c(uram) a(gente) Iulio Can|dido c(enturione) leg(ionis) I Italicae* | *v.s.l.l.m.* (*Britannia.*1970, #20).
    Altar. Found in a ditch west of the fort's northeast corner. AD 193–211. Possibly a New Year's *votum*: E. Birley, "Altar from Old Kilpatrick;" A. Birley, *People*, 63–64.
    Maternus: A Romanized Celt?

Auchendavy

225. *I(ovi) O(ptimo) M(aximo)* | *Victoriae* | *Victrici pro salu|te imp(eratoris) n(ostri) et sua* | *suorum* | *M. Coccei(us)* | *Firmus* | *c(enturio) leg(ionis) II Aug(ustae)* (*CIL* VII 1111; *ILS* 4831: *RIB* 2176).
    Altar. Found in a pit southwest of the fort. AD 138/61? M. Cocceius Firmus: #46, 283, 301.

Duntocher

226. *I(ovi) O(ptimo) [M(aximo)* | *---* (*CIL* VII 1134; *RIB* 2201).
    Altar. Jug and knife on the left; patera on the right. Found in marshy ground near the fort.

Juno

Alauna (Maryport)

227. *I[un]on[i]* | *[---|* *---]iana Q. f(ilia) Hermione* (*RIB* 813).
    Altar. Found with debris at the foot a cliff northwest of the fort. Haverfield, Collingwood, and E. Birley ("Deities," 18, n. 20) read this altar as a dedication to Jupiter Optimus Maximus.
    Hermione: #107.

Minerva

Novimagus (Chichester)

228. *[N]eptuno et Minervae* | *templum* | *[pr]o salute dom[us] divinae* | *[ex] auc-toritat[e Ti(beri)] Claud(i)* | *[To]gidubni r(egis) lega[ti] Aug(usti) in Brit(annia)* | *[colle]gium fabror(um) et qui in eo* | *[sun]t d(e) s(uo) d(ederunt) donante aream* | *---]ente Pudentini fil(io)* (*CIL* VII 11, *addit.* 305; *RIB* 91).
    Marble dedication slab. AD 44/68.

Togidubnus: Barrett, "Cogidubnus," 227–42; Bogaers, "Cogidubnus," 243–54. See also Murgia, "Review: Minor Works of Tacitus," 339. "Tog"— is common in Celtic names, while "Cog"—lacks adequate attestation: e.g. Caratacus' brother Togodumnus (Dio 60.20–21).

Segontium (Caernarvon)
229. *Deae | Minervae | Aur(elius) Sabini | anus act(arius) | v.s.l.m.* (*RIB* 429).
  Altar. Found in third century debris of the *aerarium*.
  For Aurelii Sabiniani: *PIR* I, 325, #1598 (AD 220/1, Egypt), 1599 (Egypt, father of #1598), 1600.

Deva (Chester)
230. *Deae M[i] | nerva[e] | Furiu[s] | Fortu | natus | Macri (filius) | v. [s.]* (*CIL* VII 169; *RIB* 457).
  Altar. Axe and knife on right side, jug and patera on left. G. Alföldy's reading, followed by E. Birley, "Deities," 32.

Vindomora (Ebchester)
231. *D[eae s(anctae) Miner] | vae Iul(ius) Gr[---] | nus actar[ius] | coh(ortis) IIII Br[eucor(um)] | Antoninian[ae v.s.] | l.l.m.* (*CIL* VII 458; *RIB* 1101).
  Dedication slab. Unrecognizable object on the left; right trimmed away. Third century.

Coriosopitum (Corbridge)
232. *Deae M[inervae] | T. Tertini[us---] | libr(arius) ex [voto pos(uit)]* (*RIB* 1134; *CSIR* 1.1.29).
  Statue base. Part of the foot of the statue survives. Second/third century.
  Librarii ab eo, quod in libros referunt rationes ad milites pertinentes (Vegetius 2.7).

Epiacum (Whitley Castle)
233. *Deae Me | nervae | et | Herculi | Victor[i]* (*CIL* VII 313; *RIB* 1200).
  Altar.

Bremenium (High Rochester)
234. *Deae Mi | nerv(a)e Iul(ius) | Carantus s(ingularis) c(onsularis)* (*CIL* VII 1033; *RIB* 1266; *CSIR* 1.1.210).
  Altar. Wheel motifs on focus. Early third century.

235. *Deae sanctae | Minervae | Flavius Se | verinus | trib(unus) aram | dedit* (*CIL* VII 1034; *RIB* 1267; *CSIR* 1.1.211).
  Altar. Stylized flowers on focus. Early third century.
  Flavius Severinus: *PME* I.379, #F.73; *CIL* XIII 8156; *ILS* 5491 for homonyms.

236. *Deae Mi | nervae et | Genio col | legi Caecil(ius) | Optatus trib(unus) | v.s.l.m.* (*CIL* VII 1035, *addit.* 312; *RIB* 1268; *CSIR* 1.1.212).
  Altar. Ca. AD 213.
  L. Caecilius Optatus: #422, 620; *PME* I.196, #C.19, a westerner: *CIL* II 4514 (*ILS* 6957).

Condercum (Benwell)
237. *Minerv(ae)* | *Primus* (*JRS*.1958 #8; *CSIR* 1.1.209).
Altar. Patera on the left, jug on the right. Found southwest of *principia*. Second/third century.

Brocolitia (Carrawburgh)
238. *Minervae* | *Quin[t]us architect(us)* | *v.s.l.m.* (*RIB* 1542).
Altar.

239. *Die M|iner|ve Ve|nico pr(o) s(alute)* | *p(osuit) s(umptu) s(uo)* (*RIB* 1543).
Altar. Found in Coventina's Well.
Venico, a Celt: Holder, *Alt-celtischer*, III, 170.

Blatobulgium (Birrens)
240. *Deae* | *Minervae* | *coh(ors) II Tungrorum* | *mil(liaria) eq(uitata) c(ivium) L(atinorum)* | *cui praeest C. Silv(ius)* | *Auspex praef(ectus)* (*CIL* VII 1071; *RIB* 2104; *CSIR* 1.4.9).
Altar. On the capital and base, dolphins and birds; ivy scrolls decorate the sides of the capital, die, and base. Found west of the 2nd century fort. Ca. AD 158.

Mars

Glevum (Gloucester)
241. *D(eo) Mar(ti)* | *---]s* (*RIB* 120).
Altar.

Stony Stratford
242. *Deo* | *Marti s(acrum)* (*CIL* VII 81; *RIB* 216).
Silver plate with a gabled top; punched lettering. Found in urn at Windmill Field.

243. *Doe Mar|[t]i san(cto)* | *s(acrum)* | *d(ono) d(edit)* (*CIL* VII 82; *RIB* 217).
Gilt bronze plate, rounded top, leaf pattern on the right. Punched lettering. Found in urn with #242.

Lindum (Lincoln)
244. *Deo* | *Ma[r]t[i]* (*RIB* 248).
Altar. Found near east wall of Roman city.

The Foss Dike
245. *Deo Mar(ti) et* | *Nu(mini)b(us) Aug(ustorum) Col|asuni Brucci|us et Caratius de suo donarunt* || *ad sester(tios) n(ummos) c(entum)* | *Celatus aerar|ius fecit et aera|menti lib(ram) donav(it) factam (denariis) III* (*CIL* VII 180; *RIB* 274).
The base of a bronze statuette. The statuette, nude with crested helmet, once held a spear and shield.
Bruccius and Caratius were Celts (Holder, *Alt-celtischer*, I, 1064–65; A. Birley, *People*, 131, 143).

Navio (Brough-on-Noe)
246. *Deo* | *Marti* | --- (*RIB* 282).
   Altar. Found in the *aerarium* of the *principia*.

Deva (Chester)
247. *Deo* | *Marti* | *Conserv(atori)* | *[---]tus* | *[---* (*RIB* 454).
   Altar. On the right side, the head of a bull, a jug on the left. Found at the fort's southeast angle.

Bremetenacum Veteranorum (Ribchester)
248. *Pacife*|*ro Marti* | *ELEGAUR*|*BA pos*|*uit ex vo*|*to* (*CIL* VII 219; *RIB* 584).
   Altar.

249. *Deo Marti* | *et Victoriae* | *PR --- NO* | *H . CC . NN* . (*CIL* VII 220; *ILS* 3162; *RIB* 585).
   Base.

Lancaster
250. *Deo* | *Mart[i]* | *Sabinu[s]* | *p(rae)p(ositus) et milit[es]* | *n(umeri) Barc(ario-rum) s(ub) c(ura) eiius po[s(uerunt)]* (*CIL* VII 285; *RIB* 601).
   Altar. Right side trimmed. Third/fourth century.

Staincross Common
251. *Deo Mar[ti]* | *pro salut[e]* | *DD(ominorum) NN(ostrorum)* | *imp(eratorum) Aug[(ustorum)---* (*RIB* 622).
   Altar. After AD 161 (#7).

Eboracum (York)
252. *Marti E[---*| --- (*RIB* 651).
   Altar. On left side, a jug, a patera on the right, a wreath on the back.

Brovacum (Brougham)
253. *[Deo Ma]rti et Victori(ae)* | *[---* (*RIB* 779).
   Altar.

Alauna (Maryport)
254. *Marti Militari* | *coh(ors) I Baetasi*|*orum c(ivium) R(omanorum) [c(ui)]* | *praeest [T. Atti]*|*us Tutor [prae]*|*fectus* |*v.s.l.l.m.* (*CIL* VII 390; *RIB* 837).
   Altar. Late second century.
   Attius Tutor: #95, 137.

255. *Marti Militari* | *coh(ors) I Baetasio*|*rum c(ivium) R(omanorum)* | *cui praeest U[l]*|*pius Titianu[s]* | *praef(ectus)* | *v.s.l.l.m.* (*CIL* VII 391; *ILS* 3155; *RIB* 838).
   Altar. Found in a pit 320m northeast of the fort. Late second century.
   Ulpius Titianus: #96.

Longovicium (Lanchester)
256. *Marti* | *Aug(usto)* | *Auffidi*|*us Aufi*|*dianus* | *d(ono)* | *d(edit)* (*CIL* VII 436; *RIB* 1077).
   Gold plate votive. Raised lettering. Found southeast of the fort.

257. *Deo M*|*arti Ascer*|*nus posu*|*it aram---* | *v.s.* (*CIL* VII 437; *RIB* 1078).

Altar.
A Celtic worshipper?

258. *Deo | Mar(ti) C. Au | r(elius) sus(cepto) vot(o)* (*CIL* VII 438, *addit.* 308; *RIB* 1079).
Altar. Jug on the left side; patera on the right. Possibly after AD 212. E. Birley suggests *Caur(us)*: "Review of *RIB*," 229. C. Aurelius without a cognomen is highly implausible.

259. *Deo | Marti | Sanci | dus l(ibenti) a(nimo)* (*RIB* 1080).
Altar. Found east of the fort.

260. *Mar | ti* (*CIL* VII 439; *RIB* 1081).
Altar. Patera on the left; jug on the right.

Vindomora (Ebchester)
261. *Deo M | ar[t]e et N(umini) | Aug(usti) n(ostri) P(ii) F(elicis)* (*CIL* VII 457; *RIB* 1100).
Altar. On the left side, a unrecognizable figure, the right bears a Z with a horizontal bar through it. The emperor might be Commodus, though most subsequent emperors styled themselves *Pius, Felix*.

Coriosopitum (Corbridge)
262. *[Deo Marti] | Ul[tori vex(illatio) leg(ionis)] | VI [Vic(tricis) P(iae) F(idelis) sub] | Cn. Iul(io) [Vero leg(ato) Aug(usti)] | per L(ucium) [O---] | trib(unum) [militum]* (*RIB* 1132).
Statue base fragment. Probably belonged to *principia*. AD 155/59.

Habitancum (Risingham)
263. *Marti | Victori | [I]ul(ius) Publi(lius) | [P]ius trib(unus) | v.s.l.m.* (*CIL* VII 992; *RIB* 1221; *CSIR* 1.1.200).
Altar. On the capital, Mars holds a spear in his right hand and a shield in his left. To his right stands Victory holding a globe in her right hand, a palm branch in her left. On the base is a bucranium. Third century.
Our Iulius Publilius was probably a tribune of the *cohors I Vangionum* (#403). Devijver (*PME* I.467, #I.102) prefers the reading *Iulius Publi(lia tribu)*. An Italian name: Kajanto, *Cognomina*, 251.

264. *Marti | Victor[i] | [---] RRON [---] | Au[r(elio)] EINV | trib(uno) [c(uram) ag(ente)* (*CIL* VII 993; *RIB* 1222).
Altar. Probably after AD 212.

265. *--- | ---Vi]ctori | ---]nius Pr[--- | --- | ---] trib(un-) libe | rtus ex v(oto) s(olvit) l(ibens) m(erito)* (*CIL* VII 657; *RIB* 1223).
Altar. The face shows fire-marks.

Condercum (Benwell)
266. *Deo M | arti | Lenu | anus | v.s.* (*CIL* VII 508; *RIB* 1332).
Altar. Found in the north part of the fort.
The worshipper has a Celtic name, which recalls that of the god Lenus (#468–9).

267. *Deo M|arti V|ictor(i) | Vind(ex) | v.s.* (*CIL* VII 509; *RIB* 1333).
Altar. Found in the north part of the fort.
Vindex may be Celtic.

Vercovicium (Housesteads)
268. *Marti[---* (*RIB* 1590).
Statue base.

269. *Deo | Marti Quint(us) | Florius Ma|ternus praef(ectus) | coh(ortis) I Tung(rorum) | v.s.l.m.* (*CIL* VII 651; *RIB* 1591; *CSIR* 1.6.63).
Altar. Globe on base. Found on Chapel Hill. Third century.
Our dedicator may be related to the Florii at Colchester (*PME* I.385, #F.86; A. Birley, *People*, 117). See #588.

270. *D[e]|o sancto M|art[i] votum | possivit Vi|[---]anus* (*CIL* VII 656; *RIB* 1592; *CSIR* 1.6.64).
Altar. The god, crudely etched, stands in an arch above the inscription. Ross (*Roman Celtic Britain*, 164, plate 57b) suggested this piece read "Antocido," a variant of Antenociticus. Second/third century.

271. *Marti | et Vic|toriae | [---* (*RIB* 1595).
Upper part of an altar. Found in the Mithraeum.

272. *Deo | [M]arti et | Victoriae | et Numinib(us) Augg(ustorum) | SUB CURALIC VI | IVIC --- II | --- V.IS VALLVTI | ALPIBAIIRISI | .I.I---SIC --- | VS --- VIVIOB | --- NDICII | --- cus(tos) arm(orum) | --- SD --- T* (*RIB* 1596; *CSIR* 1.6.65).
Altar. Mars in panoply appears on the left; a goose stands at his left foot. Right side plain. After AD 161 (#7).

273. *Deo M(arti) | Calve(---) | Ger(manus)* (*RIB* 1597).
Altar. Found on a flagged floor in the northeast corner of the fort.
The dedicator claims a German origin.

Vindolanda (Chesterholm)
274. *Marti Victor[i | coh(ors) III Nervioru]m | [cui] praeest [T.] Caninius [---| ---.MI[I]IUS* (*CIL* VII 706; *RIB* 1691).
Panel. Second/third century.
Caninius: *PME* I.222, #C.75

Banna (Birdoswald)
275. *Deo Ma|rt(i) c(o) h|ortis | pri(mae) [A]e|l(iae) Dac(orum) V | P V | CVI tri[b(unus)]* (*CIL* VII 826; *RIB* 1898).
Altar. Third/fourth century.

276. *Deo Marti | et Victor|[ia]e Aurel(ius) Maximu[s] | s(acrum) s(umptu) s(uo) v.s.l.m.* (*CIL* VII 827; *RIB* 1899).
Altar. Third century?
Aurelii Maximi: *PME* I.156, #A.244 (*CIL* VI 3549, Rome, third century); 245 (*CIL* III 14927, Dalmatia, second century).

277. *Deo Ma|rti Au[g(usto)] | [---* (*RIB* 1900).

Altar.

Mars Augustus: *CIL* VIII 895, 12425 (*ILS* 5074), *CIL* VIII 2635 (*ILS* 3157).

278. *Mar]ti Pat[ri* (*RIB* 1901).

Fragment from the top of a molded panel, perhaps from a screen which surrounded a shrine. Found on fort's west side.

Mars Pater: *feriale duranum* I.9, 19–20, II.9; *CIL* III 10109.

Camboglanna (Castlesteads)

279. *Deo Sang(to) M | arti Venustin[i] | us Lupus v.s.l.m.* (*CIL* VII 884; *RIB* 1986).
Altar.

A fabricated Celtic *nomen* (A. Birley, *People*, 110).

280. *[De]o Marti | [s(ancto) e]t N(umini) Aug(usti) | [---] Paco | [ni]us Satu | [rni]nus | [praef(ectus)] eq(uitum) posuit* (*CIL* VII 885; *RIB* 1987).
Altar. Part of left side removed. Third century?

Paconius Saturninus, perhaps African: *CIL* VIII 4245 (Numidia); *PME* II.625, #P.6.

Blatobulgium (Birrens)

281. *Marti et Victo | riae Aug(usti) c(ives) Rae | ti milit(antes) in coh(orte) | II Tungr(orum) cui | praeest Silvius | Auspex praef(ectus) | v.s.l.m.* (*CIL* VII 1068; *ILS* 2555; *RIB* 2100; *CSIR* 1.4.7).
Altar. Ca. AD 158. These soldiers were recruited in Raetia.

Croy Hill

282. *Mar[t]i | C. D(---) B(---) v.s.* (*RIB* 2159).
Altar. Found in a quarry 91.5m south of fort.

Auchendavy

283. *Marti | Minervae | Campestri | bus Herc(u)l(i) | Eponae | Victoriae | M. Coccei(us) | Firmus | c(enturio) leg(ionis) II Aug(ustae)* (*CIL* VII 1114; *ILS* 4831c; *RIB* 2177).
Altar. Found in the *vallum*. Ca. AD 158?
M. Cocceius Firmus: #46, 225, 301.

Balmuildy

284. *Dio | [Ma]rti san[cto---* (*RIB* 2190; *CSIR* 1.4.130).

Fragments of an altar. Found, together with fragments of statues of Mars and Victory, in the annex southeast of the fort. Antonine in date.

Aesculapius

Calacum (Overborough)

285. *Deo sanc[to] | Asclep[i]o [et] Hygiaeae [p(ro) s(alute) s] | ua cum su[is] | Iul(ius) Saturn[inus]* (*RIB* 609).
Altar. Right side trimmed. Probably from the fort at Overborough.

The dedicator favors the Greek form of the god's name but uses a Latin dative for Hygieia (Collingwood and Wright, *RIB*, 204). Iulii Saturnini: *PIR* IV.3, 269–270, #547–548.

Alauna (Maryport)
286. *Asklepio(i)* | *A(ulos) Egnatios* | *Pastor etheken* (*CIL* VII 85; *RIB* 808).
Dedication slab, flanked by peltae.

Vinovia (Binchester)
287. *[Aesc]ulapio* | *[et] Saluti* | *[pro salu]te alae Vet\[tonum] c(ivium) R(omanorum)*
M. Aure\[lius ---]ocomas me\[dicus v.s.l.m. (*RIB* 1028).
Slab. Late second/early third century.

Arbeia (South Shields)
288. *D(eo) Esculap(io)* | *P. Viboleius* | *Secundus* | *aram* | *d(ono) d(edit)* (*RIB*
1052; *CSIR* 1.1.181).
Altar. Wreath on back, patera on left, jug on right. Found near east
gate inside the fort. Second/third century.
Viboleius may be variant of Vibuleius: *CIL* IX 1324 (Aeclanum), X
4153, 4410 (Capua), XIV 3013 (*ILS* 5667; Praeneste).

Longovicium (Lanchester)
289. *[Aescula]\pio* | *T. Fl(avius) Titianus* | *trib(unus)* | *v.s.l.l.m.* (*CIL* VII 431,
addit. 308; *RIB* 1072).
On the back: *[Asklep]io* | *[Ti]t(os) Phlaou\[i]os Titiano\[s] che[i]liar\[ch]os.*
Altar. AD 175/8.
Flavius Titianus: #32.

Apollo

Castra Exploratorum (Netherby)
290. *[De]o Apollini* | *[---] Aurelius M[a]\te[r]nus pro* | *s[a]lu[t]e [s]ua et [se] --*|
--- v.s.l.m. (*RIB* 965).
Altar.

Concangis (Chester-le-Street)
291. *Deo Apoll[i]\ni Tertiu[s]* | *v.s.l.m.* (*CIL* VII 452; *RIB* 1043).
Altar. Patera on right side, jug on left.

Epiacum (Whitley Castle)
292. *D[e]o* | *Apo[lli]n[i] C.* | *[---]ius* | *---* | *---] coh(ortis) [II] Ne\r(viorum)]* |
[--- (*CIL* VII 309; *MMM* ii 162, #488, 432 #318; *RIB* 1198).
Altar. Found 91.5m northeast of the fort. Third century.
The panels are elaborately sculptured. On the front is Apollo Citha-
roedus, his cloak pinned at the shoulders hangs on his back. He holds a
plectrum in his right hand. A harp rests on the ground at his left hand.
On the left panel, the sun god wears a radiate crown and holds a whip
in his left hand. A cloak hangs from his shoulders. On the back, a draped
central figure stands on a rock, holding a scepter in his right hand. Torch
bearers stand on either side. One torch is raised, the other lowered. The
scene recalls Mithraic iconography. On the right panel, a bearded man
dressed in a tunic, facing left, holds out a cup with his right hand and a
jug at his left side, perhaps about to offer a libation to a figure standing
on a low platform. The figure, also dressed in a tunic, with a cloak over

his shoulders, holds a scepter in his right hand (Wright, "Severan Inscription," 36). This last sceptered figure might represent Apollo as Maponus (#460–66).

Vercovicium (Housesteads)
293. *Diis deabusque se | cundum interpre | tationem oracu | li Clari Apollinis | coh(ors) I Tungrorum* (*CIL* VII 633; *ILS* 3230; *RIB* 1579).
  Slab. Early third century.
  CIL III 2880 (*ILS* 3230a), VIII 8351 (*ILS* 3230b), *AE* 1929 #156; E. Birley, "*Cohors I Tungrorum*;" Fishwick, *ICLW* 596–7.

Cawfields Milecastle (42)
294. *Deo Apol | l(i)n(i) Melonius | Senilis dupl(icarius) | Ger(mania) Sup(eriore) | (votum) s(usceptum) s(olvit) | l(aetus) l(ibens) m(erito)* (*CIL* VII 632; *RIB* 1665; *CSIR* 1.6.2).
  Altar. Found next to a spring, now dry. Second/third century.
  Dedicator from Upper Germany.

Trimontium (Newstead)
295. *Deo | Apollini | L. Maximius | Gaetulicus c(enturio) | leg(ionis)* (*RIB* 2120; *CSIR* 1.4.46).
  Altar. On the right side, a bow. A defaced figure on the left might be a lyre. Found in a pit with pottery of Antonine date.
  The *gentilicium* suggests a Celtic origin; the *cognomen* suggests an African origin (A. Birley, *People*, 78; see #407).

Bar Hill
296. *[Deo Apoll]i | n[i..]CO--- | E[---] | C[---] | S---* (*CIL* VII 1061; *RIB* 2165; *CSIR* 1.4.92).
  Altar, much weathered. A wreath on the back, a bow on the right, and a quiver with arrows on the left.

Diana

Isca (Caerleon)
297. *T. Fl(avius) Postumius | [V]arus v(ir) c(larissimus) leg(atus) | templ(um) Dianae | restituit* (*CIL* VII 95, *addit.* 306; *RIB* 316).
  Slab. Found with part of a statue of Diana near the fortress, probably from the amphitheater (Boon, *Caerleon*, 41).

Coriosopitum (Corbridge)
298. *ara(m) | Dian(ae) | posui(t) | N[---* (*RIB* 1126).
  Altar. Both sides molded, but original surface was chiseled off for cutting this (second) text.

Habitancum (Risingham)
299. *Deae | Dianae sa | cru(m) Ael(ia) | Timo p(osuit) | v.s.[l.]l.m.* (*CIL* VII 981, 999; *RIB* 1209).
  Altar.
  Perhaps a soldier's wife or daughter. Celtic (Holder, *Alt-celtischer*, 1851).

Trimontium (Newstead)

300. *Dianae Regi|nae o[b] pros|pero[s] eventus | C. Arrius | Domitianus | c(enturio) leg(ionis) XX V.V. | v.s.l.l.m. (RIB* 2122).

Altar. Found in ditch at east annex of Trimontium. Ca. AD 158. See #222, 368.

Auchendavy

301. *Dianae | Apollini | M. Cocce[i(us)] | Firmus | c(enturio) leg(ionis) II Aug(ustae)* (*CIL* VII 1112; *ILS* 4831a; *RIB* 2174; *CSIR* 1.4.115).

Altar. Domaszewski, *Religion*, 53, notes Diana and Apollo as the primary deities of Thrace, represented as their Roman counterparts. Found, with a mutilated bust and 2 large iron mallets (also with #370), in a pit southwest of the fort.

M. Cocceius Firmus, #46, 225, 283.

Bellona

Maglona (Old Carlisle)

302. *Deae Bel|lonae Rufi|nus prae[f(ectus)] | eq(uitum) a[l]ae Aug(ustae) et Lat[i]nia|nus fil(ius)* (*CIL* VII 338; *RIB* 890).

Altar. Found near the fort.

Etruscan goddess of war (Ovid *Fasti* 6.199–208; Lloyd-Morgan, "Nemesis and Bellona," 124–126).

303. *et civitatem veniens cum rem divinam vellet facere, primum ad Bellon(a)e templum ductus est errore hauruspicis rustici* (*SHA Sev.* 22,6).

The *civitas* may be Luguvalium (Carlisle) or York: A. Birley, *Septimius Severus*, 185, considers York more likely because a palace is mentioned: *quod cum esset aspernatus atque ad Palatium se reciperet* (*SHA Sev.* 22,7).

Hercules

Eboracum (York)

304. *Hercul[i---] | T. Perpet[uus?---] | Aeter[nus---] | Ebur[---] | res[itu---]* (*CIL* VII 236; *RIB* 648; *CSIR* 1.3.8).

Fragment of dedicatory tablet. Suggests a temple to Hercules. Second/third century.

Haile, south-east of Whitehaven

305. *Dibus | Herculi | et | Silvano | f(ecit) | Primus cu(stos) ar(morum) | pro se et | vex(il)latione | v.s.l.m.* (*ILS* 3471; *RIB* 796).

Altar. Base chiseled off, capital broken.

Maglona (Old Carlisle)

306. *Herculi | sortes Sigi|lius emerit(us) | d(edit) d(e) s(ua) p(ecunia)* (*RIB* 892).

Rectangular base. Found 91.5m east of the fort.

Luguvalium (Carlisle)

307. *Dei Herc[ulis ---In]|victi Con[---]|tibus pro sa[lute ipsius et] | commiliton[um caesa manu] | barbaroru[m ab ala Augusta] | ob virtu[tem appellata] | P. Sextantiu[s*

--- *praef(ectus) e civi] | tat(e) Traia[nens(ium) v.s.l.m.]* (*CIL* VII 924, *addit.* 311; *RIB* 946).

Dedication slab.

Rostovtseff, "Commodus-Hercules," 97, suggested that the god Hercules may represent Commodus and so dated the inscription to 180/92 (N.b. Dio 72.15.5–6, 72.17.4; *SHA Com.* 7.5, 9.2; *CIL* XIV 3449; *ILS* 400; Cohen, iii, 251ff, nos. 180–210). See E. Birley ("Deities," 27–8) who argued that the condition of the stone forces the question to remain open.

For P. Sextantius, from Germania Inferior: *PME* II.740, #S.47 (Devijver dated this stone to Commodus).

Epiacum (Whitley Castle)
308. *Deo | Herculi | C. Vitellius | Atticianus | c(enturio) leg(ionis) VI | V(ictricis) P(iae) F(idelis)* (*CIL* VII 308; *RIB* 1199).

Pedestal base. On the left side, the infant Hercules strangles the serpents. On the right, Hercules and the serpent in the garden of the Hesperides. Found at the northeast corner of the fort.

Habitancum (Risingham)
309. *[Deo] | Hercu | li Iul(ius) | Paullus | trib(unus) | v.s.* (*CIL* VII 985; *RIB* 1213).

Altar. Third century.

Iulius Paullus was a tribune of *cohors I Vangionum* (*RIB* 1241; *PME* I.472, #I.93).

310. *[D]e[o] | (H)e[r]cul[i C.] | V[al(erius)] Lon | [g]inu[s] | trib(unus) | [---* (*RIB* 1214).

Altar.

C. Valerius Longinus, #71.

311. *Deo Invicto | Herculi sacr(um) | L. Aemil(ius) Salvianus | tr[i]b(unus) coh(ortis) I Vangi(onum) | v.s.l.m.* (*CIL* VII 986; *RIB* 1215; *CSIR* 1.1.190).

Altar. On the left, a bull, decked with sacrificial fillets, faces right; on the right, a swag. AD 205/7.

L. Aemilius Salvianus was Numidian: *RIB* 1234; *CIL* VIII 2758 (*primipilus leg. III Aug.*, the brother of our man: *PIR* I, 65, #385); *AE* 1939, 37; *PME* I.86, #A.89.

Bremenium (High Rochester)
312. *Deo | Hercu | lenti* (*CIL* VII 1032; *RIB* 1264; *CSIR* 1.1.191).

Altar. Hercules' club appears on the right side. Found inside northwest angle of fort. Second/third century.

Vercovicium (Housesteads)
313. *Herculi | coh(ors) I Tu[ng]ror(um) | mil(liaria) | cui pr[a]eest P. Ael(ius) | Modes[t]us prae(fectus)* (*CIL* VII 635; *RIB* 1580; *CSIR* 1.6.28).

Altar. Third century.

Aelius Modestus: *PME* I.68, #A.49.

Magnis (Carvoran)
314. *D(e)o | (H)erc(u)l[i] [---* (*CIL* VII 751; *RIB* 1781).

Inscription.

Aballava (Burgh-by-Sands)
315. *Herculi et | Numini | Aug(usti) coh(ors) | [--- (CIL VII 936, addit. 311; RIB 2040).*
  Altar. Capital and sides chiseled off. Found near fort's northwest corner. Mid third-century.

Brancaster
316. *DEO | HER(CULI) (Britannia.1974 #2).*
  Bronze plaque. Found in the Saxon Shore fort. Late third century or later.

Navio (Brough-on-Noe)
317. *Herculi [Au]g(usto) [ob] restitutionem --- Proculus praef(ectus) posuit idemque dedica|vit (Britannia.1980 #3).*
  Altar.

Lamiae

Condercum (Benwell)
318. *Lamiis | tribus (CIL VII 507; RIB 1331).*
  Altar.

Mercury

Isca (Caerleon)
319. *Deo Mercurio | Cur(---) d(ono) d(edit) Sever(us) p(osuit) (RIB 321; CSIR 1.5.5).*
  Statuette. Only the base, the feet of the god, and traces of the feet of a cock, Mercury's sacred bird, survive. Found near the fort's center. Third century?

Eboracum (York)
320. *Deo | Mer(curio) (RIB 655; CSIR 1.3.7).*
  Relief above small altar. Mercury holds a purse in his right hand and a caduceus in his left. The god is flanked by a goat and a cock.

Coriosopitum (Corbridge)
321. *[D]e[o] | Merc(urio) (RIB 1133).*
  Relief. Found in the Theodosian road-metalling south of the east granary.

Segedunum (Wallsend)
322. *Deo M(ercurio) s[igil(lum) (?)] d(edicavit) et p(osuit) coh(ors) | II Ner[vioru]m pago | ---]diorum (RIB 1303; CSIR 1.1.202).*
  Fragmentary slab. On the left a goat, on the right Mercury's feet. Found 274m west of fort. Second century.

323. *D(eo) M(ercurio) [---]DIA | NE[--- (RIB 1304).*
  Sculpted slab. To the right of Mercury stands a cock on an altar, to his left a goat. Found 274m west of fort.

Blatobulgium (Birrens)
324. *Deo Mercu|rio Iul(ius) Cres|cens sigill(um) | collign(io) cult(orum) | eius d(e) s(uo) d(edit) | v.s.l.m.* (*CIL* VII 1069, *addit,* 313; *ILS* 7316a; *RIB* 2102; *CSIR* 1.4.8).
    Statue base, cock and rosette on the left side, jug and patera on the right. Found outside the fort. First/second century.

325. *Num(ini) Aug(usti) | deo Merc(urio) | sign(um) posu|erunt cu[l|t]ores col|ligni eius|dem dei cur(ante) | Ing(enuio) Rufo | v.s.l.m.* (*CIL* VII 1070, *addit.* 313; *ILS* 7316; *RIB* 2103).
    Statue base. Found outside the fort.

Castlecary
326. *Deo | Mercurio | milites leg(ionis) VI | Victricis Pie F(idelis) | (a)ed(em) et sigillum | cives Italici | et Norici | v.s.l.l.m.* (*CIL* VII 1095; *RIB* 2148).
    Altar. Antonine in date. The late appearance of Italian soldiers serving in a legion is significant: E. Birley, "Noricum," 178.

Nemesis

Isca (Caerleon)
327. *Dom(i)na Ne|mesis do ti|bi palleum | et galliculas | qui tulit non | redimat ni | vita Sanguinei | sui* (*RIB* 323).
    Lead *defixio*. Found in the amphitheater.

Deva (Chester)
328. *Deae Nemesi | Sext(ius) Marci|anus ex visu* (*JRS*.1967 #5).
    Altar from the amphitheater.

Hadrian's Wall, Provenance Unknown
329. *Deae | Nem[es]i | Apollon|ius sace|rdos fec(it)* (*CIL* VII 654; *RIB* 2065).
    Altar. Apollonius is a Greek name.

Neptune

Portus Lemanis (Lympne)
330. *N]eptu[no] | aram | L. Aufidius | Pantera | praefect(us) | clas(sis) Brit(annicae)* (*CIL* VII 18; *RIB* 66).
    Altar. Reused in the fort's east gate.
    L. Aufidius Pantera, Italian (Sassina): *CIL* III, 1978 (*CIL* XVI 76, Pannonia Superior), which diploma Starr (*Roman Imperial Navy*) dates AD 135; *PME* I.137, #A.198.

Alauna (Maryport)
331. *[--- | ---] | Neptuno | L. Cass(ius) | [---* (*RIB* 839).
    Altar. Found west of the fort.

Pons Aelius (Newcastle)
332. *Neptuno le(gio) | VI Vi(ctrix) | P(ia) F(idelis)* (*ILS* 9265a; *RIB* 1319; *CSIR* 1.1.213).

Altar, on front panel, dolphin entwined around a trident. Dates to Hadrian.

#332 and #346 were set up in a shrine on the bridge built at the point where the river (under Neptune) and the tidal currents (under Oceanus) meet, making the protection of both necessary.

Vindolanda (Chesterholm)

333. *Deo* | *Neptuno* | *aram [p]o|s(uit)* --- *NO* (*CIL* VII 708; *RIB* 1694).
Altar. Probably Hadrianic.
Neptune, intended as a river god. Note the river/ocean distinction in #332, 346.

Banna (Birdoswald)

334. *[D]eo* | *Nep[t]uno* | *Reginius* | *Iustinus* | *tribunus* | *[v]otum* | *libens* | *solvit* | *me[rito]* (*Britannia*.1974 #9; *CSIR* 1.6.89).
Altar. Decorative band on the front, jug on right. Axe on the right side of the die, cleaver to the left. Third century.
Reginius Iustinus, a fabricated *nomen*, suggesting a Celtic northwestern origin: *PME* II.704, #R.6.

Camboglanna (Castlesteads)

335. *Deo* | *[N]ep|[t]uno* | *[---* (*CIL* VII 893; *RIB* 1990; *CSIR* 1.6.90).
Altar fragment. Second/third century.

Blatobulgium (Birrens)

336. *D(eo) Nept|[un]o Cl(audius)* | *[---* (*RIB* 2105).
Altar. Found in the fort.

Castlecary

337. *Deo* | *Neptuno* | *cohors I* | *Fid(a) Vardul(lorum)* | *c(ivium) R(omanorum)* *eq(uitata) m(illiaria)* | *cui pra(e)est* | *Trebius* | *Verus pr|aef(ectus)* (*CIL* VII 1096; *RIB* 2149; *CSIR* 1.4.77).
Altar. Within the capital, a recessed shell. Found at the fort's west side. AD 138/61.
Trebius Verus: *PME* II.792, #T.38.

Nymphs

Deva (Chester)

338. *Nymphis* | *et Fontibus* | *leg(io) XX* | *V(aleria) V(ictrix)* (*CIL* VII 171; *RIB* 460).
Altar. The same inscription repeated on the front and back.
Deva is known for fine springs. The altar may have marked a source of the water supply for Deva (Collingwood and Wright, *RIB*, 153).

Habitancum (Risingham)

339. *Somnio prae|monitus* | *miles hanc* | *ponere ius|sit aram quae* | *Fabio nup|ta est Nym|phis vene|randis* (*CIL* VII 998; *RIB* 1228).
Plain sided altar. Two hexameters. Found near a spring.

Brocolitia (Carrawburgh)
340. *[Nymp]his | [vexi]llatio | [leg(ionis) VI] Vic(tricis)* (*CIL* VII 623; *RIB* 1547).
    Altar. Found near Coventina's well. Hadrianic.
    For the nymph Coventina: #444–5.

341. *Nymphis et Gen(io) | loci M. Hispanius | Modestinus praef(ectus) | Coh(ortis)*
I Bat(avorum) pro se | et suis l(ibens) m(erito) (*JRS*.1961 #9; *CSIR* 1.6.92).
    Altar. Found about 3.8m southwest of the Mithraeum. AD 200/213.
    Hispanius Modestinus: *PME* I.425, #H.20.

Magnis (Carvoran)
342. *Deabus Nym|phis Vetti[a] | Mansueta e[t] | Claudia Turi[a]\nilla fil(ia) v.s.l.*
[m.] (*CIL* VII 757; *RIB* 1789).
    Altar. A soldier's family?

Westerwood
343. *Silvanis [et] | Quadruis Ca[e]\lestib(us) sacr(um) | Vibia Pacata | Fl(avi)*
Verecu[nd]i | c(enturio) leg(ionis) VI Vic(tricis) | cum suis | v.s.l.m. (*CSIR* 1.4.86).
    Altar. Probably Severan.
    Caelestibus might imply an African connection.

Croy Hill
344. *Nymphis | vexillatio | leg(ionis) VI Vic(tricis) | P(iae) F(idelis) sub Fa|[b]io*
L[i]bera|[li] (*CIL* VII 1104, *addit.* 313; *RIB* 2160; *CSIR* 1.4.87).
    Altar. Found at the foot of Croy hill. AD 138/61.
    Our Fabius Liberalis may be the same T. Fabius Liberalis, prefect of
cohors I Aquitanorum at Stockstadt (Drexel, *Obergermanisch-Raetische Limes*
B iii, #33, 95; Macdonald, *Roman Wall in Scotland*, 423, pl. lxxii 4; Miller,
Southwestern Scotland) who dedicated an altar to Jupiter Dolichenus (*CIL* XIII
11780; M#303): *PME* I.351, #F.8.

Oceanus

Eboracum (York)
345. *Okeanoi | kai Tethui | Demetri[os]* (*CIL* VII 62; *RIB* 663).
    Bronze plate, originally silver-plated. Demetrios: #30.

Pons Aelius (Newcastle)
346. *Ociano Leg(io) | VI Vi(ctrix) Pia F(idelis)* (*ILS* 9265; *RIB* 1320; *CSIR* 1.1.216).
    Altar. Blank panels on sides. Anchor on front. N.b. #332. Hadrianic?

Parcae

Lindum (Lincoln)
347. *Parcis Dea|bus et Nu|minibus Aug(ustorum) | C. Antistius | Frontinus | cura-*
tor tert(ium) | ar(am) d(e) s(uo) d(edicavit) (*ILS* 3768; *RIB* 247; *CSIR* 1.8.70).
    Altar. Patera on left, jug on right. No earlier than AD 161 (nb #7).
    The *Parcae* are rare in Britain: compare *RIB* 953 (Carlisle) to the
Parcae for the recovery of a son from a serious illness. See 484, 488.

Priapus

Blatobulgium (Birrens)
  348. *[P]riapi m(entula)* (*CIL* VII 1079; *RIB* 2106; *CSIR* 1.4.11).
    Slab. Horned god is etched above the dedication. Found near the
  camp.

Regina

Longovicium (Lanchester)
  349. *Reginae | votum | Misio v.l.m.* (*CIL* VII 434, *addit.* 308; *RIB* 1084).
    Altar.
    The wild boar engraved on the left side does not necessarily suggest
  a connection with *legio XX V.V.* The boar is also sacred to and popular
  among the Celts (Ross, *Celtic Britain*, esp. 308–321).
    Our worshipper is possibly a semi-Romanized native.

Romulus

Custom Scrubs
  350. *Deo Rom[u]lo | Gulioepius | donavit | Iuuentinus | fecit* (*CIL* VII 74; *RIB*
  132).
    Gabled relief, 38.1 × 45.7 × 12.7cm. The god in panoply faces front.
  To his right, an altar with offerings.
    The dedicator is Celtic.

Hadrian's Wall
  351. *deo R[omulo?]* (*RIB* 2067).
    Base. Provenance unknown.

Silvanus

West Kington
352a. *O---M.N* (*JRS*.1969 #1).
    Altar; primary inscription.

352b. *Silva[no] et | Numini [A]ug(usti) n(ostri) | [A]ur Pu[---*
    Reused in furnace chamber in building XVIII at Nettleton Scrub.

Somerdale Keynsham
  353. *Num(inibus) Divor(um) | Aug(ustorum) C. Indutius | Felix Silvano | v.s.l.m.
  con(sulibus) Vic(torino) Ga(uio)* (*RIB* 181).
    Statue base.
    The consular date, AD 155, is impossible in that dating by suffect
  consuls is rare, at best. A. Birley suggests: *con(ductor) vic(I) Ga( )*: *People*,
  141.
    Indutius Felix, a Gaul or Briton (Holder, *Alt-celtischer*, II, 44). The
  genticilicum is fabricated.

Eboracum (York)

354. *D[eo sancto]* | *Silva[no s(acrum)]* | *L. Celerin[i]us* | *Vitalis corni(cularius)* | *leg(ionis) VIIII His(panae)* | *v.s.l.l.m.* | *et donum hoc donum* | *adpertiniat cautum attiggam* (*RIB* 659).

Altar. Capital and top of die are missing. Must predate 122, by which time the *Legio IX Hispana* was transferred from Britain.

Celerinius Vitalis' *nomen* is fabricated; the man was probably a Celt, and perhaps a Briton (A. Birley, *People*, 83). Vitalis: #75, 474, 538.

Bravoniacum (Kirkby Thore)

355. *Deo Si[l]van[o]* | --- | *Ael[---]* | *vo[tum* | *s]olvit* (*CIL* VII 304; *RIB* 763).

Altar. Axe and knife on left side; jug and patera on right.

Voreda (Old Penrith)

356. *Deo Silvano* | *votum l(a)et(us)* | *[p]osuu[it]* (*RIB* 923).

Fragment, probably an altar.

357. --- | *sa(n)cto* | *Silvan[o* --- (*RIB* 924).

Altar fragment.

Castra Exploratorum (Netherby)

358. *Deo* | *Silv(ano)* (*CIL* VII 959; *RIB* 972).

Altar.

Bollihope Common, Weardale, near Binchester

359a. *[Numinibus August]orum* | *et [---* (*CIL* VII 451, *addit.* 309; *ILS* 3562; *RIB* 1041).

Altar. First inscription.

359b. *Silvano Invicto sacr(um)* | *C. Tetius Veturius Micia|nus pr[(a)e]f(ectus) alae Sebosian|nae ob aprum eximiae* | *formae captum quem* | *multi antecesso|res eius praedari* | *non potuerunt v(oto) s(uscepto) l(ibens) p(osuit)*.

Third century. Secondary text.

Micianus, whose *ala* was in garrison at Lancaster, seems to have been on a hunting trip. An Italian (*CIL* XIV 4144 [*ILS* 6173], Ostia, AD 147; *PME* II.780, #T.14)?

Eastgate

360. *Deo* | *Silvano* | *Aurelius* | *Quirinus* | *pr(aefectus) f(ecit)* (*CIL* VII 450, *addit.* 309; *RIB* 1042).

Altar.

M. Aurelius Quirinus, prefect of *cohors I Lingonum* at Lancaster, AD 238–244 (Gordian III; *RIB* 1091, 1092; *PME* I.158, #A.250).

Longovicium (Lanchester)

361. *Deo* | *Silvano* | *Marc(us) Didius* | *Provincialis* | *b(ene)f(iciarius) co(n)s(ularis)* | *v.s.l.l.m.* (*CIL* VII 441; *RIB* 1085).

Pedestal.

Coriosopitum (Corbridge)

362. *Deo san(cto) Silvan[o* | *milite]s vexil|[lat(ionis) leg(ionis)] II Aug(ustae) et c(unei)* |

[---]vaniano|rum aram de suo pos(uerunt) | vol(entes) lib(entes) (*RIB* 1136).
     Altar.

Bremenium (High Rochester)
363. *Silvano | [P]antheo | [p]ro sal(ute) | [Ru]fini trib(uni) et | [L]ucillae eius |
Eutychus | lib(ertus) c(um) s(uis) v.s.l.m.* (*CIL* VII 1038; *RIB* 1271; *CSIR* 1.1.217).
     Altar. Bolsters terminate in rosettes. Found at the fort's northwest
angle. Third century.
     Rufinus served in *cohors I fida Vardullorum* (*RIB* 1288). Eutychus, a
Greek name.

Pons Aelius (Newcastle)
364. *D(e)o | Silvano | C. Val(erius) | [---* (*CIL* VII 500; *RIB* 1321).
     Altar.

Vindolanda (Chesterholm)
365. *[--- | ---] Silvan(o) | [M.] Aure|lius Mo|destus b(ene)|f(iciarius) co(n)s(ularis)
pr|ovinciae | super[i]or[i]s | leg(ionis) II Aug(ustae)* (*RIB* 1696).
     Altar. Dates to after 211, the division of Britain into two provinces.

Magnis (Carvoran)
366. *Silvano | Vellaeus | [---* (*RIB* 1790).
     Altar. Found 0.8km south of the fort.
     Vellaeus recalls a place-name in the Tungrian territory (*pagus Vellaus*:
Holder, *Alt-celtischer*, III, 151; See #698).

Banna (Birdoswald)
367. *Deo sancto | Silvano ve|natores | Banniess(es)* (*CIL* VII 830; *ILS* 3548;
RIB 1905; *CSIR* 1.6.95).
     Altar. Found inside the fort.
     Perhaps a local hunting club.

Trimontium (Newstead)
368. *Deo Silva|no pro sa|lute sua et | suorum C. Ar|rius Domiti|anus c(enturio)
leg(ionis) XX | V.V. v.s.l.l.m.* (*CIL* VII 1081; *RIB* 2124).
     Base. Found 59m southeast of the fort. AD 138/61. See #222,
300.

Bar Hill
369. *[D]eo Silv[ano | C]aristan[ius | I]ustianu[s] | praef(ectus) | [c]oh(ortis) I
Ham[ior(um)] | v.s.l.l.m.* (*RIB* 2167; *CSIR* 1.4.94).
     Altar. On the right side, a bow; left side blank. Found 219m north-
east of the fort. AD 158/163.
     The family of the Caristanii is known at Antioch in Pisidia (Chees-
man, "Caristanii at Antioch," 253; E. Birley, "Prosopographical Method,"
163, 169). Cf. *PME* I.226, #C.83; Devijver assigns our man's origin to
Antioch.

Auchendavy
370. *Silva|no | [---* (*CIL* VII 1115; *RIB* 2178).
     Altar. Found with #301.

Cadder

371. *Deo | Silvano | L. Tanicius | Verus | praef(ectus) v.s.l.l.m.* (*CIL* VII 1124; *RIB* 2187).
    Altar.
    Our Verus might be L. Tanicius Verus, a centurion of *legio III Cyrenaica*, stationed in Upper Egypt in AD 80–81 (*CIL* III 34, *ILS* 8759b): Haverfield, "Agricola," 178. Agricola established garrison posts on the Forth-Clyde line, and pottery, glass, and coins of first century date have surfaced at Mumrills, Castlecary, Cadder, Balmuildy, and Old Kilpatrick (Robertson, *Antonine Wall*, 19). Clarke (*Cadder*) and E. Birley ("M. Cocceius Firmus," 366) suggest that the Scottish Verus may be a grandson of the Egyptian Verus, a likelier assumption since most of the epigraphic evidence from the Scottish Wall dates to the Antonine occupation. Devijver (*PME* II.775, #T.1) assigns the family origin to Gallia Narbonensis.

Vulcan

Barkway

372. *Nu(mini) V(o)lc(an)o* (*CIL* VII 86; *RIB* 220).
    Silver votive leaf. Vulcan wears a cap, tunic, breeches, and boots. He holds a cloak over his left arm, a hammer in his left hand and a pair of tongs and a small anvil in his right. He stands, his head turned left, in a gabled shrine.

Alauna (Maryport)

373. *Helstri|us Novel|lus prae|fectus | numini | Volcan[i] | [p]o[s(uit)]* (*CIL* VII 398; *RIB* 846).
    Altar. Found in a pit 320m northeast of the fort.
    Helstrius Novellus: #129.

Vindolanda (Chesterholm)

374. *Pro domu | divina et Nu|minibus Aug|ustorum Volc|ano sacrum vicani Vindol|andesses curam | agente [---]o[---]| v.s.l.[m.]* (*RIB* 1700).
    Altar. Found 110m west of the fort.

Di deaeque

Alauna/Alone (Watercrook)

375. *[Dis] deab[us|que] sacru[m | ---] Valens | [---] Aug(usti) v.s.l.m.* (*RIB* 752).
    Altar.

Alauna (Maryport)

376. *Dis deabusq(ue) | P. Postumius | Acilianus | praef(ectus) | coh(ortis) I Delm(atarum)* (*CIL* VII 367, *addit.* 308; *RIB* 810).
    Altar. On the right side, Hercules with his club in his right hand and lion skin over his left shoulder. On the left, Mars with a shield at his right side, a spear at his left. AD 138/63.
    For P. Postumius Acilianus: #139, 140, 142, *RIB* 847.

377. *[Dis et | d]eabus | [om]nibus | [--- (CIL* VII 368; *RIB* 811).
Altar fragment.

Arbeia (South Shields)
378. *Dis Conservato|rib(us) pro salut(e) | imp(eratoris) C(aesaris) M. Aurel(i) | Antonini Aug(usti) Brit(annici) Max(imi) | [et imp(eratoris) C(aesaris) P. Sep(timi) | Getae Aug(usti) Brit(annici) | ---]rens | ob reditu(m) | v.s. (CIL* VII 496, *addit.* 309; *RIB* 1054; *CSIR* 1.1.182).
Altar. An axe and knife on the left side, jug and patera on the right, vase with stylized flowers on the back. Erased after 212.

Habitancum (Risingham)
379. *Dis culto|ribus huiu[s] | loci Iul(ius) | Victor trib(unus) (CIL* VII 980; *RIB* 1208).
Found in the bath house. Third century.
Reminiscent of dedications to the local *genii*. Iulius Victor: #160, 483, 493.

Vercovicium (Housesteads)
380. *Diis deabusque se|cundum interpre|tationem oracu|li Clari Apollinis | coh(ors) I Tungrorum (CIL* VII 633; *ILS* 3230; *RIB* 1579).
Dedication slab. Septimius Severus: E. Birley, "*Cohors I Tungrorum,*" 189.

Aesica (Great Chesters)
381. *Deo (CIL* VII 648; *RIB* 1732).
Altar.

Hadrian's Wall, Provenance Unknown
382. *Deo | [--- (CIL* VII 770; *RIB* 2070).
Altar. Found in west Northumberland. Perhaps from Carvoran.

Blatobulgium (Birrens)
383. *Di(bus) De|ab(us)q(ue) | omnib(us) | Frumen|tius mil(es) coh(ortis) II | Tungr(orum) (CIL* VII 1074; *RIB* 2109; *CSIR* 1.4.1).
Altar. Ca. AD 158.
The dedicator is German (A. Birley, *People,* 95).

EASTERN DEITIES

Astarte

Coriosopitum (Corbridge)
384. *Ast[ar]tes | bomon m' | esoras | Poulcher m' | anetheken (CIL* VII, 97; *RIB* 1124; *CSIR* 1.1.47).
Altar, jug on the right, patera on the left side. Third century.

Dea Hammia

Magnis (Carvoran)
385. *De(a)e Ha|mmi(ae) Sabi(nus) | f(ecit)* (*CIL* VII 750; *RIB* 1780).
Altar. This goddess was probably brought to Britain by *cohors I Hamio-rum* garrisoned at Carvoran under Hadrian and from 163 on.

Dea Panthea

Coriosopitum (Corbridge)
386. *B(ona) F(ortuna) | Deae | Pantheae | [---* (*RIB* 1135; *CSIR* 1.1.58).
Altar. On the left side, head and shoulders of a figure in mourning, wearing a cloak and Phrygian cap. A similar figure on the left. Winged head of Mercury on the back. The goddess is Cybele, the mourning figure, Attis. Hermes Hegemonius is associated with that cult (*CIL* VI 499). Found in the ventilation chamber in east granary. Third century?

Dea Syria

Cataractonium (Catterick)
387. *Deae | Suria|e ara(m) | C. N(---) O(---) | b(ene)f(iciarius)* (*CIL* 272; *RIB* 726).
Altar.

Magnis (Carvoran)
388. *Imminet Leoni Virgo Caeles|ti situ spicifera iusti in|ventrix urbium conditrix | ex quis muneribus nosse con|tigit deos: ergo eadem mater divum | Pax Virtus Ceres dea Syria | lance vitam et iura pensitans | in caelo visum Syria sidus edi|dit Libyae colendum inde | cuncti didicimus | ita intellexit numine inductus | tuo Marcus Caecilius Do|natianus militans tribunus | in praefecto dono principis* (*CIL* VII 759; *RIB* 1791).
Rectangular panel. The lettering is rustic capitals without ligatures or contractions. Iambic senarii. Found in the fort's northeast corner. The singular *princeps* suggests a Caracallan date (Wright, *RIB*, *loc. cit.*; Allason-Jones, *Guide*, #49).
Severan coins depict Septimius Severus' wife, Julia Domna, as Caelestis riding on a lion. The statue accompanying the poem depicts the empress with a wreath of corn ears, riding a lion, and holding a balance. Julia Domna was honored at Moguntiacum as Caelestis (*CIL* XIII 6671). E. Birley, "Beaumont Inscription, the *Notitia Dignitatum*," 217, connected M. Caecilius Donatianus with the Hamii, worshippers of the dea Syria; see also *PME* I.194, #C.13, Devijver offers an African origin for the worshipper, which is quite plausible as reference to Libya may mean Northern Africa. The worshipper probably identified the Dea Syria of the Syrian soldiers with his own Juno Caelestis (= Tanit). The piece could date to 170's or 180's: Kettenhofen, *syrischen Augustae*, 98ff.; Mundle, "Dea Caelestis," 228–237.

389. *Deae Suri|ae sub Calp|urnio Ag[r]|ico[la] leg(ato) Au[g(usti)] | pr(o) pr(aetore) Lic[in]ius | [C]lem[ens praef(ectus) | co]h(ortis) I Ha[miorum]* (*CIL* VII 758; *RIB* 1792; *CSIR* 1.6.134).

Altar. AD 163/66.

The worship of Dea Syria in Britain seems to have been restricted to *cohors I Hamiorum* at Carvoran (Richmond, "Corbridge," 203). Licinius Clemens: *RIB* 1809; *PME* II.525, #L.9.

One might ask if this unit still included native Syrians. Haynes, "Romanisation of Religion," 149, suggests that this cult was not necessarily restricted to ethnic worship since the goddess was known well enough at Rome to be familiar to army officers.

Hercules Tyrius

Coriosopitum (Corbridge)

390. *Heraklei | Turio(i) | Diodora | archiereia* (*CIL* VII, 97; *RIB* 1129; *CSIR* 1.1.49).

Altar. Knife and bucranium on the left, wreath on the right. The verse is hexameter. Third century.

The dedicator's name is Greek.

Isis

Augusta Londinium (London)

391. *Londini ad fanum Isidis* (*JRS* 12 [1922], 283).

Pottery jug.

392. *In h(onorem) d(omus) d(ivinae) | M. Martian|[n]ius Pulch|er V(ir) C(larissimus) leg(atus) Aug(ustorum) pro|praet(ore) templ(u)m Isidis C [---] | TIS vetustate collabsum | restitui prae|cepit* (*Britannia*.1976 #2).

Altar. AD 221–2 or 235–8? A. Birley, *Fasti*, 176–178.

Pulcher may have governed Britannia Superior during the third century (Wright, Hassall, and Tomlin, "Roman Britain in 1975," 379; *PIR* V.2, 216, #337).

Jupiter Dolichenus

Isca (Caerleon)

393. *Iovi O(ptimo) M(aximo) Dolich[e]n[o --- | Fronto Aemilianus [--- | Calpurnius [--- | Rufilianus [l]eg[atus] | Augustorum | monitu* (*CIL* VII 98, *addit*, 306; Merlat, *Dolichenus*, #269; *RIB* 320; *CCID* 586).

Altar. AD 161/9.

Aemilianus was probably commander of the second legion and not a Roman governor of Britain: A. Birley, *Fasti*, 258.

Eboracum (York)

394. *[I(ovi) O(ptimo) M(aximo) D(olicheno)] et Genio Loci | [et N(uminibus) Au]g(ustorum) L. Viducius | [L. f(ilius) Pla]cidus domo | civit(ate)] Veliocas[s]ium | [sevir n]egotiator | [cret(arius) a]rcum et fanum | [d(ono) d(edit) l(oco) d(ato)] d(ecreto) [d(ecurionum)] Grato et | [Seleuco co(n)s(ulibus)]* (*Britannia*.1977 #18).

Dedication slab, AD 221.

Placidus was a *cives Veliocassinius* and *negotiator Britannicianus*, who dedicated an altar to Nehalennia (Stuart and Boagers, *Nehalenniae*, #45).

Maglona (Old Carlisle)

395. *I(ovi) O(ptimo) M(aximo) [D(olicheno)] | pro salut[e] imp(eratoris) L(uci) Sept[i]m[i] | Severi Aug(usti) n(ostri) | equites alae | Aug(ustae) curan[t]e | Egnatio Vere|cundo pra|ef(ecto) posuerunt* (*CIL* VII 342; *RIB* 895).

    Altar. Found 183m east of the fort. AD 197.

    Egnatius Verecundius: *PME* I.342, #E.4.

Voreda (Old Penrith)

396. *In h(onorem) d(omus) d(ivinae) I(ovi) O(ptimo) M(aximo) D(olicheno) [templum] | vetustate co[nlapsum] | Aurel[i]us At[tianus] | [praef(ectus) c]oh(ortis) II [Gall(orum) rest(ituit)]* (*CIL* VII 316; Merlat, *Dolichenus*, #270; *RIB* 916; *CCID* 577).

    Dedication slab. AD 225/35.

    In honorem domus divinae, a rare formula in Britain (but common on the Rhine); e.g. *RIB* 89, 916; *Britannia*.1976 #2. Aurelius Attianus: *RIB* 929; *PME* I.144, #A.214.

Castra Exploratorum (Netherby)

397a.*I(ovi) O(ptimo) M(aximo) | D(olicheno) Iu[n(oni)] (A)et|er(nis) sanct(is) F|ortuna|[tus---] | v.[s.l.]m.* (*CIL* VII 956; Merlat, *Dolichenus*, #355; *RIB* 969; *CCID* 556).

    Altar.

397b. *d(eo) Hv[e]ter(i) sanct(o) | Fortunat[us* (E. Birley, "Deities," 63).

    Recut dedication.

Fanum Cocidi (Bewcastle)

398. *I(ovi) O(ptimo) M(aximo) | Dolicheno --- | templum a so[lo | fecit] | pro s[alute---* (*CIL* VII 976; Merlat, *Dolichenus*, #280; *RIB* 992; *CCID* 559).

    Dedication.

Piercebridge

399. *[I(ovi)] O(ptimo) M(aximo) | Dolychen[o] | Iul(ius) Valentin[us] | ord(inatus) Ger(mania) Su[p(eriore)] | ex iussu ipsius | posuit pro se et | suis l(aetus) l(ibens) m(erito) | [Pr]aesente et Extricato II co(n)[s(ulibus)]* (*CIL* VII 422, addit. 308; Merlat, *Dolichenus*, #272; *RIB* 1022; *CCID* 576).

    Altar fragment. On the right, an eagle with a wreath in its beak. AD 217.

    Merlat speculates that Iulius Valentinus may have come to Britain to propagate the cult (*Dolichenus*, 265).

400. *[I(ovi) O(ptimo)] M(aximo) Dol[icheno | Po]mpeius C[ornutus]* (*CIL* VII 419; Merlat, *Dolichenus*, #271; *RIB* 1023; *CCID* 574).

    Fragment. Hübner's conjectural reading.

Coriosopitum (Corbridge)

401. *Iovi aeterno | Dolicheno | et Caelesti | Brigantiae | et Saluti | C. Iulius Ap|-*

olinaris | c(enturio) leg(ionis) VI iuss(u) dei (*ILS* 9318; Merlat, *Dolichenus*, #273; *RIB* 1131; *CSIR* 1.1.51; *CCID* 565).

Altar. Crowned Genius with right hand above an altar on the left side. His left hand holds a cornucopia. On the right, a winged Cupid with sickle in his right hand, grapes (to indicate fertility and prosperity) in his left. Used as kerbstone to latest road-level south of site XI. Third century.

The inclusion of *Salus* parallels Dolichenus' association with *Hygieia* in Africa (*CIL* III 558, 7291, 7837).

Habitancum (Risingham)
402. *I(ovi) O(ptimo) M(aximo) D[olicheno pro salute ---] | imp(eratorum) C[aes(arum)* --- (*CIL* VII 990; *RIB* 1219).

Dedication slab. Reused in the fort's bath house. Third century.

403. *[I(ovi) O(ptimo) M(aximo)] | Dolocheno | C. Iul(ius) Publ(ilius) | Pius trib(unus) | v.s.l.m.* (*CIL* VII 991; Merlat, *Dolichenus*, #281; *RIB* 1220; *CCID* 557).

Altar fragment. See #263. Third century.

Condercum (Benwell)
404. *I(ovi) O(ptimo) [M(aximo) Dolic]he|no et N[u]minibus | Aug(ustorum) pro salute imp(eratoris) | Caesaris T(iti) Aeli Hadr(iani) | Antonini Aug(usti) Pii p(atris) p(atriae) | et leg(ionis) II Aug(ustae) | M. Libernius Fron|to c(enturio) leg(ionis) eiusdem | v.s.l.m.* (*CIL* VII 506; Merlat, *Dolichenus*, #274; *RIB* 1330; *CSIR* 1.1.221; *CCID* 564).

Altar. Axe and knife on the left side, jug and patera on the right. AD 139–161.

E. Birley, "Three New Inscriptions," 107 and "Building Records," 236 suggests that this Fronto may be Liburnius Fronto, a centurion of *legio XX V.V.* on Hadrian's Wall (*RIB* 2077).

Cilurnum (Chesters)
405. *I(ovi) O(ptimo) [M(aximo)] Dolic]heno | pro sal(ute) [Au]gg(ustorum) NN-(ostrorum) | Gal(erius) Ver[ecundus---* (Merlat, *Dolichenus*, #275; *RIB* 1452; *CCID* 562).

Dedication slab. Found on the east side of the fort. AD 198–208.

406. *[B]onae Deae | Reginae Cae[l\esti | [---* (*RIB* 1448; *CSIR* 1.6.128).

Altar; patera on left, jug on right. Caelestis is Dolichenus' consort. Found 0.8km west of the fort. Second/third century.

Bona Dea Caelestis: CIL X 4849; XIV 3530; *Bona Dea Regina: CIL* XI 3243.

Aesica (Great Chesters)
407. *I(ovi) O(ptimo) M(aximo) | D[ol]ic(h)eno Lu|cius Maxim|ius Gaetulic|us c(enturio) leg(ionis) XX V.V. | v.[s.l.]m.* (Merlat, *Dolichenus*, #278; *RIB* 1725; *CSIR* 1.6.120; *CCID* 561).

Altar. Built into a wall of a room in the *praetorium*. AD 138/61. See #295.

408. *[I(ovi)] O(ptimo) M(aximo) D(olicheno) | ---] Sabini fil(ia) | ---]ina Regulus | [---] Publi[---* (*CIL* VII 725; Merlat, *Dolichenus*, #277; *RIB* 1726; *CSIR* 1.6.119; *CCID* 560).

Altar fragment. On the capital, an animal, perhaps a cow, approaches a small altar. Second century.

Magnis (Carvoran)
409. *I(ovi) O(ptimo) M(aximo) D(olicheno) | H(eliopolitano?) ---* (*CIL* VII 753; Merlat, *Dolichenus*, #279; *RIB* 1782; *CCID* 573).

Altar.

Banna (Birdoswald)
410. *I(ovi) O(ptimo) M(aximo) [D(olicheno)] | coh(ors) I A[el(ia) Dac(orum)] | c(ui) p(raeest) Flavi[us Ma]|ximia[nus] | trib(unus) ex [evoc(ato) c(ohortis)] | I pr(aeto-riae) Ma[ximin(ianae)* (*CIL* VII 810; *RIB* 1896; *CSIR* 1.6.52; *CCID* 572).

Altar. AD 235/8 (Maximiniana: *CIL* XVI 146; VIII 2675; III 10375).

Croy Hill
411. *[I(ovi)] O(ptimo) M(aximo) Dolic]heno | [---* (Merlat, *Dolichenus*, #283; *RIB* 2158; *CSIR* 1.4.88; *CCID* 554).

Two fragments. The torso of the god, wearing a tunic and sword belt over his right shoulder, remains. The sword's pommel can be seen at the left arm, and the scabbard is visible at the right side. The bull on which Dolichenus would stand and the usual double-axe and thunderbolt have not survived. Above the inscribed panel is part of a cow and part of Juno Regina's foot. Found in a ditch outside the fort's northeast corner.

Birrens (Blatobulgium)
412. *[I(ovi) o(ptimo) m(aximo)] | Dol[iche] | no sac(rum) | Magun|na v. s.* (Merlat, *Dolichenus*, #282; *CCID* 555).

Altar.

Magunna, a Celtic name: *CIL* V 4155 (Magunnus) and 4609 (Magonus).

Jupiter Heliopolitanus

Magnis (Carvoran)
413. *I(ovi) O(ptimo) M(aximo) | Helio|polit(ano) | Iul(ius) Po|llio [---* (*CIL* VII 752; *RIB* 1783).

Altar. Probably dedicated by the Hammian archers stationed at Carvoran. An engraved gem from Corbridge shows Jupiter Heliopolitanus: Henig, *Corpus*, #351.

Magna Mater

Brocolitia (Carrawburgh)
414. *D(eae) M(atri) D(eum) Tranquil|a Severa | pro se et sui|s v.s.l.m.* (*CIL* VII 618; *RIB* 1539).

Altar. Third century.

Mithras

Augusta Londinium (London)

415. *Ulpi | us Silva | nus | emeri | tus leg(ionis) | II Aug(ustae) | votum | solvit | fac | tus | Arau | sione* (*MMM* ii 160, #471; 389, #267; *CIMRM* #811, fig. 218; *RIB* 3).

Marble relief of tauroctony. The torchbearers Cautes and Cautopates flank Mithras. Also visible are the dog, serpent, scorpion, and traces of a raven. A circular frame with the zodiac signs encircles the relief. In the corners are the quadriga of the sun (upper left), the chariot of the moon pulled by a pair of bulls (upper right), bearded winds (lower left and lower right).

Aurasio: Orange.

416. *[Pro salute d(ominorum) n(ostrorum) Au]gggg(ustorum) | [et nob(ilissimi) Caes(aris) | deo Mithrae et Soli] Invicto | [ab oriente] ad [occid]entem* (*CIMRM* #825; *RIB* 4).

Marble panel. A likely date is AD 310/311 when Constantine, Galerius, Licinius, and Maximinus were joint Augusti.

Isca (Caerleon)

417. *[In]victo | [Mit]hrae | [---]s Iustus | [---le]g(ionis) II Aug(ustae) | [b(ene)] m(erenti) f(ecit)* (*CIL* VII 99; *MMM* ii 160, #472; *CIMRM* #809; *RIB* 322).

Base. Left side cut away. Reused in baths.

Eboracum (York)

418. *Vol(usius) Iren[aeus] | Arimani v.[s.l.m.] | d(ono) [d(edit)]* (*MMM* ii 160, #474; *CIMRM* #833, 834; *RIB* 641; *CSIR* 1.3.22).

Statue. Winged deity holds two keys in left hand. A serpent appears at the deity's right knee.

Irenaeus: Greek.

Luguvalium (Carlisle)

419. *Deo Cauti Iu[lius] | Archietus [d(ono) d(edit)]* (*MMM* ii 473 #485a; *CIMRM* #875; *RIB* 943; *CSIR* 1.6.483).

Pedestal for statue. The right foot survives. Third century.

For Archietus as a *cognomen*: *CIL* VI 148 (*ILS* 3776).

Longovicium (Lanchester)

420. *Deo M(ithrae) | C(auto)p(ati) S(oli) I(nvicto)* (*CIL* VII 1344c; *ILS* 4257; *MMM* ii 160, #473; *CIMRM* #836; *RIB* 1082).

Altar.

Coriosopitum (Corbridge)

421. *Soli Invicto | vexillatio | leg(ionis) VI Vic(tricis) P(iae) F(idelis) f(ecit) | sub cura Sex(ti) | Calpurni Agrico | lae leg(ati) Aug(usti) pr(o) pr(aetore)* (*CIMRM* #870; *RIB* 1137; *CSIR* 1.1.59).

Dedication slab. Inscription was flanked by two Victories supporting *peltae*. Only the forearms remain. Built into roadway of AD 369 south of site XI. AD 162–3.

Bremenium (High Rochester)

422. *Deo Invicto et Soli soc(io) | sacrum pro salute et | incolumitate imp(eratoris)*

Caes(aris) | *M. Aureli Antonini Pii Felic(is)* | *Aug(usti)* L. *Caecilius Optatus* | *trib(unus) coh(ortis) I Vardul(lorum) cum con[se]|craneis votum deo [---]* | *a solo extruct[um ---* (*CIL* VII 1039, *addit.* 312; *ILS* 4234; *MMM* ii 162, #486; *CIMRM* #876; *RIB* 1272).

Slab. Caracalla.

L. Caecilius Optatus: #236, 620.

This stone recalls a similar dedication from the Eisack valley in the Tyrol, dedicated to the Unconquered God Mithras and his companion the Sun (*CIL* V 5082; *MMM* II no. 186; *CIMRM* no. 730).

Vindobala (Rudchester)

423. *Deo Invicto* | *Mytrae P. Ael(ius)* | *Titullus prae(fectus)* | *v.s.l.l.m.* (*CIL* VII 541; *MMM* ii 160, #475; *CIMRM* #841; *RIB* 1395; *CSIR* 1.1.222).

Altar. Bolsters are decorated with "St. Andrew's crosses," triangular pediment between them. Found in the Mithraeum. Third century.

Titullus, a widely attested Celtic name: *PME* I.76, #A.67.

424. *Deo Soli Invic(to)* | *Tib(erius) Cl(audius) Dec(i)mus* | *Cornel(ius) Anto|nius praef(ectus)* | *templ(um) restit(uit)* (*CIL* VII 542; *MMM* ii 161, #476; *CIMRM* #842; *RIB* 1396; *CSIR* 1.1.225).

Altar. A palm-leaf motif decorates the capital; stylized six-petalled flowers garnish the front ends of the bolsters. Found in the Mithraeum. Third century.

425. *Soli* | *Apollini* | *Aniceto* | *[Mithrae]* | *Apon[i]us* | *Rogatianus* | *[--- (CIL* VII 543; *MMM* ii 161, #477; *CIMRM* #843; *RIB* 1397; *CSIR* 1.1.224).

Altar. Found in the Mithraeum. Early third century.

Aniceto, the Greek equivalent of *invictus*, paralleled in Dacia (*CIL* III 1436).

Aponius Rogantianus, African: *PME* I.116, #A.152; *CIL* VI 1057, VIII 3038; E. Birley in Gillam and MacIvor, "Rudchester," 212–213.

426. *Deo* | *L. Sentius* | *Castus* | *(centurio) leg(ionis) VI d(ono) p(osuit)* (*CIL* VII 544; *MMM* ii 161, #478; *CIMRM* #839–40; *RIB* 1398; *CSIR* 1.1.223).

Altar. Garlanded bucranium at the capital's left side. Phrygian cap at the right side. The relief on the face of the capital is heavily weathered but may represent Mithras emerging from the rock. On the die *DEO* is enclosed by a wreath (compare the chi-rho monogram etched within a wreath in Christian iconography as a symbol of the resurrection and victory over death). On the right side of the base, three daggers. On each side, a palm branch. On the base, Mithras seizing the bull. Found in the Mithraeum. Third century.

Cumont thought that the wreath and daggers commemorated initiation into the grade of *miles*.

Brocolitia (Carrawburgh)

427. *Deo Inv(icto) M(ithrae)* | *L. Antonius* | *Proculus* | *praef(ectus) coh(ortis) I Bat(avorum) Antoninianae* | *v.s.l.m.* (*CIMRM* #845; *RIB* 1544; *CSIR* 1.6.121).

Altar. Found in the Mithraeum. AD 212/22 (*Antoniniana*).

Antonius Proculus, perhaps Spanish in origin: *PME* I.111, #A.142; *CIL* II 3729.

428. *D(eo) In(victo) M(ithrae) s(acrum)* | *Aul(us) Cluentius* | *Habitus pra(e)f(ectus)* | *coh(ortis) I Batavorum* | *domu Ulti|n(i)a Colon(ia)* | *Sept(imia) Aur(elia) L(arino)* | *v.s.l.m.* (*CIMRM* #846; *RIB* 1545; *CSIR* 1.6.123).

Altar. A row of three eggs on the capital. The top is roughly chiseled, perhaps to hold a container for water or fire. Found in the Mithraeum. Larinum (Southern Italy).

An Aulus Cluentius Habitus of Larinum was defended by Cicero in 66 BC: E. Birley, *Roman Britain*, 172–174; *PME* I.143, #A.210.

429. *Deo Invicto* | *Mitrae M. Sim|plicius Simplex* | *pr(a)ef(ectus) v.s.l.m.* (*CIMRM* #847; *RIB* 1546; *CSIR* 1.6.122).

Altar. Traces of red paint still visible in lettering and the cloak and hair of the god in low relief. On the die, Mithras' upper body faces front, a cloak covers body and left arm, he holds a whip in his right hand. His radiate crown is pierced so that light could shine through. A hole for a lamp appeared at the back of the altar. Found in the Mithraeum. Third century.

The dedicator is a Romanized Celt, perhaps a Briton (E. Birley in Richmond and Gillam, "Carrawburgh," 176–178; *PME* II.744, #S.55; A. Birley, *People*, 67) who served with the *Cohors I Batavorum*.

Vercovicium (Housesteads)
430. *Deo* | *Soli Invi|cto Mytrae* | *Saeculari* | *Litorius* | *Pacatianus* | *b(ene)f(icia-rius) co(n)s(ularis) pro* | *se et suis v.s.|l.m.* (*CIL* VII 645; *ILS* 4230; *MMM* ii 161, #479; *CIMRM* #864; *RIB* 1599; *CSIR* 1.6.129).

Altar. Jug on the right side, patera on the left. Found in the Mithraeum. Early third century.

431. *Deo Soli* | *Invicto Mit|rae Saeculari* | *Publ(icius) Proculi|nus c(enturio) pro se* | *et Proculo fil(io)* | *suo v.s.l.m.* | *DD(ominis) NN(ostris) Gallo et* | *Volusi(a)no co(n)s(ulibus)* (*CIL* VII 646; *MMM* ii 161, #480; *CIMRM* #863; *RIB* 1600).

Altar. Found in the Mithraeum. AD 252.

432. *D(eo) Soli* | *Herion* | *v.l.m.* (*CIL* VII 647; *MMM* ii 161, #481, 395 #273e; *CIMRM* #858–859; *RIB* 1601; *CSIR* 1.6.130).

Altar. On the capital, the sun god with a radiate crown, whip in hand. Found in the Mithraeum. Third century.

Herion: an Oriental name.

Camboglanna (Castlesteads)
433. *[Deo] Soli* | *[I]nvicto* | *Sex(tus) Seve|rius Sa|lvator* | *[pr]aef(ectus)* | *[v.s.] l.m.* (*CIL* VII 889; *MMM* ii 162, #490; *CIMRM* #874; *RIB* 1992; *CSIR* 1.6.133).

Altar. Third century.

Our prefect, of *cohors II Tungrorum*, a Westerner (*PME* II.739, #S.46).

434. *De[o] Soli* | *[Invi]cto* | *M[ith]r[a]e M[ar]|cus Liciniu[s]* | *Ripanus* | *praef(ectus)* | *v.s.[l.m.]* (*CIL* VII 831; *MMM* ii 162, #489; *CIMRM* #872; *RIB* 1993; *CSIR* 1.6.132).

Altar. Patera on the capital, a row of three jugs across the capital on the front. Found "near some fort." Third century.

This prefect, of *cohors II Tungrorum*, a Westerner (*PME* II.529, #L.15).

435. *Deo Soli Mitr|[ae ---] VIS | [---]COR | [---]* (*CIL* VII 890; *MMM* ii 162, #485; *CIMRM* #873; *RIB* 1994).

Altar. Severely damaged.

Serapis

Eboracum (York)

436. *Deo sancto | Serapi | templum a so|lo fecit Cl(audius) Hierony|mianus leg(atus) | leg(ionis) VI Vic(tricis)* (*CIL* VII 240; *ILS* 4384; *RIB* 658; *CSIR* 1.3.21).

Dedication slab.

Hieronymianus, a senator who persecuted Christians (Tertullian *ad Scap.* 3; Ulpian *Digest* 33, 7, 12, 40), was in York in the 190's; he became governor of Cappadocia after 202: *PIR*, II, 206, #888; E. Birley, "Roman Law," 51; A. Birley, *Fasti*, 263–5.

Bravoniacum (Kirkby Thore)

437. *Iovi Serapi | L. Alfenus Pal[---* (*CIL* VII 298; *ILS* 4392; *RIB* 762).

Altar. On the capital, a row of three 6-rayed stars.

A Severan connection might explain #437 and the temple at York (Fishwick, "Imperial Cult in Roman Britain," 225; Richmond, "Corbridge," 208).

CELTIC DEITIES FOUND ON THE CONTINENT

Apollo Anextlomarus

Arbeia (South Shields)

438. *Apollini Anextlomaro M.A. Sab(inus)* (*RIB* II.2415.55).

Bronze patera.

This god may have been imported from Lugdunum (Lyon) where he is attested on a marble tablet (*CIL* XIII 3190). A goddess Anextlomara, "great protectress" is attested at Avenches: Stähelin, *Schweiz*, 480; E. Birley, "Deities," 44.

Apollo Grannus

Coria (Inveresk)

439. *Apollini | Granno | Q. Lusius | Sabinia|nus | proc(urator) | Aug(usti) | v.s.l.m.* (*CIL* VII 1082; *ILS* 4646; *RIB* 2132).

Altar. Probably 138/50. *Britannia*.1977 #30, dedicated by the same man.

Apollo Grannus is attested at Trier (*ILS* 4647), Autun (*CIL* XIII 2600 [*ILS* 4648]), with the nymphs in the area of the Danube (*CIL* III 3861 [*ILS* 4650]), with *Sancta Hygieia* at Faimingen in Raetia (*CIL* III 3873 [*ILS*

4651]), and with *Sancta Sirona* at Rome (*CIL* VI 36 [*ILS* 4652]). Apollo Grannus Mogounus is known at Horburg (*CIL* XIII 5315 [*ILS* 4649]). Caracalla, furthermore, consulted this god (nb *Sancta Hygieia*) during an illness: E. Birley, "Cohors I Tungrorum," 513; Euzennat, "l'Apollon de Claros," 63–68.

Coventina

Brocolitia (Carrawburgh)
440. *deae | Conventi|nae | Bellicus | v.s.l.m.p.* (*RIB* 1522).
    Altar. #440–453 recovered from Coventina's well, west of the fort.
    Nothing suggests that the cult site predates the fort (AD 133: Allason-Jones and McKay, *Coventina*, 12). Numismatic and archaeological evidence indicates that the cult reached its height of popularity in the late second, early third centuries and probably fell off in conjunction with Theodosius' edicts against "paganism" (the latest coins from the site date to AD 378–88).
    For the name, see chapter 4, note 69.

441. *De(ae) Conveti(nae) | v(otum) ret(t)u|lit Maus(aeus) | optio c(o)ho(rtis) | p(rimae) Frixiau(onum)* (*RIB* 1523; *CSIR* 1.6.142).
    Altar. Wreath and fillets on the left side, a set of writing tablets and a carrier handle on the right, recognizable accoutrements for an *optio* (e.g. *RIB* 492). Second/third century.
    Cohors I Frisiavonum need not have been garrisoned at Carrawburgh, since it is attested there only by this inscription (Holder, *Roman Army*, 117).

442. *Deae Co|ventine coh(orti) I Cube|morum | Aur(elius) Camp|ester | v.p.l.a.* (*RIB* 1524).
    Altar. Late second century.
    Aurelius Campester, a Celtic name? Compare the *Campestres* (#512, 515–17).

443. *Die Cove|ntine A|urelius | Crotus | German(us)* (*RIB* 1525; *CSIR* 1.6.144).
    Altar with patera-shaped focus.
    Crotus, claiming a German origin, has a Celtic name (A. Birley, *People*, 92). Our man is probably not to be confused with the Crotus of *RIB* 620.

444. *Deae Nim|fae Coven|tine Mad|uhus Germ(anus) | pos(uit) pro se et suis | v.s.l.m.* (*ILS* 4726; *RIB* 1526; *CSIR* 1.6.145).
    Altar. In relief, three Naiads each hold a goblet in one raised hand; water flows from a flagon in the lowered hands. The nymphs attend Coventina. Second/third century.
    For goddesses qualified as nymphs: Brigantia (#574) and Neine (*RIB* 744); Allason-Jones and McKay, *Coventina*, 14.

445. *[Ni]mphae Coventinae | [---]tianus dec[u]ri(o) | ---] SLE[.]V | [---] m(erito)* (*RIB* 1527).
    Dedication slab.

446. *D(e)ae Coven(tinae)* | *Vinomath|us v.s.l.m.* (*RIB* 1528; *CSIR* 1.6.146).
Altar. Above the inscription is a female face in relief. The face is circular with Celtic characteristics set on a thin neck and is recessed into the front panel (Allason-Jones and McKay, *Coventina* #8). Second/third century.
Vinomathus, Celtic: Holder, *Alt-celtischer*, III, 354.

447. *Deae Coven|tine P[---]a|nus m(i)l(es) c(o)ho(rtis) [---| ---TTOIN---|---]
v(otum) [li]|bes animo | r(eddidit) et posivit* (*RIB* 1529; *CSIR* 1.6.147).
Altar. A tree on the left side; on the right a kilted figure (perhaps the goddess) holds a wreath in her right hand, a branch or a cornucopia in her left. The incised vertical lines of the knee length tunic suggest pleats rather than folds (Allason-Jones and McKay, *Coventina* #7). Second/third century.
The dedicator was probably from an auxiliary cohort.

448. *C(o)v(entinae)* | *(Au)g(u)st(ae)* | *Sa|tu|r|ni(nus)* | *Gabin|ius f(ecit)* (*RIB* 1530).
Incense burner.
The epithet Augusta is most commonly associated with the cults of imperial virtues (#70, 72, 78, 95, 96, 99, 103, 104), but the epithet is not unknown for water deities: Nymphae Augustae (*CIL* III 3116 [*ILS* 3869]; *CIL* V 3915 [*ILS* 6706]).

449. *Cove|ntina(e) A(u)|gusta(e)* | *votu(m)* | *man|ibus suis* | *Satu|rni|nus* | *fecit* | *Gabi|nius* (*RIB* 1531).
Incense burner.

450. *Deae Co|vetine Cr|otus v(o)t(um) l(i)b|e(n)s s[o]lui pro m(ea) sa(lute)* (*RIB* 1532; *CSIR* 1.6.148).
Altar. Elaborately carved focus. Four circles are carved into the left side of the capital. On the right, a small circle is incised between two semi-circles, perhaps suggesting a wreath with ribbons (Allason-Jones and McKay, *Coventina* #11). The stone has been discolored by copper. Second/third century.
Crotus, #443, identified himself as *Germanus*.

451. *Deae sanc(tae)* | *Covontine* | *Vincentius* | *pro salute sua* | *v(oto) l(aetus) l(ibens) m(erito) d(edicavit)* (*RIB* 1533; *CSIR* 1.6.149).
Altar. On the left, knife with a curved back; long-handled patera on the right. On the front of the base, a pair of lightly incised dolphins face each other. Second/third century.
Because of the dolphins on this altar, Ross (*Celtic Britain*, 351) saw a strong connection between Coventina and Neptune (n.b. #332). But dolphins are also depicted on dedications to Minerva (240), Cocidius (587), Veteris (682), and *Disciplina Augusti* (51) (Allason-Jones and McKay, *Coventina* #12).
Vincentius may have been African (E. Birley, "Deities," 46).

452. *Deae* | *Covventinae* | *T. D(---) Cosconia|nus pr(aefectus) coh(ortis) I Bat(avorum) l(ibens) m(erito)* (*ILS* 4725; *RIB* 1534; *CSIR* 1.6.150).

Pedimented stele. Above the inscription, the goddess reclines and holds in her right hand a tree branch, perhaps of a palm or a water-lily. Hübner, "Procolitia," 262, dated the altar to ca. AD 140.

It is usually suggested that the goddess is reclining on a water-lily (Toynbee, *Art in Roman Britain*, #75). Allason-Jones and McKay, *Coventina* #4, suggested that the engraving resembles waves lapping against a stream bank more closely than "the smooth lines of such a leaf." Consider a capital from Corbridge on which two nymphs recline on a stream bank (Toynbee, *Art in Roman Britain*, #94). Both the Carrawburgh and Corbridge monuments use the same convention of wavy, rippling lines to illustrate water.

453. *Covven[ti(nae)]* | *Aelius [---]* | *pius p[ref(ectus)]* | *coh(ortis) I Bat(avorum)* | *v.s.l.m. (RIB* 1535).

Altar. Third/fourth century.

The double "v" in this and the previous inscription may be accidental or intended to give greater emphasis to the syllable (Clayton, "Procolitia," 11).

Digenis

Concangis (Chester-le-Street)

454. *Deo Di[g[eni] Gaubannai [---] (CIL* VII 453; *RIB* 1044).

Altar; patera on the right side. E. Birley's ("Deities," 46, note 218) reading.

Digenis is attested in the plural at Baeterrae, Narbonensis: *Digenibus* | *v.s.l.m. Licini[a Terentulla (CIL* XII 4216) and at Cologne: *Diginibus* | *sacrum* | *Sex. Comminius* | *Sacratus et* | *Cassia Vera* | *ex imp(erio) ips(orum) (CIL* XIII 8176).

Milecastle 3, Hadrian's Wall

455. *Iul(ius) Maximus sac(erdos) d(ei) Di[genis] o[---] pe[c(unia) sua] qu[---]* | *--- (RIB* 1314).

Altar. E. Birley's reading ("Deities," 46, note 219).

Possibly instructions given by a priest. The cult has no strong military associations.

Iulius Maximus of the *cohors II Delmatarum* in Britain is attested on a diploma for AD135 (*CIL* XVI 82; *PME* I.467, #I.83). Q. Iulius Maximus: #173, 174, *RIB* 1580 (Antoninus Pius).

Epona

Castra Exploratorum (Netherby)

456. *d(eae) s(anctae) E[ponae]* | *---* | *Monime* |---|---|---|---*posuit (CIL* VII 955; *RIB* 967).

Altar. E. Birley's restoration ("Deities," 47, note 222). See Linduff, "Epona," for a discussion of the cult.

Magnis (Carvoran)
457. *Deae | Epon|ae P. So(---)* (*CIL* VII 747; *RIB* 1777; *CSIR* 1.6.151).
Altar; knife and axe on the right side, a jug on the left.
E. Birley, "Deities," 47, note 223, suggests the expansion *So(llemnis)*.

Alauna (Alcester, Warws.)
458. *Eponae* (*JRS*.1966 #55).
Buff jar.

Ialonus

Lancaster
459. *Deo | Ialono | Contre(bi) | sanctiss[i]|mo Iuliu[s] | Ianuarius | em(eritus)
ex dec(urione) v.[s.]* (*CIL* VII 284; *RIB* 600).
Altar; knife on the right, axe on the left. Found at a perennial spring
1.6km north of the fort. This might suggest a healing cult.
Richmond, "Ialonus," 45, interprets Ialonus as "the god of the mead-
owland," a name related to the Celtic *ialo-* "clearing, glade." A goddess
Ialona is attested at Nîmes (*CIL* XII 3057, *addit.*, 834). Contrebis: #599.

Maponus

Bremetenacum Veteranorum (Ribchester)
460. *Deo san(cto) | [A]pollini Mapono | [pr]o salute D(omini) N(ostri) | [et] n(umeri)
eq(uitum) Sar|[m(atarum)] Bremetenn(acensium) | [G]ordiani | [A]el(ius) Antoni|nus
c(enturio) leg(ionis) VI | Vic(tricis) domo | Melitenis | praep(ositus) n(umeri) et r(egio-
nis) | ---| ---| ---| ---| ---* (*CIL* VII 218; *RIB* 583).
Shaft of rectangular pedestal which may have held a cult statue. The
left side had broken away. On the right side, a nude Apollo in relief wears
a cloak draped from his shoulders and a Phrygian cap. The quiver can be
seen on his back, but there remains no trace of his bow. Apollo Maponus
leans against his lyre. On the back is a relief of two female figures each
standing in a niche and facing each other. The left figure, a personification
of *Britannia Inferior*, wears a mural crown with no veil. She is young with
flowing locks, and her shoulders and back are draped. The right figure,
personifying *Regio Bremetennacensis*, also wears a mural crown but with a veil
and is fully draped.
The title *Gordianus* dates the inscription to the reign of Gordian III
(AD 238–244) or later. Melitene on the Euphrates was the garrison site of
Legio XII Fulminata.
Maponus survived in Welsh tradition as Mabon, the mighty hunter
in the *Mabinogion*. The name may derive from the Celtic *maqono-s*, "youth."
E. Birley, "Deities," 57–8, fig. 4 and note 291, suggested that the god's
cult center was at Lochmaben in Dumfriesshire. See also Radford, "Locus
Maponi," 35–38.
Maponus is attested at Chamalières: E. Birley, "Deities," 55, note 286a.

Coriosopitum (Corbridge)

461. *Apollini* | *Mapono* | *Q. Terentius* | *Q. f(ilius) Ouf(entia)* | *Firmus Saen(a)* | *praef(ectus) castr(orum)* | *leg(ionis) VI V(ictricis) P(iae) F(idelis)* | *d(edit) d(edicavit)* (*CIL* VII 1345; *ILS* 4639; *RIB* 1120).
Altar. Capital, base, and sides trimmed.

462. *[Ap]ollini* | *Mapon[o* | *Calpu]rnius* | *[---] trib(unus)* | *dedicavit* (*CIL* VII 471; *RIB* 1121; *CSIR* 1.1.60).
Altar. On the left side Apollo is depicted as a harpist holding a lyre in his left hand, a laurel in his right (compare #460). The right side shows Diana with a quiver, holding a bow in her left hand. On the back, a damaged figure, wearing a short tunic, could be Maponus. Late second century.
The name is far from certain: *Abu]rnius; Libu]rnius.*
The worshipper was probably a tribune of the sixth legion.

463. *[Deo* | *M]apo[no]* | *Apo[llini]* | *P. Ae[---]* | *lus c(enturio) [leg(ionis) VI V]ic(tricis) v.[s.l.m.* (*CIL* VII 483; *RIB* 1122).
Altar.

Vindolanda (Chesterholm)

464. *deo Mapono* (*Britannia.*1971 #12).
Silver lunula. Found at site XXII in the *vicus* west of the third century fort. Third century.

Provenance Unknown

465. *Deo* | *Mapono* | *et n(umini) Aug(usti)* | *Durio et Ramio* | *et Trupo* | *et Lurio* | *Germa|ni v.s.l.m.* (*CIL* VII 332; *ILS* 4640; *RIB* 2063; *CSIR* 1.6.158).
Altar. Second/third century.
Voreda: Bruce (*LS* 793); Uxellodunum: Haverfield, "Voreda," 194; or Old Church, Brampton (a Roman civilian site): Wright, "Severan Inscription," 37, #19.
Durio (Holder, *Alt-celtischer,* I, col. 1380), a name also attested at Amiens (*RA,* n.s., 40 [1880], 325); Ramio (Holder, *Alt-celtischer,* II, col. 1072); Trupo, possibly a German name (Holder, *Alt-celtischer,* II, col. 1973; *CIL* VI 10319).

Blatobulgium (Birrens)

466. *Cistumuci lo(co) Maboni* (*CSIR* 1.4.14).
Slab. An incised animal faces right, ears erect, a collar around its neck.
Cistumus may be from the *locus Maponi,* or the dedication may refer to the god.

Mars

Mars Camulus:
Bar Hill

467. *Deo Mar|ti Camulo* | *[leg(io)] II [Au]g(usta)* | *[---| --- | --- v.s.* (*CIL* VII 1103; *RIB* 2166; *CSIR* 1.4.93).

Altar. Knife on the left side; patera on the right side. Found near the fort.

Mars Camulus is known as among the Remi in connection with the imperial cult (*CIL* XIII 8701 [*ILS* 235], Rindern; *AE* 1935, 64, Riems; *CIL* XIII 3980, Arlon; *CIL* XIII 11818, Mainz).

Camulus is found often in strictly military contexts, as at Salona which names Camulus and Epona together (*CIL* III 6871). This important god recalls several place names including Camulodunum, (the fort of Camulus, now Colchester), and a town now called Almondbury in Yorkshire. The Romans called a site in the Scottish Lowlands Camulosessa. This altar attests that Camulus was known on the Antonine Wall. An inscription from Croy Hill (#282) may have been intended for the same Celtic deity (Ross, *Celtic Britain*, 180).

Mars Lenus:
Chedworth
468. *[L]en(o) M[arti]* (*RIB* 126).
Altar. The god is represented on the panel, crudely carved, facing front, holding a spear in his right hand and an axe in his left.

Venta Silurum (Caerwent)
469. *[Deo] Marti Leno | [s]ive Ocelo Vellaun(o) et Num(ini) Aug(usti) | M. Nonius Romanus ob | immunitat(em) collegni | d(onum) d(e) s(uo) d(edit) | Glabrione et H[om]ulo co(n)s(ulibus) (a(nte) d(iem)) X K(alendas) Sept(embres)* (*ILS* 9302; *RIB* 309; *CSIR* 1.5.13).
Statue base. August 23, 152, the day of the Vulcanalia (Snyder, "Public Anniversaries," 284).

Of the statue only the god's feet of and the webbed feet of a bird survive, perhaps a goose, bird of war in Celtic myth (Ross, *Celtic Britain*, 173). Mars Ocelus, a god of the Silures, is known only in Britain (*RIB* 310, 949). Lenus Mars, however, is represented at Trier, where a hybrid Celtic-classical temple stood in his honor (*CIL* XIII 3654, 3970, 4030). The god seems to be intimately connected with these people (Haverfield, *EE* 9 1009). One of these dedications was made at Trier by a man from Chester: *Leno Marti | et Ancamnae | Optatius | Verus Devas | ex voto | posuit* (*AE* 1915, #70). Vellaunus is applied to Mercury at Gallia Narbonensis (*CIL* XII 2373).

Mars Loucetius:
Aquae Sulis (Bath)
470. *Peregrinus | Secundi fil(ius) | civis Trever | Loucetio | Marti et | Nemetona | v.s.l.m.* (*CIL* VII 36; *ILS* 4586a; *RIB* 140).
Altar.

Mars Loucetius (or Leucetius, "lightning:" Ross, *Celtic Britain*, 174), was associated with the Treveri (our man claims Treveran citizenship) and other Celts on the Rhine. His worshippers included a trooper of the *Ala Petriana* stationed in Upper Germany (*CIL* XIII 11605 [*ILS* 9136]).

Loucetius was worshipped with Nemetona (*CIL* XIII 6131 [*ILS* 4586], the Rhine; *CIL* XIII 7412 [*ILS* 4586b], Großkrotzenburg). Nemetona's

name means "of the sacred grove." Trees or groves were the preferred
place for the Druidic rites (Lucan 1.4, 50–8). The stem occurs in numerous place names including Drunemeton, the oak sanctuary where the Gala-
tians in Asia Minor met (Strabo 12.52), Nemetodurum (Nanterre) in Gaul,
Nemeton at Vaison (Vaucluse) in honor of Belasama, Nemetacum in the
territory of the Atrebates, and Nemetobriga in Galicia (Ross, *Celtic Britain*,
36, 159). The form Nemetona could be a Celtic dative (Hübner, *CIL* VII
36), or a mason's error (Dessau, *ILS* 4586a). Also #619.

Mars Olludius:
Custom Scrubs
471. *Marti Olludio* (*CIL* VII 73; *RIB* 131).
    Relief. The god faces front and wears high boots and a tunic falling
below the knees. He holds in his right hand a patera over a small altar
and a fruit laden cornucopia in his left. A herring-boned cloak lays over
his left shoulder and reaches to the hem of his tunic.
    Mars Olludius is attested at Antibes (*CIL* XII 166). Ross, *Celtic Britain*,
37, 172, interprets the name as meaning "great tree," a name suitable for
the war god of a people who venerated trees and compared their warriors
to them.

Mars Rigisamus:
West Coker
472. *Deo Marti* | *Rigisamo* | *Iuentius* | *Sabinus* | *v.s.l.l.m.* (*CIL* VII 61, *addit.*
306; *RIB* 187).
    Bronze plate.
    Foundations of a temple are visible at the site. Also found there were
tesserae, tiles, pottery, and a bronze statuette of Mars (Lewis, *Temples*, 127).
This Celtic god is known at Bourges (*CIL* XIII 1190 [*ILS* 4581]). Rigisamus
means "most kingly" (Tolkien in Collingwood, *Roman Britain*, 262; Ross,
Celtic Britain, 175).

Mars Toutates:
Barkway
473. *Marti* | *Toutati* | *Ti. Claudius Primus* | *Attii liber(tus)* | *v.s.l.m.* (*CIL* VII
84; *ILS* 4540; *RIB* 219).
    Leaf-shaped silver plate. Found with seven other leaf-shaped silver
plates. On one, Mars stands in front of his temple. Vulcan appears on two
others.

Cumberland
474. *Riocalat(i)* | *[T]outat(i) M*|*[ar(ti)]* *Cocid(i)o* | *[vo]to feci*|*[t]* *Vita*|*[lis]* (*CIL*
VII 335, *addit.* 307, 314; *RIB* 1017).
    Altar. Left side cut away.
    The god Toutatis, "ruler of the people" (Ross, *Celtic Britain*, 172), is
well represented on the continent: Toutatis (*CIL* III 5320 [*ILS* 4566];
VI 31182 [*ILS* 4691]), Teutatis (*M Annaei Lucani Commenta Bernensia* I 445),
Totatis (*EE* III, 313, #181), and Tutatis. Riocalatis is attested only here.

Rio is an alternate spelling for Rigo, according to K. Jackson, *Language*, 457. For Vitalis: 75, 354, 538.

Matres

Dubris (Dover)

475. *St(rator) co(n)s(ularis)* | *Ol(us) Cor[dius]* | *Candid(us) [Mat]* | *rib(us) Italic[is] aedem [fe]cit v.s.[l.m.]* (*Britannia*.1977 #4).

Altar. E. Birley, "Deities," 51, n. 252a, read *Cor(nel)*.

The votary was a transport officer of the governor. Olus, Aulus as pronounced by the Lower Orders? (Holder, *Alt-celtischer*, II, 847).

Venta Belgarum (Winchester)

476. *Matrib(us)* | *Italis Ger* | *manis* | *Gal(lis) Brit* | *(annis)* | *[A]ntonius* | *[Lu]cretianus* | *[b(ene)]f(iciarius) co(n)s(ularis) rest(ituit)* (*CIL* VII 5; *ILS* 4786; *RIB* 88).

Altar. Compare #481.

Deva (Chester)

477. *Deae* | *Mat* | *rib(us) do* | *num* (*CIL* VII 168a; *RIB* 456).

Altar. The stonecutter may have intended *deab(us)* (Wright and Richmond, *Grosvenor Museum*, 14–15, #8).

Heronbridge, Claverton (Cheshire)

478. *Deabus* | *Matribus* | *Ollototis* | *Iul(ius) Secun* | *dus et Ae* | *lia Augusti* | *na* (*RIB* 574).

Altar. Jug on right, patera on left. Found with second century material on the Roman site.

See #489–90. Ollototae, attested only in Britain, "of a great people:" Holder, *Alt-celtischer*, II, 847.

Bremetenacum Veteranorum (Ribchester)

479. *[Deab(us) Ma]trib[us]* | *M. Ingenui* | *us Asiati[cus]* | *dec(urio) al(ae) II As[t(urum)]* | *[v.]s.l.l.m.* (*CIL* VII 221; *RIB* 586).

Altar. Late first/early second century.

Ingenuius, a fabricated *gentilicium* suggesting an origin from Gaul or the Rhineland (A. Birley, *People*, 92).

Eboracum (York)

480. *C. Iuliu(s)* | *Crescens* | *Matri* | *bus Do* | *mesticis* | *v.s.m.l.* (*RIB* 652; *CSIR* 1.3.25).

Altar. Sides fluted.

The *Matres Domesticae* are known also at Bonn (*CIL* XIII 8022–8026).

481. *Matr(ibus) Af(ris) Ita(lis) Ga(llis)* | *M. Minu(cius) Aude(n)s* | *mil(es) leg(ionis) VI Vic(tricis)* | *guber(nator) leg(ionis) VI* | *v.s.l.l.m.* (*CIL* VII 238; *ILS* 4787; *RIB* 653).

Altar. After AD 122.

The three epithets reflect the different origins of fellow soldiers: #476.

482. *[M]atribus | suis Marcus | Rustius v.s.l. | Massa l.m.* (*CIL* VII 1342; *RIB* 654).
Altar.

Cataractonium (Catterick)
483. *Matribus Domesticis | Iu(lius) Victor pro se | et suis v.s.l.l.m.* (*JRS*.1960 #6; *CSIR* 1.3.29).
Altar. Found inside the Roman town.
Iulius Victor: #160, 379, 493.

Skinburness, Cumbria
484. *Matribu[s] | Par(cis) VITI |VACI* (*CIL* VII 418; *RIB* 881).
Altar. See #347, 488.

Maglona (Old Carlisle)
485. *[Dea]bus Ma[tribus | pro s]alute M. [Aur(eli) | Alexa]ndri [P(ii) F(elicis) | Aug(usti) et Iu]liae M[am\eae matr(is) d(omini)] n(ostri) et c[astr(orum) |---] pu[---* (*CIL* VII 348; *RIB* 901).
Dedication slab, in fragments. Found southeast of the fort. AD 222/235.

Voreda (Old Penrith)
486. *Deabus Matribus Tramarinis | et N(umini) imp(eratoris) Alexandri Aug(usti) et Iul(iae) Mam\meae matr(i) Aug(usti) n(ostri) et castrorum to|[tique eorum] domui divinae ae|[dem ruina dilapsam vexil]latio M[a]r|[sacorum---* (*CIL* VII 319; *RIB* 919).
Dedication slab. AD 222/235.
The Marsaci/Marsacii lived near the Rhine in Zeeland.

487. *Deabus Ma\tribus Tramari(nis) | vex(illatio) Germa[no]r(um) V[o]r[e]d(ensium) pro sa\lute R. F v.s.l.m.* (*CIL* VII 303, addit. 307; *RIB* 920).
Altar. Third century.
The unit seems to have taken on the name of its fort.

Luguvalium (Carlisle)
488. *Matrib(us) Parc(is) pro salut(e) | Sanctiae Geminae* (*CIL* VII 927, addit. 311; *RIB* 951).
Base, probably once held a relief of the three Mother goddesses.
For *Matres Parcae*: *CIL* XIII 6223 (Weis-Oppenheim); #347, 484.

Vinovia (Binchester)
489. *Deab(us) | Matrib(us) O[l]lot(otis) | T[i]b(erius) Cl(audius) Quin\tianus b(ene)f(icia-rius) co(n)s(ularis) | v.s.l.m.* (*CIL* VII 424; *RIB* 1031).
Altar.
The *Matres Ollototae* are attested only in Britain (#154, 478, 490).

490. *[M]atrib(us) O[lloto(tis)] | CARTO VAL | MARTI Vetto(num) | GENIO LOCI | LIT . IXT* (*CIL* VII 425; *RIB* 1032).
Altar.
Perhaps set up by the *Ala Hispanorum Vettonum CR.*

491. *Mat(ribus) | sac(rum) | Geme\llus | v.s.l.m.* (*CIL* VII 426; *RIB* 1033).
Altar.
Gemellus: Kajanto, *Cognomina*, 75, 295.

492. *Mat[ribus ---| trib(unus) [--- | inst(ante) [--- | IRI [--- (RIB* 1034).
Altar. Patera on the left. Right side trimmed away. The votive is probably legionary (tribune). Third century.

Habitancum (Risingham)
493. *Matribu|s Trama|rinis Iul(ius) | Victor v.s.l.m.* (*CIL* VII 994; *RIB* 1224;
CSIR 1.1.242).
Altar. A six-petal wheel on each corner of upper portion of capital.
On each side, a whorl-wheel disc. Found in the south gateway, badly
weathered. Third century.
Iulius Victor: #160, 379, 483.

Pons Aelius (Newcastle)
494. *Dea(bus) | Matribus Tramarinis | Patri(i)s Aurelius Iuvenalis | s(acrum)* (*CIL*
VII 499; *ILS* 4784; *RIB* 1318).
Dedication. Above the inscription are the three Mother Goddesses
each enthroned in a separate niche, their arms folded.

495. *Matribus | [---] G[.]O | [---] Leg | [---]V | [---* (*Britannia*.1978 #13).
Altar.

Milecastle 19, Hadrian's Wall
496. *Matrib(us) | templ(um) cum ara | vex(illatio) coh(ortis) | I Vard(ullorum) |
instante P. D. V. | v.s.l.m.* (*RIB* 1421; *CSIR* 1.1.239).
Altar. Knife on right side, axe on left. Found in second century level
in the milecastle. Ca. 138/150.

Onnum (Halton Chesters)
497. *Deabus | [M]atribu|[s---E.* (*CIL* VII 559; *RIB* 1424; *CSIR* 1.1.238).
Altar fragment. On the front of the capital, two Victories support a
wreath decorated with ribbons. Portion of patera visible on left side, fragment of jug visible on right. Second/third century.

Cilurnum (Chesters)
498. *[Mat]ribus Com|[mun(ibus) p]ro salute de|[cur(iae) A]ur(eli) Severi | [--- (RIB*
1453).
Dedication slab. Found in the baths. 222/35?

Brocolitia (Carrawburgh)
499. *Matribus | Albinius | Quart(us) mil(es) d(edicavit)* (*RIB* 1540; *CSIR* 1.6.165).
Altar. A festoon on the right side. Reused a bench in the nave of
Mithraeum III. Its inscribed face was deliberately hidden. Mithraeum II
was destroyed ca. 296/7, and subsequently completely rebuilt: Richmond
and Gillam, "Mithras at Carrawburgh," 28–29, 33.

500. *Mat|ribu|s Com|mun(ibus)* (*RIB* 1541).
Altar.

Vercovicium (Housesteads)
501. *[Ma]tribus | coh(ors) I Tungr|[or]u[m]* (*CIL* VII 653; *RIB* 1598).
Altar. Third/fourth century.

Vindolanda (Chesterholm)
502. *Matribus et Nu|mini d(omini) n(ostri) [---|.]ini [---* (*RIB* 1692).
Altar. Found 27m north of north guard chamber of west gate.
According to Collingwood and Wright (*RIB* 533), *Maxi|mini* does not
fit the traces of the lettering. Some dedications to the emperor's *numen*,
however, do not specify the emperor, e.g. *RIB* 193 (Colchester).

503. *Deab[us] | [s]uis Ma[t]|[ribus--- | --- | --- | [v.] s.l.m.* (*Britannia*.1970 #16).
Altar. Found at the south gate of the Constantinian fort.

Magnis (Carvoran)
504. *Matrib[us|---]ntius[---* (*CIL* VII 756; *RIB* 1785; *CSIR* 1.6.178).
Altar. A female figure stands in a niche at the left of a small altar.
Second/third century.

Banna (Birdoswald)
505. *Matr[ib]|us PRNV --- | VVSCO [v.s.] | l.m.* (*CIL* VII 832; *RIB* 1902).
Altar.

Camboglanna (Castlesteads)
506. *[Deabu]s | [Mat]ribu[s] | omnium | gentium | templum | olim vetus|tate con-
lab|sum C. Iul(ius) Cu|pitianus c(enturio) | p(rae)p(ositus) restituit* (*CIL* VII 887,
addit. 310; *ILS* 4788; *RIB* 1988).
Altar. Reused in south jamb of east gate.
E. Birley, "Some Roman Military Inscriptions," 70 suggested that the
omnes gentes were, in fact, the various peoples comprising the Roman army.
This temple was restored early in the third century; but the structure
is unknown (Lewis, *Temples*, 120).
Cupitianus: *CIL* III 4442, 4452, 4733, 5221 (Egypt, Illyricum); Holder,
Alt-celtischer, I, col. 1197.

507. *Matri|bus Tr[a]|mar[inis* (*RIB* 1989).
Altar fragment.

Uxelodunum (Stanwix)
508. *Matribu[s D]|omesticis [s]|uis Asin[ius] | S[e]nili[s] v.s.l.m.* (*CIL* VII 915;
RIB 2025).
Altar. On the right side, a jug; patera on the left.

Dykesfield
509. *Matri(bus) | Dom(esticis) | vex(illatio) | [l]eg(ionis) VI | [V(ictricis)] P(iae)
F(idelis)* (*CIL* VII 939; *RIB* 2050).
Altar. Found southwest of milecastle 73 on Hadrian's Wall. After
AD 122.

Milecastle 79
510. *Matri|bus suis | milite[s | ---* (*CIL* VII 950; *RIB* 2055).
Altar fragment Found on the Wall east of the milecastle.

Hadrian's Wall, Provenance Unknown
511. *Ma[tribus] | Ger[manis] | M. Senec[i]|a]nius V[---* (*CIL* VII 652; *RIB* 2064).
Altar.
A German worshipper? Holder, *Alt-celtischer*, II, col. 1472–73.

Cramond

512. *Matrib(us) Ala|tervis et Matrib(us) Cam|pestribu(s) coh(ors) I | Tungr(orum) ins(tante) | VERSCARM | [c(enturione)] leg(ionis) XX V.V.* (*CIL* VII 1084; *ILS* 4801; *RIB* 2135).
Altar.

The *cohors I Tungrorum* was not mounted; the *cohors II Tungrorum*, however, was *equitata*. Both units are attested in the Antonine Wall area early in the reign of Antoninus Pius. The *Matres Campestres* are appropriate to a mounted unit (E. Birley, "Deities," 49 and note 237).

The *Alatervae* might be related to the Mother Goddesses attested on the Lower Rhine as *Alaferhuiae* (*CIL* XIII 7862, 12012; *RGKBer* #303) and as *Alateiviae* (*CIL* XIII 8606). Alatervae may be a fusion of the two attested Germanic forms or a misreading of Alafervis (Collingwood and Wright, *RIB*, 656): Davies, "Training Grounds," 96.

Mumrills

513. *Cassius | sign(ifer) | Matribus---* (*RIB* 2141).
Altar. Found 146m east of the fort.

The *signifer* could be of the *Ala I Tungrorum* (*RIB* 2140) or the *cohors II Thracum eq.* (*RIB* 2142), both at Mumrills under Antoninus Pius.

Castlecary

514. *Matrib(us) | milites | vexill[at]io(n---) | [---* (*CIL* VII 1094; *RIB* 2147).
Altar. AD 138/50.

A vexillation of *legio II Augusta* or *legio VI Victrix Pia Fidelis* (*RIB* 2146).

Matres Campestres

Gloster Hill

515. *[Ca]mpestri|[bus c]oh(ors) I | [---]* (*CIL* VII 1029, addit. 312; *RIB* 1206).
Altar. Second/third century.

Perhaps *cohors I Vangionum* or *cohors I Fida Vardullorum* whose *equites* trained on the Northumberland coast (Davies, "Training Grounds," 73–75). Mother Goddesses of the parade grounds were worshipped by mounted units and recall Epona (Domaszewski, *Religion*, 51). Elsewhere the goddesses are addressed as *Campestres* without the further definition *Matres* (E. Birley, "Campestres," 109; "Religion of Roman Army," 1529) and as *diis/dis Campestribus* in Lambaesis (*CIL* VIII 2635, 10760): Baradez, *Sud-Algérien*, 104 (Lambaesis).

Trimontium (Newstead)

516. *Campestr(ibus) | sacrum Ael(ius) | M. | dec(urio) alae Aug(ustae) | Vocontio(rum) | v.s.l.l.m.* (*CIL* VII 1080; *RIB* 2121).
Altar. Found 183m east of the fort. AD 142/55.

Castlehill

517. *Campes|tribus et | Britanni(ae) | Q. Pisentius | Iustus Pr(a)ef(ectus) | coh(ortis) IIII Gal(lorum) | v.s.l.l.m.* (*CIL* VII 1129; *ILS* 4829; *RIB* 2195).
Altar. Found a few hundred meters east of the fort. It seems to have been buried intentionally. AD 138/50.

The *cohors IV Gallorum* was mounted (*RIB* 1979). Pisentius Iustus, perhaps Italian: *PME* II.643, #P.36.

Mogons

Voreda (Old Penrith)
518. *deo | Mog(on)ti* (*CIL* VII 320; *RIB* 921).
Altar.
Mogons, from Upper Germany. His name recalls Mogontiacum (Mainz) and the goddess Mogontia at Metz (*CIL* XIII 4313 [*ILS* 4706]). A graffito found at Saalburg seems to invoke this god: *Mogont(i?) Narci(ssus)* (*RGKBericht* 1909, 59). Ross, *Celtic Britain*, 201, 375, defines the name as "powerful" or "great one;" see Jackson, *Language*, 444.

Castra Exploratorum (Netherby)
519. *Deo | Mogont(i) | Vitire san(cto) | Ael(ius) [Secund(us)] | v.s.l.m.* (*CIL* VII 958; *ILS* 4733; *RIB* 971).
Altar.
The name seems Romanized.

Habitancum (Risingham)
520. *[D]eo | Mogonti Cad(---) | et N(umini) N(omini) n(ostri) Aug(usti) | M. G(auius?) Secundinus | [b(ene)]f(iciarius) co(n)s(ularis) Habita|nci prima stat(ione) | pro se et suis posu[it]* (*CIL* VII 996, addit. 311; *ILS* 4728; *RIB* 1225).
Altar. Found in the River Rede just north of the fort. Third century?
Cad. may be a territorial epithet, perhaps a German pagus: Richmond, "Redesdale," 86; cf. #524.

Vindolanda (Chesterholm)
521. *deo Mo|gunti et | Genio lo|ci | Lupul(us) [v.]s.m.* (*Britannia*.1973 #10).
Small altar. Found in the *vicus* west of the Diocletianic fort.

Mountis

Voreda (Old Penrith)
522. *Deo | Mounti | [p]ro salu(t)e | [---]sti v.s.|l.m.* (*CIL* VII 321; *RIB* 922).
Altar. Perhaps a variant of Mogons/Mounus.

Bremenium (High Rochester)
523. *Dis | Mounti|bus Iul(ius) | Firmin|us dec(urio) f(ecit)* (*CIL* VII 1036; *RIB* 1269).
Altar.

Mounus

Habitancum (Risingham)
524. *Deo | Mouno Cad(---) | Iuuent[i]us Do|[---| v.s.* (*CIL* VII 997; *RIB* 1226).
Altar. Found in the Rede, north of the fort.
Mounus, attested in Gaul on a piece of Samian ware (*CIL* XIII 10012,

19), might be an alternate of Mogons (E. Birley, "Deities," 54–55). For *Cad(---)*, #520.

Sucellus

Eboracum (York)
525. *deo Sucello* (*EE* III 181a).
    Silver ring.
    Sucellus was identified with Jupiter (Jupiter Sucaelus) at Mainz (*CIL* XIII 6730), where he is depicted as a bearded middle-aged deity (recalling the classical Jupiter) and carrying a hammer (indicating his function as a Celtic smith god). His consort, Nantosvelta, commonly carries a model house set on a long pole. Their attributes include ravens (symbolic of war), dogs, barrels and pots.
    Reliefs from East Stoke, Nottinghamshire (Frere, *Britannia*, 318) and Corbridge in the late second century suggest the smith god (Leach, "Smith God," 35–39). Literature (e.g., Caesar, *BG* VI.21.2) further reflects the Celtic smith god's importance.

Sulis

Aquae Sulis (Bath)
526. *[D]eae Suli | pro salute et | incolumita[te] Mar(ci) Aufid[i | M]aximi c(enturionis) leg(ionis) | VI Vic(tricis) | [A]ufidius Eu | tuches leb(ertus) v.s.l.m.* (*CIL* VII 40; *RIB* 143).
    Altar. After AD 122.
    Outside Bath, Sulis is attested only at Alzey: *dea(e) Sul(i) | Attonius Lucanus* (*CIL* XIII 6266). A native British deity, her cult was exported to the Rhineland by a visitor to the Romano-British resort. The freedman's name is Greek. See pp. 166–171 (Chapter 5) for discussion of the site and cult.

527. *Deae Suli | [p]ro salute et | [i]ncolumitate | Aufidi Maximi | c(enturionis) leg(ionis) VI Vic(tricis) | M. Aufidius Lemnus | libertus v.s.l.m.* (*CIL* VII 41; *RIB* 144).
    Altar.
    Lemnus: *CIL* VI 8499 (*ILS* 1489), *CIL* VI 8450 (*ILS* 1490).

528. *Deae S[uli] | Ti(berius) Cl(audius) T[i(beri) fil(ius)] | Sollem[nis | --- (*CIL* VII 44; *RIB* 145).
    Dedication slab.

529. *Deae Su | li Min(ervae) et Nu | min(ibus) Augg(ustorum) C. | Curatius | Saturninus | c(enturio) leg(ionis) II Aug(ustae) | pro se su | isque | v.s.l.m.* (*CIL* VII 42; *RIB* 146).
    Altar. AD 161–169 or later (#7).

530. *Dea[e] Suli | [o]b s[alutem] sac(rum) | G. Iau[oleni Sa]tur[n | al]is [--- | i]m[a]g[i]n(iferi) leg(ionis) II | Aug(ustae) L. Manius | Dionisias libe(r)t(us) | v.s.l.m.* (*RIB* 147).

Altar.

Iavolenus: *PIR*, IV.3, 108, #13.

531. *Q. Pompeius | Anicetus | Suli* (*RIB* 148).
Altar.
A Greek cognomen (A. Birley, *People*, 139).

532. *Priscus | Touti f(ilius) | lapidariu[s] | cives Car[nu]|tenus Su[li] | deae
v.[s.l.m.]* (*ILS* 4661; *RIB* 149).
Dedication stone.
The worshipper is from Chartres.

533. *Deae | Suli Mi|nervae | Sulinus | Matu|ri fil(ius) | v.s.l.m.* (*CIL* VII 43;
ILS 4660; *RIB* 150).
Altar.
A Celtic name which curiously resembles the goddess'.

Tanarus

Deva (Chester)
534. *I(ovi) O(ptimo) M(aximo) Tanaro | L. [Bruttius ?)] Galer(ia tribu) | Praesens
[Cl]unia | pri(nceps) leg(ionis) XX V.V. | Commodo et | Laterano co(n)s(ulibus) |
v.s.l.m.* (*CIL* VII 168; *ILS* 4622; *RIB* 452).
    Altar. A flower with six petals appears on the right, a jug on the left,
and a rosette encircled by a wreath on the back. Found at a depth of
20.3cm. AD 154: E. Birley, "Some Military Inscriptions," 207.
    The Celtic epithet Tanarus means "the roarer" (Tolkien in Colling-
wood, *Roman Britain*, 262). Probably a variant of Taranis: deo Taranunco
(*CIL* XIII 6478 [*ILS* 4624]; XIII 6094 [*ILS* 4625]); Iovi Taranuco (*CIL* III
2804 [*ILS* 4623]); Tarnis ara (Lucan 1.446). Equivalent to the Germanic
Donan: Heichelheim, "Vitiris," 414.

CELTIC DEITIES FOUND ONLY IN BRITAIN

Antenociticus

Condercum (Benwell)
535. *Deo | Antenocitico | et Numinib(us) | Augustor(um) | Ael(ius) Vibius | c(entu-
rio) leg(ionis) XX V.V. | v.s.l.m.* (*CIL* VII 503; *ILS* 4714; *RIB* 1327; *CSIR*
1.1.230).
    Altar. Elaborately decorated with foliage, a vase with vine tendrils on
the left side of the capital, a loose vine scroll on the right. A garland suspended above a knife on the left side of the shaft, a garland above a jug
on the right. Found in the ruins of temple outside the fort. Third century?
    The god's name has defied interpretation. See pp. 111–112 (chapter 3).

536. *Deo An[t]enocitico | sacrum | coh(ors) I Va[n]gion(um) | quib(us) praeest |*

[---] c(ius) Cassi|[anus p]raef(ectus) | [v.s.l.]m. (CIL VII 515; *ILS* 9316; *RIB* 1328).

Altar. Found in the temple. AD 161/80.

537. *Deo Anocitico | iudiciis Optimo|rum Maximorum|que Imp(eratorum) N(ostrorum) sub Ulp(io) | Marcello co(n)s(ulari) Tine|ius Longus in p[re]\fectura equitu[m] | lato clavo exorna|tus et q(uaestor) d(esignatus) (CIL* VII 504; *ILS* 4715; *RIB* 1329; *CSIR* 1.1.231).

Altar. Triangle motifs on sides of capital. Three scallops on the base. Found in the temple. AD 180/5.

Arciaco

Eboracum (York)

538. *Deo | Arciacon(i) | et N(umini) Aug(u)st(i) | Mat(---) Vitalis | ord(inatus) v.s.l.m. (CIL* VII 231; *RIB* 640; *CSIR* 1.3.24).

Altar. Dates possibly to early second century since clearly only one Augustus is being honored.

The expansion of Mat. is uncertain (*RIB*, 215). No comment has been made on the deity's name or nature. Vitalis: #75, 354, 474.

Arecurius

Coriosopitum (Corbridge)

539. *Deo | Arecurio | Apollinaris | Cassi | v.s.l.m (RIB* 1123; *CSIR* 1.1.61).

Statue. Head missing. Carved in the round, the god clasps something in his left hand (a cup?) and holds his right hand over an urn above an altar at his right leg. Found on the northeast side of site XI. Second/third century.

Arecurius is otherwise unattested. The god's name seems Celtic, his form classical.

Arnomecta

Navio (Brough-on-Noe)

540. *Deae | Arnomecte | Ael(ius) Motio |v.s.l.l.m. (RIB* 281).

Altar. The inscription is enclosed in a circular wreath with ribbons. Found in the *aerarium* of the *principia.*

Arnomecta might be a variation of Arnemetia who presided over the curative waters and the sacred spring at Aquae Arnemetiae (Buxton) where there may have been a Roman thermal establishment (Richmond and Crawford, "Ravenna Cosmography," 23; Richmond, *Roman Britain*, 76). Her name, derived from Arnemetiae (Arnemeze in the Ravenna Cosmography) might mean "at the sacred grove." Compare "nemeton," "sacred grove" (Richmond and Crawford, "Ravenna Cosmography," 23, #107; Ross, *Celtic Britain*, 36). There is no epigraphic evidence to Arnemetia.

Belatucadrus

Bravoniacum (Kirkby Thore)
541. *Deo Belatucad|ro lib(ens) votu|m fecit | [---]iolus* (*CIL* VII 294; *RIB* 759).
    Altar. Crude lettering.

Brocavum (Brougham)
542. *Deo | B[a]latu(cadro) | --- [po]|sivit [---]|tinus | ex cune(o) | [--- | --- |
    ---] |rum* (*ILS* 4544; *RIB* 772).
    Altar. Lettering very crude and weathered.
    Brougham may have been a cult center.

543. *Deo Balatucai|ro Baculo pr|o se et suis v.|l.s.* (*RIB* 773).
    Altar.
    Baculo, a Celtic name: Holder, *Alt-celtischer*, I, col. 325.

544. *Deo | Blatucairo | Audagus | v(otum) s(olvit) p(ro) s(ua) s(alute)* (*CIL* VII
    295; *ILS* 4545; *RIB* 774).
    Altar.
    Audagus, a Celtic name: Holder, *Alt-celtischer*, I, col. 283.

545. *[Deo] Belatu| [ca]dro Iu|[l]ianus a[r]|am v.s.l.m.* (*RIB* 775).
    Altar.

546. *[Deo Belat|uca]dr[o | ---]inam | [a]ram v.|s.l.m.* (*RIB* 776).
    Altar fragment.

547. *Sancto deo Belatucadro* (*RIB* 777).
    Part of a statue. Now lost. Reported to resemble Belinus or Apollo.
He possibly wore a radiate crown.

548. *Deo Bela|tucabro| v.s.* (*JRS*.1969 #7).
    Altar.

Alauna (Maryport)
549. *Belatu|cadro | Iul(ius) Ci|vilis | opt(io) | v.s.l.m.* (*CIL* VII 369; *RIB* 809).
    Altar.

Maglona (Old Carlisle)
550. *Deo | Belatuca|dro sancto | Aur(elius) Tasulus | vet(eranus) v.s.l.[m.]* (*RIB* 887).
    Altar. Found 1.6km southwest of the fort.
    Tasulus: Holder, *Alt-celtischer*, II, col. 1751.

551. *Deo | sancto Bela|tucadro | Aurelius | Diatova ara(m) e|x voto posuit | l.l.m.
    M* (*CIL* VII 337; *RIB* 888).
    Altar.
    A Celtic worshipper (Holder, *Alt-celtischer*, I, col. 1281).

552. *Deo | Belatu|cauro | [---]cipa [---]* (*RIB* 889).
    Altar.

Voreda (Old Penrith)
553. *Deo san|cto Bel|[a]tuca(dro) | aram* (*CIL* VII 314; *RIB* 914).
    Altar.

554. *Deo* | *Marti* | *Belatucad*|*ro et Numini*|*b(us) Augg(ustorum)* | *Iulius Au*|*gustalis* | *actor Iul(i) Lu*|*pi pr(a)ef(ecti)* (*CIL* VII 318; *RIB* 918).
Altar. Uneven capitals. Found inside the fort, near the east wall.
Iulius Lupus may have been connected with *cohors II Gallorum* at Old Penrith during the third century (#151, 152, 396, *RIB* 929).

555. *Deo Bala*|*toca*|*dro* (*Britannia*.1978 #7).
Altar. Roughly cut capitals. Found unstratified in *vicus* south of the fort.

556. *Deo sa*|*ncto* | *Belat*|*ucai*|*ro po(suit)* (*Britannia*.1978 #8).
Altar. Capitals roughly incised, some with cursive form.

Luguvalium (Carlisle)
557. *Deo Marti Belatucadro* (*RIB* 948).
Altar.

Castra Exploratorum (Netherby)
558. *Deo Marti* | *Belatucadro* | *RO [A]ur(elius) [Ni]ca[n]* | *or v.s.[l.l.]m.* (*CIL* VII 957; *RIB* 970).
Altar.

Brocolitia (Carrawburgh)
559. *Deo* | *Belleti*|*cauro* | *Lunaris* (*CIL* VII 620; *RIB* 1521).
Altar.
A rare name, fewer than ten examples altogether, three of which occur in Britain (A. Birley, *People*, 113; *RIB* 786; *AE* 1922 116).

Magnis (Carvoran)
560. *Deo* | *Balit*|*icau*|*ro v*|*otu(m)* (*RIB* 1775).
Altar. Found at the north side of the fort.

561. *D(e)o Blatu*|*cadro* | *votu(m) s(olutum)* (*CIL* VII 745; *RIB* 1776; *CSIR* 1.6.135).
Altar. Pediment on the capital frames a jug carved into a niche. Second/third century.

562. *D(e)o Marti* | *Belatu*|*cairo* (*CIL* VII 746; *RIB* 1784; *CSIR* 1.6.136).
Altar. Second/third century.

Camboglanna (Castlesteads)
563. *Deo* | *Belat*|*ugag*|*ro ar(am)* | *Minerv(alis)* (*CIL* VII 873; *RIB* 1976).
Altar.

564. *Deo s(ancto) Be*| *[l]atuca[d*|*r]o AVDO* | *[---]ullinus* | *v.s.* (*CIL* VII 874; *RIB* 1977).
Altar. E. Birley expands the reading: *deo s(ancto) Belatuca[d]ro a(r)u(llam) do[n(avit) I]ullinus v(oto) s(oluto)*: "Deities," 61, n. 319.

Aballava (Burgh-by-Sands)
565. *Deo* | *Bela*|*tuca(dro)* (*CIL* VII 934; *RIB* 2038).
Altar.

566. *Deo Belato|cadro Antr(onius)* | *Auf(idianus) posuit ar|am pro se et s|uis* (*CIL*
VII 935, *addit*, 311; *RIB* 2039).
　　　Altar.

567. *Marti* | *Belatu|cad(ro) sa(n)ct(o)* | *MATVSI* (*RIB* 2044).
　　　Altar.

568. *[B]alatucadro S(ancto)* | *Censorinus* | *[pro] salute sua [et suorum] pos(uit)*
(*CIL* VII 941; *RIB* 2045).
　　　Altar. E. Birley's reading ("Deities," 61, n. 320).
　　　Censorinus: #603. The same man?

Kirkbride
569. *Deo Belato|cairo Peisi|us M. solv|it votu|m l(ibens) m(erito)* (*CIL* VII 333,
addit., 307; *RIB* 2056; *CSIR* 1.6.137).
　　　Altar. Zigzag incised into front of capital. Second/third century.

Bregans

Slack
570. *Deo* | *Breganti* | *et N(umini) Aug(usti)* | *T. Aur(elius) Quintus* | *d(ono) d(edit)*
p(ecunia) et s(umptu) s(uo) (*ILS* 4716; *RIB* 623).
　　　Altar. Found 2.4km east of the fort. Third century.
　　　Bregans is perhaps a masculine form of Brigantia (Richmond in Wheeler
Stanwix fortifications, 61) and perhaps Brigantia's consort (E. Birley, "Dei-
ties," 66).
　　　Aurelius Quintus: *PME* I.157, #A.249.

Brigantia

Greetland
571. *D(eae) Vict(oriae) Brig(antiae)* | *et Num(inibus) Augg(ustorum)* | *T. Aur(elius)*
Aurelian|us d(edit) d(edicavit) pro se | *et suis s(e) mag(istro) s(acrorum)* (*CIL* VII
200; *ILS* 4719; *RIB* 627; *CSIR* 1.3.33).
　　　Antonin[o] | *III Geta II* | *co(n)s(ulibu)s* inscribed on the right side.
　　　Altar. AD 208.
　　　Brigantia is the patron deity of the Brigantes.

Lagentium (Castleford)
572. *Deae Vic|toriae* | *Brigant(iae)* | *a(ram) d(edicavit) Aur(elius) S|enopianus* (*ILS*
4720; *RIB* 628).
　　　Altar. Found in the river Calder. Third century.
　　　Senopianus: Holder, *Alt-celtischer*, II, col. 1499.

Arbeia (South Shields)
573. *Deae Bri|gantiae* | *sacrum* | *Congenn(i)c|cus v.s.l.m.* (*ILS* 4717; *RIB* 1053;
CSIR 1.1.233).
　　　Altar. Patera on the right side; jug on the left; a bird on the back.
Fluted pilaster at each corner. Found 91.5m south of fort's southwest angle.
Third century.

Congennicus attested in Gaul (*CIL* XII 4883, 5793; Holder, *Alt-celtischer*, I, col. 1099). Our man is probably of the *cohors V Gallorum*.

Cumberland, provenance unknown
574. *Deae Nymphae Brig(antiae)* | *quod [vo]verat pro* | *sal[ute et incolumitate]* | *dom(ini) nostr(i) Invic(ti)* | *imp(eratoris) M. Aurel(i) Severi* | *Antonini Pii Felic[i]s* | *Aug(usti) totiusque do|mus divinae eius* | *M. Cocceius Nigrinus* | *[pr]oc(urator) Aug(usti) n(ostri) devo|[tissim]us num[ini* | *maies]tatique eius v.[s.]l.l.m.* (*CIL* VII 875; *ILS* 9317; *RIB* 2066).
Altar. AD 212–217. Severus, however, is not usually part of Caracalla's imperial nomenclature.
The altar has been attributed to Castlesteads. Jolliffe "Dea Brigantia," 58, suggests that the dedication was offered for the emperor's health in 213, as demanded by Caracalla; E. Birley, "Roman Milestone," 61, argues that this dedication was made in 212 "as soon as the news had come to hand of the emperor's escape from his brother Geta."

Blatobulgium (Birrens)
575. *Brigantiae s(acrum): Amandus* | *Arc(h)itectus ex imperio imp(eratum fecit)* (*CIL* VII 1062; *ILS* 4718; *RIB* 2091; *CSIR* 1.4.12).
Statuette. The goddess, carved in high relief and equated with Minerva Victrix (Jolliffe, "Dea Brigantia," 36, 48, pl. 1), stands in a gabled niche. She is winged, wears a Medusa head on her breast, and on her head a plumed helmet and turreted crown, denoting her hegemony over the Brigantes. She holds a spear in her right hand, a globe in her left. Her shield is at her left, an omphaloid stone to her right. Found in the *vicus* outside the fort.
Amandus might be identifiable with *Val. Amandus discens (architectus)* of the *Legio I Minerva* (*CIL* XIII 7945 [*ILS* 2459], AD 209, Iversheim, Lower Germany). Amandus may have belonged to the sixth legion, based in York.

Britannia

Eboracum (York)
576. *Britanniae* | *Sanctae* | *p(osuit) Nikomedes* | *Augg(ustorum) nn(ostrorum)* | *libertus* (*CIL* VII 232; *RIB* 643; E. Birley, "Deities," 66, n. 344).
Base. After AD 161 (#7).
The freedman has a Greek name.

Cocidius

Lancaster
577. *Deo* | *sancto Marti* | *Cocidio Vibenius* | *Lucius b(ene)f(iciarius) co(n)s(ularis)* | *v.s.l.m.* (*CIL* VII 286; *RIB* 602).
Altar.

Castra Exploratorum (Netherby)
578. *Deo* | *sancto* | *Cocidio* | *Paternius* | *Maternus* | *tribunus coh(ortis)* | *I*

Nervan(a)e | *ex evocato* | *Palatino* | *v.s.l.m.* (*CIL* VII 953; *ILS* 4724a; *RIB* 966).
   Altar. Late third century: E. Birley, "Building Records," 219 (*ex evocato Palatino*).
   Paternius Maternus, a German or Gaul: *PME* II.630, #P.16.

Fanum Cocidi (Bewcastle)
579. *Deo* | *sancto* | *Cocidio* | *Annius* | *Victor* | *centur(io)* | *legioni[s]* | *E* --- (*RIB* 985).
   Altar. Found 0.8km south of the fort.
   Bewcastle is very likely the *fanum Cocidi* of the Ravenna Cosmography
(a late seventh century compilation): Collingwood, *Roman Britain*, 265;
E. Birley, "Deities," 59; Richmond and Crawford, "Ravenna Cosmography," 1–50.

580. *Deo Cocidio* (*RIB* 986).
   Silver plaque. Cocidius, standing within a shrine, faces front. He holds
in his right hand a long spear, a shield in his left. Recovered from the *aerarium principiorum* with third century debris, sealed by the fourth century floor.

581. *Deo* | *D(e)o Coc(i)dio* | *Au(e)ntinus f(ecit)* (*RIB* 987).
   Silver plaque. In crude relief, the god holds a spear in his left hand.
The god wears a pleated garment in two layers hung around his shoulders, similar to the garment worn by a horned god from Moresby: Ross,
Celtic Britain, 170. The pleated garment may be the type of cloak worn by
the northern Britons. Found with #580.

582. *Sancto Co|cideo Aurunc(eius)* | *Felicesse|mus tribun(us)* | *ex evocato* | *v.s.l.m.*
(*CIL* VII 974; *RIB* 988).
   Altar.
   Aurunceius Felicessemus, an Italian? *PME* I.162, #A.261. *Cohors I
Nervia Germanorum?*

583. *Deo sancto Cocidio* | *Q. Peltrasi[u]s* | *Maximus trib(unus)* | *ex corniculario* |
praef(ectorum) pr[a]etorio e|m(inentissimorum) v(irorum) v.s.l.m. (*ILS* 4721; *RIB*
989).
   Altar. Late third/early fourth century.
   Peltrasius Maximus, perhaps German or Gallic in origin: *PME* II.631,
#P.17. *Cohors I Nervia Germanorum?*

584. *Deo Ma|[rt]i Cocid(io)* | *sancto Aeliu[s]* | *Vitalianus* | *d(ono) d(edit) l(ibens)
m(erito)* (*CIL* VII 977; *RIB* 993).
   Altar.
   Aelius Vitalianus, perhaps governor of Mauretania Caesariensis (235/6):
PME I.77, #A.70.

Vindomora (Ebchester)
585. *Deo* | *Verno|stono* | *Cocidi|o Viri[l]is* | *Ger(manus) v.s.l.* (*CIL* VII 9; *RIB*
1102).
   Altar. Found 0.8km south of the fort.
   Vernostonus, a Celtic deity. The worshipper claims a German origin.

Habitancum (Risingham)
586. *Deo Cocidio et | Sil[vano ---] Seu| [---]IOV | [---a]ram | [--- | ---| ---| v.]s.l.m.* (*RIB* 1207; *CSIR* 1.1.234).
　　Altar. On the capital, a hunter (the god?) with a hound hunts a stag. On the right side are a doe, hind, and tree. Second/third century.

Vercovicium (Housesteads)
587. *Cocidio [et] | Genio pr[ae]|sidi Vale|rius m(iles) l[e]|g(ionis) VI V(ictricis) P(iae) F(idelis) v(oto) p(osuit)* (*CIL* VII 644; *RIB* 1577; *CSIR* 1.6.138).
　　Altar. A patera on the left side, a jug on the right. On the front of the base, two dolphins, each in separate rectangular panels, face each other. Found east of the Mithraeum. AD 122/6.

588. *Deo | Silvano | Cocidio | Q. Florius | Maternus | praef(ectus) coh(ortis) | I Tung(rorum) | v.s.l.m.* (*CIL* VII 642; *ILS* 4723; *RIB* 1578).
　　Altar. Found at the southwest corner of the fort. Third/fourth century. Q. Florius Maternus: #269.

589. *Deo | Cocidio | Vabrius | [v.]s.l.m.* (*CIL* VII 643; *RIB* 1633; *CSIR* 1.6.139).
　　Altar. Found at the crag below Milecastle 37.
　　Vabrius, a Celtic name: Holder, *Alt-celtische*, III, col. 71.

Hardriding
590. *Deo | Cocidio | Decimus | Caerelli|us Victor | pr(aefectus) coh(ortis) II Ner(viorum) v.s.l.m.* (*CIL* VII 701; *RIB* 1683).
　　Altar.
　　There is no independent evidence for this cohort at Vindolanda. The altar might have belonged to a local shrine of the god (E. Birley, "Maponus," 41, note 5). D. Caerillius Victor may have been Italian or African (*PME* I.203, #C.35).

Banna (Birdoswald)
591. *Deo Cocidio | coh(ors) I Aelia | [Dacorum c(ui) p(raeest) | Tere]ntius Valerianus | [trib(unus) v.s.l.m.* (*CIL* VII 803; *RIB* 1872).
　　Altar. Third/fourth century.
　　The tribune may have been Italian (*PME* II.780, #T.13).

Milecastle 52
592. *Deo | Cocidio | milites | l[eg(ionis)] II Aug(ustae) | v.s.l.m.* (*CIL* VII 800; *RIB* 1955).
　　Altar. Found in the milecastle's foundations. AD 122/6.

593. *Deo | Cocidio | milites | leg(ionis) XX V.V. | v.s.l.m. | Apr(---) et Ruf(---) co(n)s(ulibus)* (*CIL* VII 802; *ILS* 4722; *RIB* 1956; *CSIR* 1.6.140).
　　Altar. Jug on the left side, patera on the right, and a wild boar (the emblem of *legio XX V.V.*) on the base. Found with #592.
　　Apr. and Ruf. were consuls of the Gallic empire between 262 and 266 (E. Birley, "Roman Altar from Bankshead," 1).

Milecastle 55
594. *Deo | Cocid[io] | vexil[(l)atio] | leg(ionis) VI V[ic(tricis) | v.s.l.m.]* (*CIL* VII 801; *RIB* 1961; *CSIR* 1.6.141).
Altar. Knife on the left; patera on the right. AD 122/6.

595. *Deo Co[cidio---* (*CIL* VII 804; *RIB* 1963).
Altar.

Milecastle 59
596. *[D]eo | Marti [C]ocidio | [---]martius | [c(enturio) c]oh(ortis) I Ba[t(avorum) | et] Genio | ---]vali | [v.s.l.]m.* (*CIL* VII 886, *addit.* 310; *ILS* 4724b; *RIB* 2015).
Altar. Left side trimmed. AD 122/6.

Milecastle 60
597. *Deo | Cocidio | milites | leg(ionis) VI Vic(tricis) P(iae) F(idelis)* (*CIL* VII 876; *RIB* 2020).
Two altar fragments. Bolsters and focus chiseled off. AD 122/6.

Milecastle 65
598. *Marti Coc(idio) m(ilites) | leg(ionis) II Aug(ustae) | c(enturia) Sanctiana | c(enturia) Secundini | d(ono) sol(verunt) sub cu|ra Aeliani c(enturionis) cura(vit) Oppius | [F]elix optio* (*CIL* VII 914, *addit.* 311; *RIB* 2024; *CSIR* 1.6.163).
Altar. AD 122/6.

Contrebis

Calacum (Overborough)
599. *Deo san(cto) | Contr|ebi Vat|ta posu(it)* (*CIL* VII 290; *RIB* 610).
Altar. On the right side is a bird, perhaps an owl; on the left a hatchet and knife.

Contrebis, who recalls the Contrebia in Hispania Citerior, was possibly, though not certainly, imported into Britain (E. Birley, "Deities," 67). According to Tolkien in Collingwood, *Roman Britain*, 266, Contrebis means "god of a fair open place dwelling among us." (Ialonus Contrebis: #459).

For the cognomen Vatta: *CIL* V 7181 (Turin); Holder, *Alt-celtischer*, III, col. 127.

Cunomaglus

West Kington
600. *Deo Apol|lini Cuno|maglo Co|rotica Iu|ti Fil(ia) v.s.l.m.* (*JRS.*1962, #4).
Altar, sides plain. Found reused as seat next to a hearth in late occupation of octagonal building.

Latis

Banna (Birdoswald)
601. *Die | Lat[i]* (*CIL* VII 1348; *RIB* 1897; *CSIR* 1.6.157).

Altar. Jug and patera on the back. Second/third century.

This deity's name is translated "goddess of the pool" or "of beer" (Ross, *Celtic Britain*, 231, 378, 422). She was probably one of the many Celtic water nymphs and survives as the divine Irish queen Mebd (from *meduos, medua*, "drunk," or "intoxicating") "the drunk-making Queen" (Ross, *Celtic Britain*, 180). Cf. #605 (Mars Braciaca).

Fallsteads
602. *Deae | Lati | Lucius | Vrsei(us)* (*CIL* VII 938; *RIB* 2043).
    Altar.
    The altar probably belonged to the fort at Burgh-by-Sands, about 4.8km northeast of Fallsteads.

Mars

Mars Alator:
Barkway
603. *D(eo) Marti Alatori | Dum(---) Censorinus | Gemelli fil(ius) | v.s.l.m.* (*CIL* VII 85; *ILS* 4541; *RIB* 218).
    Silver plate.
    The god's name means "he who rears or nourishes" (Ross, *Celtic Britain*, 174) or "huntsman" (Roscher, *Lexicon*, s.v. "Mars," 2396). #603 and cult objects were contained in a shrine to a Celtic Mars and Vulcan (Leach, "Smith God," 41).
    Censorinus: #568.

Arbeia (South Shields)
604. *Mar(ti) Ala(tori) | C. Vinicius | Celsus | pro se et [---] | v.s.l.m.* (*RIB* 1055; *CSIR* 1.1.198).
    Altar. Patera and jug on the left side. Found west of the fort. Third century lettering.
    Mars Alator was invoked primarily as warrior (Ross, *Celtic Britain*, 174).

Mars Braciaca:
Bakewell
605. *Deo | Marti | Braciacae | Q. Sittius | Caecilian(us) praef(ectus) coh(ortis) | I Aquitano(rum) | v.s.* (*CIL* VII 176; *RIB* 278).
    Altar.
    The Celtic name, from the Welsh "brag" (malt), may indicate "the god of intoxication." The connection between drink and Mars follows from the Celtic tradition of liberally providing alcoholic drink to heroes setting out into battle as a stimulus to their efforts (Ross, *Celtic Britain*, 180–1, 201, 377).
    Sittius Caecilianus seems to be Numidian (*PME* II.745, #S.57; A. Birley, *People*, 67).

Mars Condatis:
Latravis (Bowes)
606. *[M]arti | Condati | Arpona|tus v.s.l.m.* (*RIB* 731).
    Altar. Found 183m east of the fort. Second century.

Condatis, "God of the Watersmeet," recalls Condate in Norwich, Cheshire (E. Birley, "Deities," 69) and Condè-sur-Itan in Gaul (Clark, "Roman Yorkshire, 1936," 224). The deity was closely associated with springs and may have had a healing cult (Ross, *Celtic Britain*, 197). As in the cult of Belatucadrus, the votaries of Mars Condatis seem to be of humble origin (Ross, *Celtic Britain*, 182–3).

Piercebridge

607. *D(eo) M(arti) | Condati | Attonius Quintianus | men(sor) evoc(atus) imp(eratum) ex ius(su) sol(vit) l(ibens) a(nimo)* (*CIL* VII 420; *RIB* 1024).

Altar. Solar symbol (swastika) on the capital. Found 1.6km east of the fort.

E. Birley, "Deities," 68, n. 357, suggested the expansion *ex cc imp(eratoris) ex ius(su)*.

Concangis (Chester-le-Street)

608. *Deo Marti | Condati V(alerius) | [P]rob[i]anus [pr]o | se et suis v.s.l.m.* (*ILS* 4557; *RIB* 1045).

Altar. Found 274m north of the fort. Mid-fourth century?

Mars Corotiacus:

Martlesham

609. *Deo Marti | Corotiaco | Simplicia | pro se v.p.l.m.* (*CIL* VII 93a, addit. 306; *ILS* 4558; *RIB* 213).

Glaucus | fecit inscribed on the back.

Bronze statue base, shield-shaped. Of the statuette, a horse's hoof, suggesting an equestrian statue, and a headless and prostrate foe have been recovered.

Mars Medocius:

Camulodunum (Colchester)

610. *Deo Marti Medocio Camp|esium et Victorie Alexan|dri Pii Felicis Augusti nos(tr)i | domum Lossio Veda de suo | posuit nepos Vepogeni Caledo* (*ILS* 4576; *RIB* 191).

Bronze plate. AD 222/35.

Medocius is otherwise unknown. *Campestrium* may have been intended. Lossio Veda is a Celtic name.

Mars Nodens:

Lydney

611. *D(eo) M(arti) Nodonti | Flavius Blandinus | armartura | v.s.l.m.* (*CIL* VII 138; *ILS* 4729; *RIB* 305).

Bronze plate.

Ross, *Celtic Britain*, 176, defines the name as "he who bestows wealth," or "the cloud maker." She offered no etymology. Irish origin: Wheeler, *Lydney Park*, 132–33.

612. *Devo | Nodenti Silvianus | anilum perdedit | demedian partem | donavit Nodenti | inter quibus nomen | Seniciani nollis | permittas sanita|tem donec perfera(t) | usque templum [No]|dentis* (*CIL* VII 140, addit. 306; *ILS* 4730; *RIB* 306).

Lead plate. Compare Sulis Minerva, a healing deity, and the recipient of similar *defixiones*.

For a Senicius at Silchester: *CIL* VII 1305.

613. *Pectillus | votum quod | promissit | deo Nudente | M(arti) dedit* (*CIL* VII 139; *ILS* 4729a; *RIB* 307).

Pentagonal bronze plate, with a circular ornament in the gable at the top. Above the inscription, a barking dog, with his feet outstretched and his rump raised, faces right.

614. *d(eo) M(arti) N(odenti) | T. Flavius Senilis pr(aepositus) rel(igionis) ex stipibus pos<s>uit | o[pitu]ante Victorino interp(r)[e]tiante* (*RIB* II.2448.3).

Mosaic pavement.

This naval officer, in charge of the fleet's supply depot, probably made a pilgrimage to the site for his health: E. Birley, "Deities," 70.

Cockersand Moss

615. *Deo Marti Nodonti Aur|elius [---] cinus sig(illum)* (*RIB* 616).

Pedestal. Found with a statuette of Mars. Second/third century.

616. *D(eo) M(arti) N(odonti) || Lucianus || colleg(ae) Aprili Viato||ris v.s.* (*RIB* 617).

Pedestal inscribed on four sides. Found with a statuette.

Mars Ocelus:
Venta Silurum (Caerwent)

617. *Deo | Marti | Ocelo | Ael(ius) A(u)gus|tinus op(tio) | v.s.l.m.* (*RIB* 310).

Altar. Found in the central block of house XVI. Second/third century.

Ocelus may have been a god of the Silures (Caerwent) transferred northward with native migrations under the pressure of Roman occupation. "His name defies interpretation" (Ross, *Celtic Britain*, 376).

Luguvalium (Carlisle)

618. *Deo Marti Ocelo et | Num(ini) imp(eratoris) [Alexandri] Aug(usti) | et Iul(iae) M[ama]eae [ma]tr(is) castr(orum) | [et senatus et patr(iae) et toti] domini | [divinae* (*ILS* 4579; *RIB* 949).

Dedication slab. Found in the Roman cemetery. AD 222–235.

Mars Rigonemetos:
Nettleham

619. *Deo Marti Rigo|nemeti et Numini|bus Augustorum | Q. Nerat(ius) Proxsi|mus arcum de suo | donavit* (*JRS*.1962 #8; *CSIR* 1.8.91).

Dedication slab. Perhaps from a local shrine to Mars. Found at a depth of 10.16cm 183m east of the Roman settlement.

Mars Rigonemetos, "king of the grove/sanctuary," is otherwise unknown in Britain. For Nemetona: #470.

Matunus

Bremenium (High Rochester)

620. *Deo Matuno | pro salute | M. [A]ur(eli) ---| --- | bono generis | humani impe|rante C. [Iulius | Marcus] leg(atus) | Aug(usti) pr(o) pr(aetore) posuit | ac dedicavit | c(uram) a(gente) Caecil(io) Optato trib(uno)* (*CIL* VII 995, addit. 311; *ILS* 4727; *RIB* 1265).

Dedication slab. AD 213.

The meaning of Matunus is disputed. Tolkien in Collingwood, *Roman Britain*, 266, suggested "the kindly one;" Ross (*Celtic Britain*, 349, 375), offering "divine bear," derived the name from *matus* (Gaulish) and *math* (Irish), both connoting "bear." Bears are significant in Irish mythology. E. Birley ("Deities" 70) suggested that Matunus had a high standing in order to attract a high-ranking senator.

L. Caecilius Optatus: #236, 422.

Ratis

Cilurnum (Chesters)
621. *Dea(e)* | *Rat(i)* | *v.s.l.* (*CIL* VII 580; *RIB* 1454; *CSIR* 1.6.181).
    Altar. Candelabras on the sides. Second/third century.
    Ross, *Celtic Britain*, 215, 231, identifies Ratis as the "goddess of the fortress" but offers no etymology.

Banna (Birdoswald)
622. *D(e)ae* | *Rati votu*|*m in* | *perp*|*etuo* (*CIL* VII 828; *RIB* 1903).
    Altar.

Sattada

Vindolanda (Chesterholm)
623. *Deae* | *Sattadae* | *curia Tex*|*touerdorum* | *v.s.l.m.* (*CIL* VII 712; *RIB* 1695; *CSIR* 1.6.182).
    Altar. Wreath on the left side; knife and patera on the right; jug and patera on the back. Found 3.2km southeast of the fort. Third century lettering.
    Jackson, *Language and History*, 325, defines Sattada as "goddess of grief." The Textouerdi are otherwise unattested.

Setlocenia

Alauna (Maryport)
624. *Deae* | *Setlo*|*ceniae* | *Labar*|*eus Ge(rmanus)* | *v.s.l.m.* (*CIL* VII 393; *RIB* 841).
    Altar.
    Setlocenia may mean "long life:" Jackson, *Language and History*, 325. A relief from Alauna might portray the goddess (Ross, *Celtic Britain*, 214).

Vanauns

Camboglanna (Castlesteads)
625. *N(umini) Aug(usti)* | *deo Vana*|*unti Aurel(ius)* | *Armiger* | *dec(urio) princ(eps)* (*CIL* VII 888; *RIB* 1991; *CSIR* 1.6.91).
    Altar. On the capital, the three central rooms of an auxiliary unit's *principia*. Found 274m north of the fort. Third/fourth century.

Verbeia

Verbeia (Ilkley)
626. *Verbeiae | sacrum | Clodius | Fronto | praef(ectus) coh(ortis) | II Lingon(um)* (*CIL* VII 208; *ILS* 4731; *RIB* 635; *CSIR* 1.3.30).
    Altar. AD 161/80.
    Verbeia may represent the local river Wharfe, or she may be a goddess of cattle: Ross (*Celtic Britain*, 217, 307) relates the Verbeia to the Irish *ferb*, "cattle." Compare Boand, "she who has white cows," a goddess who personifies the river Boyne in Ireland. A relief from this site depicts a goddess, possibly Verbeia, grasping two serpents, associated with water cults (Ross, *Celtic Britain*, 232).
    Clodius Fronto: *PME* I.279, #C.200.

Veteris

Eboracum (York)
627. *Deo Ve|teri | Primul|us vo(vit) l(ibens) | m(erito)* (*RIB* 660; E. Birley, "Review of *RIB*," 228).
    Altar. *RIB* expands *vol* as *Vol(usianus)*.

Cataractonium (Catterick)
628. *Deo sa|ncto V|heteri | pro sal(ute) | Aur(eli) Muci|ani v.s.l.m.* (*RIB* 727).
    Altar. Third century?
    The worshipper's name is Romanized.

Voreda (Old Penrith)
629. *Vicri[b]us T.S. v.|s.l.m.* (*CIL* VII 710; *RIB* 925).
    Altar.

Castra Exploratorum (Netherby)
630. *Deo | Hue|tiri* (*RIB* 973; *CSIR* 1.6.189).
    Altar. On left side, the tree of the Hesperides with dragon; on right side, head of Erymanthian boar with tree in the background. Elaborate moldings. Second/third century.

Concangis (Chester-le-Street)
631. *Deo | Vitiri D|uihno v.s.* (*RIB* 1046).
    Altar. Found in a Roman well. Deliberately hidden? Cf. Coventina (#440–453).
    The worshipper is, perhaps, Celtic: Holder, *Alt-celticsher*, I, col. 1365.

632. *Daeab[u]|s Vitir|ibus | Vitalis | [v.]s.l.m.* (*RIB* 1047).
    Altar. Capitals of irregular size.

633. *Deab[u]s | Vit(iri)bus | VIAS | VADRI* (*CIL* VII 454, *addit.* 309; *RIB* 1048).
    Altar.

Arbeia (South Shields)
634. *Deo | ANSU (sancto?) | Vitiri Cr[---]* (*Britannia*.1987 #7).

Buff sandstone altar. Reused in fourth century restoration of ditch in front of southwest gate. Letters are crudely cut.

Longovicium (Lanchester)

635. *Deo | Vit(iri)* (*CIL* VII 442; *RIB* 1087).
   Altar.

636. *Deo | Vitir[i] | VNTHAV[.] | pr(inceps) pos(uit) | [p]ro se e[t] sui[s]* (*CIL* VII 444; *RIB* 1088).
   Altar.

Vindomora (Ebchester)

637. *Deo | Vitiri | Maximu|s v.s.* (*CIL* VII 459, *addit*. 309; *ILS* 4734; *RIB* 1103).
   Altar. Boar on the right side; bird on the left.

638. *Deo | Vitiri | I . IT* (*RIB* 1104).
   Altar. Crude lettering.

Piercebridge

639. *Deo | Vet|eri* (*Britannia*.1974 #3).
   Buff sandstone altar. Found with debris in stoke hole of hypocaust.

Coriosopitum (Corbridge)

640. *Deo | Veteri* (*RIB* 1139).
   Altar. Found east of site XI.

641. *Deo | Vit|iri* (*CIL* VII 472; *RIB* 1140; *CSIR* 1.1.64).
   Altar. Base decorated with incised zigzag. Second/third century.

642. *Vit(iri) | M|iti(us)* (*RIB* 1141).
   Altar. Roughly cut capitals. Found in the late road level east of site **XXXIX**.

643. *V M D(eo)* (*RIB* 1145; *CSIR* 1.1.65).
   Altar. The piece is similar in size to other Corbridge altars to Veteris but could have been intended for Vulcan. "M" probably signified a local deity with whom "V" was equated (or vice versa). On the right, a male figure stands, his left hand at his side. The head fits within an arch on the capital. Found on site XI. Second to fourth century.

Condercum (Benwell)

644. *Deo | Vetri | sangto* (*CIL* VII 511; *RIB* 1335; *CSIR* 1.1.245).
   Altar. Patera and jug on left; axe and knife on right. Found at the north part of the fort. Second/third century.

645. *Vit|ir(i)b|us* (*CIL* VII 512; *RIB* 1336; *CSIR* 1.1.244).
   Base. Found at the north part of the fort. Second/third century.

Cilurnum (Chesters)

646. *Deo sanc|to Vitiri | Tertulus | v.s.l.m.* (*CIL* VII 581; *RIB* 1455; *CSIR* 1.6.183).
   Altar. Smashed. Second/third century.

647. *Dibus | Veteri | bus* (*CIL* VII 582; *RIB* 1456).
Altar. Found near the fort's east gate.

648. *[Di]bus | Vitiri | bus* (*RIB* 1457).
Altar. Found near the Roman bridge over the North Tyne.

649. *SVACNV | SVOTVI | d(eo) Vot | ri v.s.* (*CIL* VII 583; *RIB* 1458).
Altar.

Brocolitia (Carrawburgh)
650. *Deo Ve | teri vo | tum Uc | cus v(ovit) l(ibens)* (*CIL* VII 619; *RIB* 1548).
Altar.
Uccus, a Celtic name (Holder, *Alt-celtischer*, III, col. 13).

651. *[Dibu]s | Huite | ribus* (*CIL* VII 502b; *RIB* 1549).
Altar.

Vercovicium (Housesteads)
652. *Deo | Hueteri | Superstes [et] | Regulu[s] | v.s.l.[m.]* (*RIB* 1602; *CSIR* 1.6.184).
Altar. Regular capitals. Incised crescent on front of capital. Found at northeast or northwest angle tower. Second/third century.

653. *Deo | Huitri | Aspuanis | pro (se) et suis | vot(um) | sol(vit)* (*RIB* 1603).
Altar. Found in the fort's southwest corner.

654. *Deo | Veterib | us votu | m* (*RIB* 1604).
Altar. Roughly cut lettering. Found in the fort's southwest corner.

655. *[Dib]us | Vete | [ri]bus* (*RIB* 1605).
Altar. Found in the granary.

656. *Veter | ibus | [p]osuuit A | ure(lius) Vict(or) v(otum)* (*RIB* 1606).
Altar. Found on the roadway south of the south gate. Second/third century.

657. *Dibus [Veteribus* (*RIB* 1607).
Altar. Crude lettering. E. Birley's reading, "Deities," 63.

Vindolanda (Chesterholm)
658. *Deo | [V]ete | [r]i* (*RIB* 1697).
Altar. Found 4.6m north of the west gate's north guard chamber.

659. *] Veteri | ---] tin[. | ---]s* (*CIL* VII 709; *RIB* 1698).
Altar fragment.

660. *Veteri | bus pos(uit) | Senacu | lus* (*CIL* VII 711; *RIB* 1699).
Altar.
Senaculus, a Celt: Holder, *Alt-celtischer*, II, col. 1466, expands Pos(tumius).

661. *Dibus Ve | teribus | pos(uit) Longi | nus* (*Britannia*.1973 #11).
Altar. Found in the fourth century storehouse.

662. *Veteri | bus po[s] | uit Sen | ilis* (*Britannia*.1973 #12).

Altar. Found in the fourth century storehouse.

Senila is attested at Carthage (*CIL* VIII 13133); Vienne (*CIL* XII 5685); and at Potiers and Trion (*CIL* XIII 10010, 1778), Amiens, Boulogne, and Douvai (Holder, *Alt-celtischer*, II, col. 1476). Probably a Celtic name.

663. --- *Deo* | *s(ancto) Ve* | *tiri pos(uit)* | --- (*Britannia*.1975 #6).
Altar. Found at the west end of the *vicus*.

664. ---*Deo Ve* | *[---]N [.]* | *[---* (*Britannia*.1975 #7).
Altar. Found south of the third century fort's south gate.

665. *Deo* | *Huiti* | *ri v.s.* (*Britannia*.1977 #22).
Altar. Found in the *vicus*.

666. *Ara Vi* | *tirum* (*Britannia*.1979 #8).
Altar. Crudely cut. Found as fallen stone from the northwest angle of the fort's wall.

Aesica (Great Chesters)
667. *Deo* | *Veti* | *ri v(otum)* (*CIL* VII 727; *RIB* 1728).
Altar. Cramped capitals.

668. *Dib[us]* | *Veteri* | *bus pos* | *sit Roma* | *na* (*CIL* VII 728; *RIB* 1729).
Altar. Roughly cut capitals.
A curious name, a proudly Romanized family?

669. *Dibus Ve* | *teribus* | *[---* (*CIL* VII 729; *RIB* 1730; *CSIR* 1.6.185).
Altar. Star on front of capital. Second/third century.

Magnis (Carvoran)
670. *Deo Vete* | *ri Nec* | *alame[s]* | *v.s.l.m.* (*CIL* VII 762; *RIB* 1793; *CSIR* 1.6.186).
Altar. Rough and cramped capitals. Knife and axe on the left side; quadruped on the right. A German (A. Birley, *People*, 107)? Second/third century.

671. *Deo Ve* | *teri Ne* | *calam* | *es v.s.l.* (*CIL* VII 761; *RIB* 1794; *CSIR* 1.6.187).
Altar. Second/third century.

672. *Deo* | *Viti* | *ri Ne[c* | *a]limes* | *[---]RO v.* | *p.l.m.* (*CIL* VII 763; *RIB* 1801).
Altar.

673. *Deo sanct[o]* | *Veteri* | *Iul(ius) Pastor* | *imag(inifer) coh(ortis) II* | *Delma(tarum) v.s.l.m.* (*CIL* VII 760; *RIB* 1795).
Altar. Third/fourth century.

674. *Deo Ve* | *tiri san* | *cto An* | *diatis v.s.l.m.f.* (*CIL* VII 960; *ILS* 4732; *RIB* 1796).
Altar. Neatly spaced lettering. Second/third century.
Andiatis: Holder, *Alt-celtischer*, I, col. 147.

675. *Deo* | *Vetiri v(otum)* (*RIB* 1797).
Altar.

676. *Deo Vite* | *ri No[---* (*CIL* VII 766; *RIB* 1798).
Altar.

677. *Deo | Vitiri | Meni(us) | Dada | v.s.l.m.* (*CIL* VII 764; *RIB* 1799).
Altar.
Dada: Holder, *Alt-celtischer*, I, col. 1214; *RIB* 1927.

678. *Deo Vitiri | Milus et | Aurides | v.s.l.m.* (*CIL* VII 765; *RIB* 1800).
Altar. Small, irregular capitals.

679. *Vete|ribus [---* (*CIL* VII 768; *RIB* 1802).
Dedication.

680. *Dibus | Veter|ibus | vot(u)m* (*RIB* 1803).
Altar. Roughly cut capitals.

681. *Dibus Vit|[eribus] IVIX|A v.s.l.m.* (*RIB* 1804).
Altar.

682. *Dibus | Vitiribus | Deccius | v.s.l.m.* (*CIL* VII 767; *ILS* 4735; *RIB* 1805; *CSIR* 1.6.188).
Altar. Boar on the left side; on the right a dolphin. Second/third century.

Hadrian's Wall, Provenance Unknown
683. *[De]o | Vete|ri* (*RIB* 2068).
Altar.

684. *Huiti|ribus | votum* (*CIL* VII 502a; *RIB* 2069).
Altar.

Thisleton, Rutland
685. *De(o) Ve|te(ri) Mo|cux[s]o|ma pa(ngit)* (*JRS*.1962 #6).
Silver votive plaque. Found in small hole at west end of nave of an apparent temple to Veteris.
Probably a Celtic artisan, but no parallels or cognates have been recorded.

Vintonus

Lavatris (Bowes)
686. *[Deo] | Vinotono | Silvano Iul(ius) | Secundus c(enturio) | coh(ortis) I Thrac(um) | v.s.l.m.* (*RIB* 732).
Altar. Found at Scargill Moor in a rectangular shrine to Vintonus 3.2km south of the Roman fort at Bowes. Third century.
Ross, *Celtic Britain*, 52, 377, suggested that Vinotonus may be related to *vino* ("vine"). Equation with Silvanus implies a god hunting and patron of the wilds.

687. *Deo Vin|otono | L. Caesius | Frontinus pr|aef(ectus) coh(ortis) I Thrac(um) | domo Parma | v.s.l.l.m.* (*RIB* 733; *CSIR* 1.3.28).
Altar. Found in the circular shrine on Scargill Moor. Good lettering, early third century.
Parma, northern Italy; see also *PME* I.206, #C.43.

688. *---]|no L. Cae[sius]* | *Frontinus [praef(ectus)]* | *coh(ortis) I Thrac(um) [v.s.l.m.]* (*CIL* VII 274; *RIB* 734).
Fragmentary dedication. Early third century.

689. *De[o]* | --- (*RIB* 735).
Altar fragment. Found in the circular shrine.

690. *D[eo]* (*RIB* 736).
Altar fragment. Found in the circular shrine.

691. *[Deo] V[inotono* (*RIB* 737).
Altar. Found in the circular shrine.
The *cohors I Thracum* may have been responsible for all these dedications.

Germanic Deities

Garmangabis

Longovicium (Lanchester)
692. *Deae Gar|mangabi* | *et N[(umini) Gor[di|ani] Aug(usti) n(ostri) pr[o]* | *sal(ute) vex(illationis) Suebo|rum Lon(gouicianorum) Gor(dianae) (vexillarii) vo|tum solverunt m(erito)* (*ILS* 4742; *RIB* 1074).
Altar. Knife and jug on the left side; patera and disk on the right. Found 247m northwest of the fort. Gordian III (238–244).

One of the earliest records of the new-style cavalry *vexillationes*: Saxer, *Vexillationes*, 131.

For Garmangabis, see Greinberger, "Dea Garmangabis," 189–95 and Ihm, "Garmangabis," 767, who suggested that the name means *grata donatrix*.

Hercules Magusanus

Mumrills
693. *Herculi* | *Magusan(o)* | *sacrum* | *Val(erius) Nigri|nus dupli(carius)* | *alae Tun|grorum* (*CIL* VII 1090; *ILS* 4628; *RIB* 2140).
Altar.

Hercules Magusanus is attested in Lower Germany, especially among the Batavians at *insula Batavorum* (*CIL* XIII 8705 [*ILS* 4629]), Rummel (*CIL* XIII 8771, 8777), Divitia (Deutz: *CIL* XIII 8492 [*ILS* 4630]), Vetera (Xanten: *CIL* XIII 8610, by an *immunis* of *legio XXX*), Bonna (Bonn: *CIL* XIII 8010, by a centurion of *leg. I Minervia*). At Tongern (Gallia Belgica) a ring was dedicated to the god (*CIL* XIII 10027, 212). At Rome, the *equites singulares* made a dedication on 29 September, 219 in honor of the safe arrival of the emperor to Rome (*CIL* VI 31162 [*ILS* 2188]). The god is also represented on the coinage of Postumus (Webb, *RIC* V 1, nos. 68 and 139–40). Haug ("Hercules") suggested that Magusanus might have been a Neptune consort of Nehalennia, and that the Medieval place name Mahusenhein might be related to this deity (Haug, "Hercules," 611).

Harimella

Blatobulgium (Birrens)

694. *Deae | Harimel|lae sac(rum) Ga|midiahus | arc(h)it(ectus) v.s.l.l.m.* (*CIL* VII 1065; *ILS* 4744; *RIB* 2096; *CSIR* 1.4.13).

Altar.

The votary has a German name; the goddess, almost certainly Germanic, may be related to Harimalla on the river Maas in Belgium (Keune, "Harimella," 2365). The Scottish inscription is the only known attestation of this deity.

Mars Thincsus

Vercovicium (Housesteads)

695. *Deo | Marti | Thincso | et duabus | Alaisiagis | Bede et Fi|mmilene | et N(umini) Aug(usti) Ger|m(ani) cives Tu|ihanti | v.s.l.m.* (*ILS* 4760; *RIB* 1593; *CSIR* 1.6.159).

Tall square pillar which may have been the left-hand jamb of a shrine's doorway (Collingwood and Wright, *RIB*, 507). On the right side of the pillar is a female figure, perhaps an Alaisiaga, in relief. The pillar was found with a sculpted arcuate lintel which portrays in its central panel Mars with sword, shield, and spear. A goose stands to his right. Cross-legged nude figures, carrying wreaths in one hand, offer palm-branches to Mars. Found on the north slope of Chapel Hill. Third century.

The epithet Thincsus seems to be cognate with "Thing" (public meeting) and is an epithet of Tziu (cf. Tuesday) who was equated with Mars. Alaisiagae might mean "the all-honored ones;" Beda may have a connection with prayer; Fimmilena may mean clever and skilful: Clayton, "Mars Thincsus," 148–50, 169–71; Hodgkin in Clayton, "Mars Thincsus," 171–72 (reporting the views of Scherer). Heinzel, "Housesteads," 165, tried to connect the names of Beda and Fimmilena with the Frisian legal terms "bodthing" and "fimelthing." Thus the two deities would represent the Valkyries. Their designation as Alaisiagae might imply that they bestowed honor or aid in battle. The Alaisiagae seemed to have been a distinct order of deities, two pairs of whom (four in all: #697) are attested.

The *cives Tuihanti* came from the district of Twenthe in Over-Yssel, Holland, thus providing a Frisian connection.

696. *Deo | Marti et duabus | Alaisiagis et N(umini) Aug(usti) | Ger(mani) cives Tuihanti | cunei Frisiorum | Ver(couicanorum) Se(ve)r(iani) Alexand|riani votum | solverunt | libent[es] | m(erito).* (*ILS* 4761; *RIB* 1594; *CSIR* 1.6.160).

Altar. Found on the north slope of Chapel Hill. AD 222/35.

697. *Deabus | Alaisia|gis Bau|dihillie | et Friaga|bi et N(umini) Aug(usti) | n(umerus) Hnau|difridi | v.s.l.m.* (*RIB* 1576).

Altar. Found on the north slope of Chapel Hill. Third century.

The second pair of Alaisiagae. Baudihillie, a Latinized form with the dative in e, might mean "battle-commanding" or "ruler of battle," while

Friagabi, a Germanic nominative, might mean "the giver of freedom" (Siebs in Bosanquet, "Alaisiagae," 192–197). Siebs interpreted Hnaudifridus as a Latinized form of the Old High German Notfried.

Ricagambeda

Blatobulgium (Birrens)

698. *Deae Ricagam\|bedae pagus | Vellaus milit(ans) | coh(orte) II Tung(rorum) | v.s.l.m.* (*CIL* VII 1072; *ILS* 4752; *RIB* 2107; *CSIR* 1.4.15).

Altar. Ca. AD 158 or Severan?

The *pagus* Vellaus may have been a subdivision of the *civitas Tungrorum* (E. Birley, "Deities," 75). The goddess' name recalls Beda (#695). She is almost certainly Germanic (Haug, "Ricagambeda," 795). See #366 (Vellaeus).

Omnes Dei Unsenis Fersomomeris

Voreda (Old Penrith)

699. *Omnibus | Dibus Unse\|nis Fersome\|ris Burcanius | Arcauius Vagda\|uarcustus Pou[.\|.]c[.]arus vex(illationis) MA\|VI --- pr]o salute | sua et suorum v.s.l.m.* (*RIB* 926).

Altar. Found 91.5m north of the fort.

A goddess Vagavercustis is known as a Batavian war deity (Schmitz, "Vagdavercustis," col. 2072–3) at Monterberg (*CIL* XIII 8662 by an *eques alae Noricorum*), Rindern (*CIL* XIII 8702 and 8703, the latter by a member of the *legio XXX*), Hemmen (*CIL* XIII 8805 [*ILS* 2536]: *deae Vagdavercusti Sim[p]li\|cius super dec alae Vocontior | exerci[t]uus Britannici*), Koln (*CIL* XIII 12057 [*ILS* 9000], by a praetorian prefect, AD 160/70), Adony (*RA* 1935, #163, by a tribune of the *cohors III Batavorum*, AD 218/222). Our Vagdauarcustus, perhaps the son of worshippers of the Batavian goddess, was thus named in her honor (E. Birley, "Deities," 76).

Domaszewski (*EE* ix 1124) cited the island of Borkum (Burcanis in Strabo *Geogr.* 7.291; Bourcanis in Stephanus Byz.) in comparison for Burcanius. A. Birley (*People*, 110) suggested that the dedication was one by six votaries, the first two with the names Unsensis and Fersomeris, to Omnes dei. The unit to which these four or six men belonged is uncertain but may have been a permanent cavalry *vexillatio* (n.b. Garmangabis #692; E. Birley, "Deities," 76).

Viradecthis

Blatobulgium (Birrens)

700. *Deae Viradec\|thi pa[g]us Con\|drustis milit(ans) | in coh(orte) II Tungror(um) sub Silvi\|o Auspice praef(ecto)* (*CIL* VII 1073; *ILS* 4756; *RIB* 2108; *CSIR* 1.4.16).

Altar. Ca. AD 158.

For Silvius Auspex: *RIB* 2100, *RIB* 2104; *PME* II.743, #S.53.

The Condrusi were a Germanic tribe within the *civitates Tungrii*, near the Eburones and the Treveri (Caesar *BG* 6.32.1). Viradecthis, native to the Condrusi, is attested also at Vechten (*CIL* XIII 8815 [*ILS* 4757]), at Mainz where she is equated with Lucena (*CIL* XIII 6761 [*ILS* 4758]), on the German *limes* near Karlsruhe in honor of the imperial house (*CIL* XIII 6486 [*ILS* 4759]), and at Starkenburg, again in conjunction with the imperial house (*CIL* XIII 4, 11944).

CATALOGUE OF MILITARY UNITS STATIONED
IN BRITAIN

This appendix is not intended as a full commentary on the garrison of Roman Britain (for which see Holder, *Roman Army*, and Jarrett, "Non-legionary Troops." All references to Holder and Jarrett cited below derive from those two works. Cross-references to the catalogue in parenthesis are possible or likely citations of the unit in question). The following list will provide essential information, including where a unit was raised, when it was sent to Britain, where it was stationed in the province, and when it was withdrawn.

Diplomas of Britain: AD 96/108 (Roxan, *RMD* II, #83)
                AD 98 (*CIL* XVI 43)
                AD 103 (*CIL* XVI 48)
                AD 105 (*CIL* XVI 51)
                AD 117/20 (*CIL* XVI 88)
                AD 122 (*CIL* XVI 69)
                AD 124 (*CIL* XVI 70)
                AD 135 (*CIL* XVI 82)
                AD 145/6 (*CIL* XVI 93)
                AD 154 or 159 (*CIL* XVI 130)

Legions

Legio II Augusta: Raised by Augustus, transferred to Britain in 43 (Ritterling, "Legio," 1249, 1459). Concentrated at Exeter after Nero, with detachments out-posted at Waddon Hill (Ritterling, "Legio," 1459–1460; Frere, *Britannia*, 58–59). Vexillations participated in the Civil War of 69 (Tacitus, *Histories* 3.22, 44); once the legion was reunited, Frontinus commanded the legion in the conquest of the Silures and built a new base at Caerleon (Ritterling, "Legio," 1460), last recorded at Caerleon, AD 253–259 (*RIB* 334). Part of the legion at Richborough in the fourth century (*NDO* XXVII.19).
    Holder, 104–105; A. Birley, *Fasti*, 219.
    Catalogue: 24, 46, 48, 52, 79, 84, 93, 150, 153, 162, 171, 172, 191, 225, 283, 301, 362, 365, (393), 404, 415, 467, (514), 529, 530, 592, 598.

Legio VI Victrix: In Spain until 68 (Ritterling, "Legio," 1599–1602; Tacitus *Histories* 3.44; *CIL* II 1442, 2983); transferred to Lower Germany (Ritterling, "Legio," 1602–1605; Tacitus, *Histories* 5.16; *CIL* XIII 8551); This legion received the title *pia fidelis Domitiana* under Domitian (*CIL* XIII 8533;

Ritterling, "Legio," 1613) in 89. *Domitiana* was dropped in 96. *Legio VI* came to Britain in 122 under Platorius Nepos to help in building Hadrian's Wall (*RIB* 1388, 1389), after which its permanent base was at York (*RIB* 653), while detachments were stationed in Scotland (*RIB* 2146, 2148, 2160) and Corbridge (*RIB* 1132) under Antoninus Pius.

Holder, 105; A. Birley, *Fasti*, 221–2.

Catalogue: 38, 49, 62, 76, 79, 84, 87, 94, 109, 158, 262, 308, 326, 340, 343, 344, 346, 401, 421, 426, 436, 460, 461, (462), 463, 481, (514), 526, 527, 594, 597.

Legio IX Hispana: Stationed in Pannonia until 43 when it was sent to Britain (Ritterling, *RE*, 1249, 1665–1666). After the revolt of Boudicca, this legion formed the garrison of Lincoln (*RIB* 254–257), but under Cerialis, it was moved to the new fortress at York (*RIB* 659, 673, 680). This legion was last recorded in Britain at York in 108 (Ritterling, "Legio," 1667–1668; *CIL* VII 241 [*RIB* 665]), perhaps removed for Trajan's Parthian war ca. 120 (Bogaers, "Nijmegen," 54), destroyed with *Legio XXII Deiotariana* in the Jewish Wars of 132–135 (E. Birley, "Britain after Agricola," 78–83), or lost in Armenia ca. 160 (Webster, *Roman Army*, 121).

Holder, 106.

Legio XIV Gemina Martia Victrix: Raised by Augustus after Actium and stationed at Mainz from AD 9 until transferred to Britain in 43 (Ritterling, "Legio," 1249, 1730–1732). The legion participated in the invasion of Anglesey in 60 and in suppressing the revolt of Boudicca (Tacitus, *Annals* 14.34, 37). Withdrawn in 66 for Nero's expedition against the Albani (Tacitus, *Histories* 2.27). Returned to Britain by Vitellius during the civil wars of 69 (Tacitus, *Histories* 2.66) but withdrawn again permanently in 70 (Tacitus, *Histories* 4.68).

Holder, 106.

Legio XX Valeria Victrix: Raised by Augustus after Actium, stationed in Illyricum and then Lower Germany after AD 9. The legion was sent to Britain in 43 (Ritterling, "Legio," 1249, 1769–1781) and based at Colchester (*RIB* 202, 203), then Usk after 49 (Holder, *Roman Army*, 106). The fortress at Deva (Chester) was built by 87 (Ritterling, "Legio," 1773). The legion received the title *Valeria Victrix* for its service during the Boudicca revolt (Holder, *Roman Army*, 107).

Holder, 106–107.

Catalogue: 8, 28, 29, 39, 48, 49, 79, 105, 110, (112), 158, 222, 300, 338, 368, (404), 407, 512, 534, 535, 593.

Alae (Auxiliary Cavalry Regiments)

Ala Agrippiana miniata: attested on diploma of 122, otherwise unattested in Roman Britain: Jarrett, 39 #2.

Ala I Asturum: Raised by Tiberius from Astures of north-west Spain. Attested on a diploma of AD 140 found at Palamarica (Roxan, *RMD* I,

#39). At Benwell, early third century (#102). Sent to Britain by Severus?
    Holder, 110.
    Catalogue: 102.

Ala II Asturum: Raised by Tiberius from Astures of north-west Spain, attested
in Pannonia (*CIL* III 14349), and sent to Britain under Cerialis. Stationed
at Ribchester late first–early second (*RIB* 586) and later formed the late
second–third/fourth century garrison at Chesters (#108; *RIB* 1462, 1465;
NDO XL.38).
    Holder, 107; Jarrett, 39, #4.
    Catalogue: 108.

Ala Augusta ob virtutem appellata: Attested at Chesters under Hadrian (#50)
and at Old Carlisle from 188–242 (*RIB* 893, 897, 903), perhaps, though
not necessarily, identical with the *ala Augusta Gallorum Proculeiana*. Its fate
after 242 is unknown.
    Holder, 109; Jarrett, 40, #5.
    Catalogue: 50, 144, 145, 307.

Ala Exploratorum: Attested at Auchendavy under Antoninus Pius (*RIB* 2179);
such *alae* were unknown elsewhere in the empire until the third century.
    Holder, 108.

Ala (Gallorum) Agrippiana miniata: Raised in Gaul under Tiberius and named
for one of its prefects, stationed in Upper Germany before Claudius (*CIL*
XIII 6235). Attested in Britain only on the diploma of 122; probably transferred to the island before 69.
    Holder, 108; Jarrett, 39, #2.

Ala Gallorum et Thracum Classiana invicta bis torquata CR: Raised in Gaul by
Tiberius and named for one of its prefects. Apparently stationed in the East
until the Civil Wars of 69 (Holder, *Roman Army*, 108). Sent to Britain with
Cerialis where it was named on the *diplomata* of 105, by which time it had
received citizenship, and 122. Attested in Lower Germany in the late sec-
ond/early third century (*CIL* XIII 8306).
    Holder, 108; Jarrett, 42, #10.

Ala Indiana Gallorum: Raised in Gaul in AD 21 and named for Julius Indus.
Stationed in Upper Germany before Claudius (*CIL* XIII 6230). At Cirencester
under Vespasian (*RIB* 108), but recorded in Lower Germany under Domitian
(*CIL* XIII 8519).
    Holder, 108; Jarrett, 40, #6.

Ala Augusta Gallorum Petriana milliaria CR bis torquata: Raised in Gaul under
Augustus, named for T. Pomponius Petra (*CIL* XI 969). Attested in Upper
Germany in the pre-Flavian period (*CIL* XIII 6820); supported Vitellius in
69. Perhaps sent to Britain with Cerialis. At Corbridge under Domitian
(*RIB* 1172) and named on the *diplomata* of 98, 122, 124, and 135 as *mil-
liaria* and may have been increased to that size by Trajan when at Carlisle.
Perhaps formed the garrison of Stanwix but not directly attested there until
the fourth century (*NDO* XL.45).
    Holder, 108; Holder, 33; Jarrett, 38, #1; cf. *RIB* 2411.84.

Ala Gallorum Picentiana: Raised in Gaul before the death of Augustus, named for its prefect L. Rustius Picens (*CIL* III 10094), stationed in Upper Germany until AD 82 (*CIL* XVI 28). First attested in Britain on the diploma of 122; attested at Malton late second century (*Britannia*.1971 #9).

    Holder, 109; Jarrett, 41, #7.

Ala Augusta Gallorum Proculeiana: Raised in Gaul under Tiberius and named for one of its prefects. Perhaps part of the invasion force 43 (not attested elsewhere). At Lancaster under Trajan (*RIB* 606). At Chesters under Hadrian (*Britannia*.1979 #7). From AD 185–242 stationed at Old Carlisle (*RIB* 897).

    Holder, 15, 109; Jarrett, 41, #8.

Ala Gallorum Sebosiana: Raised in Gaul before Tiberius, attested in Upper Germany during the pre-Flavian period (*CIL* XIII 1709, 6239). Supported Vitellius in 69. Probably sent to Britain with Cerialis but not recorded in Britain until the diploma of 103. Possibly at Carlisle under Agricola (Tomlin, *Britannia*.23 [1992] 153). Attested at Lancaster (*RIB* 605, 2465.1), and Brough-under-Stainmore (*RIB* 2411.89) in the third century; last recorded in 262/5.

    Holder, 109; Jarrett, 41, #9.

    Catalogue: 359b.

Ala Herculea: Raised by or renamed for Maximian between 295 and 305. Perhaps sent to Britain with Constantius Chlorus. At Elslack (Olenacum) in the fourth century (*NDO* XL.55).

    Holder, 109; Jarrett, 42, #10a.

Ala I Hispanorum Asturum: Raised from the Astures of Spain before 43 and probably sent to Britain in 43. Recorded on the *diplomata* of 98, 122, 124, 135, and 146. Attested at South Shields (*RIB* 1064) and Wallsend (*Britannia*. 1976 #48). Stationed at Benwell under Ulpius Marcellus, AD 211/212 (*RIB* 1329; A. Birley, *Fasti*, 142, n. 12, 166 n. 12), and in the third/fourth centuries (#36; *RIB* 1337; *NDO* XL.35).

    Holder, 110; Jarrett, 39, #3.

    Catalogue: 36.

Ala Hispanorum Vettonum CR: Raised in central Spain from the Vettones; sent to Britain in 43, where it is recorded on the *diplomata* for 103 and 122. Attested at Brecon Gaer late first century (*RIB* 403). At Binchester during the late second/early third century (#287; *RIB* 1028, 1029, 1032, 1035).

    Holder, 30–31, 110; Jarrett, 44, #17.

    Catalogue: 65, 287, (490).

Ala I Pannoniorum Sabiniana: Raised in Pannonia, sent to Britain in 43. Listed on the *diplomata* of 122 and 146. Formed third/fourth century garrison of Halton Chesters (*RIB* 1433; *NDO* XL.37).

    Holder, 110; Jarrett, 43, #11.

Ala I Pannoniorum Tampiana Victrix: Raised in Pannonia, sent to Britain in 43. Sent to the Danube (Carnutum) under Domitian (probably 85, *CIL* III 4466). Returned to Britain by AD 98, recorded on *diplomata* of 103 and

122. Transferred to Noricum, where it was recorded on the diploma for 128/38 (*CIL* XVI 174).
Holder, 110–111; Jarrett, 43, #12.

Ala Sarmatarum: Attested at Ribchester (*RIB* 594, 595), presumably identical to the *cuneus Sarmatarum* (*NDO* XL.54) and *numerus equitum Sarmatarum Bremeten-nacensium* at Ribchester, third century (*RIB* 587 [AD 222–35]; *RIB* 583 [AD 238–44]). See Dio LXXXI.16 for Sarmartian hostages taken in 175 and subsequently sent to Britain, some, perhaps, forming this unit.
Holder, 111; Jarrett, 43, #14.

Ala I Thracum: Raised in Thrace and sent to Britain in 43, where it is recorded on the *diplomata* for 103 and 124. At Colchester under Claudius (*RIB* 201) and at Cirencester under Nero (*RIB* 109). Transferred to Lower Germany by the mid-second century (*CIL* XIII 8818, 12058).
Holder, 111; Jarrett, 44, #15.

Ala I Tungrorum: Raised in Gallia Belgica from the Tungri after the revolt of Civilis. Sent to Britain with Cerialis. Sent to the Danube (Carnuntum) by Domitian (*CIL* III 6485). Returned to Britain by AD 98 and listed on the *diplomata* for 98, 105, 122, and 135. Attested at Mumrills under Antoninus Pius (#693; cf., 513).
Holder, 111; Jarrett, 44, #16.
Catalogue: 693.

Ala Augusta Vocontiorum CR: Raised in Gallia Narbonensis from the Vocontii by AD 14. Attested in Lower Germany until AD 96 (*CIL* XIII 8655). Recorded in Britain on the *diplomata* of 122, by which time it had received citizenship *en bloc*, and 178. Attested at Newstead under Antoninus Pius (#516). Possibly at Lancaster, late first or early second century; Leicester (*Britannia*.1978 #46; *RIB* 2411.90) and South Shields (*RIB* 2411.70), third century?
Holder, 111–12; Jarrett, 45, #18.
Catalogue: 516.

Cohorts (Infantry Auxiliary Regiments)

Cohors I Afrorum CR eq.: Raised in Africa, recorded on the diploma of 122, by which time it had received citizenship *en bloc*. Perhaps the same cohort attested in Dacia later in the same century (*CIL* VI 3529).
Holder, 112; Jarrett, 51, #8.

Cohors I Alpinorum eq.: Raised in Aquitania under Augustus and stationed in Upper Germany. Probably sent to Britain in 43. Perhaps the same unit attested at Gallia Aquitania before Claudius (*CIL* XIII 922) and on the British diploma for 103 as *Cohors I Alpinorum*.
Holder, 112; Jarrett, 52, #9.

Cohors I Aquitanorum: Recorded on the *diplomata* of 117/20, 122, 124. Attested at Carrawburgh under Hadrian (*RIB* 1550). Attested at Brough-on-Noe in

Julius Verus' governorship (AD 158; *RIB* 238). Stationed at Brancaster, early third century (*RIB* 2466) and later replaced by the *Equites Dalmatae Branodunenses*.

 Holder, 112; Jarrett, 52, #10.
 Catalogue: 605.

Cohors I Asturum eq.: Raised from the Astures in north-west Spain early in the principate. It seems probable that there existed two series of *cohortes Asturum* (Roxan, "Pre-Severan Auxilia," 63–64). Transferred probably from Noricum. Recorded in Britain first on the career inscription of Q. Gargalius Martialis (*ILS* 2767; before 260). Possibly garrisoned at Great Chesters, fourth century (*NDO* XL.42).

 Holder, 112; Jarrett, 52, #11.

Cohors II Asturum eq.: Raised from the Astures early in the principate and stationed in Lower Germany, where it is recorded on the *diploma* for 80 (*CIL* XVI 158). Recorded in Britain in 105 and on the *diplomata* of 122 and 124. Attested at Llanio in the second century (*RIB* 407, 408) and at Great Chesters in the third (*RIB* 1738). The entry in the *Notitia* citing the *cohors I Asturm* at Aesica (*NDO* XL.42) may be a scribal error for *II Asturum*.

 Holder, 112–13; Jarrett, 53, #12.

Cohors I Baetasiorum CR ob virtutem et fidem: Raised from the Baetasii of Lower Germany after Civilis and sent to Britain with Cerialis. Recorded on the *diplomata* of 103, 122, 124 and 135. Stationed at Bar Hill under Antoninus Pius (*RIB* 2170). Stationed at Maryport, probably late second century (#137). Stationed at Old Kilpatrick, possibly under Severus (#224). Transferred to Reculver early in the third century (*JRS*.1961 #30; *JRS*.1969 #37) and was placed there in the fourth century (*NDO* XXVIII.18).

 Holder, 113; Jarrett, 53, #13.
 Catalogue: 95, 96, 137, 224, 254, 255.

Cohortes I–VIII Batavorum: This series of cohorts was raised from the Batavi of Lower Germany in accordance with their treaty with Rome, commanded by their own nobles (e.g. Julius Civilis). Sent to Britain in 43. Withdrawn in 66/67, together with *Legio XIV Gemina*, by Nero for his expedition against the Albani of the Caucuses (Tacitus, *Histories* I.6, I.59, II.27).

Cohortes I–IX Batavorum: Raised in Lower Germany after the revolt of Civilis. Sent to Britain with Cerialis. Four *cohortes* present at Mons Graupius (Tacitus, *Agricola* 36).

Cohors I Batavorum eq.: Perhaps one of the four present at Mons Graupius (Tacitus, *Agricola* 36). Recorded on the *diplomata* of 122, 124, 135, and 178. Attested at Carvoran (*RIB* 1823, 1824) and Castlesteads (*RIB* 2015) in the second century. Stationed at Carrawburgh in the third/fourth centuries (*RIB* 1553; *NDO* XL.39).

 Holder, 114; Jarrett, 55, #14.
 Catalogue: 74, 341, 427, 428, (429), 452, 453.

Cohors II Batavorum: destroyed with Cornelius Fuscus after transfer from Britain (*CIL* III 14214).

Cohors III Batavorum: Attested at Vindolanda, under Cerialis: Bowman and Thomas, *Vindolanda: II*, 263, 311.
   Jarrett, 56, #15.

Cohors IIII Batavorum: attested in Dacia early in the second century (*AE* 1964 n 229; *AE* 1975 n 725).

Cohors VIII Batavorum: Recorded at Vindolanda (ca. AD 100) and perhaps stationed there (Bowman and Thomas, *Vindolanda: II*, #127, 130, 134, 135, 137, 140, 143, 151, 242, 263, 281, 282, 284).
   Holder, 114; Jarrett, 56, #15A.

Cohors IX Batavorum: attested in Dacia, early second century (*AE* 1964 n 229; *AE* 1975 n 725).

Cohors III Bracaraugustanorum: Raised from the Bracares of Portugal by the reign of Claudius. Perhaps sent to Britain in 43. Recorded on the *diplomata* of 103, 122, 124, and 146. Recorded on building tiles at Manchester (*CIL* VII 1230; *EE* IX 1277) and Melandra (*Britannia*.1974 #14) in the second century.
   Holder, 114; Jarrett, 57, #18.

Cohors IIII Breucorum: Raised from the Brecci of Pannonia. Probably sent to Britain in 43. Recorded on the diploma of 122. Attested on building tiles at Grimescar (*JRS*.1957 #30), Castleshaw (*EE* IX 1278) and Slack (*CIL* VII 1231) in the early second century. Attested at Bowes during Julius Severus' governorship (AD 130–33; *RIB* 739). At Ebchester, third century (#231; *JRS*.1964 #26, *JRS*.1965 #47).
   Holder, 114; Jarrett, 57, #19.
   Catalogue: 231.

Cohors I Celtiberorum eq.: Raised in north-east Spain. Recorded in Britain first in 105, then on the *diplomata* of 122, 146, and 178. Possibly known at Caersws on building tiles (*RIB* 2471.1).
   Holder, 114; Jarrett, 57, #20.

Cohors I Aelia classica: Raised from *classiarii* before the death of Hadrian (*CIL* XIV 5347). First recorded in Britain on the diploma of 146. Attested on a lead seal at Ravenglass in the third century but not necessarily in garrison there (Potter, *Romans in Northwest England*, 73; *RIB* 2411.94). Stationed at Burrow Walls in the fourth century (*NDO* XL.51).
   Holder, 114–15; Jarrett, 57, #21.

Cohors I Cornoviorum: The only unit which was raised from a single British tribe. Known only at Newcastle in the fourth century (*NDO* XL.34). Possibly at Caerws, date uncertain (*RIB* 2471.1).
   Holder, 115; Jarrett, 58, #22.

Cohors I Cubernorum: #442 (Carrawburgh, late second century).

Cohors I Ulpia Traiana Cugernorum CR: Raised from the Cugerni of the Lower Rhine after Civilis and sent to Britain with Cerialis. Recorded on the *diplomata* of 103 and 122, when it gained citizenship and honorific titles, and 124. At Cramond in 140/44 (*RIB* 2131; *Britannia*.1973, 336). Perhaps in garrison at Carrawburgh, late second century (*RIB* 1524). At Newcastle under Caracalla (#17), after whom nothing further is known of this unit.
  Holder, 115; Jarrett, 58, #23.
  Catalogue: 17.

Cohors I Aelia Dacorum milliaria: Raised in Dacia under Hadrian and sent to Britain to help build the *vallum* of Hadrian's Wall (*RIB* 1365). This unit received the title *Aelia* in 146 (*CIL* XVI 93). At Bewcastle (#153) under Hadrian. Garrisoned at Birdoswald, early third/fourth centuries (*RIB* 1909; *NDO* XL.44; Holder, *Roman Army*, 115).
  Holder, 115; Jarrett, 45, #1.
  Catalogue: (4), 153, 185–207, 275, 410, 591.

Cohors I Delmatarum: Raised in Dalmatia by the reign of Claudius. Recorded on the *diplomata* of 122, 124, and 135. Attested at Maryport under Antoninus Pius (#139, 376) and at Chesters, late second century (*JRS*.1957 #14).
  Holder, 115–16; Jarrett, 59, #24.
  Catalogue: 138–143, 376.

Cohors II Delmatarum eq.: Raised in Dalmatia and stationed in Germany until sent to Britain in 43. Recorded on the *diplomata* of 105, 122 and 135. Attested at Carvoran, third/fourth centuries (#673; *NDO* XL.43).
  Holder, 116; Jarrett, 59, #25.
  Catalogue: (455), 673.

Cohors IIII Delmatarum: Raised in Dalmatia, sent to Britain either in 43 or 61. Recorded on the *diplomata* of 103 and 122. Attested at Hardknot under Hadrian (*JRS*.1965 #7).
  Holder, 116; Jarrett, 59, #26.

Cohors I Frisiavonum: Raised in Lower Germany after Civilis and sent to Britain with Cerialis. Recorded on the *diplomata* of 105, 122, 124, and 178. Attested at Manchester (*RIB* 577–579) and Melandra (*RIB* 279), perhaps garrisoned at one of these forts under Hadrian. Stationed at Rudchester, third/fourth centuries (*RIB* 1395, 1396; *NDO* XL.36), cited in the *Notitia* as the *Cohors I Frixagorum*.
  Holder, 116; Jarrett, 59, #27.
  Catalogue: 441.

Cohortes I–V Gallorum: Raised in Gaul by 43, probably part of the invasion force. I and III not attested but must have existed, likely part of Claudius' invasion force.

Cohors II Gallorum eq.: Raised in Gaul by 43, probably part of the invasion force. Recorded on the *diplomata* of 122, 146, and 178. Attested at Old Penrith in the third century (#151; *RIB* 929).

Holder, 116–17; Jarrett, 60, #28.
Catalogue: 151, 152, (554).

Cohors IIII Gallorum eq.: Raised in Gaul by 43, probably part of the invasion force. Attested at Templeborough under Trajan (*RIB* 619, 620). Recorded on the *diplomata* of 122, 146, and 178. Stationed at Castlehill under Antoninus Pius (#517). Garrisoned at Risingham, late second century (#11; *RIB* 1249), at Castlesteads—possibly third century or Hadrian—(#208, 209), at Vindolanda, third/fourth centuries (*RIB* 1705; *NDO* XL.41).
Holder, 117; Jarrett, 60, #29.
Catalogue: 11, 37, 179–181, (184), 208, 209, 218, 517.

Cohors V Gallorum (eq.?): Raised in Gaul by 43, probably part of the invasion force. Recorded on the *diplomata* of 122, 124, and 135. At Cramond, perhaps under Septimius Severus (#223). Stationed at South Shields, third century (*RIB* 1060).
Holder, 117; Jarrett, 61, #30.
Catalogue: (10), (14), 223, (573).

Cohors I Hamiorum sagittariorum: Raised from the Hamii of Syria and possibly sent to Britain in 43. Recorded on the *diplomata* of 122, 124, and 135. At Carvoran in 136–8 (#78); at Bar Hill, mid-second century (#367; *RIB* 2172); and at Carvoran again from 162/3 (#389, *RIB* 1809, 1810; A. Birley, *Fasti* 127–129).
Holder, 117; Jarrett, 61, #31.
Catalogue: 78, 369, (385), 389.

Cohors I Hispanorum eq.: Raised in Spain and stationed in Galatia under Augustus. Sent to Britain with Cerialis. Attested at Ardoch under Agricola (*RIB* 2213). Recorded on the *diplomata* of 98, 103, 105, 122, 124, 146, and 178. Stationed at Axelodunum (Uxeloduno), fourth century (*NDO* XL.49).
Holder, 118; Jarrett, 46, #32.

Cohors I Aelia Hispanorum milliaria eq.: Raised by Hadrian about 119. Cited on the *diplomata* of 98, 103, 105, 122, 124, 146, 178 (as *Aelia*). This unit built the fort at Alauna (Maryport) and was its first garrison (#121). The cohort was split about 130, with a detachment sent elsewhere. The unit at Alauna was equivalent in size to a *cohors quingenaria* and was commanded by a prefect instead of a tribune. Under Antoninus Pius, the unit, returned to full strength, earned the honorific title *Aelia* for the conquest of Scotland. Stationed at Netherby in the third century (#9, 15; *RIB* 977, 979). At Axelodeuno (Uxelodunum) in the fourth century (*NDO* XL.49).
Holder, 118; Jarrett, 46, #3.
Catalogue: 9, 15, 88, 121–136.

Cohortes I–V Lingonum: Raised in Upper Germany after the revolt of Civilis and sent to Britain with Cerialis.

Cohors I Lingonum eq.: Raised in Upper Germany after the revolt of Civilis, sent to Britain with Cerialis. Recorded on the *diplomata* of 105 and 122.

Attested at High Rochester between 139 and 143 (*RIB* 1276). Stationed at Lanchester, third century (#33; *RIB* 1091, 1092).
    Holder, 118; Jarrett, 61, #33.
    Catalogue: 33, (70), 157, (360).

Cohors II Lingonum (eq.?): Raised in Upper Germany after the revolt of Civilis, sent to Britain with Cerialis. Recorded on the *diplomata* of 98, 105?, 122, 124, and 178. Attested at Ilkley under Marcus Aurelius (#626; *RIB* 636). Stationed at Moresby sometime in the second century (*RIB* 798, 800). Attested at Brough-under-Stainmore on third century leaden seals (*RIB* 2411.106, 108). Stationed at Drumburgh, fourth century (*NDO* XL.48).
    Holder, 118–19; Jarrett, 62, #34.
    Catalogue: 626.

Cohors III Lingonum: Raised in Upper Germany after the revolt of Civilis, sent to Britain with Cerialis. Attested on the *diplomata* of 103?, 122, 117–26, and 178.
    Holder, 119; Jarrett, 62, #35.

Cohors IIII Lingonum (eq.): Raised in Upper Germany after the revolt of Civilis, sent to Britain with Cerialis. Recorded on the *diplomata* of 103?, 122 and 146. Stationed at Wallsend, third/fourth centuries (#162–164; *NDO* XL.33).
    Holder, 119; Jarrett, 62, #36.
    Catalogue: 162–164.

Cohors V Lingonum is not attested in Britain but is recorded on the *diploma* of 110 for Dacia (*CIL* XVI 163).

Cohors I Menapiorum: Raised in Gallia Belgica from the Menapii after Civilis and sent to Britain with Cerialis. Recorded on the *diplomata* of 122 and 124. Possibly at Vindolanda in 97–103 (*RIB* 2445.1).
    Holder, 119; Jarrett, 62, #37.

Cohors I Morinorum et Cersiacorum: Raised from two tribes in Gallia Belgica after the revolt of Civilis and sent to Britain with Cerialis. Attested as *Cohors I Morinorum* on the *diplomata* of 103 and 122. Possibly at Vindolanda in 97–103 (*RIB* 2445.1). Garrisoned at Ravenglass, fourth century (*NDO* XL.52).
    Holder, 119; Jarrett, 62–63, #38; cf. *AE* 1972, 148.

[Cohors I Me]n(apiorum) Naut(arum)?: Recorded in Britain on the *diploma* of 135. Perhaps the same cohort attested at Cemenelum (Alpes Maritimae) in 69: *CIL* V 7892.
    Holder, 119; Jarrett, 63, #39.

Cohors I Nervia/Nervana Germanorum milliaria eq.: Raised by Nerva in 97 and sent directly to Britain. Recorded on the *diplomata* of 122 and 178. Stationed at Birrens under Antoninus Pius (*RIB* 2093, 2097). Known at Burgh-by-Sands (*RIB* 2041), probably second century. Attested at Netherby (*RIB* 966) and possibly Bewcastle (582, 583) during the third century.
    Holder, 117; Jarrett, 46, #2.

Cohortes I–VI Nerviorum: Raised in Gallia Belgica after the revolt of Civilis, sent to Britain with Cerialis. Possibly raised for service in Britain.

Cohors I Nerviorum milliaria: Recorded on the *diplomata* of 105 and 178 and attested at Caer Gai (*RIB* 418, undated). At Birrens, mid-second century (#81, 219), by which time it became *milliaria*. At Burgh-by-Sands in third century (#215).
  Holder, 119; Jarrett, 63, #40.
  Catalogue: 81, 215, 219, 578.

Cohors II Nerviorum CR: Recorded on the *diplomata* of 96/114?, 98, 122, 124, and 146. Attested at Wallsend, second century (#322), Carrawburgh (#45), and Vindolanda (#590), but did not necessarily form a garrison at any of these sites. This cohort was stationed at Whitley Castle, early third century (*RIB* 1202).
  Holder, 119–20; Jarrett, 63, #41.
  Catalogue: 45, 292, 322, 590.

Cohors III Nerviorum: Recorded on the *diplomata* of 122, 124, 117–26?, and 135?. Attested at Newstead, second century (*RIB* 2411.142), and Chesterholm (#274). Stationed at Alione (uncertain location) during the fourth century (*NDO* XL.53).
  Holder, 120; Jarrett, 64, #42.
  Catalogue: 274.

Cohors IIII Nerviorum: Recorded on the *diplomata* of 117–126?, 135?, and 140–54.
  Holder, 120; Jarrett, 64, #43.

Cohors V Nerviorum: not attested in Britain.
  Jarrett, 64, #43A.

Cohors VI Nerviorum: Recorded on the *diplomata* of 122, 124, 117–26?, 135?, and 146. Attested at Great Chesters during the reign of Hadrian (#103) and at Rough Castle in Scotland under Antoninus Pius (#105; *RIB* 2145). In garrison at Bainbridge, third/fourth centuries (*RIB* 722, *JRS*.1961 #4; *NDO* XL.56).
  Holder, 120; Jarrett, 64, #44.
  Catalogue: 103, 105.

Cohors I Pannoniorum eq.: Raised in Pannonia between Trajan's death and Septimius Severus' accession (*CIL* IX 2649 [*ILS* 2732]) and recorded in Britain near Great Chesters on a tombstone on which the unit's numeral is missing, second century (*RIB* 1667).
  Holder, 120; Jarrett, 65, #45.

Cohors II Pannoniorum eq.: Raised in Pannonia by the reign of Claudius. Recorded on the *diplomata* of 105 and 124. Attested on a lead seal at Vindolanda (*RIB* 2411.143), though not necessarily in garrison there. Stationed at Beckfoot in the second century (*RIB* 880). *RIB* 1667 could refer to this cohort.
  Holder, 120; Jarrett, 65, #46.

Cohors V Pannoniorum: Attested at Brough-under-Stainmore (*RIB* 2111.144).
  Holder, 120–21; Jarrett, 65, #47.

Cohors V Raetorum eq.: Raised in Raetia in the early principate and stationed
in Germany. Recorded in Britain on the diploma of 122. In garrison in
Egypt in the fourth century (*NDO* XXVIII.30).
  Holder, 121; Jarrett, 65, #48.

Cohors VI Raetorum (eq.?): Raised in Raetia in the early principate, stationed
in Germany, where it is recorded on tiles of Flavian date from Vindonissa
in Upper Germany (*CIL* XIII 12456). Attested at Great Chesters around
166/7 (*RIB* 1737) and on lead seals at Brough-under-Stainmore, third century (*RIB* 2411.147–151). Possibly the same as the *Cohors VI Valeria Raetorum*
in Raetia, fourth century (*NDO* XXXV.27).
  Holder, 121; Jarrett, 65, #49.

Cohors I Sunucicorum: Raised in Lower Germany either by Civilis (Tacitus,
Histories 4.66) or under Trajan. Recorded on the *diplomata* of 122 and 124.
In the vicinity of Holt, second century (*RIB* 2491.96). The unit was build-
ing an aqueduct at Caernarvon in the Severan period (*RIB* 430).
  Holder, 121; Jarrett, 66, #50.

Cohors I Thracum CR: Raised in Thrace. Possibly attested on the *diplomata*
of 122, and 178. At Birdoswald, 205/8 (*RIB* 1909), but probably not garrisoned there. Possibly identical to *cohors I Thracum CR* attested in Pannonia
Superior ca. 154 (*CIL* XVI 104) and perhaps to the *cohors I Thracum eq.*,
though Breeze and Dobson (*Hadrian's Wall*, 256–257) argue against this.
  Holder, 121–22; Jarrett, 66, #51.
  Catalogue: 65, 686, 687, 688.

Cohors I Thracum eq.: Stationed in Lower Germany (*CIL* XIII 7803) under
Claudius. The unit, transferred to Britain by 61, was stationed at Wroxeter
until 69 (*RIB* 291). Cited possibly on the *diplomata* of 122 and 178. The
unit formed a second century garrison at Newcastle (*RIB* 1323) and a third
century garrison at Bowes (*RIB* 740).
  Holder, 121; Jarrett, 66, #51A.

Cohors II Thracum eq.: Stationed in Germany where it is recorded on the
diploma for 80 (*CIL* XVI 158). Transferred to Britain by 103 where it is
recorded on the *diplomata* of 103, 122, and 178. Attested at Mumrills, third
century (*RIB* 2142). The unit formed the third–fourth century garrison of
Moresby (#120; *RIB* 803, 804; *NDO* XL.50).
  Holder, 122; Jarrett, 67, #52.
  Catalogue: 120, (513).

Cohors VI Thracum eq.: This unit was sent to Britain either in 43 or 61.
Attested at Kingsholm (*RIB* 121) under Nero. Recorded on third-century
lead seals from Brough-under-Staimore (*RIB* 2411.152–158).
  Holder, 122; Jarrett, 67, #53.

Cohors VII Thracum eq.: Sent to Britain in 43. It is recorded on the *diplomata* of 122, 135, and 178. Attested on third century lead seals from Brough-under Stainmore (*RIB* 2411.159–240).
   Holder, 122; Jarrett, 67, #54.

Cohors I Tungrorum milliaria: Raised in Gallia Belgica from the Tungri after the revolt of Civilis and sent to Britain with Cerialis. Recorded on the *diplo-mata* of 103, 122, 124, 135, 146. Attested at Vindolanda before Hadrian (Bowman and Thomas, *Vindolanda*, 47–50 [ca. 90], 117–119 [ca. 105]). A *diploma* for 128 indicates that a vexillation was detached (*CIL* XVI 174). The unit remaining in Britain was active at Carrawburgh under Hadrian (*JRS*.1966 #5). Soon afterwards the full strength of the unit was in garrison at Castlecary (*RIB* 2155). A soldier of the cohort is recorded on a *diploma* fragment, dating to 146, found at Vindolanda (cf. Bowman and Thomas, *Vindolanda: II*, #154, 295). Garrisoned at Housesteads, third/fourth century (293, 313, 380, 588; *NDO* XL.40).
   Holder, 122–23; Jarrett, 48, #4.
   Catalogue: 173, (177), 269, 293, 313, 380, (439), 501, 512, 588.

Cohors II Tungrorum milliaria eq. CL: Sent to Britain with Cerialis. Part of the cohort was sent to Raetia where it is recorded on the *diplomata* for 121/5 (Roxan, *RMD* I #25), 147 (*CIL* XVI 94) and 153 (*CIL* XVI 101). Under Antoninus Pius, part of the unit was stationed at Cramond (*RIB* 2135). The cohort was reunited by 158 and is recorded at Birrens (281). It formed a third and fourth century garrison at Castlesteads (210; *NDO* XL.44). For *CL (c[oram] l[audata]?)*, see H. Wolff, "Cohors II Tungrorum," 267–288.
   Holder, 123; Jarrett, 49, #5.
   Catalogue: (13), 56, 82, 210–212, 240, 281, 383, (433), (434), 698, 700.

Cohors Usiporum: Raised in Upper Germany from the Usipi and sent to Britain for training during Agricola's sixth campaign. The cohort mutinied and escaped by ship (Tacitus *Agricola* 28). The *cohors Usiporum* was subsequently disbanded.
   Holder, 123.

Cohors I Vangionum milliaria eq.: Raised in Upper Germany from the Vangiones after the revolt of Civilis. This cohort was sent to Britain with Cerialis where it is recorded on the *diplomata* of 103, 122, 124, and 135. Attested at Benwell under Marcus Aurelius (#515, *RIB* 1350) and at Chesters in the third century (*RIB* 1428). The cohort formed the third century garrison at Risingham (*RIB* 1234).
   Holder, 123–24; Jarrett, 50, #6.
   Catalogue: 16, (71), (119), 159, (263), (309), 311, (515), 536.

Cohors I Fida Vardullorum milliaria eq. CR: Raised under Claudius in Spain from the Vardulli, first recorded in Britain by 98, by which time it had received citizenship *en bloc* and its honorific title, possibly for service on the Rhine during the revolt of Civilis. The unit may have came to Britain with

Cerialis (Holder, *Roman Army*, 124). Between 105 and 122, it was enlarged to *milliaria*. It is recorded on the *diplomata* for 105, 122, 124, 135, 146, 154 (159?), and 178. *Equites Vardulli* are also known at Vindolanda under Hadrian (Bowman and Thomas, *Tab. Vind. II.* #181.13). Attested at Castlecary during the first occupation of the Antonine Wall (#337) where it was under the command of a prefect. A vexillation of the same unit is attested on Hadrian's Wall at about the same time (#496). Known at Corbridge, probably under Marcus Aurelius and Verus (*RIB* 1128). The cohort is attested at Lanchester late second century (#32, 156) and formed, in detachments, the third century garrison of High Rochester (#422).

Holder, 124; Jarrett, 50, #7.
Catalogue: 19, 32, 34, 35, 53, 156, 337, (363), 422, 496, (515).

Cohors II (Hispana) Vasconum CR eq.: During the reign of Galba, this cohort was raised from the Vascones of Northern Spain, whence it was sent to fight in Lower Germany in 70 (Tacitus, *Histories* 4.33), and probably transferred to Britain under Cerialis. It won citizenship by 105 and is recorded on the *diplomata* for 105 and 122.

Holder, 124; Jarrett, 68, #56.

Numeri (Specialized regiments raised from tribes within and outside the empire)

Cuneus Frisiorum Aballavensium: Raised from the Frisii of Holland, attested at Papcastle under Philip (#2, 3), and was previously in garrison at Aballava (Burgh-by-Sands), according to its epithet (Holder, *Roman Army*, 124).

Holder, 124; Jarrett, 68, #1.
Catalogue: 2, 3.

Cuneus Frisionum Ver(covociensium): Raised from the Frisii of Holland, attested at Vercovicium (Housesteads) during the reign of Severus Alexander (#696).

Holder, 124; Jarrett, 68, #2.
Catalogue: 696.

Cuneus Frisiorum Vinoviensium: Raised from the Frisii of Holland, attested at Vinovia (Binchester), third century (*RIB* 1036, undated).

Holder, 124; Jarrett, 69, #3.

Cuneus Sarmatarum: Formed from the Sarmatians, this *cuneus* was sent to Britain by Marcus Aurelius in 175, attested at Ribchester in the third century (#460) where it was still in garrison in the fourth (*NDO* XL.54).

Holder, 124–25; Jarrett, 43, #14.
Catalogue: 460.

Numerus Barcariorum: Attested at Lancaster in the third century (#250), where it was used for transportation, lighterage, and inshore military operations. Probably still in garrison at Lancaster in the fourth century.

Holder, 125; Jarrett, 69, #13.
Catalogue: 250.

Numerus Barcariorum Tigrisensium: Originally stationed on the river Tigris, this *numerus* is recorded at South Shields in the fourth century (*NDO* XL.22). Recorded with the epithet of its original posting in the *Notitia*, this *numerus* may be identical to the *Numerus Barcariorum*, though Jarrett finds this unlikely (69, #13).
 Holder, 125.

Numerus Exploratorum Bremeniensium: Attested at High Rochester under Gordian (#34) and perhaps identical with the *numerus exploratorum* recorded at Portchester (*NDO* VII.110).
 Holder, 126.
 Catalogue: 34.

N(umerus) Con(cangensium): Attested at Binchester on stamped bricks and tiles (*RIB* 2480.1–2).
 Jarrett, 70, #14.

Numerus Exploratorum Habitancensium: Attested at Risingham in AD 213 (#16) and perhaps identical with the *numerus exploratorum* recorded at Portchester (*NDO* VII.110).
 Holder, 126.
 Catalogue: 16.

Numerus Hnaudifridi: Attested at Housesteads in the third century (#697) and named after its commander Hnaudifridus.
 Holder, 126; Jarrett, 71, #17.
 Catalogue: 697.

Numerus Magnesium: Attested at Carvoran (*RIB* 1825).
 Jarrett, 71, #18A.

Numerus Maurorum Aurelianorum: Raised from the Moors of Africa under Marcus Aurelius, it came to Britain with Septimius Severus and is attested at Burgh-by-Sands under Valerian and Gallienus (#216) where it was still stationed in the fourth century (*NDO* XL.47; E. Birley, "Beaumont Inscription, the *Notitia Dignitatum*," 193).
 Holder, 126; Jarrett, 71, #23.
 Catalogue: 216.

Numerus equitum Stratonicianorum: Attested at Brougham, third century (*RIB* 780). Stratonicaea was a city in Asia Minor.
 Holder, 126; Jarrett, 69, #10.

Numerus militum Syrorum sagittariorum: This unit of Syrian archers is attested at Kirkby Thore, third century (#67).
 Holder, 126; Jarrett, 71, #19.
 Catalogue: 67.

Venatores Bannienses: A unit of hunters attested at Birdoswald, third century (#367).
 Holder, 126; Jarrett, 72, #33.
 Catalogue: 367.

Vexillatio Gaesatorum Raetorum: Raetian spearmen attested at Great Chesters in the third century (#77), and attested as *Vexillatio Raetorum Gaesatorum* at Risingham (#159, 160, 221), probably third century.
    Holder, 127; Jarrett, 73, #36.
    Catalogue: 77, 159, 160, 221.

Vexillatio Germanorum V[o]r[e]d(ensium): RIB 920 (find-spot unrecorded). Perhaps a variant of *vexillatio Marsacorum*.
    Jarrett, 73, #34.

Vexillatio Mar[sacorum]: Attested at Old Penrith under Severus Alexander. The Marsaci/Marsacii, a German tribe, lived at the mouth of the Rhine in Zeeland (Byvanck, *Nederland*, I.199, fig. 7; Pliny *NH* 4.101, 106; Tacitus *Histories* 4.56; *CIL* VI 3263; *CIL* XIII 8303, 8317; *AE* 1954, 78).
    Holder, 126–27; Jarrett, 73, #35.

Vexillatio Sueborum Longovicianorum: Raised from the Suebi, this vexillation is attested at Lanchester, whence it took its name, under Gordian III (#692). Possibly the *numerus Longovicanorum* of *NDO* XL.30.
    Holder, 127; Jarrett, 73, #37.

Field Army

Equites Catafractarii Iuniores: A field army under the command of the *comes Britanniarum* (*NDO* VII.200).
    Holder, 127; Jarrett, 69, #5A.

Equites Honoriani Seniores: A field army under the command of the *comes Britanniarum* (*NDO* VII.171).
    Holder, 127; Jarrett, 69, #7.

Equites Honoriani Taifali Seniores: A conflation of the *Equites Honoriani Seniores* (*NDO* VII.202) and *Equites Taifali* (*NDO* VII.205), under the command of the *comes Britanniarum*. Raised by Honorius and sent to Britain with Stilicho.
    Holder, 127.

Equites Scutarii Aurelaici: under the command of the *comes Britanniarum* (*NDO* VII.201).
    Holder, 128; Jarrett, 69, #9.

Equites Stablesiani: under the command of the *comes Britanniarum* (*NDO* VII.203).
    Holder, 128.

Equites Syri: Under the command of the *comes Britanniarum* (*NDO* VII.204).
    Holder, 128; Jarrett, 69, #11.

Equites Taifali: Under the command of the *comes Britanniarum* (*NDO* VII.205).
    Holder, 128.

Batavi Iuniores Britanniciani: Raised by Stilicho (AD 399/400) and sent to Britain. Removed from the island by Constantine III in 407, whence recorded as part of the field army in Gaul (*NDO* VII.72–73).
    Holder, 128.

Exculcatores Iuniores Britanniaci: Raised by Stilicho (AD 399/400) and removed from Britain in 407, hence recorded under the command of the *magister peditum* (*NDO* VII.127).
Holder, 128–129.

Invicti Iuniores Britanniciani: Probably raised by Stilicho (AD 399/400) and removed from Britain in 407, hence recorded as part of the field army in Spain (*NDO* VII.127).
Holder, 129.

Primani Iuniores: Under the command of the *comes Britanniarum* (*NDO* VII.155).
Holder, 129; Jarrett, 72, #31.

Secundani Iuniores: Under the command of the *comes Britanniarum* (*NDO* VII.156).
Holder, 129.

Seguntienses: Probably in garrison at Caernarvon, removed by Stilicho (400/402), and promoted to field army status to serve in Illyricum (*NDO* VII.49).
Holder, 129.

Victores Iuniores Britanniciani: Under the command of the *comes Britanniarum* (*NDO* VII.154). Probably raised by Stilicho.
Holder, 129; Jarrett, 72, #32.

Limitanei

Equites Catafractarii: The fourth century garrison at Morbium (Yorkshire or Durham) (*NDO* XL.21).
Holder, 130; Jarrett, 69, #5.

Equites Crispiani: Raised or renamed for Crispus Caesar in Gaul (317–26) or from the place-name Crispiana in Pannonia. Garrisoned at Doncaster (*NDO* XL.20).
Holder, 130; Jarrett, 69, #6.

Equites Dalmatae Branodunses: Stationed at Brancaster (*NDO* XXVIII.16). Raised by Gallienus and probably transferred to Britain after 274.
Holder, 130.

Equites Stablesiani Gariannonenses: Recorded at Burgh Castle (*NDO* XXVIII.17). Raised by Gallienus and probably sent to Britain after 274.
Holder, 130.

Milites Anderetiani: Under the command of the *dux Mogontiacensis* (*NDO* XLI.17), moved from Pevensey (Anderida) to Gaul after 367.
Holder, 130–131.

Milites Tungrecani: This unit, which proclaimed for Procopius in 365 (Ammianus XXVI.6.12), was demoted from field army status and sent to Britain after 367. Stationed at Dover under the command of the *comes litoris Saxonici* (*NDO* XXVIII.14).
Holder, 131; Jarrett, 71, #21.

Numerus Abulcorum: This unit had supported Magnentius (Zosimus II.51). It was transferred to Britain after 351 and stationed at Pevensey (*NDO* XXVIII.20) until transfer to Gaul and promotion to field army status in the early fifth century (*NDO* VII.109).
   Holder, 131; Jarrett, 69, #12.

Numerus Defensorum: Transferred to Britain after 367 and stationed at Kirkby Thore (*NDO* XL.27).
   Holder, 131; Jarrett, 72, #25.

Numerus Directorum: Stationed at Brough-under-Stainmore (*NDO* XL.26).
   Holder, 131; Jarrett, 70, #15.

Numerus Fortensium: In garrison at Othonae (Bradwell?: *NDO* XXVIII.13).
   Holder, 131; Jarrett, 71, #22.

Numerus Longovicianorum: Garrisoned at Lancaster (Longovicium: *NDO* XL.30).
   Holder, 131; Jarrett, 71, #18.

Numerus Nerviorum Dictensium: Sent to Britain after 367. Stationed at Dictis (Wearmouth?: *NDO* XL.23).
   Holder, 132; Jarrett, 71, #20.

Numerus Pacensium: Sent to Britain after 367. Stationed at Magis (*NDO* XL.29).
   Holder, 132; Jarrett, 72, #26.

Numerus Solensium: This unit arrived with Theodosius after 367 and was in garrison at Maglone (Old Carlisle?: *NDO* XL.28).
   Holder, 132; Jarrett, 72, #27.

Numerus Supervenientium Petueriensium: Presumably stationed at Brough-on-Humber (Petuaria) until transfer to Malton after 367 (*NDO* XL.31).
   Holder, 132; Jarrett, 71, #24.

Numerus Turnacensium: Stationed at Lympne (*NDO* XXVIII.15), but presumably transferred from Turnacum after 367.
   Holder, 132; Jarrett, 72, #28.

Numerus Vigilum: In garrison at Chester-le-Street (*NDO* XL.24).
   Holder, 132; Jarrett, 72, #29.

Fleet

Classis Britannica: Created 40 or 43. Stationed at Richborough and Boulogne until a new base was built at Dover (early second century). By the end of the third century, the fleet was split into smaller units stationed along the Saxon shore.
   Holder, 132–133.

Classis Anderetiana: Moved from Pevensey (Anderida) to Paris after 367.
   Holder, 133.

APPENDIX II

THE GOVERNORS OF UNDIVIDED BRITAIN

(see A. Birley, *Fasti, passim*)

A. Plautius A. f. Ani. (cos. 29)	43–47
P. Ostorius Q. f. Scapula (cos. 41/45)	47–52
A. Didius Gallus (cos. 36)	52–57
Q. Veranius Q. f. Clu. (cos. ord. 49)	57–58
C. Suetonius Paullinus (cos. 42?)	58–61
P. Petronius P.f. Turpilianus (cos. ord. 61)	61–63
M. Trebellius Maximus (cos. 55)	63–69
M. Vettius Bolanus (cos. 66)	69–71
Q. Petillius Cerialis Caesius Rufus (cos. 70, cos. II 74)	71–73/4
Sex. Julius Frontinus (cos. by 74, cos. II 98, cos. III ord. 100)	73/4–77
Cn. Julius L. f. Ani. Agricola (cos. 77)	77–84
Sallustius Lucullus (cos. by 96)	85/96?
P. Metilius Nepos (cos. 91)	98
T. Avidius Quietus (cos. 93)	98
L. Neratius M. f. Volt. Marcellus (cos. 95, cos. II ord. 129)	103
Atilius Metilius Bradua (cos. ord. 108)	111/117?
Q. Pompeius Sex. f. Quir. Falco (cos. 108)	122
A. Platorius Nepos (cos. 119)	122–124
Sex. Julius Severus (cos. 127)	130?
P. Mummius Sisenna (cos. ord. 133)	135
Q. Lollius M. f. Quir. Urbicus (cos. by 138)	139, 140, 142
Cn. Papirius Gal. Aelianus Aemilius Tuscillus (cos. by 139?)	146
Cn. Julius Cn. f. Verus (cos. 151, cos. II ord. 180)	158
M. Statius Priscus (cos. ord. 159)	161/1612
Sex. Calpurnius Agricola (cos. 158/159)	163
Q. Antistius Adventus (cos. by 168)	160's?
Ulpius Marcellus (cos. by 184)	184
P. Helvius Pertinax (cos. 175, cos. II ord. 192)	185?
D. Clodius Albinus (cos. by 192, cos. II ord. 194)	192–197
Virius Lupus (cos. by 196)	197
C. Valerius Prudens (cos. 194)	205
L. Alfenus Senecio (cos. by 200)	205/207?
Ulpius Marcellus (cos. by 211?)	211/212?
C. Julius Marcus (cos. ?)	213

Some Governors of Britannia Superior

M. Martiannius Pulcher (cos. ?)	221–2; 235–8?
Desticius Juba (cos. by 253/258)	253–258?

Some Governors of Britannia Inferior

M. Antonius Gordianus Sempronianus Romanus (cos. ?)	216
Modius Julius (cos. ?)	219?
Ti. Claudius Paulinus (cos. ?)	220
Marius Valerianus (cos. ?)	221–222
Claudius Xenophon (cos. ?)	223
Maximus (cos. ?)	225
Calvisius Rufus (cos. ?)	225–235?
Valerius Crescens Fulvianus (cos. ?)	225–235?
Claudius Apellinus (cos. ?)	235?
Tuccianus (cos. ?)	237
Maecilius Fuscus (cos. ?)	238–244?
Egnatius Lucilianus (cos. ?)	238–244?
Nonius Philippus (cos. ?)	242
Octavius Sabinus (cos. ?)	263–268?
Aurelius Arpagius (cos. ?)	296–305?

THE EMPERORS OF ROME DOWN TO HONORIUS

Imp. Caesar Divi f. **Augustus**	27 BC–AD 14
Tiberius Caesar Augustus	14–37
Gaius Caesar Germanicus Aug. (Caligula)	37–41
Ti. **Claudius** Caesar Aug. Germanicus	41–54
Nero Claudius Caesar Aug. Germanicus	54–68
Ser. **Galba** Imp. Caesar Aug.	68–69
Imp. M. **Otho** Caesar Aug.	69
Vitellius Germanicus Imp.	69
Imp. Caesar **Vespasianus** Aug.	69–79
Imp. **Titus** Caesar Vespasianus Aug.	79–81
Imp. Caesar **Domitianus** Aug.	81–96
Imp. Caesar **Nerva** Aug.	96–98
Imp. Caesar Nerva **Trajanus** Aug.	98–117
Imp. Caesar Trajanus **Hadrianus** Aug.	117–138
Imp. Caesar T. Aelius Hadrianus **Antoninus** Aug. **Pius**	138–161
Imp. Caesar **Marcus Aurelius** Antoninus Aug.	161–180
Imp. Caesar **Lucius** Aurelius **Verus** Aug.	161–169
Imp. Caesar M. Aurelius **Commodus** Antoninus Aug.	180–192
Imp. Caesar P. Helvius **Pertinax** Aug.	193
Imp. Caes. M. Didius Iulianus Aug.	193
Imp. Caes. C. **Pescennius Niger** Iustus Aug. [Syria]	193–194
Imp. Caes. D. **Clodius Albinus** Aug. [Britain]	193–197
Imp. Caes. L. **Septimius Severus** Pertinax Aug.	193–211
Imp. Caes. M. Aurelius Antoninus Aug. (**Caracalla**)	211–217
Imp. Caes. P. Septimius **Geta** Aug.	211–212
Imp. Caes. Opellius Severus **Macrinus** Aug.	217–218
Imp. Caes. M. Aurelius Magni Antonini f. Antoninus Aug. (**Elagabalus**)	218–222
Imp. Caes. M. Aurelius **Severus Alexander** Aug.	222–235
Imp. Caes. C. Iulius Verus **Maximinus** Aug. (**Maximinus Thrax**)	235–238
Imp. Caes. M. Antonius **Gordianus** Aug. (**Gordian I**)	238
Imp. Caes. M. Antonius **Gordianus** Aug. (**Gordian II**)	238
Imp. Caes. M. Clodius **Pupienus** Maximus Aug.	238
Imp. Caes. D. Caelius Calvinus **Balbinus** Aug.	238
Imp. Caes. M. Antonius **Gordianus** Aug. (**Gordian III**)	238–244
Imp. Caes. M. Iulius **Philippus** Aug. (**Philippus Arabs**)	244–249

Imp. Caes. C. Messius Q. Traianus **Decius** Aug.	249–251
Imp. Caes. C. Vibius **Trebonianus Gallus** Aug.	251–253
Imp. Caes. C. Vibius Afinius Gallus Veldumnianus **Volusianus** Aug.	253
Imp. Caes. M. Aemilius **Aemilianus** Aug.	253
Imp. Caes. P. Licinius **Valerianus** Aug.	253–259
Imp. Caes. P. Licinius Egnatius **Gallienus** Aug.	253–268
Imp. Caes. M. Aurelius **Claudius** Aug. **Gothicus**	268–270
Imp. Caes. L. Domitius **Aurelianus** Aug.	270–275
Imp. Caes. M. Claudius **Tacitus** Aug.	275–276
Imp. Caes. M. Annius **Florianus** Aug.	276
Imp. Caes. M. Aurelius **Probus** Aug.	276–282
Imp. Caes. M. Aurelius **Carus** Aug.	282–283
Imp. Caes. M. Aurelius **Carinus** Aug.	283–285
Imp. Caes. M. Aurelius **Numerianus** Aug.	283–284
D.n. Imp. Caes. C. Aurelius Valerius **Diocletianus** Aug.	284–305
D.n. Imp. Caes. M. Aurelius Valerius **Maximianus** Aug.	285–305
D.n. Flavius Valerius **Constantius** Aug. (**Constantius I**)	293–306
D.n. C. **Galerius** Valerius Maximinianus Aug.	293–311
D.n. Imp. Caes. Flavius Valerius **Constantinus** Aug. (**Constantine I**)	306–337
D.n. Imp. Caes. Valerius Licinianus **Licinius** Aug.	308–324
D.n. Imp. Caes. Flavius Iulius **Constans** Aug.	337–350
D.n. Imp. Caes. Flavius Iulius **Constantius** Aug. (**Constantius II**)	337–361
D.n. Imp. Caes. Flavius Claudius **Iulianus** Aug. (**Julian the Apostate**)	360–363
D.n. Imp. Caes. Flavius **Iovianus** Aug.	363–364
D.n. Imp. Caes. Flavius **Valentinianus** Aug. (**Valentinian I**)	364–375
D.n. Imp. Caes. Flavius **Valens** Aug.	364–378
D.n. Imp. Caes. Flavius **Gratianus** Aug.	375–383
D.n. Imp. Caes. Flavius **Valentinianus** Iun. Aug. (**Valentinianus II**)	375–392
D.n. Imp. Caes. Flavius **Theodosius** Aug. (**Theodosius I**)	379–395
D.n. Imp. Caes. Flavius **Honorius** Aug.	395–423

BRIEF LIST OF EVENTS INVOLVING
THE ROMAN ARMY IN BRITAIN

55–54 BC Julius Caesar invades (*BG* 4.20–36). A few fiercely fought battles occur. Caesar accepts offers of submission. Caesar's second invasion in 54 (*BG* 5.1–23) results in the defeat of the Celtic chieftain Cassivellaunus and the tenuous conquest of the southeast.

31 BC–AD 43 Trade between Rome and Britain increases (Strabo 4.5.3).

AD 40 Gaius contemplates an invasion of Britain (*Agricola* 13.2), suddenly called off (Suetonius *Caligula* 44). Gaius considers the island conquered and orders his troops to gather seashells as booty for his triumphal procession (Dio 59.25.3).

AD 43 Claudius sends Aulus Plautius with an invasion force of 40,000 troops from four legions (*II Augusta, IX Hispana, XIV Gemina*, and *XX Valeria Victrix*) and numerous auxiliary units (Suetonius *Claudius* 17; Dio 60.19). The conquest creates a new Roman province in Britain, its capital at Camulodunum (Colchester), formerly the tribal capital for the Trinovantes. On the occasion of the victory, Claudius visits the island for 16 days, celebrates a grand triumph at Rome, and renames his son "Britannicus" in honor of his win in Britain.

AD 43–47 Aulus Plautius extends Roman occupation westward towards the Severn and the Wash, and good relations are established with the Regni (Tacitus *Agricola* 14, *RIB* 91), with the Iceni (north of Colchester) under Prasutagus, and with the Brigantes (in northern England: Northumbria, Westmorland, and Cumbria) under Cartimandua. The future emperor Vespasian serves in Britain as a legionary legate (Suetonius *Vespasian* 4) and is instrumental in the early conquest.

AD 47–52 P. Ostorius Scapula subdues tribes south of the Fosse Way (Tacitus *Annals* 12.31–39). Caratacus, one of Cunobelinus' heirs, attacks the Dubonni and the Atrebates, whose king Verica appealed to Rome for help. As Ostorius fights Caratacus, the latter finds refuge among the Silures. Caratacus escapes northward, finding asylum among the Ordovices and then with the Brigantes, whose queen Cartimandua hands him over to the Romans (Tacitus *Annals* 12.31–9). Claudius, however, impressed with Caratacus' courage and determination, pardons Caratacus and allows him to live comfortably in exile at Rome.

AD 58–61 Suetonius Paulinus conducts campaigns in South Wales.

AD 57–58   Veranius (57–58) conducts raids against the Silures, in Wales.

AD 60   The Icenian king Prasutagus dies. Although the king named Nero co-heir with his family (Tacitus *Annals* 14.31). However, centurions plunder the kingdom, flog Boudicca, rape her daughters, and strip the Icenian nobility of their estates. Roman veterans, who had settled in Colchester, drive natives from their estates and enslave them. In response, the Iceni, the Trinovantes, and other tribes rise in revolt under Boudicca and sacked Colchester—including the temple of the Divine Claudius—St. Albans, and London. The uprising comes to an end as Roman troop reinforcements arrive and as Boudicca falls in a pitched battle. Without her strength of leadership and organization, the rebellion soon falls apart (Tacitus *Annals* 14.38–9).

AD 67/8   *Legio XIV Gemina* is withdrawn for Nero's intended expedition to the Caspian Sea (Tacitus *Agricola* 16, *Hist.* 2.66).

AD 69   Britain supports Vitellius against Otho by sending troops (Tacitus *Histories* 2.57). After victory in Italy, Vitellius returns the *XIV Gemina* to Britain. Vespasian recalls *legio XIV Gemina* from Britain to fight the Batavi (Tacitus *Histories* 4.68).

AD 71–73   Petilius Cerialis is governor. *Legio IX Hispana* is transferred from Lincoln to York. The Brigantes are subdued in 71 (Tacitus *Agricola* 17).

AD 74–78   Sextus Julius Frontinus defeats the Silures (in southeastern Wales; Tacitus *Agricola* 17). *Legio II Augusta* is transferred from Gloucester to Caerleon, and numerous forts and roads are built throughout Wales.

AD 78–84   Agricola and the Roman army push northward into Scotland. Agricola defeats the Ordovices (Tacitus *Agricola* 18) and the Brigantes (Tacitus *Agricola* 20), whose territory he regarrisons. By 79, he reaches the Tyne-Solway line and occupies the Scottish lowlands by 80. In 81, his troops build roads and forts. Agricola advances into the highlands by 83, where the legionary fortress at Inchtuthil is established (Tacitus *Agricola* 25–27). In 84, the Romans are successful against the Caledonians at Mons Graupius (Tacitus *Agricola* 29–38).

AD 84/85   Agricola is recalled to Rome (84/85; Tacitus *Agricola* 39). Scottish highlands are abandoned.

AD 105   Scottish lowlands are abandoned, as troops are transferred to Cumbria. The Trajanic border runs along the Stangate (between the Tyne and the Solway).

AD 122   Hadrian visits Britain (*SHA Hadr.* 11, *RIB* 1051, 1340). *Legio VI Victrix* replaces *legio IX Hispana* in garrison at York. Platorius Nepos oversees construction of Hadrian's Wall, along the Tyne-Solway line.

AD 138   Lollius Urbicus reoccupies southern Scotland and begins building the Antonine Wall (*SHA Ant. Pius* 5.4; *RIB* 1147), perhaps in response to unrest from the barbarian tribes to the north.

AD 150s   The Antonine *limes* is temporarily abandoned because of revolts in northern Britain (Pausanias 8.43.4).

AD 158   Julius Verus with reinforcements from Germany crushes these revolts, and the Roman army once again occupies the Antonine *limes* (ca. 158–163; *RIB* 2110).

AD 163   Unsettled tribes in the north (*SHA Marcus Aur.* 8.7) and general unrest in the province (perhaps rebellions among the Brigantes, as implied by coin issues of 154/5) force the Roman troops to abandon the highlands. Hadrian's Wall is refortified (*RIB* 1137, 1149).

AD 180s   Tribes from the north overrun Hadrian's Wall.

AD 193   Clodius Albinus declares himself emperor (Dio 73.14.3; 73.4.1).

AD 196   Albinus crosses into northern Gaul (*SHA Sev.* 10.1–2), with British troops, leaving the island unprotected. Tribes from the north overrun the Hadrianic *limes*.

AD 197   Septimius Severus defeats and kills Clodius (Dio 75.6–7).

AD 200   Britain is divided into *Britannia Superior* and *Inferior* (Dio 55.23. 2–6).

AD 197–202   Virius Lupus quells the unrest in northern Britain (Herodian 3.8.2).

AD 205–207   Under Alfenius Senecio, troops restore Hadrian's Wall and advance towards Aberdeen, reoccupying Scotland.

AD 208/9   Septimius Severus visits Britain (Dio 76.11–15; Herodian 3.14).

AD 211   Severus dies at York (Dio 76.15.1–2; Herodian 3.15.1–3). Scotland is evacuated, perhaps because further expenditures of men and material to secure progressively poorer land seems pointless (Keppie, *Scotland's Roman Remains*, 69).

early to mid-third century:
   Britain remains peaceful. Rebuilding and refortification occur.

Late third century:
   Britain is divided into four provinces—with a *dux Britanniarum* stationed at York—perhaps for the purposes of civil administration and contemporary with Diocletian's administrative division of the empire.

AD 286/7   Carausius, commanding a navy in the English channel, establishes an independent rule in Britain and northern Gaul (Aurelius Victor, *Liber de Caesaribus* 39.20–21; Eutropius 9.21).

AD 293/4   Allectus overthrows Carausius.

AD 296   Constantius Caesar defeats Allectus, recovers Britain for Rome (*Panegyric on Constantius Caesar* 13–20), and repairs damages to Hadrian's Wall.

AD 306   Constantius, as Augustus, returns to Britain to campaign in Scotland (*Panegyric on Constantine* 7.1–2). Constantius dies at York. Constantius' troops proclaim Constantine emperor (Aurelius Victor 40.2–4; Eutropius 10.1.3 and 2.2; Zosimus 2.8.2 and 9.1). Troops in Britain support Constantine against Maxentius, the son of Maximian, for whom the praetorian guard in Rome declared after Constantius' death (Zosimus 2.15.1).

ca. AD 343   The emperor Constans visits Britain in response to disturbances from tribes north of Hadrian's Wall (Firmicus Maternus, *de Errore Profanum Religionum* 28.6; Libanius, *Oration* 59.139, 141).

AD 350   Magnentius, in his claim to the throne, withdraws troops from Britain (Ammianus Marcellinus 14.5.6–8), leaving the island vulnerable.

AD 353   Constantius II vanquishes Magnentius.

ca. AD 360   Raids from Picts, Saxons, and Scots increase (Ammianus Marcellinus 26.4.5).

AD 367   The father of the future emperor Theodosius quells barbarian threats to Britain in a series of naval expeditions (Claudian *de Consulatu Honorii* 51–6, *de Consulatu Stilichonis* 24–33; Pacatus *Pan. Theod.* 5.2; Ammianus Marcellinus 28.3).

AD 383   Magnus Maximus, is declared emperor by his troops in Britain and withdraws troops to fight on the continent (Orosius 7.34.9–10; Zosimus 4.35–37; Gildas *de Excidio Britanniae* 14–15).

AD 388   Theodosius besieges and defeats Maximus at Aquileia (Prosper Tiro *Chronicon* 1191; Orosius 7.35.3–4).

AD 396–398   Britain is reinforced as Stilicho, Honorius' general, campaigns against the sea-borne incursions of Scots, Picts, and Saxons (Claudian *de Consulatu Stilichonis* 2.247–255).

ca. AD 400   Hadrian's Wall is abandoned, and troops are withdrawn from Britain to fight against the Visigoth Alaric (Zosimus 6.1).

AD 407   Constantine III crosses over to the continent with troops from Britain (Zosimus 6.2–5), once again leaving the island vulnerable to the Saxon invasion of 408.

AD 410   Britons appeal to Honorius who tells them to look to their own defenses (Zosimus 6.10.2; Gildas *de Excidio Britanniae* 18).

BIBLIOGRAPHY

Abramic, M. *Poetovio.* Vienna, 1925.

Alcock, J.P. "Celtic Water Cults in Roman Britain." *Arch J* 112 (1965): 1–12.

——. "Classical Religious Belief and Burial Practice in Roman Britain." *Arch J* 137 (1980): 50–85.

——. "The concept of *genius* in Roman Britian." In *Pagan Gods and Shrines of the Roman Empire* (M. Henig and A. King, edd., Oxford, 1986): 113–134.

Alföldi, A. "A Bronze Mace from Willingham Fen, Camb." *JRS* 39 (1949): 19–22.

——. Review of: H. Gesche, *Die Vergottung Caesars* (Kallmünz, 1968). *Phoenix* 24 (1970): 166–170.

——. *Die monarchische Repräsentation im römischen Kaiserreiche.* Darmstadt, 1970.

——. Review of: Stefan Weinstock, *Divus Julius* (Oxford, 1971). *Gnomon* 47 (1975): 154–179.

Alföldi, G. *Noricum,* trans. A. Birley, London and Boston, 1974.

Allason-Jones, Lindsay. "A lead Shrine from Wallsend." *Britannia* 15 (1984): 231–232.

——. *A Guide to the Inscriptions and Sculptured Stones in the Museum of Antiquities of the University and Society of Antiquaries of Newcastle upon Tyne.* Newcastle-upon-Tyne, 1989.

——. *Women in Roman Britain.* London, 1989.

——. "Visions and Dreams in Roman Britain." *AA* 25, ser. 5 (1997): 21–25.

——. *Roman Jet in the Yorkshire Museum.* York, 1996.

Allason-Jones, Lindsay, and McKay, Bruce. *Coventina's Well: A Shrine on Hadrian's Wall.* Chesters, Northumberland, 1985.

Allen, D.F. "Celtic Coins from the Romano-British Temple at Harlow, Essex." *BNJ* 32 (1964): 1–6; 36 (1967): 1–7; 38 (1968): 1–6.

——. *The Coins of the Ancient Celts.* Edinburgh, 1988.

Altheim, F. "Altitalische Götternamen." *Studi e Materiali di Storia delle Religioni* 8 (1932): 146–165.

Alvar, J. "El culto de Mitra en Hispania." *MHA* 5 (1981): 51–72.

Ambrose, T. and Henig, M. "A New Roman Rider-relief from Stragglethorpe, Lincolnshire." *Britannia* 11 (1980): 135–138.

Anati, E. *Camonica Valley: A Depiction of Village Life in the Alps from Neolithic Times to the Birth of Christ as Revealed by Thousands of Newly Found Rock Carvings.* trans. L. Asher. New York, 1961.

Andreae, B. "Zum Triumphfries des Trajansbogens von Benevent." *MDAI (R)* 86 (1979): 325–329.

Ankersdorfer, Hans. *Studien zur Religion des römischen Heeres von Augustus bis Diokletian.* Diss. Konstanz, 1973.

Anonymous. *Die Kelten in Mitteleuropa.* Salzburg 1980.

Anthony, I.E. "Excavations in Verulum Hills Field, St. Albans, 1963–4." *Herfordshire Archaeology* 1 (1968); 9–50.

ApSimon, A.M. "The Roman Temple on Brean Down, Somerset." *Proceedings of the University of Bristol Spelaeological Society* 10 (1965): 195–258.

Askew, G. *The Coinage of Roman Britain.* London, 1951.

Atkinson, Donald. "The Governors of Britain from Claudius to Diocletian." *JRS* 12 (1922): 60–73.

Austen, P.S. *Bewcastle and Old Penrith.* Kendal, 1990.

Austen, P.S. and Breeze, D.J. "A New Inscription from Chesters on Hadrian's Wall." *AA* ser. 5, 7 (1979): 114–126.

Bailey, Geoff. "A Roman Shrine near Laurieston?" *Calatria* 2 (1992): 1–4.
Baillie-Reynolds, P.K. "Excavations at the Site of the Roman Fort at Caerhun: Second Interim Report, 1927." *ArchCam* 82 (1927): 292–332.
———. *Excavations on the Site of the Roman Fort of Kanovium.* Cardiff, 1938.
Baradez, J. *Vue Aérienne de l'Organisation romaine dans le Sud-Algérien.* Paris, 1949.
Barley, M.W. and Hanson, R.P.C., edd. *Christianity in Britain, 300–700.* Leicester, 1968.
Barnard, Sylvia. "The *Matres* of Roman Britain." *ArchJ* 142 (1985): 237–245.
Barrett, A.A. "Knowledge of the Literary Classics in Roman Britain." *Britannia* 9 (1978): 307–313.
———. "The Career of Cogidubnus." *Britannia* 10 (1979): 227–242.
Bartholomew, Philip. "Fifth-Century Facts." *Britannia* 13 (1982): 261–270.
Bassett, Steven. "Churches in Worcester before and after the Conversion of the Anglo-Saxons," *AntJ* 69 (1989): 225–256.
Bathhurst, W.H. "Roman Antiquities at Lydney Park, Gloucestershire." In *Roman Antiquities* (ed. C.W. King. London, 1879): 44–47.
Beaujeau, J. *La religion romaine à l'apogée de l'empire.* Paris, 1955.
Beck, R. "Mithraism since Franz Cumont." *ANRW* II.17.4 (1984): 2002–2115.
———. *Planetary Gods and Planetary Orders in the Mysteries of Mithras.* Leiden, 1988.
Behn, F. *Das Mithrasheiligtum zu Dieburg.* Berlin, 1928.
Benoît, F. "Des chevaux de Mouriès aux chevaux de Roquepertuse." *Préhistoire* 10 (1948): 137–210.
———. *Les mythes de l'outre-tombe: Le cavalier à l'Anguipède et l'ecuyère Epona.* Bruxelles, 1950. (Coll. Latomus 3).
———. *Art et Dieux de la Gaule.* Paris, 1970.
Béranger, J. *Recherches sur l'aspect idéologique du Principat. Schweizerische Beiträge zur Altertumswissenschaft* 5.6 Basel, 1953.
———. "Der *Genius Populi Romani* in der Kaiserpolitik." *BJ* 165 (1965): 72–87.
Berger, Pamela C. *The Insignia of the Notitia Dignitatum.* New York, 1981.
Bergquist, Anders and Taylor, Timothy. "The Origin of the Gundestrup Cauldron." *Antiquity* 61 (1987): 10–24.
Bianchi, U., ed. *Mysteria Mithrae: Proceedings of the International Seminar on the Religio-historical Character of Roman Mithras with Particular Reference to Roman and Ostian Sources.* Leiden, 1979.
Bidwell, Paul. *Roman Forts in Britain.* Batsford and London, 1997.
Bieler, L. "St. Patrick and the British Church." In *Christianity in Britain: 300–700* (edd. M.W. Barley and R.P.C. Hanson, Leicester, 1968): 123–130.
Birchall, A. "Roman Forts Revealed in Scotland." *ILN* 273 (1985): 62.
Birkner, H. "Denkmäler des Mithraskultes vom Kastell Rückingen." *Germania* 39 (1952): 349–362.
Birley, A.R. "Celts, Romans and Picts." *Northern History* 3 (1968): 188–192.
———. "The Roman Governors of Britain." *ES* 4 (1967): 63–81.
———. *The People of Roman Britain.* London, 1979.
———. "An Altar from Bremenium." *ZPE* 43 (1981): 13–23.
———. *The Fasti of Roman Britain.* Oxford, 1981.
———. *Septimius Severus: The African Emperor.* 2nd edition. New Haven and London, 1988.
Birley, Eric. "Materials for the History of Roman Brougham." *TCWS* ser. 2, 32 (1932): 124–139.
———. "Three New Inscriptions." *AA* ser. 4, 10 (1933): 102–108.
———. "A Note on the Second Cohort of Tungrians." *TCWS* ser. 2, 35 (1935): 56–60.
———. "Marcus Cocceius Firmus: An Epigraphic Study." *PSAS* 70 (1935–1936): 363–377; repr. in E. Birley, *Roman Britain and the Roman Army: Collected Papers.* Kendal, 1953: 87–103.

———. "An Inscription from Beaumont and the *cohors I Nervia Germanorum.*" *TCWS* 36 (1936): 61–68.

———. "A Roman Altar from Bankshead, and the *Imperium Gallorum.*" *TCWS* 36 (1936): 1–7; repr. in E. Birley, *Roman Britain and the Roman Army: Collected Papers.* Kendal, 1953: 58–63.

———. "Centurial Stones from the Vallum West of Denton Burn." *AA* ser. 4, 14 (1937): 227–242.

———. "Building Records from Hadrian's Wall." *AA* ser. 4, 16 (1939): 219–236.

———. "Die *cohors I Tungrorum* und das Orakel des Klarischen Apollo." *Germania* 23 (1939): 189–190.

———. "The Beaumont Inscription, the *Notitia Dignitatum* and the Garrison of Hadrian's Wall." *TCWS* ser. 2, 39 (1939): 190–226.

———. Review of: Walter Wagner, *Die Dislokation der Römischen Auxiliarformationen in den Provinzen Noricum, Pannonien, Moesien, und Dakien von Augustus bis Gallienus* (Berlin, 1938). *JRS* 32 (1942): 138–140.

———. "Roman Law and Roman Britain." *DUJ* (1947): 58–63; repr. in E. Birley, *Roman Britain and the Roman Army: Collected Papers.* Kendal, 1953: 48–58.

———. "The Roman Site at Burrow in Londsdale." *TCWS* ser. 2, 46 (1947): 138.

———. "Britain after Agricola and the end of the ninth legion." *DUJ* (1948): 78–83; repr. in E. Birley, *Roman Britain and the Roman Army: Collected Papers.* Kendal, 1953: 20–30.

———. "The Origins of equestrian officers: prosopographical method." *DUJ* (1951): 86–95; repr. in E. Birley, *Roman Britain and the Roman Army: Collected Papers.* Kendal, 1953: 154–171.

———. Review of: John Clarke, J.M. Davidson, and Anne Robertson, *The Roman Occupation of South-Western Scotland* (Glasgow, 1952). *TDGS* 30 (1951–2): 198–200.

———. "Noricum, Britain, and the Roman Army." In *Festschrift für R. Egger.* (Klagenfurt, 1952): 175–188.

———. *Roman Britain and the Roman Army: Collected Papers.* Kendal, 1953.

———. "The Roman Milestone at Middleton in Lonsdale *TCWS* 53 (1953): 52–62.

———. "The Roman Fort at Netherby." *TCWS* ser. 2, 54 (1954): 6–39.

———. "Maponus, the Epigraphic Evidence." *TDGS* ser. 3, 31 (1954): 39–42.

———. *Research on Hadrian's Wall.* Kendal, 1961.

———. "Review and Discussion of *RIB*," *JRS* 56 (1966): 226–231.

———. "Troops from the Two Germanies in Roman Britain." *ES* 4 (1967): 103–7.

———. "*Cohors I Tungrorum* and the Oracle of the Clarian Apollo." *Chiron* 4 (1974): 511–513.

———. "An Inscription from Cramond and the *Matres Campestres.*" *ArchJ* 4 (1976): 108–110.

———. "The Religion of the Roman Army: 1895–1977." *ANRW* II.16.2 (1978): 1506–1541.

———. "A Roman Altar from Old Kilpatrick and interim commanders of auxiliary regiments." *Latomus* 42 (1983): 73–83. Repr. E. Birley, *The Roman Army: Papers 1929–1986* (Amsterdam, 1988): 221–231.

———. "The Deities of Roman Britain." *ANRW* II.18.1 (1986): 1–112.

———. "Some Military Inscriptions from Chester." *ZPE* 44 (1986): 201–208.

Birley, E. and Charlton, J. "3rd Report on Excavations at Housesteads." *AA* ser. 4, 11 (1934): 185–206.

Birley, R.E. *Discoveries at Vindolanda.* 2nd edition. Newcastle-upon-Tyne, 1975.

———. *Vindolanda: A Roman Frontier Post on Hadrian's Wall.* London, 1977.

Bishop, M.C. and Dore, J.N. *Corbridge: Excavations of the Roman Fort and Town 1947–1980.* London, 1988. (Historic Buildings and Monuments Commission for England, Archaeological Report, #8).

Blagg, T.F.C. "The Votive Column from the Roman Temple Precinct at Springhead." *ArchCant* 95 (1979): 223–229.
———. "The Cult and sanctuary of Diana Nemorensis." In *Pagan Gods and Shrines of the Roman Empire* (M. Henig and A. King, edd., Oxford, 1986): 211–220.
Blagg, T.F.C. and King, A.C., edd. *Military and Civilian in Roman Britain: Cultural Relationships in a Frontier Province.* Oxford, 1984. (*BAR* British Series 136).
Bloch, H. "The Pagan Revival in the West at the end of the Fourth Century," in A. Momigliano, ed. *The Conflict between Christianity and Paganism in the Fourth Century.* Oxford, 1963: 193–218.
Bober, J.J. "Cernunnos: Origin and Transformation of a Celtic Divinity." *AJA* 55 (1951): 13–51.
Bogaers, J.E. "Die Besatzungstruppen des Legionslagers von Nijmegen im 2 Jahrhundert nach Christus." *Studien zu Militärgrenzen Roms* (1967): 54–76.
———. "King Cogidubnus in Chichester: another reading of *RIB* 91." *Britannia* 10 (1979): 243–254.
Bömer, F. *P. Ovidius Naso: Die Fasten.* 2 vols. Heidelberg, 1957.
Bonner, C. *Studies in Magical Amulets.* Ann Arbor, 1950.
Boon, G.C. "A Temple of Mithras at Caernarvon-Segontium." *ArchCamb* 99 (1960): 136–172.
———. "Serapis and Tutela: A Silchester Coincidence." *Britannia* 4 (1973): 107–141.
———. "Mensa Dolenda—a Caerleon Discovery of 1774." *BBCS* 25 (1973): 346–358.
———. "*Genius* and *Lar* in Celtic Britain." *Jahr. RGZM* 20 (1973): 265–269.
———. *Silchester: The Roman Town of Callava.* Newport Abbot, 1974.
———. "A Richly Inlaid Strigil from the Fortress Baths, Caerleon." *AntJ* 60 (1980): 333–337.
———. "Vessels of Egyptian Alabaster from Caerwent and Silchester." *BBCS* 29 (1981): 354–356.
———. *The Legionary Fortress of Caerleon—Isca.* Caerleon, 1987.
———. "A Roman Sculpture Rehabilitated: The Pagan's Hill Dog." *Britannia* 20 (1989): 201–217.
Bosanquet, R.C. "The Temple of Mithras: Excavations at Housesteads." *AA* ser. 2, 25 (1904): 255–263.
———. "On an Altar Dedicated to the *Alaisiagae*." *AA* ser. 3, 19 (1922): 185–197.
Bowersock, G.W. *Augustus and the Greek World.* Oxford, 1953.
Bowman, A.K. "Roman Military Records from Vindolanda." *Britannia* 5 (1974): 360–373.
Bowman, A.K. and Thomas, J.D. *Vindolanda: The Latin Writing Tablets.* Gloucester, 1984.
———. *The Vindolanda Writing-Tablets: Tabulae Vindolandensis II.* London, 1994.
———. "New writing-tablets from Vindolanda." *Britannia* 27 (1996): 299–328.
Bradford Welles, C., Fink, R.O., and Gilliam, J.F. "The Feriale Duranum." In *The Excavations at Dura-Europus. Final Report. Part 1: the Parchments and Papyri* (ed. M. Rostovtseff, New Haven, 1959): 191–212.
Brand, C.E. *Roman Military Law.* Austin, 1968.
Braund, David. *Ruling Roman Britain: Kings, Queens, Governors and Emperors from Julius Caesar to Agricola.* London and New York, 1996.
Breeze, D.J. "A Note on the Use of the Titles *Optio* and *Magister* below the Centurionate during the Principate." *Britannia* 9 (1979): 127–133.
Breeze, David and Dobson, Brian. "Fort Types on Hadrian's Wall." *AA* ser. 4, 47 (1969): 15–32.
———. *Hadrian's Wall.* 3rd edition. London, 1987.
Brown, F.E., and Wells, C.B. *The Excavations at Dura-Europus: Preliminary Report of the Sixth Season of Work.* New Haven, 1937.
———. *The Excavations at Dura-Europus: Preliminary Report of the Seventh and Eighth Seasons of Work.* New Haven, 1939.

Brown, P.D.F. "The Church at Richborough." *Britannia* 2 (1971): 225–231.
Bruce, J.C. *LS: Lapidarium Septentrionale.* Newcastle-upon-Tyne, 1870–1875.
——. "Roman Altar from Byker." *PSAN* ser. 2, 1 (1884): 357–360.
——. *Handbook to the Roman Wall.* Newcastle-upon-Tyne, 1966.
Brunt, P.A. "Pay and Superannuation in the Roman Army." *PBSR* 18 (1950): 50–71.
Budge, E.A.W. *An Account of the Roman Antiquities preserved in the Museum at Chesters.* Newcastle-upon-Tyne, 1907.
Burdeau, F. "L'empereur d'après les panégyriques latins," in F. Burdeau, ed. *Aspects de l'Empire romaine.* Paris, 1964: 25–29.
Burgess, R.W. "The Dark Ages Return to Fifth-Century Britain: The 'Restored' Gallic Chronicle Exploded." *Britannia* 21 (1990): 185–195.
Burkert, Walter. *Rendiconti dell'Accademia Nazionale dei Lincei.* VII 26 (1971).
——. "Buzyge und Palladion." *ZRGG* 22 (1970): 356–368.
——. *Rendiconti dell'Accademia Nazionale dei Lincei VII 26 (1971).*
——. *Structure and History in Greek Mythology and Ritual.* Berkeley and Los Angeles, 1979.
——. *Homo Necans: The Anthropology of Ancient Greek Sacrificial Ritual and Myth.* trans. Peter Bing. Berkeley and Los Angeles, 1983.
——. *Greek Religion.* trans. John Raffan. Cambridge, MA, 1985.
Burn, A.R. *The Romans in Britain: An Anthology of Inscriptions.* Oxford, 1932; second edition, Columbia, SC, 1969.
Burnham, Barry C. and Wacher, John. *The Small Towns of Roman Britain.* Berkeley and Los Angeles, 1990.
Bury, J.B. "The Notitia Dignitatum." *JRS* 10 (1920): 131–154.
Bushe-Fox, J.P. *Third Report on the Excavations of the Roman fort at Richborough, Kent.* Oxford, 1932.
——. *Fourth Report on the Excavations of the Roman fort at Richborough, Kent.* Oxford, 1949.
Byvanck, A.W. *Nederland in den romeinschen tijd.* Leiden, 1945.
Cagnat, R. *L'armée romaine d'Afrique et l'occupation militaire de l'Afrique sous les empereurs.* 2nd edition. Paris, 1913.
Camden, William. *Britannia.* London, 1607.
Campbell, Leroy A. *Mithraic Iconography and Topography.* Leiden, 1968.
Caruana, I. "An Altar to Victory from the Birdoswald Sector of Hadrian's Wall." *TCWS* 86 (1986): 260–264.
Casey, P.J. *Carausius and Allectus: The British Usurpers.* London, 1995.
Catalogue of the Collection of London Antiquities in the Guildhall Museum. 2nd edition. London, 1908. (Now the Museum of London).
Cesano, L. "Genius." *Dizionario Epigraphico* 3 (1922): 449–481.
Charlesworth, M.P. "The Virtues of a Roman Emperor: Propaganda and the Creation of Belief," *Proceedings of the British Academy* 23 (1937): 105–133.
——. *Documents Illustrating the Reigns of Claudius and Nero.* Cambridge, 1939.
——. "The Refusal of Divine Honors." *PBSR* 15 (1939): 1–10.
——. "Pietas and Victoria: The Emperor and the Citizen." *JRS* 33 (1943): 1.
Charlesworth, D. "Excavations at Papcastle, 1961–2." *TCWS* 65 (1965): 102–114.
Charlton, Beryl and Mitcheson, Margaret. "Yardhope. A Shrine to Cocidius?" *Britannia* 14 (1983): 143–153.
Cheeseman, G.L. "The Family of the Caristanii at Antioch in Pisidia." *JRS* 3 (1913): 253–266.
Cichorius, C. "Cohors." *RE* 3 (1900): 231–356.
——. *Die Reliefs der Traianssäule.* Berlin, 1900.
Clark, M.K. "Roman Yorkshire in 1936." *The Yorkshire Archaeological Journal* 33 (1938): 224–226.
Clarke, J. *The Roman Fort at Cadder.* Glasgow, 1933.
Clauss, Manfred. *Mithras: Kult und Mysterien.* Munich, 1990.

Clayton, J. "Description of Roman Remains Discovered near to Procolitia, a Station on the Wall of Hadrian." *AA* ser. 2, 8 (1880): 1–49.

——. "On the Discovery of Altars to Mars Thincsus." *AA* ser. 2, 10 (1885): 148–150; 169–171.

Cleere, Henry. "The Roman Iron Industry of the Weald and its Connexions with the *Classis Britannica.*" *ArchJ* 131 (1974): 172–199.

Collingwood, R.G. "Excavations at Brough-by-Bainbridge in 1926." *Proceedings of the Leeds Philosophical and Historical Society* 1 (1925–28): 261–284.

——. "Catalogue of the Roman Inscriptions and Sculptures Belonging to the Society of Antiquaries of Newcastle-upon-Tyne." *AA* ser. 4, 2 (1926): 52–110.

——. "Roman Britain in 1935." *JRS* 26 (1936): 236–267.

Collingwood, R.G. and Myers, J.N.L. *Roman Britain and the English Settlements.* 2nd edition. Oxford, 1937.

Collingwood, R.G. and Richmond, I.A. *The Archaeology of Roman Britain.* London, 1969.

Collingwood, R.G. and Taylor, M.V. "Roman Britain in 1923." *JRS* 12 (1923): 240–287.

——. "Roman Britain in 1927." *JRS* 17 (1927): 184–219.

——. "Roman Britain in 1933." *JRS* 24 (1934): 196–221.

Collingwood, R.G. and Wright, R.P. *The Roman Inscriptions of Britain: Inscriptions on Stone.* Oxford, 1965.

——. *The Roman Inscriptions of Britain: II.1: Instrumentum Domesticum.* Gloucester, 1989.

Collins-Clinton, J. *A Late Antique Shrine of Liber Pater at Cosa. Etudes prélominaire aux religions orientales dans l'Empire Romaine.* Leiden, 1977.

Coulanges, Fustel de. *La Cité Antique.* 2 vols. Paris, 1882.

Crawford. *Roman Republican Coinage.* Cambridge, 1974.

Croon, Johan H. *The Herdsman of the Dead: Studies on some cults, myths and legends of the Ancient Greek Colonization Era.* Utrecht, 1954.

——. "Die Idelologie des Marskultes unter dem Principat und ihre Vorgeschichte." *ANRW* II.17.1 (1981): 246–275.

Crow, James. *Book of Houseteads.* Bath, 1995.

Crummy, P. "The Temples of Roman Colchester." In *Temples, Churches, and Religion in Roman Britain.* (ed. W. Rodwell, Oxford, 1980): 243–284. (*BAR* British Series, 77).

——. "The Roman theatre at Colchester." *Britannia* 13 (1982): 299–302.

Cumont, Franz. *Textes et monuments figurés relatifs aux mystères de Mithra.* 2 vols. Bruxelles, 1896–1899.

——. "Jupiter Dolichenus." *RE* 5 (1903): 1276–1281.

——. *Les mystères de Mithra.* Bruxelles, 1913.

——. "Groupe de marbre du Zeus Dolichènos." *Syria* 1 (1920): 185–189.

——. *Les religions orientales dans le paganisme romain.* 4th edition. Paris, 1929.

——. "Un bas-relief mithraique du Louvre." *RA* 25 (1946): 183–195.

——. *Lux Perpetua.* Paris, 1949.

——. *The Oriental Religions in Roman Paganism.* New York, 1956.

Cunliffe, B.W. *Fifth Report on the Excavations of the Roman Fort at Richborough, Kent.* London, 1968.

——. *Roman Bath.* London, 1969.

——. *Fishbourne: A Roman Palace and its Garden.* London, 1971.

——. "The Sanctuary of Sulis Minerva at Bath: A brief review." In *Pagan Gods and Shrines of the Roman Empire* (M. Henig and A. King, edd., Oxford, 1986): 1–14.

——. *The Temple of Sulis Minerva at Bath: II: The Finds from the Sacred Spring.* Oxford University Committee for Archaeology Monograph #16, 1988.

Cunliffe, B.W. and Davenport, P., edd. *The Temple of Sulis Minerva at Bath: I: The Site.* Oxford University Committee for Archaeology Monograph #7, 1985.

Cunnington, M.E. "Wiltshire Exhibits in an Essex Museum." *Wiltshire Archaeology and Natural History Magazine* 50 (1942–4): 289.

Curle, J. *A Roman Frontier Post and Its People: The Fort of Newstead in the Parish of Melrose.* Glasgow, 1911.

Daniels, C. "Mithras Saecularis, the Housesteads Mithraeum and a Fragment from Carrawburgh." *AA* ser. 4, 40 (1962): 105–115.

———. "The Role of the Army in the Spread and Practice of Mithraism." In *Mithraic Studies: Proceedings of the First International Congress of Mithraic Studies* (ed. John R. Hinnells, Manchester, England, 1975): 249–274.

———. *Mithras and his Temples on the Wall.* 3rd edition. Newcastle-upon-Tyne, 1989.

Dark, K.R. "A Sub-Roman Re-Defence of Hadrian's Wall?" *Britannia* 23 (1992): 111–120.

Davidson, H.R. Ellis, "Mithraism and the Gundestrup Bowl." In *Mithraic Studies: Proceedings of the First International Congress of Mithraic Studies* (ed. John R. Hinnells, Manchester, England, 1975): 494–506.

Davies, Jeffrey L. "Soldiers, Peasants and markets in Wales and the Marches." In *Military and Civilian in Roman Britain: Cultural Relationships on a Frontier Province* (T.F.C. Blagg and A.C. King, edd., Oxford, 1984): 93–127.

Davies, R.W. "The Chursh in Wales." In *Christianity in Britain: 300–700* (edd. M.W. Barley and R.P.C. Hanson, Leicester, 1968): 131–150.

———. "The Training Grounds of the Roman Cavalry." *ArchJ* 125 (1968): 73–100.

———. "*Singulares* and Roman Britain." *Britannia* 7 (1976): 134–44.

———. "Some Cumbrian Inscriptions." *ZPE* 22 (1976): 179–183.

———. "The *ala I Asturum* in Roman Britain." *Chiron* 6 (1976): 357–380.

Deininger, J. "Die Provinziallandtage der römischen Kaiserzeit von Augustus bis zum Ende des dritten Jahrhunderts n. Chr." *Vestigia* 6 (1965): 102–104.

———. "Numinibus Augustorum: Anmerkung zur Datierung der Trierer Bronzeprora." *Germania* 44 (1966): 138–142.

Delehaye, H. "Sanctus Silvanus." *AB* 25 (1906): 158–162.

———. "Sanctus." *AB* 28 (1909): 145–200.

Deman, A. "L'identification des stations occidentales (à l'ouest de Birdoswald) du Mur d'Hadrien." *Latomus* 13 (1954): 577–589.

Demougeot, Ém. "La Notitia Dignitatum et l'histoire de l'Empire d'Occident au début du vᵉ siècle." *Latomus* 34 (1975): 1079–1134.

Dent, John S. "The Impact of Roman Rule on Native Society in the Territory of the Parsi." *Britannia* 14 (1983): 35–44.

Deyts, S. *Le Sanctuaire des Sources de la Seine.* Dijon, 1985.

Dillon, M. and Chadwick, Nora K. *The Celtic Realms.* 2nd edition. London, 1972.

Dobson, Brian. *Die Primipilares.* Köln, 1978.

Dodds, E.R. *The Greeks and the Irrational.* Berkeley, 1951.

Dolenz, H. "Zur Verehrung des Jupiter Dolichenus in Kärnten." *Carinthia* 144 (1954): 139–155.

Domaszewski, A. von. "Die Fahnen in römischen Heere." *Abh. d. Arch. Epigr. Seminars der Univers. Wien.* 5 (1885).

———. *Die Religion des römischen Heeres.* Trier, 1895.

———. "Der Truppensold der Kaiserzeit." *Neue Heidelberger Jahrbücher* 10 (1900): 218–241.

———. *Die Randgordnung des Römischen Heeres.* Bonn, 1908. (*Beihefte der Bonner Jahrbücher* 14). 2nd ed. revised by B. Dobson. Köln/Graz, 1967.

Donaldson, G.H. "A Reinterpretation of *RIB* 1912 from Birdoswald." *Britannia* 21 (1990): 206–214.

Dorcey, Peter F. *The Cult of Silvanus: A Study in Roman Folk Religion.* Leiden, 1992.

Dore, J.N. and Gillam, J.P. *The Roman Fort at South Shields.* Newcastle, 1979.

Downy, G. "Tiberiana." *ANRW* 2.2 (1975): 98–105.

Drexel. *Obergermaische-Raetische Limes des Roemerreiches*. Heidelberg, 1894–1937. (*Auftrage der Reichs-limeskommission*).

Drury, P.J. "The Temple of Claudius at Colchester Reconsidered." *Britannia* 15 (1984): 7–50.

Duchesne-Guillemin, J., Lecof, Pierre, and Kellens, Jean, edd. *Études Mithriaques: Actes du 2e Congrès International Téhéran, du 1er au 8 Septembre 1975*. Leiden, 1978.

Dumézil, Georges. *Archaic Roman Religion*. trans., Philip Krapp. Baltimore and London, 1996, repr.

Durry, M. *Les cohortes prétoriennes*. Paris, 1938.

Eck, W. "Die religiösen und kultischen Aufgaben der römischen Statthalter in der hohen Kaiserzeit," in Mayer, M., ed. *Religio deorum. Actas del Coloquio Internacional de Epigrafía. Culto y Sociedad en Occidente*. Sabadell, 1993: 151–156.

Ekwell, E. *English River Names*. Oxford, 1928.

Edmonson, J.C. "Mithras at Pax Julia. A Re-examination." *Conimbriga* 23 (1984): 69–86.

Egger, R. "Genius Cucullatus." *Wiener praehistorische Zeitschrift* 19 (1932): 311–323.

Ehrenberg, V.L. and Jones, A.H.M. *Documents Illustrating the Reigns of Augustus and Tiberius*. 2nd edition. Oxford, 1955.

Erikesen, Roy T. "Syncretic Symbolism and the Christian Roman Mosain at Hinton St. Mary: A Closer Reading," *Proceedings of the Dorset Natural History and Archaeological Society* 52 (1980): 43–48.

Erkell, H. *Augustus, Felicitas, Fortuna: Lateinische Wortstudien*. (Diss. Göteborg) Gothenburg, 1952.

Espérandieu, É. *Recueil général des Bas-Relief, Statues et Bustes de la Gaule Romaine*. Paris, 1907–1966.

Etienne, R. *Le Culte impériale dans la pèninsule ibérique d'Auguste à Dioclétien*. Paris, 1958.

Etienne, R., Piso, I., and Diaconescu, A. "Les deux forums de la Colonia Ulpia Traiana Augusta Dacica Sarmizegetusa. *REA* 92 (1990): 273–296.

Euzennat, "Une dédicae Volubilitaine à l'Apollon de Claros." *Antiquités Africaines* 10 (1976): 63–68.

Evans, D. Ellis. "Language Contact in Pre-Roman and Roman Britain." *ANRW* II.29.2 (1983): 949–987.

Evans, R.F. "Pelagius, Fastidius, and the Pseudo-Augustinian de Vita Christiana." *JTS* 13 (1962): 72–98.

———. *Pelagius*. London, 1968.

Faider-Feytmans, G. "Enseigne Romaine découverte à Flobecq." *Helinum* 20 (1980): 3–43.

Fairless, K.J. "Three Religious Cults from the Northern Frontier Region." In *Between and Beyond the Walls* (R. Miket and C. Burgess, edd., Edinburgh, 1984): 224–242.

Fantham, Elaine, Foley, Helene Peet, Kampen, Natalie Boymel, Pomeroy, Sarah B., and Shapiro, Alan H. *Women in the Classical World: Image and Text*. New York and Oxford, 1994.

Farnell, L.R. *Greek Hero Cults and Ideas of Immortality*. Oxford, 1921.

Farrar, R.A.H. "A Bronze Hanging-Bowl and Model Axe-head from the Roman Cemetary at Poundbury, Dorchester." *Dorset Natural History and Archaeological Society* 74 (1952): 98.

Fauth, W. "Simia." *RE* Suppl. 14 (1974): 679–701.

Fears, J.R. "The Cult of Jupiter and Roman Imperial Ideology." *ANRW* II.17.1 (1981): 3–141.

———. "The Cult of Virtues and Roman Imperial Ideology." *ANRW* II.17.2 (1981): 827–948.

———. "The Theology of Victory at Rome: Approaches and Problems." *ANRW* II.17.2 (1981): 736–826.

Ferguson, J. *Pelagius*. Cambridge, 1956.
——. *The Religions of the Roman Empire*. London, 1970.
Fink, R.O. "Lucius Seius Caesar, 'Socer Augusti'," *AJP* (1939): 326–332.
——. "Feriale Duranum I.1 and *Mater Castrorum*," *AJA* 48 (1944): 17–19.
——. "Hunt's Pridianum: BM Papyrus 2851." *JRS* 48 (1958): 102–116.
——. *Roman Military Records on Papyrus*. Cleveland, 1971. (Philological Monographs of the APA, no. 26).
Fink, R.O., Hoey, A.S., and Snyder, W.S. "The Feriale Duranum." *YCS* 7 (1940): 1–222.
Finke, H. *Neue Inschriften. Römisch-Germanische Kommission*, Berichte 17 (1927): 1–107, 198–231.
Firebaugh, W.C. *The Inns of Greece and Rome and a History of Hospitality from the Dawn of Time to the Middle Ages*. Chicago, 1928.
Fishwick, D. "The Imperial Cult in Roman Britain." *Phoenix* 15 (1961): 159–73; 213–29.
——. "The origin of the ROTAS-SATOR square." *HTR* 57 (1964): 39–53.
——. "The *Cannophori* and the March Festival of Magna Mater." *TAPA* 97 (1966): 193–202.
——. "*Genius* and *Numen*." *HTR* 62 (1969): 356–367.
——. "The Imperial *Numen* in Roman Britain." *JRS* 59 (1969): 76–91.
——. "Numina Augustorum." *CQ* 59 (1970): 191–197.
——. "Templum Divo Claudio Constitutum." *Britannia* 3 (1972): 164–181.
——. "The Development of Provincial Ruler Worship in the Western Empire." *ANRW* II.16.2 (1978): 1201–1253.
——. *ICLW: The Imperial Cult in the Latin West: Studies in the Ruler Cult of the Western Provinces of the Roman Empire*. 2 vols. Leiden, 1987.
——. "Imperial Sceptre Heads in Roman Britain." *Britannia* 19 (1988): 399–400.
——. "Numen Augusti." *Britannia* 20 (1989): 231–234.
——. "Votive Offerings to the Emperor?" *ZPE* 80 (1990): 121–130.
——. "*Sanctissimum Numen*: Emperor or God?" *ZPE* 89 (1991): 196–200.
——. "Seneca and the Temple of Divus Claudius." *Britannia* 22 (1991): 137–141.
——. "Prayer and the Living Emperor." In *The Two Worlds of the Poet: New Perspectives on Vergil* (R.M. Wilhelm and H. Jones, edd., Detroit, 1992): 343–355.
——. "Soldier and Emperor." *AHB* 6 (1992): 63–72.
——. "Numinibus Aug(ustorum)." *Britannia* 25 (1994): 127–141.
——. "The Temple of Divus Claudius at Camulodunum." *Britannia* 26 (1995): 11–27.
——. "The provincial centre at Camulodunum: towards an historical context." *Britannia* 28 (1997): 31–50.
Fitz, J. "Der Besuch des Septimius Severus in Pannonien im Jahre 202 u.Z." *Acta archaeologica academie scientiarum Hungaricae* 2 (1959): 237–263.
Flattery, David and Schwartz, Martin. *Haoma and Harmoline*. Berkeley, 1989.
Fonterose, J. *Python*. Berkeley, 1959.
Forster, R.H. and Knowles, W.H. "Corstopitum: Report on the Excavations in 1913." *AA* ser. 3, 11 (1914): 278–310.
Foucart, P. "Le culte des héros chez les grecs." *Mémoires de l'Académie des Inscriptions* 42 (1918): 1–15.
Fowler, W. Ward. *The Roman Festivals of the Period of the Republic*. London, 1899.
Frazer, J.G. *The Fasti of Ovid Edited with a Translation and Commentary*. London, 1929.
——. *The Golden Bough*. London, 1913.
Frend, W.C.H. "Religion in Roman Britain in the Fourth Century." *JBAA* 3 ser. 18 (1955): 1–18.
——. "The Christianization of Roman Britain." In *Christianity in Britain: 300–700* (edd. M.W. Barley and R.P.C. Hanson, Leicester, 1968): 37–49.

——. "Ecclesia Britannica: Prelude or Dead End?" *Journal of Ecclesiastical History* 30 (1979): 129–144.

——. "Romano-British Christianity in the West: Comparison and Contrast." In *The Early Church in Western Britain and Ireland* (ed. Susan M. Pearce, Oxford, 1982): 5–16.

——. "Pagans, Christians, and 'the Barbarian Conspiracy' of AD 367 in Roman Britain." *Britannia* 23 (1992): 121–131.

Frere, S.S. "A Romano-British Votive relief from Witham." *Britannia* 1 (1970): 267.

——. "The Silchester Church: Excavation by Sir Ian Richmond in 1961." *Archaeologia* 126 (1975): 277–302.

——. *Verulamium Excavations Vol. II.* London, 1983. (*Reports of the Research Committee of the Society of Antiquaries of London*, #41).

——. "*RIB* 1322." *Britannia* 17 (1986): 329.

——. *Britannia: A History of Roman Britain.* 3ʳᵈ edition. London, 1987.

Furlonger, Tracy A. "RIB 508: Christian not Pagan," *ZPE* 97 (1993): 225–226.

Gagè, J. "La victoria Augusti et les auspices de Tibère." *RA* 32 (1930): 1–35.

——. "La théologie de la Victoire impériale." *RH* 171 (1933): 1–34.

——. "L'empereur Romain devant Sérapis" *Ktema* 1 (1976): 145–168.

Ganz, J. *Early Irish Myths and Sagas.* London, 1981.

Gentili, G.V. *La villa romana di Piazza Armerina.* Roma, 1951. (Itinerari dei Musei e Monumenta d'Italia, no. 87).

——. "I mosaica della villa romana del casale di Piazza Armerina." *Bolletino d'Arte* ser. 4, 37 (1952): 33–46.

——. *La villa erculia di Piazza Armerina: I mosaici figurati.* Roma, 1959.

Gesche, H. *Die Vergottung Caesars.* Kallmünz, 1968.

Gilliam, J.F. "The Roman Military Feriale." *HTR* 47 (1954): 183–196.

Gillam, J.P. and Daniels, C. "The Roman Mausoleum on Shorden Brae, Beaufront, Corbridge, Northumberland." *AA* ser. 4, 32 (1952): 176–219.

Gillam, J.P. and MacIvor, I. "The Temple of Mithras at Rudchester." *AA* ser. 4, 32 (1954): 176–219.

Gimpera, P. Bosch. "Katalonien in der Kaiserzeit." *ANRW* 2.3 (1975): 572–600.

Girard, Jean-Louis. "Domitien et Minerve: Une prédilection impériale." *ANRW* II.17.1 (1981): 233–245.

——. "La place de Minerve dans la religion romaine au temps du principat." *ANRW* II.17.1 (1981): 203–245.

Goodburn, R. "The Farley Heath Sceptre Binding." *AntJ* 27 (1947): 83.

——. *The Roman Villa, Chedworth.* London, 1979.

Goodburn, R. and Bartholomew, Philip, edd. *Aspects of the Notitia Dignitatum.* Oxford, 1976. (*BAR* Supplementary Series, 15).

Goodchild, R.G. "A Priest's Sceptre from the Romano-Celtic Temple at Farley Heath, Surrey." *AntJ* 18 (1938): 391–396.

——. "The Farley Heath Sceptre." *AntJ* 27 (1947): 83–85.

Goodchild, R.G. and Kirk, J.R. "The Romano-Celtic Temple at Woodeaton." *Oxoniensia* 19 (1954): 15–37.

Gordon, R.L. "Franz Cumont and the Doctrines of Mithraism." In *Mithraic Studies: Proceedings of the First International Congress of Mithraic Studies*, (ed. John R. Hinnells, Manchester, England, 1975): 215–248.

——. "Authority, salvation and mystery in the Mysteries of Mithras." In J. Huskinson, M. Beard, and J. Reynolds, edd. *Image and Mystery in the Roman World: Three Papers Given in Memory of Jocelyn Toynbee.* Cambridge, 1988.

——. "Jupiter Dolichenus." In *The Oxford Classical Dictionary* 3ʳᵈ edition (Simon Hornblower and Anthony Spawforth, edd. Oxford, 1996): 802.

Grant, M. *Roman Anniversary Issues.* Cambridge, 1950.

Green, C.W. "A Romano-Celtic Temple at Bourton Grounds, Buckingham." *Records of Buckinghamshire* 17 (1965): 356–366.

Green, M.J. *A Corpus of Religious Materials from the Civilian Areas of Roman Britain.* Oxford, 1976. (*BAR* British Series, 24).

———. *Small Cult Objects from the Military Areas of Roman Britain.* Oxford, 1978. (*BAR* British Series, 52).

———. "The Worship of the Romano-Celtic Wheel God in Britain Seen in Relation to Gaulish Evidence." *Latomus* 38 (1979): 345–367.

———. "A Celtic God from Netherby, Cumbria." *TCWS* 83 (1983): 41–47.

———. *The Wheel as a Cult Symbol in the Romano-Celtic World: with special reference to Gaul and Britain.* Collection Latomus, vol. 183. Bruxelles, 1984.

———. *Gods of the Celts.* Phoenix Mill, England, 1986.

———. "The Iconography and Archaeology of Romano-British Religion." *ANRW* II.18.1 (1986): 113–162.

———. "Jupiter, Taranis and the Solar Wheel." In *Pagan Gods and Shrines of the Roman Empire* (M. Henig and A. King, edd., Oxford, 1986): 65–76.

———. *Symbol and Image in Celtic Religious Art.* London, 1989.

———. "The Celtic Goddess as Healer," in Billington, S. and Green, M.J., edd. *The Concept of the Goddess* (London and New York, 1996); 26–40.

Greenfield, E. "The Romano-British Shrines at Brigstock, Northants." *AntJ* 43 (1963): 228–263.

Greep, S. "Antler Roundel Pendants from Britain and the North-Western Provinces." *Britannia* 25 (1994): 79–97.

Greinberger, Th. "Dea Garmangabis." *Zeitschrift für Deutsches Altertum und Deutsche Litteratur* 38 (1894): 189–195.

Grenier, A. *Manuel d'Archéologie Gallo-Romaine: III L'Architecture.* Paris, 1958.

Grew, F.O. "Roman Britain in 1980, I: Sites Explored." *Britannia* 12 (1981): 314–368.

Grimes, W.F. EMRL: The Excavation of Roman and Medieval London. London, 1968.

Groag, E. and Stein, A. edd. *Prosopographia Imperii Romani.* 2nd edition. Berlin, 1933–.

Grosso, F. *La lotta politica al tempo di Commodo.* Turin, 1964.

Güterbock, B.G. *Bemerkungen über die lateinischen Lehnwörter im Irischen.* Dissertation Univerisät Königsberg. Leipzig, 1882.

Haarmann, H. *Der lateinische Lehnwortschatz im Kymrischen.* Bonn, 1970.

———. *Der lateinische Lehnwortschatz im Bretonischen.* Hamburg, 1973.

Haeselgrove, Colin. "'Romanization' before the conquest: Gaulish precedents and British consequences." In *Military and Civilian in Roman Britain: Cultural Relationships on a Frontier Province* (T.F.C. Blagg and A.C. King, edd., Oxford, 1984): 5–63.

Halsberghe, G.H. "Sol Invictus Elagabal tegenover Sol Indiges en Sol Invictus Mithra." *Philologische Studien* 9 (1939–40): 29–41.

———. "Le Culte de Dea Caelestis." *ANRW* 2.17.4 (1984): 2203–2223.

Hanson, W.S. and Maxwell, G.S. *Rome's Northwest Frontier: The Antonine Wall.* 2nd edition. Edinburgh, 1986.

Harnack, Adolf. *Militia Christi: Die Christliche Religion und der Soldatenstand in den ersten drei Jahrhunderten.* Tübingen, 1905.

Harper, R.P. "An Excavation at Chesters, 1960." *AA* ser. 4, 39 (1961): 31–35.

Harris, J.R. "Conventina's Well." *AA*, ser. 3, 21 (1924): 162–172.

Harris, E., and Harris, J.R. *The Oriental Cults in Roman Britain.* Leiden, 1965.

Harrison, J.E. *Themis: a study of the social origins of Greek Religion.* Cambridge, 1927.

Hart, George. *A Dictionary of Egyptian Gods and Goddesses.* London, 1986.

Hassall, M.W.C. Review of: Dietrich Hoffmann, *Das spätrömische Bewegungsheer und die Notitia Dignitatum* (Düsseldorf, 1969). *Britannia* 4 (1973): 344–346.

———. "Britain in the Notitia." In *Aspects of the Notitia Dignitatum.* (edd., R. Goodburn and P. Bartholomew, Oxford, 1976): 103–118. (*BAR* Supplementary Series 15).

———. "The Inscribed Altars." In *The Roman Riverside Wall and Monumental Arch in London.* (edd., C. Hill, M. Millett, and T.F.C. Blagg, edd., London, 1980): 195–198.

——. "Altars, Curses, and other Epigraphic Evidence," in Rodwell, W., ed. *Temples, Churches, and Religion in Roman Britain*. Oxford, 1980. (*BAR* British Series, 77): 79–89.

Hauschild, Th. "Tarraco en la epoca augustea." *Ciudades Augusteas de Hispania, Bimilenario de la Colonia Caesaraugusta*, Universidad de Zaragoza: Dept. de prehistoria y arqueologia I (1976): 213–218.

Haug, F. "Hercules." *RE* 8.1 (1913): 550–612.

——. "Ricambeda." *RE* 2A.1 (1920): 795.

Haverfield, F., "The Mother Goddesses." *AA* ser. 2, 15 (1892): 314–339.

——. "A New Altar from Wallsend Dedicated to Jupiter." *AA* ser. 2, 16 (1892): 76–80.

——. "Roman Inscriptions in Britain II." *ArchJ* 49 (1892): 215–234.

——. "On Two Marble Sculptures and a Mithraic Relief of the Roman Period Found in London." *Archaeologia* 60 (1906): 43–48.

——. "Roman London." *JRS* 1 (1911): 141–172.

——. "Voreda, the Roman Fort at Plumpton Wall." *TCWS* ser. 2, 13 (1913): 177–198.

——. "Roman Britain in 1914." in *British Academy Supplemental Papers*, no. 13, 1915.

——. "Newly Discovered Roman Altars." *AA* ser. 3, 12 (1915): 201–205.

——. "Agricola and the Antonine Wall." *PSAS* 52 (1917–18): 174–181.

——. "Early Northumbrian Christianity and the Altars to the *Di Veteres*." *AA* ser. 3, 15 (1918): 22–43.

Haverfield, F., Forster, B.H., Craster, H.H.E., Knowles, W.H., and Meek, A. "Corstopitum: Report of the Excavations in 1907." *AA* ser. 3, 4 (1908): 205–303.

——. "Corstopitum: Report of the Excavations in 1910." *AA* ser. 3, 7 (1910): 143–267.

Haverfield, F., Forster, B.H., Knowles, W.H., and Newbold, P. "Corstopitum: Report of the Excavations in 1912." *AA* ser. 3, 9 (1913): 230–280.

Haverfield, F. and Jones, H. Stuart. "Some Representative Examples of Romano-British Sculpture." *JRS* 2 (1912): 121–152.

Haynes, I.P. "The Romanisation of Religion in the *Auxilia* of the Roman Imperial Army from Augustus to Septimius Severus." *Britannia* 24 (1993): 141–157.

Heichelheim, F.M. "Genii Cucullati." *AA* ser. 4, 12 (1935): 187–194.

——. "Viradecthis." *RE* 2A.9 (1961): 174–175.

——. "Vitiris." *RE* 9A.1 (1961): 408–415.

Heinzel. "Roman Inscribed Altars at Housesteads." *AA* ser. 2, 10 (1885): 164–171.

Helgeland, John. "Roman Army Religion."*ANRW* II.16.2 (1978): 1470–1505.

——. "Christians and the Roman Army."*ANRW* II.23.1 (1985): 724–834.

Henig, M. "The Veneration of Heroes in the Roman Army." *Britannia* 1 (1970): 249–67.

——. "Roman Gemstones: Figuretype and Adaptation." In *Roman Life and Art in Britain*. (edd. J. Munby and M. Henig, Oxford, 1977): 341–346. (*BAR* British Series, 41).

——. *A Corpus of Roman Engraved Gemstones from British Sites*. 2nd edition. Oxford, 1978. (*BAR* British Series, 8).

——. "Art and Cult in the Temples of Roman Britain," in Rodwell, W., ed. *Temples, Churches, and Religion in Roman Britain*. Oxford, 1980. (*BAR* British Series, 77): 91–113.

——. *Religion in Roman Britain*. New York, 1984.

——. "Throne, altar, and sword: civilian religion and the Roman army in Britain." In *Military and Civilian in Roman Britain: Cultural Relationships on a Frontier Province* (T.F.C. Blagg and A.C. King, edd., Oxford, 1984): 227–248.

——. "An Inscribed Intaglio." *Britannia* 16 (1985): 241–242.

——. "Ita intellexit numine inductus tuo: some personal interpretations of deity in Roman religion." In *Pagan Gods and Shrines of the Roman Empire* (M. Henig and A. King, edd., Oxford, 1986): 159–170.

——. *The Art of Roman Britain.* Ann Arbor, 1995.

——. Review of B.W. Cunliffe. *Roman Bath*, third edition. Batsford and London, 1996: *JBAA* (1996): 101–102.

——. "Sculptors from the West in Roman London." In *Interpreting Roman London: Papers in Memory of Hugh Chapman.* (Joanna Baird, Mark Hassall, and Harvey Sheldon, edd., Oxford, 1996): 97–103. (Oxbow Monograph #58).

Henig, M. and King, A., edd. *Pagan Gods and Shrines of the Roman Empire.* Oxford, 1986. (Oxford University Committee for Archaeology Monograph, #8).

Herter, Hans. "Theseus." *RE* suppl. 13 (1973): 1045–1238.

Heurgon, Jacques. "The Amiens Patera." *JRS* 41 (1951): 22–24.

Higham, N.J. "Literary Evidence for Villas, Towns, and Hillforts in Fifth-Century Britain." *Britannia* 25 (1994): 229–232.

Hildyard, E.J.W. "A Roman and Saxon Site at Catterick." *Yorkshire Archaeological Journal* 38 (1953): 241–245.

——. "Cataractonium, fort and town." *Yorkshire Archaeological Journal* 39 (1957): 224–265.

Hill, C., Millett, M., and Blagg, T.F.C. *The Roman Riverside Wall and Monumental Arch in London.* London, 1980. (London and Middlesex Archaeological Society, Special Paper No. 3).

Hill, P.R. "The Maryport Altars: some First thoughts," in R.J.A., ed., *Roman Maryport and its Setting.* Maryport, 1997.

Hill, P.V. *The Coinage of Septimius Severus and his Family in the Mint of Rome AD 193–217.* London, 1964.

Hind, John. "Whose Head on the Bath Temple-Pediment?" *Britannia* 27 (1996): 358–60.

Hinnells, John R., ed. *Mithraic Studies: Proceedings of the First International Congress of Mithraic Studies.* Manchester, 1975.

Hobley, B. "Excavations in the City of London: First Interim Report, 1974–1975." *AntJ* 57 (1977): 31–66.

Hodgson, J. *History of Northumberland.* Newcastle-upon-Tyne, 1827–1840.

——. "Housesteads." *AA* 1 (1822): 273–291.

Hoey, Allan S. "Rosaliae Signorum." *HTR* 30 (1937): 15–35.

——. "Official Policy towards Oriental Cults in the Roman Army." *TAPA* 70 (1939): 456–481.

Holder, A. *Alt-celtische Sprachschatz.* Leipzig, 1896–1907.

Holder, P.A. *The Roman Army in Britain.* New York, 1982.

Home, G. *Roman York.* London, 1924.

Honigmann, E. and Maricq, A. *Recherches sur les Res Gestae Divi Saporis.* Bruxelles, 1952.

Hönn, K. *Quellenuntersuchungen zu den Viten des Heliogabalus und des Severus Alexander im Corpus der Scriptores Historiae Augustae.* Leipzig und Berlin, 1911.

Hooke, R., ed. *Philosophical Transactions: Giving Acount of the Present Undertakings, Studies and Labours of the Ingenious in many Considerable Parts of the World.* London, 1600. (Repr. New York, 1965).

Hooppell, R.E., "On the Roman Altar to the Goddess Garmangabis Found at Lanchester (Co. Durham) on the 15th July, 1893." *AA* ser. 2, 16 (1893): 313–327.

Hope, W.H. St. John and Fox, G.E., "Excavations at the Site of the Roman City at Silchester, Hants., in 1899." *Archaeologia* 57 (1900): 87–112.

Hopkins, Keith. *Conquerors and Slaves.* Cambridge, 1978.

Hörig, M. "Jupiter Dolichenus," *ANRW* 17.4 (1984): 2136–2179.

Hübner, E. "Der Fund von Procolitia." *Hermes* 12 (1877): 257–262.
Hull, M.R. "An Epona Sculpture in the Colchester and Essex Museum." *Transactions of the Essex Archaeological Society* 2 (1938): 19, 198.
———. *Roman Colchester.* Colchester, 1958.
Hunt, A.S. "Register of a Cohort in Moesia." in *Raccolta di Scritti in Onore di Giacomo Lumbroso* (ed. P. Bonfante, Milan, 1925): 265–272.
Huskinson, J. "Some Pagan Mythological Figures and their Significance in Early Christian Art." *PBSR* 42 (1974): 68–97.
Hutchinson, Valerie Jean. *Bacchus in Roman Britain: Archaeological Evidence for his Cult.* Ann Arbor, 1983.
———. "The Cult of Bacchus in Roman Britain." In *Pagan Gods and Shrines of the Roman Empire* (M. Henig and A. King, edd., Oxford, 1986): 135–145.
Ihm, Max. "Matres Ollototae." *BJ* 92 (1892): 256–259.
———. "Garmangabis." *RE* 7 (1912): 767.
Ingholdt, H. "Parthian Sculptures from Hatra." *Memoirs of the Connecticut Academy of Arts and Sciences* 12 (1954): 5–46.
Instinsky, H. "Kaiser und Ewigkeit," *Hermes* 77 (1942): 313–355.
Irby-Massie, G.L. "The Roman Army and the Cult of the Campestres." *ZPE* 113 (1996): 293–300.
———. "Horned Gods in Britain and Greek Hero Cult," *Latomus*, forthcoming.
Ireland, S. *Roman Britain: A Sourcebook.* New York, 1986.
Jackson, H. "The Leontocephaline in Roman Mithraism." *Numen* 32 (1985): 17–45.
Jackson, K.H. *Language and History in Early Britain: A Chronological Survey of the Brittonic Languages, First to Twelfth Century AD.* Edinburgh, 1953.
James, Simon. "Britain and the Late Roman Army." In *Military and Civilian in Roman Britain: Cultural Relationships on a Frontier Province* (T.F.C. Blagg and A.C. King, edd., Oxford, 1984): 161–186.
Jardé, A. *Études critiques sur la vie et le règne de Sévère Alexandre.* Paris, 1925.
Jarrett, M.G. "Album of Equestrians in North Africa." *ES* 9 (1972): 153.
———. *Maryport, Cumbria: A Roman Fort and its Garrison.* Kendal, 1976.
———. "Non-Legionary Troops in Roman Britain: Part One, the Units." *Britannia* 25 (1994): 35–77.
Jenkins, F. "Nameless or Nehalennia." *ArchCant* 70 (1956): 192–200.
———. "The role of the dog in Romano-Gaulish Religion." *Latomus* 16 (1957): 60–76.
———. "The Cult of the Dea Nutrix in Kent." *ArchCant* 71 (1957): 38–46.
———. "The Cult of the 'Pseudo-Venus' in Kent." *ArchCant* 72 (1958): 60–76.
Johns, C. "A Roman Bronze Statuette of Epona." *BMQ* 36 (1971): 37–41.
———. *The Jewellery of Roman Britain: Celtic and Classical traditions.* Ann Arbor, 1996
Johnson, Anne. *Roman Forts of the 1ˢᵗ and 2ⁿᵈ centuries in Britain and the German Province.* London, 1983.
Johnson, Stephen. *The Roman Forts of the Saxon Shore.* London, 1976.
———. *Later Roman Britain.* London, 1980.
Jolliffe, N. "Dea Brigantia." *ArchJ* 98 (1941): 36–61.
Jones, A.H.M. "The Western Church in the Fifth and Sixth Centuries." In *Christianity in Britain: 300–700* (edd. M.W. Barley and R.P.C. Hanson, Leicester, 1968): 9–18.
———. *Prosopography of the Later Roman Empire.* Cambridge, 1971.
Jones, G.D.B. "'Becoming Different without knowing it:' The role and development of vici." In *Military and Civilian in Roman Britain: Cultural Relationships on a Frontier Province* (T.F.C. Blagg and A.C. King, edd., Oxford, 1984): 75–91.
Jones, Michael E. *The End of Roman Britain.* Ithaca, N.Y., 1996.
Jones, Michael E. and Casey, John. "The Gallic Chronicle Restored: A Chronology for the Anglo-Saxon Invasions and the End of Roman Britain." *Britannia* 19 (1988): 366–398.
de Jubainville, Arbois. "Esus, Tarvos Trigaranus: la Légende de Cuchulainn en Grand-Bretagne." *RevCelt* 19 (1898): 245.

Kähler, H. *Die Villa des Maxentius bei Piazza Armerina.* Rome, 1973. (Monumentis Artis Romanae 12).

Kajanto, I. *The Latin Cognomina.* Helsinki, 1965.

Kan, A.H. *Jupiter Dolichenus: Sammlung der Inschriften und Bildwerke.* Leiden, 1943; repr. Chicago, 1979.

Kantorowicz, E.H. "The Gods in Uniform." *PAPhS* 105 (1961): 368–98.

Kaul, F. *Gundestrupkedelen.* Copenhagen, 1991.

Kenyon, K. *Excavations in Southwark: 1945–1947.* Surrey, 1959. (Occasional Papers of the Surrey Archaeological Society, no. 5).

Keppie, L.J.F. "Roman Inscriptions in Scotland. Some Additions and Corrections to *RIB* I." *PSAS* 113 (1983): 391–404.

——. *Scotland's Roman Remains.* Edinburgh, 1986, rev. 1990.

——. *The Origins and Early History of the Second Augustan Legion.* Sixth Annual Caerleon Lecture. Caerleon, 1993.

Kerényi, K. "Altitalische Götterverbindungen." *Studi e Materiali di Storia della Religioni* 9 (1933): 17–28.

——. "Telesphoros." *Egyetemes Philologiai Koezloeny* 57 (1933): 7–11.

Kettenhofen, E. *Die syrischen Augustae in der historischen Überlieferung: Ein Beitrag zum Problem der Orientalisierung.* Bonn, 1979.

Keune. "Harimella." *RE* 7.2 (1912): 2365–2366.

Kirk, G.S. *The Nature of Greek Myths.* London, 1974.

Kirk, J. "Bronzes from Woodeaton." *Oxoniensia* 14 (1949): 1–45.

Kirkman, J.S. "Canterbury Kiln Site, the Pottery." *ArchCant.* 53 (1941): 118–136.

Kleburg, T. *Hôtels, resteraunts et cabarets dans l'antiquité romaine.* Upsala, 1957.

Klein, W.G. "The Roman Temple at Worthington, Kent." *AntJ* 8 (1928): 76–86.

Kotula, T. "Die zwei Frauen des Severus Alexander." In *Romanitas-Christianitas: Festschrift Johannes Straub.* (G. Wirth, ed. Berlin-New York, 1982): 293–307.

Krumbacher, Karl. *Geschichte der Byzantinischen Litteratur von Justinian bis zum Ende des Oströmischen Reiches.* New York, 1958.

Kruse, H. *Studien zur offiziellen Geltung des Kaiserbildes im römischen Kaiserreiche.* Paderborn, 1934.

Kubitschek, W. "Signa." *RE* 2A.2 (1923): 2325–2347.

Kunckel, H. *Der römische Genius.* Heidelberg, 1974.

Laing, L.R. *Coins and Archaeology.* New York, 1970.

Lambrechts, P. *Contributions à l'étude des divinités Celtiques.* Brugge, 1942.

Lambrino, S. "La déesse Coventina de Parga (Galice)." *Revue da Faculdade de Letras, Lisboa.* 18 (1953): 74–87.

Lane-Fox, Robin. *Pagans and Christians.* New York, 1986.

Latte, K. *Römische Religionsgeschichte.* München, 1960.

Leach, John. "The Smith God in Roman Britain." *AA* ser. 4, 40 (1962): 35–45.

Leech, Roger. "The Excavation of a Romano-Celtic Temple of Laymott Beacon." *Britannia* 7 (1976): 73–95.

Lehner, H. "Orientalische Mysterienkult in römischen Rheinland." *BJ* 129 (1924): 36–91.

Lepelley, Claude. *Les Cités de l'Afrique Romaine au Bas-Empire.* 2 vols. Paris, 1979.

Lendon, J.E. *Empire of Honour: The Art of Government in the Roman World.* Oxford, 1997.

Lestaw, M. "The Symbolism of Minerva on the Coins of Domitian." *Klio* 59 (1977): 185–193.

Levick, B. "Mercy and Moderation on the Coinage of Tiberius." In *The Ancient Historian and his Materials: Essays in Honour of C.E. Stevens on his seventieth Birthday.* (B. Levick, ed. Farnborough, 1975): 123–137.

Lewis, M.J.T. *Temples in Roman Britain.* Cambridge, 1966.

Liebenam, E. "Equites Singulares." *RE* 6 (1909): 312–321.

Lietzmann, Hans. *A History of the Early Church.* trans. Bertram Lee Woolf. New York, 1949–53.

Linduff, K.M. "Epona, A Celt Among Romans." *Latomus* 38 (1979): 817–837.
Lindgren, C. *Classical Art Forms and Celtic Mutations: Figural Art in Roman Britain.* Park Ridge, NJ, 1980.
Ling, Roger. "Further Thoughts on Fourth-Century Mosaics." *Britannia* 12 (1981): 292–293.
Liversidge, Joan. *Britain in the Roman Empire.* New York, 1968.
Lloyd-Morgan, Glenys. "Roman Venus: public worship and private rites." In *Pagan Gods and Shrines of the Roman Empire* (M. Henig and A. King, edd., Oxford, 1986): 179–188.
Lloyd-Morgan, Glenys. "Nemesis and Bellona: a preliminary study of two neglected goddesses," in Billington, S. and Green, M.J., edd. *The Concept of the Goddess* (London and New York, 1996): 120–128.
Lonigan, P.R. *The Druids: Priests of the Celts.* London, 1996.
L'Orange, H.P. *Apotheosis in Ancient Portraiture.* Oslo, 1947.
Loth, J. *Les mots latins dans les langues brittoniques (gallois, armoricain, cornique) phonétique et commentaire.* Paris, 1892.
Lorenz, T. *Leben und Regierung Trajans auf dem Bogen von Benevent.* Amsterdam, 1972.
Lorimer, H.L. *Homer and the Monuments.* London, 1950.
Luck, G. *Arcana Mundi: Magic and Occult in the Greek and Roman Worlds.* Baltimore and London, 1985.
Lysons, D. and Lysons, S. *Magna Britannia: IV (Cumberland).* London, 1816.
MacCana, Proinsias. *Celtic Mythology.* New York, 1985.
MacCormick, S. *Art and Ceremony in Late Antiquity.* Berkeley and Los Angeles, 1981.
Macdonald, G. "Notes on Some Fragments of Imperial Statues and a Statuette of Victory." *JRS* 16 (1926): 1–16.
Macdonald, G. "Maponi." *RE* 14.2 (1930): 1413.
———. "Notes on the Roman Forts at Old Kilpatrick and Croy Hill, and on a Relief of Jupiter Dolichenus." *PSAS* 66 (1932): 219–276.
———. *Roman Wall in Scotland.* 2nd edition. Oxford, 1934.
Mackintosh, Marjorie. *The divine Rider in the Art of the Western Roman Empire.* Oxford, 1995. (*BAR* International Series 607).
MacMullen, R. *Paganism and the Roman Empire.* New Haven, Conn., 1981.
———. *Christianizing the Roman Empire: AD 100–400.* New Haven, 1984.
Magnen, R. *Epona déesse gauloise des chevaux, protectrice des cavaliers.* Bordeaux, 1955.
Mancini, R. "Deo-Deae nelle iscrizioni di Roma." *MGR* 2 (1980): 173–178.
Mann, J.C. "Spoken Latin in Britain as Evidenced in the Inscriptions." *Britannia* 2 (1973): 218–224.
———. "A Note on the Maryport Altars." In *Roman Maryport and Its Setting.* (R.J.A. Wilson, ed. Maryport, 1997): 90–91.
Mann, J.C. and Penman, R.G., edd. "Literary Sources for Roman Britain." *Britannia* 10 (1979): 377–378.
Mannsperger, D. "ROM ET AUG. Die Selbstdarstellungdes Kaisertums in der römischen Reichsprägung." *ANRW* 2.1 (1974): 919–996.
Maricq, A. *Classica et Orientalia: Extrait de Syria 1955–1962 revu et corrigé.* Paris, 1965.
Marsh, G. "Nineteenth and Twentieth Century Antiquities Dealers and Arretine Ware from London." *Transactions of the London and Middlesex Archaeological Society* 30 (1979): 125–129.
Mastino, A. *Le Titolature di Caracalla e Geta attraverso le Inscrizioni.* Studi di Storia Antica 5. Bologna, 1981.
Mattingly, Harold. *Roman Imperial Coinage.* London, 1923.
———. "The Consecration of Faustina the Elder and her Daughter." *HTR* 41 (1948): 147–151.
Mau, A. *Pompeii: Its Life and Art,* tr. Francis W. Kelsey. New York, 1899.
Mawer, Frances. *Evidence for Christianity in Roman Britain: the small Finds.* Oxford, 1995 (*BAR* British Series, 243).

Maxfield, V.A. *The Military Decorations of the Roman Army*. London, 1981.
Mayer, Max. *Vexillum und vexillarius: Ein Beitrag zur Geschichte des römischen Heerwesens*. Dissertation Straßburg, 1910.
McCann, A.M. "*The Portraits of Septimius Severus*." *Memoirs of the American Academy at Rome* 30 Rome, 1968.
Meates, G.W. *Lullingstone Roman Villa*. London, 1955.
———. *The Roman Villa at Lullingstone, Kent: Vol. I, the Site*. Kent, 1979.
Megaw, J.V.S. *Art of the European Iron Age*. New York, 1970.
Mellor, R. "The Goddess Roma." *ANRW* II.17.2 (1981): 950–1030.
Merkelbach, R. *Mithras*. Hain, 1984.
Merlat, Pierre. "Jupiter Dolichenus, Sérapis et Isis." *RA* 27 (1947): 10–31.
———. *Repertoire des inscriptions et monuments figures de culte de Jupiter Dolichenus*. Paris, 1951.
———. *Jupiter Dolichenus: Essai d'interprétation et de synthèse*. Paris, 1960.
Merrifield, R. "Art and Religion in Roman London—An Inquest on the sculptures of Londinium." In *Roman Life and Art in Britain* (J. Munby and M. Henig. Oxford, 1977; *BAR* British Series, 41): 375–406.
———. *London: City of the Romans*. London, 1983.
———. "The London Hunter God." In *Pagan Gods and Shrines of the Roman Empire* (M. Henig and A. King, edd. Oxford University Committee for Archaeology Monograph, #8, 1986): 85–92.
Meuli, K. *Gesammelte Schriften*. Basel, 1975.
———. "Greichische Opferbräuche." In *Phyllobolia Festschrift P. Von der Mühll*. (Basel, 1946): 185–288.
Millar, F. "Emperors, Frontiers, and Foreign Relations: 31 BC–AD 378." *Britannia* 13 (1982): 1–23.
Miller, S.N., ed. *The Roman Occupation of South-Western Scotland*. Glasgow, 1952.
Millett, M. "Forts and Origins of Towns: cause or effect?" In *Military and Civilian in Roman Britain: Cultural Relationships on a Frontier Province* (T.F.C. Blagg and A.C. King, edd., Oxford, 1984): 65–74.
———. *The Romanization of Britain*. Cambridge, 1990.
Mitard, P.-H. "La Sculpture gallo-romaine dans le Vexin Francais." *Histoire et Archéologie* 76 (1983): 56–71.
Mohen, J.P., Duval, A., and Eluère, C. edd. *Trésors des princes celtes*. Paris, 1987.
Mommsen, Th. *Gesammelte Schriften iv (Historische Schriften i)*. Berlin, 1906.
Morris, J.R. "Pelagian Literature." *JTS* 16 (1965): 26–60.
———. "The date of St. Alban." *Hertfordshire Archaeology* 1 (1968): 1–8.
———. *The Age of Arthur: A History of the British Isles from 350 to 650*. New York, 1973.
———. "The Literary Evidence." In *Christianity in Britain: 300–700* (edd. M.W. Barley and R.P.C. Hanson, Leicester, 1968): 55–73.
Munby, J. and Henig, M. *Roman Life and Art in Britain: A Celebration in Honour of the eightieth birthday of Jocelyn Toynbee*. Oxford, 1977. (*BAR* British Series, 41).
Mundle, I. *Untersuchungen zur Religionspolitik des Septimius Severus (Herkules, Bacchus, Jupiter, Juno)*. Diss. Freiberg, 1957.
———. "Dea Caelestis in der Religionspolitik des Septimius Severus und der Julia Domna." *Historia* 10 (1961): 228–237.
Murgia, Charles E. Review Article of: *The Minor Works of Tacitus: A Study in Textual Criticism*. *CPh* 72 (1977): 323–343.
Murray, A.S. "On a Bronze Statuette of Hercules." *Archaeologia* 55 (1896): 199–202.
Myres, J.N.L. "Pelagius and the End of Roman Rule in Britain." *JRS* 50 (1960): 21–36.
———. "Introduction," In *Christianity in Britain: 300–700* (edd. M.W. Barley and R.P.C. Hanson, Leicester, 1968): 1–8.
Nash-Williams, V.E. *The Roman Frontier in Wales*. 2nd edition. Cardiff, 1969.
Neilson, K.P. "The *Tropaion* in the *Aeneid*." *Vergilius* 29 (1983): 27–33.

Nicholson, Oliver. "The Corbridge Lanx and the Emperor Julian." *Britannia* 26 (1995): 312–315.

Nillson, M.P. "Rosalia." *RE* 2A.1 (1914): 1111–1115.

——. *Homer and Mycenae*. London, 1933.

——. *Geschichte der griechischen Religion II*. 2 vols. 3rd edition. München, 1974.

Nock, Arthur Darby. "Studies in the Graeco-Roman Beliefs of the Empire." *JHS* 45 (1925): 92–93.

——. Review of: Lily Ross Taylor: *The Divinity of the Roman Emperor* (Middleton, Conn., 1931). *Gnomon* 8 (1932): 513–518.

——. Review of: Ludwig Deubner: *Attische Feste* (Berlin, 1932). *Gnomon* 10 (1934): 289–295.

——. "Genius of Mithraism." *JRS* 27 (1937): 108–113.

——. "Lucius Seius Caesar, *Socer Augusti*." *AJP* 60 (1939): 326–332.

——. "The Emperor's Divine *Comes*," *JRS* 37 (1947): 102–116.

——. "The Roman Army and the Roman Religious Year." *HTR* 45 (1952): 187–252.

Norman, A.F. "Religion in Roman York." In *Soldier and Civilian in Roman Yorkshire* (ed. R.M. Butler, Leicester, 1971): 143–154.

Nutt, Alfred. *Cuchulainn, the Irish Achilles, Popular Studies*. Mythology, Romance and Folklore, no. 8, London, 1900.

Oaks, Laura S. "The Goddess Epona: Concepts of sovereignty in a changing landscape." In *Pagan Gods and Shrines of the Roman Empire* (M. Henig and A. King, edd., Oxford, 1986): 77–84.

Olmstead, G.S. "The Gundestrup Version of Tain bo Cuailnge." *Antiquity* 50 (1976): 95–103.

L'Orange, H.P. *Apotheosis in Ancient Portraiture*. Oslo, 1947.

Otto, W.F. "Fortuna." *RE* 7 (1912): 11–42.

——. "Genius." *RE* 7 (1910): 1155–1170.

Pace, B. *I mosaica di Piazza Armerina*. Rome, 1955.

Painter, K.S. "The Roman Site at Hinton St. Mary, Dorset." *BMQ* 32 (1968): 15–31.

——. "Villas and Christianity in Roman Britain." *BMQ* 35 (1971): 156–175.

——. *The Water Newton Early Christian Silver*. London, 1977.

Palmer, R.E.A. *Roman Religion and the Roman Empire*. Philadelphia, 1974.

——. "Silvanus, Sylvester, and the Chair of St. Peter." *PAPhS* 122 (1978): 222–247.

Paris, P. "Restes du culte de Mithra en Espagna." *Revue Archéologique* 24, ser. 4 (1914).

Parker, H.M.D. *The Roman Legions*. Oxford, 1921.

Pascal, C.B. *The Cults of Cisalpine Gaul*. Bruxelles, 1964. (Collection Latomus vol. 75).

Payne, George, "Catalogue of the Kent Archaeological Society's Collections at Maidstone." *ArchCant* 19 (1892): 1–66.

Pearce, Susan M. *The Early Church in Western Britain and Ireland*. Oxford, 1982 (*BAR* British Series 102).

Pedersen, H. *Vergleichende Grammatik der keltischen Sprachen*. 2 vols. Göttingen, 1909–1913.

Pekàry, T. "Das Opfer vor dem Kaiserbild." *BJ* 186 (1986): 81–103.

Petch, J.A. "Excavations at Benwell (Condercum)." *AA* ser. 4, 4 (1927): 135–193.

——. "Roman Durham." *AA* ser. 4, 1 (1925): 28.

Petrikovits, H. von. "*Sacramentum*." (translated by David Parsons). In *Rome and her Northern Provinces* (edd. B. Hartley and J. Wacher, 1983): 178–201.

Pfister, F. *Der Reliquienkult im Altertum*. Geissen, 1909–1912.

Pflaum, H.-G. *Les Carrières procuratoriennes équestres sous le haut-empire romain*. Paris, 1961.

Piccottini, Gernot. *Mithrastempel in Virunum*. Klagenfurt, 1994.

Pickin, J. "A Bronze Head of Jupiter from Bidford-on-Avon, Warwickshire." *Britannia* 20 (1989): 241–243.

Piggot, S. *The Druids*. New York, 1968.

Pippidi, D.M. "Le *numen Augusti*: Observations sur une forme occidentale du culte impérial." *REL* 9 (1931): 83–112.

———. "La Date del'Ara Numinis Augusti de Rome." *REL* 11 (1933): 435–456.

Pittes, L.F., and St. Joseph, J.K. *Inchtuthil, the Roman Legionary Fortress.* London, 1985.

Potter, T.W. *Romans in Northwest England: Excavations at the Roman Forts of Ravenglass, Watercrook, and Bowness-on-Solway.* Kendal, 1975. (Cumberland and Westmorland Antiquarian Society and Archaeological Society. Research Series 1).

Potts, I.D. "Mithraic Converts in Army Service: A Group with Special Privileges." *Proceedings of the African Classical Association* 17 (1983): 114–117.

Premerstein, A. "Die Buchführung einer ägyptischen Legionsabteilung." *Klio* 3 (1903): 1–46.

Price, S.R.F. "Gods and Emperors: The Greek Language of the Roman Imperial Cult." *JHS* 104 (1984): 79–95.

———. *Rituals and Power: The Imperial Cult in Asia Minor.* Cambridge, 1984.

"Proceedings of the Central Committee." *ArchJ* 1 (1845): 385.

Raepsaet-Charlier, M. "La datation des inscriptions latines dans les provinces occidentales de l'empire romain d'après les formules in h(onorem) d(omus) d(ivinae) et 'deo-deae'." *ANRW* II.3 (1975): 232–282.

———. "A propos des premiers emplois datés de Deo-Deae dans les trois Gaules et les Germanies." *ZPE* 61 (1985): 204–208.

Radford, C.A.R. "Locus Maponi." *TDGS* ser. 3, 31 (1954): 35–38.

———. "Christian Origins in Britain." *Medieval Archaeology* 15 (1971): 1–12.

Radke, G. *Die Götter Altitaliens.* Münster, 1949.

Rahtz, P.A. "The Roman Temple at Pagan's Hill, Chew Stoke, north Somerset." *Proceedings of the Somerset Archaeological and Natural History Society* 96 (1951): 112–142.

Rahtz, P.A. and Watts, L. "The end of Roman Temples in the West of Britain." In *The End of Roman Britain* (ed. J. Casey, Oxford, 1979): 183–201. (*BAR* British Series 71).

———. "Pagans Hill Revisited." *ArchJ* 146 (1989): 330–371.

Rau, R. "Zur Geschichte des pannonisch-dalmatischen Krieges der Jahre 6–9 nach Christus." *Klio* 19 (1925): 313–346.

Reece, Richard. "Mints, markets and the military." In *Military and Civilian in Roman Britain: Cultural Relationships on a Frontier Province* (T.F.C. Blagg and A.C. King, edd., Oxford, 1984): 143–160.

Rees, B.R. *Pelagius: A Reluctant Heretic.* Woodbridge, 1988.

Reinach, S. "Epona." *RA* 1 (1895): 163–195.

———. "Encore Epona." *RA* 2 (1898): 187–200.

———. "Divinites Equestres." *RA* 3 (1902): 225–238.

Renel, Ch. *Cultes militaires de Rome: Les enseignes.* Lyon, 1903.

Rhys, John. "Welsh Words borrowed from Latin, Greek, and Hebrew." *ArchCamb*, 4th ser. 4 (1873): 258–270, 355–365; 5 (1874): 52–59, 224–232, 297–313.

———. *Studies in the Arthurian Legend.* Oxford, 1901.

Richmond, I.A. "Roman Leaden Sealings from Brough-under-Stainmore." *TCWS* ser. 2, 36 (1936): 104–125.

———. "The Romans in Redesdale." *History of Northumberland*, vol. 15. Newcastle-upon-Tyne, 1940.

———. "Roman Legionairies at Corbridge: Their Supply Base, Temples, and Religious Cults." *AA* ser. 4, 21 (1943): 127–224.

———. "Roman Britain in 1943." *JRS* 34 (1944): 76–85.

———. "Mithraism in Roman Britain." *DUJ* n.s. 5 (1943–1944): 1–8.

———. *Archaeology and the After-Life in Pagan and Christian Imagery.* University of Durham, Riddell Memorial Lecture, 1950.

———. "On Ialonus." *Transactions of the Historic Society of Lancashire and Cheshire* 105 (1953): 45.

——. "Roman Britain in 1953." *JRS* 44 (1954): 83–103.
——. "Excavations on the Site of the Roman Fort at Lancaster, 1950." *Transactions of the Historic Society of Lancashire and Cheshire* 105 (1954): 1–23.
——. "Roman Britain in 1954." *JRS* 45 (1955): 121–145.
——. "Two Celtic Heads in Stone from Corbridge, Northumberland." In *Dark Age Britain: Studies Presented to E.T. Leeds* (ed. D.B. Harden, London, 1956): 11–15.
——. "A Statue of Juno Regina from Chesters." In *Fritz Saxl, 1890–1948* (ed. D.J. Gordon. Edinburgh, 1957): 47–52.
——. "Roman Britain in 1958." *JRS* 49 (1959): 102–135.
——. "The Roman Army and Roman Religion." *Bulletin of the John Rylands Library* 45 (1962/3): 185–197.
——. *Roman Britain.* 2nd edition. Oxford, 1963.
——. *Roman Art and Archaeology.* London, 1969.
Richmond, I.A. and Crawford, O.S.G. "The British Section of the Ravenna Cosmography." *Archaeologia* 93 (1949): 1–50.
Richmond, I.A. and Gillam, J.P. "The Temple of Mithras at Carrawburgh." *AA* ser. 4, 29 (1951): 1–92.
Richmond, I.A. Hodgson, K.S., and Joseph, K. "The Roman Fort at Bewcastle." *TCWS* ser. 2, 38 (1938): 195–237.
Richmond, I.A. and McIntyre, J. "A New Altar to Cocidius and the 'Rob of Risingham'." *AA* ser. 4, 14 (1937): 103–109.
Richmond, I.A. and Simpson, F.G. "The Roman Fort on Hadrian's Wall at Benwell." *AA* ser. 4, 19 (1941): 1–43.
Ritterling, E. "Legio." *RE* 12 (1924/25): 1211–1829.
Rivet, A.L.F. and Smith, Colin. *The Place Names of Roman Britain.* Princeton, NJ, 1979.
Robertson, Anne. *The Antonine Wall.* Keppie, L.F.J., rev. and ed. Glasgow, 1990.
Robins, Gay. *Women in Egypt.* Cambridge, MA, 1993.
Rodwell, W., ed. *Temples, Churches, and Religion in Roman Britain.* Oxford, 1980. (*BAR* British Series, 77).
Rohde, E. *Psyche: Seelencult und Unsterblichkeitsglaube der Griechen.* Freiburg, 1898.
Rose, H.J. *The Roman Questions of Plutarch.* Oxford, 1924.
——. "Numen Inest: 'Animism' in Greek and Roman Religion." *HTR* 28 (1935): 237–257.
——. "Numen and Mana." *HTR* 44 (1951): 109–120.
——. *Ancient Roman Religion.* London, 1948.
Ross, Anne. "The Horned God of the Brigantes." *AA* ser. 4, 39 (1961): 63–85.
——. *Pagan Celtic Britain: Studies in Iconography and Tradition.* London, 1967.
Rostovtseff, M. "Commodus-Hercules in Britain." *JRS* 13 (1923): 91–109.
——. *Città Carovaniere.* Laterza, 1934.
——. "Das Militärarchiv von Dura." *Münchener Beiträge zur Papyrusforschung* 19 (1934): 351–378.
——. *Dura-Europus and its Art.* Oxford, 1938.
——, ed. *The Excavations at Dura-Europus: Preliminary Report of the Seventh and Eighth Seasons of Work, 1933–4 and 1934–5.* New Haven, 1939.
——. "Vexillum and Victory." *JRS* 32 (1942): 92–106 and plates iv–vi.
Rouse, W.H.D. *Greek Votive Offerings.* Cambridge, 1902.
Rouselle, A. "Du Sanctuaire au thaumaturge: le gúerison en Gaule au ive siècle." *Annales, Economies, Sociétés, Civilisations* 6 (1976): 1085–1107.
Roxan, M.M. "Pre-Severan *Auxilia* named in the *Notitia Dignitatum*." In *Aspects of the Notitia Dignitatum.* (R. Goodburn and P. Bartholomew, edd., Oxford, 1976: *BAR* Supplemental Series 15): 59–80.
——. *Roman Military Diplomas Published between 1954 and 1977.* London, 1978. (*Institute of Archaeology Occasional Publications* 2).
——. *Roman Military Diplomas Published between 1978 and 1984.* London, 1985. (*Institute of Archaeology Occasional Publications* 9).

Rüger, C.B. "A Husband for the Mother Goddesses—Some Observations on the *Matres Aufaniae*." In *Rome and her Northern Provinces: Papers presented to S. Frere in honor of his retirement from the Chair of Archaeology of the Roman Empire, University of Oxford, 1983* (edd. B. Hartley and J. Wacher, Gloucester, 1983): 210–221.
Russu, I.I. "Elementele Syriene in Dacia Carpatica." *Acta Musei Napocensis* 6 (1969): 167–186.
Ryberg, I.S. *Rites of the State Religion in Roman Art.* New Haven, 1955.
Salway, Peter. *The Oxford Illustrated History of Roman Britain.* Oxford, 1993.
Sanders, H.A. "Some Papyrus Fragments from the Michigan Collection." *Memoirs of the American Academy at Rome* 9 (1931): 81–85.
Saur, E. *The End of Paganism in the North-Western Provinces of the Roman Empire: The Example of the Mithras Cult.* Oxford, 1996. (*BAR* International Series 634).
Saxer, Robert. *Untersuchen zu den Vexillationes des römischen Kaiserheeres von Augustus bis Diokletian.* Köln, 1967.
Saxl, Fritz. *Mithras: Typengeschichtliche Untersuchungen.* Berlin, 1931.
Schmitz, H. "Vagdavercustis." *RE* 2A.7 (1943): 2072–2073.
Scholz, U.W. *Studien zum altitalischen und altrömischen Marskult und Marsmythos.* Heidelburg, 1970.
Schultze, R. "Die römischen Legionslazarette in Vetera und anderen Legionslagern." *BJ* 139 (1934): 54–63.
———. *Zur Geschichte der Lateinischen Eigennamen.* Berlin, 1933, repr.
Scullard, H.H. *Roman Britain: Outpost of the Empire.* London, 1979.
———. *Festivals and Ceremonies of the Roman Republic.* Ithaca, New York, 1981.
Seeck, Otto. *Notitia Dignitatum.* Berlin, 1876, repr. Frankfurt am Main, 1962.
Sellner, Edward C. *Wisdom of the Celtic Saints.* Notre Dame, IN, 1993.
Sergent, Bernard. "Celto-Hellenica IV: La Ruse." *L'Initiation: Actes du colloque international de Montpellier, 11–14 Avril, 1991: Tome I: Les Rites d'Adolescence et les Mystères.* (Alan Moreau, ed., Montepellier, 1992): 39–50.
Sheldon, H. "Recent Developments in the Archaeology of Greater London." *Royal Society of Arts Journal* 124 (1976): 411–425.
Shepherd, John D., ed. *The Temple of Mithras London: Excavations by W.F. Grimes and A. Williams at the Walbrook.* London, 1998. (English Heritage Archaeological Report 12).
Shotter, David. *Romans and Britons in North-West England.* Lancaster, 1993.
Sieburg, M. "Ein gnostisches Goldamulet aus Gellup." *BJ* 103, (1898): 123–53.
Simpson, C.J. "The date and dedication of the Temple of Mars Ultor." *JRS* 76 (1977): 91–94.
———. "Real Gods." *Britannia* 24 (1993): 264–265.
———. "The Statue of Victory at Colchester." *Britannia* 27 (1996): 386–387.
Simpson, F.G. and Richmond, I. "The Roman Fort on Hadrian's Wall at Benwell." *AA* ser. 4, 19 (1941): 25–33.
Smith, Colin. "Vulgar Latin in Roman Britain: Epigraphic and Other Evidence." *ANRW* II.29.2 (1983): 893–948.
Smith, C. Roach. *Illustrations of Roman London.* London, 1859.
———. "The Roman Wall: Procolitia." *Collectanea Antiqua* 7 (1880): 115–135.
Smith, D.J. "The Shrine of the Nymphs and the Genius Loci at Carrawburgh." *AA* ser. 4, 40 (1962): 59–81.
Smith, R.E. *Service in the Post-Marian Roman Army.* Manchester, 1958.
Snyder, W.F. "Public Anniversaries in the Roman Empire: The Epigraphical Evidence for their Observation during the first three Centuries." *YCS* 7 (1943): 223–317.
Sommer, C. Sebastian. *The Military Vici in Roman Britain: Aspects of their Origins, their Location and Layout, Administration, Function and End.* Oxford, 1984. (*BAR* British Series 129).
Speidel, M.A. "Roman Army Pay Scales." *JRS* 82 (1992): 87–106.
Speidel, M.P. "The Pay of the Auxilia." *JRS* 63 (1973): 141–147.

——. "Eagle Bearer and Trumpeter." *BJ* 176 (1976): 124–126.

——. *The Religion of Jupiter Dolichenus in the Roman Army.* Leiden, 1978.

——. "An Altar to the Healer Gods and Jupiter Dolichenus." *AArchSlov* 31 (1980): 182–185.

——. *Mithras-Orion: Greek Hero and Roman Army God.* Leiden, 1980.

——. *Roman Army Studies.* Amsterdam, 1984.

——. "The Shrine of the Dii Campestres at Gemellae." *Antiquités Africaines* 27 (1991): 111–118.

——. *Riding for Caesar: The Roman Emperor's Horse Guard.* Cambridge, MA, 1994.

Speidel, M.P., and Dimitrova-Milceva, Alexandra. "The Cult of the *Genii* in the Roman Army." *ANRW* II.16.2 (1978): 1542–1553.

Sprockhoff, Ernst. "Central European Urnfield Culture and Celtic La Tène." *Proceedings of the Prehistoric Society* 21 (1955): 257–282.

Squarciapino, M.F. *I culti orientali ad Ostia.* Leiden, 1962.

——. *Leptis Magna.* Basel, 1966.

Squire, Charles. *Celtic Myth and Legend.* London, 1911.

Stähelin, F. *Die Schweiz in römischer Zeit.* 2nd edition. Basel, 1931.

Starr, C.G. *The Roman Imperial Navy 31 BC to AD 324.* 2nd edition. Cambridge, 1960.

Stephens, G.R. "A Note on the Martyrdom of St. Albans." *St. Albans and Hertforshire Architectural and Archaeological Society* 9 (1983–86): 20–21.

Stephens, G.R. and Jarrett, M.G. "Two Altars of *Cohors IV Gallorum* from Castlesteads." *TCWS* 85 (1985): 77–80.

Stewart, P.C.N. "Inventing Britain: The Roman Creation and adaptation of an image." *Britannia* 26 (1995): 1–10.

Stokes, W. "The Prose Tales in the Rennes Dindshenchas." *RevCelt* 15 (1894): 272–336.

Stuart, P. and Bogaers, J. *Deae Nehalenniae.* Leiden, 1971.

Stupperich, Reinhard. "Reconsideration of some fourth-century British Mosaics." *Britannia* 11 (1980): 289–301.

Swoboda, E. *Carnuntum: Seine Geschichte und seine Denkmäler.* 4th edition. Graz, 1964.

Syme, Ronald. *The Roman Revolution.* Oxford, 1939.

——. *Roman Army Papers IV.* Oxford, 1988.

Taeger, F. *Charisma: Studien zur Geschichte des antiken Herrscherkultes.* Stuttgart, 1960.

Taylor, Lily Ross. "The Worship of Augustus during his Lifetime." *TAPA* 51 (1920): 132.

——. "Tiberius' Refusal of Divine Honors." *TAPA* 60 (1929): 87–101.

——. "Tiberius' *Ovatio* and the *Ara numinis Augusti*." *APA* 58 (1937): 189.

——. *The Divinity of the Roman Emperor.* Middleton, Conn., 1931.

Thévenot, E. *Inventaire des Monuments.* Bordeux, 1955.

Thomas, C. "The animal art of the Scottish Iron Age and its Origins." *ArchJ* 118 (1963): 14–25.

——. "The Evidence from North Britain." In *Christianity in Britain: 300–700* (edd. M.W. Barley and R.P.C. Hanson, Leicester, 1968): 93–121.

——. *Christianity in Roman Britain to AD 500.* London, 1981.

Thompson, D.B. *Ptolemaic Oinochoai and Portraits in Faience: Aspects of the Ruler Cult.* Oxford, 1973.

Thompson, E.A. "Britain, AD 406–410." *Britannia* 8 (1977): 303–318.

——. "Fifth-century Facts?" *Britannia* 14 (1983): 272–274.

Thompson, F.H. *Roman Cheshire.* Chester, 1965.

Thornborrow, J. "Report on the Excavations at Beacon Street, South Shields, 1959." *Papers of the South Shields Archaeology and History Society* 1 (1959): 8–25.

Todd, Malcolm. "A Relief of a Romano-British Warrior God." *Britannia* 2 (1971): 238.

——. "Famosa Pestis and Britain in fifth century." *Britannia* 8 (1977): 318–325.

Tomlin, R.S.O. "The Date of the 'Barbarian Conspiracy'." *Britannia* 5 (1974): 303–309.

——. "The Identity of Ignotus in *CIL* viii 1578." *ZPE* 74 (1988): 145–147.

——. "A Roman Altar from Carlisle Castle." *TCWS* 89 (1989): 71–91.

Tóth, I. "Sacerdotes Iovis Dolicheni." *Studium* 2 (1971): 23–28.

——. "Ornamenta Iovis Dolicheni." *ACD* 9 (1973): 105–109.

Toutain, J. *Les cultes païens dans l'empire romain. Première partie: Les provinces latines: Vol. 1: Les cultes officiels; les cultes romains et gréco-romains.* Paris, 1907.

Toynbee, J.M.C. "Christianity in Roman Britain." *JBAA* ser. 3, 16 (1953): 1–24.

——. "The Ara Pacis Reconsidered and Historical Art in Roman Italy." *PBA* 39 (1953): 67–95.

——. "Genii Cucullati." In *Hommages à W. Deonna* (Bruxelles, 1957): 456–469. (*Collection Latomus* vol. 28).

——. *Art in Roman Britain.* London, 1962.

——. *A Silver Casket and Strainer from the Walbrook Mithraeum in the City of London.* Leiden, 1963.

——. *Art in Britain under the Romans.* Oxford, 1964.

——. "Pagan Motifs and Practices in Christian Art and Ritual in Roman Britain." In *Christianity in Britain: 300–700* (edd. M.W. Barley and R.P.C. Hanson, Leicester, 1968): 177–192.

——. "Two Romano-British Genii." *Britannia* 9 (1978): 329–330.

——. *The Roman Art Treasures from the Temple of Mithras.* London, 1986. (Special Paper no. 7 of the London and Middlesex Archaeological Society).

Toynbee, J.M.C. and Clarke, R.R. "A Roman Decorated Helmet and Other Objects from Norfolk." *JRS* 38 (1948): 20–27.

Toynbee, J.M.C. and Wilkins, Alan. "The Vindolanda Horse." *Britannia* 13 (1982): 245–251.

Tudor, D. *Corpus Monumentorum Religionis Equitum Danuvinorum.* Leiden, 1969.

Ulansey, David. *The Origins of the Mithraic Mysteries.* Oxford, 1989.

Usener, H. *Götternamen, Versuch einer Lehre von der religiösen Begriffsbildung.* Frankfurt, 1948.

Vaglieri, D. "Deus." *DE* 22 (1910): 1716–1726.

van der Leeuw, G. *La Religion dans son Essence.* Paris, 1948.

Vári, R. "Zur Überlieferung mittelgriechischer Taktiker." *Byzantinische Zeitschrift* 15 (1915): 84.

Vendryes, J. *Die Hibernicis Vocabulis qaue a Latina Lingua Originem Duxerunt.* Paris, 1902.

Vermaseren, M.J. *Corpus Inscriptionum et Monumentorum Religionis Mithriacae.* 2 vols. The Hague, 1956–1960.

——. *Mithras, ce dieu mystérieux.* Paris and Brussels, 1960.

——. *Mithras: The Secret God.* New York, 1963.

——. *Matrem in leone sedentem.* Leiden, 1970.

——. *Cybele and Atys: The Myth and the Cult.* London, 1977.

——, ed. *Die orientalischen Religionen im Römerreich (OrRR)* Leiden, 1981.

Vermaseren, M.J. and van Essen, C.C. *The Excavations in the Mithraeum of the Church of Santa Prisca in Rome.* Leiden, 1965.

Vermeule, C.C. *The Goddess Roma in the Art of the Roman Empire.* Cambridge, Mass., 1959.

de Vries, J. *La Religion des Celtes.* Paris, 1963.

de Waal, Esther. *Every Earthly Blessing: Celebrating a Spirituality of Creation.* Ann Arbor, MI, 1991.

Wacher, J. *The Towns of Roman Britain.* London, 1974.

Wagner, W. *Die Dislokation der römischen Auxiliartruppen in den Provinzen Noricum, Pannonien, Mösien und Dazien von Augustus bis Gallienus.* Berlin, 1938.

Walbank, F.W. *The Hellenistic World.* Brighton and New Jersey, 1981.

Wall, John. "Christian Evidences in the Roman Period: The Northern Counties." *AA* ser. 4, 43 (1965): 201–225.

Wallace-Hadrill, Andrew. "The Emperor and his Virtues." *Historia* 30 (1981): 298–323.

Walters, Bryn, Mortimer, Catherine, Henig, M. "Two Busts from Littlecote." *Britannia* 19 (1988): 407–410.

Walters, V.J. *The Cult of Mithras in the Roman Provinces of Gaul.* Leiden, 1974.

Wardman, Alan. "Pagan Priesthoods in the Later Empire." In *Pagan Gods and Shrines of the Roman Empire* (M. Henig and A. King, edd., Oxford, 1986): 257–262.

Watkin, W.T. "Roman Inscriptions Discovered in Britain in 1878." *ArchJ* 36 (1879): 154–168.

——. *Roman Cheshire.* Liverpool, 1886.

Watson, G.R. "Christianity in the Roman Army in Britain." In *Christianity in Britain: 300–700* (edd. M.W. Barley and R.P.C. Hanson, Leicester, 1968): 51–54.

——. *The Roman Soldier.* Ithaca, NY, 1969.

Webster, Graham. *Rome Against Caratacus: The Roman Campaigns in Britain AD 48–58.* Totowa, NJ, 1981.

——. "The Possible Effects on Britain of the Fall of Magnentius." In *Rome and her Northern Provinces: Papers presented to S. Frere in honor of his retirement from the Chair of Archaeology of the Roman Empire, University of Oxford, 1983* (edd. B. Hartley and J. Wacher, Gloucester, 1983): 240–254.

——. *Boudica. The British Revolt against Rome AD 60.* London, 1978.

——. "The British under Roman Rule: A Study in Colonialism." *HT* 30 (1980): 18–24.

——. *The Roman Invasion of Britain.* London, 1980.

——. *Rome Against Caratacus.* London, 1981.

——. "The Function of Chedworth Roman Villa." *Bristol and Gloucestershire Archaeological Society Transactions* 101 (1983): 5–20.

——. *The Roman Imperial Army of the first and second centuries AD.* 3rd edition. Totowa, NJ, 1985.

——. *Celtic Religion in Roman Britain.* Totowa, NJ, 1986.

——. "What the Britons required from the gods as seen through the pairings of Roman and Celtic deities and the character of votive offerings." In *Pagan Gods and Shrines of the Roman Empire* (M. Henig and A. King, edd., Oxford, 1986): 57–64.

Webster, J. "Interpretatio: Roman word power and the celtic gods." *Britannia* 26 (1995): 153–161.

Wedlake, W.J. *The Excavation of the Shrine of Apollo at Nettleton, Wiltshire, 1956–1971.* London, 1982.

Welch, M.G. "Late Romans and Saxons in Sussex." *Britannia* 2 (1971): 232–237.

Welsby, Derek A. *The Roman Military Defence of the British Provinces in its Later Phases.* Oxford, 1982. (*BAR* British Series, 101).

Wehrli, F. "Orion." *RE* 18 (1942): 1065–1082.

Weinstock, Sefan. Review of: H.J. Rose, *Ancient Roman Religion* (London, 1948). *JRS* 39 (1949): 166.

——. "Victor and Invictus," *HTR* 50 (1957): 211–247.

——. "Victor and Victoria," *RE* 8A.2 (1958): 2485–2542.

——. *Divus Julius.* Oxford, 1971.

Welles, C. Bradford, Fink, R.O., and Gilliam, J.F. *The Excavations at Dura-Europos: Final Report V part 1: Parchments and Papyri.* New Haven, CT, 1959.

Wenham, L.P. "Notes on the Garrisoning of Maryport." *TCWS* ser. 2, 39 (1939): 19–30.

Werle, G. *Zeitschrift für deutsche Wortforschung.* Straßburg, 1910.

Westhall, P. "The Romano-British Cemetary at The Grange, Welwyn, Herts." *St. Albans and Hertsfordshire Architectural and Archaeological Transactions* 1930: 37–45.

Wheeler, R.E.M. *Segontium and the Roman Occupation of Wales*. Cardiff, 1923.
———. "A 'Romano-Celtic' Temple near Harlow, Essex and a note on the type." *AntJ* 8 (1928): 300–326.
———. *London in Roman Times*. London, 1930.
———. *Verulamium: A Belgic and two Roman Cities*. Oxford, 1936. (*Reports of the Research Committee of the Society of Antiquaries of London*, XI).
———. *The Stanwix Fortifications: North Riding of Yorkshire*. Oxford, 1954. (*Society of Antiquarian Research Report* 17).
Wheeler, R.E.M. and Wheeler, T.V. *Report on the Excavation of the Prehistoric, Roman, and Post-Roman Site in Lydney Park, Gloucestershire*. Oxford, 1932. (*Reports of the Research Committee of the Society of Antiquaries of London*, IX).
Wikander, S. "Études sur les mystères de Mithras." *Yearbook of the New Society of Letters at Lund* (1950): 3–46.
Wilcken, Robert L. *The Christians as the Romans Saw Them*. New Haven, CT, 1984.
Wilcken, U. "Hupomnematismoi." *Philologus* 53 (1894): 80–126.
Will, E. *Le relief cultuel gréco-romain: Contribution à l'histoire de l'art de l'empire Romain*. Paris, 1955.
Williams, H. *Christianity in Early Britain*. Oxford, 1912.
Wilmott, Tony. *Birdoswald: Excavations of a Roman fort on Hadrian's Wall and its successor settlements: 1987–1992*. London, 1997. (English Heritage Archaeological Report #14).
Wilson, R.J.A. *A Guide to the Roman Remains in Britain*. 3rd edition. London, 1988.
———, ed. *Roman Maryport and its Setting*. Maryport, 1997.
Wissowa, G. *Apophoreton der Graeca Halensis*. München, 1903.
———. *Religion und Kultus der Römer*. 2nd edition. München, 1912.
Witt, R.E. *Isis in the Graeco-Roman World*. Ithaca, NY, 1971.
Wolff, H. "Die Cohors II Tungrorum milliaria equitate c(oram?) l(audata?) und die Rechtsform des ius Latii." *Chiron* 6 (1976): 267–288.
Wood, Ian. "The Fall of the Western Empire and the End of Roman Britain." *Britannia* 18 (1987): 251–262.
Woodfield, C. "Six Turrets on Hadrian's Wall." *AA* ser. 4, 43 (1965): 87–201.
Woodward, Ann and Leach, Peter, edd. *The Uley Shrines: Excavation of a ritual complex on West Hill, Uley, Gloucestershire 1977–9*. London, 1993 (English Heritage Archaeological Report #17).
Woolley, C.L. "Corstopitum: Provisional Report of the Excavations in 1906." *AA* ser. 3, 3 (1907): 161–186.
Wright, R.P. "New Readings of a Severan Inscription from Nicopolis, near Alexandria." *JRS* 33 (1943): 33–38.
———. "Roman Britain in 1961, II: Inscriptions." *JRS* 52 (1965): 190–199.
———. "Roman Britain in 1964, II: Inscriptions." *JRS* 55 (1965): 220–228.
Wright, R.P., Hassall, M.W.C., and Tomlin, R.S.O. "Roman Britain in 1975, II: Inscriptions." *Britannia* 7 (1976): 378–392.
Wright, R.P., and Phillips, E.J. *Roman Inscribed and Sculptured Stones in Carlisle Museum*. Carlisle, 1975.
Wright, R.P., and Richmond, I.A. *The Roman Inscribed and Sculptured Stones in the Grosvenor Museum, Chester*. Chester, 1955.
Zaehner, R.C. *The Dawn and Twilight of Zoroastrianism*. London, 1961.
Zanker, Paul. *The Power of Images in the Age of Augustus*. trans. Alan Shapiro. Ann Arbor, MI, 1990.

I. GENERAL INDEX

Achilles, 121, 124, 126, 127, 128, 129, 130
actarius, cat. #24, 231
Adonis, 128
Aelius (nomen), cat. #27, 116, 145, 313, 453, 584
Aelius Caesar, L., 34 n.124, 35, 215
Aelius Secundus, 158 n.3
Aelius Seius, L., 15
Aeneas, 18, 122, 130
Aeon, 95
Aesculapius (Asclepius), 142 n.2, 143, 144, 150, 166, 169, 170, 208, 214, cat. #90, 285–289
Agamemnon, 55, 124, 127
Agricola, 212
Agrippina II, 25 n.61, 43 n.164
Ahriman, 76, 77, 87, 211, cat. #418
Ahura, 72, 76, 95
Ajax, 125 n.93
Alaisiagae, 30, 153, 214, cat. #695–697
Alaric, 185
Alban, 197, 198, 200
Albiorix, 124
Alemanni, 187
Alexander, 55, 75, 176
Alexandria, 25
Allectus, 3, 52 n.206, 183
Ambrosius Aurelianus, 188
Ammon, 172, 180–181
Andraste, 173
Anicetus, 211, cat. #425
Annius Victor, 115, cat. #579
Antenociticus, 30, 101, 104, 111–120, 121, 159, 206, 207, 213, cat. #535–537
Antoninus Pius, 3, 29, 30, 32, 35, 47, 53, 57, 68, 148, 162, 203, cat. #139, 142, 404
Anubis, 178
Apis, 62, 172, 176, 177, 190
Apollo, 13, 68, 69, 89, 103, 108, 116, 120, 121 n.75, 129, 144 n.15, 145, 158, 191, 211, cat. #290–296, 301, 380, 460–463
    Apollo Anextlomarus, cat. #438

Apollo Cunomaglus, 144 n.12, 169, 216, cat. #600
    Apollo Grannus, cat. #439
Aponius Rogatianus, 89, cat. #425
Apulum, 66
aquila, 38, 44 n.166
aquilifer, 9
architectus, 173
Arciaco, 30, 213, cat. #538
Arecurius, 211, cat. #539
Ares, 152
Armilustrium, 37, 38, cat. #2, 3
Arnomecta, cat. #540
Arrius (nomen), cat. #222, 300, 368
Artemis, 62, 128, 144 n.5, 170 n.66
Aspuanis, 210, cat. #653
Astarte, cat. #384
Athena, 152
Attis, 87, 116 n.63, 174–176
Attonius Quintianus, 143, cat. #607
Audagus, 210, cat. #544
Augustine of Canterbury, 9, 197, 198 n.72, 200
Augustine of Hippo, 189
Augustus, 14 n.5, 15, 16, 18, 19, 23, 24, 28 n.87, 32 n.113, 35, 39, 40 n.148, 41 n.150, 48, 62, 128, 168 n.56, 177
Augustus/a (epithet), 20, 35, 49, 50, 51–53, 54, 165 n.38, 207, 208, 214, cat. #59, 70, 72, 78, 95–97, 102–104, 107–110, 121, 256, 277, 281, 317, 449, 610
Aurelian, 27, 63
Aurelius (nomen), cat. #9, 19, 26, 58, 88, 110, 188, 207, 211, 229, 258, 276, 287, 290, 360, 365, 396, 442, 494, 550, 551, 570–572, 615, 628, 656
Aurelius Diotava, 114 n.57, cat. #551
Aurelius Nicanor, 114 n.57, 210, cat. #558
Aurelius Tasulus, 114 n.57, cat. #550
Aurelius Victor, 210, cat. #656

Babdh, 152
Bacchus (Dionysus/Liber), 84 n.125, 85, 86, 160, 162–163, 172 n.70, 177, 192, 204

Livia, 32 n.113, 33 n.114
Loki, 107
Ludi Genialici, 27
Ludi Saeculares, 33 n.114, 174 n.84
Lug, 19 n.29, 99
Luna, 68, 69, 77, 82, 94, 153 n.55
Lunaris, 210, cat. #559
Lurio, 210, cat. #465

Mabon, 117, 145
Macha, 148, 152
Maduhus, 210, cat. #444
Magna Mater, 13, 44 n.169, 174 n.82, 175, 176, cat. #414
Magnentius, 184, 196
Magnus Maximus, 34, 183, 185
Manes, 26 n.74, 120
Maponus, 145, 207, 210, 213, cat. #460–466
Marcius Memor, L., 167
Marcus Aurelius, 33 n.114, 35, 47, 57, 111, 112
Mars, 13, 20, 27 n.77, 31, 36, 37, 38, 39 n.142, 41, 50, 51, 52 n.204, 53, 55, 74, 95, 98, 100, 108, 111, 119, 121 n.75, 123 n.125, 142–144, 145 n.24, 153, 158 n.2, 160, 164–165, 182, 192, 205, 207, 208, 209, 211, cat. #110, 241–284, 554, 557, 558, 562, 567, 577, 584, 596, 598
Mars Alator, 142, cat. #603, 604
Mars Braciaca, 183 n.5, 211, cat. #605
Mars Camulus, 142, 207, cat. #467
Mars Condatis, 120, 143, 215, cat. #606–608
Mars Coroticus, cat. #609
Mars Lenus, 30, 142, 143, 213, cat. #468, 469
Mars Loucetius, 101, 124, 126, 142, 143, 169, cat. #470
Mars Medocius, cat. #610
Mars Nodens, 99, 100, 108, 143–144, 169, 190, 204, 206, 213, cat. #611–616
Mars Ocelus, 30, 213, cat. #617, 618
Mars Olludius, 164, cat. #471
Mars Rigisamus, 124, 142, cat. #472
Mars Rigonemetis, 144, 213, cat. #619
Mars Thincsus, 214, cat. #695, 696
Mars Toutates, 142, cat. #473, 474
Mater Castrorum, 33
Matres (Mother Goddesses), 30, 47, 57, 80, 91–92, 95, 99, 105, 116 n.63, 131, 146–149, 151, 153, 174,

176, 207, 208, 209, 210, 213, 216, cat. #475–514
Matunus, 214, cat. #620
Maximianus, 76, 96, 183
Maximinius, 91 n.155
Maximinus Thrax, 65, 68
Men, 175
Menelaus, 124
Menologia Rustica, 37 n.132
Mens, 48
Mercury, 27 n.77, 31, 59, 83–84, 85, 98, 99, 104, 116 n.63, 120 n.74, 121 n.75, 122, 123, 142, 149, 151, 160, 164–166, 169, 170, 171, 176, 178, 182, 191–193, 204, 207, 209, cat. #319–326
miles, 58, 78, 114, 194 n.43, 209, 210, cat. #53, 171, 172, 250, 281, 326, 339, 362, 383, 481, 499, 510, 514, 592, 593, 597
Minerva, 19, 20, 21, 22, 37 n.132, 50, 52 n.204, 55, 83, 85, 145 n.24, 149, 166–171, 177, 205, 208, 211, 213, cat. #110, 228–240, 283, 529, 533
Mithras, 5, 7, 35, 44 n.169, 63, 65, 68, 70, 72–97, 102 n.13, 113, 114, 116, 130, 131, 147 n.28, 154, 159, 163, 203, 204, 205–206, 207, 208, 209, 211, 216, cat. #415–435
Mitius, 210, cat. #642
Mogons, 30, 105, 108, 112–120, 124, 158 n.3, 161, 206, 209, 213, cat. #518–521
Mórrígan, 152
Mountis, cat. #522, 523
Mounus, cat. #524

Narbo, 18, 23, 28
Natalis Urbis Romana, 17
Necalames, 210, cat. #670–672
Nemesis, 153, 170, 211, 215, cat. #327–329
Nemetona, 101, 169, cat. #470
Neptunalia, 17
Neptune, 19, 20, 21, 22, 50, 103, 169, 205, 208, 216, cat. #228, 330–337
Nerio, 37 n.133
Nero, 3, 19, 43 n.164, 50, 55, 56, 177
Nerva, 35, 49
Nestor, 127
Ninian, 199
Notitia Dignitatum, 186, catalogue *passim*
Nuada, 144

II. SITES IN BRITAIN

III. GARRISONS STATIONED IN BRITAIN

(See also Appendix I for cross references to the Catalogue of Inscriptions)

Ala I Asturum, 148
Ala II Asturum, 208
Ala Augusta Gallorum Petriana milliaria CR bis torquata, 43
Ala Herculea, 187
Ala Hispanorum Vettonum CR, 167 n.47

Cohors I Baetasiorum CR ob virtutem et fidem, 165
Cohors I Batavorum eq., 91, 157, 208
Cohors IX Batavorum, 39 n.143
Cohors I Cornoviorum, 186
Cohors I Cubernorum, 208
Cohors I Aelia Dacorum milliaria, 114, 208
Cohors II Delmatarum eq., 114, 210
Cohors I Frisiavonum, 208
Cohors IIII Gallorum eq., 39 n.143
Cohors I Hamiorum sagittariorum, 205, 208
Cohors I Nerviorum milliaria, 208
Cohors II Nerviorum CR, 114, 208
Cohors I Suncicorum, 87 n.135
Cohors I Tungrorum milliaria, 148, 208
Cohors II Tungrorum milliaria eq. CL, 210
Cohors I Fida Vardullorum milliaria eq. CR, 31, 39, 148, 208
Cuneus Frisiorum Aballavensium, 187
Cuneus Frisionum Ver(covociensium), 30 n.98

Legio II Augusta, 39, 40, 45, 46, 82, 114, 161, 167 n.47, 207, 209
Legio VI Victrix, 47, 51, 114, 145, 161, 168, 173, 207, 209
Legio XX Valeria Victrix, 39, 46, 47, 50, 60, 114, 118, 161, 167 n.47, 207, 209

Numerus Barcariorum, 187, 209
Numerus Exploratorum Bremeniensium, 31, 187

Vexillatio Mar[sacorum], 30 n.98
Vexillatio Sueborum Longovicianorum, 30 n.98, 187

SUPPLEMENTS TO MNEMOSYNE

EDITED BY J. M. BREMER, L. F. JANSSEN, H. PINKSTER
H. W. PLEKET, C. J. RUIJGH AND P. H. SCHRIJVERS

72. CAMPBELL, M. *Echoes and Imitations of Early Epic in Apollonius Rhodius.* 1981. ISBN 90 04 06503 2
73. MOSKALEW, W. *Formular Language and Poetic Design in the Aeneid.* 1982. ISBN 90 04 06580 6
74. RACE, W.H. *The Classical Priamel from Homer to Boethius.* 1982. ISBN 90 04 06515 6
75. MOORHOUSE, A.C. *The Syntax of Sophocles.* 1982. ISBN 90 04 06599 7
77. WITKE, C. *Horace's Roman Odes.* A Critical Examination. 1983. ISBN 90 04 07006 0
78. ORANJE, J. *Euripides' 'Bacchae'.* The Play and its Audience. 1984. ISBN 90 04 07011 7
79. STATIUS. *Thebaidos Libri XII.* Recensuit et cum apparatu critico et exegetico instruxit D.E. HILL. 1983. ISBN 90 04 06917 8
82. DAM, H.-J. VAN. *P. Papinius Statius, Silvae Book II.* A Commentary. 1984. ISBN 90 04 07110 5
84. OBER, J. *Fortress Attica. Defense of the Athenian Land Frontier, 404-322 B.C.* 1985. ISBN 90 04 07243 8
85. HUBBARD, T.K. *The Pindaric Mind.* A Study of Logical Structure in Early Greek Poetry. 1985. ISBN 90 04 07303 5
86. VERDENIUS, W.J. *A Commentary on Hesiod: Works and Days,* vv. 1-382. 1985. ISBN 90 04 07465 1
87. HARDER, A. *Euripides' 'Kresphontes' and 'Archelaos'.* Introduction, Text and Commentary. 1985. ISBN 90 04 07511 9
88. WILLIAMS, H.J. *The 'Eclogues' and 'Cynegetica' of Nemesianus.* Edited with an Introduction and Commentary. 1986. ISBN 90 04 07486 4
89. McGING, B.C. *The Foreign Policy of Mithridates VI Eupator, King of Pontus.* 1986. ISBN 90 04 07591 7
91. SIDEBOTHAM, S.E. *Roman Economic Policy in the Erythra Thalassa 30 B.C.-A.D. 217.* 1986. ISBN 90 04 07644 1
92. VOGEL, C.J. DE. *Rethinking Plato and Platonism.* 2nd impr. of the first (1986) ed. 1988. ISBN 90 04 08755 9
93. MILLER, A.M. *From Delos to Delphi.* A Literary Study of the Homeric Hymn to Apollo. 1986. ISBN 90 04 07674 3
94. BOYLE, A.J. *The Chaonian Dove.* Studies in the Eclogues, Georgics and Aeneid of Virgil. 1986. ISBN 90 04 07672 7
95. KYLE, D.G. *Athletics in Ancient Athens.* 2nd impr. of the first (1987) ed. 1993. ISBN 90 04 09759 7
97. VERDENIUS, W.J. *Commentaries on Pindar.* Vol. I. Olympian Odes 3, 7, 12, 14. 1987. ISBN 90 04 08126 7
98. PROIETTI, G. *Xenophon's Sparta.* An introduction. 1987. ISBN 90 04 08338 3
99. BREMER, J.M., A.M. VAN ERP TAALMAN KIP & S.R. SLINGS. *Some Recently Found Greek Poems.* Text and Commentary. 1987. ISBN 90 04 08319 7
100. OPHUIJSEN, J.M. VAN. *Hephaistion on Metre.* Translation and Commentary. 1987. ISBN 90 04 08452 5
101. VERDENIUS, W.J. *Commentaries on Pindar.* Vol. II. Olympian Odes 1, 10, 11, Nemean 11, Isthmian 2. 1988. ISBN 90 04 08535 1
102. LUSCHNIG, C.A.E. *Time holds the Mirror.* A Study of Knowledge in Euripides' 'Hippolytus'. 1988. ISBN 90 04 08601 3
103. MARCOVICH, M. *Alcestis Barcinonensis.* Text and Commentary. 1988. ISBN 90 04 08600 5
104. HOLT, F.L. *Alexander the Great and Bactria.* The Formation of a Greek Frontier in Central Asia. Repr. 1993. ISBN 90 04 08612 9
105. BILLERBECK, M. *Seneca's Tragödien; sprachliche und stilistische Untersuchungen.* Mit Anhängen zur Sprache des Hercules Oetaeus und der Octavia. 1988. ISBN 90 04 08631 5
106. ARENDS, J.F.M. *Die Einheit der Polis. Eine Studie über Platons Staat.* 1988. ISBN 90 04 08785 0
107. BOTER, G.J. *The Textual Tradition of Plato's Republic.* 1988. ISBN 90 04 08787 7
108. WHEELER, E.L. *Stratagem and the Vocabulary of Military Trickery.* 1988. ISBN 90 04 08831 8
109. BUCKLER, J. *Philip II and the Sacred War.* 1989. ISBN 90 04 09095 9
110. FULLERTON, M.D. *The Archaistic Style in Roman Statuary.* 1990. ISBN 90 04 09146 7
111. ROTHWELL, K.S. *Politics and Persuasion in Aristophanes' 'Ecclesiazusae'.* 1990. ISBN 90 04 09185 8
112. CALDER, W.M. & A. DEMANDT. *Eduard Meyer.* Leben und Leistung eines Universalhistorikers. 1990. ISBN 90 04 09131 9

113. CHAMBERS, M.H. *Georg Busolt. His Career in His Letters.* 1990. ISBN 90 04 09225 0
114. CASWELL, C.P. *A Study of 'Thumos' in Early Greek Epic.* 1990. ISBN 90 04 09260 9
115. EINGARTNER, J. *Isis und ihre Dienerinnen in der Kunst der Römischen Kaiserzeit.* 1991. ISBN 90 04 09312 5
116. JONG, I. DE. *Narrative in Drama.* The Art of the Euripidean Messenger-Speech. 1991. ISBN 90 04 09406 7
117. BOYCE, B.T. *The Language of the Freedmen in Petronius'* Cena Trimalchionis. 1991. ISBN 90 04 09431 8
118. RÜTTEN, Th. *Demokrit — lachender Philosoph und sanguinischer Melancholiker.* 1992. ISBN 90 04 09523 3
119. KARAVITES, P. (with the collaboration of Th. Wren). *Promise-Giving and Treaty-Making.* Homer and the Near East. 1992. ISBN 90 04 09567 5
120. SANTORO L'HOIR, F. *The Rhetoric of Gender Terms.* 'Man', 'Woman' and the portrayal of character in Latin prose. 1992. ISBN 90 04 09512 8
121. WALLINGA, H.T. *Ships and Sea-Power before the Great Persian War.* The Ancestry of the Ancient Trireme. 1993. ISBN 90 04 09650 7
122. FARRON, S. *Vergil's Æneid: A Poem of Grief and Love.* 1993. ISBN 90 04 09661 2
123. LÉTOUBLON, F. *Les lieux communs du roman.* Stéréotypes grecs d'aventure et d'amour. 1993. ISBN 90 04 09724 4
124. KUNTZ, M. *Narrative Setting and Dramatic Poetry.* 1993. ISBN 90 04 09784 8
125. THEOPHRASTUS. *Metaphysics.* With an Introduction, Translation and Commentary by Marlein van Raalte. 1993. ISBN 90 04 09786 4
126. THIERMANN, P. *Die* Orationes Homeri *des Leonardo Bruni Aretino.* Kritische Edition der lateinischen und kastilianischen Übersetzung mit Prolegomena und Kommentar. 1993. ISBN 90 04 09719 8
127. LEVENE, D.S. *Religion in Livy.* 1993. ISBN 90 04 09617 5
128. PORTER, J.R. *Studies in Euripides'* Orestes. 1993. ISBN 90 04 09662 0
129. SICKING, C.M.J. & J.M. VAN OPHUIJSEN. *Two Studies in Attic Particle Usage.* Lysias and Plato. 1993. ISBN 90 04 09867 4
130. JONG, I.J.F. DE, & J.P. SULLIVAN (eds.). *Modern Critical Theory and Classical Literature.* 1994. ISBN 90 04 09571 3
131. YAMAGATA, N. *Homeric Morality.* 1994. ISBN 90 04 09872 0
132. KOVACS, D. *Euripidea.* 1994. ISBN 90 04 09926 3
133. SUSSMAN, L.A. *The Declamations of Calpurnius Flaccus.* Text, Translation, and Commentary. 1994. ISBN 90 04 09983 2
134. SMOLENAARS, J.J.L. *Statius*: Thebaid VII. A Commentary. 1994. ISBN 90 04 10029 6
135. SMALL, D.B. (ed.). *Methods in the Mediterranean.* Historical and Archaeological Views on Texts and Archaeology. 1995. ISBN 90 04 09581 0
136. DOMINIK, W.J. *The Mythic Voice of Statius.* Power and Politics in the *Thebaid.* 1994. ISBN 90 04 09972 7
137. SLINGS, S.R. *Plato's Apology of Socrates.* A Literary and Philosophical Study with a Running Commentary. Edited and Completed from the Papers of the Late E. DE STRYCKER, s.j. 1994. ISBN 90 04 10103 9
138. FRANK, M. *Seneca's* Phoenissae. Introduction and Commentary. 1995. ISBN 90 04 09776 7
139. MALKIN, I. & Z.W. RUBINSOHN (eds.). *Leaders and Masses in the Roman World.* Studies in Honor of ZVI YAVETZ. 1995. ISBN 90 04 09917 4
140. SEGAL, A. *Theatres in Roman Palestine and Provincia Arabia.* 1995. ISBN 90 04 10145 4
141. CAMPBELL, M. *A Commentary on Apollonius Rhodius* Argonautica III 1-471. 1994. ISBN 90 04 10158 6
142. DeFOREST, M.M. *Apollonius'* Argonautica: A Callimachean Epic. 1994. ISBN 90 04 10017 2
143. WATSON, P.A. *Ancient Stepmothers.* Myth, Misogyny and Reality. 1995. ISBN 90 04 10176 4
144. SULLIVAN, S.D. *Psychological and Ethical Ideas.* What Early Greeks Say. 1995. ISBN 90 04 10185 3
145. CARGILL, J. *Athenian Settlements of the Fourth Century B.C.* 1995. ISBN 90 04 09991 3
146. PANAYOTAKIS, C. *Theatrum Arbitri.* Theatrical Elements in the *Satyrica* of Petronius. 1995. ISBN 90 04 10229 9
147. GARRISON, E.P. *Groaning Tears.* Ethical and Dramatic Aspects of Suicide in Greek Tragedy. 1995. 90 04 10241 8

148. OLSON, S.D. *Blood and Iron*. Stories and Storytelling in Homer's *Odyssey*. 1995. ISBN 90 04 10251 5
149. VINOGRADOV, J.G.& S.D. KRYŽICKIJ (eds.). *Olbia*. Eine altgriechische Stadt im Nordwestlichen Schwarzmeerraum. 1995. ISBN 90 04 09677 9
150. MAURER, K. *Interpolation in Thucydides*. 1995. ISBN 90 04 10300 7
151. HORSFALL, N. (ed.) *A Companion to the Study of Virgil*. 1995 ISBN 90 04 09559 4
152. KNIGHT, V.H. *The Renewal of Epic*. Responses to Homer in the *Argonautica* of Apollonius. 1995. ISBN 90 04 10386 4
153. LUSCHNIG, C.A.E. *The Gorgon's Severed Head*. Studies of *Alcestis*, *Electra*, and *Phoenissae*. 1995. ISBN 90 04 10382 1
154. NAVARRO ANTOLÍN, F. (ed.). *Lygdamus*. Corpus Tibullianum III. 1-6: Lygdami elegiarum liber. Translated by J.J. Zoltowski. 1996. ISBN 90 04 10210 8
155. MATTHEWS, V.J. *Antimachus of Colophon*. Text and Commentary. 1996. ISBN 90 04 10468 2
156. TREISTER, M.Y. *The Role of Metals in Ancient Greek History*. 1996. ISBN 90 04 10473 9
157. WORTHINGTON, I. (ed.). *Voice into Text*. Orality and Literacy in Ancient Greece. 1996. ISBN 90 04 10431 3
158. WIJSMAN, H.J.W. *Valerius Flaccus*, Argonautica, *Book V*. A Commentary. 1996. ISBN 90 04 10506 9
159. SCHMELING, G. (ed.). *The Novel in the Ancient World*. 1996. ISBN 90 04 09630 2
160. SICKING, C.M.J. & P. STORK. *Two Studies in the Semantics of the Verb in Classical Greek*. 1996. ISBN 90 04 10460 7
161. KOVACS, D. *Euripidea Altera*. 1996. ISBN 90 04 10624 3
162. GERA, D. *Warrior Women*. The Anonymous Tractatus *De Mulieribus*. 1997. ISBN 90 04 10665 0
163. MORRIS, I. & B. POWELL (eds.). *A New Companion to Homer*. 1997. ISBN 90 04 09989 1
164. ORLIN, E.M. *Temples, Religion and Politics in the Roman Republic*. 1997.ISBN 90 04 10708 8
165. ALBRECHT, M. VON. *A History of Roman Literature*. From Livius Andronicus to Boethius with Special Regard to Its Influence on World Literature. 2 Vols.Revised by G.Schmeling and by the Author. Vol. 1: Translated with the Assistance of F. and K. Newman, Vol. 2: Translated with the Assitance of R.R. Caston and F.R. Schwartz. 1997. ISBN 90 04 10709 6 (Vol. 1), ISBN 90 04 10711 8 (Vol. 2), ISBN 90 04 10712 6 (Set)
166. DIJK, J.G.M. VAN. Αῖνοι, Λόγοι, Μῦθοι. Fables in Archaic, Classical, and Hellenistic Greek Literature. With a Study of the Theory and Terminology of the Genre. 1997. ISBN 90 04 10747 9
167. MAEHLER, H. (Hrsg.). *Die Lieder des Bakchylides*. Zweiter Teil: Die Dithyramben und Fragmente. Text, Übersetzung und Kommentar. 1997. ISBN 90 04 10671 5
168. DILTS, M. & G.A. KENNEDY (eds.). *Two Greek Rhetorical Treatises from the Roman Empire*. Introduction, Text, and Translation of the Arts of Rhetoric Attributed to Anonymous Seguerianus and to Apsines of Gadara. 1997. ISBN 90 04 10728 2
169. GÜNTHER, H.-C. *Quaestiones Propertianae*. 1997. ISBN 90 04 10793 2
170. HEINZE, T. (Hrsg.). *P. Ovidius Naso. Der XII. Heroidenbrief: Medea an Jason*. Einleitung, Text und Kommentar. Mit einer Beilage: Die Fragmente der Tragödie *Medea*. 1997. ISBN 90 04 10800 9
171. BAKKER, E.J. (ed.). *Grammar as Interpretation*. Greek Literature in its Linguistic Contexts. 1997. ISBN 90 04 10730 4
172. GRAINGER, J.D. *A Seleukid Prosopography and Gazetteer*. 1997. ISBN 90 04 10799 1
173. GERBER, D.E. (ed.). *A Companion to the Greek Lyric Poets*. 1997. ISBN 90 04 09944 1
174. SANDY, G. *The Greek World of Apuleius*. Apuleius and the Second Sophistic. 1997. ISBN 90 04 10821 1
175. ROSSUM-STEENBEEK, M. VAN. *Greek Readers' Digests?* Studies on a Selection of Subliterary Papyri. 1998. ISBN 90 04 10953 6
176. McMAHON, J.M. *Paralysin Cave*. Impotence, Perception, and Text in the *Satyrica* of Petronius. 1998. ISBN 90 04 10825 4
177. ISAAC, B. *The Near East under Roman Rule*. Selected Papers. 1998. ISBN 90 04 10736 3
178. KEEN, A.G. *Dynastic Lycia*. A Political History of the Lycians and Their Relations with Foreign Powers, c. 545-362 B.C. 1998. ISBN 90 04 10956 0
179. GEORGIADOU, A. & D.H.J. LARMOUR. *Lucian's Science Fiction Novel* True Histories. Interpretation and Commentary. 1998. ISBN 90 04 10667 7

180. GÜNTHER, H.-C. *Ein neuer metrischer Traktat und das Studium der pindarischen Metrik in der Philologie der Paläologenzeit.* 1998. ISBN 90 04 11008 9
181. HUNT, T.J. *A Textual History of Cicero's* Academici Libri. 1998. ISBN 90 04 10970 6
182. HAMEL, D. *Athenian Generals.* Military Authority in the Classical Period. 1998. ISBN 90 04 10900 5
183. WHITBY, M. (ed.). *The Propaganda of Power.* The Role of Panegyric in Late Antiquity. 1998. ISBN 90 04 10571 9
184. SCHRIER, O.J. *The Poetics of Aristotle and the* Tractatus Coislinianus. A Bibliography from about 900 till 1996. 1998. ISBN 90 04 11132 8
185. SICKING, C.M.J. *Distant Companions.* Selected Papers. 1998. ISBN 90 04 11054 2
186. P.H. SCHRIJVERS. *Lucrèce et les Sciences de la Vie.* 1999. ISBN 90 04 10230 2
187. BILLERBECK M. (Hrsg.). *Seneca.* Hercules Furens. Einleitung, Text, Übersetzung und Kommentar. 1999. ISBN 90 04 11245 6
188. MACKAY, E.A. (ed.). *Signs of Orality.* The Oral Tradition and Its Influence in the Greek and Roman World. 1999. ISBN 90 04 11273 1
189. ALBRECHT, M. VON. *Roman Epic.* An Interpretative Introduction. 1999. ISBN 90 04 11292 8
190. HOUT, M.P.J. VAN DEN. *A Commentary on the Letters of M. Cornelius Fronto.* 1999. ISBN 90 04 10957 9
191. KRAUS, C. SHUTTLEWORTH. (ed.). *The Limits of Historiography.* Genre and Narrative in Ancient Historical Texts. 1999. ISBN 90 04 10670 7
192. LOMAS, K. & T. CORNELL. *Cities and Urbanisation in Ancient Italy.* ISBN 90 04 10808 4 *In preparation*
193. MALKIN, I. *History of Greek Colonization.* ISBN 90 04 09843 7 *In preparation*
194. WOOD, S.E. *Imperial Women.* A Study in Public Images, 40 B.C. - A.D. 68. 1999. ISBN 90 04 11281 2
195. OPHUIJSEN, J.M. VAN & P. STORK. *Linguistics into Interpretation.* Speeches of War in Herodotus VII 5 & 8-18. 1999. ISBN 90 04 11455 6
196. TSETSKHLADZE, G.R. (ed.). *Ancient Greeks West and East.* 1999. ISBN 90 04 11190 5
197. PFEIJFFER, I.L. *Three Aeginetan Odes of Pindar.* A Commentary on *Nemean* V, *Nemean* III, & *Pythian* VIII. 1999. ISBN 90 04 11381 9
198. HORSFALL, N. *Virgil,* Aeneid 7. A Commentary. 2000. ISBN 90 04 10842 4
199. IRBY-MASSIE, G.L. *Military Religion in Roman Britain.* 1999. ISBN 90 04 10848 3
200. GRAINGER, J.D. *The League of the Aitolians.* 1999. ISBN 90 04 10911 0
201. ADRADOS, F.R. *History of the Graeco-Roman Fable.* I: Introduction and from the Origins to the Hellenistic Age. Translated by L.A. Ray. Revised and Updated by the Author and Gert-Jan van Dijk. 1999. ISBN 90 04 11454 8